Psychoeducational Assessment
of Preschool Children

Psychoeducational Assessment
of Preschool Children

Fourth Edition

Edited by

Bruce Bracken and Richard Nagle

LEA LAWRENCE ERLBAUM ASSOCIATES, PUBLISHERS
2007 Mahwah, New Jersey   London

Senior Acquisitions Editor: Naomi Silverman
Cover Design: Tomai Maridou
Full-Service Compositor: MidAtlantic Books & Journals, Inc.

This book was typeset in 10/12 pt Bookman BT, Italic, Bold, and Bold Italic. Headings were typeset in Lyndian BT and Lyndian Italic.

Lawrence Erlbaum Associates, Inc., Publishers
10 Industrial Avenue
Mahwah, New Jersey 07430
www.erlbaum.com

CIP information for this volume can be obtasined by contacting the Library of Congress.

ISBN   0-8058-5263-8 (case)

Books published by Lawrence Erlbaum Associates are printed on acid-free paper, and their bindings are chosen for strength and durability.

Printed in the United States of America
10 9 8 7 6 5 4 3 2 1

*This book is dedicated with love to Bruce Jr. who was
a preschooler when this book was conceived and who increased my
interest and fascination with preschool children, their development, and the means
by which to accurately assess them. The book is also dedicated with love to
Mary Jo Bracken, Bruce's mother and my wife of 35 years.(BAB)*

*This book is dedicated to my wife Pat and the loving memory
of my mother, Aurelia, who both taught me all about love, and to my sons
Brian and Greg, my most cherished possessions. . . . It is not that
I own them, but rather they possess my heart. (RJN)*

Contents

Preface

The first edition of *The Psychoeducational Assessment of Preschool Children* was conceived in 1979 at an APA conference in New York City. That first edition was intended primarily to meet the needs of the editors, who were entering their first academic positions and were tasked with teaching preschool assessment. To acquaint students and practitioners with the idiosyncratic behavior of preschool children and address the pertinent issues related to the assessment of this unique population, the editors identified and invited a nationally prominent multidisciplinary team of professionals to write chapters that would serve as the foundation for sound psychoeducational assessment of preschool children for the decade to come. Rich Nagle, who joined Bruce Bracken to edit this current edition, was among those nationally prominent scholars who consulted in the development of the first edition. The first edition, published in 1983, was quickly adopted nationally as the standard text in preschool assessment courses and served professionals as the only comprehensive preschool assessment text available at that time.

As the 1980s progressed into the 1990s, many changes influenced the practice of psychology, with new public laws mandating appropriate assessment and remedial services for exceptional preschool children. Some venerable preschool instruments were transitioning into use with far less frequency (e.g., McCarthy Scales of Children's Abilities, Illinois Test of Psycholinguistic Abilities) and other tests had been revised and restandardized. Many new instruments were developed and added to the repertoire of those individuals who assess young children (e.g., the Bracken Basic Concept Scale, which more than 20 years later has become one of the established preschool tests). New theoretical orientations expanded the focus of preschool assessment and combined assessment with instruction and brought about an awareness of such approaches as curriculum-based assessment/intervention and dynamic assessment/intervention. Throughout the 1980s and 1990s, universities increased their graduate and undergraduate offerings in early childhood regular and special education, assessment, and therapeutic interventions. Local, state, regional, and national professional organizations and institutions sponsored an amazing number and array of preschool assessment skill-building workshops.

The goal for the second edition of the book was to incorporate the many advances and changes that occurred in the field and to serve further as a catalyst for future advances in preschool assessment. The second edition continued to be appropriate for school, child clinical, and pediatric psychologists, early childhood educators and diagnosticians, speech and language pathologists, and other professionals who observe and assess preschool children. As with the first edition, the second edition was designed as a text for undergraduate and graduate courses devoted to the psychoeducational assessment of preschool children and as a best practices resource for the practicing professional. Given the legal, ethical, practical, and professional mandates facing those professionals who assess preschool children, the second edition remained in the vanguard as a reliable resource throughout the 1990s.

The third edition of the book was designed to cross over to the twenty-first century and provide professionals with state-of-the-art information about assessing preschool children. That edition of the book discontinued chapters which focused on outdated instrumentation (e.g., the McCarthy Scales) or practices and introduced some new authors who were on the cutting edge of practice and science (e.g.,. play-based assessment).

The editors of this fourth edition had three primary goals in mind during the revision process. The first goal was to maintain the popular content and focus of the three earlier editions. The second goal was to update the content of all chapters and to add chapters with new content-specialization in order to provide coverage of topics necessary to meet the needs of contemporary best practice. The final goal for this fourth edition of the book was to continue to provide academics and practitioners with one comprehensive guide for conducting psychoeducational assessments with preschool children by combining the experiences and knowledge of this dual-editor team and list of contributing authors.

Psychoeducational Assessment
of Preschool Children

I

FOUNDATIONS

1

History of Preschool Assessment

Michael F. Kelley
Arizona State University, West

Elaine Surbeck
Arizona State University, Tempe

Preschool assessment, within the broader context of psychoeducational assessment, is a relative newcomer in the history of testing. Although its history is recent, preschool assessment issues, practices, and techniques have links to practices that began in Europe and America roughly 200 years ago. This chapter is designed to survey the evolution of the testing movement as it developed over the course of two centuries and show how this movement impacted the current field of preschool assessment in America.

Historians have shown that life in Europe and America during the eighteenth and nineteenth centuries was difficult for all but a few (Aries, 1962; De Mause, 1974). Disease and famine were commonplace, afflicting young and old alike. Work conditions were difficult and particularly deadly for child laborers. Those who suffered most were young children, the economically poor, and individuals considered mentally deficient and insane. Schooling was nonexistent for the majority of young people since most schools were private and established for the elite. Virtually all decisions related to societal work or access to educational opportunity were linked to personal or family wealth. Demographically, between 1820 and 1860 American cities grew at a faster rate than at any other period in history, adding an average of 125,000 new immigrants annually to urban areas (U.S. Congress, Office of Technology Assessment, 1992). Many of the cities were overwhelmed by the sheer numbers of people needing education, jobs, and housing.

One of the central educational issues raised during the nineteenth century was the lack of any selection or classification scheme for determining those who might benefit from a

Michael F. Kelley, Ed.D. is an associate professor in Early Childhood Education and Chair, Department of Elementary Education at Arizona State University at the West campus. He has professional experience with families and children ranging from infants through the early childhood years. His current scholarship is focused on studying the effects of restructuring early childhood education programs within private and public settings.

Elaine Surbeck, Ed.D. is a professor in Early Childhood Education and Interim Associate Dean, College of Education at Arizona State University at the Tempe campus. She has professional experience with families and children ranging from infants through the early childhood years. Her current scholarship is focused on Constructivism and its application to teacher preparation, and on interprofessional collaboration among human service personnel.

proper education and those who were considered uneducable. It was precisely the need for some form of classification of human ability that impelled the great scientists of France, England, Germany, and America to formulate the early versions of our present day assessment devices.

A central theme undergirding the history of assessment is how the early scientists' view of the nature of human development and mental activity influenced the school-aged and subsequent preschool testing movement. What is evident in examining the historical antecedents of the preschool testing movement is that each major scientific improvement resulted from cycles of interactions between sociocultural and educational needs of society at a point in time and the prevailing scientific conception of human functioning and ability. As new views of human functioning and intelligent activity were proposed and challenged during these cycles of intense sociocultural tension and controversy, concomitant changes were reflected in the policies, instruments, and procedures used to measure such ability. In the course of roughly 200 years, current day methodological issues such as test validity and reliability, sophisticated sampling techniques, the use of elaborate statistical analyses, and decision utility emerged. These developments can be traced to the pioneering efforts of the nineteenth century scientists.

NINETEENTH CENTURY INFLUENCES ON PRESCHOOL ASSESSMENT

The contributions of the great philosophers and educators who lived prior to the twentieth century were instrumental in the formulation of early theories of mental activity and various conceptions of intelligence (Goodenough, 1949). However, because preschool assessment didn't begin until the early twentieth century, the focus on the nineteenth century contributions will be limited to those most directly related to contemporary issues of assessment. (For the contributions of the early philosophers and educators, see Braun & Edwards, 1972; Lascarides & Hinitz, 2000; Osborn, 1991; and, Ulich, 1945, 1947). Different purposes and methodological issues related to assessment of human functioning were raised and studied in countries around the world. Foundational contributions came from work done in France, England, Germany, and the United States.

In France, the study and treatment of the insane and the mentally deficient received considerable attention from Esquirol, Itard, Sequin, and Binet. Their contributions included establishing the need for a classification system to diagnose mental retardation, experimenting with sensory training for the mentally deficient, and developing practical diagnostic classification systems for admission to special schools and for selection into professional civil service (Goodenough, 1949; Johnson, 1894).

In England, scientists were struggling with the assessment of inherited mental ability. Sir Francis Galton, a second cousin to Charles Darwin, constructed very simple tests of memory, motor, and sensory functions to differentiate between high and low achievers. Moreover, he advocated studying individual differences between twins and was one of the first scientists to use quantitative methods derived from mathematics and astronomy in analyzing data (Anastasi, 1982), earning him the title "the father of mental testing" (Goodenough, 1949).

Charles Darwin suggested that the early behaviors of young children might provide relevant information concerning the ontogenesis of human development. Thus, numerous studies of infant behavior were conducted (Darwin, 1877; Preyer, 1882; Shinn, 1900; Stern, 1914, 1924). These early baby biographies were important to the preschool testing movement in that they demonstrated a sequence of early behavioral development and individual differences regarding the rate of development (Goodenough, 1949). Furthermore, the baby biographies extended the span of research to include an age previously neglected. This resulted in a beginning awareness of the importance of infancy and the early childhood years to later development. Some protocols used in early preschool assessment devices to establish developmental sequences were derived, in part, from the work of the baby biographers.

In contrast, German scientists such as Wundt and Cattell were directing their attention toward sensation, perception, and individual differences. Their efforts influenced the emerging testing movement by clearly demonstrating the need for uniform experimental procedures and, more importantly, the existence of age-related individual variation in performance (Goodenough, 1949). The issue of individual differences and instability in test performance among young children proves to be a continuing problem in preschool assessment and educational decision making yet today.

In the United States a pressing social problem directed investigations of a different nature. Educators were beginning to recognize that the huge population influx of immigrants necessitated new institutional demands for educational efficiency and accountability. What was needed was a system for accurate identification and classification of students that would result in effective mass education. Unfortunately, the American educational institutions of the time were hampered in their goal by the lack of discriminating assessment instruments. Virtually all of the tests constructed were of a highly sensory nature and failed to differentiate individuals of various levels of ability (Goodenough, 1949; Stott & Ball, 1965).

It can thus be seen that the activity of the social scientists during the nineteenth century raised many issues concerning the assessment of children and adults. A primary tension that surfaced was how to respond to the need for efficiency in classification while respecting the need for valid measures that ensured fairness. Questions about test validity and the link to prevalent theories of mental development and human functioning were raised. The changing context of the work during this period is important to recognize. In contrast to earlier periods, the theories generated by the nineteenth century scientists about intelligence and behavior were more closely linked to phrenology (where "good" or base character traits were attributed to physical endowments), experimental psychology, and the systematic study of humans rather than metaphysical notions derived from philosophy and religion. The most prevalent belief was that mental ability was fixed genetically, unalterable from an environmental perspective. Methodological issues such as the need for controlled testing conditions, useful sampling techniques, and test reliability surfaced during the latter part of this period. Finally, how to assess the nonschool-age child began to emerge as a question of study (Senn, 1975).

EARLY TWENTIETH CENTURY INFLUENCES ON PRESCHOOL ASSESSMENT

The early twentieth century witnessed dramatic developments in technology, medicine, and the behavioral sciences. The major universities in the United States opened psychological clinics with the study of child development as their primary focus (Sears, 1975).

In France and the United States, the establishment of compulsory school attendance laws resulted in numerous school admission problems. Children from all backgrounds and ability levels were rapidly filling American schools, such that by the turn of the century, almost 80% of children ages 5 to 17 were enrolled in some kind of school (Katz, 1972). Questions about appropriate selection and classification of individuals were being raised, with school personnel relying on best guesses and personal judgments regarding proper academic placement. Eventually, the governments of both France and the United States commissioned groups of scientists to devise tests of mental ability that would assist in differentiating school-age children and allow for appropriate school placement (Goodenough, 1949). The seminal work of Alfred Binet ensued.

THE BINET SCALES AND THEIR INFLUENCE ON PRESCHOOL ASSESSMENT

Alfred Binet and several of his colleagues were asked by the Paris Minister of Public Instruction to construct a means for identifying children in need of special education. Binet, who published numerous studies related to perception and reasoning, eventually became interested in qualitative differences in functioning displayed by young children and adults (Pollack & Brenner, 1969).

As previously mentioned, the commonly held belief of the time was that intelligence (or mental functioning) was a genetically fixed entity manifested behaviorally through the sensory functions of the body. Most of the early influential scientists argued for such a position and constructed sensory tests based on that premise. Binet was one of the first scientists to challenge that belief (Goodenough, 1949). He argued that complex mental functioning could not be determined by a simple test of sensory functioning. Moreover, he believed that intelligence was fluid, shaped by environmental and cultural influences (Fancher, 1985). In contrast, he suggested judgment, reasoning, and comprehension were more adequate dimensions of intellectual ability (Binet & Simon, 1905). With the assistance of Theodore Simon, Binet developed a 30-item test that was administered to a small sample of subnormal and normal children in Paris. The main objective of the test was to determine general mental development rather than simple sensory functioning. The items were arranged in ascending order of difficulty and were scored on a pass/fail basis. Although by today's standards the 1905 scale was quite crude, several important methodological issues were raised by Binet and Simon (1905). They argued that tests of mental ability must be simple to administer and score, must have standard procedures to follow, and should provide results that distinguish the retarded from the normal (Pinter, 1923).

In 1908, Binet and Simon reported the results of a second test series. They introduced the qualitative notion of "mental level" and described the test standardization procedures to determine item placement. Moreover, their work influenced a number of colleagues and former students (including Jean Piaget) to raise substantive methodological questions and pursue them with vigor and scrutiny (Wolf, 1973). In 1911, the year Binet died, a third revision was reported. The 1911 scale was a further refinement of the previous scale, with new items added and some of the original items dropped because they did not measure general intelligence.

Numerous translations of the Binet Scale appeared, including the English translations provided by Henry Goddard in 1908 and 1910. In response to interest in the scale, Goddard and his associates at Vineland Training School established test administration seminars for teachers and championed the importance of early diagnosis (Goddard, 1920). He advocated the systematic testing of children and the special placement of limited-abilities students in classes especially created and staffed with trained teachers. Thus, the seeds of special education classrooms were planted some 70 years prior to the passage of Public Law (P.L.) 94-142, the Education of All Handicapped Act (Kelley, Sexton, & Surbeck, 1990). As can be seen by the following quote, Goddard enthusiastically endorsed the power of systematic testing and its potential impact on human progress and the creation of social order:

> . . . it is no longer possible for anyone to deny the validity of mental tests, even in the case of group testing; and when it comes to an individual examined by a trained psychologist, it cannot be doubted that the mental level of the individual is determined with marvelous exactness. The significance of all this for human progress and efficiency can hardly be appreciated at once. Whether we are thinking of children or adults it enables us to know a very fundamental fact about the human material. The importance of this in building up the cooperative society such as every community aims to be, is very great. (Goddard, 1920, pp. 28–29).

In addition to the flurry of activity by Goddard and his associates, Kuhlmann (1912, 1914) published two versions of the Binet scales, and it was his second version that extended the test items downward to address intelligent activity at 2 months of age. This was one of the first revised editions designed to test children younger than 3 years of age (Goodenough, 1949).

The work of Binet and Simon, along with the revised scales designed by others such as Lewis Terman (1916), contributed greatly to the impetus for early testing, and more importantly, the emerging preschool assessment efforts. These individuals challenged the widely held beliefs regarding the static nature of intelligent activity. In addition, they described standardization procedures for item placement, documented age-related score variations and other sources of error in test administration, and discussed difficulties in reporting meaningful test results (Goodenough, 1949). Even though Goddard's vision about the benefits of systematic testing was not realized, significant progress was made in establishing the scientific acceptability of psychometric testing (Kelley, Sexton, & Surbeck, 1990). While these important scientific gains were made in Europe, related issues were afoot in America.

CHILD STUDY MOVEMENT

In the United States, the child study movement of the early 1900s gained momentum under the leadership of G. Stanley Hall at Clark University. Several influential scientists (Kuhlmann, Goddard, and Terman) studied under Hall; Arnold Gesell was another influential figure who was his student (Senn, 1975).

Because the vast majority of the tests developed in the early 1900s were for school-age children, it became increasingly apparent to those individuals at Clark University, and to others at Cornell University (Pauline Park and Wilson Knapp), Yale University (Arnold Gesell), the University of Minnesota (John Anderson), the University of Iowa (Bird Baldwin), Teachers College, Columbia (Lois Meeks), Merrill-Palmer Institute in Detroit (Edna Noble White), and the University of California at Berkeley (Herbert Stolz and Nancy Bayley) that additional revisions were needed for the preschool years. This work was facilitated by Lawrence K. Franks, who, through funding provided by the Laura Spelman Rockefeller Memorial, was instrumental in establishing institutes of child welfare for the study of child development in many of these universities. Thus, the preschool assessment movement began in earnest with the study of young children as the primary thrust.

During the years between 1920 and 1940, considerable time and effort went into formulating answers to three major questions in regard to preschool assessment. First, what are the characteristics of normal young children? Second, is intelligent behavior deter-mined by heredity or environment? Third, what can be done to improve assessment de-vices designed to test the ability of young children? These questions were raised not only by the scientists and academicians of the time, but also by the public. In order to under-stand what occurred during this period of time, consider the sociocultural context and events leading to the intense study of children.

Demographic statistics continued to reflect high infant and maternal mortality among the poor, and the World War I recruits displayed a strikingly poor educational and physical preparedness (Senn, 1975). Moreover, the proliferation of day care, nursery, and kinder-garten facilities led to the realization that little was known about the overall development of young children (Sears, 1975).

The baby biographies written in the latter part of the nineteenth century represented the first real attempt at organizing and describing child growth and development. The vast majority of the early scientists and educators directed their attention toward school-age children and the mentally deficient. Although constrained by the theoretical perspective of genetically "fixed" mental ability, several important psychologists and educators of the early 1900s recognized the social and scientific need for relevant information regarding the growth and development of normal young children (For review, see Sears, 1975, and Senn, 1975).

In 1916, Lucy Sprague Mitchell and several of her colleagues began a series of exper-iments at the Bureau of Educational Experiments (currently the Bank Street College of Education) in New York. The research conducted at the Bureau consisted of studying child development and experimental schools. Techniques of recording children's behavior and analyzing and interpreting the data in ways that displayed the interdependent complexities within each child became a primary focus. These efforts were in direct contrast to the work of John B. Watson and colleagues who chose to ignore the issue of context effects for the science of objective observation and measurement (Senn, 1975).

In addition to the work of Mitchell and her colleagues, the behaviorist work of both Thorndike (1921) and Watson (Watson & Watson, 1928) legitimized the study of children by demonstrating that the right stimuli and environment improved children's ability to learn. However, data regarding the typical pattern and sequence of normal behavior of young chil-dren were still unavailable. Although testing of school-age children was well established by 1910 (Goodenough, 1949), the preschool child received little attention until Burt (1921), Yerkes and Foster (1923), and Kuhlmann (1914) published versions of intelligence tests that extended downward into the preschool years. Unfortunately, these early tests were consid-ered methodologically lacking in that standardization procedures were poorly defined and re-liability and validity data usually were not reported (Stott & Ball, 1965).

GESELL AND THE MATURATIONAL PERSPECTIVE

Perhaps the earliest significant interest in understanding the development of preschool-age children was shown at the Yale Clinic for Child Development. Exceptional children were observed in the Yale Clinic as early as 1911, but by 1916 Gesell had undertaken a project to explore developmental change and growth of normal children under 5 years of age. Op-erating under the belief that growth and development were biologically predetermined, Gesell (1925) and his colleagues argued for a maturational perspective that incorporated time-bound qualitative change ("ages and stages") in development. This theoretical viewpoint had support among scientists disenchanted with the views and experiments of

Watson, and significantly influenced the child study movement and later debates about the impact of environment on intelligent activity (Senn, 1975).

Gesell (1925), a pediatrician by training, began his study with 50 "representative" children; they were examined at each of 10 age levels: birth, 4, 6, 9, 12, 18, 24, 36, 48, and 60 months. A psychological examination and an observational survey of the child's behavior at home were made at each level. Although little attention was paid to precise methodology, the initial results were presented as a "developmental schedule" and contained approximately 150 items in four areas: motor development, language development, adaptive behavior, and personal-social behavior. Gesell's work continued for more than 40 years. Several of the subsequently developed tests for infants and preschoolers used information derived from the Gesell profiles (Stott & Ball, 1965). Innovative techniques for observing children, such as the use of the one-way observation booth, were also developed by Gesell.

While Gesell and his colleagues were gathering normative data on young children at the Yale Clinic, several other assessment instruments were being developed for use with infants and preschoolers. The most notable among these were the Merrill-Palmer Scale of Mental Tests (Stutsman, 1931), the Minnesota Preschool Scale (Goodenough, 1926; Goodenough, Maurer, & Van Wagenen, 1940), the California First Year Mental Scale (Bayley, 1933), and the Iowa Test for Young Children (Fillmore, 1936). (See Stott & Ball, 1965, and Brooks & Weinraub, 1976, for reviews).

While the reliability and validity data for these early scales would be considered questionable by contemporary standards, the formulation of these tests and their subsequent publication generated considerable research activity on their use as adequate measures (Goodenough, 1949); of central concern were test reliability, predictive validity, and stability of test scores. Moreover, individuals such as Kurt Lewin were proposing naturalistic, ecologically sensitive observational approaches as scientific tools of investigation that would parallel laboratory methods (Senn, 1975).

Although most of these early test developers did not focus on intelligence per se, they were concerned with the mental and physical growth of normal children. Influenced by the theory of maturation of Hall and Gesell, the underlying assumption made by the majority of the test developers and child developmentalists of this period was that mental ability or intelligence was stable and unmodifiable (Stott & Ball, 1965). These assumptions of predetermined development and genetically fixed intelligence established the climate for perhaps one of the best known controversies in developmental psychology. This controversy was the prelude to major shifts in thinking about the nature of intelligent activity and concomitant preschool test construction.

WELLMAN–GOODENOUGH CONTROVERSY

With the formation of university child development laboratories in the United States, researchers were afforded sizable numbers of preschoolers on which to conduct studies of growth and development. Wellman and her colleagues at the Iowa Child Welfare Research Station administered intelligence tests to the preschool children enrolled in the program. Over a period of several years, Wellman (1932b) observed an increase in the IQ's of the children and attributed these increases to the stimulating environment in the program. In 1932, Wellman (1932a) published the first of several articles (1932b, 1934, 1940) that challenged the fixed intelligence assumption so prevalent at the time. Several other investigators subsequently conducted longitudinal studies with young children and reported findings that suggested that environment could either increase or decrease IQ's (Crissey, 1937; Skeels, 1938; Skodak, 1939). The results of these studies were fiercely attacked by proponents of the fixed intelligence view (Stott & Ball, 1965).

Primary among those who vehemently disagreed with the view of modifiable intelligence were Simpson (1939) and Goodenough (1939). Although Goodenough had earlier (1928) found IQ increases in a study of nursery school children, she dismissed the findings by concluding that the test (1922 Kuhlmann-Binet) was poorly standardized and that any changes in IQ could not be attributed to actual increases in intelligence. In a similar manner, Goodenough (1940) also dismissed the Wellman studies as poorly controlled and methodologically unsound. Finally, Goodenough and Maurer (1940) published another research report that compared IQ changes among nursery school children and non-nursery school children. The result displayed an average IQ gain of 4.6 points for both groups. Thus, as far as Goodenough was concerned, the notion that environment influenced mental development was not tenable. Lewis Terman had reached similar conclusions in his own research (Senn, 1975).

Controversy ensued throughout psychological circles. New studies were designed and conducted with environmentally deprived children (Bradway, 1945). Eventually, evidence that supported the conclusion that environment was, indeed, a factor in mental development, began to accumulate. The evidence suggested a need for a reevaluation of the structure of intelligence (Stott & Ball, 1965) and the manner in which intelligent activity was assessed.

INTELLIGENT ACTIVITY RECONCEPTUALIZED

While the heredity-environment controversy was raging, Terman and Merrill (1937) published the 1937 revised edition of the 1916 Stanford-Binet. Additional items for the preschool child, coupled with more elaborate and carefully designed standardization procedures, were introduced. The test incorporated more nonverbal items, had additional memory tests, reported high-reliability coefficients, and could be administered in either of two forms. The 1937 revision was criticized on several grounds (Flanagan, 1938; Krugman, 1939). It took longer to administer than previous editions, it still reflected mostly verbal ability, the standard error of measurement could not be determined, and the notion of one global IQ score did not accommodate the emerging conceptualization of multifactoral approaches to intelligence.

Individuals (Hotelling, 1933; Kelley, 1935; Thurstone, 1935) conducted factor analytic studies on the most widely used tests of the day and reported a number of recognizable group factors related to intelligence. These factors included verbal ability, numerical ability, mechanical ability, and attention. Thurstone (1938) reported six primary mental abilities: verbal comprehension, word-fluency, space, memory, number, and induction. Thus, it became apparent that the global structure of intelligence was in need of reconceptualization.

The 1930s and 1940s represented a major turning point in the preschool testing movement. Demographically, universal public schooling was prevalent for almost all children. Socially and politically, there was widespread belief that tests would aid in the efficient management of schools. Scientifically, shifts occurred in how intelligent activity was defined and how that information could be used to benefit children. For example, the inherent limitations of the Stanford-Binet concept of global intelligence and the findings of primary mental abilities led Wechsler (1949) to develop the Wechsler Intelligence Scale for

Children (WISC), which incorporated subtests to measure the various aspects of intelligence. Subtests allowed for differentiation and interpretation of results leading to greater analysis of performance. Furthermore, social upheaval such as the economic depression and World War II created the need for additional programs for young children, including child care facilities (Osborn, 1991). These conditions led to the conduct of longitudinal research programs to investigate the effects of the environment on intelligence. Finally, the older intelligence scales underwent revisions. Throughout the 1940s and into the 1950s, the emphasis shifted from intelligence testing to the study of personality, social, and motoric factors related to general functioning.

THE YEARS 1940–1960

Although the previous 20 years had seen increased test construction for preschool-age children and infants, during the years 1940–1960 there was concern over the lack of predictive validity of the existing instruments (Stott & Ball, 1965). Numerous studies reported little correlation between infant and preschool assessment ratings with those gathered at later school-age years (DeForest, 1941; Escalona, 1950; Gallagher, 1953; Goodenough & Maurer, 1942; Mowrer, 1934). These results raised doubts about the generally accepted view of mental development as being genetically endowed, inherently stable, and quantitative in nature (Stott & Ball, 1965). However, these doubts did not stop the designers of tests from continuing their test construction efforts.

NEW TEST DEVELOPMENTS

During the 1940s, several tests were published for infant and preschool assessment. These included the Cattell Infant Intelligence Scale (Cattell, 1940), the Northwest Infant Intelligence Scale (Gilliland, 1948), the Leiter International Performance Scale (Leiter, 1948), and the Full Range Picture Vocabulary Test (Ammons & Ammons, 1948). (See Stott & Ball, 1965, for a description of each scale or test). The Cattell scale and the Northwest test were devised to assess infant abilities, while the Leiter scale and the Full Range Vocabulary Test were concerned with the abilities of preschoolers 2 years of age and older.

The Leiter (1948) scale was devised as a non-language mental test to be as culture fair as possible. This represented a significant advance in test construction because the Leiter scale proved to be more culture free than the widely accepted Stanford-Binet (Stott & Ball, 1965). However, this finding did not change public opinion; the Stanford-Binet continued to be the most widely used test of mental ability (Goodenough, 1949).

The Full Range Picture Vocabulary Test was novel in that it was a test with high reliability and validity. In addition, care was taken to standardize the test on a sample of preschoolers considered representative of the general population (Ammons & Holmes, 1949). One serious drawback in the standardization procedure, however, was the fact that the entire group of 120 "representative" children was Caucasian.

In 1949, Wechsler published the WISC. The WISC contained 12 subtests applicable to children between 5 and 15 years of age. The subtests included Arithmetic, Vocabulary, Similarities, Picture Completion, Block Design, and Object Assembly, to name a few. Although the WISC was intended for use with children, its application for preschool-age children raised questions. Most of the criticism of the WISC was concerned with its level of difficulty for young children. In spite of this criticism, the WISC was listed as one of the five most frequently used tests to measure mental functioning in preschoolers (Stott & Ball, 1965). This questionable downward extension of tests designed for school-age children into the preschool years was a common practice during this period of time.

During the 1950s, two more tests were published, one for infants and another for young children about to enter first grade. The Griffiths Mental Development Scale (Griffiths, 1954) was designed to measure infant mental ability. Constructed under the premise that intelligence is general ability, Griffiths' test consisted of 260 items in five subscales. Although the test-retest reliability coefficient reported was .92 based on 52 cases, no predictive validity coefficients were reported (Stott & Ball, 1965).

The Brenner Gestalt Test (Brenner, 1959) was designed as a screening device to evaluate children's readiness for first grade. The tasks included copying dots, drawing a man, recognizing numbers, and copying sentences. The test correlated .81 with teacher ratings of children's functioning and was easy to administer. It is instructive to point out that during this period of time in the United States, many children were denied public school access based on race and/or assessment of potential school success. The questionable ethical and social impact of using screening and readiness tests to determine school placement will be more fully addressed in later sections of this chapter.

Although the tests just mentioned were developed with far greater precision than their earlier counterparts, they still proved inadequate in predicting later mental development. Although factors such as test resistance (Rust, 1931) and individual temperament (Stutsman, 1931) were considered partly responsible for the lack of predictive validity, the idea that intelligence is qualitative in nature was gaining acceptance and a following in the literature.

THEORETICAL REVISIONS REGARDING THE NATURE OF DEVELOPMENT

In the late 1940s and early 1950s, Escalona (1950), Garrett (1946), and Piaget (1952), among others, proposed that mental development and intelligent activity was qualitative in nature. Piaget (1952), in his classic work on the origin of intelligence in young children, postulated a fixed sequence of "structures or schemas" that were qualitatively different in composition, yet functionally related, in that each developed out of the earlier structure. Central to Piaget's theory was the importance of experience. To Piaget, mental development was dependent on the organism's active construction of the invariant aspects of the environment. Thus, the quality of the environment and the nature of the organism's activity were of vital importance. With the publication of *Intelligence and Experience* by J. McVicker Hunt (1961), and the pioneering replication research of Piaget's concepts conducted by David Elkind (Senn, 1975), American psychologists were confronted with a new conceptualization of human experience and intelligent activity. Called into question were the theoretical approaches that viewed intelligent activity as passive and stable.

This alternative view of development, coupled with multiple-factor analytical models of intelligence (Guilford, 1956, 1957, 1959), significantly altered the nature of test construction. No longer could intelligence be considered a general unitary ability. Instead, primary mental abilities were seen as constituting a part of intelligence. In addition, it was becoming increasingly apparent that an individual's level of functioning was not dependent solely on mental activity. With the popularization of Freudian theory, psychologists and educators began considering personal and social variables as important components of overall functioning (Stott & Ball, 1965).

The ideas proposed by Piaget (1952) and others (e.g., Escalona, 1950; Hunt, 1961) concerning the qualitative nature of development directly affected subsequent research and educational thought. Research studies demonstrated that the quality of the environment was an important factor in development (Bayley, 1954, 1955; Bradway, Thompson, and Cravens, 1958; Dennis & Najarian, 1957). Educators began calling for social intervention and early education for the economically disadvantaged and for the children of working mothers (Frank, 1938; Hunt, 1964; Hymes, 1944). These ideas were, no doubt, a result of the successes of the war nurseries and child care centers established by the 1940 Lanham Act (Braun & Edwards, 1972). With the successful launching of the Russian spacecraft Sputnik in 1957, the United States federal government began providing additional education funds for science and math programs (Osborn, 1991). All of these factors contributed to the development of the compensatory early childhood education programs of the 1960s and 1970s. Unfortunately, the previously designed infant and preschool assessment instruments were considered too subjective, culturally outdated, of poor validity, and inadequate in characterizing a child's level of functioning (Stott & Ball, 1965). Hence, new assessment devices that would reflect current theoretical concepts of the qualitative nature of development, contain a child- and family-oriented approach, and provide sufficient diagnostic applications were needed. The next period of major developments in preschool assessment was underway.

THE YEARS 1960–1980

Until the 1960s, the primary focus of the testing movement was the assessment of school-age children and military inductees (Parker, 1981). Beginning in the early 1960s, remarkable growth occurred in the testing of preschool children. This was primarily because of the significant role the federal government began to play in education. The most influential events were the funding of the 1964 Maternal, Child Health and Mental Retardation Act, the 1964 Educational Opportunity Act, and the 1965 Elementary and Secondary Education Act (Osborn, 1991). These programs provided improved educational and social opportunities for the children of poor families.

Although the period of social and educational concern of the late 1950s and early 1960s generated a few privately funded intervention programs, Head Start and Follow Through programs were the most widely recognized educational experiments. These programs directed attention to the need for effective program evaluation and adequate preschool assessment instruments.

HEAD START AND TEST DEVELOPMENT

Program orientation and goals in the Head Start Models usually reflected one of three philosophies: an emphasis on maturational principles that stressed a nurturing social-emotional environment; a behaviorist approach that emphasized highly structured didactic methods; or a cognitive-interactionist approach that focused on the child's construction of knowledge.

The original Head Start model programs varied in theoretical and instructional orientations; however, they were all required to establish the effectiveness of their program. Primarily through the efforts of Senator Robert Kennedy, a provision was made that federally funded programs have a performance-based evaluation design (Hoepfner, Stern, Nummedal, et. al., 1971). The continuation of funding was dependent on gains in intelligence scores, academic achievement, or some other measurable dimension. Because most of the measures discussed earlier were imprecise or inappropriate for young children (Stott & Ball, 1965) and often did not reflect program goals, many new measures were developed between 1965 and 1975. Some of the more notable measures included the McCarthy Scales of Children's Abilities (MSCA) (McCarthy, 1972), the Wechsler Preschool and Primary Scale of Intelligence (WPPSI) (Wechsler, 1967), and the Caldwell Preschool Inventory (CPI). The CPI formed the basis for curriculum objectives and was a forerunner of the criterion-referenced movement (Hoepfner et. al., 1971). With program evaluation as a central concern of early childhood education programs in the 1960s and 1970s, the majority of preschool assessment instruments were developed to measure the various goals of the programs. Thus, tests were devised to measure outcomes in the affective domain, the intellectual domain, the psychomotor domain, and the subject-achievement domain. These developments represented a significant shift because overall functioning was seen as a composite of numerous skills, abilities, and aptitudes.

In reviewing several listings of preschool instruments, one can see the impact of the early Head Start movement on preschool test construction (Dykes, Strickland and Munyer, 1979; Frost & Minisi, 1975; Hoepfner et al., 1971). More than 200 assessment instruments were constructed and published in the years 1960–1980. In 1971, the Center for the Study of Evaluation and the Early Childhood Research Center of the UCLA Graduate School of Education published a comprehensive evaluation guide of more than 120 preschool and kindergarten tests (Hoepfner et al., 1971). Their primary objective was to provide teachers, supervisors, and early childhood specialists with relevant information as to the validity, examinee appropriateness, administrative utility, and normed technical excellence of each test. Of 120 tests comprised of 630 subtests, only 7 subtests were rated as providing *good* validity. The ratings for examinee appropriateness and administrative utility were generally higher for most of the tests; however, the general ratings for normed technical excellence were either *poor* or *fair*.

Although additional preschool test construction continued (Barnes, 1982; Dykes et al., 1979; Wolery, 1994), there were still the age old measurement problems of inadequate test validity (content, construct, predictive) and inadequate standardization procedures. Such findings, coupled with identified myths of measurement and the social and cultural implications of testing (Bersoff, 1973; Houts, 1977; Laosa, 1991; Meisels, 1987; White, 1977) have raised concern about using test performance as the sole criterion for educational decision making. Indeed, major concerns have been raised about the use of invalid and unreliable screening and readiness tests for early childhood education placement (Meisels, 1987, 1992; Sheppard, 1992). These issues will be addressed later in this chapter.

IMPACT OF ADDITIONAL FEDERAL SUPPORT AND SPECIAL EDUCATION THROUGH THE 1990S

With the appropriation of federal funds for Head Start, Follow Through, and the Education Acts, university undergraduate and graduate teacher training programs began to proliferate. In addition, the government saw the need for expanding personnel training grants to the field of special education. Prior to 1960, few universities were adequately staffed with professors for training special education personnel (Meyen, 1978). By 1975, 61 federal laws related to the handicapped had been passed (Weintraub, Abeson, Ballard, & La Wor, 1976), with P.L. 94-142 serving as the cornerstone.

P.L. 94-142 mandated a free and appropriate public education for handicapped children in the least restrictive environment possible. Included within the provisions were parental input and the requirement that an Individual Education Program (IEP) be developed and maintained for each handicapped child. Integral to the development of the IEP is the evaluation and diagnosis of each child's level of functioning. The assessment devices for special education range from informal behavioral checklists to standardized tests (Rotatori, Fox, Sexton & Miller, 1990). In addition, the special education personnel rely on anecdotal information provided by parents and former teachers and observation of the child's behavior in the classroom. Once an adequate diagnosis of functional level has been ascertained, the instructional program is developed based on clearly stated educational objectives.

The mandate for IEPs holds for all exceptional children ages 3 to 21 at various levels of functioning. These include the mentally retarded, hard of hearing, deaf, speech impaired, visually impaired, severely emotionally disturbed, and the gifted and talented. The passage of the 1986 Education of the Handicapped Amendments (P.L. 99-457), required that all handicapped preschool children and infants and toddlers with special needs must be served by the states. Furthermore, identified preschoolers with special needs (including developmental delay) must be placed in the least restrictive environment possible, preferably with nonhandicapped peers (Wolery & Wilbers, 1994). This provision led many of the states to create interagency agreements between Head Start and child care centers and the public schools to serve handicapped preschool children.

Unfortunately, some states refused to allow Head Start and child care centers to contract with public school agencies based on the argument that those settings do not meet *regular* educational requirements (Weiner & Koppelman, 1987). Another problem centered on the definition of handicapped status used by the public schools. By holding to stringent definitions of handicapping conditions and requiring significant assessment data, public schools were able to exclude some mildly to moderately handicapped preschool children from being served.

In 1990, P.L. 101-576 reauthorized the Education for all Handicapped Children Act (P.L. 94-142) and renamed it the Individuals with Disabilities Education Act (IDEA); autism and traumatic brain injury were also established as two new categories. This reauthorization clarified special education as specially designed instruction that could be offered in the classroom, in hospitals and institutions, in the home, and in other settings such as community-based early childhood programs. While the states are required to ensure that the services provided are done so by "qualified personnel" who meet state-approved licensing, certification, or other comparable requirements that apply (Bruder, 1994), considerable flexibility is provided to the states in revising or expanding occupational and professional standards for personnel. With the most recent P.L. 108-446 reauthorization of IDEA in 2004 (Butler, 2004), the federal government has significantly increased the expectations for "highly qualified" teachers who will teach in the public schools.

The federal government's involvement in establishing educational program guidelines for Head Start and special education and providing substantial dollars for those programs has contributed significantly to the development of assessment devices for the early childhood years. Additionally, this involvement has helped to shape some very important legal parameters related to educational programs, testing, and to parents' rights to participate in the development of educational programs.

The 1975 passage of P.L 94-142 and subsequent reauthorizations (including the most recent of 2004) specifically established that a free, appropriate public education must be made available to all handicapped children between birth and age 21. These educational opportunity legislative acts mandated formal due process procedures for schools and service entities to follow. These included formal involvement of parents in planning, developing and implementing educational programs for their children, notice to parents and the children of educational programming changes, the right of the parents and the child to outside legal representation and mediation to resolve disputes, the right to refuse placement without a full and individual evaluation of the child's educational status and needs (including family needs for children younger than 3 years), and the right to seek outside testing if desired (Prasse, 1983; Wolery & Wilbers, 1994; Butler, 2004).

With regard to testing specifically, the trends in legislation and regulations (P.L. 94-142, P.L. 99-457, P.L 101-336 [Americans with Disabilities Act] P.L. 101-576, P.L. 105-17 and P.L. 108-446 [IDEA]; Office of Civil Rights, 2000), and court cases (Hobson vs. Hansen, 1967; Diana vs. State Board of Education, 1970; Guadalupe Organization, Inc. vs. Tempe School District No. 3, 1971; Covarrubias vs. San Diego Unified School District, 1971; Larry P. vs. Riles, 1979; PASE vs. Hannon, 1980) have shown clear expectations for special educational assessment requirements. These include:

- Tests and accompanying materials/procedures must be void of racial and/or cultural bias. Additionally, the child's native language must be considered when administering assessments.
- Tests and accompanying materials/procedures must be valid and administered by trained personnel. This requires the capacity to carefully interpret test results and observed behavior from a culturally and linguistically sensitive perspective (Shaw, Goode, Ringwalt, & Ayankoya, 2005).
- Tests and accompanying materials/procedures must be capable of assessing educational needs and yield academic outcome results.
- Appropriate educational programming for a child must consider multiple assessment procedures including obtaining information from the parent(s) and other relevant individuals. These assessments must be aligned with state standards and yield academic, developmental and functional information.
- A multidisciplinary team or group of persons that includes both special and regular education teachers, as well as the parent(s), must be a part of the evaluation.
- The child must be assessed in all areas related to the suspected disability. This is particularly crucial for those children designated as developmentally delayed.

Although these requirements relate to special education, the specific assessment requirements hold utility for all early childhood assessment. As evidence of this, they are in congruence with the Standards for Educational and Psychological Testing (American Educational Research Association, American Psychological Association, National Council on Measurement in Education [AERA, APA, NCME], 1999) for educational testing and the curriculum and assessment position statement of the National Association for the Education of Young Children and the National Association of Early Childhood Specialists in State Departments of Education (NAEYC, NAECS/SDE; 2003). In addition, the Revised Developmentally Appropriate Practices (Bredekamp & Copple, 1997) suggests similar assessment requirements.

Several changes to both the NCLB Act (Guddemi & Case, 2004; Jorgensen & Hoffman, 2003) and IDEA legislation (Butler, 2004) have increased the focus on standards, standards-based assessments, and educational accountability that extend even into the preschool years (Shore, Bodrova & Leong, 2004). Educational services offered under both initiatives require the use of scientifically based instructional practices that have been peer reviewed for acceptability. There is an increased focus on school readiness that incorporates preliteracy, language, and numeracy skills. All assessments must be aligned with state standards that display challenging academic content. For preschool children with disabilities, the assessments used must yield information on what the child knows and can do academically, developmentally, and functionally. This federal push for academically rigorous programming is clearly evident in the new program standards for Head Start and the numerous performance measures in the Head Start Family and Child Experiences Survey (FACES; Administration for Children and Families Office of Planning, Research & Evaluation, 2003).

THE GROWTH OF PUBLIC SCHOOL PRESCHOOL PROGRAMS AND THE DEVELOPMENTAL ASSESSMENT DEBATES

Considerable debate has been focused on the implementation of preschool programs within public schools (Strother, 1987). A number of national politicians and state legislatures are calling for increased investment in preschool education, while public commitment to early childhood education programs grew considerably during the late 1980s and continues to grow at a rapid rate (Barnett & Yarosz, 2004). Some of the major policy issues that define this high-growth period include the matter of funding, where the programs should be located, and which children should be served and by whom (Barnett & Yarosz, 2004; Kelley, 1996; Kelley & Surbeck, 1991; Schweinhart, Koshel, & Bridgeman, 1987).

The issue of which children should be served has raised numerous concerns. It has been argued that preschool programs are most beneficial for economically disadvantaged children and those "at risk of school failure" (Schweinhart et al., 1987; Zigler & Styfco, 1996 (the reference has 1994)). However, Barnett and Yarosz (2004) reported that less than half of children in poverty attend preschool at age 3 and 4. Moreover, they noted that, "The children with the least access to preschool education are those whose family incomes rest somewhat above the eligibility levels for targeted programs" (p. 1). How one determines the "at risk of school failure" child has fueled a major debate in early childhood circles that continues into the twenty-first century.

In several publications, Samuel Meisels (1987, 1992; 1998) raised a number of important issues pertinent to uses and abuses of preschool assessment devices. Specifically, Meisels argued that far too many children are being assessed with screening and readiness tests that have little or no validity and reliability data to support their use. As a result, children are being labeled as developmentally immature or not ready for school placement. Meisels argues, "Tests that exclude children from public education services or that delay their access to the educational mainstream . . . are antithetical to legal and constitutional rights to free education and equal protection. In addition, such tests and practices are incompatible with the belief systems, theoretical perspectives, and best practices of most early childhood educators" (Meisels, 1987, p. 71).

Specifically, Meisels challenged the use of the Gesell School Readiness Screening Test (Ilg & Ames, 1972), which is linked to the Gesell Preschool Examination (Haines, Ames,

& Gillespie, 1980) and the Developmental Assessment (Walker, 1992). Although thousands of public and private schools subscribed to the use of these tests, the Gesell tests have failed to display adequate psychological properties of validity and reliability. Furthermore, the developers of the tests use a concept of developmental age that has never been tested empirically (Meisels, 1987; 1998).

The Gesell tests are derived from a theoretical perspective (maturational) that focuses on time as the most important variable in behavior change. Hence, from a Gesellian perspective young immature children need only "the gift of time" to develop. This leads to the claim that, "perhaps 50% of school failures could be prevented or cured by proper placement based on a child's behavior age" (Ames, Gillespie, Haines, & Ilg, 1979, p. 182). Often as many as one third of children tested are recommended for "extra time" arrangements such as developmental kindergarten or transitional first grade (Walker, 1992).

The Gesell Institute cites several studies to support its claim that the readiness assessments are reliably predictive of school success (Lichtenstein, 1990; Walker, 1992; Wood, Powell, & Knight, 1984). However, according to Meisels (1987; 1992; 1998) and Shepard (Shepard & Smith, 1986; Shepard, 1992), the tests are fraught with error including judgmental bias of examiners, poor predictive power, and lack of evidence of any differential validity. These reviews and others (Bradley, 1985; Kaufman, 1985; Naglieri, 1985) question the use of the tests and cite the potential misuse and misinterpretation that could lead to serious placement problems.

Shepard and Smith (1986) and Shepard (1992) address the issue of assessing readiness. The authors state, "Scientific knowledge underlying readiness assessment is such that none of the existing tests is sufficiently accurate to justify removing children from their normal peer group and placing them in special two-year programs. In part the lack of high correlations with later school success is caused by the instability of the very traits we are seeking to measure (Shepard & Smith, 1986, p. 83)." Thus, extra-year schooling has not shown the achievement-related benefits that many thought would result, and, in some cases, children suffer socio-emotional harm (Shepard, 1992). Any achievement differences that are shown tend to level off by third grade (Shepard & Smith, 1986).

Unfortunately, the evidence obtained from controlled studies on the lack of academic benefits of extra-year placements does not always coincide with the beliefs of teachers and parents. In a study conducted by Kelley and Surbeck (1987), a small public school district was interested in examining the effects of a developmental kindergarten and first grade program. Specifically, the Early Prevention of School Failure Program (EPSF) was evaluated to determine if children tested for placement in an extra year of schooling benefited academically. School-related test data obtained on children placed in developmental kindergarten were compared to a random sample of children enrolled in regular kindergarten programs. The test results showed that the extra year of schooling did not benefit the developmental kindergarten children academically, yet 90% of the teachers and 76% of the parents surveyed believed that the EPSF program had helped the young children improve their academic performance. Moreover, most of the teachers and a majority of the parents believed that the children were carefully and accurately identified when placed in the developmental kindergarten. The lack of congruence between teacher and parent perceptions of program placement and impact and actual pupil academic benefits is intriguing. When further probed, the teachers and parents reported being unaware of the research and literature critical of the widespread and unwarranted use of developmental testing devices for placement purposes. Furthermore, in a national sample of kindergarten teachers' views about readiness, Meisels (1998) reported that there is no common view of readiness amongst teachers that can serve to support the use of most readiness tests. Without evidence that assessment results in direct benefits to the child, then the ritual use of even good tests is to be discouraged (Epstein, Schweinhart, DeBruin-Parecki, & Robin, 2004).

As suggested earlier, public school preschool programs for both typical and atypical young children are a reality in virtually every state in this country. According to the 2000 state-by-state census data on early education and care enrollments, there were 7,701,024 children ages 3 and 4 with 3,795,049 or 49.3% "enrolled in school" throughout the United States (Barnett & Yarosz, 2004). A significant portion of this enrollment is due to the 1997 and 2004 reauthorization of federal legislation covering children through the Individuals with Disabilities Education Act (IDEA), the federal support for Head Start, Even Start, and Reading First programs linked to the No Child Left Behind Act of 2001, and through state-funded prekindergarten programs. However, there are regional and ethnic differences in preschool education participation rates. Young Hispanic children, whose parents have the least education and income, and who live in the western region of our country, have a much lower rate of participation than other children (Barnett & Yarosz, 2004). These children are less likely to enter into kindergarten with the necessary knowledge and skills to succeed. Thus, the need for well-developed early childhood assessments and processes is apparent. Additionally, with services mandated for infants and toddlers with special needs and their families, the demand for well-designed birth-to-age-three assessments and family needs assessments continues to grow.

FUTURE ISSUES IN PRESCHOOL ASSESSMENT

The past few decades have witnessed significant interest in preschool children. Extensive longitudinal research on the effects of the Abecedarian Study, Chicago Parent Study, and the High/Scope Perry Preschool Project has shown significant benefits of high-quality early childhood programs for poor children that extend well into the adult years (Barnett, 2003; Zigler & Styfco, 1994). Moreover, several scientists have extended thinking about intelligent activity that includes multiple information processing components (Sternberg, 1988) and the possibility of separate multiple intelligences that are relatively autonomous and independent of one another (Gardner, 1983). While these efforts and those of others within the "intelligence" arena may assist in furthering the development of appropriate preschool assessment devices, it is becoming increasingly apparent that we must concentrate on developing an array of reliable and valid indices of social competence that include motivational history, personality, and socioemotional factors (Weinberg, 1989). Preschool children are qualitatively different from young infants and school-aged children. Thus, preschool assessment instruments of the 1980s and 1990s were designed in an attempt to capture that uniqueness and to interpret the findings within contexts of normal preschool development.

Some of the continued work in preschool assessment during this time included the following. During the 1980s, Kaufman and Kaufman (1983) developed the Kaufman Assessment Battery for Children (K-ABC). The K-ABC is designed to measure mental processing and achievement of children ages 2½ to 12½. This test has undergone another revision and is now the K-ABC II (see Kaufman and Lichtenberger, this edition).

In 1986, the Stanford-Binet Intelligence Scale was revised to produce a Fourth Edition (Thorndike, Hagen, & Sattler, 1986). This edition assesses the intelligence of children, adolescents, and adults in an age range of 2 years through 24 years. It, too, has undergone a recent revision and is now the Stanford-Binet Intelligence Scales, Fifth Edition (see Alfonso and Flanagan, this edition).

Additional preschool instruments included the Battelle Developmental Inventory (Newborg et at., 1984), the Bracken Basic Concept Scale (Bracken, 1984), the Early Screening Inventory (Meisels & Wiske, 1983), and the Peabody Picture Vocabulary Test-Revised (Dunn & Dunn, 1981) to name a few. Virtually all of these instruments and others have undergone recent revisions.

Each of these tests serves appropriate functions, yet limitations are also evident. As an example, Bracken (1987) examined many of the earlier versions of commonly used preschool instruments for their technical adequacy. In his study, Bracken examined the subtest internal consistencies, total test internal consistencies, test-retest reliabilities, subtest floors, item gradients, total test floor, and various forms of validity for each of the preschool instruments. By using these criteria, Bracken displayed the psychometric strengths and weaknesses of the various tests. He concluded ". . . preschool assessment below the age of 4 years seems to present the greatest psychometric problems. Selection of tests for use with low-functioning children below age 4 needs to be made with special care. As can be seen, many of these tests designed for preschool use are severely limited in floor, item gradient, and reliability, especially at the lower level" (Bracken, 1987, p. 325). In addition to the technical inadequacies, Meisels (1998) is highly critical of most preschool and kindergarten tests due to his conclusion that the research shows that only one fourth of early academic or cognitive performance is predicted from information obtained from those tests. Thus, he (Meisels, 1998) and others (Epstein et al., 2004) are encouraging the development of "systems of analyses so that test scores are interpreted as part of a broader authentic assessment that may include observations, portfolios, or ratings from teachers and/or parents" (p. 1).

Much of the work throughout the 1990s and into the new century has focused on revising many of the standard preschool assessment tests in an attempt to broaden their use with language minority children from other cultures and those children with special needs (Santos de Barona & Barona, 1991; Wolery, 1994; Shaw et al., 2005). The bulk of the newly revised instruments that are reviewed in this edition have also addressed many of the technical inadequacies that Bracken highlighted earlier. Moreover, revised versions of tests such as the Early Screening Inventory–Revised (Meisels, Marsden, Wiske, & Henderson, 1997) and the Work Sampling System (Meisels, Liaw, Dorfman, & Nelson, 1995) have demarcated the preschool years separate from the kindergarten period. Furthermore, standardization, reliability, and validity data are presented separately for the two groups, thereby increasing the utility of the inventories for comparative purposes. Finally, the new versions of the revised instruments are taking a more holistic and authentic view of children within a family, school and cultural context, and typically include parents, other family members, and teachers as viable and important sources of information (Henderson & Meisels, 1994; Meisels, 1997).

Since the field of early childhood education is evolving into a collaborative enterprise where multiple human service and educational programs work together to meet the comprehensive needs of children and families (Kagan, Goffin, Golub, & Pritchard, 1995; Kelley, 2004; Kelley, 1996; Kelley & Surbeck, 1991; Surbeck, 1995), the future trends for preschool assessment will undoubtedly focus on a multi-method, multi-disciplinary assessment process that includes significant family input. In addition to the use of multi-methods and measures, there is an increasing push at the federal and state levels for the use of scientifically based instructional practices and intervention services that are based on peer-reviewed research (Butler, 2004). As highlighted earlier, the Bush Administration's Good Start, Grow Smart initiative to strengthen Head Start and other early education programs (Early Reading First) requires a significant focus on achievements in preliteracy, language, and numeracy skills. Thus, well-designed individual and program evaluation measures become very important in these initiatives (Guddemi & Case, 2004).

The young children of the future who will enter our early care and education settings will be increasingly minority given the immigration and demographic changes occurring in the United States (Barnett & Yarosz, 2004). This will increase the burden on test authors and publishers to fully consider culture, language, and the role of prior experience and knowledge when crafting their assessment tools and processes. For children with disabilities, there are ethical and legal reasons for providing test accommodations or alternate assessments (Braden & Elliott, 2003). In addition, both the No Child Left Behind Act (NCLB), and the Individuals with Disabilities Education Act (IDEA) address the need for alternate assessments and test accommodations. According to Braden and Elliott (2003), these accommodations may include "altering the presentation format of test items and directions, altering the response format expected from a child, modifying timing elements of tests, selecting portions of a test based on the type of disability, altering the test setting and conditions, and substituting tests or alternate assessments" (p. 2).

Technology, in a variety of forms, is playing an increasing role in comprehensive preschool assessment measures. Many of the assessment tools have specialized web-based and CD-ROM software for scoring and producing customized reports. Others incorporate hand-held portable devices for use in classrooms. In addition to technical systems capabilities, questions raised by advancements in brain and neurological research offer intriguing ethical and professional challenges as scientists delve further into evidence, collected as early as in utero of precursors of intelligent and adaptive functioning. These advances in brain research were specifically acknowledged by the United States Congress in its most recent reauthorization of IDEA (Butler, 2004). Hence, the increases in our knowledge of how children develop and learn, joined with the policies that we implement to provide educational services and the measures we create to assess achievement and developmental status, all serve as complementary components in a comprehensive psychoeducational assessment program.

SUMMARY

Many of the theoretical and technical issues that have surfaced within the past 20 years were not seriously considered nor envisioned by individuals engaged in the early stages of development of preschool assessment. Although the primary concern in assessment initially was the identification and classification of those capable and incapable of learning, the tests were of a highly sensory nature. They focused predominately on the school-age child, and ultimately proved incapable of discriminating various levels of functioning. With the development of the Binet scales and the subsequent construction of related instruments, interest began to shift to the younger child; the issues of simple test validity, reliability, standardization procedures, and the assessment of higher mental abilities were also of concern. Many of the early tests and those that followed were constrained by a view that intelligence and its behavioral manifestations were static. This view of genetically fixed intelligence and performance was predominant until well into the 1950s; resultant test construction reflected this view. Eventually, new theories were proposed that posited a qualitative dimension to intelligent activity. Within this new arena, a child's environment and socio-cultural experiences were shown to be powerful influences on learning. These changes in social science also mirrored changes occurring in the broader socio-political realm. Equity and access to economic and educational opportunities were values espoused by citizens and politicians. Eventually, these values became principles of law, and there followed a decade of compensatory programs and educational intervention.

With millions of dollars in federal support, hundreds of new assessment instruments were constructed to measure the "whole child." Tests were developed to measure achievement, personality, cognitive functioning, adaptive behavior, and specific skills in a variety of areas including music and the arts. However, the majority of these assessment instruments continued to reflect questionable psychometric properties of validity and reliability as well as inadequate standardization procedures.

Today, with the complexities of child and family needs, the demand for additional comprehensive preschool assessment tools and procedures is apparent. Because the educational programs of the recent past were mandated to operate under new social, legal and educational conditions, it appears that diversity and variation in educational practice will necessitate changes in assessment techniques. Whereas in the past, large segments of the population under 5 years of age were typically ignored, current federal and state initiatives now mandate that the needs of children from birth to 5 years be addressed. Although the psychometric concerns for validity, reliability, standardization, and utility will continue to be important, the primary thrust for future activity will be how well the assessment instruments and processes assist in planning, monitoring, and evaluating human service and educational programs for children and families. States are under significant federal scrutiny to close the academic achievement gaps among ethnic groups and those children who are disabled as compared to typically developed children.

Because advanced medical breakthroughs are offering new insights into the functioning of the human brain, the media, politicians, and general population have, in a sense, rediscovered the importance of early care and education for our most vulnerable children. At this juncture, there are intriguing possibilities for genetic, surgical, environmental, and educational manipulations of human potential, giving new meaning to the phrase "early intervention." Such possibilities are fraught with educational, social, and political concerns. It is clear that new comprehensive, multimodal approaches to the psychoeducational assessment of preschool children (and younger) must reflect the dynamic nature of the young child and his/her socio-cultural contexts while respecting the inherent discontinuities in culture, language, and development that prove so difficult to measure. This elusive goal will remain a major challenge for the field of psychoeducational assessment as it proceeds through the twenty-first century.

REFERENCES

Administration for Children and Families, Office of Planning, Research & Evaluation (2003). *Head Start FACES 2000: A whole child perspective on program performance fourth progress report*. Retrieved (Ed: do you have a retrieval date?) from http://www.acf.hhs.gov/programs/opre/hs/faces/index.html

American Educational Research Association, American Psychological Association, & National Council on Measurement in Education (AERA, APA, NCME). (1999). *Standards for educational and psychological testing* (3rd ed.). Washington, D.C.: American Educational Research Association.

Ames, L. B., Gillespie, C., Haines, J., & Ilg, F. (1979). *The Gesell Institute's child from one to six.* New York: Harper & Row.

Ammons, R. B., & Ammons, H. S. (1948). *The Full Range Vocabulary Test.* New Orleans: Authors.

Ammons, R. B., & Holmes, J. C. (1949). The Full-Range Picture Vocabulary Tests: III, Results for a preschool age population. *Child Development, 20*, 5–14.

Anastasi, A. (1982). *Psychological testing* (5th ed.). New York: Macmillan.

Aries, P. (1962). *Centuries of childhood.* New York: Knopf.

Barnes, K. E. (1982). *Preschool screening: The measurement and prediction of children at-risk.* Springfield, IL: Thomas.

Barnett, W. S. (2003). High quality preschool: Why we need it and what it looks like. *Preschool Policy Matters*, Issue 1, New Brunswick, NJ: National Institute for Early Education Research.

Barnett, W. S., & Yarosz, D. J. (2004). Who goes to preschool and why does it matter? *Preschool Policy Matters*, Issue 8, New Brunswick, NJ: National Institute for Early Education Research.

Bayley, N. (1933). *The California First Year Mental Scale.* Berkley, Calif.: University of California Press.

Bayley, N. (1954). Some increasing parent-child similarities during the growth of children. *Journal of Educational Psychology, 45*, 1–21.

Bayley, N. (1955). On the growth of intelligence. *American Psychologist, 10*, 805–818.

Bersoff, D. N. (1973). Silk purses into sow's ears: The decline of psychological testing and a suggestion for its redemption. *American Psychologist, 28*, 892–899.

Binet, A., & Simon, T. (1905). Méthods nouvelles pour le diagnostic du niveau intellectuel des anormaux. *L'Année Psychologique, 11*, 191–244.

Bracken, B. A. (1984). *Bracken Basic Concept Scale.* San Antonio, TX: The Psychological Corporation.

Bracken, B. A. (1987). Limitations of preschool instrumentations and standards for minimal levels of technical adequacy. *Journal of Psychoeducational Assessment, 5*, 313–326.

Braden, J. P., & Elliott, S. N. (2003). *Accommodations on the Stanford-Binet Intelligence Scales, Fifth Edition.* (Stanford-Binet Intelligence Scales, Fifth Edition Assessment Services Bulletin No. 2). Itasca, IL: Riverside Publishing.

Bradley, R. H. (1985). Review of Gesell School Readiness Tests. In J. Mitchell, Jr. (Ed.). *The ninth mental measurements yearbook (Vol. I).* Lincoln, NE: The University of Nebraska Press.

Bradway, K. P. (1945). An experimental study of the factors associated with Stanford-Binet IQ changes from the preschool to the junior high school. *Journal of Genetic Psychology, 66*, 107.

Bradway, K., Thompson, C. W., & Cravens, R. B. (1958). Preschool IQ's after twenty-five years. *Journal of Educational Psychology, 49*, 278–281.

Braun, S., & Edwards, E. (1972). *History and theory of early childhood education.* Worthington, Ohio: Jones.

Bredekamp, S. & Copple, C. (Eds.). (1997). *Developmentally appropriate practice in early childhood education programs: Revised edition.* Washington, D.C.: National Association for the Education of Young Children.

Brenner, A. (1959). A new gestalt test for measuring readiness for school. *Merrill-Palmer Quarterly, 6*, 1–25.

Brooks, J., & Weinraub, M. (1976). A history of infant intelligence testing. In M. Lewis (Ed). *Origins of intelligence.* New York: Plenum Press.

Bruder, M. B. (1994). Working with members of other disciplines: Collaboration for success. In M. Wolery & J.S. Wilbers (Eds.). *Including children with special needs in early childhood programs.* Washington, D.C.: National Association for the Education of Young Children.

Burt, C. (1921). *Mental and scholastic tests.* London: King.

Butler, J. (2004). *H.R. 1350 Individuals with Disabilities Education Improvement Act of 2004 compared to IDEA '97.* Warrenton, VA: The Council of Parent Attorneys and Advocates, Inc.

Cattell, P. (1940). *The measurement of intelligence of infants and young children.* New York: Psychological Corporation.

Covarrubias vs. San Diego Unified School District. Civ. No. 70-394-S. (S.D. Cal., filed Feb. 1971).

Crissey, O. L. (1937). Mental development as related to institutional residence and educational achievement. *University of Iowa Studies in Child Welfare, 13*, 1.

Darwin, C. (1877). A biographical sketch of an infant. *Mind, 2*, 285–294.

DeForest, B. (1941). A study of the prognosis value of the Merrill-Palmer Scale of Mental Tests and the Minnesota Preschool Scale. *Journal of Genetic Psychology, 59*, 219–223.

De Mause, L. (1974). *The history of childhood*. New York: Psychohistory Press.

Dennis, W., & Najarian, P. (1957). Infant development under environmental handicap. *Psychological Monographs, 71* (7, Whole No. 436).

Diana vs. State Board of Education. C.A.N. C-70-37 R.F.P. (N.D. Cal., filed Feb. 3, 1970).

Dunn, L. M., & Dunn, L. M. (1981). *Peabody Picture Vocabulary Test–Revised*. Circle Pines, MN: American Guidance Service.

Dykes, J. K., Strickland, A. M., & Munyer, D. D. (1979). *Assessment and evaluation instruments for early childhood programs*. Gainesville, Fla.: Florida Educational Research and Development Council (Eric Document No. ED 171 378).

Epstein, A. S., Schweinhart, L. J., DeBruin-Parecki, A., & Robin, K. B. (2004). Preschool assessment: A guide to developing a balanced approach. *Preschool Policy Matters*, Issue 7, New Brunswick, NJ: National Institute for Early Education Research.

Escalona, S. K. (1950). The use of infant tests for predictive purposes. *Bulletin of the Meninger Clinic, 14*, 117–128.

Fancher, R. E. (1985). *The intelligence men: Makers of the IQ controversy*. New York: W.W. Norton & Co.

Fillmore, E. A. (1936). Iowa Tests for Young Children. *University of Iowa Studies in Child Welfare, 22*, 4.

Flanagan, J. S. (1938). Review of Measuring Intelligence by Termin and Merrill. *Harvard Educational Review, 8*, 130–133.

Frank, L. (1938). The fundamental needs of the child. *Mental Hygiene, 22*, 353–379.

Frost, J., & Minisi, R. (1975). *Early childhood assessment list*. Hightstown, N.J.: Northeast Area Learning Resource Center (ERIC Document NO. ED 136 474).

Gallagher, J. J. (1953). Clinical judgment and the Cattell Intelligence Scale. *Journal of Consulting Psychology, 17*, 303–305.

Gardner, H. (1983). *Frames of mind: The theory of multiple intelligence*. New York: Basic Books.

Garrett, H. E. (1946). A developmental theory of intelligence. *American Psychologist, 1*, 372–378.

Gesell, A. (1925). *The mental growth of the preschool child: A psychological outline of normal development from birth to the sixth year*. New York: Macmillan.

Gilliland, A. R. (1948). The measurement of the mentality of infants. *Child Development, 19*, 155–158.

Goddard, H. H. (1920). *Human efficiency and levels of intelligence*. Princeton: Princeton University Press.

Goodenough, F. L. (1926). *Measurement of intelligence by drawings*. Chicago: World Book.

Goodenough, F. L. (1928). A preliminary report on the effects of nursery school training upon intelligence test scores of young children. *27th Yearbook of the National Society for the Study of Education*, pp. 361–369.

Goodenough, F. L. (1939). Look to the evidence: A critique of recent experiments on raising the IQ. *Educational Methods, 19*, 73–79.

Goodenough, F. L. (1940). New evidence on environmental influence on intelligence. *39th Yearbook of the National Society for the Study of Education* (Part I), pp. 307–365.

Goodenough, F. L. (1949). *Mental testing*. New York: Rinehart.

Goodenough, F. L., & Maurer, K. M. (1940). The mental development of nursery school children compared with that of non-nursery school children. *39th Yearbook of the National Society for the Study of Education* (Part II), pp. 161–178.

Goodenough, F. L. & Maurer, K. M. (1942). *The mental growth of children from two to fourteen years*. Minneapolis: University of Minnesota Press.

Goodenough, F. L., & Maurer, K. M., & Van Wagenen, M. J. (1940). *Minnesota Preschool Scales: Manual of instructions*. Minneapolis: Educational Testing Bureau.

Griffiths, R. (1954). *The abilities of babies*. London: University of London Press.

Guadalupe Organization, Inc. vs. Tempe School District No. 3. Civ. No. 71-435 (D. Ariz., filed Aug. 9, 1971).

Guddemi, M., & Case, B. J. (2004). *Assessing young children*. (Harcourt Assessment Report). San Antonio, TX: Harcourt Assessment.

Guilford, J. P. (1956). The structure of intellect. *Psychological Bulletin, 53*, 267–293.

Guilford, J. P. (1957). *A revised structure of intellect* (Report No. 19). Los Angeles: University of Southern California, Psychology Laboratory.

Guilford, J. P. (1959). Three faces of intellect. *American Psychologist, 14*, 469–479.

Haines, J., Ames, L. B., & Gillespie, C. (1980). *The Gesell Preschool Test manual*. Lumberville, PA: Modern Learning Press.

Henderson, L. W., & Meisels, S. J. (1994). Parental involvement in the developmental screening of their young children: A multiple-source perspective. *Journal of Early Intervention, 18*(2), 141–154.

Hobson vs. Hansen. 209 F. Supp. 401 (D. D.C. 1967).

Hoepfner, R., Stern, C., Nummedal, S. G., et al. (1971). *CSE-ERIC preschool/kindergarten test evaluations*. Los Angeles: UCLA Graduate School of Education.

Hotelling, H. (1933). Analysis of a complex of statistical variables into principal components. *Journal of Educational Psychology, 24*, 417–520.

Houts, P. L. (Ed.). (1977). *The myth of measurability*. New York: Hart.

Hunt, J. McV. (1961). *Intelligence and experience*. New York: Ronald.

Hunt, J. McV. (1964). The psychological basis for using preschool enrichment as an antidote for cultural deprivation. *Merrill-Palmer Quarterly, 10*, 209–248.

Hymes, J. L. (1944). Who will need a post-war nursery school? *Kaiser Child Services Center Pamphlet for Teachers*, (No. 3).

Ilg, F. L., & Ames, L. B. (1972). *School Readiness*. New York: Harper & Row.

Johnson, G. E. (1894). Contributions to the psychology and pedagogy of feebleminded children. *Pedagogical Seminars, 3*, 246–301.

Jorgensen, M. A., & Hoffmann, J. (2003). *History of the No Child Left Behind Act of 2001 (NCLB)*. (Harcourt Assessment Report). San Antonio, TX: Harcourt Assessment, Inc.

Kagan, S., Goffin, S., Golub, S., & Pritchard, E. (1995). *Toward systemic reform: Service integration for young children and their families*. Falls Church, VA: National Center for Service Integration.

Katz, M. B. (1972). *Class, bureaucracy, and schools*. New York: Praeger.

Kaufman, A. S., & Kaufman, N. L. (1983). *Kaufman Assessment Battery for Children*. Circle Pines, MN: American Guidance Service.

Kaufman, N. L. (1985). Review of Gesell Preschool Test. In J. Mitchell, Jr. (Ed.). *The ninth mental measurements yearbook* (Vol. I). Lincoln, NE: The University of Nebraska Press.

Kelley, M. F. (1996). Collaboration in early childhood education. *Journal of Educational and Psychological Consultation, 7*(3), 275–282.

Kelley, M. F. (2004). Reconciling the philosophy and promise of Itinerate Consultation with the realities of practice. *Journal of Educational and Psychological Consultation, 15*(2), 183–190.

Kelley, M. F., Sexton, D., & Surbeck, E. (1990). Traditional psychometric assessment approaches. In A. F. Rotatori, R. A. Fox, D.Sexton, & J. Miller. (Eds.). *Comprehensive assessment in Special Education: Approaches, procedures and concerns*. Springfield, IL: Thomas.

Kelley, M. F., & Surbeck, E. (1987). *Evaluation report of the Littleton School District Early Prevention of School Failure Program*. Phoenix, AZ: Michael F. Kelley & Associates.

Kelley, M. F., & Surbeck, E. (1991). *Restructuring early childhood education*. Bloomington, IN: Phi Delta Kappa Educational Foundation.

Kelley, T. L. (1935). *Essential traits of mental life*. Cambridge, MA.: Harvard University Press.

Krugman, M. (1939). Some impressions of the revised Stanford-Binet scale. *Journal of Educational Psychology, 30*, 594–603.

Kuhlmann, F. (1912). A revision of the Binet-Simon system for measuring the intelligence of children. *Journal of Psycho-Asthenics Monographs Supplement, 1*(1), 1–41.

Kuhlmann, F. (1914). *A handbook of mental tests*. Baltimore: Warwick & York.

Laosa, L. M. (1991). The cultural context of construct validity and the ethics of generalizability. *Early Childhood Research Quarterly, 6*, 313–321.

Larry P. vs. Riles. 495 F. Supp. 96 (N.D. Cal. 1979).

Lascarides, V. C., & Hinitz, B. F. (2000). *History of early childhood education*. New York: Falmer Press.

Leiter, R. G. (1948). *International Performance Scale*. Chicago: Stoelting Co.

Lichtenstein, R. (1990). Psychometric characteristics and appropriate uses of the Gesell School Readiness Screening Test. *Early Childhood Research Quarterly, 5*, 359–378.

McCarthy, D. (1972). *The McCarthy Scales of Children's Abilities*. San Antonio, TX: The Psychological Corporation.

McHugh, G. (1943). Changes in IQ at the public school kindergarten level. *Psychological Monographs, 55*, 2.

Meisels, S. J. (1987). Uses and abuses of developmental screening and school readiness testing. *Young Children, 42*(2), 4–6, 68–73.

Meisels, S. J. (1992). The Lake Wobegon effect reversed: Commentary on "The Gesell Assessment: Psychometric properties. *Early Childhood Research Quarterly, 7*, 45–46.

Meisels, S. J. (1997). Using Work Sampling in authentic performance assessments. *Educational Leadership, 54*, 60–65.

Meisels, S. J. (1998). *Assessing reading* (CIERA Report # 3–002). Ann Arbor, MI: Center for the Improvement of Early Reading Achievement.

Meisels, S. J., Liaw, F. R., Dorfman, A. B., & Nelson, R. (1995). The Work Sampling System: Reliability and validity of a performance assessment for young children. *Early Childhood Research Quarterly, 10*(3), 277–296.

Meisels, S. J., Marsden, D. B., Wiske, M. S., & Henderson, L. W. (1997). *Early Screening Inventory–Revised: Examiner's Manual*. Ann Arbor, MI: Rebus.

Meisels, S. J., & Wiske, M. S. (1983). *Early Screening Inventory*. New York: Teachers College Press.

Meyen, E. L. (1978). *Exceptional children and youth: An introduction*. Denver: Love.

Mowrer, W. M. C. (1934). Performance of children in Stutman tests. *Child Development, 5*, 93–96.

Naglieri, J. A. (1985). Review of Gesell Preschool Tests. In J. Mitchell, Jr. (Ed.). *The ninth mental measurements yearbook* (Vol. I). Lincoln, NE: The University of Nebraska Press.

National Association for the Education of Young Children & National Association of Early Childhood Specialists in State Departments of Education. (2003). *Early childhood curriculum, assessment and program evaluation*. (Position statement). Washington, DC: NAEYC. Retrieved from *http://www.naeyc.org/about/positions/pdf/pscape.pdf* (available from the Web only).

Newborg, J., Stock, J. R., Wnek, L., Guidubaldi, J., & Svinicki, J. (1984). *Battelle Developmental Inventory*. Allen, TX: DLM/Teaching Resources.

Office of Civil Rights. (2000). *The use of tests as part of high stakes decision-making for students: A resource guide for educator and policy makers*. Washington, DC: U.S. Department of Education.

Osborn, D. K. (1991). *Early childhood education in historical perspective (3rd ed.)*. Athens, GA: Daye Press.

Parker, F. (1981). Ideas that shaped American Schools. *Phi Delta Kappan, 62*(5), 314–319. *PASE vs. Hannon*. No. 74-C-3586 (N.D. Ill., July 16, 1980).

Piaget, J. (1952). *The origins of intelligence in children* (M. Cook, trans.). New York: Holt.

Pinter, R. (1923). *Intelligence testing*. New York: Holt.

Pollack, R. H., & Brenner, M. W. (1969). *The experimental psychology of Alfred Binet*. New York: Springer.

Prasse, D. P. (1983). Legal issues underlying preschool assessment. In K. D. Paget & B. A. Bracken (Eds.). *The psychoeducational assessment of preschool children*. Orlando, FL: Grune & Stratton.

Preyer, W. (1882). *The mind of the child*. New York: Springer.

Rotatori, A. F., Fox, R. A., Sexton, J. D., & Miller, J. H. (Eds.). (1990). *Comprehensive assessment in Special Education: Approaches, procedures and concerns*. Springfield, IL: Thomas.

Rust, M. M. (1931). The effects of resistance on intelligence scores of young children. *Child Development Monographs*, (No. 6).

Santos De Barona, M., & Barona, A. (1991). The assessment of culturally and linguistically different preschoolers. *Early Childhood Research Quarterly, 6*, 363–376.

Schweinhart, L. J., Koshel, J. J., & Bridgeman, A. (1987). Policy options for preschool programs. *Phi Delta Kappan, 68*(7), 524–529.

Sears, R. R. (1975). Your ancients revisited: A history of child development. In E. M. Heatherington (Ed.). *Review of child development research* (Vol. 5). Chicago: University of Chicago Press.

Senn, M. J. E. (1975). Insights on the child development movement in the United States. *Monographs of the Society for Research in Child Development, 40*(3–4. Whole No.161).

Shaw, E., Goode, S., Ringwalt, S., & Ayankoya, B. (2005). *Early identification of culturally and linguistically diverse children (Aged 0–5)*. Chapel Hill, NC: NECTAC Clearinghouse on Early Intervention & Early Childhood Special Education.

Shepard, L. A. (1992). Psychometric properties of the Gesell Developmental Assessment: A critique. *Early Childhood Research Quarterly, 7*, 47–52.

Shepard, L. A., & Smith, M. L. (1986). Synthesis of research on school readiness and kindergarten retention. *Educational Leadership, 44*(3), 78–86.

Shinn, M. (1900). *The biography of a baby*. Boston: Houghton Mifflin.

Shore, R., Bodrova, E., & Long, D. (2004). *Child outcome standards in pre-K programs: What are standards; what is needed to make them work?* Preschool Policy Matters, Issue 5, New Brunswick, NJ: National Institute for Early Education Research.

Simpson, B. R. (1939). The wandering IQ: Is it time to settle down? *Journal of Psychology, 7*, 351–367.

Skeels, H. M. (1938). Mental development of children in foster homes. *Journal of Consulting Psychology, 2*, 33–34.

Skodak, M. (1939). Children in foster homes: A study of mental development. *University of Iowa Studies in Child Welfare, 16*, 1.

Stern, W. (1914). *The psychological methods of testing intelligence*. Baltimore: Warwick & York.

Stern, W. (1924). *Psychology of early childhood up to the sixth year of age*. New York: Henry Hal. (Originally published, 1914).

Sternberg, R. J. (1988). Intellectual development: Psychometric and information-processing approaches. In M. H. Bornstein & M. E. Lamb (Eds.). *Developmental psychology: An advanced textbook* (2nd ed.). Hillsdale, NJ: Lawrence Erlbaum Associates.

Stott, L. H., & Ball, R. S. (1965). Infant and preschool mental tests: Review and evaluation. *Monographs of the Society for Research in Child Development, 30*(3, Whole No. 101).

Strother, D. B. (1987). Preschool children in the public schools: Good investment? Or bad? *Phi Delta Kappan, 69*(4), 304–308.

Stutsman, R. (1931). *Mental measurement of preschool children*. New York: World Book.

Surbeck, E. (1995). Professionalism in early childhood teacher education: Service integration and interprofessional education. *Journal of Early Childhood Teacher Education, 16*(3), 15–17.

Terman, L. M. (1916). *The measurement of intelligence: An explanation of and a complete guide for the use of the Stanford revision and extension of the Binet-Simon Intelligence Scale*. Boston: Houghton Mifflin.

Terman, L. M., & Merrill, M. A. (1937). *Measuring intelligence*. Boston: Houghton Mifflin.

Thorndike, E. L. (1921). Intelligence and its measurement. *Journal of Educational Research, 12*, 124–127.

Thorndike, R. L., Hagen, E. P., & Sattler, J. M. (1986*). Stanford-Binet Intelligence Scale, Fourth Edition*. Chicago: Riverside.

Thurstone, L. L. (1935). *The vectors of the mind*. Chicago: The University of Chicago Press.

Thurstone, L. L. (1938). *Primary mental abilities*. Chicago: The University of Chicago Press.

Ulich, R. (1945). *History of educational thought*. New York: American Book.

Ulich, R. (1947). *Three thousand years of educational wisdom*. Cambridge, MA: Harvard University Press.

U.S. Congress, Office of Technology Assessment. (1992). *Testing in American schools: Asking the right questions*. OTA-SET-519. Washington, D.C: Government Printing Office.

Walker, R. N. (1992). The Gesell Developmental Assessment: Psychometric properties. *Early Childhood Research Quarterly, 7*, 21–43.

Watson, J. B., & Watson, R. R. (1928). *The psychological care of the infant and child*. New York: Norton.

Wechsler, D. (1949). *Manual for the Wechsler Intelligence Scale for Children*. New York: The Psychological Corporation.

Wechsler, D. (1967). *Wechsler Preschool and Primary Scale of Intelligence*. San Antonio, TX: The Psychological Corporation.

Weinberg, R. A. (1989). Intelligence and IQ: Landmark issues and great debates. *American Psychologist, 44*(2), 98–104.

Weiner, R., & Koppelman, J. (1987). *From birth to five: Serving the youngest handicapped children*. Alexandria, VA: Capitol Publications.

Weintraub, F. J., Abeson, A., Ballard, J., & La Wor, M. L. (Eds.). (1976). *Public policy and the education of exceptional children*. Reston, VA: Council for Exceptional Children.

Wellman, B. L. (1932a). Some new bases for interpretation of the IQ. *Journal of Genetic Psychology, 41*, 116–126.

Wellman, B. L. (1932b). The effects of preschool attendance upon the IQ. *Journal of Experimental Education, 1*, 48–49.

Wellman, B. L. (1934). Growth of intelligence under different school environments. *Journal of Experimental Education, 3*, 59–83.

Wellman, B. L. (1940). The meaning of environment. *39th Yearbook of the National Society for the Study of Education* (Part I), pp. 21–40.

White, S. H. (1977). Social implications of IQ. In P. Houts (Ed.). *The myth of measurability*. New York: Hart.

Wolery, M. (1994). Assessing children with special needs. In M. Wolery & J. S. Wilbers (Eds.). *Including children with special needs in early childhood programs*. Washington, D.C.: National Association for the Education of Young Children.

Wolery, M., & Wilbers, J. S. (Eds.). (1994). *Including children with special needs in early childhood programs*. Washington, D.C.: National Association for the Education of Young Children.

Wolf, T. H. (1973). *Alfred Binet*. Chicago: University of Chicago Press.

Wood, C., Powell, S., & Knight, R. C. (1984). Predicting school readiness: The validity of developmental age. *Journal of Learning Disabilities, 17*, 8–11.

Yerkes, R. M., & Foster, J. C. (1923). *The point scale for measuring mental ability*. Baltimore: Warwick & York.

Zigler, E., & Styfco, S. J. (1994). Is the Perry Preschool better than Head Start? Yes and no. *Early Childhood Research Quarterly, 9*, 269–287.

2

Issues in Preschool Assessment

Richard J. Nagle
Appalachian State University

For the past several decades, there has been increasing emphasis on the assessment of preschool children. Many factors have influenced this movement, including the effectiveness of preschool and early intervention programs, the national agenda of having all children ready for school, and research with young children that has demonstrated the importance of early experiences for later development. Without question the most important influence has been federal legislation. In 1975 the Education for All Handicapped Children Act (Public Law 94-142)) was passed and mandated that all school-age children with disabilities must receive a free and appropriate education in the least restricted environment. Under Public Law (P.L.) 94-142, schools were also required to provide services to preschool children with disabilities, 3 to 5 years old, to the extent that they served their age mates with disabilities.

P.L. 94-142 was later amended in 1986 with the passage of P.L. 99-457. This legislation required states to provide a free and appropriate public education to children with disabilities from ages 3 to 5 (Part B, Section 619). Regulations that governed practices with school-age children were then applied to the assessment of preschool children (McLean, 1996). An additional component of this legislation, Part H, established incentives for states to voluntarily develop services to infants and toddlers with special needs. More recent legislation has reauthorized and changed some portions of the law. P.L. 101-476 (1990) renamed P.L. 94-142 to the Individuals with Disabilities Education Act (IDEA) and P.L. 99-457 and amended both Parts B and H of Section 619.

Under IDEA, Part B, preschool children are eligible for special and related services under the same disabilities categories as older children. These categories include mental retardation, hearing impairments including deafness, speech or language impairments, visual impairments including blindness, serious emotional disturbance, orthopedic disabilities, autism, traumatic brain injury, other health impairments, or specific learning disabilities. Considerable concerns have been raised in the professional community about how applicable these disability categories are for very young children (Danaher, 1995). According to Danaher, the developmental domains in preschoolers are so interrelated that a disability resulting in developmental delays may not be readily determined. The requirement to identify a disability may also lead to misdiagnosis and inappropriate services. Furthermore, the inherent dangers of premature labeling may have a stigmatizing effect despite appropriate progress in an early intervention program. In view of these concerns, P.L.

102-119 gives states the option of incorporating an additional category for children, ages 3 to 5, who have developmental delays (Danaher, 1995). This preschool-specific organization includes children experiencing developmental delays in one or more of the following areas: physical development, cognitive development, communication development, social or emotional development, or adaptive development. These developmental delays are defined by the state and are measured by appropriate diagnostic instruments and procedures. The 1997 reauthorization of IDEA extends the definition of preschool children to 9 years for the purpose of providing noncategorical services to these children. The IDEA Improvement Act of 2004 clarified that the age range for developmental delay is ages 3 to 9, or any subset of that range, including 3 to 5 years (Danaher, 2005).

In order to ascertain how states are using the disability categorizations and whether they have incorporated a preschool-specific eligibility category, Danaher (1995) has surveyed special education coordinators in each state and the District of Columbia. She found that only seven states use all Part B categories and no preschool-specific category. Another additional 21 states use Part B categories and a preschool-specific category that frequently replaces the omitted Part B category. Finally, eight states do not use any Part B categories for preschoolers and have adopted either noncategorical criteria or preschool-specific categories exclusively. These overall findings suggest the increasing use of the preschool-specific category when compared to previous similar surveys conducted in the early 1990s (McLean, 1996). Because states may also develop their own criteria for what constitutes a significant developmental delay that may require special education or related services, a broad range of qualitative and quantitative eligibility requirements has been developed across the country.

In a more recent survey, Danaher (2005) was interested in examining current state eligibility policies for young children under Part B of IDEA to determine if they had evolved to reflect best practice and responsiveness to revisions in federal legislation. She found that all 50 states and the District of Columbia now include a disability category unique to young children. It was also observed that 36 states use "developmental delay" or a similar term such as "significant developmental delay" as a disability category for eligible children in addition to other Part B categories. Twenty-one of these states extend the developmental delay category beyond age 5. Eligibility criteria for developmental delay were also found to vary across states as in previous surveys. Danaher noted that 43 states use quantitative criteria such as scores on developmental tests. Most states using norm-referenced criteria (35 of 38) use 2 standard deviations below the mean in one developmental area or 1.5 standard deviations below the mean in two or more developmental domains. It was also found that 14 states permitted clinical/professional judgment or informed team consensus in lieu of test scores to determine eligibility.

These historical and legislative developments have created the need for assessment activities in various areas of early childhood education programming. Nevertheless, issues related to premature labeling, rapid developmental change, and the need to assess within a context of situational specificity make the process of meeting the requirements of legislative mandates for very young children challenging (Paget & Nagle, 1986). Therefore, professionals must enter the assessment process with the understanding that assessments of preschool children are conducted for reasons beyond classification.

The expansion of educational services to young children with disabilities has expanded the role of the school psychologist to include preschool assessment activities (Kelley & Surbeck, 1991; Paget & Nagle, 1986). In 1991, The National Association of School Psychologists (NASP), recognizing the importance of early identification and intervention for young children's psychological and developmental difficulties, adopted a position statement on early childhood assessment to guide the fair and accurate identification of the developmental needs of young children (Bracken, Bagnato, & Barnett, 1991). This position statement was later revised in 2005 (National Association of School Psychologists, 2005).

The current NASP position endorses multidisciplinary team assessments within an ecological model that includes multiple procedures, multiple sources of information, across multiple settings, and across time in order to yield a comprehensive viewpoint of the child's abilities. These multidimensional assessments should be linked to intervention strategies and should be conceptualized using more than a single methodology or theoretical framework. Furthermore, the position also underscores the importance of the full integration of parents and/or caretakers into the assessment process, including systematic data gathering in the natural environment.

The foundation of the NASP statement on early childhood assessment practices is based on evidence garnered through research and professional practice. This chapter will discuss several critical issues that have emerged as psychologists in preschool settings strive to promote best practice during assessment activities.

PURPOSES OF PRESCHOOL ASSESSMENT

Assessments in educational settings are conducted to gather information, which can be used to make appropriate decisions about children that will promote their educational and Psychological development. Within preschool settings, the process of assessment is appropriate when it is systematic, multidisciplinary, and based on the everyday tasks of childhood (Mindes, Ireton, & Mardell-Czudnowski, 1996, p. 10). These assessments should be comprehensive and include information across the developmental areas of motor skills, temperament, language, cognition, and social/emotional development. A preschool child may be assessed for many specific reasons, including eligibility for special programs for developmentally disabled children, kindergarten screening, placement in educationally competitive environments, and evaluation of a community program. For these and other reasons, the purposes of preschool assessment may be grouped into several general areas that include screening, diagnosis, evaluation of the child's progress, and program evaluation (Boehm & Sandberg, 1982). According to Bagnato and Neisworth (1991), these major goals or purposes should be viewed as a continuous process culminating with individualized programming or intervention and ongoing monitoring of the child's progress in the intervention program.

Screening

Screening involves the evaluation of large groups of children with brief, low-cost procedures to identify those children who may need further, diagnostic assessment to qualify for special programs or early intervention services from those who do not require follow-up. Because screening activities are designed not to provide an extensive or in-depth evaluation, a primary concern involves the accuracy of decisions based on screening test information. Specifically, these include identifying a child "at risk" when no significant problem exists (false positive) or failing to identify a child with a problem (false negative). The validity of screening devices is usually described in terms of the ratios of sensitivity and specificity. Sensitivity refers to the proportion of those children requiring further services and identified as such, whereas specificity is defined as the proportion of children in the non target group who are correctly classified (Lichtenstein & Ireton, 1991). Several recent validity analyses of screening tests (Carran & Scott, 1992; Gredler, 1997) have indicated better specificity than sensitivity indexes. In other words, a high proportion of children performing well at follow-up were children not identified as at risk, but a considerable portion of children identified as at risk at screening were performing adequately at follow-up. Beyond validity issues, the impact of misclassifications on children and their parents should be a major concern for professionals. The occurrence of a false positive classification may create substantial anxiety among parents and may result in unnecessary worry and time as well as the expense of further diagnostic work. Perhaps more serious outcomes are involved in cases of false negatives in which the children in need of services lose the opportunity of participating in early intervention services (Lichtenstein & Ireton, 1991).

Diagnosis

Diagnostic assessment usually involves the follow-up evaluation of children identified as having a potential problem during the screening process. The level of assessment is quite comprehensive and should include a broad range of methods, including formal and informal types of data collection, obtained from multiple sources across different settings (Bagnato & Neisworth, 1991; Meisels & Provence, 1989). These procedures usually include norm-based standardized instruments across multiple behavioral domains. The primary objectives of these diagnostic activities are to determine whether a problem or special need exists, ascertain child and family strengths and weaknesses, determine causes of the problem, and to decide what services, interventions, or programs best meet the individual needs of the child (Paget & Nagle, 1986).

Diagnostic assessment may also be focused on determining eligibility for early intervention services. Information gleaned during diagnostic evaluation may also be used to guide in the selection and formulation of intervention programming. Because diagnostic decision making is done prior to entry into early intervention services (Bagnato & Neisworth, 1991) and because preschoolers show rapid developmental changes, frequent reevaluation is commonplace. Consequently, initial diagnostic information and the results from periodic reevaluation are compared to monitor the child's progress and the effectiveness of the child's program in meeting his or her needs (Paget & Nagle, 1986).

Individual Program Planning and Monitoring

It has been stated that intervention starts with the first step in the assessment process (Bagnato & Neisworth, 1991). The link between assessment and intervention is necessary in order to formulate goals and procedures to meet the child's needs. Information gleaned from assessment activities is, therefore, used for program planning, and the child's progress is monitored continually by examining the level of attainment of curricular objectives. When the child's progress is summated over the course of the program, these assessment data may be used to document program effectiveness. There is growing support for the use of curriculum-based testing for these activities (Bagnato & Neisworth, 1991, 1994) as reflected in position statements of professional organizations (i.e., NASP) and changes in federal law. Losardo and Notari-Syverson (2001) provide excellent discussions on ways to develop assessment systems which are keyed to the educational and intervention settings.

Program Evaluation

Program evaluation is the "process which the quality of a program is assessed" (Benner, 1992, p. 300). According to Benner, both accountability and documentation of program efficacy are essential components to program evaluation. A primary focus of program evaluation should be to show which specific features of the program impact program effectiveness. Therefore, not only should emphasis be placed on outcome assessment but also on reasons why changes may have occurred. By studying the processes that underlie program success, evaluations can begin to suggest causal links between program activities and behavior change so that successful preschool programs could be replicated in a variety of settings (Carta & Greenwood, 1985). Program evaluation efforts are also conducted for program justification and improvement (Fitzgibbon & Morris, 1987; Vandiver & Suarez, 1980). Information resulting from program evaluations may be used by agency decision-makers to continue funding and to identify and address elements of the program that require modification.

UNIQUENESS OF PRESCHOOL CHILDREN

Preschool assessment is a complex and challenging professional task (Bracken & Walker, 1997; Lidz, 1991). Effective assessment activities may be bounded by a limited understanding and conceptualization of the growth and development of preschool children (Bailey, 1996). Preschool children comprise a very unique population that is qualitatively different from their school-age counterparts. Many of the characteristics that are typical of preschool children make reliable and valid assessment difficult. One of the most distinguishing features of preschool children is rapid developmental change (Kelley & Melton, 1993). Research suggests that this rapid growth across various domains may be discontinuous and unstable (Bailey, 1996), that many children will show highly diverse rates of maturation (Romero, 1992), and spurts in development are common observations during the preschool years (Culbertson & Willis, 1993). A critical point derived from these developmental issues is understanding the importance of emerging skills as extensions of and complements to acquired skills, and learning processes as vital adjuncts to products of learning (Barnett, 1984; Paget & Nagle, 1986).

The behavior of young children within the testing situation may also affect the accuracy of test results. Preschoolers typically have short attention spans, high levels of activity, high distractibility, low tolerance for frustration, and are likely to fatigue easily. They approach the test session with a different motivational style than older children and tend not to place importance on answering questions correctly, persisting on test items, pleasing the examiner, or responding to social reinforcement. For most preschool children, the test situation represents new surroundings with an unfamiliar adult. Preschool children vary considerably in their experiential and cultural backgrounds and in their levels of exposure to persons and environments outside the home (Romero, 1992). Some children may have prior experience in preschool environments while others have not had comparable experiences. Because of this, the assessor must be vigilant to individual differences in response style and must be sensitive to potential problems with shyness, verbal facility, and interpersonal discomfort (Ulrey, 1982). Several authors (Bracken & Walker, 1997; Paget, 1991; Romero, 1992) provide excellent discussions on facilitating child performance in assessment settings.

The issues of developmental change, emerging skills, behavioral fluctuation, situational variables, and experiential background all strongly influence the psychometric integrity of procedures used at the preschool level. Because of these influences, lower estimates of stability across settings and test intervals (Boehm & Sandberg, 1982; Bracken & Walker, 1997) are more likely to be obtained among preschool populations. These stability data should be viewed as reflections of the rapid developmental change that is characteristic of this population and underscore the necessity of expanding the scope and time frame of assessments to measure these changes. Multimethod-multisource assessments should, therefore, be designed and conducted periodically.

The lower stability estimate of preschool assessment tools also affects the manner in which inferences should be made about future developmental functioning. Because many tests have inherent inadequacies with stability, particularly measures of cognitive ability, test scores are most appropriately interpreted as reflecting current developmental levels (Flanagan & Alfonso, 1995).

ISSUES IN PRESCHOOL INSTRUMENTATION

Technical Adequacy of Preschool Instruments.   Selecting assessment devices with adequate psychometric properties is another challenge for professionals involved in the assessment of preschoolers. With changing legal mandates, the number of young children who are referred for psychoeducational assessments will increase. Furthermore, assessors will need to be attentive to the quality of the instruments they use in these activities (Bracken, 1987). Several studies have been directed at evaluating the psychometric properties of commonly used preschool instruments of the post-P.L. 99-457 era.

Bracken (1987) examined 10 preschool instruments. Five instruments that were commonly used for educational placement decisions included the Battelle Developmental Inventory (Newborg, Stock, Wnek, Guidubaldi, & Svinicki, 1984), the Stanford-Binet Intelligence Scale: Fourth Edition (S-B IV; Thorndike, Hagen, & Sattler, 1986), the Kaufman Assessment Battery for Children (K-ABC; Kaufman & Kaufman, 1983), the McCarthy Scales of Children's Abilities (MSCA; McCarthy, 1972), and the Wechsler Preschool and Primary Scale of Intelligence (WPPSI; Wechsler, 1967). Five individual diagnostic instruments used to assess specific skills and/or abilities included the Bracken Basic Concept Scale (BBCS; Bracken, 1984), the Columbia Mental Maturity Scale (Burgemeister, Blum, & Lorge, 1972), the Miller Assessment for Preschoolers (MAP; Miller, 1982), the Peabody Picture Vocabulary Test–Revised (PPVT–R; Dunn & Dunn, 1981), and the Token Test for Children (DiSimoni, 1978).

The technical adequacy of these instruments was evaluated through various indexes of reliability (median subtest reliability, total test internal consistency, and total test stability coefficients), subtest and total test floors, subtest item gradients, and provision of validity information. For each of these areas, Bracken (1987) delineated minimal standards of technical adequacy. These areas were selected because of their central importance in test selection and the interpretation of assessment results.

The reliability of a test refers to the degree to which a child's score is consistent (internal consistency) and stable (test-retest reliability) across time (Anastasi & Urbina, 1997). Adequate internal consistency for subtest and total test scores allows the assessor to assume that the items that comprise the test are highly related and measure a similar domain of behavior. During the assessment process, this permits a more concise and clear interpretation of test scores (Flanagan & Alfonso, 1995). Test-retest reliability or stability is extremely important because it places constraints or limits on the validity of the test. Test-retest reliability for preschool instruments can be affected by a number of variables (Bracken & Walker, 1997). According to Bracken and Walker, the variables that need to be considered in evaluating test-retest reliability include the expected duration of the stability of assessed behavioral levels, whether all assessed skills should be similarly stable over time, the degree that intervening environmental influences will affect the stability of different behavioral domains, and the extent to which normal developmental progression may affect stability.

Another dimension of technical adequacy involves test floors. Test floors refer to the availability of standard scores that are at least two standard deviations below the mean or the presence of a sufficient number of easy items to allow differentiation between levels of test performance. For example, in the assessment of intellectual ability, tests that do not have adequate floor would not be able to discriminate between children with normal abilities from those with mental retardation based on the criteria of the American Association on Mental Retardation (1992), Adequate test floor is also needed to be able to differentiate average, low-average, borderline, and other functioning on a given assessment tool. In instances when poor floor exists, scores may become unduly inflated and, consequently, provide misleading information (Bracken & Walker, 1997). This potential shortcoming is particularly germane for preschool children because many preschool assessment cases have the goal of determining developmental delay based on a significant discrepancy between the referred child's test performance and that of same-age peers.

Item gradients are an additional technical quality that is crucial in preschool assessment. An item gradient refers to "how rapidly standard scores increase as a function of a child's success or failure on a single test item" (Bracken, 1987, p. 322). If a single item results in a substantial increment in the child's standard score, the test instrument may not be sensitive to minor differences in the child's ability in the domain being assessed. An acceptable item gradient requires a sufficient number of nonredundant test items placed throughout the test (Bracken & Walker, 1997). Problems with item gradients and floor effects should be considered in conjunction with the mean of the test to guide the interpretation of differentiations in the child's scores. If most of the item gradient violations occur within one standard deviation of the mean, then the test will probably show little sensitivity to differences in ability within the average range of functioning (Flanagan & Alfonso, 1995). This again complicates the accurate detection of children suspected of exhibiting a developmental delay.

Bracken's (1987) analysis of the 10 preschool tests revealed a pattern of psychometric shortcomings, particularly for children below the age of 4 years. Most of the tests evaluated were noted to have problems with limited floor, item gradients, and reliability. Thus, selection of tests needs to be done with considerable care and attention to the inadequacies of each instrument.

Examining many of the same psychometric properties, Flanagan and Alfonso (1995) sought to determine whether certain technical limitations of previous instruments were improved with the publication of new or recently revised intelligence tests for preschool children. These authors reviewed the following tests: Wechsler Preschool and Primary Scale of Intelligence–Revised (WPPSI–R; Wechsler, 1989); Differential Ability Scale (DAS; Elliott, 1990); Stanford-Binet Intelligence Scale: Fourth Edition (S-B IV; Thorndike, Hagen, & Sattler, 1986); Woodcock-Johnson Psycho-Educational Battery: Tests of Cognitive Ability (WJ-R: COG; Woodcock & Mather, 1989, 1990), and the Bayley Scales of Infant Development–Second Edition (BSID–II; Bayley, 1993).

Similar to Bracken (1987), Flanagan and Alfonso (1995) found that most of the tests showed some of the same inadequacies at the lower end of the preschool age range. Problems with test floors and item gradients, in particular, continued to be evaluated as weaknesses for children below the age of 4 years. Although test-retest reliabilities reported in the respective test manuals appeared satisfactory, Flanagan and Alfonso have pointed out a number of methodological concerns about the design of these test-retest reliability studies. These include small sample sizes as well as the use of samples that were either not representative of preschoolers, were comprised of too broad an age range, and/or included children beyond preschool age. According to the authors, stability data should be collected on age-stratified samples that approximate the age ranges for which the test is intended to be used.

Unlike Bracken's findings, Flanagan and Alfonso (1995) found two tests, the BSID–II and the WJ–R: COG, to be technically adequate across most criteria below the age of 4 years. Additionally, the technical qualities of the selected instruments appeared to be superior to those summarized by Bracken. Thus, overall, the technical qualities of the new and recently revised tests for preschoolers have shown improvement. Despite the increase in the number of reliable and valid measures of cognitive abilities for preschool children, more empirical work is needed to formulate a theory-driven framework to interpret intelligence tests, as well as the development of more developmentally appropriate and culturally relevant measures with ecological validity and treatment utility (Ford & Dahinten, 2005).

These evaluative studies (Bracken, 1987; Flanagan & Alfonso, 1995) were limited to tests of cognitive ability. Bracken, Keith, and Walker (1994) examined the quality of 13 commonly used or newly developed instruments designed to assess preschool behavior and social-emotional functioning. Using the same criteria as Bracken (1987), Bracken et al. (1994) found that the 13 social-emotional, third-party assessment devices had more psychometric limitations than preschool cognitive ability measures. When comparing more recently published instruments to others with older publication dates, it was found that the newer instruments were generally more technically sound. This latter finding parallels the work of Flanagan and Alfonso (1995), who also reported a general improvement in quality among newer instruments measuring cognitive abilities. Despite the substantial limitations among existing preschool instruments, there may be some optimism for improved quality assessment tools developed in the future.

Traditional versus Alternative Methods.   Considerable debate exists in the professional literature about the most appropriate approaches to be used in preschool assessment activities. In view of the technical inadequacies of many preschool instruments, it has been argued that standardized, norm-based assessment methods should be replaced by a wide range of methods that more clearly meets the various purposes of early childhood assessment (Bagnato & Neisworth, 1991, 1994). These alternative methods may include play-based assessment, direct observation, parent interviews, parent-child interactions, clinical judgment rating scales, and curriculum-based assessment. The strongest criticism lodged by Bagnato and Neisworth (1994) involves the continued use of intelligence tests because of their limited utility in treatment planning. They argue that such testing should be discontinued and replaced by the more dynamic and flexible alternative assessment approaches.

In response to these criticisms, Bracken (1994) acknowledges the technical inadequacies of many preschool instruments, particularly for children younger than 4 years old, and the need for psychologists to use a broad range of techniques in their assessment of preschool children. Bracken argues that the problem is not with intelligence testing but with practices that mandate the administration of an intelligence test when it is incompatible with the nature of the child or the reason for referral. Because standardized assessment data are required by most states in determining eligibility for services, the continued use of measures of intellectual functioning is likely to remain despite arguments against this practice (Flanagan & Alfonso, 1995; Harbin, Gallagher, & Terry, 1991). The discontinuance of mandated practices would allow psychologists to utilize the full armament of their techniques, procedures, and practices in an unconstrained manner so that assessors can employ all their psychological skills and expertise in promoting the needs of the child (Bracken, 1994).

According to Bracken (1994), preschool assessment does not require choosing between intellectual (traditional) or alternative assessments. He states that rather than conceptualizing these forms of assessment as being mutually exclusive, a better strategy would be to view them as complementary procedures that form a constellation of skills and methods for the psychologist. Gyurke (1994) likewise supports the combined use of both models of assessment but suggests that both approaches are useful for answering different referral questions. If the assessment question focuses on how a child compares to his or her age-mates on a set of defined criteria, then a norm-referenced approach is indicated. In other situations, if the aim of the assessment question is to ascertain the child's relative pattern of strengths and weaknesses or performance limits, alternative strategies are more appropriate.

The development of alternative strategies has been driven by the shortcoming of standardized testing. Many of these procedures were developed with the direct application of creatively meeting the needs of practitioners in early intervention. Losardo and Notari-Syverson (2001) have provided a framework consisting of three categories of alternative assessment models labeled embedded models, authentic models, and mediated models. Embedded approaches to assessment include opportunities to observe children's behavior which are embedded within the natural environment. In this approach, children are provided opportunities to perform various skills under different circumstances (i.e., methods, people) in multiple environments. With authentic assessments, profiles of the child's abilities are gathered based on the completion of "real-life" tasks. The primary goal of authentic assessment is to provide information which helps explicate the "how" and "why" of a child's responsiveness to instructional procedures to achieve goals in learning and development. Finally, mediated assessment approaches involve assessments in which guided teaching is utilized to gather information about the child's response to instruction and the use of language skills in instructional contexts.

Although many acknowledge the value of such procedures, there is a need to empirically validate these methods (Bracken, 1994; Bracken & Walker, 1997; Flanagan & Alfonso, 1995; Gyurke, 1994). What is needed is evidence that alternative procedures are "technically adequate, promote meaningful interventions, enhance child development, improve the alliance between parents, educators, professionals, and children" (Bracken, 1994, p. 104) before they can be adopted for widespread application in clinical practice. These research findings would also clarify more fully which relevant dimensions and conditions under these procedures are most efficacious.

ISSUES OF PARENTAL INVOLVEMENT DURING THE ASSESSMENT PROCESS

Although P.L. 102-119 only required IFSP development for children up to the age of 2, many service providers opt to maintain the family focus through the age of 5, rather than switching to a strict IEP format when the child turns 3. Therefore, parents of preschool children may be more effectively included if the psychologist interacts with them as they would interact with a parent of an infant (Bailey, 1996; Linder, 1993). From the time of the initial referral, P.L. 102-119 provides opportunities for parents to participate in assessment, interpretation, and intervention planning for their child.

One of the most important ways to include parents in the assessment process is to contact them prior to the evaluation and ascertain their perspective on the child's areas of strength and weakness (Praetor & McAllister, 1995). Abilities that are targeted as weaknesses in a preschool or day care setting may be stronger at home. Additionally, the parent may have concerns that the referring agent has not expressed due to lack of importance in that environment or lack of opportunity to see those other skills.

In addition to gathering information about the level of functioning of the child and family, psychologists should be aware that the current evaluation may be the first contact that parents have had with the diverse professionals who work with young children. Three goals may be accomplished during these initial conversations with psychologists. First, early contacts with parents can serve as educational experiences in which the psychologist explains the parents' rights to participate fully in the assessment and intervention process (Linder, 1993). Few parents will be familiar with the extent and nature of their possible participation in their child's evaluation, nor will they recognize the importance of their input in designing interventions. During preliminary conversations, empowering the parents can improve the quality and accuracy of the evaluation process.

A second function of the initial parent contact is to explain the identity and role of the various professionals who may be in contact with the child during the evaluation and intervention phases. A brief summary of the differences between occupational and physical therapists may enlighten parents who are unfamiliar with these professionals. Additionally, parents may not understand the functions of a psychologist in an early childhood assessment. Explaining the types of skills that are likely to be assessed allows parents to offer suggestions about the best way to obtain such information about the child (e.g., if communication will be assessed, parents may know that the child talks a lot with books but less during free play; if motor skills are assessed, parents may report that the child prefers to use his or her right hand for fine motor skills, so the psychologist can present tasks to that hand). Describing the roles of the many professionals who may be present at the evaluation serves to lessen potential feelings of being overwhelmed by the experts.

The third function of the initial contact is to discuss aspects of the evaluation setting that may affect the child's performance (Linder, 1993; Praetor & McAllister, 1995). Parents will be able to report on the child's ability to adapt to new people and materials, allowing the psychologist to prepare for a successful approach to the child and to pace the evaluation appropriately. Parents can also suggest methods of maintaining the child's interest in activities, such as sitting the child at a table or taking breaks to eat a favorite snack. Furthermore, the decision of whether to have the parent present in the room during the evaluation may be explored. Infants and some toddlers perform better when a parent is present; many preschoolers do better if the parent is out of the room or out of sight.

In some cases, the initial contact can serve as the first piece of assessment. Interviewing the parent about the child's adaptive behavior will offer information about specific strengths and weaknesses in the child's daily routine. Parents may also describe physical considerations that could influence test selection. For example, sensory impairments or physical limitations may influence the decision to use a particular measure or to have supportive equipment the child needs in order to complete the tasks.

During the evaluation, parents can serve as valuable sources of information about the representativeness of the child's performance (Bayley, 1993; Linder, 1993). For example, the Behavior Scale of the Bayley Scales of Infant Development: II provides two exemplary questions to be asked of the parents. First, parents are asked if the child's overall behavior was typical, and then parents are asked if the child's performance on the tasks was consistent with what the parents believe the child can do. These two questions are critical because they inform the psychologist of potential problems with the validity of the evaluation results as well as the likelihood that behavioral observations during the session are applicable to intervention planning.

Including a parent in the evaluation process also permits the psychologist to observe parent-child interactions. The child's attachment to the parent, the parent's responsiveness to the child's needs, and the verbal and physical interaction between the two provide information about their relationship and the parent's ability to respond effectively. These observations may influence the intensity or breadth of interventions advocated by the assessment team, such as parent training or reliance on the parent to carry out interventions at home.

If the parents are not present during the child's evaluation, they may still provide extensive information about the child's behavior and skills in multiple domains. Checklists and rating scales may give information about adaptive and maladaptive behaviors, temperament, emotional expressiveness, coping skills, and peer relationships that may not be evident during a clinic-based evaluation (see Martin, 1991).

After the evaluation, the psychologist needs to deliver feedback to parents in a way they can understand. With very young children, that feedback session may be the first explicit report of a deficit in their child's functioning. Therefore, psychologists need to present test results clearly and compassionately. The standard scores used in nearly all evaluation scales may confuse most parents. A brief explanation of average scores and cutoffs for significantly impaired performance may help clarify parents' understanding of their own child's relative level of functioning.

Furthermore, parents may need to hear results more than once if they are overwhelmed by test results from multiple professionals and cannot digest everything at once (Parker & Zuckerman, 1990). As a final note, although preschoolers are not required by law to carry a diagnosis in order to be eligible for special services in the schools, it is likely that a specific diagnosis will be applicable to a child after the evaluation. Although sensitivity to parents' feelings is important, psychologists must be honest in their report of the child's abilities. Terms such as *mentally disabled* or *autistic* will most likely upset the parents initially, but psychologists should not avoid using these terms when appropriate. A candid report of the child's status is a first step in the parents' process of accepting their child's disability and later will allow them to participate fully in designing interventions.

PROFESSIONAL COLLABORATION

The development of collaborative relationships during the assessment process is essential for effective program planning and intervention. The problems confronting preschool children with disabilities and vulnerabilities are quite diverse, and the range of possible services required to meet these needs is likewise diverse. Because of this, collaborative relationships between disciplines and agencies must be built (McLean & Crais, 1996). Additionally, both the legal mandates and professional guidelines (Bracken, Bagnato, & Barnett, 1991) require that assessment be multidisciplinary in nature. Many disciplines may be involved in the assessment process (Bondurant-Utz, 1994; Mowder, Widerstrom, & Sandall, 1989), including education, medicine, nursing, psychology, physical therapy, occupational therapy, speech-language pathology, audiology, social work, and nutrition. Professionals in each discipline may have specific questions about the child's level of functioning in their area of specialty, and they may all wish to complete some evaluation with the child. Psychologists must understand the services that each of these professionals can provide and be able to work with them on a team during assessment and intervention planning. In many cases, psychologists will need to become familiar with the terminology used by each profession to describe specific disabilities, therapy techniques, and assistive technology (Praetor & McAllister, 1995). The determination of which professionals to include on the team should be made based on the individual needs of the child and family that originated out of their unique home and community environments (Benner, 1992). Although the degree of specific professional involvement will vary, parents should always be central members of the team (Bagnato & Neisworth, 1991; McLean & Crais, 1996).

Three models of team functioning have emerged in the early intervention literature. These models have been labeled multidisciplinary, interdisciplinary, and transdisciplinary, and they vary considerably in the degree of interaction among disciplines represented in the team.

Models of Team Functioning

Multidisciplinary Model.   The multidisciplinary model is the most widely used approach in early assessment settings (Bagnato & Neisworth, 1991). The origins of this approach are rooted in the medical model in which the main premise is that specialists evaluate in areas of their own expertise that parallel suspected areas of dysfunction (Benner, 1992). In the multidisciplinary approach, professionals from each discipline carry out independent assessments and formulate the part of the service plan that is related to their discipline (Bondurant-Utz, 1994). There is little interaction among the disciplines and the results of these independent assessments are reported to the families by each professional separately. This requires family members to meaningfully integrate the information and suggestions given by the different professionals (McLean & Crais, 1996). In the absence of group synthesis, families may find recommendations redundant, confusing, and even conflicting (Bagnato & Neisworth, 1991). The multidisciplinary approach of meeting with professionals separately is also very time consuming for families. Even in instances when the team provides the assessment results to one professional to summarize the findings and formulate recommendations, the quality of this outcome will be a function of the designated professional's biases and ability to accurately interpret the findings of other professionals (Benner, 1992). The lack of professional communication does not allow for a comprehensive and integrated conception of the child and family. Because many of the .developmental problems identified in preschool children are multifaceted and often extend beyond the expertise of any one discipline, professional collaboration is essential (Paget & Barnett, 1990).

Interdisciplinary Model.   In the interdisciplinary model, professionals also carry out assessments independently. Unlike the multidisciplinary approach, there is a strong emphasis on communication and consultation among team members so that the outcome of the assessment and program planning is more integrated and unified (McLean & Crais, 1996). Interdisciplinary team functioning involves formal channels of communication in which the results of assessment activities across disciplines are shared and used to develop intervention plans. This model also emphasizes group decision making and goal setting with parents as part of the team. Interdisciplinary teamwork results in a more unified view of the needs of the child and family. Interventions are prescribed so that common goals are developed as part of each discipline's program (Bagnato & Neisworth, 1991). The effectiveness of the interdisciplinary model may be limited by communication difficulties across disciplines (Benner, 1992). According to Benner, professionals familiar with the language and terminology of their specialty area may experience difficulty understanding and being understood by other professionals on the interdisciplinary team. Furthermore, disagreement among team members may also emerge over priority areas of intervention. Unlike the multidisciplinary model, the interdisciplinary model represents a true team approach to assessment and program planning (Bagnato & Neisworth, 1991), but team members must be in continual communication with each other to minimize conflict and to ensure that well-coordinated services are received for the child and family.

Transdisciplinary Model. This model attempts to optimize the level of communication and collaboration among team members by crossing disciplinary boundaries (McLean & Crais, 1996). These assessments are frequently conducted as arena assessments. This format of assessment requires considerable pre-assessment planning by the team members. Typically only one or two of the team members work directly with the child and parent while other team members observe these interactions. During the preassessment phase, team members who will serve as observers consult with the person designated to conduct or facilitate the assessment. At this stage, team members coach the facilitator and share information across disciplines to guide the structure of the evaluation. As the assessment is conducted by the facilitator, observers attend to all aspects of the child's behavior and interactions between the child and parent. Team members observe and record across all developmental areas outlined in the assessment plan. Rather than having each professional conduct an assessment independently, they observe each other's assessments and take turns administering items specific to their domain. When possible, a single facilitator may administer items from all domains to take advantage of the rapport established with the child.

In many cases, items from one measure are sufficiently similar to another measure so that more than one person can score an item from a single administration. For example, the psychologist may ask the child to put a block into a cup for the Bayley Scales. The occupational therapist may pay close attention to the child's coordination, grip, and release. The physical therapist may observe the child's ability to balance his or her torso while sitting on the floor during the task. The speech therapist may listen for babbling or attempts at communication. Thus, a single item may provide a wealth of information for multiple professionals. This multidisciplinary approach saves time and reduces stress on the child by minimizing redundancy. Additionally, arena assessments allow the family to answer questions about the child's recent and current performance in one session rather than answering the same questions repeatedly. Following the assessment, team members meet to discuss the results and plan for needed services or interventions. Professionals who undertake arena assessments convey that they are time efficient and with proper training can observe what is needed for their discipline-specific evaluation, as well as observe the child's general functioning in other domains (Bondurant-Utz, 1994).

Arena assessments may not be the most appropriate method for some children and families. Bondurant-Utz (1994) has pointed out that some families may feel uncomfortable being in the presence of more than one professional because certain child characteristics such as distractibility or shyness may affect the outcome of the assessment. Before planning an arena assessment, the format should be explained to the parent in order to ascertain the likelihood of the child performing successfully in that environment (McLean & Crais, 1996). A potential drawback of the transdisciplinary model is that it requires a considerable time commitment from multiple professionals (Benner, 1992). According to Benner, professionals are required to attend team meetings, participate in preassessment planning, observe or facilitate the assessment, and attend the final meeting to synthesize the results and formulate recommendations. Thus, this approach can be costly and time consuming. Myers, McBride, and Peterson (1996) found that transdisciplinary assessments were more time efficient than standardized multidisciplinary assessments. They cited several reasons why multidisciplinary evaluations took longer to complete, including the need to schedule multiple appointments, appointment cancellations, and child health issues. The transdisciplinary approach should be viewed as family friendly because the family is usually only needed once to complete the assessment. This approach to assessment shows considerable promise for early intervention activities. Whether the assessment takes on an arena format or a more serial format, there will still be opportunities to take advantage of other professionals' skills (Bagnato & Neisworth, 1991). During evaluations for children with physically disabling conditions, a physical therapist may be able to provide appropriate support during testing to optimize the child's ability to complete a task. Occupational therapists are likely to have relevant information for test administration such as handedness, grip strength, and coordination. Speech therapists often have tips for increasing verbalizations during testing by using preferred toys or verbal cues. Physicians or nurses can offer advice on how to work with children who have assistive medical devices such as tracheotomy tubes or gastrointestinal tubes. An initial interview with the parent prior to the evaluation may reveal information that affects evaluation procedures, and psychologists can seek recommendations from relevant colleagues.

Some children may already be receiving therapeutic services from a variety of professionals. They may be accustomed to working with unfamiliar adults and may perform better without their parents present. In these cases, the therapists can answer questions about the representativeness of the child's behavior and task performance during testing.

PROFESSIONAL TRAINING IN PRESCHOOL ASSESSMENT

Preschool assessment is a complex and multifaceted process requiring a broad range of skills to meet the purposes of screening, diagnosis, monitoring child progress, intervention design, and program evaluation (Paget & Nagle, 1986). With the passage of federal mandates, it has become apparent that there is a critical shortage of well-trained early interventionists (Klein & Campbell, 1990) and school psychologists (Mowder, 1996). Unfortunately, the availability of training programs has not kept pace with personnel needs. There are few school psychology programs that provide both the didactic and field components of training necessary to prepare school psychologists for their roles in early intervention activities (Epps & Jackson, 1991; McLinden & Prasse, 1991). In addition to school psychology, the application of the discipline of psychology to infants and young children can be found in a small number of specialty areas in university-based training programs such as pediatric psychology, applied developmental psychology, and child-clinical psychology

(Poulsen, 1996). In order to meet the challenges of preschool service delivery, professional psychologists will need additional training, and training programs will need to provide specialized coursework and field experiences.

Meisels and Provence (1989) have suggested that extensive and comprehensive training is needed for assessors of very young children. Given the diversity of interlocking roles that psychologists working in preschool settings must assume, a broad range of content and training experiences has been suggested (Flanagan, Sainato, & Genshaft, 1993; Meisels & Provence, 1989; Mowder 1996; Paget & Nagle, 1986; Poulsen, 1996).

Training should include mastery of the broad spectrum of techniques involving test and nontest assessment in order to perform comprehensive evaluations that accurately identify child and family strengths and weaknesses to provide useful information in intervention planning. With the proliferation of new preschool methods, it is also important that preschool psychologists be able to evaluate the technical adequacies of assessment tools (Bracken, 1987; Flanagan et al. 1993). Strong psychometric training will ensure that assessors will make sound decisions regarding test selection and interpretation to avoid making misdiagnoses (Bracken, 1987).

Psychologists working in preschool settings also need a background in typical and atypical child development, developmental disabilities, biological and environmental correlates of risk and resilience status, preschool service delivery models for normal children and children with developmental delays, and curriculum programs for preschoolers with disabling conditions. Given the central importance of the family in preschool programming, family systems theory, family life cycles, child-family interactions, and family structure are critical curricular components (Meisels & Provence, 1989). Within this area, it is essential that psychologists develop the skills to build successful relationships with families throughout the assessment and program planning process. It is likewise important that psychologists working in preschool settings develop a firm understanding of the contributions of other disciplines in early childhood programs. In order to develop the groundwork for future collaboration and interdisciplinary functioning, the curriculum should include extensive discussion of the discipline-specific skills of other professionals involved in early intervention programs (Klein & Campbell, 1990; Mowder, 1996). Furthermore, it is also imperative that the skills to establish collaborative relationships with community agencies and programs when seeking additional needed services should be acquired.

Several authors (Mowder, 1996; Paget & Nagle, 1986; Poulsen, 1996) have underscored the importance of field-based practicum and internship experiences. Such experiences are the core to the professional preparation because they afford the opportunity to integrate theory with practice (Mowder, 1996). These activities may also take place across a variety of school, clinical, and medical settings.

Mowder (1996) has discussed several important issues related to the manner in which training may be carried out as a preservice activity or through service, continuing professional development, or postgraduate training formats. With regard to pre-service models, it is unclear the time at which specialty training should be introduced. The alternatives involve specialty training following the completion of general training, specialty training in place of program electives, or postgraduate training after the completion of the specialist or doctoral degree. Although Mowder reports that much of the literature supports pre-service preparation, postgraduate and in-service training experiences will continually need to be developed to meet the needs of practitioners in the field who are presently being asked to provide services to preschoolers. NASP (2005) has advocated for pre-service and in-service education for school psychologists and other professionals in the area of preschool assessment. Therefore, it is imperative that training programs and professional organizations develop models of training for practitioners.

As significant advances and innovations are made within the field of early childhood programming, revisions of training content will be necessary to meet the challenges of these new developments. The efficacy of current and future models of training will need to be demonstrated through research (Mowder, 1996) to ensure the delivery of high-quality services to young children and their families.

SUMMARY

The majority of research in preschool assessment has been amassed over the past three decades. The national agenda of having all children ready for school, the effectiveness of early intervention and prevention programs, and legal mandates requiring services to preschool children with disabilities have forced professionals to examine their assessment practices as they relate to the accuracy of identification and the utility of assessment findings for treatment planning and evaluation. As the field of early intervention has advanced, new assessment methods and processes have been developed.

The development of new methods, sometimes referred to as alternative or nontraditional methods (i.e., play-based assessment, judgment-based assessment, etc.), has spawned considerable professional debate over the validity and utility of more traditional assessment approaches such as norm-referenced assessment tools. The selection of which techniques to use in preschool assessment activities must be matched to the purpose for which the assessment is being conducted (Mindes et al., 1996). Why the assessment is being conducted and how the assessment data will be used are critical issues in method selection. Assessment activities should be viewed as a general problem-solving process aimed at identification and intervention. It is time to drop such descriptors as "traditional," "alternative," and so on and view the different methods and approaches to assessment as options the well-trained professional can use to answer the referral problem and to design appropriate interventions based on the child and family needs. Future research should focus on the validity of different assessment approaches with particular emphasis on the comparative validity of different methodologies across various age, sociocultural, and health conditions. This type of research would be especially relevant to support possible changes in eligibility criteria for intervention services.

Training professionals for early child assessment activities will continue to be a critical issue in maintaining high-quality early intervention programs. As discussed earlier, the assessor will need to acquire clinical expertise over a broad range of techniques and knowledge of the contextual influences on child and family development. Progress of our theoretical understanding of early development will also require ongoing specialized training.

REFERENCES

American Association on Mental Retardation. (1992). *Mental retardation: Definition, classification, and systems of supports* (9th ed.). Washington, DC: Author.

Anastasi, A., & Urbina, S. (1997). *Psychological testing* (7th ed.). Upper Saddle River, NJ: Prentice Hall.

Bagnato, S. J., & Neisworth J. T. (1991). *Assessment for early intervention: Best practices for professionals*. New York: Guilford.

Bagnato, S. J., & Neisworth, J. T. (1994). A national study of the social and treatment "invalidity" of Intelligence testing for early intervention. *School Psychology Quarterly, 9*(2), 81–102.

Bailey, D. B. (1996). Assessment and its importance in early intervention. In D. B. Bailey & M. Wolery (Eds.), *Assessing infants and preschoolers with special needs* (pp. 1–21). Columbus, OH: Merrill.

Bailey, D. B. (1996). Assessing family resources, priorities, and concerns. In M. McLean, D. B. Bailey, & M. Wolery (Eds.), *Assessing infants and preschoolers with special needs* (pp. 202–233). Englewood Cliffs, NJ: Prentice Hall.

Barnett, D. W. (1984). An organizational approach to preschool services: Psychological screening, assessment, and intervention. In C. Maher, R. Illback, & J. Zins (Eds.), *Organizational Psychology in the schools: A handbook for practitioners* (pp. 53–82). Springfield, IL: C.C. Thomas.

Bayley, N. (1993). *Bayley Scales of Infant Development–II*. San Antonio, TX: Psychological Corporation.

Benner, S. M. (1992). *Assessing young children with special needs: An ecological perspective*. New York: Longman.

Boehm, A., & Sandberg, B. (1982). Assessment of the preschool child. In C. R. Reynolds & T. B. Gutkin (Eds.), *Handbook of School Psychology* (pp. 82–120). New York: Wiley.

Bondurant-Utz, J. A. (1994). The team process. In J. A. Bondurant-Utz & L. B. Luciano (Eds.), *A practical guide to infant and preschool assessment in special education* (pp. 59–72). Boston: Allyn & Bacon.

Bracken, B. A. (1984). *Bracken Basic Concept Scale*. San Antonio, TX: Psychological Corporation.

Bracken, B. A. (1987). Limitations of preschool instruments and standards for minimal levels of technical adequacy. *Journal of Psychoeducational Assessment, 4*, 313–326.

Bracken, B. A. (1994). Advocating for effective preschool assessment practices. A comment on Bagnato and Neisworth. *School Psychology Quarterly, 9*(2), 103–108.

Bracken, B. A., Bagnato, S. J., & Barnett, D. W. (1991). *Early Childhood Assessment. Position statement adopted by the National Association of School Psychologists Delegate Assembly*, March 24, 1991.

Bracken, B. A., Keith, L. K., & Walker, K. C. (1994). Assessment of preschool behavior and socioemotional functioning: A Review of thirteen third-party instruments. *Assessment in Rehabilitation and Exceptionality, 1*, 331–346.

Bracken, B. A., & Walker, K. C. (1997). The utility of Intelligence tests for preschool children. In D. P. Flanagan, J. L. Genshaft, & P. C. Harrison (Eds.), *Contemporary intellectual assessment: Theories, tests, and issues* (pp. 484–502). New York: Guilford.

Burgemeister, B. B., Blum, L. H., & Lorge, I. (1972). *Columbia Mental Maturity Scale*. New York: Harcourt Brace Jovanovich.

Carran, D. T., & Scott, K. G. (1992). Risk assessment in preschool children: Research implications for the early detection of educational handicaps. *Topics in Early Childhood Special Education, 12*, 196–211.

Carta, J. J., & Greenwood, C. R. (1985). Ecobehavioral assessment: A methodology for expanding the evaluation of early intervention programs. *Topics in Early Childhood Special Education, 5*, 88–104.

Culbertson, J. L., & Willis, D. J. (1993). Introduction to testing young children. In J. L. Culbertson & D. J. Willis (Eds.), *Testing young children: A reference guide for developmental, psychoeducational, and psychosocial assessments* (pp. 1–10). Austin, TX: PRO-ED.

Danaher, J. (1995). *Preschool special education eligibility classifications*. Chapel Hill, NC: National Early Childhood Technical Assistance System.

Danaher, J. (2005). *Eligibility policies and practices for young children under part B of IDEA* (NECTTAC Notes No. 15). Chapel Hill: The University of North Carolina, FPG Child Development Institute, National Early Childhood Technical Assistance Center.

DiSimoni, F. (1978). *The Token Test for Children*. Allen, TX: DLM/teaching Resources.

Dunn, L. M., & Dunn, L. M. (1981). *Peabody Picture Vocabulary Test–Revised*. Circle Pines, MN: American Guidance Service.

Elliot, C. D. (1990). *Differential Ability Scales: Introductory and technical handbook*. San Antonio, TX: Psychological Corporation.

Epps, S., & Jackson, B. J. (1991). Professional preparation of Psychologists for family-centered service delivery to at-risk infants and toddlers. *School Psychology Review, 8*, 311–318.

Fitzgibbon, C. T., & Morris, L. L. (1987). *How to design a program evaluation*. Newbury Park, CA: Sage.

Flanagan, D. P., & Alfonso, V. C. (1995). A critical Review of the technical characteristics of new and recently revised Intelligence tests for preschool children. *Journal of Psychoeducational Assessment, 13*, 66–90.

Flanagan, D. P., Sainato, D. M., & Genshaft, J. L. (1993). Emerging issues in the assessment of young children with disabilities: The expanding role of school psychologists. *Canadian Journal of School Psychology, 9*(2), 192–203.

Ford, L., & Dahinten, V. S. (2005). Use of intelligence tests in the assessment of preschoolers. In D. Flanagan & P. Harrison (Eds.), *Contemporary intellectual assessment: Theories, tests, and issues* (2nd ed., pp. 487–503). New York: Guilford Press.

Gredler, G. R. (1997). Issues in early childhood screening and assessment. *Psychology in the Schools, 24*, 99–106.

Gyurke, J. S. (1994). A reply to Bagnato and Neisworth: Intelligent versus Intelligence testing of preschoolers. *School Psychology Quarterly, 9*, 109–112.

Harbin, G. L., Gallagher, J. J., & Terry, D. V. (1991). Defining the eligibility population: Policy issues and challenges. *Journal of Early Intervention, 15*, 13–20.

Kaufman, A. S., & Kaufman, N. L. (1983). *Kaufman Assessment Battery for Children*. Circle Pines, MN: American Guidance Service.

Kelley, M. P., & Melton, G. B. (1993). Ethical and legal issues. In J. L. Culbertson & D. J. Willis (Eds.), *Testing young: A reference guide for developmental, psychoeducational, and psychosocial assessments* (pp. 408–426). Austin, TX: Pro-Ed.

Kelley, M. E., & Surbeck, E. (1991). History of preschool assessment. In B. A. Bracken (Ed.), *The psychoeducational assessment of preschool* (2nd ed., pp. 1–17). Boston: Allyn & Bacon.

Klein, N. K., & Campbell, P. (1990). Preparing personnel to serve at-risk and disabled infants, toddlers, and preschoolers. In S. J. Meisels & J. P. Shonkoff (Eds.), *Handbook of early childhood intervention* (pp. 679–699). New York: Cambridge University Press.

Lichtenstein, R., & Ireton, H. (1991). Preschool screening for developmental and educational problems. In B. A. Bracken (Ed.), *The psychoeducational assessment of preschool children* (2nd ed., pp. 486–513). Boston, MA: Allyn & Bacon,

Lidz, C. S. (1991). Issues in the assessment of preschool children. In B. A. Bracken (Ed.), *The psychoeducational assessment of preschool* children (2nd ed., pp. 18–31). Boston: Allyn & Bacon.

Linder, T. W. (1993). *Transdisciplinary play-based assessment: A functional approach to working with young children*. Baltimore: Paul H. Brookes.

Losardo, A., & Notari-Syverson, A. *Alternative approaches to assessing young children*. Baltimore: Paul H. Brookes.

Martin, R. D. (1991). Assessment of social and emotional behavior. In B. A. Bracken (Ed.), *The psychoeducational assessment of preschool children*. (2nd ed., pp. 450–464). Boston: Allyn & Bacon.

McCarthy, D. (1972). *The McCarthy Scales of Children's Abilities*. San Antonio, TX: Psychological Corporation.

McLean, M. (1996). Assessment and its importance in early intervention/early childhood special education. In M. McLean, D. B. Bailey, & M. Wolery (Eds.), *Assessing infants and preschoolers with special needs* (pp. 1–22). Englewood Cliffs, NJ: Prentice Hall.

McLean, M., & Crais, E. R. (1996). Procedural considerations in assessing infants and preschoolers with disabilities. In M. McLean, D. B. Bailey, & M. Wolery (Eds.), *Assessing infants and preschoolers with special needs* (pp. 46–68). Englewood Cliffs, NJ: Prentice Hall.

McLinden, S. E., & Prasse, D. P. (1991). Providing services to infants and toddlers under P.L. 99-457: Training needs of school psychologists. *School Psychology Review, 20*, 37–48.

Meisels, S. J., & Provence, S. (1989). Screening and assessment: *Guidelines for identifying young disabled and developmentally vulnerable and their families*. Washington, DC: National Center for Infants, Toddlers and Families.

Miller, L. J. (1982). Miller Assessment for Preschoolers. Littleton, CO: Foundation for Knowledge and Development.

Mindes, G., Ireton, H., & Mardell-Czudnowski, C. (1996). *Assessing young* . New York: Delmar.

Mowder, B. A. (1996). Preparing school psychologists. In D. Bricker & A. Widerstrom (Eds.), *Preparing personnel to work with infants and young children and their families: A team approach*. Baltimore: Paul H. Brookes.

Mowder, B. A., Widerstrom, A. H., & Sandall, S. R. (1989). School psychologists serving at-risk and handicapped infants, toddlers, and their families. *Professional School Psychology, 4*, 159–172.

Myers, C. C, McBride, S. L., & Peterson, C. A. (1996). Transdisciplinary, play-based assessment in early childhood special education: An examination of social validity. *Topics in Early Childhood Special Education, 16*(1), 102–126.

National Association of School Psychologists. (2005). *Position statement on early childhood assessment*. NASP: Bethesda, MD.

Newborg, J., Stock, J. R., Wnek, L., Guidubaldi, J., & Svinicki, J. (1984). *Battelle Developmental Inventory*. Allen, TX: DLM Teaching Resources.

Paget, K. D. (1991). The individual assessment situation: Basic considerations for preschool-age children. In B. Bracken (Ed.) *The psychoeducational assessment of preschool children* (pp. 32–39). Boston: Allyn & Bacon.

Paget, K. D., & Barnett, D. W. (1990). Assessment of infants, toddlers, preschool children, and their families: Emergent trends. In T. B. Gutkin & C. R. Reynolds, (Eds.) *The handbook of school Psychology* (2nd ed., pp. 458–486). New York: Wiley.

Paget, K. D., & Nagle, R. J. (1986). A conceptual model of preschool assessment. *School Psychology Review, 15*(2), 154–165.

Parker, S. J., & Zuckerman, B. S. (1990). Therapeutic aspects of the assessment process. In S. J. Meisels & J. P. Shonkoff (Eds.), *Handbook of early childhood intervention* (pp. 350–369). New York: Cambridge University Press.

Poulsen, M. K. (1996). Preparing pediatric psychologists. In D. Bricker & A. Widerstrom (Eds.), *Preparing personnel to work with infants and young children and their families: A team approach*. Baltimore: Paul H. Brookes.

Praetor, K. K., & McAllister, J. R. (1995). Assessing infants and toddlers. In A. Thomas & J. Grimes (Eds.), *Best practices in school Psychology–III* (pp. 775–788). Washington, DC: National Association of School Psychologists.

Romero, I. (1992). Individual assessment procedures with preschool children. In E. Vazqez-Nuttal, I. Romero, & J. Kalesnik (Eds.), *Assessing and screening preschoolers: Psychological and educational dimensions* (pp. 55–66). Boston: Allyn & Bacon.

Thorndike, R. L., Hagen, E. P., & Sattler, J. M. (1986). *Stanford-Binet Intelligence Scale, Fourth Edition*. Chicago: Riverside.

Ulrey, G. (1982). Influence of preschooler's behavior on assessment. In G. Ulrey & S. J. Rogers (Eds.), *Psychological assessment of handicapped infants and handicapped children* (pp. 25–34). New York: Thiemme-Stratton.

Vandiver, P., & Suarez, T. M. (1980). An evaluator's resource handbook. Chapel Hill, NC: Technical Assistance Development Center.

Wechsler, D. (1967). *Wechsler Preschool and Primary Scale of Intelligence*. San Antonio, TX: Psychological Corporation.

Wechsler, D. (1989). *Manual for the Wechsler Preschool and Primary Scale of Intelligence–Revised*. San Antonio, TX: Psychological Corporation.

Woodcock, R. W, & Mather, N. (1989, 1990). WJ–R Tests of Cognitive Ability-Standard and Supplemental Batteries: Examiner's Manual. In R. W. Woodcock & M. B. Johnson, *Woodcock-Johnson Psychoeducational Battery–Revised*. Allen, TX: DLM Teaching Resources.

3

Early Childhood Screening and Readiness Assessment

Candace H. Boan, Lydia Aydlett, and Nichole Multunas
Western Carolina University

Is five-year-old Taylor old enough for school? Should Tessa's parents keep her in preschool for another year so she will be ahead of her class? Does Tommy need special services? Is a program for at-risk four- and five-year-olds appropriate for Jane? These are some of the questions addressed by the implementation of developmental screening and readiness assessment in the lives of young children, their families, and their schools. As indicated by these questions, developmental screening and readiness assessment are integral to the decision-making process regarding the educational well-being of preschool children. However, their use is fraught with controversy, primarily centering around the misapplication of instruments, the misuse of resultant data, and the inadequacy of research on the predictive validity of assessment tools. The purpose of this chapter is to provide a context for understanding screening and readiness assessment in early childhood. The first section of the chapter is an overview of the political context for screening and readiness assessment in young children.

CONTEXT FOR EARLY CHILDHOOD ASSESSMENTS

The assessment of preschool children's developmental status and school readiness has become a politically and theoretically sensitive topic for educators and social policy makers alike (Maxwell & Clifford, 2004; Meisels, 1987; Saluja, Scott-Little, & Clifford, 2000). In 1975 the passage of Public Law (P.L.) 94-142 (later called the *Individuals with Disabilities Education Act*) mandated the early identification of children with developmental delays, and in 1986 P. L. 99-457 created a downward extension of the *Individuals with Disabilities Education Act* (IDEA) services to children ages 3 through 5 years. Although the latest amendments to IDEA require the early identification of developmental delay and the provision of services to those children who need them, there have been several specific initiatives and public policies that have shaped the practices in early childhood assessment.

In 1989, President George Bush and the governors of the United States conducted an education summit which resulted in a renewed national commitment to students, teachers, and schools. The commitment manifested in the creation of six national *Education Goals*.

The first of these goals had direct bearing on the practice of testing young children and spawned numerous conferences, papers, policies, and research in an effort to understand and meet this goal (Meisels, 1999). The goal simply stated that all children should start school ready to learn (National Education Goals Panel, 1991).

In 2002, President George W. Bush called for the assessment of all three- and four-year-old children in Head Start programs (Doherty, 2002). Although Head Start children are the youngest of the nation's children to be subjected to assessment, preschool assessment is congruent with the measurement-based accountability required of public schools. The *No Child Left Behind Act* (2001) required publicly funded education programs to monitor the effectiveness of their programs. The complementary early childhood initiative, *Good Start, Grow Smart* (2002) specifically addressed accountability in early education programs. As a result of this initiative, Head Start has been charged with assessing performance across domains such as literacy, language, and numeracy.

CONCEPTUAL ISSUES IN SCREENING AND READINESS ASSESSMENT

The socio-political context for early childhood assessment suggests a stronger need for tools to examine whether children are ready to learn when they enter school. However, determining what is meant by being "ready to learn" and determining how best to identify children who are at risk for academic difficulties have generated considerable interest in the use of readiness assessment and developmental screening. The increased emphasis on the ability of publicly funded agencies to monitor the effectiveness of their programs and to ultimately be held accountable for failure to close achievement gaps between "at-risk" children and "non-at-risk" children has also spawned interest in early childhood assessment. The types of assessments central to these public policies described are developmental screening and school readiness. Both are used at school entry under a general rubric of determining whether children are ready to learn. The next section will discuss developmental screening and readiness assessment with regard to conceptual and pragmatic issues.

Definition of Developmental Screening

Since the 1970s, developmental screening has become an accepted part of the early childhood experience. Over the years considerable evidence has accumulated for the efficacy of intervening educationally with children at risk for developmental problems, and many schools recognize that children's problems can be remediated if they are identified early. The research has specifically suggested that the cognitive, emotional, and social functioning of young children can be positively influenced by developmentally appropriate curricula (e.g., Campbell, Pungello, Miller-Johnson, Burchinal, & Ramey, 2001; Campbell, Ramey, Pungello, Sparling, & Miller-Johnson, 2002; Campbell & Ramey, 1994, 1995; Marcon, 1999; Ramey et al.,2000; Ramey & Campbell, 1991; Schweinhart & Weikart, 1998). The well-established Abecedarian Project has demonstrated that children from early intervention programs show higher scores on cognitive tests, demonstrate higher scores on measures of reading and math, and complete more years of education than children who do not participate in early intervention (Frank Porter Graham Child Development Institute, 2005). The demonstrated efficacy of early intervention programs makes a strong case for assessment that facilitates early identification of children at risk for educational difficulties.

Developmental screening evaluations are designed to provide cursory information about preschool children. Screening attempts to identify children who are eligible for mandated services, children who, if they do not receive services, are at risk for school failure (Thurlow & Gilman, 1999). This type of evaluation leads to decisions based on a pass or fail model. Children who pass screening evaluations are identified as not needing additional assessment; children who fail screening evaluations are identified as needing additional assessment.

Developmental screening is the first step in the process of identifying children who have or are at risk for having developmental or behavioral problems (Kenny & Culbertson, 1993). Although screening neither diagnoses nor plans treatment for a disorder, it assists in early identification and referral for diagnostic evaluation and intervention services. Based on a medical model, developmental screening theoretically provides a quick assessment of significant developmental domains and helps detect risk for delays or disorders.

The developmental screening serves as a preliminary component to a comprehensive diagnostic assessment. In order to determine the need for additional assessment, screening instruments generally compare a specific child to standards or norms of other children the same age. It is believed that through screening, aspects of children's health or development which are problematic can be distinguished from those that are non-problematic (Luehr & Hoxie, 1995). Screenings can be administered individually or in a group setting. Similar to medical screenings, developmental screenings are ideally quick, reliable, and cost-efficient.

Definition of Readiness Assessment

School readiness is widely accepted as an important goal for children (e.g., National Education Goals Panel, 1991); however, readiness is a poorly defined construct (Kagan, 1990). School readiness has been historically defined as readiness to learn specific material and be successful in a typical school context. It has been used to assess young children before kindergarten, at kindergarten entry, or early in the kindergarten year for skills believed to be related to academic tasks and predictive of school success. The practice of readiness assessment has been greatly influenced by educational philosophy, educational history, and definitions of readiness.

Theoretical models of readiness vary on a continuum, from ones that assert that readiness allows for identifying children that are developmentally in need of an alternative educational program (The Gesell Institute of Child Development, 1987) to others that assert that readiness assessment allows for identification of skills specifically related to the curriculum of a given program (Meisels, 1999). For the purposes of this chapter, readiness assessment is designed to assess the child's current development across five domains which are health and physical functioning, social and emotional development, approaches to learning, language and communication, and cognition and general knowledge (Rhode Island KIDS COUNT, 2005). Readiness assessment can be used to develop curricula and to establish individualized programming (Mehaffie & McCall, 2002) and it incorporates three key elements: child readiness across the five domains (physical, social-emotional, learning approaches, language, and cognitive), school readiness (transitional plans between home and school), and the existence of family and community support.

Domains Assessed in Screening and Readiness Assessment

There are clear conceptual differences between developmental screening and readiness assessment. Readiness instruments are designed to assess areas related to school tasks, while developmental screenings help identify children needing additional assessment. The screening instruments provide for a quick evaluation of domains that may need further, diagnostic assessment. Readiness assessment provides an indication of curriculum-related skills that the child demonstrates during the evaluation.

The domains of readiness assessment are not considered mutually exclusive, and a child's development in one domain may show a strong relationship to his or her development in another domain (Rhode Island KIDS COUNT, 2005). The physical domain focuses on things such as impairments in sensory functioning, gross and fine motor skills, illnesses or medical conditions, growth, and overall physical well-being. The social and emotional domain focuses on things such as age-appropriate social skills, psychological well-being, self-perceptions, and interpersonal interactions. The learning domain includes attention, curiosity, and enthusiasm for learning activities. The language domain focuses on verbal communication skills, nonverbal communication skills, and early literacy skills. The cognitive and general knowledge domain emphasizes problem-solving skills, abstract reasoning, early mathematical skills, and overall fund of knowledge.

Most measures of readiness assess facets of the five domains identified above. Cognitive and general knowledge are assessed by examination of basic concepts such as color and shape identification, quantity and time, and problem-solving abilities. Language development is often assessed through an examination of expressive and receptive skills, understanding of syntax, and ability to demonstrate basic phonological skills. These two domains are well represented on most measures of readiness because they are clearly connected to curriculum-related skills. Areas assessing social and emotional functioning tend to be less well represented across measures of readiness, although some instruments include qualitative or observational opportunities for identifying social awareness, self-reference, and social skills. The lack of social and emotional areas on readiness instruments is particularly interesting, given the finding that teachers typically identify this domain as critical for readiness in school. Physical functioning is primarily assessed in the form of gross or fine motor skill performance by examining things such as the ability to copy pictures or engage in behaviors such as skipping. The connection between physical functioning, especially gross motor skills, and curriculum-related skills is less apparent than in the other domains mentioned. Finally, although approach to learning provides for an understanding of the process skills that children demonstrate, very few instruments provide for direct assessment of these skills. Instruments that do include process skills typically focus on things such as ability to maintain attention and ability to follow directions.

Although there are clear conceptual differences between developmental screening instruments and readiness assessment instruments, there is considerable overlap in content and domains assessed (Lichenstein & Ireton, 1991; Meisels, 1994). Niemeyer & Scott-Little, (2002) reviewed screening instruments, diagnostic instruments, and instructional instruments across several variables. In their review, they identified 12 screening instruments that measure multiple domains. All of the screening instruments reviewed provided some measure of cognitive development or general knowledge. The majority of screening instruments also measured aspects of language (91.7%) and health and physical functioning (83.3%). Developmental screening instruments have a primary function of identifying children that need additional assessment. Historically, it has been accepted that

children who perform poorly on measures of cognitive development, language development, and physical functioning need a more comprehensive examination of their abilities
in these areas.

Half of the screening instruments reviewed measured social and emotional functioning,
and only one instrument measured aspects of approaches to learning (Niemeyer & Scott-
Little, 2002). Although developmental screening instruments assess multiple domains,
they do not consistently assess social and emotional functioning. Additionally, there tend to
be fewer referrals for diagnostic assessment solely related to social and emotional functioning in preschool children as a result of the wide variations in experiences and opportunities for development in these domains that are provided across contexts. It is interesting
to note that several of the screening instruments identified in this compendium of assessment tools also were identified as instruments with instructional benefits (and one of the
screening instruments actually included the word *readiness* in the title).

The difference between screening instruments and readiness instruments appears to
be primarily conceptual. The cognitive and general knowledge domain and the language
domain both appear to be widely represented on both types of assessment instruments.
Differences in content for a given domain and breadth of coverage are likely to show more
variability across developmental screening and readiness instruments. Screening instruments are more likely to focus on measures of physical functioning that may need further
evaluation through physical therapy or occupational therapy services. Neither screening instruments nor readiness assessments consistently assess the social and emotional domain
or the approach to learning domain. Given the overlap in domains assessed, the next sections will integrate discussions on screening and readiness.

Methods of Screening and Readiness Assessment

Assessment techniques that are utilized in screening and assessing readiness vary across
school systems. The assessment techniques differ with regard to several variables including, development of items, administration of the assessment tool, recommended method
for interpretation, and psychometric robustness. The assessment techniques range from
traditional norm-referenced methods to alternative methods that focus on evaluations in an
authentic context.

Norm-referenced instruments for preschool children provide the most formal method
for assessing areas of concern. Content development for norm-referenced, standardized instruments may include a review of the theoretical population of items to assess a given domain, item analysis with the selection of individual items that demonstrate the highest possible discrimination indexes, factor analysis of items to determine loadings, examination of
coefficient alpha reliabilities for domain scores, and extensive pilot testing. Norm-referenced
instruments typically require adherence to standardized administration procedures, and
higher levels of training for scoring and interpreting results on instruments. Interpretation
involves consideration of normative data and ipsative performance. Norm-referenced instruments use measures of reliability and validity to demonstrate the utility of the instrument. Examples of norm-referenced measures used with preschool children include the
Early Screening Profile (Harrison, 1990) and the *Bracken Basic Concept Scale, Revised*
(Bracken, 1998).

Rating scales or checklists are intended to ask knowledgeable individuals (parents,
teachers) about whether or not a child has demonstrated a specific skill (Scott-Little &
Niemeyer, 2001). Some rating scales that are used to screen preschool children or assess

readiness utilize similar test construction methods, interpretation procedures, and evidence for psychometric soundness; other rating scales and checklists involve item development through a more informal sampling of behaviors or attributes observed in a specific setting, and are interpreted using clinical judgment or a specific criterion that is related to the classroom, and demonstrate value through social utility. An example of a formal rating scale is the *Social Skills Rating System* (Gresham & Elliott, 1990).

The use of mastery tasks involves having children complete tasks that demonstrate specific skills (Scott-Little & Niemeyer, 2001). These could include things such as having a child use scissors to cut on a line or having a child catch something tossed to them. This type of criterion-referenced assessment allows for an examination of curriculum-related skills in an authentic assessment. Items are selected based on their direct relevance to the curriculum, results are interpreted with regard to mastery of individual skills, and individual progress can be charted as a means of monitoring a specific intervention.

Observational techniques can be used to provide a picture of the child's behavior in classroom (Scott-Little & Niemeyer, 2001). Observations can be structured and involve examining specific behaviors, such as how a child responds to a contrived situation, or can be unstructured and involve examining general behavioral functioning. The observational data obtained can be used to examine mastery of the skill that is relevant to the curriculum, or to examine developmental concerns that warrant further investigation. Observational methods can also take advantage of naturally occurring situations such as play and parent-child interactions to examine specific skills and functioning across domains.

Portfolio assessments involve collecting work samples from the child and observing their behavior in a natural setting (such as the classroom) (Meisels, 1989; Scott-Little & Niemeyer 2001). The portfolio approach is useful when the types of information that are being collected are clear and consistent with teachings in the curriculum. The portfolio assessment allows for examination of a child's skills over time and is directly relevant to the classroom curriculum. It allows examination of the individual child as he or she acquires mastery over specific skills.

There is considerable debate about the appropriate method for evaluating the functioning of young children. Proponents of standardized, norm-referenced assessment value the ability to compare results with a standardized group and the increased support for the technical adequacy of instruments (Flanagan & Alfonso, 1995). Opponents to standardized, norm-referenced assessment suggest that evaluating preschool children in a non-authentic context renders results useless and cite problems with psychometrics as a major cause for concern (Bagnato & Neisworth, 1994). Some specific criticisms center on standardized instruments that emphasize the product rather than the process, fail to differentiate between current level of performance and potential level of performance, and do not demonstrate a connection between assessment results and interventions (Meltzer & Reid, 1994).

Advocates for criterion-referenced and informal assessment techniques stress the importance of authentic assessments that allow for a relevant to context (such as the classroom curriculum and environment) to understanding readiness skills, and the ability of alternative methods of assessment to provide information about mastery of specific skills that are relevant to the classroom curriculum. There is considerable value in the information provided by both traditional and alternative assessment methods, and an integration of the approaches is most likely to allow examination of skills across all five readiness domains. However, there are several issues that need to be considered when selecting the assessment methods that are utilized in screening and readiness evaluations.

ISSUES IN EARLY CHILDHOOD ASSESSMENT

Evaluation of young children offers many unique challenges to the assessment process. Their development often involves rapid changes that are greatly affected by the environments the children encounter. They may also demonstrate uneven development of skills across domains (National Educational Goals Panel, 1998). This means that a child may demonstrate at-risk functioning in some domains while showing no areas of concern in other domains. Young children demonstrate considerable variations in behavior that can impact the results of assessment (Gredler, 1997). Behavioral problems may be apparent during a screening assessment that is conducted early in the school year. These same behavioral problems may not be found in assessments conducted later during the school year.

Assessment of young children also makes the assumption that potential for success in school is being sampled. It is possible that poor performance on an assessment may result from a lack of previous experiences (National Education Goals Panel, 1998). Some young children have experience working with unfamiliar adults in day care settings, while other young children have been limited in their interactions with unfamiliar adults. Preschool children with little experience may demonstrate problems with attention, activity level, threshold for frustration, and motivation (Nagle, 2000). Although consideration must be given to the uniqueness of preschool children when conducting developmental screenings or readiness assessments, additional issues must be addressed. These issues include technical adequacy and social validity of instruments, decision-making models used with instruments, and misapplications of information from instruments.

Technical Adequacy and Social Validity of Instruments

The technical adequacy and social validity of an instrument are important for several reasons. They provide a means by which an evaluator can select the appropriate instrument in a given situation. Technical adequacy relates to the psychometric properties of instruments and includes examination of validity and reliability. Instruments are selected for use with individuals based on technical adequacy (e.g., Does this instrument have enough easy items to assess a child that is presumed to be relatively low functioning?) and for use with program evaluation (e.g., Is the method that Head Start is using to screen for children at risk accurate in identifying children that need diagnostic assessments?). The social validity of an instrument is indicated by the ability to identify specific needs of an individual child within the curriculum (e.g., a child that has difficulty differentiating between comparative concepts). Reliability and validity have been major issues for screening and readiness assessments. Research has demonstrated that many instruments lack sound psychometric properties (Bredekamp & Shephard, 1989; Meisels, 1987; Meisels, 1992; Shepard, 1992; Wodtke, Harper, Schommer, & Brunelli, 1989).

Floor Effects and Item Gradients.   The floor of an instrument provides information about whether or not the sampling of items provides a low enough range of standard scores. An examination of the lowest standard scores provided for each age range in the standardization sample allows for an appropriate examination of the floor. If the floor is too high, poor performance on the domain being measured will result in an inflated standard score. This is particularly important to pay attention to when assessing preschool children where there is a concern. If the child obtains a raw score of one on a particular domain which translates into a standard score that is in the average range, it is likely that this child will not be identified as being at risk. However, the average classification is the result of construct-irrelevant factors that are inflating the score (Bracken, 2000). The child obtained an average score without getting any items correct not because the child is functioning in the average range, but because the instrument does not sample enough easy items. In this situation, the instrument selected cannot possibly provide any information about children in this age range that are at risk.

Item gradients provide information about the range of content that has been sampled across all difficulty levels. If item gradients are steep, standard scores are dramatically increased as a result of relatively small changes in raw scores. When there is a steep gradient between standard scores and raw scores, subtle facets of a domain are not being adequately assessed. In this situation, the instrument introduces construct-irrelevant variation that does not allow for a valid assessment of the child's ability (Bracken, 2000). Research that has examined preschool instruments identifies significant problems with floor effects and steep item gradients (Bracken, 1987; Flanagan & Alfonso, 1995).

Construct Validity.   Construct validity assesses the degree to which an instrument is measuring the construct of interest. Most screening and readiness assessment instruments demonstrate adequate evidence for overall construct validity. However, assessment with these instruments can be confounded by the interrelationship among constructs widely assessed in young children such as, language development, cognitive functioning, and social-emotional functioning (National Education Goals Panel, 1998). Measures of cognitive functioning may require advanced expressive language or receptive language skills. A child that demonstrates difficulties with expressive language or receptive language may be identified as being at risk for problems with cognitive functioning as a function of the overlap in way the constructs are measured or defined.

Standardized tests that involve the use of paper and pencil are rarely appropriate for young children and typically offer limited information (Shepard, Kagan, & Wurtz, 1998). Most young children have not completed these types of standardized tests, are unable to use pencils, and are unable to read at the level required by the test (National Education Goals Panel, 1998). The children may be able to demonstrate the skills that they possess, but have a difficult time with demonstrating skills because of the language or writing demands of standardized tests. In this situation, the construct that is being assessed by the standardized instrument is confounded by construct-irrelevant variables such as lack of experience with the administration techniques.

Predictive Validity.   The use of screening and readiness for young children assumes that learning and behavioral problems can be accurately and reliably predicted (Gredler, 1997). The ability to use information from screening measures or readiness measures to predict some criterion is one way in which instruments are evaluated.

The primary purpose of screening is to identify children who require more comprehensive evaluation. The utility of a screening instrument can be determined by comparing the outcome on the screening measure (e.g., requires additional assessment, does not require additional assessment) with some criterion. The criterion for comparison could be the results of a comprehensive evaluation, eligibility for special services, or success in an academic setting. Determining the *hit rate* (correct identification of children that do or do not need in-depth assessment) of a screening instrument involves comparing the results of the screening with those of some criterion.

There are four possible outcomes when a child is evaluated using a screening instrument: *true positive*, *false positive*, *true negative*, or *false negative* (see Figure 3.1). A *true positive* involves correctly identifying a child that needs additional assessment. A *false positive* involves identifying a child as needing additional assessment when the child does not actually need additional assessment. A *true negative* involves correctly identifying a child that does not need additional assessment. A *false negative* involves failing to identify a child as needing assessment when the child does actually need additional assessment.

Evaluation of screening instruments typically involves examining the *sensitivity*, the *specificity*, and the *agreement index* (see Figure 3.2). *Sensitivity* is determined by looking at the number of true positives divided by the number of true positives plus the number of false positives. *Specificity* is determined by examining the number of true negatives divided by the number of true negatives plus the number of false negatives. Research that has examined the indexes of screening tests, has suggested adequate levels of specificity (average of .91 across eight instruments) and inadequate levels of sensitivity (average of .48 across eight instruments) (Carran & Scott, 1992).

A screening instrument that aids in the identification of children that are at risk for having learning problems is useful. In examining data from screening instruments, Kingslake (1983) suggested that information from screening instruments demonstrate a minimum criterion of 75% accuracy on two questions: (1) for children that fail on the domain assessed, what percentage were identified as at risk by the screening instrument and (2) for the children that were identified as at risk by the instrument, what percentage actually fail on the domain assessed? Gredler (2000) re-analyzed data on several screening instruments and found the following: the percentage of children identified as at risk on the screening instrument that later performed poorly ranged from 46% to 66%, suggesting that not all the children identified as at risk actually fail on the domain assessed. Gredler also found that the percentage of children that actually performed poorly on the domain, but were missed by the screening instrument, ranged from 9% to 60%.

Research that has specifically examined the predictive validity of readiness assessments has not yielded more positive findings. La Paro and Pianta (2001) conducted a meta-analysis of several longitudinal studies that examined readiness on the domains of

---

Screening Outcomes

(a) True positive—A child that needs additional assessment is identified. This is a correct decision for referral.

(b) False negative—A child that needs additional assessment is not identified. This reflects an under-referral decision.

(c) False positive—A child that does not need additional assessment is identified as needing additional assessment. This reflects an over-referral decision.

(d) True negative—A child that does not need additional assessment is not identified. This reflects a correct non-referral decision.

FIGURE 3.1.   Possible outcomes of screening assessments

Outcome Decision from Screening		
Needs Referral	Does Not Need Referral	Indices
(a) True positive	(b) False negative	$Sensitivity$ $\dfrac{a}{a + b}$
(c) False positive	(d) True negative	$Specificity$ $\dfrac{d}{c + d}$

FIGURE 3.2.   Indices for evaluating screening instruments

cognitive/language development and social and emotional functioning. Their results demonstrated that readiness assessment in cognitive/language functioning and social and emotional functioning only predicted a small to moderate amount of variability on outcome measures during early school years. The results demonstrated the limited utility of readiness assessments in predicting later school functioning. Not all research has suggested difficulties with predictive validity in readiness assessment; preliminary findings about the use of CBM probes for assessing readiness in kindergarten children suggest the ability to identify deficits in reading, math, and writing (van der Heyden, Witt, Naquin & Noell, 2001). Overall, research on the predictive validity of both screening and readiness assessments suggests considerable problems that need to be considered when evaluating programs and selecting instruments for individual assessments.

Decision-Making in Screening and Readiness Assessment

Instruments that are useful in the planning and evaluation of an intervention are considered to have *social utility* (Meisels & Atkins-Burnett, 2000). These instruments provide information that can be directly related to intervention. When evaluating readiness instruments, social utility should be a top priority. Readiness instruments should provide an indication of specific concepts or skills that are relevant for intervention within the child's curriculum. Decisions about labeling should be based on current accepted practices with regard to young children, and efforts should be made to avoid any negative effects related to labeling young children. Additionally, the use of developmental screening and readiness assessment in accountability decisions and "high-stakes" testing need to be closely examined.

Accountability.   There are two primary reasons preschool children are assessed: accountability and intervention (Scott-Little & Maxwell, 2000). Accountability assessment is focused on demonstrating that a program is effective in meeting the needs of the individuals it serves. Programs such as Head Start have been mandated to assess performance across important areas. Assessment of children when they enter kindergarten or Head Start programs can serve as a pre-test on specific domains that are included in the curriculum. Aggregate data from cohorts of children in a program provide repeated measures design that can be used to examine changes on specific domains as a result of the intervention program being utilized. With regard to screening and readiness assessment, accountability is a particular important issue.

In order to adequately assess the efficacy of a treatment program, the readiness construct that is being assessed must be operationalized relative to the goals of the intervention program. Kagan (2005) stresses the importance of accountability assessment that includes physical, social and emotional, and cognitive approaches to learning and language development to provide a comprehensive picture of children's readiness skills. She further suggests that if these domains are indications of readiness that need to be assessed, instrument development will need to advance to include more domains than are currently assessed. This means that careful selection of instruments for program evaluation should include consideration of predictive validity, content sampling, and other important psychometric principles.

The assessment of readiness has been influenced by the trend in education for greater levels of accountability. Saluja, Scott-Little and Clifford (2000) examined state definitions of school readiness, methods used for assessing school readiness, use of data from school readiness assessments, and specific methods for assessing children with diverse difficulties (e.g., disabilities, emotional/behavioral problems, economic disadvantages, . . .). Results of the survey suggested that readiness assessment is a major consideration for most states; however, the focus in most states is not on placement decisions. States are using data from readiness to examine the needs of children as they enter school and to design curriculum based on the needs of the children. There is a more cogent link between readiness assessment and accountability in classroom instruction. Saluja, Scott-Little, and Clifford found that only one state evaluates the readiness of schools for children in their assessment system. They concluded that most school systems are not examining the readiness of the school. A second trend they noted as a concern is that most of the decisions about readiness assessment are made at the district level and that there is considerable variability in the assessment models that are being used at the district level (e.g., from use of standardized assessment tools to use of instruments with no established validity or reliability).

Misapplications.   Assessment data for young children can provide important information about child characteristics and experiences that influence learning (Scott-Little & Neimeyer, 2001). The identification of strengths and weakness allows for the development of a learning environment that will enhance a child's learning. The information from assessments may also serve as baseline data to evaluate the effectiveness of curricula. "High-stakes" assessment involves making decisions that have serious implications for individual children. Examples of "high-stakes" assessment include decisions about tracking into ability groups, labeling children, retaining children, and using data from assessment to deny entry into school (Shepard, Kagan, & Wurtz, 1998).

Readiness assessment has been misused to deny children entrance into school or to place them into specific classes without completion of more comprehensive evaluations (Gredler, 1992; May & Kundert, 1992). Results are sometimes misinterpreted to suggest that some children are not ready for school (National Research Council, 2000). The result in the school system is that children who are identified as not being ready for a particular program would be likely to benefit from the learning opportunities provided in the setting (Shepard, Kagan, & Wurtz, 1998). An additional result is that instead of seeing decreases in achievement gaps between groups such as boys and non-English speaking students when compared with girls and English speaking students, the gap between these groups increases because of the inadequacy of the alternative program provided.

Several important panels have stressed that readiness data should not be used to keep children out of kindergarten or to suggest that some children are not ready for school (e.g., National Educational Goals Panel Goal 1 Ready Schools Resource Group, 1997). As a result of misapplications of readiness assessment in relation to "high-stakes" testing, Meisels (1989) recommended that readiness assessment be the initial step in diagnostic assessment, that school policymakers recognize the importance of careful consideration when selecting instruments for individual children, and that the alternative program options provided to children who fail readiness assessment be closely scrutinized.

BEST PRACTICES IN DEVELOPMENTAL SCREENING AND READINESS ASSESSMENT

Previous research has suggested that the cognitive, emotional, and social functioning of young children can be positively influenced by developmentally appropriate curricula (e.g., Campbell, Pungello, Miller-Johnson, Burchinal, & Ramey, 2001; Campbell, Ramey, Pungello, Sparling, & Miller-Johnson, 2002; Campbell & Ramey, 1994, 1995; Marcon, 1999; Ramey et al., 2000; Ramey & Campbell, 1991; Schweinhart & Weikart, 1998). The empirical research base that supports early intervention also provides a strong impetus for assessment during early childhood. Assessment with preschool children serves three primary functions: (a) screening for suspected disabilities or for comprehensive evaluation, (b) providing specific information about strengths and weaknesses that can be used to individualize instruction provided by teachers, and (c) providing one component of data for program evaluation (Scott-Little & Niemeyer, 2001).

Developmental screening is designed to identify children that are at risk for failure in the academic environment without interventions. The children that are identified using screening instruments are administered diagnostic assessment batteries to examine more specific areas of concern. Screening measures typically assess children on domains such as cognitive functioning and general knowledge, language development, and physical functioning. Children who are likely to fail screening instruments in one of these domains are also likely to demonstrate curriculum-related deficits in these areas. This overlap in target population perhaps suggests that a continuum of assessment functions (ranging from screening to diagnostic) is probably the best way in which to conceptualize early childhood assessment.

The National Educational Goals Panel (1991) identified four potential benefits of readiness assessment: identifying children with special needs and health conditions, individualizing and improving instruction, evaluating program effectiveness, and obtaining benchmark data on the status of children at the local, state, and community level. These identified benefits suggest considerable overlap in the functions of developmental screening instruments, readiness assessment instruments, and diagnostic assessment instruments. If a screening function is included in readiness assessment, the opportunity to identify conditions that have not been previously detected (Muenchow, 2003) is greatly enhanced.

The goals of the screening programs and readiness assessment should not be to exclude certain children from kindergarten or to place certain children into programs for children with disabilities. The goals should focus on curriculum planning and on identifying children who need comprehensive evaluations. The assessment techniques selected should be based on the goals of the school. If the school is interested in the child's readiness to take advantage of specific components within the school curriculum, then a readiness tool that is used must assess skills associated with the curriculum. The assessment tool should be matched with the curriculum that is being utilized. Readiness assessments may often include a criterion-referenced component. If the goal is to identify children that need special services, a screening instrument may provide an index of which children need to be referred for additional assessment. Screening tests are typically designed to measure a child's potential for acquiring skills and are often norm-referenced.

In general, screening and readiness assessment programs should take into consideration the following: (1) ensuring appropriate goals, (2) selecting assessment techniques that correspond to program goals, (3) using psychometrically sound instruments, (4) utilizing findings from research to guide screening program development, (5) including information from multiple sources, and (6) monitoring to make sure that follow-up assessment and program evaluation are conducted (Rafoth, 1997). The considerations can be discussed in terms of best practices in defining goals and constructs, selecting assessment tools, examining the technical adequacy of assessment tools, using a multidimensional, multifaceted approach to assessment, and providing data that is of benefit to the individual child as well as the community.

Construct Definitions

When developing a screening or readiness assessment program, it is important to clearly define the goals of the evaluation. Goals can range from being focused on identifying individual children that need additional assessment or that show specific skill deficits to being focused on examination of the effectiveness of intervention programs within a school system or the effectiveness of the methods used for identifying groups of children that need additional assessment. It is also important to provide clear definitions of important constructs such as "at risk" or "readiness."

Research on screening and readiness assessment must take into consideration the difficulty of defining constructs such as "at-risk" and "readiness." At-risk definitions assume that the children identified are likely to have difficulties that place them at risk for academic failure or behavioral problems, while readiness assessment assumes that there are specific skills that children need to have before they enter formal schooling. The manner in which academic failure and behavioral problems are defined has a tremendous impact on the use of outcome data. For readiness assessment, the expectation for what these skills are varies considerably across readiness assessment tools and across actual school systems.

Consideration of Technical Properties

The technical properties of an instrument are considerably important. They determine how much confidence an examiner can have in the results of the assessment. Historically, school systems have demonstrated little concern for using assessment tools with strong technical properties. For norm-referenced developmental screening and readiness assessment instruments, it is important to pay attention to several things. Examiners should examine the range of standard scores provided across all domains assessed and for all age ranges. Floor effects have been problematic with screening and readiness assessment and suggest too few easy items to get an accurate picture of an individual that is low functioning.

Item gradients allow examination of how well an instrument assesses subskills within a domain. Instruments with poor item gradients show a steep increase in standard scores with relatively small increases in raw scores. Instruments that are the most useful will be able to discriminate between more subtle subskills within a domain. This is particularly important for readiness assessment when an error analysis might shed some light onto specific skills that need intervention.

Examination of the standardization sample should also be a concern when selecting instruments for screening or readiness assessment. If a primary concern for screening is to be able to identify individuals that are at risk or need additional assessment, it is important for the normative sample for the selected instrument to include individuals with a range of disabilities. Additionally, the standardization sample needs to reflect the situation and population representative of the examiners setting, especially if the examiner is working with children with cultural or linguistic differences.

Predictive validity of the instruments needs to be well documented when making important decisions about a child's functioning. The predictive validity establishes a basis for accepting the results of one's findings. For both screening and readiness instruments, it is important to have a well-defined criterion that is going to be used to evaluate the instrument. Measures of sensitivity and specificity are important concepts for screening instruments and can provide specific information about the effectiveness of the instrument in identifying a target group. Screening is most useful when it is cost efficient and does not over- or under-identify children who need additional assessment. Criteria that are useful for readiness assessments may focus on specific aspects of curriculum such as decoding skills. For program evaluation, readiness assessment criteria involve aggregating data across children and looking for the ability to predict skill areas warranting curriculum adjustments. Accountability assessment, by nature of being an assessment that is used to make significant decisions such as program evaluation or success of individual teachers, must utilize instruments that have demonstrated the highest indexes of being psychometrically robust.

Multidimensional, Multifaceted, and Multisource Assessments

The National Education Goals Panel recommended that school readiness include five dimensions: health and physical development, emotional well-being and social competence, approaches to learning, communication skills, and cognition and general knowledge (Kagan, Moore, & Bredekamp, 1995). Indicators for measuring readiness on each of these standards are not well defined (Saluja, Scott-Little, & Clifford, 2000). There are also no standardized procedures for how to accurately assess each of these domains. As previously mentioned, assessment of these areas is confounded by the limitations inherent in evaluating young children. Additionally, Meisels (1999) suggested that there may be important considerations beyond the five dimensions.

Assessments with children should focus on multiple dimensions (i.e., cognitive, socioemotional, language, physical), include multiple sources of information (parents and teachers), use multiple assessment tools (authentic, standardized, observational, rating scales . . .), and sample behavior in multiple settings (classroom and school). When attempting to assess the domains that have been identified as being critical for assessing readiness, it is important to utilize instruments that sample broadly across content domains and that take into account the high correlations between domains such as cognitive, language, and socioemotional functioning (Scott-Little & Niemeyer, 2001). Given the interrelationship between these domains, assessment should examine as many different domains as possible. This will allow for a better understanding of the child's strengths and weaknesses.

Developmental screening and readiness assessment should not rely solely on information from one instrument, rely on information from one source, or utilize information from one type of assessment technique. Standardized norm-referenced instruments provide valuable information for comparing children to their same age peers. However, additional valuable information can be obtained from the use of rating scales and checklists. These instruments are particularly useful for examining the domains such as social and emotional functioning and approaches to learning that are not necessarily included on other types of instruments.

Authentic assessments require children to complete "real-life" tasks in natural settings. They may involve examining work samples or observing children in classrooms. The use of authentic assessment minimizes behavioral changes as a reaction to strangers and allow for observation of the demands that exist within the classroom. Observational systems can be used to examine social and emotional development with a focus on interactions with parents and interactions with other children. Curriculum-based instruments that focus on mastery of skills can provide valuable information about readiness skills.

An extension of curriculum-based assessment involves the collection of work samples over time. These work samples can be documented in a portfolio that allows for monitoring of attainment of specific skills. Assessments that focus on work samples are designed to document skills and behaviors of young children across domains (Meisels, 1995). Work samples allow for curriculum-based assessment that can occur multiple times throughout a year. This model for work sampling proposes checklists to examine personal and social development, language and literacy, mathematics, scientific thinking, social studies, the arts, and physical development. It is designed to examine performance based on accepted standards in the curriculum according to national, state, and local norms. The sampling involves a collection of work that is displayed in a child's portfolio. The work sampling also includes a summary report that is based on the evidence presented in the portfolio and on the checklists. This model has been recommended as a replacement for standardized, group-administered assessments that are commonly used in early intervention programs such as Head Start.

It is also important to consider the readiness of the school to receive children, not just the readiness of individual children as they enter the school environment (Saluja, Scott-Little, & Clifford, 2000). The components that have been identified as indicating schools are ready for children include: (1) knowledge of typical and atypical growth and development of children, (2) knowledge of the individual strengths, interests, and needs of the child, (3) understanding of the context (social and cultural) in which the family lives, and (4) the ability to utilize the knowledge to foster an environment that is developmentally appropriate (North Carolina School Improvement Goal Panel Ready for School Goal Team, 2000).

Social Utility of Instruments

Assessment data gathered from young children should not serve as the sole piece of information used for high-stakes decisions (Scott-Little & Niemeyer, 2001). The data should not be used to determine whether or not a child can start kindergarten (or continue into first grade). These decisions should be made using authentic assessments (work samples and observations), parent and teacher feedback, evaluations from other professionals (such as speech language pathologists), knowledge of empirical research, and any information from standardized assessments.

Saluja, Scott-Little, and Clifford (2000) examined several position statements regarding readiness assessment in young children and identified eight important considerations for readiness assessment: (1) the assessment should benefit both the children and the adults working with the children, (2) assessment tools should be used only for the intended purpose expressed by the test developer, (3) the validity and reliability of the assessment technique should be well established, (4) naturalistic observations that are age appropriate and involve interaction in a "real-life" context should be utilized, (5) the assessment should involve data collection across developmental domains, (6) the assessment techniques should take into consideration linguistic and cultural factors, (7) multiple sources and multiple tools should be utilized when collecting assessment data, and (8) the assessment data gathered should guide instructional practice.

SUMMARY

This chapter has provided a context for understanding developmental screening and readiness assessment. The current political agenda is focused on accountability in education, including early childhood intervention programs. In this regard, developmental screening and readiness assessment have a significant role in early childhood assessment. They have been targeted as methods for identifying children that are "at risk" for school failure, for identifying whether or not children are "ready to learn" when they enter school, and for identifying children that need a more comprehensive evaluation. Although there is considerable utility in the use of developmental screening and readiness assessment, there needs to be caution in determining the best way to evaluate preschool children. Selection of an instrument should take into consideration the importance of assessing functioning across multiple domains, the importance of having robust psychometric properties and technical adequacy, and the importance of authentic assessment when evaluating young children. These considerations should be useful in both developing an assessment protocol for an early intervention program to measure accountability as well as for developing an assessment plan to determine what curriculum-based interventions are needed for a given child.

REFERENCES

Bagnato, S. J., & Neisworth, J. T. (1994). A national study of the social and treatment "invalidity" of intelligence testing for early intervention. *School Psychology Quarterly, 9*, 81–102.

Bracken, B. A. (1987). Limitations in preschool instruments and standards for minimal levels of technical adequacy. *Journal of Psychoeducational Assessment, 4*, 313–326.

Bracken, B. A. (1998). *Bracken Basic Concept Scale, Revised*. San Antonio, TX: The Psychological Corporation.

Bracken, B. A. (2000). Maximizing construct relevant assessment: The optimal preschool testing situation. In B. A. Bracken (Ed.), *The psychoeducational assessment of preschool children* (3rd ed., pp. 33–44). Boston: Allyn & Bacon.

Bredkamp, S., & Shepard, L. (1989). How to best protect children from inappropriate school expectations, practices, and policies. *Young Children, 44*, 14–24.

Campbell, F. A., Pungello, E. P., Miller-Johnson, S., Burchinal, M., & Ramey, C. T. (2001). The Development of Cognitive and Academic Abilities: Growth Curves from an Early Childhood Educational Experiment. *Developmental Psychology, 37*, 231–242.

Campbell, F. A., & Ramey, C. T. (1994). Effects of early intervention on intellectual and academic achievement: A follow-up study of children from low-income families. *Child Development, 65*, 684–698.

Campbell, F. A., & Ramey, C. T. (1995). Cognitive and school outcomes for high-risk African-American students at middle adolescence: Positive effects of early intervention. *American Educational Research Journal, 32*, 743–772.

Campbell, F. A., Ramey, C. T., Pungello, E. P., Sparling, J., & Miller-Johnson, S. (2002). Early Childhood Education: Young Adult Outcomes from the Abecedarian Project. *Applied Developmental Science, 6*, 42–57.

Carran, D. T., & Scott, K. G. (1992). Risk assessment in preschool children: Research implications for the early detection of educational handicaps. *Topics in Early Childhood Special Education, 12*, 196–211.

Flanagan, D. P., & Alfonso, V. C. (1995). A critical review of the technical characteristics of new and recently revised intelligence tests for preschool children. *Journal of Psychoeducational Assessment, 13*, 66–90.

Frank Porter Graham Child Development Institute. (2005). *The Carolina Abecedarian project: Executive summary*. Retrieved January 6, 2005, from http://www.fpg.unc.edu/,abc/

Gesell Institute of Child Development. (1987). The Gesell Institute responds. *Young Children, 42*, 7–8.

Gredler, G. (1992). *School readiness: Assessment and educational issues*. Brandon, VT: Clinical Psychology Publishing Company.

Gredler, G. R. (1997). Issues in early childhood screening and assessment. *Psychology in the Schools, 34*(2), 99–106.

Gredler, G. R. (2000). Early childhood screening for developmental and educational problems. In B. A. Bracken (Ed.), *The psychoeducational assessment of preschool children* (3rd ed., pp. 399–411). Boston: Allyn & Bacon.

Gresham, F. M., & Elliott, S. N. (1990). *Social Skills Rating System manual*. Circle Pines, MN: American Guidance Services.

Harrison, P. L. (1990). *AGS Early Screening Profiles manual*. Circle Pines, MN: American Guidance Service.

Kagan, S. (1990). Readiness in 2000: Rethinking rhetoric and responsibility. *Phi Delta Kappan, 72*, 272–279.

Kagan, S. L. (2005). Assessing young children: A matter of head, heart, and hand. *Social Policy Report: Giving Child and Youth Development Knowledge Away, 19*, 14–15.

Kagan, S. L., Moore, E., & Bredekamp, S. (Eds.). (1995). *Reconsidering children's early development and learning: Toward common views and vocabulary*. Report of the National Education Goals Panel, Goal 1 Technical Planning Group. Washington, DC: Government Printing Office.

Kenny, T. J., & Culbertson, J. L. (1993). Developmental Screening for preschoolers. In J. L. Culbertson & D. J. Willis (Eds.), *Testing Young Children: A reference guide for developmental, psychoeducational, and psychosocial assessments* (pp. 73–100). Austin, TX: Pro-Ed.

Kingslake, B. (1983). The predictive (in)accuracy of on-entry to school screening procedures when used to prevent learning difficulties. *British Journal of Special Education, 10*, 24–26.

La Paro, K. M., & Pianta, R. C. (2001). Predicting children's competence in the early school years: A meta-analytic review. *Review of Educational Research, 70*, 443–484.

Lichenstein, R., & Ireton, H. (1991). Preschool screening for developmental and educational problems. In B. A. Bracken (Ed.), *Psychoeducational assessment of preschool children* (pp. 486–513). Boston: Allyn & Bacon.

Luehr, R. E., & Hoxie, A. (Eds.). (1995). *Early childhood screening: Program administration manual*. St. Paul. MN: Minnesota Department of Education.

Marcon, R. A. (1999). Differential impact of preschool models on development and early learning of inner-city children: A three cohort study. *Developmental Psychology, 2*, 358–375.

May, D. C., & Kundert, D. K. (1992). Kindergarten screenings in New York state: Tests, purposes, and recommendations. *Psychology in the Schools, 29*, 35–41.

Mehaffie, K. E., & McCall, R. B. (2002). *Kindergarten readiness: An overview of issues and assessment* (Special Report). University of Pittsburgh, Office of Child Development.

Meisels, S. J. (1987). Uses and abuses of developmental screening and school readiness tests. *Young Children, 42,* 68–73.

Meisels, S. J. (1989). High-stakes testing. *Educational Leadership, 40,* 16–22.

Meisels, S. J. (1992). Doing harm by doing good: Iatrogenic effects of early childhood enrollment and promotion policies. *Early Childhood Research Quarterly, 7,* 155–174.

Meisels, S. J. (1994). *Developmental screening in early childhood: A guide* (4th ed.). Washington, DC: National Association for the Education of Young Children.

Meisels, S. J. (1995). Performance assessment in early childhood education: The Work Sampling System. *ERIC Clearinghouse on Elementary and Early Childhood Education.* ED382407.

Meisels, S. J. (1999). Assessing readiness. In R. C. Pianta, & M. J. Cox (Eds.), *The transition to kindergarten.* Baltimore: Paul H. Brookes.

Meisels, S. J., & Atkins-Burnett, S. (2000). The elements of early childhood assessment. In J. P. Shonkoff & S. J. Meisels (Eds.), *The handbook of early childhood intervention* (2nd Edition) (pp. 231–257). New York: Cambridge University Press

Meltzer, L., & Reid, D. K. (1994). New directions in the assessment of students with special needs: The shift toward a constructivist perspective. *The Journal of Special Education, 28,* 338–355.

Muenchow, S. (2003). *A risk management approach to readiness assessment: Lessons from Florida.* In C. Scott-Little, S. L. Kagan, & R. M. Clifford (Eds.), *Assessing the state of state assessments: Perspectives on assessing young children* (pp. 13–23). Greensboro, NC: SERVE.

Nagle, R. J. (2000). Issues in preschool assessment. In B. A. Bracken (Ed.), *The psychoeducational assessment of preschool children* (3rd ed., pp. 19–32). Boston: Allyn & Bacon.

National Education Goals Panel (1991). *The national education goals report: Building a nation of learners.* Washington, DC: U.S. Government Printing Office.

National Education Goals Panel. (1998). *Principles and recommendations for early childhood assessment.* Washington, DC: Government Printing Office.

Niemeyer, J., & Scott-Little, C. (2002). *Assessing kindergarten children: A compendium of assessment instruments.* Greensboro, NC: SERVE.

North Carolina School Improvement Goal Panel Ready for School Goal Team. (2000). *School readiness in North Carolina: Strategies for defining, measuring, and promoting success for all children.* Raleigh, NC: North Carolina State Board of Education.

Rafoth, M. A. (1997). [Electronic Version]. Guidelines for developing screening programs. *Psychology in the Schools, 34,* 129–137.

Ramey, C. T., & Campbell, F. A. (1991). Poverty, early childhood education, and academic competence: The Abecedarian experiment. In A. Huston (Ed.), *Children reared in poverty* (pp. 190–221). New York: Cambridge University Press.

Ramey, C. T., Campbell, F. A., Burchinal, M., Skinner, M. L., Gardner, D. M., & Ramey, S. L. (2000). Persistent effects of early intervention on high-risk children and their mothers. *Applied Developmental Science, 4,* 2–14.

Rhode Island KIDS COUNT. (February, 2005). *Getting reading: Findings from the National School Readiness Indicators Initiative: A 17 state partnership.* Author.

Saluja, G., Scott-Little, C., & Clifford, R. M. (2000). [Electronic Version]. Readiness for school: A survey of state policies and definitions. *Early Childhood Research and Practice, 2*(2). Retrieved from http://ecrp.uiuc.edu/v2n2/saluja.html

Schweinhart, L., & Weikart, D. (1998). Why curriculum matters in early childhood education. *Educational Leadership, 55,* 57–60.

Scott-Little, C., & Maxwell, K. (2000). *School readiness in North Carolina: Strategies for defining, measuring, and promoting success for all children.* Greensboro, NC: SERVE.

Scott-Little, C., & Niemeyer, J. (2001). *Assessing kindergarten children: What school systems need to know.* Greensboro, NC: SERVE.

Shepard, L. (1992). Psychometric properties of the Gesell Developmental Assessment: A critique. *Early Childhood Research Quarterly, 7,* 47–52.

Shepard, L., Kagan, S. L., & Wurtz, E. (Eds.). (1998). *Principles and recommendations for early childhood assessments*. Washington, DC: National Education Goals Panel.

Thurlow, M. L., & Gilman, C. J. (1999). Issues and practices in the screening of preschool children. In E. V. Nuttall, I. Romero, & J. Kalesnik (Eds.), *Assessing and screening preschoolers: Psychological and educational dimensions* (2nd ed., pp. 59–71). Boston: Allyn & Bacon.

van der Heyden, A. M, Witt, J. C., Naquin, G., & Noell, G. (2001). The reliability and validity of curriculum-based measurement readiness probes for kindergarten students. [Electronic Version]. *School Psychology Review, 30*, 1–17.

Wodtke, K., Harper, F., Schommer, M., & Brunelli, P. (1989). How standardized is school testing? An exploratory observational study of standardized group testing in kindergarten. *Educational Evaluation and Policy Analysis, 2*, 223–235.

4

Assessing Multicultural Preschool Children

Maryann Santos de Barona and Andrés Barona
Arizona State University, Tempe

The need for appropriate evaluation of culturally different preschool children continues to increase. This need is a result of two major developments in the United States. The first development was federal involvement in education in the 1960s and 1970s that resulted in legislation affecting preschool and school-age children. The 1964 Maternal Child Health and Mental Retardation Act and the 1964 Educational Opportunity Act required that educational and social opportunities be provided for all children, while Public Law (P.L.) 94-142 mandated that a free and appropriate education be provided to children with disabilities from the age of 3 (Kelley & Surbeck, 1983). Later legislation in the form of P.L. 94-457 and the Individuals with Disabilities Act (IDEA; P.L. 102-119) further authorized special education and related services to eligible preschool children. Federally funded educational programs designed to implement the terms of these acts were required to implement performance-based evaluations to demonstrate that participating children improve in the areas of achievement, intelligence, or other measurable dimensions (Kelley & Surbeck, 1983). Appropriate preschool assessment instruments, therefore, became necessary not only to determine eligibility but also to measure and demonstrate gains in the specified areas.

The second development that creates an increased need for assessment of culturally different preschoolers is the population shift occurring in the United States. The rate of growth in the number of children has increased since 1990, and in 2002 children under age 18 constituted 25% of the total U.S. population (Federal Interagency Forum on Child and Family Services (FIFCFS; 1997, 2004). Currently, approximately 64% of the U.S. population can be considered to be white and non-Hispanic and it is projected that this percentage will be reduced to 53% by the year 2020 (America's Children, 2004a). In 2003, 20% of children under the age of 18 had at least one foreign-born parent. (America's Children, 2004b). Thus, it can be seen that the number of persons from minority cultures in this country is sizable and growing. The increase in the minority population is perhaps most evident when examining the statistics of school-age and younger children; the number of Hispanic children has increased faster than any other racial group, growing from 9% of the child population in 1980 to 19% in 2004 (America's Children, 2004a). By 2020, it is projected that more than one in five children in the U.S. will be of Hispanic origin. Additionally, the overall percentage of children of Asian descent in the United States doubled from 2% to 4% from 1980 to 2000 and is projected to increase to 6% by 2020. The growth is particularly evident at the younger ages; whereas only about 7% of the total U.S. population is under 5 years of age (U.S. Census, 2003), for Hispanics the percentage is over 10% (Ramirez, 2004). In July 2003, 21% of all children under age 5 were Hispanic (Collins & Ribeiro, 2004).

By definition, a culturally different child is one who comes "from an ethnic group having sociocultural patterns that differ from those of the predominant society. These groups may include "Blacks, Hispanic-Americans, American Indians, and Asian-Americans" (Sattler, 1992, p. 592). Within each group, "there are differences in values, motivation, social organization, ways of speaking and thinking, and life styles that vary with education, income, class status, geographic origin, assimilation patterns, religious background, and age. (Sattler, 2001, p. 636). A child of preschool age who is a member of a culturally different family might share few common experiences with age peers of the dominant American culture. For this young age group, it is expected that the family will be the primary socializing influence because preschool programs reach only about 34% of the total population (U.S. Census, 1997), with white children enrolled in nursery schools at a rate twice that of Hispanic children (U.S. Department of Commerce and Management Planning Research Associates, Inc., 1992; cited in Prince & Lawrence, 1993). Among ethnic groups, Hispanic children in particular have the lowest preschool participation rates. Additionally, although there has been a substantial increase in the number of 3 and 4 year olds attending, state-funded preschool programs in 2002 reached only 10% of the children in this age group. This is significant as "the children least likely to attend preschool are those whose parents have the least education and least income . . ." (Barnett & Yarosz, 2004, p. 12).

The values, behaviors, experiences, and attitudes of these culturally different families vary significantly from those of the typical American acculturated middle-class family. These differences can be highlighted by contrasting two cultures' perceptions of giftedness. In mainstream America, a gifted middle-class child is commonly thought to demonstrate high achievement or potential in general intellectual ability, or academic, creative, or psychomotor aptitude (EAC West, 1996; Marland, 1972). In American subcultures, this perspective can vary dramatically. The results of at least one study (Bernal, 1974) indicate that the traits of obedience, common sense, responsibility, respectfulness, independence, self-reliance, and the ability to influence others were emphasized as much as the trait of intelligence when Mexican Americans identified gifted children. Similar findings were noted by Hartley (1991) who reported that a gifted Navajo child may consider family and spiritual activities to take precedence over school activities, be reluctant to compete with peers for leadership roles, and be modest about personal accomplishments. Traditionally oriented Navajos markedly differed from both white and acculturated Navajos in their concept of giftedness; interestingly, the Navajo language contains no single word for gifted. From these examples, it can be seen that not only do experiences differ for preschool children of different cultures, but also that certain abilities and characteristics not commonly recognized by U.S. society as reflective of outstanding talent are likely to be selectively reinforced among U.S. minority cultures. In support of this, Hartley (1991) suggests that Navajo traits such as not being competitive or assertive and not asking questions or challenging incorrect statements make identification of gifted and talented Navajo children difficult. The growing awareness of these differences led Christensen (1991) to call for definitions of gifted and talented to include a cultural stance.

Similarly, cultural differences can affect the way learning occurs as well as what information is learned. Evidence suggests that individuals of different cultures will recall and understand those aspects of a lesson that are most relevant to their own culture. In a cross-cultural study of reading comprehension conducted be Steffensen, Joag-Dev, and Anderson (1979), American and Indian students read passages describing weddings in both cultures. Members of each culture recalled more information related to the wedding within their own culture. In addition, each culture focused on different aspects of the passages; Americans emphasized the romantic, whereas Indians highlighted the monetary exchange between families. Results of these studies suggest that culturally different students might need assistance in learning information with which they have had little or no prior experience (Fradd, 1987). Additional work by Razi (2004) found that students provided with a nativized short story demonstrated significantly better comprehension than those provided with the original version. Finally, Wang and Leichtman (2000) found social, emotional, and cognitive content differences between 6-year-old American and Chinese children's stories and memory narratives which were "associated with cultural value systems established through divergent socialization processes during the early years of life (p. 1331).

Additionally, differences in language socialization practices may result in different levels of vocabulary acquisition (Peña & Quinn, 1997). Specifically, Latino American, African American, and European American mothers used very different verbal interaction styles with their young children (Anderson-Yockel & Haynes, 1994; Heath, 1986; Langdon & Cheng, 1992; Peña, Quinn, & Iglesias, 1992). Whereas European American children often were asked to respond to questions broached with a "wh" format (who, where, when, what, why), this questioning style did not occur often with Latino children, who rarely were asked to provide rehearsed information or information that the adult already knew, or with African American children, who were asked to compare, explain, or respond nonverbally rather than provide a succinct one-word response. Such cultural variations in language socialization may inadvertently affect performance on standardized tests which often incorporate labeling tasks to evaluate vocabulary Using a test format that is unfamiliar to the children may provide results that are more reflective of how well the child is acculturated rather than what they may know or are capable of doing.

Many individuals from culturally different groups often come from linguistically different backgrounds, specifically non-English-language backgrounds. Approximately 17% of children in the United States between 5 and 17 years of age speak a language other than English at home (FIFCFS, 2004), and it is estimated that this proportion may be higher for children younger than 5 years because school may be their first formal encounter with English (Prince & Lawrence, 1993) (Author; please provide reference). Although the majority of non-English speakers (i.e., 59.9%) speak Spanish as their primary language, many other languages also are represented (Shin & Bruno, 2003).

Young children who speak a language other than English as their primary language may exhibit academic problems if placed in monolingual English classes upon school entry. Their lack of exposure to the English language greatly increases the probability that they will not understand much of the information that is being communicated to them. Unable to process information provided in English and unaware of what is being said to them, Limited English Proficient (LEP) children can easily become inattentive and distractible. Such behaviors may lead school personnel to conclude that these young children lack school readiness because they do not demonstrate the type of attention span, motivation, or maturity desired and expected in mainstream U.S. school settings. These children can be considered to be at risk for learning academic content such as reading, writing, and arithmetic, as well as for knowing what behaviors are expected in their new, unfamiliar, and structured environment (Bryen & Gallagher, 1983).

It also is suggested that LEP preschool children might experience additional difficulties with the way in which information is conveyed in group situations. Whereas parents of young children often use repetition, emphasis, and the context of the physical environment to assist the child in learning new words, classroom teachers often interact with the entire group and are unable to use repetitive and context-based clues (Bryen & Gallagher, 1983). Information also can be conveyed in more abstract forms. Unfortunately, preschoolers of limited English proficiency are largely unable to benefit fully from these approaches until their English skills are better developed. Instead, they often must rely on the aid of the physical context or the actions of their peers to understand and produce language. Without these aids, learning and possibly behavior problems will occur.

As one might imagine, defining normal development and behavior, as well as being able to identify mild learning problems in young children, is a difficult task given the rapid and variable rate of development among preschool children. For some children, the acquisition rate of cognitive, physical, social, emotional, and motor skills is sudden—one moment the skill is not observable while the next it is clearly present. For other children, skill acquisition is a gradual process. Given the recognition that the rate of development is unique for each child (Guddemi & Case, 2004), the definition of normal development and behavior is even more difficult when a culturally different or LEP preschool child is involved; school personnel often are unaware that aspects of school readiness may be strongly influenced by culture (Prince & Lawrence, 1993), with different ethnicities varying in their rates of development in or emphasis on specific areas (Peña & Quinn, 1997; Prince, 1992).

THE PURPOSES OF ASSESSMENT

Assessment of the preschool child serves several purposes. First, assessment can be used to screen children for potential learning problems by a normative comparison to same-age peers. This technique quantifies differences between individuals by describing the child's performance in light of the average performance of a relevant comparison group. Second, it can be diagnostically useful to determine if deficiencies exist in any one of a number of areas. Preschool assessment can measure competencies in either developmental areas or readiness skills (McLoughlin & Lewis, 1986; Paget & Nagle, 1986). Criterion-referenced measures also can be included here, with scores on such measures interpreted relative to an established standard of performance. Finally, assessment can be used to monitor progress that is the result of an intervention (Garber & Slater, 1983). Generally, assessment can be viewed as a means of confirming or denying the presence of a problem for an individual. During the assessment process, information is obtained that specifies the individual's level of functioning and identifies areas of strength and weakness. This information then is used to make intervention decisions to facilitate the development of that individual.

THE PROBLEMS OF ASSESSMENT

Problems Related to the Preschool Child

Obtaining the appropriate information with which to make decisions to assist in further development is likely to be a challenge when preschool children are tested. Generally, preschoolers' social behaviors are not conducive to psychoeducational assessments.

Preschool children often follow their own impulses and may be unaccepting of the constraints of the testing situation (Bagnato & Neisworth, 1991; Bondurant-Utz & Luciano, 1994; Gelman, 1979; Ulrey, 1981). Young children often express their feelings easily and can be quite uninterested in their own performance. In addition, test performance can be affected by biological drives such as the need to nap or rest, and behavior can vary significantly over short periods of time. Thus, the examiner needs special skills and understanding to work with the preschooler. Patience and creativity are essential and it is necessary to be both positive and confident in interactions with the child. Finally, the examiner must be able to modify the assessment to accommodate any changes in a child's behavior. These requirements generally represent a departure from the more traditional methods followed for school-age children (Bagnato & Neisworth, 1991; Paget, 1983; Romero, 1992).

Problems Related to Differences in Culture

In the most ideal circumstances, assessment is a complicated process. It is made even more complex when the individual to be evaluated is from a culturally diverse or limited English-speaking background (Barona & Santos de Barona, 1987). When the unique age-related problems inherent to testing preschool children are added, it becomes crucial to conduct an assessment with even greater care given to both accuracy and an awareness of those social, cultural, and linguistic factors that can influence test performance because "unrecognized diversity . . . can generate behaviors that interfere with learning and mimic those generated by disabilities" (Barrera, 1995, p. 54). Certainly, the fact that the number of children in special education who are culturally and linguistically diverse is higher than expected highlights the need to proceed carefully to avoid error in the assessment process (McLean, 1998).

The culturally different preschooler can differ from a mainstream American peer on a number of important dimensions. If from an economically disadvantaged environment, the minority child might be less attentive and less persistent on tasks because of differences in the demand characteristics between home and school (Garber & Slater, 1983) and, therefore, less likely to do well on tasks with an academic orientation. Solutions to social intervention problems can be both more limited in variety and more aggressive (Spivack & Shure, 1976). It should be noted, however, that when provided with learning environments that reinforced more appropriate learning styles, improvements in reflection and in problem-solving strategies were noted (Garber, 1977; Slater & Heber, 1979; Spivack & Shure, 1976).

Expressive skills and style of interaction with an adult also can differ among culturally different preschoolers (McLaughlin, Gesi Blanchard, & Osanai, 1995). Vocabulary for preschoolers revolves around their experiences. To the extent that a culturally different child has experienced significantly different events from either the mainstream American child or from what the assessment materials cover, that child might be unable to respond in the same manner as his or her peers who have had more exposure with the general subject matter.

Even more significant are the differences in styles of interaction that exist among children of varying cultures. Early social development for Asian Americans and Native Americans differs from the American mainstream (Prince, 1992). Furthermore, in some cultures it is considered impolite and even challenging for eye contact to be maintained between a child and an adult, for a child to contradict an adult or to express an opinion that might differ, or to speak to an adult unless spoken to directly. A well-mannered Vietnamese child, for instance, will speak only when spoken to. As a result, voluntary responses in a classroom might be interpreted as showing off or even rude. Respect is shown by sitting quietly and listening attentively. Much can be communicated non-verbally—thankfulness or apology can be conveyed with silence or a smile. Indeed, within the Vietnamese culture, a verbal expression of thanks would reflect a lack of modesty (Huynh, 1987). In a similar vein, preschool Chinese children frequently are passive participants in a classroom setting and do not compete with other children (Garber & Slater, 1983). After completing a task, they rarely proceed automatically to other work (Tikunoff, 1987). A teacher or evaluator unfamiliar with such cultural characteristics might, unfortunately, conclude that a child who demonstrates any of the preceding characteristics is dull, sullen, unmotivated, or even developmentally delayed.

In still another culture, eye contact has very different connotations than in U.S. society. Unlike American parents and teachers, who when scolding a child might say, "Look at me when I speak to you," Hispanic adults would interpret sustained direct eye contact as an act of defiance. This cultural characteristic holds throughout life. Prolonged eye contact between adolescent or even adult males in the Hispanic culture can lead to fighting because it is read as a challenge. An often-used phrase among adolescent Mexican males is "soy o me paresco?" or "is it me—or do I look like him?" with the implication being, "is it me that you are looking for (to fight) or do I just look like him?"

Related to this issue is an important point: individuals must not be lumped together because of apparent physical similarities. For example, it must be recognized that great diversity in cultural patterns and values exists among Asian cultures. Whereas the parameters of social situations are carefully defined within Cambodian society (Chhim, 1987), Lao adults avoid overt guidance. Rather, Lao children learn through observation and modeling (Luangpraseut, 1987). A lack of awareness of such variations between cultures, that to many Americans appear strikingly similar because of physical similarities, again can result in erroneous conclusions about the culturally different child.

In the preschool assessment situation in particular, these differences may require special intervention or the selection of alternative assessment procedures to maximize the usefulness of the obtained information. Such procedures may supplement or, if necessary, replace more formal or traditional approaches. The process of assessment of multicultural preschool children has the potential for error or problems in a number of arenas and requires considerable skill, sensitivity, and collaboration. We briefly discuss specific areas that may be problematic and of which evaluators should make special note.

Test Administration Style/Examiner Approach.   It has been suggested that when a culturally different child is assessed, the examiner might need to initiate conversation or even prod the child to respond (Cummins, 1980). Strategies such as the alternation of test items (Zigler & Butterfield, 1968) or the location of the assessment (Silverman, 1971) have had significant and positive effects on test performance. It also is possible that the style and tempo of the examination might need to be modified. The examiner might need to adopt a more facilitative style. As the situation demands, the examiner might need to become more nurturing, affectionate, soft-spoken, directive, "laid back," or reserved. Thus, it is extremely important that the examiner be tolerant and accepting, aware of basic styles of interaction considered appropriate to the specific child's background and equipped with a variety of strategies to get the child to demonstrate skill and knowledge.

Language.   Assessing language development issues in a nondiscriminatory manner may pose particular difficulty in light of the scarcity of bilingual professionals qualified to perform assessments and the lack of appropriate assessment tools for both established and less well-established minority populations (Hernandez, 1994). In particular, it is necessary to determine if a child's communication difficulties are due to limited English skills, the process of second language acquisition, or a communication disorder that requires special education intervention (Hernandez, 1994). Young children with linguistic differences are at risk for communication, social, and academic problems (Leung, 1990). Limited proficiency only in English is not sufficient cause for a referral to special education. Age-appropriate skills in the home language indicate that language learning abilities are not compromised. With the exception of stuttering, a language disorder will not be specific to only one language but will be present across languages (Barrera, 1995). Thus, language skills must be evaluated in both English and the child's native language (Dodd, Nelson, & Spint, 1995; Hernandez, 1994), and it cannot be assumed that limited proficiency in English means that the child is proficient in the native home language. Limited comprehension in both English and the child's home language may indicate a true communication disorder, especially if the confounding effects of chronic poverty or trauma are ruled out (Barrera, 1995).

Making this determination, however, may be a difficult task. First, those involved in the evaluation process should be skilled in the child's primary language and also should be aware of language development milestones and patterns. Second, although it may be relatively easy to identify language problems in monolingual preschool children (Dodd et al., 1995), the task becomes increasingly complex when there are skills in both languages. Language development is in a continuous state of flux and is highly dependent on the continuity and richness of a child's language environment. Although cognitive and social development may be enhanced through bilingualism (Bialystok, 1999; Bialystok & Martin, 2004; Hakuta, 1986; McCardle, Kim, Grube & Randall, 1995), children developing bilingually may lag 4 to 5 months behind children developing monolingually because of the increased complexity of the learning process (Swain, 1972). In addition, the rate of second language acquisition "can vary considerably, depending on factors such as age, strength of native language skills, amount of exposure to the second language, attitude, and language aptitude (Prince & Lawrence, 1993, p. 8). Complicating this issue is the possibility that very young children who are learning English as a second language may lose the ability to speak and understand their home Language (Schiff-Meyers, 1992; Wong-Fillmore, 1992).

Knowledge of social, linguistic, and cultural differences is vital for the appropriate interpretation of test results. Knowledge of such differences alone, however, will not ensure a valid assessment. It is necessary to be aware of the limitations of many of the commonly used assessment instruments as well as the issues and controversies surrounding assessment (Bracken, 1987).

Problems Related to Traditional Assessment Methods and Instruments

As is widely known, much criticism has been leveled at the use of traditional assessment instruments with minority populations. One criticism has been that traditional methods of assessment have made little allowance for cultural differences. Methods that incorporate standardized administration procedures limit the amount and nature of interaction between child and examiner. These methods also permit only a narrow repertoire of acceptable responses, many of which can be completely unknown to a child of a U.S. subculture. Because such a child might respond to an examiner or to the testing situation in a nontraditional way, information related to the child's knowledge base and/or ability level might not be adequately demonstrated. Much of the material in traditional standardized tests is geared primarily toward white, middle-class homes and values (Reynolds & Clark, 1983). Indeed, it is quite likely that an examiner in a nontraditional standardized assessment situation would make erroneous conclusions about a culturally different child's level of functioning and cognitive or educational strengths and weaknesses, when in reality a lack of exposure to pertinent stimuli might be the reason for poor performance.

Although in the past many traditional assessment instruments included standardization samples in which many culturally different groups were underrepresented, this problem largely has been eliminated in recent tests. A review of new and recently revised intelligence tests for preschool children (Flanagan & Alfonso, 1995) indicated that the standardization samples of five frequently used norm-referenced tests all closely matched population estimates based on U.S. census data and were rated as adequate or good. In addition, more recently published cognitive measures such as the Wechsler Preschool and Primary Scales of Intelligence–III (WPPSI–III; Wechsler, 2002), the Kaufman Assessment (KABC–II; Kaufman & Kaufman, 2004), LEITER–R (Roid & Miller, 1997) have attempted to de-emphasize culture-laden verbal skills and acquired knowledge and instead focus on fluid reasoning and processing speed.

Traditional assessment methods also have been plagued with an inability to uniformly predict outcomes for children from diverse backgrounds. Traditional measures typically are most accurate in prediction when White, middle-class children are involved, but are generally unacceptable in their level of predictive ability for minority children (Reynolds & Clark, 1983). Thus, diagnosis and long-range planning are hampered when children from U.S. subcultures are involved.

The tests might not measure the same underlying constructs for all children (Bracken et al.,1990). As an example, the factor structure of one popular test of intelligence for school-age children was found to differ for White, Black, and Hispanic children (Santos de Barona, 1981) and it has been hypothesized that using intelligence tests with minorities might measure only the degree of acculturation (Mercer, 1979) rather than level of ability. Similarly, constructs can be measured differently at different ages within the same instrument (Bracken, 1985), thus further limiting the ability to validly interpret test results.

One of the major criticisms aimed at the assessment of all preschool children involves limitations in the reliability and validity of the available assessment instruments (Ulrey, 1981), particularly the ability of these measures to satisfactorily evaluate, diagnose, and classify children between the ages of 3 and 5 years. These concerns continue for most of the new and recently revised instruments (Flanagan & Alfonso, 1995) despite the fact that the technical adequacy of these measures has improved and they are superior to "preschool measures that measure language, behavior, and social-emotional functioning" (Flanagan & Alfonso, 1995, p. 86). Indeed, evaluators of preschool children reported that early intelligence tests did not successfully determine eligibility for services 43% of the time (Bagnato & Neisworth, 1994). Some differences have been noted, however, by the targeted ages of the instruments and by the level of ability of the young child. Infant assessment instruments such as the original Bayley Scales of Infant Development (Bayley, 1969) or the Apgar Scale (Apgar, 1953) are poor predictors of intelligence and neurological dysfunction, respectively (Thurman & Widerstrom, 1985). Such infant scales are considered to be limited in their ability to estimate future levels of functioning. An exception to this, however, is when low-functioning children are assessed for intelligence; in this case, measured IQs tend to remain relatively stable (Brooks-Gunn & Lewis, 1983; Goodman & Cameron, 1978; Keogh, 1970; Lewis, 1976; McCall, Appelbaum, & Hogarty, 1973; Meisels & Atkins-Burnett, 1999; Pollitt & Triana, 1999; Sattler, 2001; Share, Koch, Webb, & Graliker, 1964).

Preschool tests appear to fare better in their ability to predict future outcomes than do infant tests. The increased predictive accuracy of the preschool tests appears in part to be a function of item content; whereas infant tests are limited largely to perceptual-motor tasks, preschool measures contain items better able to tap the cognitive domain (Sattler, 2001). However, stability of test scores and prediction of future academic performance also appear related to the age at which the initial assessment occurs (Bayley, 1969; McCall, Hogarty, & Hurlburt, 1972; Sattler, 2001). IQs obtained before age 5 must be interpreted cautiously (McCall et al., 1973) because "many of the indicators of later learning difficulties and behavior problems simply are not measurable before the age of 6" (Ulrey, 1981, p. 486).

Although numerous screening, diagnostic, and prescriptive measures that target the preschool population exist, many are unacceptable because of their poor psychometric characteristics (Arffa, Rider, & Cummings, 1984; Bracken, 1987; Rubin, Balow, Dorle, & Rosen, 1978). Test results might lack utility for numerous reasons. First, instruments that utilize norms for comparison purposes might be unacceptable because standardization samples are inadequate in overall size or are unrepresentative of the population for which they are used. For example, many developmental scales developed before 1986 were normed on White, middle-class populations (Garber & Slater, 1983; Pavri & Fowler, 2001) and, therefore, provide little valid data for interpretation among diverse populations. At the very least, the standardization sample should include a sampling of variables such as age, sex, ethnicity, SES, and geographic region in adequate numbers so that interpretation of test results can occur along these dimensions.

Second, the test might not be able to predict equally well for individuals of all ethnic, socioeconomic, or ability groups. The content of test items might favor a particular group or groups through disproportionate representation of a group, stereotyping, or the use of concepts or materials that are more familiar to some groups than others (Wiersma & Jurs, 1985).

Third, insufficient technical information might be provided, making it difficult to determine a test's utility and soundness; moreover, reliability and validity studies might not have been conducted or might be limited in scope. Reliability refers to consistency of measurement and might take several forms. Test-retest reliability studies, which examine the consistency of measurement or stability of a construct across time (Wiersma & Jurs, 1985), might be difficult to conduct given the rapid rate of development that occurs at the preschool level. Such studies would need to determine a retest period that would reduce the probability of practice effects as well as the likelihood that any change in scores really is because of the child's acquisition of knowledge and skills (Goldman, L'Engle Stein, & Guerry, 1983). Indeed, Flanagan and Alfonso (1995) point out that some test manuals report test-retest information for individuals who were not preschoolers or provide interpretive information useful only to older preschoolers. Equivalence reliability, which involves the consistency of measurement across parallel test forms and can involve a measure of internal consistency (Wiersma & Jurs, 1985), can be obtained in an easier manner (see Bracken, 1987 for suggested technical standards).

A fourth criticism is the fact that many assessment measures fail to provide enough specificity to enable useful decision making regarding service delivery or educational programming. As a result, areas of deficit might not receive adequate prescriptive attention. These limitations have resulted in some reluctance to refer children for formal evaluation to avoid problems caused by premature labeling or possible misclassification. Because labeling or classification can create a negative and lasting stigma, many professionals have avoided assessment at early ages to avoid the negative consequences that occur as a result of this process. This concern has been tempered somewhat by P.L. 99-457, which permits young children with special needs to be served with the general classification of developmental delay. In addition, federal guidelines also permit an at-risk classification, although it is unclear how many states actually use this option.

Finally, early intelligence tests have been criticized for failing to accommodate a child's response limitations and requiring that specific responses to narrowly defined tasks be demonstrated in an unfamiliar setting (Bagnato & Neisworth, 1994).

A PROCESS FOR THE ASSESSMENT OF CULTURALLY
DIFFERENT PRESCHOOL CHILDREN

The complexity involved in the assessment of culturally different children makes it necessary to devote a great deal of time to the assessment process. Traditionally, evaluation has taken a client-centered approach in which data are collected through the use of standardized instruments and observations made in the testing situation. Although the rationale for this approach is valid and ample evidence supports this notion of testing, the approach has a number of shortcomings when culturally different preschool children are involved. A number of areas require close attention and monitoring to ensure that a clear understanding of the child emerges; these areas generally extend the limits of the traditional assessment.

When traditional standardized instruments are used in isolation for culturally different preschoolers, the possibility for confounding test results is great. The unique characteristics of the preschool period, which often is marked by uneven development and growth spurts, combined with the effects of cultural variations in style of interaction, language issues, and problems associated with the assessment instruments, create significant difficulties when interpreting test results. This development culture-instrument interaction in preschool assessment makes it difficult to determine if test findings are attributable to cultural, language, environmental, developmental, or measurement factors.

What is needed, therefore, are additional methods to obtain valid information about the culturally different preschooler. These methods should provide the opportunity to systematically assess areas of strength and deficit without fear of immediate classification. Thus, the assessment of the culturally different preschooler must allow for sufficient interaction with the child so that conclusions regarding the child's capacity to learn are arrived at with confidence. This strategy should allow for adequate time to identify the relevant factors in the child's learning style as well as effective teaching strategies for that child.

In recent years considerable attention has been given to alternative methods of assessing preschool children. In particular, it has been widely acknowledged that no one assessment method or instrument is appropriate for every child (Bracken, 1994). Rather, it is necessary to identify the unique concerns related to the child and then determine the information that is necessary to address these concerns. Once this information is specified, there should be an awareness of the limitations of the information to be obtained along with how the information can be used to plan appropriate interventions (Gyurke, 1994).

Evaluation of the culturally different preschooler should utilize a family-centered team approach (Meisels & Provence, 1996) that includes at least one member knowledgeable about the child's language and culture. Parents and family members should be involved from the outset, and the model used in evaluation should permit maximum input from them as well as from a variety of assessment professionals. Both the interdisciplinary model, which involves parents as partners on the team yet utilizes separate assessment by team members, and the transdisciplinary model, in which team members and parents work actively together with the child in arena-style assessments (Bagnato & Neisworth, 1991;

Bondurant-Utz & Luciano, 1994; Kilgo et al., 2003; Losardo, A., & Notari-Sylverson, A., 2001; McWilliam, 2000; Vacc & Ritter, 1995) are appropriate.

What follows is a suggested process for the assessment of culturally different preschool children. This method uses a number of strategies to obtain comprehensive information about the child.

Pre-assessment Data

Information obtained prior to the actual assessment is extremely important. Federal guidelines mandate parental involvement in the evaluation and prescriptive process. Parental input is particularly critical for the culturally different preschooler because the child's experiences often occur almost exclusively within the family environment. Parents also are very capable of providing accurate information about their children's development (Squires, 1996). Thus, it is important for the parents not only to communicate basic birth, medical, and developmental information but also to provide their perspective on their child's functioning within the family milieu. More specifically, parents should be asked to provide impressions about how the child's skills and behavior compare to other children in the family and community.

Although it is possible to obtain this information through written questionnaires, parent interviews are preferred for the following reasons. First, written communication may be difficult in English or the home language and, therefore, information provided may be minimal. Similarly, the formality of responding on paper may be threatening and overwhelming for a parent with minimal education or poor writing skills. Second, the interview provides an opportunity to begin to build a relationship of trust between parents and team members, to orient the parents and family members to the evaluation process and their critical role within it, and to empower them to become participants in the process. Finally, contact with the parents provides the evaluator(s)/team with critical information regarding parental awareness of their child's functioning, skill in navigating the frequently complex assessment and referral system, degree of financial/economic risk, available support system, degree of acculturation, and other resources. Such information can assist the evaluating team in determining the family's ability to participate in aspects of their child's intervention as well as the degree of assistance the family will need in such activities; indeed, the selection of particular intervention strategies may depend on the types of information obtained through the interview.

The interview should explore in depth the reasons for referring the child for evaluation. Parental concerns about the child, the evaluation process, and its potential consequences regarding further education should be discussed and clarified. Other referral agents, if applicable, also should be contacted for information. Information gathered during this phase should be comprehensive and include language, motor, and social developmental histories. Medical information and data from day care or preschool settings, if available, also are important. In addition, information related to the family composition, status within the community, and level of acculturation can add significantly to a more complete understanding of the culturally different child.

This information should be compiled to develop an evaluation plan that will identify the types of data to be collected, the individual(s) responsible for obtaining data, and the settings in which the various assessment components will take place. The assessment should be planned to be developmentally and culturally appropriate and consider "the unique cultural aspects that affect how children learn and relate to other people"

(McLaughlin et al., 1995, p. 6). Although it is expected that norm-referenced measures may be administered, the degree to which such measures can be validly administered and the results determined to be useful will vary according to the child's language and other skills. Generally, norm-referenced measures will yield less valuable information when children are less acculturated and/or English proficient. Rather, it is probable that evaluation will be ecological and will identify critical environmental settings and performance expectations as well as the child's ability to function according to expectations within those settings (Lowenthal, 1991). Indeed, the value of ecological assessments for preschool children is being increasingly recognized (Bagnato & Neisworth, 1994).

Language Assessment

Language assessment must be a major focus in the evaluation of culturally different children. Potential or ongoing problems related to limited English proficiency must be separated from language disorders, limited experiences, or slow development so that appropriate planning and intervention can occur. This can be difficult unless the evaluator is both skilled in the assessment of language and a proficient speaker of the relevant language.

The purpose of this language assessment "is not merely to determine whether the child can communicate well enough to be tested in English but rather to determine the actual levels of skill and fluency in each language spoken and the role that language may play in potential learning problems" (Barona & Santos de Barona, 1987, p. 194). Although all young children through age 5 are involved in language acquisition, second language acquisition during this critical period may present unique challenges (McLean, 2001). Bilingual development is a complex process that is dependent on the degree to which a child is exposed to and has the opportunity and motivation to use a second language. A child who hears both languages from birth will develop language skills differently from a child who learns a second language after the first has been established. A child learning two languages simultaneously will proceed linguistically in a developmental pattern similar to monolingual speakers, although there may be a slower rate of vocabulary development. A child who establishes skills in one language and then proceeds to learn a second will progress through four distinct developmental stages that include a nonverbal period in which the child begins to crack the code of the second language (McLaughlin et al., 1995).

Because developmentally children may be losing aspects of their first language as the second language is acquired, their performance on tests of language proficiency may be misleading . . . even though a bilingual child's performance in either language may lag behind that of monolingual speakers of the language in some point of development, the child may actually possess a total vocabulary and total linguistic repertoire that is quite similar to that of monolingual speakers (McLaughlin et al., 1995, p. 5).

Because vocabulary often is used as an indicator of cognitive functioning (Lidz & Peña, 1996), it is important to recognize varying language development patterns and avoid erroneous interpretation.

In addition to determining home language and the degree, if any, to which the child has been exposed to English, it is necessary to assess language structure and the child's ability to make functional use of language (Barona & Santos de Barona, 1987). Vocabulary, comprehension, and syntax should be examined within both receptive and expressive aspects of language; however, since some measures of English language proficiency have been found to not reliably discriminate between native and non-native preschoolers (Stephenson, Jiao, & Wall, 2004), children should be given the opportunity to demonstrate their language skills if necessary in a non-standardized manner (McLaughlin et al., 1995). It has been shown that normally developing preschoolers demonstrated more complex language features when assessed thematically instead of in a standardized fashion (Fagundes, Haynes, Haak & Morgan, 1998). It also may be useful to use language tasks that are processing dependent rather than knowledge-based; these tasks, which place greater emphasis on psycholinguistic processes, have been found to minimize the effect of experience (Campbell, Dollaghan, Needleman, & Janosky, 1997; Jacobs, 2001). Rather than use a formal language instrument, consideration should be given to the use of alternative technique. One example is the California Early Language Assessment Process which emphasizes ongoing observations and data collection and explores how children use language over pronunciation, grammar, and vocabulary. Specifically, assessing the child's ability to use language to express feelings and ideas, ask for help, provide information, solve problems, and gain attention can provide valuable insight into the level of language skills as well as direction for future language development.

Language assessment should enable a decision regarding the language or languages with which to conduct the remainder of the assessment. Generally, clear dominance in one language would lead to assessment in that language. However, frequently dominance is not clearly established and in these instances evaluation in both English and the home language is recommended to ensure that an adequate sampling of abilities is obtained (Barona & Santos de Barona, 1987).

When concerns about language skills exist, it may be advisable to select a cognitive assessment instrument that will permit nonverbal assessment. Such instruments include the LEITER–R (Roid & Miller, 1997) and the Universal Nonverbal Intelligence Test (Bracken & McCallum, 1998); in addition, the KABC–II (Kaufman & Kaufman, 2004) and the DAS (Elliott, 1990) contain nonverbal scales which may be useful.

In the event that a child cannot be evaluated in English, a number of important questions must be addressed. First, a decision must be made as to whether the child should be evaluated only in the home language or if a combination of English and the home language should be used. Often, a monolingual evaluation, even if it is in the home language, is not appropriate because the language familiar to the child is actually a combination of the home language and English. Second, it must be determined if a translated version of the test is available in the child's language. If so, technical information related to the translation should be examined and a determination of the adequacy of its psychometric properties should be made. In particular, attention should be paid to whether norms exist for the translated version as well as to the specific composition of the standardization sample. In addition, some attention should be paid to whether the test is a direct translation of English (Bracken et al., 1990) and if it allows for dialectical differences. Exact equivalents of English concepts might not exist and the difficulty level of both concepts and test items can change in the translation. Also, within the same language, it is possible that multiple acceptable answers can exist depending on the child's region of origin (Barona & Santos de Barona, 1987; Bracken et al., 1990; Bracken & Fouad, 1987; Wilen & Sweeting, 1986).

If a formal translation of the desired test is not available, it might be necessary to create one for the local area. Such a translation should be developed carefully prior to the actual testing session. Standardized procedures should be established for use by all evaluation personnel. Both the translation and the procedures should be reviewed by several proficient speakers of the language to ensure the most accurate translation possible (Bracken & Fouad, 1987; Wilen & Sweeting, 1986).

Although not a preferred option, in the event that a bilingual evaluator is not available, it might be necessary to use an interpreter not related to the child, who is fluent in standard English and the home language and who has had some formal education. This interpreter should receive training in such general aspects of the assessment process establishing rapport, using standardized test administration procedures, objective observation, and the precise recording of verbal and nonverbal behaviors during the assessment process (Wilen & Sweeting, 1986).

Finally, it should be clearly understood that the primary goal is the collection of useful information for decision making and planning. Thus, flexibility and creativity are essential regardless of the techniques used.

The Formal Evaluation Phase

A number of reviews of various standardized instruments have been written (Bracken, 1985; McLoughlin & Lewis. 1986; Schakel, 1986) and that information will not be reiterated. Rather, the purpose of this section is to provide guidelines for using information derived from such instruments.

Although to this point only the problems associated with standardized assessment instruments have been dealt with as they pertain to culturally different individuals, it must be recognized that standardized instruments do have a useful function. Standardized instruments provide a systematic way to collect data about the child in various domains. Even though the value of specific test items might not be equivalent, because of the problems of representation and exposure that have been discussed earlier, the fact that the test was administered under relatively uniform conditions creates some basis for comparison, as well as a means with which to judge interactive styles.

When a culturally different child is involved, results of standardized intelligence tests should not be used as an absolute index of cognitive functioning. Rather, such results should be viewed as a general estimate of the child's current level of measurable functioning in which information has been obtained about the level and types of skills and knowledge that the child has demonstrated relative to other children. As such, it should serve as a marker from which to begin to build for further assessment, if needed, or for making educational recommendations. Depending on the child's unique characteristics, it is possible that a standardized test administration will not be appropriate.

The results of assessment with standardized instruments should provide crucial information regarding the culturally different preschooler. Based on the assessment, the examiner should determine the relative level of functioning and whether either overall test performance or specific responses might be related to factors other than ability or achievement. The examiner should have a sense of the validity of test results by evaluating the degree to which the child invested energy and effort in the evaluation tasks. The examiner also should determine how well the child appeared to understand the language in which the assessment was conducted and whether language appeared to affect test results as well as the ability to perform specific tasks.

During the formal evaluation phase, the examiner must bring together all data gathered in earlier stages and evaluate test findings with those data in mind. For example, if a child appeared to attend more when test items were communicated in the home language than in English, the examiner might conclude that the distractibility was primarily because of a language factor. Similarly, a newly immigrated Vietnamese child would not be expected to engage in elaborate or animated verbal interactions in any language. An examiner who encountered such a child would need to conduct an additional investigation to determine why the child was not behaving in the manner expected. Thus, the traditional assessment phase should serve as a forum in which information about the child is integrated, hypotheses are generated and explored, and strategies for either educational recommendation or further assessment are developed.

Increasingly, evaluation personnel are recognizing the value of conducting arena-style assessments in which parents and evaluation team members simultaneously participate in the gathering of data. The advantage of this procedure is that participants witness the same behavior and are able to use the common observations to share information, discuss concerns, and generate hypotheses in a more natural context.

As noted earlier, differences in language socialization and styles of interaction may create difficulty in determining whether test performance reflects a disorder or differential exposure to information. The finding that tasks that were congruent with home-trained skills were better able to differentiate those who were normally developing from those with lower ability led to the recommendation that assessment tasks be presented in a manner familiar to the child (Peña & Quinn, 1992). Specifically, the use of mediated learning experiences (Feuerstein, 1979), which provides the child with the opportunity to first understand the task, has been demonstrated to be a valuable adjunct to more standardized procedures (Peña, Iglesias, & Lidz, 2001).

Increasingly, tests are integrating procedures which enable the examiner to determine whether the child understands the nature of the task. However, in the event that the measure being used lacks such features or is insufficient for such a determination, it may be helpful to use testing-of-limits procedures. These are modifications from standard procedures which are undertaken to gain additional information about the child's "ability to learn and the type and amount of assistance needed to raise the child's level of performance" (Sattler, 2001, p. 209).

Diagnostic Placement

Even though modified procedures may have been used to increase the validity of evaluation results, a decision might be made that insufficient information exists with which to make recommendations about the child. There might be several possible reasons for this realization. First, language, developmental, or cultural factors can appear to have influenced the standardized test results. As noted earlier, normal preschool behavior, such as distractibility, easy fatigue, shyness, difficulty in separating from mother, lack of familiarity with or inability to successfully work with a specific cultural interaction style, or concern over language involvement can raise questions as to the reliability of test findings. Second, the examiner might feel that the assessment procedures just did not provide an adequate arena in which to sample the child's repertoire of skills and knowledge. It also is possible that more information is needed concerning the way in which the child learns to get clearer ideas regarding future planning for the child.

To avoid the constraints and pitfalls of both cultural and developmental variables and yet obtain useful information, it is necessary that culturally different children be sufficiently acclimated to and comfortable within the assessment setting. To accomplish this goal, it is suggested that the child first undergo a diagnostic placement, particularly if the child has not been enrolled in a preschool program. This consists of an already established preschool enrichment program in which children of various ethnic and cultural backgrounds are cared for on a daily basis and in which bilingual/bicultural personnel are available to assist children with their communication needs. This setting ideally should serve a high proportion of children with apparently normal development who can facilitate socialization and model appropriate behavior, as well as provide an informal means of comparison. Such a program can provide, within a nurturing atmosphere, age-appropriate activities geared toward facilitating the child's growth in motor, social, and cognitive areas. As part of its curriculum, mediated learning experiences (Feuerstein, 1979) can be incorporated which emphasize encouraging children to explore a variety of ways to obtain information and solve problems in all dimensions of development and in which the child's progress in accomplishing these tasks can be monitored and measured. Such procedures have been found to provide insight into learning and language functioning for non-English dominant preschoolers and preschoolers with disabilities (Lidz & Peña, 1996; Missiuna & Samuels, 1989).

It is expected that the child's involvement in a diagnostic placement setting will last for an extended period, ranging from 3 to 6 months. During this time, the child should be encouraged to participate in activities, and opportunities for appropriate social interactions should be provided.

This diagnostic placement can serve several purposes. For those children who demonstrated difficulty in separation from a significant adult, the routine of daily attendance will accustom the child to interaction with a number of adults. Assessments, when performed, will be less emotionally charged and will occur in an environment with which the child is familiar, resulting in increased responsiveness and attention to task.

While in attendance, the child will come to view learning activities and the presentation of new information as a regular part of the daily routine. The actual measurement of skills, learning styles, and progress often can be accomplished either unobtrusively or with minimal fanfare.

Participation in an ongoing diagnostic setting has a number of advantages. It provides personnel with the opportunity to observe the child in group situations and to assess preferential language and learning styles as well as effective teaching strategies over time. In addition, social adjustment can be monitored because preschool teacher–pupil ratios are relatively small and it is possible to have a greater awareness of the child's overall personality and needs.

Diagnostic placement also permits an assessment of the effects of culture because in many cases an enrichment facility will have children in attendance of both same and different cultures as well as some personnel with similar language skills. The rate at which the child acquires new skills and concepts can be measured and monitored throughout the child's attendance and personnel can identify effective reinforcing conditions to provide the child. Diagnostic placement assessment also will permit a judgment as to the amount of effort that will be needed to work successfully with one child relative to other children in the center.

Several methods of assessment can be used in this setting to obtain other useful information. These include observations, criterion-referenced tests, and dynamic assessment techniques. Observations of the child can assist in assessing social skills and in describing patterns of behavior and styles of interaction in both individual and group settings. Knowledge of information that can facilitate the culturally different child's attending to tasks and responding is extremely useful in the design of effective teaching strategies. For example, if an examiner in the traditional phase of assessment had difficulty getting a culturally different child to invest in the evaluation, one goal of observation might be to determine if the preschooler interacts differently with the adults in the diagnostic setting. If interaction is limited only to adults of similar culture, or if the child has established rapport with some other subset of adults, then goals can be set to broaden the child's interaction patterns. Similarly, it also would be useful to observe the child's interactions with other children and to determine those conditions under which such interactions occur. Information related to whether the child interacts only with a particular child or group of children, whether most interactions occur during free play or in structured activities, how the child communicated with others in the diagnostic placement setting, and the nature of the interactions that do occur are all helpful in identifying relevant factors in instructional programming.

Criterion-referenced testing measures "the performance levels of examinees in relation to a set of well-defined objective competencies" (Hambleton, 1982, p. 352). Whereas norm-referenced measures generally allow comparisons among examinees, criterion-referenced measures do not make comparisons among examinees or groups as a primary purpose. Rather, criterion-referenced tests describe what a child specifically knows or can do and therefore are useful when planning additional instructional activities.

For example, an examiner might have noted in the standardized assessment that a preschooler had difficulty following directions communicated in either the home language or in English and as a result performed poorly on a number of tasks. During the diagnostic placement, a criterion-referenced measure focusing on basic readiness skills indicated that the child was deficient in demonstrating knowledge of directional concepts such as through, beside, beneath, right, left, and so on, and, in addition, had difficulty remembering and executing directions consisting of more than two parts. Remedial planning for this child, therefore, would involve two components. First, the child would receive direct training in directional concepts. Second, a number of strategies could be interspersed throughout the day in a variety of formal and informal situations to facilitate the child's memory, ability to follow directions, and use of the newly acquired directional concepts.

Dynamic assessment (Feuerstein, 1979) modifies traditional assessment practice in three ways. First, the nature of the interaction between examiner and examinee is shifted from one in which the examiner is neutral and adheres to a standardized script to one in which the examiner assumes the role of teacher and provides mediated learning experiences. In this role, the examiner-turned-teacher intervenes, provides advance organizers and explanations for problems and activities, summarizes experiences, and interjects insightful and clarifying remarks whenever and wherever necessary. Second, training is considered an important part of the assessment and the child is provided not only the principles, skills, and techniques to accomplish a task, but also with the opportunity to apply these functions to novel tasks. Finally, dynamic assessment results are not interpreted within a product modality in which emphasis is on what is known, but rather the results are viewed from a process orientation in which how learning occurs is considered important. In this final phase, both unique responses and strategies toward learning are examined to provide direction for both remediation and further education.

Using a test-train-retest paradigm (Sattler, 1992), the child's ability to perform specific tasks and/or solve particular problems first is measured with unfamiliar stimuli. After the initial testing is conducted, the child is taught to solve the task through a variety of methods aimed at helping the child develop appropriate problem-solving strategies. Upon completion of the training phase, the child is again tested on either the original task or on one of its alternate forms.

Contrary to traditional assessment in which the goal is to determine how much and what is known, the dynamic assessment or process-oriented approach seeks to determine the degree to which cognitive structures can be modified, the amount and type of teaching effort that is needed to bring about such modification, the areas of functioning that require intervention to produce the desired effects, as well as to identify the child's preferential learning strategies. Thus, in the course of the total assessment, data related to the rate of acquisition of strategies, skills, and concepts, as well as the generalizability of these strategies, are obtained through interaction with the child and systematic observation (Feuerstein, 1979; Feuerstein, Rand, Haywood, Hoffman, & Jensen, undated; Sattler, 1992). Although appropriate for use during the evaluation phase, the ongoing use of these techniques can increase understanding of the child's needs.

Presently, process-oriented techniques for preschool children are in a relatively early stage of development; however, dynamic techniques increasingly are being incorporated as they "offer the potential of more accurate and less discriminatory diagnostic information, more relevant to an educational or treatment setting than norm-referenced assessment" (Lidz, 1983, p. 60). Although there does not yet exist a well-developed or widely accepted standardized dynamic preschool measure (Lidz, 1983), at least one technique (Brown & Ferrara, 1985) has been suggested to be useful for children from a variety of cultures. This technique involves giving children "a set of increasingly explicit hints toward solution of a problem until they are able to solve it" (Schakel, 1986, p. 109). Furthermore, the use of mediated learning experiences also shows promise with language-minority children (Lidz & Peña, 1996).

Diagnostic assessment placement should continue until assessment and program personnel conclude that sufficient information has been obtained with which to make a set of educational recommendations about the child. At that time, a meeting should be convened of all program personnel who have been involved in various aspects of assessment, including the parents and appropriate school and/or agency representatives. During this meeting, all data obtained throughout the assessment process should be thoroughly reviewed and recommendations for the most appropriate way to meet the child's educational needs should be generated. For those children for whom an ongoing education placement is suggested, an individualized education plan specifying those areas requiring remediation should be developed. In addition, the placement setting should be specified. It should be noted that it is entirely possible that a placement recommendation would be to continue participation in the preschool enrichment program in which the diagnostic placement occurred. In such cases, emphasis would shift from assessment to teaching.

SUMMARY

The process of assessing culturally different preschool children is complex. The problems associated with working with young children include: relatively little exposure to U.S. culture, vastly different ways of interacting with adults, and measurement instruments with a limited degree of psychometric soundness that cause considerable concern regarding the degree of confidence with which test results can be interpreted, as well as the implications for instructional planning. Assessment of the culturally different preschooler, therefore, must be approached with a great deal of care and with sufficient opportunity to obtain accurate and relevant information.

A suggested procedure for assessment expands the standard assessment process. First, pre-assessment data should go beyond the typical social, medical, and developmental data generally obtained and should include relevant information from all significant individuals involved with the child. Information regarding the family's assimilation into U.S. society is crucial. Second, in-depth investigation of the child's communicative competence must occur.

This should include determining the language or combination of languages that the child uses, as well as the level of skill and fluency demonstrated in each. During the formal evaluation phase, assessment with standardized measures should take place to enable a general estimate of the current level of measurable functioning and to determine a relative level of performance compared to age-equivalent peers. During this phase of assessment, the examiner should develop a sense for potential effects of cultural factors in the testing process and should determine the degree of validity of test results. Alternative assessment procedures should be incorporated to ensure that children have been given every opportunity to demonstrate their abilities. Diagnostic placement in an established preschool enrichment program should be conducted if questions arise concerning the validity of test results or if it is believed that additional information is needed to make educational decisions. A variety of techniques is appropriate for this phase of assessment. Finally, parents, assessment personnel, and appropriate school and agency representatives should review all assessment data in a review meeting and together develop educational recommendations for the child.

REFERENCES

America's Children (2004a). Table POP3 Racial and ethnic composition: Percentage of U.S. children under age 18 by race and Hispanic origin, selected years 1980–2002 and projected 2003–2020. Retrieved April 28, 2005 at http://childstats.gov/ac2004/tables/pop3.asp

America's Children (2004b). Table POP4 Children of at least one foreign-born parent: Percentage of children under 18 by nativity of child and parents[a] by parent's education, poverty status, and other characteristics, selected years 1994–2003. Retrieved April 28, 2005 at http://childstats .gov/ac2004/tables/pop4.asp

Anderson-Yockel, J., & Haynes, W. (1994). Joint book-reading strategies in working-class African American and White mother-toddler dyads. *Journal of Speech and Hearing Research. 37*(3): 583–593.

Apgar, V. (1953). A proposal for a new method of evaluation of the newborn infant. *Anesthesia and Analgena, 32*, 260–267.

Arffa, S., Rider, L. H., & Cummings, J. A. (1984). A validity study of the Woodcock-Johnson Psychoeducational Battery and the Stanford-Binet with Black preschool children. *Journal of Psychoeducational Assessment, 2*, 73–77.

Bagnato, S. J., & Neisworth, J. T. (1991). *Assessment for early intervention: Best practices for professionals*. New York: Guilford.

Bagnato, S. J., & Neisworth, J. T. (1994). A national study of the social and treatment "invalidity" of intelligence testing for early intervention. *School Psychology Quarterly, 9*, 81–102.

Barnett, W. S., & Yarosz, D. J. (2004). Who goes to preschool and why does it matter? *Preschool Policy Matters, 8*, 1–16.

Barona, A., & Santos de Barona, M. (1987). A model for the assessment of limited English proficient students referred for special education services. In S. H. Fradd & W. J. Tikunoff (Eds.), *Bilingual education and bilingual special education: A guide for administrators* (pp. 183–210). Boston: College Hill Press.

Barrera, I. (1995). To refer or not to refer: Untangling the web of diversity, "deficit," and disability. *New York State Association for Bilingual Education Journal, 10*, 54–66.

Bayley, N. (1969). *Bayley Scales of Infant Development*. New York: Psychological Corporation.

Bayley, N. (1993). *Bayley Scales of Infant Development–II*. San Antonio, TX: Psychological Corporation. (Author: do you have a citation for this reference?)

Bernal, E. M. (1974). Gifted Mexican-American children: An ethnoscientific perspective. *California Journal of Educational Research, 25*, 261–273.

Bialystok, E. (1999). Cognitive complexity and attentional control in the bilingual mind. *Child Development, 70*(3), 636–644.

Bialystok, E., & Martin, M. M. (2004). Attention and inhibition in bilingual children: Evidence from the dimensional change card sort task. *Developmental Science, 7*(3), 325–339.

Bondurant-Utz, J. A., & Luciano, L. B. (1994). *A practical guide to infant and preschool assessment in special education.* Boston: Allyn and Bacon.

Bracken, B. A. (1985). A critical review of the Kaufman Assessment Battery for Children (K-ABC). *School Psychology Review, 14*, 21–36.

Bracken, B. A. (1987). Limitations of preschool instruments and standards for minimal levels of technical adequacy. *Journal of Psychoeducational Assessment, 5*, 313–326.

Bracken, B. A. (1994). Advocating for effective preschool assessment practices: A comment on Bagnato & Neisworth. *School Psychology Quarterly, 9*, 103–108.

Bracken, B. A., & Fouad, N. A. (1987). Spanish translation and validation of the Bracken Basic Concept Scale. *School Psychology Review, 16*, 94–102.

Bracken, B. A., & McCallum, R. S. (1998). *Universal nonverbal intelligence test examiner's manual.* Itasca, IL: Riverside.

Bracken, B. A., Barona, A., Bauermeister, J., Howell, K. K., Poggioli, L., & Puente, A. (1990). Multinational validation of the Spanish Bracken Basic Concept Scale for Cross-Cultural Assessments. *Journal of School Psychology, 28*(4), 325–341.

Brooks-Gunn, J., & Lewis, M. (1983). Screening and diagnosing handicapped infants. *Topics in Early Childhood Special Education, 3*, 14–28.

Brown, A. L., & Ferrara, R. A. (1985). Diagnosing zones of proximal development. In J. Wertsch (Ed.), *Culture, communication, and cognition—Vygotskian perspectives.* London: Cambridge University Press.

Bryen, D. N., & Gallagher, D. (1983). Assessment of language and communication. In K. D. Paget & B. A. Bracken (Eds.), *The psychoeducational assessment of preschool children* (pp. 81–144). New York: Grune & Stratton.

Campbell, T., Dollaghan, C., Needleman, H., & Janosky, J. (1997). Reducing bias in language assessment: Processing-dependent measures. *Journal of Speech, Language, and Hearing Research, 40*, 519–525.

Chhim, S. (1987). *Introduction to Cambodian culture.* San Diego, CA: Multifunctional Resource Center, San Diego State University.

Christensen, R. A. (1991). A personal perspective on tribal-Alaska native gifted and talented education. *Journal of American Indian Education, 31*(1), 10–14.

Collins, R., & Ribeiro, R. (2004). Toward an Early Care and Education Agenda for Hispanic Children. *Early Childhood Research and Practice, 6*(2). Retrieved from http://ecrp.uiuc.edu/

Cummins, J. (1980). *Psychological assessment of minority language students.* Unpublished manuscript of Ontario Institute for Studies in Education, Toronto, pp. 1–91.

Dodd, J. M., Nelson, J. R., & Spint, W. (1995). Prereferral activities: One way to avoid biased testing procedures and possible inappropriate special education placement for American Indian students. *The Journal of Educational Issues for Language Minority Students, 15.* Retrieved July 8, 1997, from *http://ncbe.gwu.edu/miscpubs/jeilms/vol15/prereferra.html*

EAC West, New Mexico State Highlands University. (1996). Evaluation and assessment for Title VII projects—handouts, Retrieved July 8, 1997, from http://www.ncbe.gwu/edu/miscpubs/eacwest/handouts/gifted/backgrnd.html

Elliott, C. D. (1990). *Differential ability scales: Introductory and technical handbook.* San Antonio, TX: Psychological Corporation.

Fagundes, D. D., Haynes, W. O., Haak, N. J., & Morgan M. J. (1998). Task variability effects on the language test performance of southern lower socioeconomic class African American and Caucasian five-year-olds. *Language, Speech, and Hearing Services in Schools, 29*, 148–157.

Federal Interagency Forum on Child and Family Statistics [FIFCFS]. (1997). *America's children: Key national indicators of well-being.* Washington, DC: U.S. Government Printing Office.

Federal Interagency Forum on Child and Family Statistics [FIFCFS]. (2004). *America's children in brief: Key national indicators of well-being*. Washington, DC: U.S. Government Printing Office.

Feuerstein, R. (1979). *The dynamic assessment of retarded performers: The learning potential assessment device theory instruments and techniques*. Baltimore: University Park Press.

Feuerstein, R., Rand, Y., Haywood, H. C., Hoffman, M. B., & Jensen, M. R. (n.d.). *L.P.A.D. Learning Potential Assessment Device manual experimental version*. Jerusalem: Hadassah-Wizo-Canada Research Institute.

Flanagan, D. P., & Alfonso, V. C. (1995). A critical review of the technical characteristics of new and recently revised intelligence tests for preschool children. *Journal of Psychoeducational Assessment, 13*, 66–91.

Fradd, S. H. (1987). Accommodating the needs of limited English proficient students in regular classrooms. In S. H. Fradd & W. J. Tikunoff (Eds.), *Bilingual education and bilingual special education–A guide for administrators* (pp. 133–182). Boston: College Hill Press.

Garber, H. (1977). Preventing mental retardation through family rehabilitation. In S. Caldwell & J. Stedman (Eds.), *Infant education: A guide for helping handicapped children in the first three years*. New York: Walker and Company.

Garber, H. L., & Slater, M. (1983). Assessment of the culturally different preschooler. In K. D. Paget & B. A. Bracken (Eds.), *The psychoeducational assessment of preschool children* (pp. 443–471). New York: Grune & Stratton.

Gelman, R. (1979). Preschool thought. *American Psychologist, 34*, 900–905.

Goldman, J., L'Engle Stein, C., & Guerry, S. (1983). *Psychological methods of child assessment*. New York: Bruner/Mazel.

Goodman, J. F., & Cameron, J. (1978). The meaning of IQ constancy in young retarded children. *The Journal of Genetic Psychology, 132*, 109–119.

Guddemi, M., & Case, B. J. (2004). *Assessing young children*. Harcourt Assessment Report. Retrieved July 25, 2006 from http://www.harcourtassessment.com

Gyurke, J. S. (1994). A reply to Bagnato and Neisworth: Intelligent versus intelligence testing of preschoolers. *School Psychology Quarterly, 9*, 109–112.

Hakuta, K. (1986). *Mirror of language: the debate on bilingualism*. New York, NY: Basic Books.

Hambleton, R. K. (1982). Advances in criterion-referenced testing technology. In C. R. Reynolds & T. B. Gutkin (Eds.), *The handbook of school psychology* (pp. 351–379). New York: John Wiley Sons.

Hartley, E. A. (1991). Through Navajo eyes: Examining differences in giftedness. *Journal of American Indian Education, 31*(1), 53–64.

Heath, S. B. (1986). Sociocultural contexts of language development. In California State Department of Education (Ed.), *Beyond language: Social and cultural factors in schooling language minority children* (pp. 143–186). Los Angeles, CA: Evaluation Dissemination and Assessment Center, California State University.

Hernandez, R. D. (1994). Reducing bias in the assessment of culturally and linguistically diverse populations. *The Journal of Educational Issues of Language Minority Students, 14*, 269–300.

Huynh, D. T. (1987). *Introduction to Vietnamese culture*. San Diego, CA.: Multifunctional Resource Center, San Diego State University.

Jacobs, E. L. (2001). The effects of adding dynamic assessment components to a computerized preschool language screening test. *Communication Disorders Quarterly, 22*(4), 217–226.

Kaufman, A. S., & Kaufman, N. L. (2004). *Kaufman Assessment Battery for Children–II*. Circle Pines, MN: American Guidance System Publishing.

Kelley, M. F., & Surbeck, E. (1983). History of preschool assessment. In K. D. Paget & B. A. Bracken (Eds.), *The psychoeducational assessment of preschool children* (pp. 1–16). New York: Grune & Stratton.

Keogh, S. V. (Ed.). (1970). Early identification of children with potential learning problems. *Journal of Special Education, 4*, 307–363.

Kilgo, J. L., Aldridge, J., Denton, B., Vogtel, L., Vincent, J., Burke, C., & Unanue, R. (2003). Transdisciplinary teaming: A vital component of inclusive services. *Focus on Inclusive Education, 1*(1). Retrieved July 25, 2006 from http://www.acei.org/inclusivefall03.htm

Langdon, H. W., & Cheng, L. L. (1992). *Hispanic children and adults with communication disorders: Assessment and intervention.* Gaithersburg, MD: Aspen.

Leung, E. K. (1990). Early risks: Transition from culturally/linguistically diverse homes to formal schooling. *Journal of Education Issues of Language Minority Students, 7,* 35–51.

Lewis, M. (1976). Infant intelligence tests: Their use and misuse. *Human Development, 16,* 108.

Lidz, C. S. (1983). Dynamic assessment and the preschool child. *Journal of Psychoeducational Assessment, 1,* 59–72.

Lidz, C. S., & Peña, E. D. (1996). Dynamic assessment: The model, its relevance as a nonbiased approach, and its application to Latino American preschool children. *Language, Speech, and Hearing Services in Schools, 27,* 367–372.

Losardo, A., & Notari-Sylverson, A. (2001). *Alternative approaches to assessing young children.* Baltimore: Brookes.

Lowenthal, B. (1991). Ecological assessment: Adding a new dimension for preschool children. *Intervention in School and Clinic, 26,* 148–162.

Luangpraseut, K. (1987). *Laos culturally speaking: Introduction to the Lao culture.* San Diego, CA: Multifunctional Resource Center, San Diego State University.

Marland, S. (1972). *Education of the gifted and talented: Report to the Congress of the United States by the U.S. Commissioner of Education.* Washington. DC: U.S. Government Printing Office.

McCall, R. B., Appelbaum, M., & Hogarty, P. S. (1973). Developmental changes in mental performance. *Monographs of the Society for Research in Child Development, 38* (3, Serial No. 150).

McCall, R. B., Hogarty, P. S., & Hurlburt, N. (1972). Transitions in infant sensorimotor development and the prediction of childhood IQ. *American Psychologist, 27,* 728–748.

McCardle, P., Kim, J., Grube, C., & Randall, C. (1995). An approach to bilingualism in early intervention. *Infants and Young Children, 7*(3), 63–73.

McLaughlin, B., Gesi Blanchard, A., & Osanai, Y. (1995). *Assessing language development in bilingual preschool children.* Washington, DC: NCELA [National Clearinghouse for English Language Acquisition].

McLean, M. (1998). Assessing young children for whom English is a second language. *Young Exceptional Children, 1*(3), 20–26.

McLean. M. (2001). Evaluation and assessment: Conducting culturally sensitive child assessments. In *Serving the underserved: A review of the research and practice in child find, assessment, and the IFSP/IEP process of culturally and linguistically diverse young children.* (ERIC Document Reproduction Service No. ED454640)

McLoughlin, J. A., & Lewis, R. B. (1986). Assessing special students (2nd ed). Columbus, OH: Merrill.

McWilliam, R. A. (2000). Recommended practices in interdisciplinary models. In S. Sandall, M. McLean, & B. Smith, (Eds.), *DEC recommended practices for early intervention/early childhood special education* (pp. 47–54). Longmont, CO: Sopris West.

Meisels, S. J., & Atkins-Burnett, S. (1999). Assessing intellectual and affective development before age three: A perspective on changing practices. *Food and Nutrition Bulletin, 20*(1). Retrieved April 15, 2005, from http://www.unu.edu/unupress/food/V201e/index.htm

Meisels, S. J., & Provence, S. (1996). *Screening and assessment: Guidelines for identifying young disabled and developmentally vulnerable children and their families.* Washington, DC: National Center for Infants, Toddlers, and Families.

Mercer, J. (1979). *Technical manual: SOMPA: System of Multicultural Pluralistic Assessment.* New York: Psychological Corporation.

Missiuna, C., & Samuels, M. T. (1989). Dynamic assessment of preschool children with special needs: Comparison of mediation and instruction. *Remedial and Special Education, 10,* 53–62.

Paget, K. D. (1983). The individual examining situation: Basic considerations for preschool children. In K. D. Paget & B. A. Bracken (Eds.), *The psychoeducational assessment of preschool children* (pp. 51–61). New York: Grune & Stratton.

Paget, K. D., & Nagle, R. J. (1986). A conceptual model of preschool assessment. *School Psychology Review, 15,* 154–165.

Pavri, S. & Fowler, S. A. (2001). Child Find, screening, and tracking: Serving culturally and linguistically diverse children and families. *Serving the underserved: A review of the research and practice in child find, assessment, and the IFSP/IEP process of culturally and linguistically diverse young children.* (ERIC Document Reproduction Service No. ED454640).

Peña, E., Iglesias, A., & Lidz, C. S. (2001). Reducing test bias through dynamic assessment of children's word learning ability. *American Journal of Speech-Language Pathology, 10*(2), 138–153.

Peña, E., & Quinn, R. (1992). The application of dynamic methods to language assessment: A non-biased procedure. *Journal of Special Education, 26*(3), 269–281.

Peña, E. D., & Quinn, R. (1997). Task familiarity: Effects on the test performance of Puerto Rican and African American children. *Language, Speech, and Learning Services in Schools, 28,* 323–332.

Peña, E., Quinn, R., & Iglesias, A. (1992). The application of dynamic methods to language assessment: A nonbiased procedure. *Journal of Special Education, 26*(3), 269–280.

Pollitt, E., & Triana, N. (1999). Stability, predictive validity, and sensitivity of mental and motor development scales and pre-school cognitive tests among low-income children in developing countries. *Food and Nutrition Bulletin, 20*(1). Retrieved April 15, 2005, from http://www.unu.edu/unupress/food/V201e/index.htm

Prince, C. D. (1992, March 27). *Reactions to the Goal 1 Technical Planning Subgroup report on school readiness: Report to the National Education Goals Panel* (Tech. Rep. No. 92–03). Washington, DC: National Education Goals Panel.

Prince, C. D., & Lawrence, L. A. (1993). *School readiness and language minority students: Implications of the first national education goal.* National Clearinghouse for Bilingual Education: Washington, D.C.

Ramirez, R. R. (2004). *We the people: Hispanics in the United States.* Washington, DC: US Census Bureau.

Razi, S. (2004). The effects of cultural schema and reading activities on reading comprehension. *Proceedings of the First International Online Conference on Second and Foreign Language Teaching and Research* (pp. 276–293). The Reading Matrix, Inc., USA. Retrieved July 26, 2006 from www.readingmatrix.com/conference/pp/proceedings/razi.pdf

Reynolds, C. R., & Clark, J. (1983). Assessment of cognitive abilities. In K. D. Paget & B. A. Bracken (Eds.), *The psychoeducational assessment of preschool children* (pp. 163–190). New York: Grune & Stratton.

Roid, G., & Miller, L. (1997). *Leiter International Performance Scale–Revised.* Wood Dale, IL: Stoelting.

Romero, I. (1992). Individual assessment procedures with preschool children. In E. Vasquez-Nuttall, I. Romero, & J. Kalesnik (Eds.), *Assessing and screening preschoolers* (pp. 55–66). Boston: Allyn and Bacon.

Rubin, R. A., Balow, B., Dorle, J., & Rosen, M. (1978). Preschool prediction of low achievement in basic school skills. *Journal of Learning Disabilities, 11,* 62–64.

Santos de Barona, M. (1981). A study of distractibility utilizing the WISC–R factors of intelligence and Bender error categories in a referred population. *Dissertation Abstracts International, 42,* 4775a.

Sattler, J. M. (1992). *Assessment of Children* (3rd revised and updated ed.). San Diego, CA: Author.

Sattler, J. M. (2001). *Assessment of children: Cognitive applications* (4th ed.). San Diego, CA: Author.

Schakel, J. (1986). Cognitive assessment of preschool children. *School Psychology Review, 15,* 200–215.

Schiff-Meyers, N. (1992). Considering arrested language development and language loss in the assessment of second language learners. *Language, Speech, and hearing Services in Schools, 23,* 28–33.

Share, J., Koch, R., Webb, A., & Graliker, B. (1964). The longitudinal development of infants and young children with Down's syndrome. *American Journal of Mental Deficiency, 68,* 689–692.

Shin, H. B., & Bruno, R. (2003). *Language use and English-speaking ability: 2000.* Washington, DC: US Census Bureau.

Silverman, E. (1971). Situational variability of preschoolers' dysfluency: Preliminary study. *Perceptual and Motor Skills, 33*, 4021–4022.

Slater, M. A., & Heber, F. R. (1979, November). *Final performance report: Modification of mother-child interaction processes in families at risk for mental retardation*. Washington, DC: Bureau of Education for the Handicapped, Grant 780012.

Spivack, G., & Shure, M. B. (1976). *Social adjustment of young children*. San Francisco: Jossey-Bass.

Squires, J. (1996). Parent-completed developmental questionnaires: A low-cost strategy for child-find and screening. *Infants and Young Children: An Interdisciplinary Journal of Special Care Practices, 9*(1), 16–28.

Steffensen, M. S., Joag-Dev, C., & Anderson R. C. (1979). A cross-cultural perspective on reading comprehension. *Reading Research Quarterly, 15*, 10–29.

Stephenson, A., Jiao, H., & Wall, N. (2004). *A performance comparison of native and non-native speakers of English on an English language proficiency test*. Harcourt Technical Report. Retrieved July 25, 2006 from http://www.harcourtassessment.com/hai/Images/resource/techrpts/NativeNonNative.pdf

Swain, M. (1972). Bilingualism as a first language. In J. Damico (1991), *Limiting bias in the assessment of bilingual students*. Austin, TX: Pro-Ed.

Thurman, S. K., & Widerstrom A. H. (1985). *Young children with special needs*. Boston: Allyn & Bacon.

Tikunoff, W. J. (1987). Mediation of instruction to obtain equality of effectivness. In S. H. Fradd & W. J. Tikunoff (Eds.), *Bilingual education and bilingual special education: A guide for administrators* (pp. 99–132). Boston: College Hill Press.

US Census Bureau. (1997). *Highlights of population profile*. Retrieved July 9, 1997, from http//www.census.gov/population/www/pop-profile/highlight.html

US Census. (2003). Retrieved July 25, 2006 from http://factfinder.census.gov

Ulrey, G. (1981). The challenge of providing psychological services for young handicapped children. *Professional Psychology, 12*, 483–491.

Vacc, N. A., & Ritter, S. H. (1995). *Assessment of preschool children*. Greensboro, NC: ERIC Clearinghouse on Counseling and Student Services. (ERIC Identifier ED389964)

Wang, Q., & Leichtman, M. D. (2000). Same beginnings, different stories: A comparison of American and Chinese children's narratives. *Child Development, 71*(5), 1329–1346.

Wechsler, D. (2002). *Wechsler Preschool and Primary Scale of Intelligence–Third Edition*. San Antonio, TX: Psychological Corporation.

Wiersma, W., & Jurs, S. G. (1985). *Educational measurement and testing*. Boston: Allyn & Bacon.

Wilen, D. K., & Sweating, C. M. (1986). Assessment of limited English proficient Hispanic students. *School Psychology Review, 15*(1), 59–75.

Wong-Fillmore, L. (1992). When learning a second language means losing the first. *Early Childhood Research Quarterly, 6*, 323–346.

Zigler, E., & Butterfield, E. (1968). Motivational aspects of changes in IQ test performance and culturally deprived nursery school children. *Child Development, 39*, 1–14.

II

ECOLOGICAL ASSESSMENT

5

Clinical Observation of Preschool Assessment Behavior

Bruce A. Bracken
The College of William & Mary

Anastasi and Urbana (1997) broadly define a psychological test as an objective and standardized measure of a sample of behavior. Psychoeducational assessment, on the other hand, encompasses much more than the mere administration of tests. Assessment is a multifaceted process that incorporates formal and informal devices, such as classroom tests and products, standardized tests, and rating scales, as well as a variety of procedures, including direct test administration, interviews, and clinical observations and judgments. The focus of this chapter is on the importance and use of clinical behavioral observations during the assessment of preschool children.

Psychological tests, as objective and standardized samples of behavior, have many assets. Typically, tests provide the examiner with several convenient bits of diagnostic information, including discernable profiles of performance, standard scores, percentile ranks, age, and grade equivalents. Tests also are expected to meet some minimal levels of technical adequacy (American Educational Research Association, American Psychological Association, National Council on Measurement in Education, 1999; Bracken, 1987; Wasserman & Bracken, 2003). Clinical observations and judgments, in comparison, are frequently less objective and standardized than tests, and they allow for much more professional disagreement and debate. Clinically derived observations generally have no published norms, standard scores, percentile ranks, or age and grade equivalents, and the reliability, validity, and interpretations of assessment observations and interpretations are frequently questioned.

Because of the lack of normative data, it is much easier for a practitioner to defend decisions made on the basis of objective test data than it is to defend judgments made on behavior observed and interpreted in a more subjective, clinical fashion. On the other hand, some concerns with psychoeducational assessment seem to have stemmed from the practice of blindly using test scores for making programmatic and placement decisions about children without the full use of clinical observations, judgments, and common sense. Therefore, it would make sense to fully use objective and subjective data in the assessment and interpretation of young children's behavior.

Clinical observations represent one critical aspect of the assessment process that can lead to a fuller understanding of the child and the child's test performance. Observations should be employed to describe and explain children's test and nontest behaviors, attest to the validity or invalidity of test scores, at least partially explain children's variable test performance, lend support for diagnoses and remediation strategies made on the basis of standardized test results, and provide the examiner with information needed to develop specific hypotheses concerning a child's learning style and individual strengths and weaknesses.

This focus on clinical observations and judgment does not imply that the issues related to subjectivity, reliability, and validity associated with observations should be ignored; rather, it is recognized that diagnosticians must develop objective, reliable, and valid observational skills. Clinical skill must complement the use of standardized tests if diagnosticians are to make accurate diagnoses, prognoses, and recommendations for the remediation of young children's deficiencies.

NORMAL PRESCHOOL BEHAVIOR

When a child is described by parents and teachers as distractible, impulsive, easily frustrated, and emotionally labile, psychologists frequently consider such tentative diagnostic hypotheses as minimal brain dysfunction, emotional disturbance, learning disabilities, or similar conditions. Although behavioral descriptors of this sort are frequently cited as soft signs for neurological impairment or severe emotional disturbance among older children, the same behaviors often characterize many normal children between the ages of 2 and 6.

Normalcy is especially difficult to define among young children and frequently even cohabiting, biological parents differ dramatically in their perceptions of their children's behavior (e.g., Bracken, Keith, & Walker, 1998; however, newer behavior rating scales with stronger psychometric qualities, such as the Clinical Assessment of Behavior (CAB; Bracken & Keith, 2005, have been developed and ameliorate some of these concerns. The CAB is one example of an instrument with very strong psychometric qualities that was normed on a population of children as young as 2 years. Such instrumentation has helped establish a benchmark of normalcy among younger children.

During the preschool years, social, physical, and cognitive development occurs at a rapid rate and the range of development among normal preschool children is great. As children increase in age, their rate of development decreases and the range of behaviors among normal children likewise becomes narrower. It is sometimes difficult to differentiate mildly handicapped preschool children from normal preschoolers due to variable rates of development (hence the preference for such descriptors as developmental delay rather than retardation), whereas older children with mild handicaps are more easily identified and stand apart from their normally functioning peers. Preschool children, for example, typically exhibit higher energy levels, less self control, and much more physical activity than socialized, school-age children. At what point then does an energetic and active preschooler cease being considered normal and begin to be considered abnormal? Because there are no norms that provide a clear indication of normal energy levels (or other behaviors) for children of various ages, the question is impossible to answer; experience and "internalized" norms guide most clinicians in the determination of whether the child's behavior is exhibited with more intensity, frequency, or in longer duration than is typical.

ENVIRONMENTAL EFFECTS

It is often assumed that a child's behavior during an evaluation is similar to the child's home or classroom behavior. In many cases this assumption is invalid. Test behavior should never be interpreted unconditionally as being representative of a child's typical behavior in any other setting. The dynamics of an evaluation are much different from those of a typical preschool, day care, kindergarten, or home environment. Even with older children, it should not be assumed that assessment behavior is typical behavior; but preschool children, especially, have had little contact with schools, teachers, authority figures other than parents, and the extensive probing, questioning, and the formality that is part of a psychoeducational evaluation. Thus, the preschool child's test behavior may often be specific to the evaluation and generalize poorly to other assessment sessions or nonassessment situations.

When teachers or parents hear a diagnostician's description of their child's behavior during an evaluation, it in not uncommon that the parents or teachers profess that the examiner must not have seen the child's typical behavior. The evaluation setting provides enough structure and personal attention to keep some children eagerly on task, while other youngsters resist the structure and formality and refuse to participate in the assessment process or participate only half-heartedly. The unfamiliar adult-child interactions, materials, and settings that are part of psychoeducational evaluations may frighten or intimidate some children, whereas other youngsters may respond positively to the novel situation and personal attention.

Psychoeducational evaluations are extremely structured events. Children are directed to do as the examiner instructs; test items, whether enjoyable or not, must be attempted, and the abundance of test rules and directions have an effect on the child's behavior. Although psychoeducational assessments are frequently described by examiners as "fun games," it becomes readily apparent to most preschool children that the examiner is more interested in the child's performance than "having fun." There are very few occasions in a preschooler's life when time and behavior are as structured and controlled as during psychoeducational evaluations. Because atypical behavior may be a common occurrence during an evaluation, test behavior should be noted and interpreted cautiously by diagnosticians so that inappropriate generalizations about the child's behavior are not made.

Situational structure and interpersonal interactions are but two possible environmental influences on a child's evaluation behavior. The examiner needs to be sensitive to the effects of a wide variety of environmental influences on the child's performance. To develop a better understanding of the child's typical behavior, the examiner should observe the child in a variety of environments and contrast the child's nonevaluation behavior with behavior observed during testing. The diagnostician should observe the child in the preschool classroom during structured and unstructured activities which require a wide range of behaviors, including quiet listening, active and passive individual and group participation, learning activities, cooperation, sharing, and interactions with peers and adults. Observations should also be made while the child is involved in free play on the playground for a more total picture of the child's typical behavior. If clinical observations are made in a variety of settings, the diagnostician will have a greater sample of behavior from which diagnostic inferences can be more reliably made.

SPECIFIC BEHAVIORS AND BEHAVIORAL TRENDS

To effectively evaluate a child's behavior, the examiner must be aware of the child's full range of specific behaviors and integrate them into meaningful behavioral trends. Because the length of the evaluation provides a relatively small sample of behavior, the observer must look carefully for noteworthy behavioral trends. Frequently, diagnosticians come away from an evaluation with a "feeling" about the child as a result of observing specific behaviors that together formed a behavioral trend. Undocumented and supported feelings about a child's behavior, however, are insufficient. It is the task of the diagnostician to observe, note, and integrate assessment and nonassessment behavior so that when behavioral trends are reported they are sufficiently supported with specific observed behaviors. Rather than merely reporting that a child was fearful during the evaluation, for example, the examiner should support this claim with instances when the child's "fearful" behavior was exhibited. If the child withdrew from the examiner's touch, began to weep silently during an attempt to build rapport, spoke hesitantly in a shaky and quiet voice, was startled when the examiner placed test materials on the table, and avoided direct eye contact with the examiner, the behavioral trend described as "fearful" would be well documented and easily supported. Most professionals would agree that a young child who exhibited these and similar behaviors indeed appeared to be frightened.

It is also important to document support of behavioral trends for later reference. If diagnosticians are questioned months later about behavioral judgments, it is much easier to support the existence of behavioral trends if the child's specific behaviors were also observed and recorded during the evaluation. Likewise, when children are reevaluated some time after the initial evaluation, it is helpful to contrast the child's specific behaviors across time. Moreover, assessment-related behaviors and behavioral trends can be triangulated and further substantiated with the perceptions of parents and teachers through the use of such formal behavioral assessment instruments as the CAB (Bracken & Keith, 2005).

Specific behaviors should not be noted to identify only trends of behavior but should also be examined carefully to identify behaviors that are inconsistent with the general trends. Inconsistent specific behaviors often form subtrends which give an indication of less obvious, yet important, strengths, weaknesses, fears, likes, dislikes, and so on. A child who smiles frequently, converses freely, jokes and teases with the examiner, readily complies with the examiner's requests, and spontaneously laughs and sings during an evaluation likely would be identified as a friendly and cooperative child. The same child, however, may at times exhibit mild resistance, express a desire to terminate the evaluation, and require occasional redirection and encouragement. If the antecedent conditions for these incongruent specific behaviors are scrutinized, a diagnostically important behavioral subtrend may emerge. For instance, the child might find the verbal exchange with the examiner enjoyable, but may have an aversion to tasks that require visual-motor integration. If the pattern of incongruent resistant behaviors is considered in the context of the tasks being performed, the examiner should see that this typically friendly preschooler becomes resistant only when faced with activities requiring visual-motor integration. Observations of this sort, combined with qualitative test data, may provide concomitant evidence for a diagnostic claim of relative weakness in that area.

INABILITY VERSUS UNWILLINGNESS

One distinction that should be made through the use of behavioral observations is whether a child failed individual test items due to an inability to complete the task successfully or due to an unwillingness to attempt the task. It is not uncommon for shy preschoolers to refuse to attempt assessment tasks, especially motor activities that require active physical participation and verbal tasks that require extensive vocalization. In such a case, the diminished subtest score will also lower the scale score as well as the total test score. In such instances, in addition to noting the detrimental effects of the child's limited vocalization on tests requiring extensive verbalization, the examiner would likely want to supplement the battery with instruments that require only receptive verbal abilities (e.g., Bracken Basic Concept Scale–III; Bracken, 2006) or nonverbal measures of ability, such as the Leiter International Performance Scale–Revised (Roid & Miller, 1997), or the Universal Nonverbal Intelligence Test (UNIT; Bracken & McCallum, 1998). Moreover, it would be important that the examiner not incorrectly identify the skill assessed by the subtest in question as an area of weakness relative to the child's other abilities because of the low score. An alternative in this instance would be to attest to the invalidity of the subtest, prorate the scale and total test scores, and suggest reevaluation of the skills at a later date.

It is imperative that the diagnostician be more that a test giver. If behavioral observations are used properly to distinguish between a child's inability and unwillingness to perform tasks, the diagnostician will avoid making foolish or embarrassing statements about the child's relative weaknesses and the need for remediation.

DESCRIBING WHAT IS SEEN

Diagnosticians frequently view the purpose of an evaluation as the identification of a child's difficulties or weaknesses so that the child can be properly serviced by the school or agency. In many instances, this is the function of diagnosticians since most preschool referrals are made by parents or preschool teachers who have perceived problems in the child's development or adjustment. However, such a deficit model of evaluation often results in a biased orientation.

Frequently, due to a deficit model of evaluation, many diagnosticians look for or observe and report on the absence of problematic behaviors—noting, for example, that the child was "neither overly active nor impulsive during the assessment process." To say that a child was "not overly active nor impulsive" provides the parent or teacher with little useful information. It is usually inferred from statements such as these that no problems were noted in the areas of concern; however, when it is reported that a specific behavior was not observed, the person informed is left to imagine where on a continuum of behavior the child actually performed. If a child is "not overly active," it cannot be safely inferred that the child was moderately active or even appropriately active. Without an accurate description of the child's actual behavior, one cannot safely infer anything except that the child was "not overly active."

Preferably, the examiner should note exactly what the child does and then describe and interpret the behavior in accurate and descriptive terms. Rather than describing a child as neither overly active nor impulsive, a more clear image of the child is communicated when the examiner notes that the child eagerly performed all tasks presented, yet waited patiently for instructions to be read, materials to be readied, and the examiner's direction to begin. In this instance the diagnostician could have characterized the child as interested and patient (or used similar descriptors), and then provided sufficient support for the positively stated clinical judgment.

BEHAVIORAL INFERENCES

Too often, psychoeducational reports contain behavioral observations that are a running chronology that fail to draw any meaningful inferences. Merely reporting what a child did during an evaluation without also providing an interpretation of that behavior in the context of the evaluation environment is insufficient. It is sometimes tempting to cite only what was actually observed during an evaluation rather than interpret the behavior because interpretations and inferences are much more subject to professional disagreement than are behavioral citings; but this temptation should be resisted. The value of behavioral interpretations by far outweighs the difficulties that arise from professional disagreement.

Eye contact, for instance, is a behavior that diagnosticians are fond of reporting, but frequently do not interpret. It is fairly common that examiners will report in a psychoeducational report that the child made, or failed to make, eye contact throughout the evaluation. What is the significance of this observation? Alone, it is meaningless; yet when coupled with an inferential interpretation this observation provides relevant and meaningful information. The possible explanations for a child's continued (or absence of) eye contact are numerous, and selecting the appropriate interpretation is important. Did the child make eye contact in an effort to secure assurance from the examiner that the child's test performance was acceptable? Was the eye contact hostile in nature and used as a nonverbal, passive-aggressive message of resistance? Was eye contact made with teary eyes, suggesting fear and a desire to terminate the evaluation session? Did the child make eye contact with eyes that expressed a lack of understanding and a need for a slower pace and greater explanation? Or, did the child's continued eye contact inform the examiner that the evaluation was viewed positively by the youngster? The answers to these questions are not found solely in the observation of eye contact, but are answered through the compilation of other specific facial and nonfacial behaviors that form a meaningful behavioral trend.

MEANINGFUL COMMUNICATION OF BEHAVIORAL OBSERVATIONS

The ability to communicate the meaning of a child's behavior to the child's parents, teachers, and others is an important and necessary assessment skill. To do this, examiners must expand their repertoire of behavioral descriptors and describe children's behavior in terms that reflect accurately not only the frequency, intensity, and duration of the child's behavior, but also the spirit in which the behavior was performed.

To report that a child walked around the room during the rapport-building phase of the evaluation only minimally describes the child's behavior. The reason for the child's walking and the intensity of the behavior are unclear. Was the child interested in exploring the new environment? Was he afraid and unready to sit? Resistant? Was he angry and walking off his anger? It is unclear what the child's intentions were without more information. There are also a host of terms that refer to the nuances in walking behavior which give a more clear indication of the child's state of being at the time. If it was reported that the child *darted* around the examining room, there is a suggestion of more energy being exerted by the child than if the child was described as *sauntering* around the room. Likewise, *skipping* suggests a lighter mood than *trudging*, *pacing* connotes a higher level of anxiety than *strolling*, and *stomping* alludes to a greater degree of emotion than *tiptoeing*.

Although there is a greater likelihood of disagreement among professionals over whether a child was sauntering or strolling, marching or stomping, diagnosticians should not hesitate to describe the behavior in terms which they believe accurately connote the nuance of emotion underlying the child's behavior or the energy with which the behavior was exhibited. As psychologists and educators, our task is to make diagnostic decisions based on the best data available at the time. As mentioned previously, test results are fairly easily defended, but clinical observations are essential for making sense of the test results and providing a clearer understanding of the child.

WHEN TO OBSERVE BEHAVIOR

Behavior is a continuous attribute that flows unendingly. Literally every moment during an evaluation the child is doing something worth noting. To make sense of the continuous behavior flow, it is necessary to study the child's behavior temporally in an ongoing manner.

Because much of the child's behavior is a reaction to the examiner or the examining situation, the child's responses to various situations should be studied meticulously to determine possible relationships between the task the child is asked to perform and the child's resulting behavior. Identification of relationships between tasks and resulting behaviors may lead to meaningful hypotheses about the child's abilities. Why might a child kneel and lean forward in anticipation when presented with a verbal memory subtest, yet recoil and become anxious when asked to repeat numbers on a numerical memory task? The child's differential response to the two similar subtests may suggest a tentative hypothesis about the child's relative comfort with verbal as opposed to numerical information.

The examiner's hypothesis should be investigated to determine whether similar responses were made to other memory and nonmemory, verbal and numerical subtests. If the child's response pattern is consistent and verbal items are continually responded to more favorably than numerical items, then information is gained which can be used, along with obtained test scores, to explain the differences in the child's verbal and numerical abilities.

Less contiguous temporal units should also be considered when analyzing trends in a child's behavior. The examiner should compare the child's behavior at the beginning of the evaluation with that near the end of the evaluation. Did the child begin eagerly, but finish frustrated? Did the child separate from her parents with difficulty, but gradually warm in mood so that by the end of the evaluation the examiner and child were mutually comfortable? Does the child work well once she gets started, but become anxious or frightened when required to cease one activity and initiate another? The child's reaction to transitions in tasks, subtests, tests, and other activities and settings should also be noted by the examiner. By considering temporal units of behavior, whether large or small, the examiner can obtain information that will not only help explain the child's test performance, but will provide parents and teachers insight into the child's variable behavior at home and in school.

WHAT TO OBSERVE

Although it would be impossible to list all behaviors that are worthy of notice during a diagnostic evaluation, behaviors that should not go unnoticed are discussed below. It is hoped that the reader will become more aware of preschool behavior, expand these suggestions as necessary, and learn to attend selectively to childhood behaviors that provide diagnostically useful information.

Appearance

During the course of an evaluation, the examiner should note with photographic clarity the child's actual physical appearance. This carefully recorded description will prove a useful aid to recall at a later date when the details of the evaluation are no longer vivid. A description of this sort is also useful for professionals who will be working with the child in the future because it provides a concrete referent. Photographic descriptions of children also humanize the assessment report, and make it clear that the report concerns an actual child, not a faceless entity. It is important that future teachers, counselors, and other school personnel see the preschooler as a living, breathing, red haired, freckle-faced youngster, for example, rather than merely a name—IQ paired association.

Height and Weight

A physical description of a child should include notes about weight and height, especially relative to the child's peers. Height and weight charts are usually available from pediatricians, but are also frequently found in books on child development. As with most traits and characteristics, variance for normal height and weight is great during the preschool years. The examiner should take care to note the interaction between the child's size and his or her performance on the assessment tests or how it relates to his rate of development. It is more meaningful, for instance, to describe a child as being seriously overweight and then discuss the ways in which the child's excess weight interfered with fine and gross motor abilities as measured on a diagnostic evaluation than to cite only that the child's weight is at the 99th percentile when compared to same-age peers.

The examiner needs to be acutely sensitive to the effects that extreme height or weight might have on a youngster's test performance, school performance, self-concept, peer relations, and so on. The question of whether a child's deviant weight is a result of a physiological problem should be investigated by a physician. The diagnostician should be aware that deviancy in a child's physical development may have implications for the emotional, social, and educational well-being of the child and should be considered within the context of the psychoeducational evaluation. As with all areas of development, early intervention for health-related problems is preferred to later interventions.

Physical Abnormalities

The diagnostician should be watchful for physical characteristics that are unusual and/or indicative of insufficient or inappropriate diet, physical or emotional abuse, lack of proper medical or dental attention, improper sleep or rest patterns, and physiological, psychological, or educational disorders.

The child should be surveyed for obvious sensory and motor abnormalities. The child should evidence fairly symmetrical motor development and functioning. While the young child's movements are typically not as smooth as an older child's, they should be neither jerky nor spasmodic. The child should be observed for tics, tremors, excessive clumsiness, and uncontrolled body movements.

The examiner should also be observant for signs of visual and/or auditory impairments. Visually, the examiner should look for obvious signs, such as red, swollen eyelids, crusty drainage around the eyes, eyes that neither track nor align properly, squinting, excessive blinking, grimacing, or evidence of impaired perception of orientation in space, size, body image, and judgment of distance. The examiner should also watch for signs of auditory impairment such as drainage from the ears, complaints of earaches or itchy ears, repeated requests for questions to be restated, tilting of the head for better reception, etc. The child's speech should be considered carefully for indications of auditory dysfunction, such as frequent auditory discrimination errors, expressed confusion when there is auditory confusion or commotion, and inappropriate responses to questions, directions, or requests.

Grooming and Dress

Observations of the child's grooming frequently provide the examiner with an indication of the care afforded the child at home. If the child's hands and face are covered with an accumulation of dirt and the clothing bears traces of compounded soil, then it might be safely inferred that little attention has been given to the child's hygiene. A diagnostician should be careful, however, to discern if the child is temporarily disheveled and dirty because of recent play or whether the observed dirt is more permanent and global.

The intent of considering a preschooler's clothing is not to attend to whether the child is stylishly dressed, but rather to infer the amount and quality of supervision given to the child's daily routines. As with grooming, a child's dress reflects somewhat the attention and care given the child at home. It would be foolish to infer necessarily that a child in old clothes does not have his or her physical needs met, however, a young boy who comes to an evaluation with his shirt buttons and buttonholes misaligned, wearing socks of different colors, and has shoes on the wrong feet obviously had little attention paid to his dress! The examiner should follow up on this observation by asking the parents and preschool teacher about the child's usual dress and dressing routine. It is possible that this situation was unique due to a rushed schedule the day of the evaluation or possibly that the parents are attempting to teach the child through natural consequences to become more independent in, and attentive to, his daily functioning. Although the potential explanations for disheveled dress are many, the examiner should pursue the reasons to rule out the possibility of parental neglect.

Children's dress can also be a valuable source of information about their level of dependence on adults. If a child's shoes become untied during the evaluation, does he immediately ask the examiner to tie them or does he attempt to tie them himself? Does the child attempt to tuck in a shirt when it comes untucked or does he obliviously leave it untucked? Does the child attempt to button buttons or snap snaps that have come undone or ask to have them done by an adult? The essence of the observation is whether the child evidences an attempt at independent functioning or is content and used to having others do for him. Obviously, the average 2-year-old would be expected to be quite dependent on adults for dressing assistance, but 3- and 4-year-olds should be evidencing attempts at independent functioning even if these attempts prove unsuccessful; 5- and 6-year-olds should be quite independent in much of their normal daily functioning, requiring assistance much less frequently than their younger peers.

Speech

A preschooler's speech yields a great deal of information about not only the quality of the child's language skills, but also the child's overall cognitive ability and level of social-emotional development. Eisenson (1978) provides a useful guide which describes qualitative characteristics of speech in children up to 36 months of age. Also, language development and basic concept attainment for preschool children are discussed in the speech and language assessment chapter of this book. Therefore, little will be added here concerning the specifics of early childhood language development; however, it is important that a child's speech be noted carefully during an evaluation for insight into the child's thought patterns, problem-solving style, tolerance to frustration, awareness and understanding of the examining situation, and ability to communicate needs and follow directions.

Although stuttering, stammering, and mild lisps caused by the loss of baby teeth and imperfect enunciation are common among young children (especially among first graders), the examiner should note the child's speech difficulties and be particularly sensitive to whether the child evidences discomfort over speech production. If the child's speech is unintelligible, is marked by severe stuttering or stammering, or causes concern to the child or parents, then the diagnostician should make a referral for a language assessment and attempt to determine in what ways and to what degree the child's imperfect speech interfered with the test results. In situations where a child's poor expressive speech results in lowered test scores, the examiner should measure the youngster's receptive vocabulary and nonverbal reasoning skills with instruments such as the Bracken Basic Concept Scale–III (Bracken, 2006) or the UNIT (Bracken & McCallum, 1998), both of which require no verbal expression and are appropriate for early childhood assessments.

Many preschoolers express their thoughts verbally while attempting to solve problems, which provides the diagnostician with insights into the processes used in obtaining the solution. Although intelligence tests have been criticized historically for measuring intellectual product but not process, the astute diagnostician can infer aspects of the child's cognitive processing from the resultant product and the child's steps taken while working toward producing that product.

During the test administration, when test items become increasingly difficult, the examiner should note the child's response to the increasingly difficult tasks and more frequent item failures. Frequently, young children remain on task as long as the task is within their ability. When the tasks become taxing, many children focus only on particular words within the test questions and respond verbally in an eluding and tangential manner. For example, the examiner who asks a young child to complete the following sentence, "This pencil is made of *wood*, this window is made of . . ." (Bracken, 2006), might get a response such as "I want to look out the window." Many preschoolers use manipulative ploys in an attempt to avoid failure, while others use verbal redirection to avoid participating in the evaluation once they discover that the examiner's "games" are not as much fun as they first seemed. A clinician's reported observations about a child's redirecting attempts infrequently astonish parents who have been manipulated successfully by their children, though some parents may be unaware that they have been redirected so effectively by their child. An awareness of this sort of observation is all some parents need to begin setting consistent limits and better managing their young children.

A child's level of verbal spontaneity often can be an indication of the child's level of comfort in the examining situation. A verbally expressive youngster who chatters happily throughout the evaluation is visibly more comfortable than a reticent child who speaks quietly, haltingly, and only when questioned. The examiner should question the validity of evaluation results when it is deemed that the child was overly inhibited during the assessment process. The examiner might contrast the child's performance on subtests that require verbal expression with subtests that require little or none for a better determination of the extent to which the child's shyness affected the test results. If the child scored consistently lower on verbal expressive measures than on verbal receptive items, the examiner should further determine whether the child is reticent due to a verbal deficiency or whether the observed verbal deficiency was a result of reticence. If the child is observed to be verbally fluent and spontaneous in nontest situations, it might be hypothesized that the child's shyness may have been the cause of the poor verbal test performance; in such a case, interventions of an entirely different sort would be warranted.

The examiner should attend to the preschooler's speech for insights into the child's overall affect. Does the child tease, joke, or attempt to be humorous verbally? Does the child use baby talk or regressive language at times of stress or frustration? When tasks become difficult, does the child utter silly nonsense phrases or respond seriously with a relevant response, whether correct or not? Does the youngster become verbally aggressive when faced with failure and petulantly inform the examiner, "I don't like you. I want to go home!"?

The diagnostician should be watchful for how the child responds verbally, as well as nonverbally, to the multitude of situations that arise during the evaluation. It is helpful, for example, if a diagnostician notes that a particular child, like many preschoolers, becomes silent when faced with failure, disappointment, embarrassment, or frustration. Many parents react to a young child's silent dejection with over-stimulating attention; the diagnostician should advise that increased attention frequently exacerbates the problem and a more relaxed, soothing, and accepting approach may be most helpful in reopening the temporarily closed lines of communication.

The content of a child's verbalizations should be considered carefully, not only to determine the relative maturity of the child's speech, but also to detect emotional projections the child is making while performing tasks during the evaluation. The examiner should listen intently to the young child's interpretations of test pictures, test items, and spontaneous comments. With a verbally expressive preschooler, the examiner frequently has available a great store of additional psychological information; preschoolers typically have not acquired the sophistication to mask their feelings and have not yet developed strong defense mechanisms. Their problems often can be readily detected by a diagnostician who observes as well as tests.

Fine and Gross Motor Skills

Since many early school experiences are motoric in nature, the examiner should pay particularly close attention to the child's motor development. Older tests such as the McCarthy Scales of Children's Abilities (McCarthy, 1972) had direct measures of gross and fine motor ability, while most other preschool tests at least indirectly measure motor skills. The Wechsler Preschool and Primary Scale of Intelligence–III (Wechsler, 2003) is heavily weighted in fine motor and perceptual speed tasks, and although the Stanford-Binet Intelligence Scale, Fifth Edition (Roid, 2003) contains fewer motor tasks than previous editions, it still includes some useful motor activities.

Formal motor assessment procedures should always be supplemented with direct behavioral observation. The examiner needs to discern the child who performs poorly on formal motor measures for reasons other than poor motor coordination. Children may score low on motor scales because of shyness, an unwillingness to attempt the task, fear of failure, embarrassment, or because motor tasks may lack the necessary structure for some children. Also, one must question whether the child understood the test directions; even subtests that are motoric in nature frequently have long and complex verbal directions (Bracken, 1986; Cummings & Nelson, 1980; Flanagan & Alfonso, 1995; Flanagan, Alfonso, Kaminer, & Rader, 1995; Kaufman, 1978). Informally, children should be watched carefully to note how well they perform nontest motor tasks as well as formal motor tasks. Children who are lacking in educational experiences may look clumsy when drawing, coloring, or cutting with scissors, yet are able to button buttons, zip zippers, and manipulate small objects with obvious facility. The nature of the remediation for a child of this sort should be to engage the child in educationally relevant motor activities as their adaptive behavior type motor skills appear to be well developed already.

When assessing preschoolers, the examiner should observe the child's gross motor abilities, including the ability to climb stairs, walk, run, skip, hop, balance on one foot, walk backwards, throw, and catch. Obvious signs of gross asymmetrical development should be noted as possible indicators of neurological impairment, and referrals should be made for a neuropsychological evaluation if warranted. As with fine motor development, the examiner should discern whether the child's gross motor difficulty is due to a lack of meaningful experiences or to a physical or perceptual limitation. While perceptual difficulties may be the cause of poor coordination in the truly awkward and clumsy child and may require educational or physical intervention, the child lacking in experience may need only additional experience to develop better motor skills.

Activity Level

How active a child is during an evaluation has direct implications for the validity of the test results. It is likely that a child who is either lethargic or extremely active is not participating in the assessment process to an optimum degree, thus reducing the test's validity. A child who must be extrinsically motivated to attempt tasks, encouraged to continue the assessment, and prodded to complete test items is problematic. The diagnostician should qualify the reports of the child's poor performance with a note about the child's diminished activity level and reluctance to participate. The examiner should contrast the child's test and nontest behaviors, search for relevant behavioral trends, and watch for instances in which the child displays isolated bursts of interest and energy before making inappropriate diagnoses based on the affected test scores. If a child actively participates in subtests of a particular nature and remains listless for others, the resultant test profile and the examiner's behavioral notes, when coupled, should lead to diagnostically useful information.

The examiner should be aware of whether a child is currently medicated and any effect such medication might have on the child's activity level. If the youngster is taking medication that has a depressant effect, the evaluation should be postponed and rescheduled to when the youngster is healthier and better able to give maximum effort. In instances of prolonged medical treatment, the diagnostician should acknowledge that it is likely that the test scores are depressed due to medication and caution the user of the results to consider judiciously the effects of the child's physical condition on the test results. Likewise, ill health may itself adversely affect the child's energy level. The examiner should note symptoms that indicate the onset of an illness and decide whether the evaluation should continue or be rescheduled for a later date.

Similarly, fatigue and drowsiness, common among preschoolers in the early afternoon, should be an indication to the examiner that optimal results on cognitive and achievement measures will not be obtained; upon observing the child's fatigue or sleepiness, the examiner should cease testing for the time being. Fatigue frequently accentuates soft signs of neurological impairment in children and the examiner should be watchful for those signs.

Attention

Artifacts in test results caused by a child's inattentiveness may bring about inappropriate remediation recommendations unless the test results are further explained through behavioral observations. For example, if a child obtains a relatively weak score on the Memory Scale of the Universal Nonverbal Intelligence Test, a diagnostician might conclude that the child's short-term memory is deficient. However, the diagnostician should be able to explain this weakness as an attention, rather than memory, issue if the child did not attend fully to the directions or the stimuli on short-term memory items. Because memory items cannot be readministered, as most other test items can, the child may consistently miss the crucial element of test items due to inattentiveness rather than poor memory. The logical recommendation based on this observation would be to ensure that the child is attending carefully before teachers or parents present information they expect the child to recall.

Distractibility

Some children, although attentive during much of the evaluation, miss crucial information because they are easily distracted. These children may be attending appropriately, but momentarily discontinue attending to the task and shift their attention to inappropriate stimuli. Distractibility interferes with successful completion of many test activities, but is particularly harmful on memory tests and tasks that are timed. The examiner should differentiate a child's failure due to inability and failure due to inconsistent attention. If the child's low scores are properly explained by the examiner, the subsequent recommendations should be more pertinent to the child's actual area of difficulty.

Impulsivity

Like inattentiveness and distractibility, impulsivity can severely limit the child's success on cognitive and achievement tests. If a child blurts out a response before the examiner completes the test question, initiates a task before the directions are finished, or says, "I know how to do it—let me try" as the examiner readies the test materials, the child is likely to fail many times and do poorly on the test overall.

Examiners need to be aware that typical preschoolers are at times inattentive, distractible, and impulsive. However, the crux of the examiner's observations should be to determine the degree to which the child's test performance was adversely affected by extreme behaviors and then judge the usefulness of the test scores. Although the diagnostician may believe that the test results are seriously deflated due to the child's test behavior and may be able to support this belief with a raft of behavioral notes, he or she should be careful when making optimistic claims about the child's likelihood of success in the classroom. If the child's behavior has interfered with his performance on the test, it may also interfere with his performance in the classroom and indeed may have been the reason for the initial referral.

Affect

Emotional lability is a common characteristic among preschool children. The examiner should become aware of the ways in which a child responds differentially to various situations. It is not uncommon for a young child to be exhilarated by success at one moment and demoralized by failure the next. Unfamiliar tasks may arouse fear and anxiety in a child who had previously completed familiar tasks calmly and confidently. An otherwise compliant and cooperative child may become "testy" and difficult during the unstructured interim between tests in a battery. A youngster who enters the examining room clinging to doors and furniture in fear may leave the room striding and exuding confidence.

The examiner should attend carefully to shifts in a child's affect as a result of changes in the environment and seek answers to the following types of questions: How does the child respond to structured versus unstructured activities? What is the child's reaction to praise, rebuke, failure, success, redirection, encouragement, etc.? What causes the child to become silent, to start crying, to withdraw, to jump up in excitement, to sing out with pleasure, or strike out in anger? To what test activity is the child most attentive and which activities arouse the least interest? How does the child react to test materials, being timed, the examiner, the examining room, the parents, verbal interaction, and nonverbal, performance-related activity?

Although the examiner may see many mild or even dramatic shifts in the child's mood, the child's general mood should be noted as well. On the whole, did the youngster seem happy? Negative? Fearful? Sullen? Confident? All of the child's affective behaviors should be drawn together diagnostically and inferences should be made about the child's overall mood, level of adjustment, areas of concern, and areas of strength.

Anxiety

Closely associated with affect is the child's level of anxiety. The diagnostician should note what causes the child to become anxious and how the child displays signs of anxiety. When asked several difficult questions near the ceiling of a test, does the youngster begin to suck his thumb while tears well in his eyes? Does the child stare at the floor in silence while sitting on her hands? Does the child giggle nervously, cry, constantly clear her throat, bite her nails, urinate, blush, block while talking, breathe unevenly, or hyperventilate?

Although a psychoeducational evaluation frequently arouses anxiety in preschoolers, some children are more affected than others. Some youngsters are aroused to an optimal level, whereas others are totally debilitated. Some are anxious throughout the evaluation, and others become anxious only in reaction to specific events or situations. By noting the child's behavior in several settings, the diagnostician is better able to determine whether the child's anxiety was specific to the evaluation, or more general in nature, and the degree to which the child's anxiety interfered with the evaluation.

Comprehension and Problem Solving

The examiner should attend to the problem-solving approach used while the child seeks solutions to puzzles, mazes, block designs, and similar problems. Such observations yield clues about the child's comprehension of the task demands and solution. Does the youngster draw directly through the maze without regard for walls? Remain between the walls, yet continually enter blind alleys? Remain within the walls and attempt to avoid blind alleys, but proceed too slowly and still fail the task? In each case, the child's earned raw score is zero, but the child's level of comprehension differs dramatically across examples. It is quite likely that the first child did not understand the nature of the task. The second child may have understood the nature of the task, but was not fully cognizant that blind alleys should be avoided. The third child seems to have fully understood the task, but was unable to complete the item successfully because of the speeded nature of the task.

The child's reaction to test materials at times provides the diagnostician with surprising insight into the child's level of understanding. In low functioning young children, it is fairly common for the child to sniff or suck the mallet of the McCarthy xylophone thinking that it is a lollipop. Similarly, the brightly colored chips that are part of the McCarthy Conceptual Grouping subtest are sometimes mistaken for candy. Observations of this sort, when added to other behavioral notes, yield valuable information about the child's maturity and level of comprehension.

The examiner should be watchful for such events as the following: Does the child make random attempts to solve problems in a trial-and-error fashion or appear to have a strategy? If an attempt is unsuccessful, does the child continue to try the same approach or try other approaches? When solving a puzzle and puzzle pieces do not fit, does the child try a second piece or try to force the first piece into place? Does the child understand that puzzle pieces must be right-side-up in order to fit properly in the puzzle? On simple two or three piece puzzles, does the child impulsively shove adjacent pieces together without regard for the total picture? Observations of this sort add a qualitative nature to the test score. Although any two children may obtain the same scores on a given subtest, no two children will exhibit exactly the same behaviors while attempting the subtest items.

Reactions to Other People and Situations

The preschool child's interactions with his or her parents together and each parent apart should be noted, as well as the manner in which the child interacts with siblings, teachers, classmates, and strangers. It should be observed whether the child interacts with others by moving forward confidently or timidly holding back. Is the youngster aggressive with classmates or bullied? Does the child seek independence from the teacher or frequently ask for help, reassurance, and support? Does the child obey one parent's commands but ignore the other parent's directions? The child's interactions with the examiner should also be noted. Overall, is the child compliant, manipulative, fearful, confident, respectful, flippant, and so on?

In many instances, children who have difficulty adjusting to assessment or classroom situations come from home or school environments that contribute to their problems. Although teachers and parents mean well and attempt to do what they believe is in the child's best interest, at times they fail to see their role in the child's lack of adjustment. Consider, for example, the father who drops his daughter off at the nursery school. At the moment the father attempts to leave his daughter in her class, she begins to cry. As the daughter cries, her father attempts to console her, yet every time he begins to leave she becomes more upset. This cycle repeats itself daily until the child begins crying before ever leaving her home, and school becomes a negative experience to which she reacts strongly. As any experienced preschool teacher knows, most young children stop crying almost immediately after their parents leave, and the best way to avoid unpleasant separations is to make departures warm yet brief.

SUMMARY

Although the administration of psychoeducational tests alone requires a great deal of skill, concentration, and coordination, an effective diagnostician must also have the resources to observe and record the preschool child's behavior. With a carefully collected sample of behavioral observations, the examiner should be able to support or refute test findings, explain a child's variable test performance, and attest to the validity or invalidity of test results. The diagnostician should also note the child's appearance and determine whether signs or symptoms of physical, emotional, or educational difficulties are present. Behaviors that indicate a child's preferred cognitive style, language abilities, problem-solving approach, level of understanding, and reasons for individual item and subtest performance must likewise be observed and interpreted. These behaviors, along with observations of the child's affect, distractibility, dependence, reactions to others, fears, likes, etc., need to be integrated with obtained test data to formulate accurate diagnoses, prognoses, and remedial recommendations.

REFERENCES

Anastasi, A., & Urbana, S. (1997). *Psychological testing*. Upper Saddle Creek, NJ: Prentice-Hall.

American Educational Research Association, American Psychological Association, and National Council on Measurement in Education (1999). *Standards for educational and psychological testing*. Washington, DC: American Psychological Association.

Bracken, B. A. (1986). Incidence of basic concepts in the directions of five commonly used American tests of intelligence. *School Psychology International, 7*, 1–10.

Bracken, B. A. (1987). Limitations of preschool instruments and standards for minimal levels of technical adequacy. *Journal of Psychoeducational Assessment, 4*, 313–326.

Bracken, B. A. (2005). *Clinical Assessment of Behavior*. Lutz, FL: Psychological Assessment of Behavior.

Bracken, B. A. (2006). *Bracken Basic Concept Scale–III*. San Antonio, TX: Harcourt Assessments.

Bracken, B. A., & Keith, L. (2005). *Clinical Assessment of Behavior*. Lutz, FL: Psychological Assessment Resources.

Bracken, B. A., Keith, L. K., & Walker, K. C. (1998). Assessment of preschool behavior and social-emotional functioning: A review of thirteen third-party instruments. *Journal of Psychoeducational Assessment*. Reprinted from *Assessment in Rehabilitation and Exceptionality, 1*, 331–346.

Bracken, B. A., & McCallum, R. S. (1998). *Universal Nonverbal Intelligence Test*. Itasca, IL: Riverside.

Cummings, J. A., & Nelson, R. B. (1980). Basic concepts in oral directions of group achievement tests. *Journal of Educational Research, 73*, 259–261.

Eisenson, J. (1978). Is my child delayed in speech? *School Psychology Digest, 7*, 63–68.

Flanagan, D. P., & Alfonso, V. C. (1995). A critical review of the technical characteristics of new and recently revised intelligence tests for preschoolers. *Journal of Psychoeducational Assessment, 13*, 66–90.

Flanagan, D. P., Alfonso, V. C., Kaminer, T., & Rader, D. E. (1995). Incidence of basic concepts in the directions of new and recently revised American intelligence tests for preschool children. *School Psychology International, 16*, 345–364.

Kaufman, A. S. (1978). The importance of basic concepts in individual assessment of preschool children. *Journal of School Psychology, 16*, 207–211.

McCarthy, D. (1972). *McCarthy Scales of Children's Abilities*. San Antonio, TX: Harcourt Assessment.

Roid, G. (2003). *Stanford-Binet Intelligence Scales, Fifth Edition*. Itasca, Il: Riverside Publishing.

Roid, G. H., & Miller, L. J. (1997). *Leiter International Performance Scale–Revised*. Wood Dale, IL: Stoelting.

Thorndike, R. L., Hagen, E. P., & Sattler, J. M. (1986). *Stanford-Binet Intelligence Scale: Fourth Edition*. Chicago: Riverside Publishing.

Wasserman, J. D., & Bracken, B. A. (2003). Psychometric considerations of assessment procedures. In J. Graham and J. Naglieri (Eds.). *Handbook of assessment psychology* (pp. 43–66). New York: Wiley.

Wechsler, D. (2003). *Wechsler Intelligence Scale for Children* (4th ed.). San Antonio, TX: Harcourt Assessment.

6

Assessment of Social and Emotional Development in Preschool Children

Jonathan M. Campbell and Carrah L. James
University of Georgia

With greater frequency than before, professionals are called upon to evaluate the social and emotional development of very young children. A few factors account for the increased frequency of early childhood evaluations. First, early entrance into child care situations provides earlier opportunity for comparison with peers who serve as a normative comparison group with regard to social development and behavioral functioning (Martin, 1991). Second, parents possess an increasing knowledge base concerning the "typical" developmental course for children, and are more frequently concerned about aspects of their child's progress at younger ages (Martin, 1991). Third, documentation of special needs is often required prior to the provision of early intervention. For example, federal mandates to serve children with special needs beginning at birth require documentation of delays as an indication of eligibility (U.S. Department of Education, 1997). Finally, increasing research into social and emotional development and functioning in preschool children has focused attention on the need for sound assessment in this area. Empirical evidence has also highlighted the efficacy of early intervention which has led to the need for earlier assessment and diagnosis (e.g., Bradley et al., 1994; White, 1985–86).

The organization of this chapter is similar to the parallel chapter in the previous edition of this volume (i.e., Keith & Campbell, 2000). First, we introduce the varied purposes for assessing social and emotional functioning in preschool children and identify major influences on social-emotional development that should inform assessment. We then provide a brief overview of several disorders of social and emotional development often diagnosed in young children. Next, we identify limitations associated with evaluating social and emotional development in preschool children and critique primary assessment techniques currently used. In our critique of primary assessment techniques, we highlight recently published third-party rating scales designed for social-emotional assessment of preschool children.

PRIMARY PURPOSES OF ASSESSMENT

The purposes of assessment can vary and may involve screening, diagnosis, treatment planning and evaluation, and detecting co-occurring conditions, among others (Kamphaus,

Reynolds, & Imperato-McCammon, 1999); therefore, the scope and activities that occur during any evaluation will be determined by its purpose. When the purpose of an assessment is to screen for a disorder, the goal is to distinguish between those persons who probably suffer from a disorder from those who probably do not (Derogatis & DellaPietra, 1994). The practice of screening "well" populations is built on the idea that early problem identification is advantageous by leading to early intervention and improved outcomes. For example, medical screening for phenylketonuria (PKU) allows for detection within the first days of life and, if detected, dietary intervention is used to prevent severe to profound mental retardation. In contrast to medical screening, screening for social and emotional problems in very young children is implemented much less frequently. For severe social developmental disorders (e.g., autism), however, several screening instruments have been created for use during well-baby visits including the Checklist for Autism in Toddlers (CHAT; Baron-Cohen, Allen, & Gillberg, 1992) and a parent-report version, the Modified CHAT (MCHAT; Robins, Fein, Barton, & Green, 2001).

A second purpose of assessment is to diagnose a specific condition, such as autism, or perhaps two (or more) co-occurring conditions, such autism and mental retardation. When the purpose of assessment is to determine the presence of a condition, a third purpose is likely to follow: recommendations for interventions to improve the functioning of the individual. Intervention may occur in a variety of domains, including environmental, medical, parental, or child-centered strategies (Keith & Campbell, 2000). For example, a young child diagnosed with autism may benefit from intervention at all four levels, including a child-focused behavior modification plan, medication, participation in an early intervention program, and parent education and support. Ideally, a comprehensive evaluation of social and emotional functioning yields information that guides decisions about intervention, including appropriate intervention goals and methods. Assessment also allows for evaluating the effectiveness of the treatment approach; that is, are interventions working to improve functioning?

Finally, assessment is an important component of research into social and emotional development and the prevention and treatment of disorders diagnosed in young children. Appropriate identification is necessary in understanding the course of disorders and treatment outcomes. In addition, a good understanding of early social and emotional development often requires assessment of current levels of functioning.

MAJOR INFLUENCES ON SOCIAL AND EMOTIONAL DEVELOPMENT

Professionals who assess social and emotional functioning in young children must have a fundamental understanding of child development in general, as well as the influences that bear on social and emotional development, specifically. These influences are far-reaching and must be considered as part of the comprehensive assessment of social and emotional functioning. Major influences include characteristics of the child (Garmezy, Masten, & Tellegen, 1984), parental style and parental characteristics (Emde & Easterbrooks, 1985), family characteristics (Bowlby, 1988), environmental influences (Bronfenbrenner, 1977; Sameroff, 1986), and the various interactions of these factors (Bowlby, 1988; Bronfenbrenner, 1977). Due to the complex interplay of factors that influence social and emotional development in preschool children, the description of any one influencing factor is somewhat artificial. It is necessary, however, to understand the components for an appreciation of their interaction.

Child Characteristics: Temperament, Appearance, and Gender

That particular child characteristics would play a significant role in development seems obvious; however, their influence was long accepted as overwhelmingly unidirectional (Grusec & Lytton, 1988). Currently, the role of child characteristics in shaping the environment, and consequently, in shaping the child's development through environmental response to the child, is well documented (Brooks-Gunn, 1985; Lewis & Rosenblum, 1974). Investigations into the relationship between infant behavior and its effects on caregivers and later peer relationships and adjustment are particularly compelling in describing the influence of child characteristics of social and emotional development (Easterbrooks & Lamb, 1979; Petit, Dodge, & Brown, 1988).

Several characteristics indigenous to the child have been collectively researched and described as temperament. Although many definitions of temperament exist, it may be specifically defined as "stable individual differences in quality and intensity of emotional reaction" (Berk, 1997, p. 397). Thomas, Birch, Chess, Hertzig, and Korn (1963) described nine dimensions of temperament including activity level, rhythmicity, approach-withdrawal, adaptability to change, threshold of responsiveness, intensity of reaction, mood, distractibility, and attention span. Further, Thomas and Chess (1977) grouped the nine descriptions of temperament into three general prototypes: easy, difficult, and slow-to-warm-up. The "easy child" is characterized by positive responsiveness to caregivers, adaptability, and playfulness, and is more likely to receive positive attention from caregivers. On average, the "difficult child" receives less supportive care giving based on the child's low degree of responsiveness. For instance, the "difficult child" is often fussy, cries more than other infants, and is difficult to comfort. The third prototype is that of the "slow-to-warm child" who is primarily described as adapting to change slowly. Therefore, this child will elicit varying degrees of attention and support from caregivers, resulting in inconsistent opportunities for positive interaction. As a result, the likelihood of a tenuous caregiver-child relationship is increased. Defining emotionality as central to defining temperament, Martin and Bridger (1999) outline important assumptions regarding the nature of temperament, including the relative stability of temperament over time and the influence of temperamental behaviors on future social and emotional development such as academic performance, moral development, personality characteristics, and psychopathology.

Of the three prototypes, the difficult child has arguably been the most researched. A difficult temperament has been shown to be associated with poorly regulated biological functions, negative responsiveness to new situations, and negative mood (Thomas & Chess, 1977). Subsequent investigations have shown evidence for a link between early difficult temperament and later behavior disorders (Graham, Rutter, & George, 1973), and difficult temperament and increased risk for child abuse (Gill, 1970). The preponderance of evidence also indicates that attributions of causality are likely from the direction of the child rather than the caregiver where "difficultness" is concerned (Grusec & Lytton, 1988).

In contrast to problems associated with a difficult temperament, research in the area of developmental psychopathology has shown that certain child characteristics serve as protective factors against stressors. For example, Garmezy (1985) identified "dispositional" attributes as protective mechanisms. Children who exhibit these characteristics demonstrate higher levels of social and emotional adjustment than children experiencing similar stressors who do not possess the identified attributes. Specifically, infants who tolerate environmental change, are easily comforted, and are physiologically regulated, are likely to be more resilient (Block & Block, 1980). Others have described resilient children as those with temperamental attributes that elicit positive responses from others (Rutter, 1978).

In addition to temperamental characteristics, a child's physical appearance has been shown to contribute to attributions made by caregivers, teachers, and peers. Specifically, Langlois, Ritter, Casey, and Sawin (1995), found that infants' physical attractiveness related to maternal behaviors and attitudes, with more attractive children receiving more affectionate attention. According to Langlois and Downs (1979), the behaviors of physically less attractive preschool children were comparable to more attractive children at age 3. At age 5, however, children rated as unattractive were more aggressive toward peers and more active in general. Finally, a strong, positive relationship exists between teacher ratings of social competence and the physical attractiveness of preschool and elementary children (e.g., Ritts, Patterson, & Tubbs, 1992).

A child's gender is also associated with a differential response from the environment that influences social and emotional development. For proponents of a biological perspective, differences in social behavior of males and females may be explained by physiological differences (Tieger, 1980). Regardless of the direction of influence, however, empirical evidence consistently supports higher levels of aggression and less effective interpersonal skills for boys compared to girls, particularly at younger ages (Berk, 1997; Maccoby, 1990).

Parental Characteristics

In addition to child characteristics, parenting characteristics and parents' approach to relating to their child are major influences on the development of social and emotional functioning. Factors influencing parental style predate the child's birth. Social learning theory points to the major role of parents' childhood experiences in the development of their parenting practices. Additionally, personal characteristics, norms of society, and religious beliefs all bear on child-rearing practices and styles (Grusec & Lytton, 1988).

Parental style has been categorized by Baumrind (1973) and others as fitting one of four styles: authoritarian, authoritative, permissive, or uninvolved, depending on two dimensions of parenting, demandingness and responsiveness. An authoritarian parenting style is characterized by high levels of demandingness and low levels of responsiveness; the authoritative style is characterized by a demanding, yet responsive, approach to parenting; the permissive parent is generally undemanding, yet responsive; while an uninvolved parent shows little commitment to parenting by exhibiting an undemanding and unresponsive style. Preschool children parented with different styles tend to exhibit different social and behavioral outcomes. For example, research has indicated that children from authoritative homes demonstrated higher levels of social responsibility in the form of positive peer interactions, a higher achievement orientation, cooperativeness with adults, and independence in terms of nonconformity and purposefulness (Baumrind, 1973). Roopnarine (1987) also found that children reared by authoritative parents engaged in fewer negative behaviors than those reared with other parenting styles.

The past three decades of research in the area of resilient children who, despite poverty, parental mental illness, and/or family discord, manage to cope successfully with chronic stressors, indicate that one close bond with a caregiver during the first years of life is crucial for achieving a basic sense of trust. Similarly, the positive results of secure early attachment versus insecure attachment to a primary caregiver have been the subject of much theory and investigation (Bowlby, 1988). Consistent with Baumrind's work, investigators also point to family cohesion and warmth (Luther & Zigler, 1991), along with reasonable structure and clear rules (Rutter, 1985), as having a positive relationship with children's ability to cope with stressors including poverty, discrimination, and lengthy childhood hospitalizations. Finally, children who were emotionally well-adjusted and socially competent despite chronic stressors were frequently provided with a sense of meaning, purpose, and opportunity by their families (Antonovsky, 1979).

Environmental Influences

Because families do not exist in isolation, societal influences play a significant role in the social and emotional development of young children. Bronfenbrenner (1986) points to the impingement of external systems on the family and the development of the child. In particular, parental employment systems and social networks, educational systems, judicial systems, and public policy are all factors that interact to affect the child's development, directly or indirectly. In the childhood resilience literature, the availability of external support systems is cited as a protective mechanism against chronic stress (Luther & Zigler, 1991). For example, Segal (1988) partially accounts for children's resilience as follows: "One factor turns out to be the presence in their lives of a charismatic adult—a person with whom they identify and from whom they gather strength. And in a surprising number of cases, that person turns out to be a teacher" (p. 2). Other influential and supportive relationships in society may include extended family, peers, and religious affiliations.

Interaction of Influences

Clearly, human development is complex and dynamic, and occurs under the influence of many factors at any given point in time. Bidirectionality and interaction are major themes in developmental theories, indicating that no single influence entirely accounts for outcomes. For example, Thomas and Chess (1977) proposed that temperamental and environmental variables, particularly parenting style, interact to affect social and behavioral development in children, the so-called "goodness-of-fit model." The goodness of fit model asserts that when harmony (i.e., a "good fit") exists between a child's temperament and environmental demands, such as parenting style, optimal social and behavioral development occurs. Conversely, when disharmony (i.e., a "poor fit") exists between temperament and environment, then social and behavioral maladjustment becomes a more likely developmental outcome. For example, the interaction between children with difficult temperaments who are parented with a punitive style (i.e., a "poor fit") results in more parent-child conflict, and more defiant and disobedient child behavior than when parenting is less punitive (Berk, 1997).

To account for factors that influence development outside of the individual and family, Bronfenbrenner (1977) outlined an ecological systems theory to organize influences on social and behavioral development. Ecological systems theory asserts that a child develops within a set of nested contexts and relationships (i.e., "systems") that vary according to the degree of immediate and direct impact on a child's development. Bronfenbrenner asserted that the individual is nested within *microsystems*, which are the interactions between the child and the child's most immediate surroundings, including immediate family members within the home, and peers and teachers within the school. The *mesosystem* represents connections between microsystems, such as interactions between parents and school professionals. Microsystems are nested within an *exosystem*, which includes peripheral influences such as parental social networks, extended family, and workplace demands. Finally, the exosystem is nested within the *macrosystem*, which is representative of indirect and far-reaching influences on development, including governmental entities, laws, cultural values, and societal customs.

FREQUENTLY DIAGNOSED DISORDERS IN EARLY CHILDHOOD

As noted earlier, one purpose of assessment is to diagnose; therefore, in the following section, we briefly introduce diagnoses that may be the focus of evaluations with young children. The brief overview of commonly diagnosed conditions will hopefully serve as a reasonable starting point for additional research into the published literature that exists for each disorder. Until recently, much more attention was given to the study of psychopathology in adults than in children. The growing knowledge of child psychopathology is based on the assumptions that: (1) many childhood disorders have lifelong consequences for the child and society; (2) adult dysfunction often has some connection to early childhood; and (3) improved diagnostic systems, intervention programs, and prevention efforts are needed (Mash & Dozois, 2003). Further, the growing knowledge base of childhood psychopathology has contributed to improved assessment of social and emotional development.

Although several classification systems exist for diagnosing childhood social and emotional problems, the *Diagnostic and Statistical Manual of Mental Disorders, Fourth Edition (DSM–IV–TR*; American Psychiatric Association (APA), 2000) is the most widely accepted standard among psychologists and psychiatrists. The *DSM–IV–TR* describes several developmental disorders as usually first diagnosed in infancy, childhood, or adolescence. Most of the childhood conditions described in *DSM–IV–TR* and "most problems identified in children are associated with their perception of reality, their interactions with adults, their interactions with other children, and the relationship between their behavior and learning" (Umansky, 1983, p. 427). We briefly review six of the most frequently diagnosed conditions in young children that have wide-ranging effects on the course of social and emotional development.

Mental Retardation

Mental retardation is defined as "significantly subaverage general intellectual functioning that is accompanied by significant limitations in adaptive functioning" (APA, 2000, p. 41) with onset prior to 18 years of age. The American Association on Mental Retardation (AAMR; Luckasson et al., 2002) definition of mental retardation, a widely recognized classification system for mental retardation, is similar to that outlined in the *DSM–IV–TR*. For both classification systems, social/interpersonal skills are included among the adaptive functioning areas listed. Although skills vary widely for children diagnosed with mental retardation, assessment often reveals concomitant deficits in social skills, language pragmatics, and disordered emotional development or psychopathology (e.g., Wallander, Dekker, & Koot, 2003). Additionally, researchers have noted a significantly higher number of infants with difficult temperaments among children with mental retardation (Bridges & Cicchetti, 1982). As with social and emotional development in children without mental retardation, Baker, McIntyre, Blacher, Crnic, Edelbrock, and Low (2003) point to a transactional influence between parenting and problem behaviors often exhibited by children with intellectual disabilities. More specifically, "maladaptive child behaviour and parenting stress have a mutually escalating effect on each other" (Baker et al., 2003, p. 227).

Pervasive Developmental Disorders

According to *DSM–IV–TR* (APA, 2000), "Pervasive Developmental Disorders (PDDs) are characterized by severe and pervasive impairment in several areas of development: reciprocal social interaction skills, communication skills, or the presence of stereotyped behavior, interests, and activities" (p. 69). Autism is the most widely recognized of the PDDs, all of which have dysfunctional social interaction as a central and common feature. Specifically, infants and young children with Autistic Disorder appear to be frequently impaired in social abilities such as formation of attachment bonds, shared attention with another person, imitation of others, perspective-taking, and imaginative play (Klinger, Dawson, & Renner, 2003). Children diagnosed with PDD frequently function in the range of mental retardation, although this is not typically the case for children identified with Asperger's disorder, which requires age-appropriate cognitive and language development for diagnosis in the current DSM classification system (e.g., Campbell & Morgan, 1998).

Attention-Deficit/Hyperactivity Disorder

The core features of Attention-Deficit/Hyperactivity Disorder (ADHD) include "a persistent pattern of inattention and/or hyperactivity—impulsivity that is more frequently displayed and more severe than is typically observed in individuals at a comparable level of development" (APA, 2000, p. 85). A child who exhibits such high levels of inattention, impulsivity, and/or hyperactivity, is also at risk for problems with social, cognitive, and emotional adjustment. Further, these children typically experience increasing difficulty compared to their peers in adapting to demands for self-regulation of behavior, affect, and organization of their environment (Barkley, 2003). For example, the lowered emotional control that is associated with ADHD may result in some of the problematic behavioral symptoms demonstrated by children with ADHD (Barkley, 2003). Parental frustration and negative parent-child interactions may be the earliest indications of a child with ADHD.

Attachment Disorders

Attachment to others may be described along a continuum from secure to unattached; thus, it is not an "all or nothing" proposition. The attachment patterns of most children lie somewhere in the middle of the continuum. Children with Attachment Disorder, however, are found at the negative extreme and are generally considered to form poor attachments as the result of early trauma, particularly in the form of severe abuse or neglect (Magid & McKelvey, 1987). Attachment disorders indicate a central disruption in social and emotional development. Specifically, *DSM–IV–TR* describes Reactive Attachment Disorder of Infancy or Early Childhood as evidenced by "markedly disturbed and developmentally inappropriate social relatedness in most contexts that begins before age five years and is associated with grossly pathological care" (APA, 2000, p. 127). Although the underlying features remain constant, one of two clinical presentations is typically dominant. *DSM–IV–TR* describes the "inhibited type" as a child who fails to initiate social interactions, or to respond appropriately to social overtures by others. Excessive inhibition, hypervigilance, resistance to comfort by caregivers, and approach-avoidance interaction styles are also frequently observed for a child with an inhibited type of presentation. The "disinhibited type," on the other hand, is characterized by lack of selectivity in attachments and indiscriminant sociability (APA, 2000). Because some of the behavioral aspects of Attachment

Disorders are similar to Attention Deficit Disorders and PDDs, including impulsivity and poor peer relations, and because pathological care is often difficult or impossible to document, misdiagnosis is common. Treatment and research surrounding these two classes of disorders, however, are quite different and necessitate careful discrimination during diagnosis (Keith, 1996). Indeed, while the number studies researching Reactive Attachment Disorder is growing, there is still a dearth of information on this disorder when compared to other disorders introduced in the chapter (Lyons-Ruth, Zeanah, & Benoit, 2003).

Mood Disorders

Over the past two decades, recognition of the existence of depression in children has resulted in theoretical reconceptualizations concerning depression and stimulated a wealth of research. Research has refuted original misconceptions about childhood depression, such as the beliefs that children cannot experience depression and that childhood depression is brief, reactive, and developmentally appropriate (Hammen & Rudolph, 2003). Although separate diagnostic categories for children are not included in *DSM–IV–TR*, special considerations for diagnosing children as opposed to adults are provided. For instance, a diagnosis of Dysthymic Disorder, a chronic mood disorder associated with fewer symptoms of depression, in adults requires the presence of symptoms for at least 2 years, whereas for children, the minimum duration is specified as 1 year (APA, 2000). Also, for a diagnosis of Major Depressive Episode in children, the mood criterion (A.1) can be met if mood presents as *irritability* or depressed mood. With depressive disorders, disruption in development may occur across affective, social, cognitive, and physical domains. Specifically, children with depression frequently exhibit irritability, sadness, aggression, and behavioral problems. Additionally, disturbed appetite and sleep patterns, and lowered academic performance may occur with depression in children.

Behavior Disorders

Defined primarily by cultural norms, antisocial behavior is classified by *DSM–IV–TR* into two primary categories of Conduct Disorder and Oppositional Defiant Disorder. According to the *DSM–IV–TR* (APA, 2000), the defining feature of Oppositional Defiant Disorder is "a recurrent pattern of negativistic, defiant, disobedient, and hostile behavior toward authority figures that persists for at least 6 months" (p. 100). While considered by some to be a milder developmental precursor of Conduct Disorder, most children diagnosed with Oppositional Defiant Disorder do not go on to develop Conduct Disorder (Hinshaw & Lee, 2003). In contrast, Conduct Disorder is characterized by more serious destructive and aggressive behavior and is generally not diagnosed in the preschool years. Given that defiance is a developmental norm for preschoolers, careful consideration is required to determine the presence of problematic behavior beyond that which is typical for peers.

GENERAL LIMITATIONS IN ASSESSING PRESCHOOLERS

At this point, it is important to introduce three unique challenges when assessing the social-emotional functioning of preschoolers. First, preschoolers demonstrate fewer cognitive and language abilities when compared to older children (Bierman & Schwartz, 1986). Second, it is more difficult to describe reliably social-emotional functioning compared to the majority of other characteristics of preschoolers, such as perceptual-motor skills, cognitive functioning, and academic achievement (Martin, 1991). Third, the range of normal developmental variability is broader for preschoolers than older children or adolescents (Wheatcraft & Bracken, 1999). The combination of these three general limitations creates special problems in the assessment of social and emotional functioning of preschool children.

Cognitive Limitations of the Preschool Child

Compared to older children and adolescents, the preschool child is cognitively limited, thereby influencing assessment practices in a variety of ways. First, most preschoolers cannot read; therefore, a host of useful instruments that require this fundamental skill cannot be used to evaluate preschoolers' social-emotional functioning (e.g., Martin, 1991). For example, widely used self-report measures of personality or social functioning are eliminated from use with the preschool child. Second, preschoolers lack the range of verbal expressivity seen in older children, adolescents, and adults. Therefore, they may have more difficulty describing thoughts, feelings, or relationships with others than older children. Also, preschoolers are usually able to provide only a general idea of what they think and feel through verbal means. Third, preschoolers are usually not aware of the purposes of assessment and often cannot adjust their behavior to meet the demands of the assessment situation, such as controlling behavior or concentrating for extended periods of time. Fourth, preschoolers are typically limited in their understanding of social-emotional concepts (Bierman, 1990), so inquiry about emotions or feelings is often misunderstood. Fifth, preschool children typically engage in rather rigid styles of thinking that are marked by egocentrism and the inability to make meaningful comparisons with others (Bierman, 1990; Martin, 1991). For example, preschoolers may identify themselves as the strongest, fastest, and smartest of their friends or simply may not be able to make such comparisons.

Limitations Related to the Content Area

Coupled with the preschool child's cognitive limitations is the problem of describing social and emotional characteristics per se. Characteristics outside of the realm of social and emotional functioning are typically described more reliably. Physical, cognitive, and academic characteristics are more stable than social and emotional traits (Martin, 1991). A primary reason that social and emotional characteristics are described less reliably is that social and emotional functioning varies across contexts. For example, a child may demonstrate social anxiety only when meeting new adults and not new peers. Preschoolers, and other persons, typically do not behave as consistently over time on social and emotional dimensions compared to other characteristics (Martin, 1991).

Increased Variability in Development

A final general limitation affecting the assessment of social-emotional functioning of preschoolers involves the large range of "normal" developmental progress in preschoolers (Wheatcraft & Bracken, 1999). That is, the range of what is considered age-appropriate social and emotional development is broader for preschoolers than older children, adolescents, or adults. This creates special problems when attempting to discriminate between preschool children who demonstrate normal social-emotional functioning versus those whose functioning is deficient or disordered (Wheatcraft & Bracken, 1999). As will be seen below, each limitation can create measurement problems when assessing social and emotional characteristics of preschool children, especially for traditional assessment procedures.

PRIMARY ASSESSMENT TECHNIQUES

Despite the aforementioned general limitations in the measurement of preschoolers' social-emotional functioning, sound assessment procedures exist. Methods for evaluating the social-emotional functioning of preschoolers include: interviewing, direct observation, third-party ratings, projective techniques, and play-based assessment. The purpose of this section is to introduce a broad range of techniques available for assessing preschoolers' social-emotional development; therefore, breadth of coverage is emphasized over depth. The rationale and content of each broad assessment category is introduced briefly and a discussion of advantages and disadvantages associated with each assessment technique follows each introduction.

Interviewing

Interviewing Preschool Children.   Interviewing is a widely used technique to gather information regarding the preschool child's social and emotional functioning (Martin, 1986). As in the case of evaluating older children and adolescents, psychologists often interview both the child and at least one adult caregiver; however, interviewing preschoolers creates special problems associated with the general limitations previously identified. First, cognitive restrictions produce limited understanding of social and emotional questions and unrealistic "all-or-none" categorizations of self and others (Bierman, 1990). For example, preschoolers typically define others as either "good" or "bad" without understanding that persons can exhibit a range of qualities. Second, formally interviewing children below the age of 6 has been discouraged due to unreliable information that young children typically provide (e.g., Martin, 1986). Third, preschool children are often shy and timid when meeting someone new; therefore, when interviewing a preschool child, traditional "formal" interviewing methods are often abandoned for alternative techniques, such as free-play sessions (Sattler, 1998).

Despite the limitations mentioned above, interviewing preschool children presents two distinct advantages. First, compared to adults, young children are not as self-conscious and often not as inhibited during an interview, which can yield valuable information about the child's perspective and concerns (Bierman & Schwartz, 1986; Martin, 1986). Furthermore, Sattler (1998) asserts that preschoolers often demonstrate the cognitive capacity to respond to *short* probing questions designed to clarify content. Second, the interview provides the means to establish rapport with the preschool child early in the evaluation of social and emotional functioning (Sattler, 1998). Based upon the limitations mentioned above, Sattler (1992) offered useful suggestions concerning how to encourage preschoolers to talk about themselves. For example, interviewing might take place in a playroom equipped with a variety of creative materials, such as paper, crayons, clay, or paints. Initial interaction with the interviewer might take the form of a game, introducing a novel toy, or some other shared creative activity.

Interviewing Caregivers.   In addition to interviewing the child, preschool assessors typically interview the child's caregivers, such as parents, teachers, or day care workers, for additional information regarding social-emotional functioning. For adults, traditional "formal" interviews are quite useful. Interviews with significant caregivers constitute an important part of any assessment procedure. Parents tend to be especially knowledgeable about their child's social-emotional functioning and are usually able to relay detailed information to the interviewer. Although parents and other caregivers often provide useful information about the child's social and emotional adjustment, a carefully conducted and thoughtful interview with parents or teachers accomplishes more than information gathering. Initial interviews constitute the first step in building rapport with family members, which will be useful in subsequent intervention efforts, if necessary. Rapport building can be accomplished if family members are actively engaged during the interview and treated as respected and valued members in the assessment process (Sattler, 1998).

Advantages of Interviewing Caregivers.   The interview holds specific advantages over other assessment techniques. First, interviews allow for flexible assessment of social-emotional functioning. For example, the interviewer can clarify unclear responses through follow-up questioning, evaluate particular strengths and/or weaknesses in detail, and change the focus of the interview as necessary. Second, interviews allow the assessor to simultaneously evaluate the veracity of reports by observing nonverbal cues, such as facial expression, change in tone of voice, or diverted eye contact (Sattler, 1992). For example, when verbal content of an answer and nonverbal cues do not match, this may suggest that the respondent is not answering questions truthfully, or that a truthful response is particularly troubling for the respondent.

Structured Diagnostic Interviews.   Structured diagnostic interviews exist for use with older preschool children, ages 6 and up, and their parents, such as: (a) the Child Assessment Schedule (CAS; Hodges, Kline, Stern, Cytryn, & McKnew, 1982), (b) the Diagnostic Interview for Children and Adolescents (DICA; Herjanic, Herjanic, Brown, & Wheatt, 1975), (c) the Diagnostic Interview Schedule for Children (DISC; Costello, Edelbrock, Dulcan, Kalas, & Klaric, 1984), and, (d) the Schedule for Affective Disorders and Schizophrenia for School Aged Children (K-SADS; Puig-Antich & Chambers, 1978). The structured diagnostic interviews are typically administered by professionals, although the DICA and DISC were specifically designed to be used by lay interviewers. Each interview includes child and parent versions that sample specific diagnostic symptoms and yield common DSM diagnoses, including ADHD, depression, and obsessive-compulsive disorder. Reliability studies that have sampled children as young as age 6 have yielded kappa statistics that range from .21 to .83, with kappas equal to or below .40 considered poor agreement (Hodges, 1993). Test-retest and inter-rater correlations range from .38 to .89. In general, validity data on these scales are limited, especially when utilized with children as young as 6 years of age (Hodges, 1993). Studies examining mother-child concordance for the CAS with both psychiatric and non-referred children have found: (a) moderate to low agreement for conduct/behavioral problems (range = .63 to .26), (b) moderate to nonsignificant agreement for affective symptoms (range = .46 to −.05), and (c) low to nonsignificant agreement for symptoms of anxiety (range = .26 to .05) (Hodges, Gordon, & Lennon, 1990; Thompson, Merritt, Keith, Murphy, & Johndrow, 1993). The correlational data point to the importance of using multiple respondents when assessing affective and behavioral problems, especially with younger children.

Often administered in interview format, caregivers may respond to measures of preschool children's adaptive functioning, which typically include information about social functioning and behavioral adjustment (e.g., Vineland Adaptive Behavior Scales (Vineland); Sparrow, Balla, & Cicchetti, 1984). The Vineland also features the Social-Emotional Early Childhood Scales (SEEC), a measure of social and emotional functioning for use with children from birth to 5 years, 11 months of age (Sparrow, Balla, & Cicchetti, 1998). The SEEC scales were derived from the Socialization domain of the Expanded Form of the Vineland. Information collected from adaptive behavior interviews may be used to support a diagnosis, such as developmental delay; however, information collected about a child's adaptive functioning is also important in establishing goals of intervention and documenting the effects of intervention.

Limitations of Interviewing Caregivers.   As with any assessment method, interviews suffer from weaknesses. First, interviewees may respond inaccurately to interview questions. Inaccurate responding may result for a variety of reasons, such as, intentional malingering, problems with remembering specific details about the child's past social and emotional functioning, or a parent's tendency to view his or her child in a positive manner. Second, estimates of reliability and validity of unstructured interviews are virtually impossible to establish (Sattler, 1992; 1998), and reliability and validity estimates for structured interviews can be quite low. Third, the interviewer can unwittingly facilitate inaccurate responding with use of subtle verbal and nonverbal cues, such as nodding in anticipation of a positive response to an interview question.

Observation Methods

A second major technique used in the assessment of preschool social-emotional functioning involves direct observation. Direct observation may occur in varied contexts, such as home, school, or day care setting. The assessor may also observe the child in more structured conditions, such as a standardized intellectual assessment or free-play session in an office. The structure required in behavioral observation can vary as well. Formal observation methods may be quite structured as in the case of interval sampling of behaviors where one records the presence or absence of a particular behavior during a specified interval of time. Other formal observation methods may require less structure by only requiring the observer to create general impressions of the child or environment. For example, the Home Observation for Measurement of the Environment (HOME; Caldwell & Bradley, 2003) requires the observer to record the presence or absence of certain behaviors or environmental characteristics, such as the presence of books or play materials at home and affective aspects of the child-parent relationship. Informal observation methods are those that occur during other interactions with the child, such as behavior observed as the child separates from parents in a clinic waiting room or during a cognitive assessment. Each type of observation is important in the evaluation of preschool children's social-emotional functioning. It is most important to observe the child across different contexts and settings, as behavior observed in one setting may not generalize to other settings (e.g., Bracken, 2000). If behavioral observation is not possible outside of the standardized assessment setting, the assessor should note that behavior observed in an office setting may not generalize well to other contexts (Bracken, 2000).

Advantages of Observing Preschool Children.   Generally, observations of preschool children enjoy improved reliability when contrasted with interviews, especially when standardized observation methods are used. For example, interobserver agreement for the HOME inventory averages approximately 90% (Bradley & Caldwell, 1988). In addition, observational methods of assessment do not require preschool children to describe their affective states or behavior as the examiner views them first-hand; therefore, observations tend to circumvent some of the cognitive and language limitations outlined earlier. Third, compared to older children, young children tend to act naturally while being observed, perhaps due to lower levels of self-consciousness than older children and adolescents (Martin, 1986). Finally, observations may take place simultaneously within the context of other assessment activities, such as during a cognitive test administration.

Limitations to Observing Preschool Children.   The overwhelming drawback to observation is the high cost in terms of time. As noted above, contextual factors influence behavior, such as physical setting and persons present. Therefore, behavior observation should take place over varied contexts, which requires additional time. In addition to these factors, mastering coding systems can also be time-consuming (Martin, 1986). Similar to informal interview methods, the psychometric properties of informal observations are not known; therefore, reliability and validity estimates are unavailable for independent scrutiny. Further, the presence of an observer can change the nature of the observation setting and introduce demand characteristics for parents, siblings, and others. This may distort observations in problematic ways. For example, family members may change behavior in response to the child due to a desire to be positively appraised. Finally, the observer may introduce his or her own biases into the observation process by systematically viewing the child in overly positive or negative ways.

Third-Party Rating Instruments

Third-party ratings are also commonly used for assessing social-emotional functioning of preschool children. Martin (1991) identified third-party ratings scales as *the* primary assessment tools in evaluating social-emotional functioning of preschool children. Typically, respondents familiar with the preschool child, such as a parent, day care worker, or teacher, respond to a list of items that describe the child across a variety of domains. Items often sample content areas of specific, and often problematic, behaviors (e.g., "Throws things at parents,"), interaction styles ("Is shy around adults,"), or affective states (e.g., "Is irritable,"). Respondents are asked to endorse items using response formats that vary slightly across scales. For example, the preschool version of the Child Behavior Checklist (CBCL; Achenbach & Rescorla, 2000) uses a three-point scale to assess "how true" 99 descriptions are for the child rated (i.e., "0"–Not True; "1"–Somewhat or Sometimes True; "2"–Very True or Often True). Other third-party rating instruments, such as the Behavior Assessment System for Children, Second Edition (BASC–2; Reynolds & Kamphaus, 2004) and the Clinical Assessment of Behavior (CAB; Bracken & Keith, 2004) require respondents to rate the frequency of behaviors, ranging from "Never" to "Always/Almost Always."

Ratings scales vary according to breadth of coverage with some designed to yield a comprehensive profile of the preschool child's social-emotional functioning, such as the BASC–2 and CAB, and others measuring fewer aspects of adjustment, such as behavioral indicators associated with ADHD, sampled by the teacher and parent short forms of the Conners' Rating Scales-Revised (CRS–R; Conners, 1997). Several rating scales consist of "systems" of assessment by offering multiple rating checklists for multiple respondents that yield scores across similar clusters of behaviors that can be compared. For example, the BASC–2, CAB, and CRS–R include parent and teacher rating forms that yield summary scores for similar behavioral clusters. Table 6.1 presents psychometric information for three

TABLE 6.1.
Brief Description of Third-party Reports Assessing the Social-Emotional Functioning of Preschool Children

Scale	Age Level	Sample of Scale Content	Avg. Median Subtest/Subscale Reliability	Avg. Total Test Reliability[7]	Avg. Test-retest Reliability[5]	Avg. Inter-rater Reliability[5]
ASEBA[1]						
Parent (CBCL)	1.5–5yr.	Anxious-obsessive; depressed-withdrawn; fears; aggressive behavior; language development survey.	.78[8]	.95	.90	.65
Caregiver–Teacher (C-TRF)	1.5–5 yr.		.80[8]	.97	.88	.72
BASC–2[1]						
Parent (PRS)	2–5 yr.	Bullying; anger control; somatization; hyperactivity; depression; adaptability; social skills.	.81	.93	.81/.84[3]	.81/.72[3]
Teacher (TRS)	2–5 yr.		.86	.96	.92/.87[3]	.76/.76 [3]
CAB						
Parent (CAB-P)	2–6 yr.	Anxiety; depression; autistic spectrum behaviors; mental retardation; bullying; gifted and talented cluster.	.86	.96	.88/.92[3]	.65/.81[3]
Parent Extended (CAB-PX)	2–6 yr.		.91	.98	.89/.94[3]	.63/.82[3]
Teacher (CAB-T)	2–6 yr.		.95	.99	.93/.94[3]	NR
CRS–R						
Parent	3–17 yr.	Conduct problems; anxiety; impulsive behavior; learning problems; inattention.	.91/.88[2]	No total test	.73/.69[2,9]	NR
Teacher	3–17 yr.		.92/.89[2]	No total test	.82/.71[2,9]	NR

TABC-R

Parent	3–7 yr.	Emotional intensity;	$.82^8$	No total test	$.70^9$	.54
Teacher	3–7 yr.	distractibility; activity.	$.90^8$	No total test	$.63^9$	NR

Vineland

Interview Edition, Survey Form	0–18 yr., 11 mo.	Communication; daily living skills, socialization; motor skills.	$.76^4$	.94	.88	.74
Interview Edition Expanded Form	0–8 yr., 11 mo.		$.86^6$	.97	NR	NR
Classroom Edition	3–12 yr., 11 mo.	Interpersonal relationships; play and leisure time; coping skills	$.84^8$	.98	NR	NR
SEEC	0–5 yr., 11 mo.		$.84^6$	.93	.75	.54

Note. ASEBA = Achenbach System of Empirically Based Assessment; CBCL = Child Behavior Checklist; C-TRF = Caregiver-Teacher Report Form; BASC–2 = Behavior Assessment System for Children, Second Edition; PRS = Parent Rating Scales; TRS = Teacher Rating Scales; CAB = Clinical Assessment of Behavior; CAB–P = CAB-Parent Rating Form; CAB-PX = CAB-Parent Extended Rating Form; CAB-T = CAB-Teacher Rating Form; CRS–R = Conner's Rating Scale–Revised; TABC-R = Temperament Assessment Battery for Children-Revised; Vineland = Vineland Adaptive Behavior Scales; SEEC = Vineland Social-Emotional Early Childhood Scales.

[1] =Preschool version; [2] = Short form/Long form; [3] =Calculated coefficient/corrected coefficient; [4] =Split-half reliability; [5] =Total-test or composite averages used when available; [6] =Stepped-up, split-half estimates; [7] =Internal consistency reliability; [8] =Median alpha coefficient; [9] =Median subtest.

of the most frequently used third-party rating scales according to Cashel (2002): the CBCL, BASC–2, and CRS–R. Psychometric data is also presented for other selected measures, such as the CAB, and the Temperament Assessment Battery for Children–Revised, a measure of temperament (TABC–R; Martin & Bridger, 1999), and the Vineland scales.

Advantages of Third-Party Ratings.   Third-party rating instruments offer two distinct advantages. Efficiency constitutes the first clear advantage. Ratings are typically completed by respondents in fewer than 20 minutes, yet yield a host of information about the social-emotional functioning of the preschool child. Additionally, rating forms are inexpensive, simple to administer and complete, and are usually easy to score. A second advantage of third-party ratings is that respondents are typically persons who have observed the child over long periods of time and constitute part of the child's natural environment. Also, parents and other caretakers of the preschool child are usually highly motivated to observe the child's behavior (Martin, Hooper, & Snow, 1986). The use of parents and teachers as respondents is particularly important because these persons often initiate referrals for children's mental health services.

Limitations of Third-Party Rating Instruments.   Third-party rating instruments suffer from two major disadvantages: (a) undesired variability in ratings, which is common to all third-party ratings instruments, and, (b) questionable technical qualities, which can be unique to preschool versions of social-emotional rating instruments (e.g., Campbell, 1999). Martin (1986; 1991) and colleagues (e.g., Martin et al., 1986) have identified four sources of "unwanted" variance produced by third-party rating instruments: rater variance, setting variance, temporal variance, and instrument variance. Rater variance is attributed to raters who view the preschool child in the same setting, such as a preschool classroom, but rate the child differently. Rater variance is common among systems of social-emotional ratings scales where low to moderate inter-rater agreement exists between respondents (e.g., Achenbach, McConaughy, & Howell, 1987; Walker & Bracken, 1996). Bracken, Keith, and Walker (1994) investigated the psychometric qualities of 13 preschool third-party measures of social-emotional functioning and found that inter-rater reliability between parents typically fell within a range of .38 to .74, while agreement between teachers ranged from .34 to .87. Similar to reliability estimates of structured interview techniques, inter-rater agreement between third-party raters appears to vary according to the type of behavior being rated, with ratings of externalizing symptoms (e.g., aggression) achieving higher levels of agreement than internalizing symptoms (e.g., withdrawal). Inter-rater disagreement in third-party scales is unavoidable. Indeed, even under ideal ratings circumstances when two biological, cohabiting parents rated their own children, median inter-rater correlations were observed to be .60 (Walker & Bracken, 1996).

Setting variance refers to variability in the child's behavior according to context. Raters familiar with the child's behavior at home may not see problematic behavior in other contexts, such as at preschool or daycare. Evidence for setting variance exists by contrasting inter-rater reliabilities for informants across different settings. For example, inter-rater agreement between teachers is often higher than inter-rater agreement between teachers and parents. Temporal variance refers to the observation that a preschool child's behavior changes over time, thus yielding differences in an identical respondent's ratings over some interval of time. Temporal variance may be particularly problematic in the assessment of preschool social-emotional functioning due to rapid developmental changes that young children experience. Instrument variance refers to observed variability that occurs when two rating instruments designed to measure similar constructs yield different results (Martin et al., 1986). Interpretation is hindered when psychometrically equal scales yield different results because the examiner cannot be sure which rating scale to interpret with confidence.

To address the problem of variability in third-party rating instruments, Martin et al. (1986) described an assessment strategy designed to help the assessor identify each source of variance. Ideally, evaluation of a preschool child's social-emotional functioning would consist of gathering third-party ratings in a multi-setting, multi-source, and multi-instrument design (Martin et al., 1986). In this assessment model, the preschool child's behavior is rated across at least two settings (e.g., home and school), by at least two raters for each setting (e.g., mother and father), and with at least two instruments for each rater (e.g., BASC–2 and CRS–R). It is easy to see how the number of ratings increases as each source of variance is accounted for in the assessment model. If one were to also account for time variance in the assessment model, a total of 16 third-party ratings would be collected in the end. Data can be aggregated over all rating scales and the subsequent value is deemed to be more reliable than any individual rating. Determining sources of rating disagreements can help to isolate situational-specific aspects of problematic social-emotional functioning. Martin and colleagues identify their assessment model as an ideal and explain that as third-party assessments deviate from the ideal, conclusions regarding the child's social-emotional functioning are weakened.

In addition to problems associated with unwanted variance in measurement, third-party preschool rating instruments have demonstrated weak psychometric properties. For example, Bracken et al. (1994) evaluated 13 third-party rating instruments according to Bracken's (1987) minimum standards of technical adequacy for preschool assessment instruments. The review pointed to limitations in third-party instrumentation such as small, regional standardization samples, subscale reliabilities less than the .80 criterion, and global scale reliabilities less than the .90 criterion. No third-party rating instrument met all specified psychometric criteria; however, many measures fell short on only one or two standards. In terms of psychometric soundness, social-emotional third-party rating instruments performed comparably to preschool cognitive tests and seemed to fare somewhat better than speech and language tests (Bracken et al., 1994). In 1994, Bracken et al. observed that newer third-party rating instruments, such as the original version of the BASC, generally demonstrated better technical characteristics when compared to older rating scales. As seen in Table 1, the trend towards improved technical properties appears to have continued. The most recently published measures of social and behavioral assessment meet or exceed most of the psychometric criteria outlined by Bracken (1987). The most frequently failed criterion consisted of temporal stability (i.e., "test-retest") reliability coefficients that did not reach the .90 threshold. In addition, the scales presented in Table 1 typically feature larger standardization samples than earlier measures, and most allow for competence-based assessment by including adaptive rating scales (e.g., BASC–2 Adaptability subscale; CAB Gifted and Talented cluster).

Projective Assessment

Projective assessment has a long history of use in the assessment of children's emotional functioning and personality (e.g., Rabin, 1968). Projective techniques are the least structured of assessment methods and typically require free expression through verbal, graphic, or written means. Projective assessment techniques share the core theoretical assumption that the respondent expresses private, covert, or, in some cases, unconscious aspects of personality or concerns during his or her response (Rabin, 1968). Of course, different assessment techniques assume that different aspects of personality or concerns are being expressed. For example, Human Figure Drawing (HFD) representations may be assumed to tap one's body image or self-concept as well as other unconscious attitudes, beliefs, and feelings (Jones, 1992), while Kinetic Family Drawings (KFD) may be assumed to assess one's attitudes towards family members and home life. Traditional projective assessment techniques include drawings, sentence completion tests, apperception tests, and the Rorschach Inkblot Test.

Advantages of Projective Techniques.   Projective assessment tasks are often enjoyable for young children. In addition, activities such as drawing, telling stories, and playing are familiar to most children, and they usually participate energetically in them. Therefore, projective techniques can be used to build rapport with young children by allowing familiar and comfortable modes of interaction with an unfamiliar adult. Projective methods can also produce a good "match" with preschool children's communication styles. For example, those who employ HFDs in the social-emotional assessment of young children have argued that drawings are the natural medium for children's communication (Koppitz, 1968).

Limitations of Projective Techniques.   Again, developmental limitations associated with preschool children also restrict the use of projective techniques in assessment of social-emotional functioning. Limitations are primarily associated with disparities between the preschool child's verbal, cognitive, and motor skills and task demands required in projective assessment. Apperception tasks, such as the Roberts Apperception Test for Children (RATC; McArthur & Roberts, 1982), require the respondent to tell stories about pictorial stimuli. Children younger than 6 often name components of the cards or offer simple descriptions about the contents of the card. This observation probably reflects the concrete style of thinking previously described and limits meaningful interpretation.

Projective drawing techniques, such as the HFD, are typically unusable with children below the age of 4 or 5 because the child's drawings are limited to single lines, circles, crosses, and squares (Chandler & Johnson, 1991; Jones, 1992; Martin, 1991). The "scribbles" are viewed as having no representational quality and are therefore not interpreted. Children ages four to seven begin to show signs of symbolic representation by drawing "tadpole people" (Chandler & Johnson, 1991). In her work on HFDs, Koppitz (1968) included children as young as 5 years old in her normative sample of 1,856 children and subsequently asserted that indicators of emotional problems (e.g., unusual omissions, shading, or added detail) could be seen in HFDs of children as young as 5. In general, critics of projective assessment have attacked the tests' psychometric properties, claiming that projective techniques lack adequate temporal and inter-rater reliability and demonstrate poor validity (Obrutz & Boliek, 1986).

Play-based Assessment

Assessing young children's social and emotional development within the context of play has a long history. This is understandable given young children's spontaneous, zealous, and often quite dramatic play activities, as well as the reality that children spend much of their time engaged in play. Play is what young children will do if given the chance; it is "what they do best and most attentively" (Reynolds & Jones, 1997, p. 3). In terms of assessing children's social-emotional development, play has meant many things to many people. For some assessors, observing play allows for sampling a child's behavior within a more natu-ralistic context than formal testing procedures completed within an office setting. For others, children's play is representational whereby children communicate about their inner expe-rience by transforming abstract experience into concrete terms. In terms of structuring so-cial-emotional assessment, play-based assessment can occur within the context of a larger assessment plan, or play-based assessment may constitute the single modality for assessing a wide range of preschool children's abilities.

Play-Based Assessment Coupled with Traditional Techniques.   Within the context of a traditional assessment strategy, play-based assessment offers a unique opportunity for social-emotional evaluation, allowing for simultaneous observation of behavior and its interpretation. Sattler (1998) outlines useful guidelines when observing young children at play, including noting how the child enters the playroom (e.g., cautious, excited), the child's energy level during play (e.g., lethargic, energetic), the child's affect and tone during play activities (e.g., ag-gressive, defiant, cooperative), and the child's attitude toward adults in play (e.g., respon-sive, compliant). Careful observations during play offer the clinician a unique opportunity to assess affect, behavior, and interpersonal style in a relatively natural setting.

Some have asserted that children represent their thoughts, feelings, and experiences through play (e.g., Reynolds & Jones, 1997). Thematic interpretation of play may occur at several levels. For example, young children's play may be interpreted: (a) at a general level of organization, which may reflect the child's perception of his or her environment (e.g., organized, scattered), (b) in terms of actual content during play (e.g., a doll described as being mad), and (c) in terms of overriding themes noted in play (e.g., heroic, destruc-tive). Themes may then be interpreted as reflecting how the child views his or her world and self, as well as general expectations about how the two interact. Comprehensive and standardized coding manuals exist for certain play-based assessments, such as the MacArthur Story-Stem Battery (MSSB; Robinson, Mantz-Simmons, & MacFie, 1997) which uses a play narrative strategy for assessment. Here, children are presented with problematic situations using plastic dolls and required to complete the story. The MSSB allows for systematic coding of content themes, (e.g., aggression), parental themes, (e.g., protection), and affective expression during play (e.g., anger or joy; Robinson et al., 1997). Inter-rater reliability has been reported to range from $r = .80$ to $r = .96$ for components of the coding system, and affective distress during play was significantly correlated with parent- and teacher-rated externalizing problems on the CBCL (Warren, Oppenheim, & Emde, 1996).

Diagnostic schedules exist that incorporate play-based activities within the context of a comprehensive assessment, such as the Autism Diagnostic Observation Schedule (ADOS; Lord, Rutter, DiLavore, & Risi, 2001), a semi-structured standardized assessment of com-munication, social interaction, and play. During the ADOS, children who are very young or language-impaired are presented with free play and social play situations, which allow for observation of shared enjoyment, aspects of reciprocal social interaction, functional play with objects, and imaginative play. For the ADOS, problematic social interaction and unusual play behaviors yield a greater likelihood of an autism spectrum disorder (Lord et al., 2001). Play-based activities may also be used to screen for social and behavioral problems in preschoolers, such as those that appear in the Screening Tool for Autism in Two-Year-Olds (STAT; Stone, Coonrod, & Ousley, 2000). Similar to the format of the ADOS for young or language-impaired children, the STAT is an interactive play-like assessment that samples toddler's play within the context of a screen for autism spectrum disorders.

Transdisciplinary Play-Based Assessment.   Linder (1993) outlines a comprehensive assessment system based entirely on play-based behaviors, Transdisciplinary Play-Based Assessment (TPBA). Within this assessment model, all aspects of the preschool child's abilities are assessed through careful observation of play-related activities. The child's abilities are assessed through a combination of structured and unstructured activities with "facilitators," parents, and another child. Cognitive, social-emotional, language, and sensorimotor development are evaluated within the context of a playroom environment. In the particular case of social-emotional assessment using TPBA, facilitators observe and rate the following: (a) characteristics of the child's temperament, (b) aspects of mastery motivation, (c) social interactions with the examiner, parents, and a peer, (d) emotional characteristics of the child's play, and (e) awareness of social conventions. For example, when evaluating the child's awareness of social conventions, TPBA observers rate the child's use of appropriate greetings, sharing behavior, and respect for adult authority (Linder, 1993).

Advantages of Play-Based Assessment Techniques.   Observing children at play is often useful because children are likely to feel more comfortable at play and behave in a more naturalistic manner than during structured assessment activities. Children usually engage in play activities attentively and with enthusiasm; therefore, the assessor can observe the child at his or her best. In the specific instance of TPBA, Linder (1993) asserted that TPBA holds advantages over traditional assessment techniques, including: (a) assessment within a natural environment, (b) ease of rapport building, (c) flexible testing procedures, (d) active participation by the parents in the assessment, and (e) improved information about qualitative aspects of the child's abilities that are useful in guiding intervention.

Limitations of Play-Based Assessment Techniques.   Play-based assessment relies primarily upon observational methods; therefore, play-based techniques and TPBA share shortcomings associated with the observational assessment methods identified earlier. For example, the ADOS and STAT require specific training for mastery of proper test administration and reliable behavioral coding. In addition to these general limitations, two specific restrictions are associated with TPBA. First, TPBA observations do not yield standardized scores which may be necessary to accurately describe current levels of functioning and to secure intervention services for young preschool children (Linder, 1993). Second, TPBA evaluates a broad range of abilities over a relatively short period of time, i.e., 60 to 90 minutes; thus, comprehensive assessment of social-emotional functioning may not occur, and follow-up evaluations may be necessary.

RECOMMENDATION FOR ASSESSMENT DESIGN

Although primary assessment techniques differ in content and method, similar recommendations guide their practical use. Despite theoretical and practical differences, consensus appears to have been reached regarding the best approach to preschool social-emotional assessment. Most authors agree that the best assessment strategy is a multidimensional one that involves evaluating preschool functioning with multiple methods, via multiple sources, across multiple settings, and over multiple occasions (e.g., Keith & Campbell, 2000; Martin et al., 1986). Thus, a multidimensional assessment strategy incorporates the various techniques introduced above with the goal of minimizing limitations associated with any single technique. Each assessment technique yields unique information and should be selected for use based upon the purpose of the assessment. For example, norm-referenced tests are most helpful when comparing the child's social-emotional adjustment against a normative criterion; other methods, such as TPBA and observation, are perhaps more useful in designing interventions (Wheatcraft & Bracken, 1999).

CHAPTER SUMMARY AND CONCLUSIONS

Increasingly, clinicians are called upon to assess preschool children's social and emotional functioning for screening, diagnosis, and intervention planning. Currently, theoretical and empirical work supports the notion that a variety of factors operate in complex ways to influence young children's social and emotional development. Such complexity causes practical problems for practitioners assigned the task of describing social and emotional characteristics of a preschool child at a single point in time. In addition to limited understanding of the complex interrelationships that seem to exist between causal factors, assessments are also hindered by preschoolers' cognitive functioning and the variable nature of social and emotional characteristics per se. Current assessment technologies hold unique strengths and weaknesses; therefore, the use of a single assessment technique for the purposes of description, diagnosis, or treatment planning is not recommended. Ideally, the best assessment approach to diagnosis and treatment planning involves: (a) sampling a variety of behaviors; (b) using varied assessment techniques, informants, settings, and instrumentation; and (c) synthesizing findings into a meaningful description of the child, the environment, and their interaction.

REFERENCES

Achenbach, T. M., McConaughy, S. H., & Howell, C. T. (1987). Child/adolescent behavioral and emotional problems: Implications of cross-informant correlations for situational specificity. *Psychological Bulletin, 101*, 213–232.

Achenbach, T. M., & Rescorla, L. A. (2000). *Manual for ASEBA Preschool Forms & Profiles*. Burlington, VT: University of Vermont, Research Center for Children, Youth, & Families.

American Psychiatric Association. (2000). *Diagnostic and statistical manual of mental disorders (4th ed., Text rev.)*. Washington, DC: Author.

Antonovsky, A. (1979). *Health, stress, and coping: New perspectives on mental and physical well-being*. San Francisco: Jossey-Bass.

Baker, B. L., McIntyre, L. L., Blacher, J., Crnic, K., Edelbrock, C., & Low, C. (2003). Pre-school children with and without developmental delay: behavior problems and parenting stress over time. *Journal of Intellectual Disability Research, 47*, 217–230.

Barkley, R. A. (2003). Attention-Deficit/Hyperactivity Disorder. In E. J. Mash & R. A. Barkley (Eds.), *Child psychopathology* (2nd ed., pp. 75–143). New York: The Guilford Press.

Baron-Cohen, S., Allen, J., & Gillberg, C. (1992). Can autism be detected at 18 months? The needle, the haystack, and the CHAT. *British Journal of Psychiatry, 161*, 839–843.

Baumrind, D. (1973). The development of instrumental competence through socialization. In A. Pick (Ed.), *Minnesota Symposia on Child Psychology: Vol. 7*, (pp. 3–46). Minneapolis: University of Minnesota Press.

Berk, L. (1997). *Child development* (4th ed.). Boston: Allyn & Bacon.

Bierman, K. L. (1990). Using the clinical interview to assess children's interpersonal reasoning and emotional understanding. In C. R. Reynolds & R. W. Kamphaus (Eds.), *Handbook of psychological and educational assessment of children: Personality, behavior, and context (pp. 204–219). New York: Guilford.

Bierman, K. L., & Schwartz, L. A. (1986). Clinical child interviews: Approaches and developmental considerations. Journal of Child and Adolescent Psychotherapy, 3, 267–278.

Block, J. H., & Block, J. (1980). The role of ego-control and ego-resiliency in the organization of behavior. In W. A. Collins (Ed.), Development of cognition, affect, and social relations: The Minnesota Symposia on Child Psychology, Vol. 13 (pp. 39–101). Hillsdale, NJ: Lawrence Erlbaum Associates.

Bowlby, J. (1988). A secure base: Parent-child attachment and healthy human development. New York: Basic Books.

Bracken, B. A. (1987). Limitations of preschool assessment and standards for minimal levels of technical adequacy. Journal of Psychoeducational Assessment, 5, 313–326.

Bracken, B. A. (2000). The clinical observation of preschool assessment behavior. In B. A. Bracken (Ed.), The psychoeducational assessment of preschool children (3rd ed., pp. 45–56). Boston: Allyn & Bacon.

Bracken, B. A., & Keith, L. K. (2004). Clinical Assessment of Behavior: Professional manual. Lutz, FL: Psychological Assessment Resources.

Bracken, B. A., Keith, L. K., & Walker, K. C. (1994). Assessment of preschool behavior and social-emotional functioning: A review of thirteen third-party instruments. Assessment in Rehabilitation and Exceptionality, 1, 331–346.

Bradley, R. H., & Caldwell, B. M. (1988). Using the HOME inventory to assess the family environment. Pediatric Nursing, 14, 97–102.

Bradley, R., Whiteside, L., Mundfrom, D., Casey, P., Kelleher, K., & Pope, S. (1994). Contribution of early intervention and early caregiving experiences to resilience in low-birthweight, premature children living in poverty. Journal of Clinical Child Psychology, 23, 425–434.

Bridges, F., & Cicchetti, D. (1982). Mothers' ratings of the temperament characteristics of Down syndrome infants. Developmental Psychology, 18, 238–244.

Bronfenbrenner, U. (1977). Toward an experimental ecology of human development. American Psychologist, 32, 513–531.

Bronfenbrenner, U. (1986). Ecology of the family as a context for human development: Research perspectives. Developmental Psychology, 22, 723–742.

Brooks-Gunn, J. (1985). Dyadic interchanges in families with at-risk children. In W. K. Frankenburg, R. N. Emde, & J. W. Sullivan, (Eds.), Early identification of children at risk: An international perspective. New York: Plenum Press.

Caldwell, B. M., & Bradley, R. H. (2003). Home Observation for Measurement of the Environment: Administration manual. Little Rock: University of Arkansas.

Campbell, J. M. (1999). [Review of the Social Skills Rating System, Preschool Version]. Journal of Psychoeducational Assessment, 17, 392–397.

Campbell, J. M., & Morgan, S. B. (1998). Asperger's disorder. In L. Phelps (Ed.), Health-related disorders in children and adolescents (pp. 68–73). Washington, DC: American Psychological Association.

Cashel, M. L. (2002). Child and adolescent psychological assessment: Current clinical practices and the impact of managed care. Professional Psychology: Research and Practice, 33, 446–453.

Chandler, L., & Johnson, V. (1991). Using projective techniques with children: A guide to clinical assessment. Springfield, IL: Charles C. Thomas.

Conners, C. K. (1997). Conners' Rating Scales–Revised: User's manual. North Tonawanda, NY: Multi-Health Systems, Inc.

Costello, A. J., Edelbrock, L. S., Dulcan, M. K., Kalas, R., & Klaric, S. H. (1984). Report on the NIMH Diagnostic Interview Schedule for Children (DISC). Washington, DC: National Institute of Mental Health.

Derogatis, L. R. & DellaPietra, L. (1994). Psychological tests in screening for psychiatric disorder. In M. E. Maruish (Ed.), The use of psychological testing for treatment planning and outcome assessment (pp. 22–54). Hillsdale, NJ: Lawrence Erlbaum Associates.

Easterbrooks, M. A., & Lamb, M. E. (1979). The relationship between quality of infant-mother attachment and infant competence in initial encounters with peers. *Child Development, 50,* 380–387.

Emde, R. N., & Easterbrooks, M.A. (1985). In W. K. Frankenburg, R. N. Emde, & J. W. Sullivan (Eds.), *Early identification of children at risk: An international perspective.* New York: Plenum Press.

Garmezy, N. (1985). Stress-resistant children: The search for protective factors. In J. E. Stevenson (Ed.), *Recent research in developmental psychopathology* (pp. 213–233). Oxford: Pergamon Press.

Garmezy, N., Masten, A. S., & Tellegen, A. (1984). The study of stress and competence in children: A building block for developmental psychopathology. *Child Development, 55,* 97–111.

Gill, D. G. (1970). *Violence against children.* Cambridge, MA: Harvard University Press.

Graham, P., Rutter, M., & George, S. (1973). Temperamental characteristics as predictors of behavior disorders in children. *American Journal of Orthopsychiatry, 43,* 328–339.

Grusec, J. E., & Lytton, H. (1988). *Social development: History, theory, and research.* New York: Springer-Verlag.

Hammen, C., & Rudolph, K. D. (2003). Childhood mood disorders. In E. J. Mash. & R. A. Barkley (Eds.), *Child psychopathology* (2nd ed., pp. 233–278). New York: Guilford Press.

Herjanic, B., Herjanic, M., Brown, F., & Wheatt, T. (1975). Are children reliable reporters? *Journal of Abnormal Child Psychology, 3,* 41–48.

Hinshaw, S. P. & Lee, S. S. (2003). Conduct and oppositional defiant disorders. In E. J. Mash & R. A. Barkley (Eds.), *Child psychopathology* (2nd ed., pp. 144–198). New York: The Guilford Press.

Hodges, K. (1993). Structured interviews for assessing children. *Journal of Child Psychology and Psychiatry and Allied Disciplines, 34,* 49–68.

Hodges, K., Gordon, Y., & Lennon, M. P. (1990). Parent-child agreement on symptoms assessed via a clinical research interview for children: The Child Assessment Schedule (CAS). *Journal of Child Psychology and Psychiatry and Allied Disciplines, 31,* 427–436.

Hodges, K., Kline, J., Stern, L., Cytryn, L., & McKnew. D. (1982). The development of a child assessment interview for research and clinical use. *Journal of Abnormal Child Psychology, 10,* 173–189.

Jones, C. J. (1992). *Human figure drawings of mildly handicapped students.* Springfield, IL: Charles C. Thomas. Kamphaus, R. W., Reynolds, C. R., & Imperato-McCammon, C. (1999). Roles of diagnosis and classification in school psychology. In C. R. Reynolds & T. B. Gutkin (Eds.), *Handbook of school psychology* (pp. 292–306). New York: John Wiley & Sons.

Keith, L. K., & Campbell, J. M. (2000). Assessment of social and emotional development in preschool children. In B. A. Bracken (Ed.), *The psychoeducational assessment of preschool children* (3rd ed., pp. 364–382). Boston: Allyn & Bacon.

Keith, R. (1996). Children at risk for reactive attachment disorder: Assessment, diagnosis and treatment. *Progress: Family Systems Research and Therapy, 5,* 83–98.

Klinger, L. G., Dawson, G., & Renner, P. (2003). Autistic Disorder. In E. J. Mash & R. A. Barkley (Eds.), *Child psychopathology* (pp. 409–454). New York: The Guilford Press.

Koppitz, E. M. (1968). *Psychological evaluation of children's Human Figure Drawings.* Boston: Allyn & Bacon.

Langlois, J. H., & Downs, C. A. (1979). Peer relations as a function of physical attractiveness: The eye of the beholder or behavioral reality? *Child Development, 50,* 409–418.

Langlois, J. H., Ritter, J. M., Casey, R. H., & Sawin, D. B. (1995). Infant attractiveness predicts maternal behaviors and attitudes. *Developmental Psychology, 31,* 464–472.

Lewis, M., & Rosenblum, L. A. (1974). *The effect of the infant on its caregiver.* New York: Wiley.

Linder, T. W. (1993). *Transdisciplinary play-based assessment: A functional approach to working with young children* (Rev. ed.). Baltimore: Paul H. Brookes.

Lord, C., Rutter, M., DiLavore, P. C., & Risi, S. (2001). *Autism Diagnostic Observation Schedule Manual.* Los Angeles: Western Psychological Services.

Luckasson, R., Borthwick-Duffy, S., Buntinx, W. H. E., Coulter, D. L., Craig, E. M., Polloway, E. A., et al. (2002). *Mental retardation: Definition, classification, and systems of supports* (10th ed.). Washington, DC: American Association on Mental Retardation.

Luther, S. S., & Zigler, E. (1991). Vulnerability and competence: A review of research on resilience in childhood. *American Journal of Orthopsychiatry, 61*, 6–22.

Lyons-Ruth, K., Zeanah, C. H., & Benoit, D. (2003). Disorder and risk for disorder during infancy and toddlerhood. In E. J. Mash, & R. A. Barkley (Eds.), *Child psychopathology* (2nd ed., pp. 589–631). New York: The Guilford Press.

Maccoby, E. E. (1990). Gender and relationships: A developmental account. *American Psychologist, 45*, 513–520.

Magid, K. & McKelvey, C. A. (1987). *High risk: Children without a conscience.* Golden, CO: M & M Press.

Martin, R. P. (1986). Assessment of the social and emotional functioning of preschool children. *School Psychology Review, 15*, 216–232.

Martin, R. P. (1991). Assessment of social and emotional behavior. In B. A. Bracken (Ed.), *The psychoeducational assessment of preschool children* (2nd ed., pp. 450–464). Needham Heights, MA: Allyn and Bacon.

Martin, R. P. & Bridger, R. C. (1999). *The Temperament Assessment Battery for Children-Revised.* Athens, GA: Author.

Martin, R. P., Hooper, S., & Snow, J. (1986). Behavior rating scale approaches to personality assessment in children and adolescents. In H. M. Knoff (Ed.), *The assessment of child and adolescent personality* (pp. 309–351). New York: Guilford Press.

Mash, E. J., & Dozois, D. J. A. (2003). Child psychopathology: A developmental-systems perspective. In E. J. Mash, & R. A. Barkley (Eds.), *Child psychopathology* (2nd ed.). New York: The Guilford Press.

McArthur, D. S., & Roberts, G. E. (1982). *Roberts Apperception Test for Children: Manual.* Los Angeles, CA: Western Psychological Services.

Obrutz, J. E., & Boliek, C. A. (1986). Thematic approaches to personality assessment with children and adolescents. In H. M. Knoff (Ed.), *The assessment of child and adolescent personality* (pp. 173–198). New York: The Guilford Press.

Petit, G. S., Dodge, K. A., & Brown, M. M. (1988). Early family experience, social problem solving patterns, and children's social competence. *Child Development, 59*, 107–120.

Puig-Antich, J., & Chambers, W. (1978). *The Schedule for Affective Disorders and Schizophrenia for School-Age Children (Kiddie-SADS).* New York: New York State Psychiatric Institute.

Rabin, A. I. (1968). Projective methods: An historical introduction. In A. I. Rabin (Ed.), *Projective techniques in personality assessment* (pp. 3–17). New York: Springer.

Reynolds, G., & Jones, E. (1997). *Master players: Learning from children at play.* New York: Teachers College Press.

Reynolds, C. R., & Kamphaus, R. W. (2004). *Behavior Assessment System for Children, Second Edition (BASC–2).* Circle Pines, MN: American Guidance Service.

Ritts, V., Patterson, M. L., & Tubbs, M. E. (1992). Expectations, impressions, and judgments of physically attractive students: A review. *Review of Educational Research, 62*, 413–426.

Robins, D. L., Fein, D., Barton, M. L., & Green, J. A. (2001). The Modified Checklist for Autism in Toddlers: An initial study investigation of the early detection of autism and pervasive developmental disorders. *Journal of Autism and Developmental Disorders, 31*, 131–144.

Robinson, J., Mantz-Simmons, L., & MacFie, J. (1997). *Memphis Narrative Coding Manual.* Unpublished manuscript.

Roopnarine, J. L. (1987). Social interaction in the peer group: Relationship to perceptions of parenting and to children's interpersonal awareness and problem-solving ability. *Journal of Applied Developmental Psychology, 8*, 351–362.

Rutter, M. (1985). Resilience in the face of adversity: Protective factors and resistance to psychiatric disorder. *British Journal of Psychiatry, 147*, 598–611.

Rutter, M. (1978). Early sources of security and competence. In Bruner, J., & A. Garton (Eds.), *Human growth and development*. New York: Oxford University Press.

Sameroff, A. J. (1986). Environmental context of child development. *The Journal of Pediatrics, 109*, 192–200.

Sattler, J. M. (1992). *Assessment of children* (3rd ed.). San Diego: Author.

Sattler, J. M. (1998). *Clinical and forensic interviewing of children and families*. San Diego: Author.

Segal, J. (1988). Teachers have enormous power in affecting a child's self-esteem. *Brown University Child Behavior and Development Newsletter, 4*, 1–4.

Sparrow, S. S., Balla, D. A., & Cicchetti, D. V. (1984). *Vineland Adaptive Behavior Scales*. Circle Pines, MN: American Guidance Service.

Sparrow, S. S., Balla, D. A., & Cicchetti, D. V. (1998). *Vineland Social-Emotional Early Childhood Scales*. Circle Pines, MN: American Guidance Service.

Stone, W. L., Coonrod, E. E., Ousley, O. Y. (2000). Brief report: Screening tool for autism in two-year-olds (STAT): Development and preliminary data. *Journal of Autism and Developmental Disorders, 30*, 607–612.

Thomas, A., Birch, H. G., Chess, S., Hertzig, C., & Korn, S. (1963). *Behavioral individuality in early childhood*. New York: New York University Press.

Thomas, A., & Chess, S. (1977). *Temperament and development*. New York: Brunner/Mazel.

Thompson, R. J., Merritt, K. A., Keith, B. R., Murphy, L. B., & Johndrow, D. A. (1993). Mother-child agreement on the Child Assessment Schedule with nonreferred children: A research note. *Journal of Child Psychology and Psychiatry and Allied Disciplines, 34*, 813–820.

Tieger, T. (1980). On the biological basis of sex differences in aggression. *Child Development, 51*, 943–963.

Umansky, W. (1983). Assessment of social and emotional development. In K. D. Paget & B. A. Bracken (Eds.), *The psychoeducational assessment of preschool children* (pp. 417–441). Orlando, FL: Grune and Stratton.

United States Department of Education, Office of Special Education and Rehabilitative Services (1997). Individuals with Disabilities Education Act Amendments of 1997. Washington, D.C.

Walker, K. C., & Bracken, B. A. (1996). Inter-parent agreement on four preschool behavior rating scales: Effects of parent and child gender. *Psychology in the Schools, 33*, 273–283.

Wallander, J. L., Dekker, M. C., & Koot, H. M. (2003). Psychopathology in children and adolescents with intellectual disability: Measurement, prevalence, course, and risk. In L. M. Glidden (Ed.), *International review of research in mental retardation* (Vol. 26, pp. 93–134). New York: Academic Press.

Warren, S. L., Oppenheim, D., & Emde, R. N. (1996). Can emotions and themes in children's play predict behavior problems? *Journal of the American Academy of Child and Adolescent Psychiatry, 35*, 1331–1337.

Wheatcraft, T. K., & Bracken, B. A. (1999). Early identification and intervention of psychosocial and behavioral effects of exceptionality. In D. H. Saklofske & V. L. Schwean (Eds.), *Handbook of psychosocial characteristics of exceptional children* (pp. 543–562). New York: Plenum.

White, K. R. (1985–86). Efficacy of early intervention. *The Journal of Special Education, 4*, 401–416.

7

Creating the Optimal Preschool Testing Situation

Bruce A. Bracken
The College of William & Mary

INTRODUCTION

The purpose for conducting psychoeducational assessments is to gain information about a child's current level of functioning within any of several important domains (e.g., cognitive, motor, language, personality, academic). Gathering such information enables examiners to accurately describe and classify children's abilities within and across the various domains. Importantly, assessment information is then used to guide decisions about the need for and types of treatments or interventions that should be implemented.

An assumption made about the psychoeducational assessment process is that examiners have made every effort to eliminate all identifiable construct-irrelevant influences on the child's performance and the resultant test scores. That is, the goal in assessment is to limit assessment as much as possible to construct-relevant attributes (e.g., intelligence), while limiting the influences of construct-irrelevant sources of variation (e.g., fatigue, lack of cooperation, emotional lability). Before important decisions can be made with confidence about a child's future educational plans, possible treatments, or medications, examiners must have confidence in the validity of the assessment results. Only when all possible sources of construct-irrelevant variation have been eliminated or optimally controlled, can an examiner attest to the validity of assessment results.

This chapter will identify common sources of construct-irrelevant influences on young children's assessment performance and will suggest means by which examiners can moderate these unwanted sources of variation by establishing and better controlling the examining situation. Many sources of construct-irrelevant variance can be effectively moderated through careful attention; however, some of these influences can never be fully controlled. Examining children's assessment performance in light of these unwanted influences will help explain young children's variable performance on psychometric evaluations and will contribute to a fuller understanding of the child's true skills and abilities.

When conducting assessments in a standardized fashion, astute clinical skill and wise selection of instruments will go a long way toward reducing major sources of construct-irrelevant variability in children's test performance. This chapter will address the issue of construct relevance and irrelevance, and suggest means by which examiners can maximize the assessment of the desired construct while controlling threats to validity. That is, this chapter will describe means by which careful attention to the examining situation can facilitate the examiner's valid assessment of preschool children.

CONSTRUCT-RELEVANT VERSUS CONSTRUCT-IRRELEVANT INFLUENCES ON YOUNG CHILDREN'S TEST PERFORMANCE

Examiners should be aware that some influences on a child's test performance may be considered construct-relevant, while in other instances the same source of variation may be considered construct-irrelevant. The examiner must decide when such variation is useful to understanding the child's performance and when it inhibits a clear understanding of the child's abilities. For example, a bilingual child's English language proficiency would be considered construct-relevant if the purpose of the evaluation was to determine the child's understanding and use of the English language. However, if the intent of the assessment was to measure the child's visual-spatial skills, use of a test that is heavily laden with verbal directions (e.g., Performance subtests of the Wechsler Primary and Preschool Scale of Intelligence–Third Edition) would produce some degree of construct-irrelevant variance related to English facility and comprehension. In an effort to control for the construct-irrelevant variance associated with limited English proficiency, the examiner would likely want to replace the WPPSI–III with a cognitive test that can be administered in Spanish and that requires no language production, such as the *Bracken Basic Concept Scale–III* (Bracken, 2006) or a nonverbal test of intelligence, such as the *Universal Nonverbal Intelligence Test* (Bracken & McCallum, 1998).

To conduct fair assessments, examiners must decide which constructs are targeted for the assessment and identify the construct-irrelevant variables that threaten the validity of the assessment. Further, examiners should consider and moderate, to whatever extent possible, the influences of these potential threats to validity. In the previous example, use of a nonverbal test of ability could reduce the language-related threat to validity and allow for a "purer" measure of the construct (i.e., visual-spatial skills) without the confounding influence of language proficiency. In a similar fashion, bi-cultural children's level of assimilation into the dominant society may constitute a construct-irrelevant influence on their test performance when instruments are heavily loaded with "cultural content" (McGrew & Flanagan, 1998)—even when the test is administered without verbal directions.

In addition to linguistic proficiency and enculturation, other variables that may be considered either construct-relevant or construct-irrelevant, depending on the context, include prior educational and life experiences, exposure to various media, physical and sensory abilities, family socioeconomic status, and many other such influences. When a variable is identified as irrelevant to the assessed construct and yet negatively influences the child's test performance, that variable should be considered as a source of test bias and should be eliminated or moderated to as great an extent as possible. For example, when assessing a visually impaired child's school-readiness skills, the examiner should strive to reduce the effects of the visual disability on the child's ability to demonstrate his or her readiness skills. Moderating the effects of the visual impairment might include such situational modifications as arranging seating and lighting to facilitate the child's view of test stimuli (e.g., reducing glare, emphasizing the contrast between light and dark), ensuring that the child wears or uses prescribed corrective devices, and modifying the test stimuli when necessary (e.g., using larger than standard print or stimulus matter).

Although a child's limited range of life experiences cannot be moderated during the assessment process, knowledge of such limitations might temper the examiner's interpretation of the child's test results. A child who has had limited previous experience with puzzles, blocks, and paper and pencil may perform poorly on any of the similar experientially oriented cognitive tasks typically found on early childhood intelligence tests. The child's poor academic motor skill, which is related at least in part to a lack of previous educational experiences, would negatively influence the child's test performance and lower the child's overall intelligence quotient. Given typical preschool and primary grade curricular experiences, the assessed experiential weakness may be easily remediated once the child is exposed to these activities in a systematic fashion. It would be a mistake to place too much emphasis on the child's artificially lowered overall intelligence, especially on tests that weight heavily educationally related visual-motor skills, when the diminished test performance was due largely to a lack of previous educational opportunity or experience.

MODERATING CONSTRUCT-IRRELEVANT INFLUENCES ON STUDENTS' TEST PERFORMANCE

There are four principal sources of construct-irrelevant influences on children's psycho-educational assessment results: 1) the examinee; 2) the examiner; 3) the environment; and 4) the instruments employed. The remainder of the chapter will address each of these four primary influences and suggest means by which examiners can moderate these unwanted influences by creating an examining situation that facilitates testing and reduces known threats to validity.

Examinee

It may seem odd that a child would be considered a possible source of construct-irrelevant influence on his or her own test performance. However, personal variables and behaviors, both within and outside the child's sphere of control, influence the child's day-to-day demonstration of his or her abilities in ways that can be observed and moderated. To whatever extent possible, these variables should be recognized and controlled during assessments, or at least considered when examiners evaluate the validity of children's assessment results.

Health.   In addition to standard examiner inquiries regarding the examinee's health, examiners should be observant of children's apparent health prior to initiating an assessment. Children who show symptoms of an illness, even an illness as mild as the common cold, may experience sluggish mental processing, slower speed of response, diminished ability to "find" the right word or produce a definition, lessened motivation, and/or decreased energy, concentration, or interest. Children who are ill or who are becoming ill often lack the physical and mental strength and acuity to perform optimally during an evaluation. Such health-related threats to assessment validity should be considered seriously and addressed.

Young children quickly develop physical symptoms, and, fortunately, their health often improves just as quickly. When children are not in optimal health or show signs or symptoms of an on-coming illness (e.g., sniffles, fever, lethargy, complaint of pains, upset stomach), examiners should consider whether these complaints are psychosomatic manifestations (e.g., internalizing behaviors, Bracken & Keith, 2004) or whether the child is becoming ill and it would be wise to postpone the evaluation until the child is free of such symptoms.

If an otherwise healthy child becomes ill within days after an assessment has been conducted, the examiner should consider whether the child's assessment-related behavior was likely representative of his or her typical behavior. If the child's assessment behavior was deemed atypical, the examiner should reconsider the validity of the assessment results.

Importantly, examiners should evaluate children's physical symptoms associated with anxiety (e.g., stomachache, nausea) when considering whether an assessment should be postponed for days or merely delayed briefly until better rapport is established. Children often report somatic complaints when they are fearful or anxious, and examiners should strive to reduce those complaints by alleviating the child's fears and anxieties. In such instances, postponement would not be appropriate, but the expenditure of a little more effort and time to establish a better rapport would be warranted. Use of behavior rating scales to gain parents' or teachers' perceptions of the typicality of such behaviors may also be useful prior to conducting the assessment with the child. The *Clinical Assessment of Behavior* (Bracken & Keith, 2004) assesses a full range of behavioral disorders and exceptionalities in children as young as 2 years of age.

Fatigue/Restfulness.   Related to overall health considerations is the child's state of restfulness. With preschool children, it is generally a good idea to conduct assessments as early in the day as possible, within reason. Because young children typically take naps (or need naps) after lunch and then wear themselves out again by late afternoon, assessments are often more easily conducted and more valid during the morning hours when children are alert and fresh.

Young children who are tired often become cranky, which can negatively affect their cooperation, motivation, and subsequent test performance. Therefore, examiners should be sensitive to signs of fatigue and postpone assessments or offer children breaks in an effort to keep their energy levels and participation at optimal levels. From a purely behavioral management standpoint, it behooves examiners to assess children who are alert and well rested—or the examiner should be prepared to struggle with the child's misbehavior and diminished effort throughout the assessment.

Fear/Anxiety.   Because young children typically are not experienced with the formal nature of psychoeducational evaluations, fear and anxiety are common examinee reactions at the beginning of assessments. An optimal level of examinee arousal is highly desired to ensure that the child is sufficiently motivated to perform tasks with his or her best effort. However, the assessment should not start or continue when the child's arousal and anxiety are at a level that debilitates or impairs the child's spontaneity, concentration, or active participation. The examiner should allay children's fears and anxiety by establishing a comfortable, safe, and engaging environment before initiating testing.

The manner by which examiners greet preschool children can do a lot to initiate a good testing situation. Examiners should meet preschool children by stooping or squatting down to the children's height and offer a warm, friendly, low-keyed greeting. If the child is reticent and not easily approached, the examiner might stand and shift his or her attention to the parent or guardian who accompanied the child to the evaluation. By addressing the parent, the examiner will allow the child an opportunity to become more familiar with the setting and the examiner, and learn a bit about the examiner through the parent-examiner interactions. Gradually, the child will become slightly bored by the interaction between the adults and will frequently become more open to interactions with the examiner.

When the child shows signs of interest in the examiner or the assessment environment, the examiner can re-engage the child by offering to show the child around a bit. Once the child's fears and anxieties have subsided, the examiner should gently "shepherd" the child to the examining room to begin the assessment. Shepherding of this sort is a process by which the examiner guides the child to the examining room by allowing the child to walk in the lead. To effectively shepherd a child, the examiner should place a hand between the child's shoulder blades and gently "steer" the child with slight hand pressure to the desired location. Because children lead the way when shepherded in this fashion, they typically do not feel forced or coerced as when they are led by the hand to the testing location.

Motivation.   Some children are not motivated to demonstrate their potential during psychoeducational assessments for a variety of reasons. Preschool children's limited motivation sometimes is due to insufficient awareness or appreciation of the importance of test results. Sometimes children do not find test materials or activities very interesting or engaging, and, on occasion, the examiner or the child's parents have not sufficiently prepared the child for the types of tasks the child will be asked to complete. Also, some children become less motivated as the assessment progresses, and they are faced with tasks that are difficult or particularly challenging, or that are not as fun as the child had expected.

To overcome initial instances of limited motivation among preschool examinees, the examiner must develop an introduction to the assessment process that prepares the child for what will occur. This introduction should be honest and 1) describe the types of tasks with which the child will be presented; 2) challenge the child to do his or her best on every task; 3) emphasize the importance of effort, persistence, and thoughtful responses; and 4) acknowledge that some of the activities may be difficult and beyond the current abilities of the child. The introduction should not suggest that the examiner and child will be playing games, because it quickly becomes apparent that the examiner is taking the game playing very seriously and that the "games" are not all that much fun. It is fair, however, to tell the child that much of what the child will do will in fact be fun. A sample introduction follows:

> Today we are going to do many interesting and exciting things together. We will work with blocks and puzzles; we'll be looking at some pictures; I'm going to ask you to draw some things for me; and, I'll ask you to tell me the answers to some questions. We'll have a good time together. I won't expect you to be able to do everything I ask you to do, because some of the things we will do are meant for older children. It's okay if you can't do some of the things I ask you to do, but I want you to try your very best anyway. Let's get going and try some of the fun things I have for you.

During the assessment, if the child's motivation begins to wane, the examiner should remind the child of the salient aspects of the previous paragraph (e.g., "Remember, I told you some of these things would be hard to do"; "That was a tough puzzle wasn't it? I like how well you worked on it even though it was hard for you."). Reinforcing the child's effort is another means of motivating the child to concentrate and continue to give full effort. It is important that the examiner reinforce the child's effort rather than his or her successes; otherwise, the reinforcement will abruptly end and become painfully absent when the child begins to fail more difficult items. It is also wise to remind the child that some of the items were intended for older children (actually, children who are more able, whether due to age or ability), and that the child isn't expected to be successful on every task or item attempted.

Preparing the child for the assessment process in such a fashion before the child begins to experience frequent failure is more timely and helpful than after the child has already failed a succession of items. Warning the child before failure can forestall frustration by challenging the child to attempt the predicted tough problems; reminding the child after failure often is seen as pardoning the child's failures, which can increase the child's frustration and sense of failure.

Temperament.   Examiners can facilitate the assessment of preschool children if they accommodate the temperament styles of their examinees. By considering each of the nine temperament characteristics identified by Thomas and Chess (1977), the examiner might better schedule the assessment, approach the examinee, address the child's needs, guide the assessment, and even select the instruments appropriate for administration. In short, the examiner should seek to create the best fit between the child and the assessment situation (Carey & McDevitt, 1995; Chess & Thomas, 1992).

Each child can be expected to demonstrate to some greater or lesser degree a *level of activity* that is different from other children the examiner has evaluated. Expecting all young children to sit cooperatively in a chair for an hour or longer and participate actively in an assessment is unrealistic. If the examiner knows before the assessment, either through parent report or observation, that the child is generally very active, the examiner can plan ahead to accommodate the child's desire or need to move about. Understanding and accommodating the needs of children by differentially allowing them to stand, move about, handle test materials, assist with the test administration, and take action breaks can go a long way toward maintaining rapport once it has been established. To be effective, the examiner must note, be sensitive to, and plan ahead for the active child.

Selecting an appropriate time to begin an assessment and being sensitive to children's biological needs should be based on the child's *rhythmicity*—that is, the predictability of a child's bodily and somatic functions (e.g., times when the child is most alert, responsivity after lunch, how the child interacts after a nap). The examiner should select a window of opportunity for assessment in which the child is predictably in his or her best form.

In addition to children's differential response to routines, children do not all respond in the same manner when approached by others. Some children respond in kind, while others withdraw. The child's *approach or withdrawal* tendency should be considered when planning how to best meet and greet the child. If the child is known to respond positively to a forward, gregarious introduction and approach, then the examiner should exude enthusiasm and excitement, and boldly introduce himself or herself. However, if the child is more reticent and timid, and typically withdraws from strangers, the examiner should proceed slowly and elicit the child's participation through subtle and indirect engagement. Again, parent or teacher reports, or behavioral observations in a classroom, can provide information about the child's typical response to being approached by others.

Although some children are very flexible and respond favorably and without comment to unanticipated changes in routines or schedules, some children are hypersensitive to even minor changes in routine or schedule, anticipated or not. Advance knowledge about the *adaptability* of children to changes in routine will forewarn the examiner about how the child will likely respond to being taken from routine activities to participate in the assessment. The examiner may identify classroom routines or activities that are viewed less favorably by the child than others, and plan the assessment at a time when the child will be "excused" from participating in the less desirable activity, and thereby lessen the intensity of the child's response to an unpredicted change in routine.

By observing a child in the classroom, examiners can consider the child's unique level of *intensity of reaction* in various situations. Once this information is known, examiners can better anticipate the child's needs and provide as much emotional support, structure, or patience as necessary when he or she begins to experience frustration and failure. Similarly, examiners should note the child's *threshold of responsiveness* to stimuli during classroom observations; that is, how much stimulation does it take to evoke a response from the child? The examiner might arrange the instruments and activities in an assessment to accommodate the child as necessary. For example, if the child is slow to warm up and does not respond initially to tasks that require active participation and verbal exchange, the examiner might begin with high-interest, less-demanding tasks (e.g., having the child draw pictures as an ice-breaking activity). Once the child becomes more comfortable, the examiner can introduce tasks that are more demanding and require more active participation and social interaction.

The nature and quality of the child's typical *mood* should be considered prior to an evaluation. That is, what sort of mood characteristically defines the child—one of sadness, anxiety, anger, apathy, happiness, and so on. Anticipating the child's typical mood should help the examiner prepare strategies for working with children who are known or observed to be difficult, as opposed to those who are typically positive and cooperative.

Although many preschool children are by nature *distractible* and have short *attention spans* and limited *persistence*, examiners should be prepared to present the assessment according to the pace of the child. By keeping the assessment sufficiently quick paced, examiners generally can minimize the effects of a child's short attention span and limited persistence. By organizing and arranging the examining room in a manner to minimize visual and auditory distractions, the examiner also can better limit the distractibility of young examinees.

Examiner Characteristics

Examiners can directly and indirectly influence the examining situation through their appearance, dress, and the manner in which they interact with the child. This section of the chapter addresses examiner characteristics that enhance the examining situation and reduce the potential threats to validity related to unwanted or undesired examiner characteristics.

Approachability/Affect. The examiner must create just the right impression to be perceived as approachable by young children. This impression is a tightrope walk that requires a balance between being formal and business-like on one hand and being fun, interesting, and humorous on the other hand. Young children often "read" examiners and respond according to the behavioral messages communicated by the examiner. When an examiner presents himself or herself in a formal manner, children may perceive the examiner as relatively cold, harsh, or unaccepting—but, importantly, as someone who cannot be easily manipulated. If the examiner comes across as lively and entertaining, the child may perceive the examiner as someone with whom it will be enjoyable to interact. But such an examiner may also be seen as a playmate with whom roles can be negotiated, requests can be refused, and who is not necessarily to be taken seriously.

It is important that the examiner balance the need to be approachable with the necessity of communicating that the examiner is the person who is "in charge." The examiner can maintain this delicate balance by pleasantly, but clearly, establishing expectations and firm limits. Clear expectations can be communicated in part by stating directives, rather making requests. Requests are polite forms of communication we tend to use with other adults, but requests imply that the other person has the right to refuse. In a testing situation, examiners should not give the impression of choice, unless choice is truly intended. For example, examiners should say to examinees, "I want you to sit here," rather than, "Would you like to sit here?" The former statement is a clear directive to be followed and implies no option, whereas the latter question permits the child to say, "No" or "I want to sit over there." The rule of thumb is that examiners should propose questions or choices only when they are willing to go along with any answer or choice made by the examinee. If the examiner intends no choice, he or she should simply state an unambiguous directive, with a warm, engaging smile.

Physical Presence.   The examiner should maintain a physical appearance that is conducive to assessing young children. Because many infant and preschool tests require active motor participation on behalf of the examiner, examiners should wear comfortable shoes and clothing that allow for easy performance of motor activities such as skipping, jumping, balancing on one foot, and so on. Also, because young children sometimes will attempt to slide under the examining table to avoid participation, examiners' dress should readily permit them to crawl, kneel, or sit on the floor.

Examiners should also limit the amount of jewelry they wear during assessments so they do not create unintended visual or auditory distractions. For example, when performing the Hand Movements subtest of the *Kaufman Assessment Battery for Children, Second Edition* (K-ABC–II; Kaufman & Kaufman, 2004), examiners should avoid the distracting clinking sounds that are made when rings, watches, or bracelets come in contact with the table top. Similarly, bright, stimulating earrings, pins, broaches, necklaces, and neckties can create attractive, but unwanted, visual distractions for young children who would be better served focusing on test materials than the examiner's apparel.

Rapport.   Establishing rapport with young children can be challenging for many reasons, but with some flexibility and effort meaningful rapport can be established fairly easily. To establish rapport with young children, examiners must overcome children's fears, trepidations, shyness, reticence, and reluctance. To overcome these negative affective conditions, it is imperative that the children quickly develop a sense of physical and emotional safety and comfort. Such conditions can be fostered by displaying a personal attitude that is both engaging and sensitive.

To facilitate the maintenance of rapport, examiners should ensure that the testing environment is prepared for a variety of potentially disruptive situations. Plans should be made to ensure that someone is available to assist young examinees use the bathroom when necessary; tissues should be at hand to dab crying eyes and wipe ubiquitous running noses; play materials should be available to develop children's interest or to motivate children when their interests have waned; and examiners should ensure that drawing paper and pencils or coloring materials are available for both informal assessment activities, as well as to create a "gift" the child can proudly hand parents when the assessment is complete. Also, hand puppets, stuffed animals, or other such engaging materials are often useful for establishing rapport or comforting younger children because these objects allow examinees and the examiner to talk indirectly through the safer medium. Examiners should anticipate possible situations that could jeopardize rapport and be prepared to deal with these situations proactively and constructively.

Behavior Management.   To conduct psychoeducational evaluations with young children, examiners need proficient behavior management skills. Examiners must know when and how to effectively ask, direct, cajole, tease, laugh, act silly, be stern, reinforce, admonish, talk, be quiet, pat the child's head or hand affectionately, slow down or speed up the administration pace, show genuine empathy, and a perform a variety of related behaviors with perfect timing and sufficient sincerity to maintain the child's motivation, cooperation, and participation.

Preschool children frequently cry when frustrated or when they wish to avoid an activity, and novice examiners often are fearful of young crying children. Knowing that a child's crying typically becomes exacerbated when one actively tries to stop the crying, it is usually better to sit back and let children cry until they are ready to stop on their own. With tissue in hand, the examiner should wait until the child stops crying, and then tenderly dab the child's final tears soothingly, and immediately redirect the child to the next assessment task without comment. Mentioning the child's crying frequently results in the child's tears flowing again.

Given the labile emotions, variable activity level, and typical distractibility of preschool children, examiners need well-developed and well-practiced behavior management skills. Examiners also need to recognize which examinee behaviors forewarn the examiner of potential problems, and the examiner should proactively and subtly change the course of the situation before the child's behavior requires direct intervention. It is always better to maintain rapport than to try to re-establish it once it has been lost.

Psychometric Skill.   Proper and well-paced administration of tests during an assessment is essential for maintaining rapport and managing young children's behavior. Whereas adolescents may sit patiently (or sullenly) and wait for the examiner to fumble through the administration of a new instrument, preschool children are not known for their patience. Idle hands do in fact make the devil's work when young children are expected to sit for even brief periods while the examiner readies materials, rereads directions, reviews scoring criteria, or searches for needed stimuli. Therefore, examiners are best served by keeping the child actively engaged in appropriately paced assessment activities.

To facilitate test administration, examiners should be very familiar with the tests they select to administer. Examiners also should prepare the assessment room prior to the child's arrival, and have test kits set up for immediate use. The pace of testing throughout the assessment should be controlled by the examiner and should match the characteristics and needs of the examinee. The pace of an assessment can be adequately controlled only when the examiner has mastered the test administration demands and is very familiar with the test's item content and stimulus materials.

Experience with Preschool Children.   Examiners who plan to assess preschool children should become familiar with the developmental characteristics of this age group. Anyone who attributes adult or adolescent motivations to preschool children's behavior simply does not understand how young children operate. If the examiner is to effectively reduce construct-irrelevant variance in preschool assessments, he or she must be both comfortable and experienced working with young children and must understand what is typical and atypical preschool behavior.

Environment

A comfortable testing environment sets the stage for a successful assessment, especially for young children. The effective assessment environment should be cheerful, convey safety, capitalize on the child's curiosity, and stimulate the child's participation. For a testing environment to do these things, it must be child-oriented and friendly, and accommodate the needs of young children.

Furniture.   Examining rooms intended for preschool children should include furniture that is appropriately child-sized. Chairs should allow children's feet to reach the floor; tabletops should be easily reached without straining; and, bookshelves should be sufficiently low that children can readily obtain the books, puzzles, or other objects that may be handled before or after the evaluation. Examining rooms should be furnished appropriately for preschool children, rather than forcing preschool children to accommodate to adult-sized furniture and an adult-oriented environment.

Using child-sized furniture is not just a thoughtful consideration, it is an important safety factor. If examinees' feet do not touch the floor while sitting, circulation to their legs will be reduced, as will the sense of feeling in their legs. Such loss of feeling and the subsequent "pins and needles" that accompanies circulation when it is restored can cause children to wriggle about and increase the risk of their falling off or out of their chairs. Some young children opt to kneel or squat when tested in adult-sized chairs so they can better reach the materials on the tabletop. Squatting and kneeling, while a suitable alternative when necessary, can also lead to a loss of balance and unwanted falls if the child is not closely watched. Also, examiners should consider that oversized chairs allow more than ample room for the child to escape the assessment by squirming between the chair and table and onto the floor beneath the table.

Decorations.   Examining rooms should be cheery, inviting places, with interesting and colorful materials and decorations. However, examining rooms should not be so stimulating that examinees will be distracted by the decor. Clean, nicely painted, appropriately furnished, and modestly decorated rooms will provide the desired environment for successful evaluations. When examining rooms include distracting decorations or window scenes, the examiner should arrange the seating to face the child away from the visual distractions. Importantly, all efforts should be made to ensure that the most stimulating aspect of the examining room is the examiner and the test materials.

Distractions.   In addition to limiting visual distractions associated with decorations (e.g., windows, pictures, posters), the examiner should ensure that other distractions are similarly subdued. For example, telephones should be set so they do not ring during assessments; a "Do Not Disturb" sign should be placed on the examining room door; noise from hallways or adjacent rooms should be controlled; and every effort should be made to ensure that the assessment will be conducted in a room that is conducive to concentration and active participation. Young children are often easily affected by visual, auditory or personal distractions, and those children who wish to terminate an evaluation require very little extraneous distraction to direct their attention away from the evaluation.

Climate Control.   Examining rooms should be maintained with temperatures that are sufficiently warm so that the children do not sit in a hypothermic stupor, and the rooms should be sufficiently cool so that the children aren't lulled into a drowsy semi-hypnotic state. Examiners are often required to use rooms (e.g., cloak rooms, closets, boiler rooms) that were not designed for educational or psychological activities, and such examining rooms are frequently too small for adequate or easily moderated climate control. When locating a more suitable room is not possible, the examiner should open windows or keep doors ajar to allow fresh cool (or warm) air to circulate.

Table/Chair Arrangement.   Much can be done to maximize behavior management through the arrangement of office furniture. When examining young, squirmy children, the examiner can maximize control by providing subtle artificial boundaries and structure. To control an active child, especially one who would choose to leave his or her seat on a whim, the examiner should place the back legs of the child's chair against a wall—thereby disallowing the child to move his or her chair backward. The table can then be slid gently against the child's abdomen and thus be used as a "friendly" barrier to keep the child from getting up or sliding down at unwanted times.

When the room is configured in such a manner that the child's chair cannot be placed against a wall, the examiner should sit across an adjacent corner of the table from the child. This position allows the examiner to sit in close proximity to the child and thereby respond easily and quickly to the child's needs or actions. Such a position also permits the examiner to reposition or reinforce the child when necessary. For example, a friendly tussle of the child's hair or a tender pat on the shoulder, when done at just the right time can subtly keep the child from rising in his or her chair. A gentle pat on the back can bring the child closer to the table top and work area. Similarly, by placing one foot behind the front leg of the child's chair, the examiner can maintain the position of a squirmy child's chair so it remains in close proximity to the table, workspace, and the examiner.

However the room is situated, the examiner should ensure that the child is positioned farther from the door than the examiner. By carefully arranging the seating arrangement, the examiner can forestall the child's efforts to separate from the testing materials and be in a better position to disallow the child to leave the room. By positioning himself or herself closer to the door, the examiner can cut off any attempts by the child to exit the room.

Psychometric Considerations

Although examiners can moderate many of the previously mentioned threats to validity by employing clinical judgment and skill, examiners have no means to control or alter the foibles associated with the various instruments they have available for use. Examiners can and should, however, select instruments for use only after carefully considering each instrument's psychometric properties and unique characteristics.

Bracken (1988) identified 10 common psychometric reasons why similar tests produce dissimilar results. The intent of that article was to reveal common psychometric threats to validity, which may or may not be obvious upon casual viewing of test manuals and materials. In an error-free world, multiple tests that purport to assess the same construct (e.g., intelligence) should produce identical results when administered to the same child. Sometimes, however, tests that purport to measure the same construct produce results that are significantly discrepant from each other, and the reasons for such discrepancies often are related to construct-irrelevant psychometric limitations of the instruments (Bracken, 1987; Wasserman & Bracken, 2002, 2003). The remainder of this section will address these construct-irrelevant conditions and recommend possible solutions to these common psychometric limitations.

Test Floors.   The floor of a test is an indication of the extent to which an instrument provides meaningful scores at very low levels of individual functioning. Given that psychoeducational assessments are conducted at times to diagnose delayed or retarded levels of functioning, it is important that examiners use tests that are capable of reliably and accurately assessing such low levels of functioning. Examiners should ensure that they use tests that are in fact capable of producing suitably low scores for the delayed children they serve. Bracken (1987) recommended that a *minimal* standard for subtest, composite, and total test floors should equal or exceed minus two standard deviations (i.e., the minimal level traditionally required to diagnose retarded functioning).

To identify the floor of a subtest, the examiner should locate the lowest possible standard score that would be obtained at every age level, if the examinee were to pass a single item on that subtest. For any age at which a subtest raw score of one fails to generate a standard score equal to or greater than minus two standard deviations, the subtest is insufficiently sensitive to accurately identify seriously delayed functioning. To determine the floors of composite or total test scores, the examiner should identify the corresponding standard score associated with an earned raw score of one on each of the subtests that contribute to the composite or total test. If five subtests contribute to the composite, the examiner would identify the corresponding standard score associated with a raw score of five. If the composite standard score is less than two standard deviations below the normative mean, the composite has an insufficient floor for identifying retarded level functioning at the age level considered.

Historically, tests frequently have insufficient floors for children below age 4 (Bracken, 1987), which results in construct-irrelevant reasons for the resulting inflated scores. That is, the child's test score would be inaccurate and an over-estimate of the child's true level of functioning due in part to the psychometric foibles of the instrument used. Examiners must be especially careful to examine floors when conducting assessments on low functioning younger children, especially those younger than 4 years. When composite and total test scores are truncated due to the construct-irrelevant limitations of the instrument employed, that test should not be used to guide decisions about the child's diagnosis and placement. Such a test should be considered biased for children of that particular age and ability level.

Ceilings.   Ceilings within tests refer to the extent to which subtest, composite, or total test scores accurately reflect upper extreme levels of functioning among examinees. Because gifted functioning is typically characterized as beginning two or more standard deviations above the normative mean, tests intended for gifted identification should provide accurate scores at and above this criterion level. Ceilings are not generally as relevant among preschool tests, as are test floors. It is easier to create suitable items for assessing the upper limits of young children's abilities than it is to develop items that discriminate between the extreme lower limits of ability at this age level. Conversely, it is more difficult to create items that accurately assess the upper extreme abilities of older adolescents than it is to develop items that assess lower limits of abilities among this older population.

Although ceiling limitations are relatively rare in preschool tests, examiners should be watchful just the same. Some tests include subtests specifically designed for younger children, which are discontinued for slightly older children. Subtests typically are discontinued within a battery when the subtests have serious ceiling or floor problems and are no longer appropriate for children at that age level.

Item Gradients.   Item gradients refer to how steeply graded standard scores are arranged in relation to their respective raw scores. Ideally, the incremental change in standard scores that results from one raw score unit to the next (e.g., a raw score of 5 versus 6) should produce a comparably small standard score increase. Unfortunately, preschool tests are notorious for having steep item gradients, with correspondingly large standard score manifestations associated with minor increases or decreases in raw scores. Whenever a test has steep item gradients, only a rough discrimination between ability levels result from that instrument. Such crude discrimination between levels of ability leads to construct-irrelevant variation in the assessed construct that is related to the instrument rather than true differences in children's individual abilities.

Examiners should carefully examine norm tables for all age levels and determine the ages at which the test or subtests have item gradients that are too steep for accurate and finely graded discrimination of abilities. Bracken (1988) recommended that an increase or decrease of a single raw score should not alter the corresponding standard score by more than one-third standard deviation. That is, a raw score of x (e.g., 25) on a given measure should not produce a standard score that is more than one-third standard deviation greater than that would result from a raw score one integer less or greater (i.e., $x+/-1$ or 24/26). Tests with item gradients that are steeper than these guidelines are too crude to accurately assess individual differences in students' ability.

Reliability.   Tests with low reliability produce proportionately large portions of subtest and composite variability that is related to measurement error rather than true differences in the construct. A test with an Alpha Coefficient of .80 will produce variance that is 80% reliable, while 20% of the variance would be related to measurement error. Obviously, error is a source of construct-irrelevant variance and examiners should selectively employ only tests which possess reasonable levels of internal consistency and stability. Bracken (1988) suggested that .90 be set as an acceptable level of internal consistency and stability for total test scores. Subtest and composite reliabilities should approximate .80, with median subtest reliabilities equal to .80 or higher. These guidelines provide a reasonable "rule of thumb" to apply when selecting tests for individual assessments.

Validity.   The sine qua non of construct-relevant assessment is test validity. Because validity is such an important element in assessment, test manuals are expected to provide thorough and convincing evidence of content, construct, and criterion-related validity (AERA, APA, NCME, 1999). Because validity is a continuous variable, rather than dichotomous variable, and ranges from the total absence of validity to perfect validity (both of these absolutes are rare), examiners must determine whether the documentation and level of demonstrated validity justifies use of the instrument for its intended purpose. Any time a test with poor validity is selected, used, and contributes to the diagnostic decision-making process, the examiner knowingly and willingly introduces variance into the decision-making equation that is to some large extent construct irrelevant. Examiners have an ethical, professional, and legal responsibility to only use instruments of the highest quality, and validity should be the most important aspect of technical adequacy considered.

Norms Tables.   Norm tables sometimes are an inadvertent contributor to construct-irrelevant variability in test scores. The norm tables of some preschool tests include age ranges that are too broad to be sensitive to the rapid growth and development that occurs during the first six years of life (e.g., 6-months or 1-year age ranges). Norm tables for preschool tests should not exceed 3-month intervals, and at the youngest age levels (i.e., birth to 2 years) norms should reflect intervals as brief as 1 or 2 months.

The easiest way to evaluate the quality of a norm table is to examine the difference in standard scores associated with a given raw score as you progress from one table to the next. If the standard score increases by large amounts (e.g., +/1 1/3 standard deviation), the test may provide too gross an estimate of ability to instill much confidence in the resultant scores. Consider the importance of norm table sensitivity for a child who is on the very upper cusp of one age level and who is about to "graduate" to the next age level. A good test should not produce a large difference in standard scores based solely on whether the child was tested yesterday, today, or tomorrow, especially when the raw score remains the same across these 3 days. If a test is sensitive to the construct being assessed, the child's obtained raw score should yield nearly identical standard scores across this hypothetical 3-day range. For example, consider a child who is 2 years 7 months and 15 days old when tested on the McCarthy Scales of Children's Abilities (MSCA; McCarthy, 1972), which is largely considered an outdated test but one that is still sold by its publisher. If this child obtains a raw score of 37 across the McCarthy's five scales (see Bracken, 1988), her total test score (i.e., GCI) would be 112. However, if the same child earned an identical score on the following day when she was 2 years 7 months and 16 days old (i.e., just one day older), her subsequent GCI would be 101—a decrease in functioning by a full two-thirds standard deviation.

Examiners should strive to eliminate or reduce such construct-irrelevant influences in the assessment of preschool children by selecting tests with appropriately sensitive norm tables. Sensitivity is needed most at the youngest age levels when children's development occurs at the fastest pace.

Age of Norms.   Examiners are ethically bound to use only the most recent editions of tests (e.g., NASP, APA Ethical Guidelines, Standards for Educational and Psychological Testing). There are several reasons for using only the most recent editions of tests, which include the benefits of improved and updated stimulus materials, the inclusion of recent perspectives and theoretical advances in the test, and the application of recent normative samples. This latter reason has direct implications for accurate assessment and decision-making.

Flynn (1984, 1987, 1999) has demonstrated that on an international level, the general intelligence of the world's population is increasing at a rate of about 3 IQ points per decade. This apparent increase in population intelligence is related to a variety of hypothesized factors, including improved diet and health care, the positive influences of various media, improved economic conditions among more individuals, and so on. Whatever the reason for this documented longitudinal improvement in intelligence, the implications for using outdated tests is clear. Outdated tests inflate the estimate of children's intelligence in direct proportion to the age of the norms.

Examiners who use tests that are 1, 2, or 3 decades old might expect test scores to be inflated by a magnitude of 3, 6, or 9 IQ points, respectively. The differential affects of test age on assessed intelligence is not related directly to the construct being assessed (i.e., intelligence), but rather to the artifactual affects of the age of the test's norms. Therefore, to avoid these artifactual affects, examiners should not only be ethically bound, but practically and professionally bound, to use only the most recent editions of instruments. When a test has not been revised within the past decade and a half, examiners should question whether to continue using the instrument. The *McCarthy Scales of Children's Abilities,* for example, was published originally in 1972 and has not been revised since. Examiners would be hard pressed to defend using such an instrument with norms that are more than 30 years old, given the construct-irrelevant influences of the age of the norms on the child's estimated level of functioning. If this example seems extreme, consider that the author, as a discussant for a recent conference paper presentation, was critical of a psychologist's continued clinical use of the 1973 *Stanford-Binet Intelligence Scale, Form L-M* (Bracken, 2004) and the author also recently served as a consultant on a legal case in which a psychologist was continuing his practice of using the 1974 WISC-R for Social Security Administration disability determination assessments.

Basic Concepts in Test Directions.   Before examiners can effectively assess children's abilities with standardized instruments, they have to ensure that the child fully understands the test's directions. If a child fails to understand what is required of him or her while taking a test, then the test may assess listening comprehension or receptive vocabulary rather than the intended construct (e.g., intelligence). Researchers have consistently shown that the past several generations of preschool instruments have test directions that are replete with basic concepts that are beyond the conceptual understanding of most young children (Bracken, 1986, 1998; Flanagan & Alfonso, 1995; Flanagan, Alfonso, Kaminer, & Rader, 1995; Kaufman, 1978). When the wording and vocabulary in test directions are more complex than the required task, the test will be more a measure of language proficiency than a measure of the intended construct.

The relevance of test direction complexity and basic concept inclusion is especially important when assessing children who speak English as a second language or who speak a nonstandard form of English. Children from these minority linguistic groups may be especially disadvantaged when administered tests with complex verbal directions, especially when the construct purportedly assessed by the instrument is not language facility, fluency, or comprehension. To avoid the construct-irrelevant influence of complex test directions, examiners should seek instruments that provide simple test directions, as well as demonstration and sample items that ensure that the child understands the nature of the task requirements before beginning task for credit. In some situations where language comprehension is a central referral issue, nonverbal tests of ability may be warranted to provide a contrast between performance on language-related tests and nonverbal measures. Comprehensive nonverbal tests of intelligence, such as the *Universal Nonverbal Intelligence Test* (UNIT; Bracken & McCallum, 1998) or the *Leiter International Performance Scale– Revised* (Roid & Miller, 1997) were designed to be used when the examinee's language skills represent a construct-irrelevant contributor to test variance.

CONCLUSION

The focus of this chapter has been on creating an examining situation that systematically reduces construct-irrelevant influences in the assessment process and maximizes the examiner's confidence in the accuracy and interpretability of the test results. Examiners should employ clinical skills to reduce threats to the validity of the assessment by creating a safe, secure, and engaging environment. Examiners should also consider the child's current physical condition and health when planning an assessment and decide whether a valid estimate of the child's true abilities can be obtained given the child's current physical state. Finally, examiners should carefully examine and consider the psychometric properties and foibles of the instruments in their psychoeducational batteries. When tests fail to meet psychometric standards that are commonly considered as essential for testing older children, adolescents and adults, these instruments should not be used for the assessment of preschool children, either.

When examiners carefully consider and address these important intrapersonal, interpersonal, environmental, and psychometric issues, they systematically reduce the construct-irrelevant variability in examinees' test scores. By reducing the variability in test scores that is attributable to measurement error, examiners can have more confidence in the test results and thereby make more defensible decisions.

REFERENCES

AERA, APA, NCME (1999). *Standards for educational and psychological testing*. Washington, DC: Author.

Bracken, B. A. (1986). Incidence of basic concepts in the directions of five commonly used American tests of intelligence. *School Psychology International, 7,* 1–10.

Bracken, B. A. (1987). Limitations of preschool instruments and standards for minimal levels of technical adequacy. *Journal of Psychoeducational Assessment, 4,* 313–326.

Bracken, B. A. (1988). Ten psychometric reasons why similar tests produce dissimilar results. *Journal of School Psychology, 26,* 155–166.

Bracken, B. A. (1998). *Bracken Basic Concept Scale–Revised*. San Antonio, TX: The Psychological Corporation.

Bracken, B. A. (2004, November). Discussant. Symposium on Intelligence Testing. Presented at the National Association of Gifted Children's annual conference. Salt Lake City, UT.

Bracken, B. A. (2006). *Bracken Basic Concept Scale–Third Edition*. San Antonio, TX: Harcourt Assessments.

Bracken, B. A., & Keith, L. (2004). *Clinical Assessment of Behavior*. Lutz, FL: Psychological Assessment Resources.

Bracken, B. A., & McCallum, R. S. (1998). *Universal Nonverbal Intelligence Test*. Itasca, IL: Riverside Publishing.

Carey, W. B., & McDevitt, S. C. (1995). *Coping with children's temperament*. New York: Basic Books.

Chess, S., & Thomas, A. (1992). Dynamics of individual behavioral development. In M. D. Levine, W. B. Carey, & A. C. Crocker (Eds.), *Developmental–behavioral pediatrics* (2nd ed., pp. 84–94). Philadelphia: Saunders.

Flanagan, D. P., & Alfonso, V. C. (1995). A critical review of the technical characteristics of new and recently revised intelligence tests for preschoolers. *Journal of Psychoeducational Assessment, 13,* 66–90.

Flanagan, D. P., Alfonso, V. C., Kaminer, T., & Rader, D. E. (1995). Incidence of basic concepts in the directions of new and recently revised American intelligence tests for preschool children. *School Psychology International, 16,* 345–364.

Flynn, J. R. (1984). The mean IQ of Americans: Massive gains from 1932 to 1978. *Psychological Bulletin, 95,* 29–51.

Flynn, J. R. (1987). Massive IQ gains in 14 nations: What IQ tests really measure. *Psychological Bulletin, 95,* 29–51.

Flynn, J. R. (1999). Searching for justice: The discovery of IQ gains over time. *American Psychologist, 54,* 5–20.

Kaufman, A. S. (1978). The importance of basic concepts in individual assessment of preschool children. *Journal of School Psychology, 16,* 207–211.

Kaufman, A. S., & Kaufman, N. L. (2004). *Kaufman Assessment Battery for Children, Second edition*. Circle Pines: American Guidance Service.

McCarthy, D. (1972). *McCarthy Scales of Children's Abilities*. San Antonio, TX: The Psychological Corporation.

McGrew, K. A., & Flanagan, D. P. (1998). *The intelligence test desk reference: Gf-Gc cross-battery assessment*. Boston: Allyn & Bacon.

Roid, G. H., & Miller, L. J. (1997). *Leiter International Performance Scale–Revised*. Wood Dale, IL: Stoelting.

Thomas, A., & Chess, S. (1977). *Temperament and development*. New York: Brunner/Mazel.

Wasserman, J. D., & Bracken, B. A. (2002). Selecting appropriate tests: Psychometric and pragmatic considerations. In J. F. Carlson & B. B. Waterman (Eds.), *Social and personal assessment of school-aged children: Developing interventions for educational and clinical settings* (pp. 18–43). Needham Heights, MA: Allyn & Bacon.

Wasserman, J. D., & Bracken, B. A. (2003). Psychometric considerations of assessment procedures. In J. Graham and J. Naglieri (Eds.). *Handbook of assessment psychology* (pp. 43–66). New York: Wiley.

8

Assessment of Home and Family Dynamics

Amanda B. Nickerson and Corrina C. Duvall
University at Albany, SUNY

Sandra G. Gagnon
Appalachian State University

Given the importance of the family for successful social and academic outcomes for preschool children, there is a need to identify assessment tools to measure home and family dynamics and to inform educational and treatment plans. This chapter provides a brief background of the importance of home and family for preschool children and discusses general issues in assessing home environments, such as building rapport, respecting cultural differences, and taking safety precautions. Critical domains in home and family dynamics are identified, and examples of relevant research demonstrating the relationship between these domains and outcomes for children are presented. The importance of an ecologically valid assessment approach is introduced, followed by descriptions of broad and specific assessment instruments useful for assessing home and family dynamics. Limitations of this type of assessment are reviewed, as are recommendations for practice and future directions.

HISTORY/BACKGROUND

The field of early childhood education has long acknowledged the importance of the family and home environment for preschool children. The implementation of the Head Start Program, recognized as one of the shaping events of the federal government's support for preschool education, emphasized the central role of parents (Gallagher, 2000). Mandates such as Goals 2000, Title I regulations, and Part H of Public Law (P.L.) 99-457 require family-school connections and emphasize the importance of family-focused service delivery systems (McBride, 1999). Family-centered practice has also been emphasized in the early intervention literature (see e.g., Barnett et al., 1997; McLean & Odom, 1996).

Visionary thinking in the assessment of preschoolers focuses on ecologically valid assessment, including an examination of the exchanges between the child and significant others (e.g., parents, grandparents) and a focus on strengths and resources (Fewell, 2000).

Obtaining information from parents is an important part of an ecological assessment, as it provides rich information about the child in his or her natural setting and estimates parents' reactions, concerns, and stresses, which may affect the child (Neisworth & Bagnato, 1996).

ISSUES IN ASSESSING HOME ENVIRONMENTS

When conducting family and home assessments, several considerations arise, such as building rapport, acting in a culturally responsive manner, and attending to safety. Establishing and maintaining rapport with family members is essential to conducting a valid assessment. Rapport can be built by conveying genuine interest and acceptance, using assessment techniques appropriate for the needs and abilities of the family that minimize their time and effort, and providing feedback in a meaningful way (Neisworth & Bagnato, 1996).

A critical part of building rapport is acting in a culturally responsive manner. It is important to be sensitive to general cultural customs regarding eye contact, personal space, and handshakes to help establish rapport (Kalesnik, 1999). It is also important to remember that many high context cultures use situational and nonverbal cues when communicating, in contrast to traditional Western cultures that rely primarily on verbal communication (Hanson & Lynch, 1990). In communicating with diverse families, asking open-ended questions in laymen's terms may encourage families to tell their stories. In some cases, it may be necessary to arrange for an interpreter who speaks the language and dialect of the family to assist with the assessment (Kalesnik, 1999).

In conducting the assessment, it is important to identify all caregivers in a child's life, such as extended family members, siblings, and tribe members (Hanson & Lynch, 1992). It is also helpful to acquire information about the roles and structure in the family (Hanson & Lynch, 1990; Kalesnik, 1999) and the family's views about issues of children/childrearing, family roles, disability and its causation, change and intervention, and medicine/healing (Hanson & Lynch, 1990). This information may vary considerably from family to family, and it is critical in conducting an assessment that will lead to the selection of interventions that will be implemented with respect and fidelity.

A thorough assessment of home and family dynamics may involve home visits, which raises safety issues. Burry (2002) suggested a number of precautions that professionals can take. When planning visits, the person conducting the assessment should talk with other professionals who have had contact with the family to assess the degree of crime in the neighborhood and the potential for violence in the home. In addition, professionals should ensure that others are aware of their plans for visits, including times, dates, and locations. Other precautions include working in pairs, leaving valuables at home, being prepared with a cellular phone, and having complete directions and enough gas to complete the trip. During visits, Burry recommends parking the car in a place that cannot be blocked from departure and, when in the home, to have a clear path to the exit. Professionals should use a calm, polite voice, and non-threatening body posture (e.g., safe physical distance, hands in lap), and, in the case of a perceived threat, the service provider should calmly and immediately end the assessment and leave.

Domains in Family and Home Dynamics: Implications for Child Outcomes.   A review of the literature on family and home dynamics reveals several domains of importance. For the purpose of this chapter, we selected four broad domains that encompass more specific variables. Selection of domains was guided by a recognition of the importance of the unique constellation of parent, child, and interaction variables within families, the extrafamilial contexts that affect the family (see Bronfenbrenner, 1986), and a focus on strengths as well as needs. These domains are (a) demographics, (b) family relationships, (c) strengths, and (d) stressors.

Demographics.   Socioeconomic status (SES) has a profound effect on children and families. Parents who are poor report reading to their children less frequently (McLennan & Kotelchuck, 2000) and children who live in poverty perform lower on cognitive ability tests (Brooks-Gunn & Duncan, 1997; Molfese & Molfese, 2002; NICD Early Child Care Research Network, 2001; Patterson & Albers, 2001) and achievement tests (Entwisle & Alexander, 1996) than do children from middle to upper SES backgrounds. Children from disadvantaged backgrounds are more likely to repeat grades, drop out of school, and be placed in special education programs (Entwisle & Alexander, 1996; McLoyd, 1998). Poverty is associated with higher levels of emotional and behavioral problems, especially externalizing behaviors (McLoyd, 1998), although the effects are not as large as those for cognitive functioning (Brooks-Gunn & Duncan, 1997; NICD, 2001). Children's health problems, such as respiratory and neurological problems, have been associated with poverty (Gersten, 1992; McLoyd, 1998), though a recent, large-scale study did not find this link (NICD).

Ethnicity is highly correlated with poverty. African Americans and Hispanics are more likely than European Americans to live in poverty (Klebanov, Brooks-Gunn, & Duncan, 1994; McLoyd, 1998; NICD, 2001). African American mothers are at increased risk for having children with adverse birth outcomes (Brooks-Gunn & Duncan, 1997) and are less likely to implement child safety practices (McLennan & Kotelchuck, 2000). Ethnicity and poverty also interact in their effects on children. For example, although poverty is associated with lower academic achievement, this is especially true for children from ethnic minority groups (Banks, 1988). Lead poisoning also affects more African Americans than Whites (McLoyd, 1998), and home environments are better for nonblack and higher income families (Klebanov et al., 1994). It is likely that the pervasive discrimination against African Americans in education, employment, and housing have contributed to the aforementioned disparities (McLoyd, 1998).

Parental education and employment also influence children's development. For instance, women with less formal education and those who drop out of high school are at increased risk of having children with lower cognitive functioning (Molfese & Molfese, 2002; Patterson & Albers, 2001). In addition, women with less education tend to have adverse birth outcomes (Brooks-Gunn & Duncan, 1997) and are less likely to engage in parental safety practices (McLennan & Kotelchuck, 2000). Higher family income is associated with better home environments and more maternal warmth (Klebanov et al., 1994). Unemployment correlates with increased depressive symptomatology in single African American mothers, which, in turn, has been associated with the use of punitive discipline strategies (McLoyd, Jayaratne, Ceballo, & Borquez, 1994).

In terms of family composition, single mothers are more likely to experience stressful life events (Gringlas & Weintraub, 1995). Children raised by single mothers are rated by teachers as having more behavior problems, lower academic performance, and less social competence than their peers from two-parent households (Gringlas & Weintraub, 1995). Klebanov et al. (1994) found that status as a single mother is not correlated with the home environment and is positively associated with maternal warmth, suggesting that it is the diminished capacity to cope with the stress of role overload, rather than single parenthood, per se, that affects these other variables. Having more than one child is associated with parents reading less to children (McLennan & Kotelchuck, 2000) and smaller household size is associated with a better home environment (Klebanov et al.).

Living in poor and high crime neighborhoods has been associated with a variety of factors. After controlling for differences in family-level measures (e.g., demographic variables), Klebanov et al. (1994) found that low-income neighborhoods were associated with inferior physical environments in the home and less maternal warmth. This effect was more pronounced for white families than for black families. There is also a significant link between exposure to community violence and reductions in children's cognitive performance and positive peer interactions (Farver, Natera, & Frosch, 1999).

In summary, there are several demographic factors that influence child outcomes. It is difficult to attribute child outcomes solely to poverty status, race/ethnicity, or family composition, as these variables are so intimately related. In addition, there are several mediating factors to consider, such as the current life situation of the parent, social support, the capacity to parent as a result of physical and mental health (Halpern, 1993), and the variability of poverty status over time (Brooks-Gunn & Duncan, 1997; McLoyd, 1998).

Family Relationships.   Theorists and researchers from diverse orientations have emphasized the importance of family relationships for child development. Family factors that promote resilience include a close relationship with at least one caregiver, effective parenting that is strict and highly structured with high levels of warmth, and access to relationships with extended family members (Doll & Lyon, 1998; Entwisle & Alexander, 1996; McLoyd, 1998). Specific aspects of the parent-child relationship, namely, attachment and childrearing, have also been linked to positive outcomes for children.

Parent-infant attachment patterns are related to children's social and cognitive development. Securely attached infants are more readily socialized and competent, in contrast to those with anxious-ambivalent attachment styles, who have slower cognitive development and problem-solving and anxious-avoidant infants, who tend to have less harmonious interactions with adults (Ainsworth & Bowlby, 1991; Ainsworth, Blehar, Waters, & Wall, 1978). There is also clear evidence of a relationship between the quality of parent-child attachment and peer competence for preschool children (Sroufe, 1988). Longitudinal studies have indicated that children with histories of secure attachment patterns score higher on broad measures of competence, emotional health, self-confidence, and social skills (Elicker, Englund, & Sroufe, 1992; Shulman, 1995).

There is also a substantial body of research linking childrearing behavior and beliefs to child development. Parents who have an authoritative style, which includes parental warmth and moderate control, have children who achieve better developmental outcomes than do parents who are either authoritarian, characterized by high parental control and little warmth, or permissive, marked by low parental control and high warmth (Baumrind, 1980; Parke et al., 1998). In addition, parents of children with aversive behavior do not tend to teach prosocial behavior, such as compliance, and often use ineffective discipline strategies, such as noncontingent punishment (Patterson, 1986; Vuchinich, Bank, & Patterson, 1992). Unskilled discipline is predictive of child maltreatment and neglect (Bank & Burraston, 2001), which is discussed in a later section on stressors.

Parental beliefs are also related to childrearing behavior and child outcomes. Negative perceptions of maternal role have been found to predict increased use of punishment (McLoyd et al., 1994). In addition, parents who have low perceptions of control or who believe they are not competent have children that are less well adjusted (Parke et al., 1998).

Strengths. The importance of recognizing family strengths has been underscored in early childhood education. It should be noted that variables mentioned in the two previous domains could be strengths for the family, such as higher SES, secure parent-child attachment, authoritative discipline, and the presence of positive extrafamilial factors, such as safe neighborhoods. Additional strengths explored in this section include internal strengths of the family as well as extrafamilial strengths, such as social support.

In addition to the previously mentioned internal strengths of families (e.g., secure attachment, effective childrearing), learning stimulation is a key variable related to children's development. Opportunities for learning experiences and stimulation have been related to children's language and reading abilities (Bradley, Corwyn, Burchinal, McAdoo, & Coll, 2001; Molfese & Molfese, 2002) and negatively correlated with behavior problems, although the latter results are more variable (Bradley et al., 2001). Home factors that relate to higher academic achievement for children from disadvantaged backgrounds include cognitive stimulation, parental expectations for children's school success, parental involvement, high levels of reading, and use of resources, such as books, tapes, and outings (Entwisle & Alexander, 1996; McLoyd, 1998).

Social support is an important extrafamilial strength. It has a beneficial effect on psychological well-being and serves a protective function in buffering against potentially negative effects of stressful events (see Cohen & Wills, 1985). Social support has a negative relationship with psychological maladjustment, such as anxiety and depression (White, Bruce, Farrell, & Kliewer, 1998). For single, unemployed, African American mothers, the increased availability of instrumental support (i.e., tangible assistance in terms of goods and services) has been associated with less negative perceptions of the maternal role and less reliance on punitive discipline strategies (McLoyd et al., 1994). In addition, maternal social support is correlated with better learning environments in the home (Klebanov et al., 1994).

Research has also examined other extrafamilial strengths, such as school and community factors. Access to relationships with positive role models, connection with at least one prosocial organization, and access to responsive, high-quality schools relate to improved outcomes for disadvantaged students (Doll & Lyon, 1998). These opportunities are closely related to the type of neighborhood in which the family lives, with high resource neighborhoods benefiting children most (McLoyd, 1998).

Stressors. This domain can encompass a wide variety of factors, depending on the circumstances of the particular family. It should be noted that many of the previously mentioned demographic variables (e.g., low socioeconomic status) and parent-child interaction variables (e.g., insecure attachment, coercive discipline) may be stressors in the family. In this section, we have organized other stressors into parenting stressors and child maltreatment.

Parenting stress is highly correlated with maternal depression (Kern et al., 2004) and behavior problems in children (Benzies, Harrison, & Magill-Evans, 2004). In addition, high stress exacerbates problems for children in single-parent households in terms of behavior problems, impaired academic performance, and problems with social competence (Gringlas & Weintraub, 1995).

Other stressors include parental mental illness and substance abuse. Maternal depression has been linked to problematic parenting, such as inept discipline practices, less sensitivity, and more pessimistic attitudes towards the child (Gelfand & Teti, 1990). Maternal depression also has an adverse impact on children's cognitive and motor development (Patterson & Albers, 2001), children's regulation of their own emotions, and risk for later academic, social, and psychological problems (Gelfand & Teti; Parke et al., 1998; Schneider, 1993). Studies using large, national databases have found that long-term depression is related to more serious consequences for children than short-lived depression (McLennan & Kotelchuck, 2000; Patterson & Albers, 2001), underscoring the importance of considering both the severity and chronicity of depression in the assessment process.

Drug and alcohol abuse have also been associated with parenting variables. For instance, maternal addiction predicted less parental involvement (Suchman & Luthar, 2000). Parental alcohol and drug use are associated with personality attributes such as poor impulse control, emotional instability, and less of a sense of relatedness, which impact the child's personality and behavior (Brook, Whiteman, Shapiro, & Choen, 1996).

Another parental stressor is marital discord. Parents who have a good marital relationship are less susceptible to depression (Rutter, 1985). Repeated exposure to unresolved marital conflict may lead to children's increased emotional arousal, sensitization to conflict, and an inability to regulate emotions and behaviors (Hetherington, 1999; Martin & Clements, 2002). These problems can occur up to 2 years after the parents divorce, especially if there was a high intensity of conflict (Zimet & Jacob, 2001).

Maltreatment, either through abuse or neglect, is a severe stressor that predicts poor long-term outcomes. Children who are maltreated are more likely to have negative social relationships (Kaplan, Pelcovitz, & Labruna, 1999) and children who are neglected are more likely to have cognitive and academic impairments (Bank & Burraston, 2001; Malinosky-Rummel & Hansen, 1993), deficits in receptive and expressive language skills (Kaplan et al., 1999), and increased risk of accidents, illnesses, and injuries (Bank & Burraston, 2001). Maltreatment in children is also predictive of a variety of maladaptive outcomes in adolescence, including antisocial behavior, a greater likelihood of arrests for violent crime (Bank & Burraston, 2001), and engagement in self-injurious behaviors (e.g., suicide attempts, sexual risk-taking, and substance abuse; Kaplan et al., 1999). Common emotional and psychological problems associated with maltreatment are diminished self-esteem, depression, anxiety, conduct disorder, multiple personality disorder, and other psychoses (Malinosky-Rummel & Hansen, 1993).

METHODS OF OBTAINING INFORMATION

These important domains can be measured through a variety of assessment techniques, including interviews, observations, and third-party rating instruments. To provide the most valid estimate of developmental functioning, Bagnato and Neisworth (1991) advocated for using a multifaceted, ecological approach to examine preschoolers' developmental skills within social, school, and family contexts, using multiple methods, traits, and sources.

Assessment strategies should be tailored to the needs of the individual child and family. Interviews are highly recommended to build rapport with families and to gather essential information about demographics, strengths, stressors, and cultural considerations. Observations of the child and family interactions are also important in order to gain direct, objective information about how the family functions in their natural environment. Administering a broad measure of home and family dynamics allows one to assess several variables that may be impacting the child, and can be followed by more specific measures.

BROAD MEASURES OF HOME AND FAMILY DYNAMICS

This section describes two of the most widely used, psychometrically sound, and useful broad measures of home and family dynamics that cover two or more of the aforementioned domains. These are the Home Observation for Measurement of the Environment Inventory (HOME; Caldwell & Bradley, 2001) and the Family Environment Scale–III (Moos & Moos, 1994). Other broad measures of home and family dynamics are also described.

Home Observation for Measurement of the Environment Inventory.   The HOME is the most widely used measure of home and family dynamics (Totsika & Sylva, 2004), and is available in four forms: Infant/Toddler (ages 0–3), Early Childhood (ages 3–6), Middle Childhood (ages 6–10) and Early Adolescence (ages 10–15). It is well researched and has been examined with many populations, such as children with disabilities (Rousey, Wild, & Blacher, 2002), White, Black and Hispanic Americans (Bradley, Mundfrom, Casey & Barrett, 1994), and families from other cultures (e.g., Bradley, Corwyn, & Whiteside-Mansel, 1996). Information is gathered in an organized manner through direct observations within the home and semi-formal interviews with the caregiver, conducted while the child is present. Some training is necessary for the assessor to accurately score items based on the information gathered. Detailed information on scoring is provided in the manual (Caldwell & Bradley, 2001).

The HOME is a comprehensive measure with strong psychometric properties used to gather information about a child's learning environment, such as available resources and language stimulation. Family relationships (e.g., family warmth, affection) and stressors (e.g., physical abuse) are assessed. Internal consistency is acceptable for each form (Infant-Toddler, $r = .80$; Early Childhood, $r = .93$), as is inter-observer agreement (Infant-Toddler, $r = .80$; Early Childhood, $r = .90$) (Bradley, 1993). Scores on the HOME are predictive of cognitive development and child IQ scores (Molfese, Dilalla, & Bunce, 1997). It has also been correlated with mother-child attachment and socio-economic status (Bradley et al., 2001). Bradley et al. (1989) found that the HOME was significantly correlated to developmental outcomes in White, Black and Mexican American children, although it was more able to discriminate among whites. The aforementioned are only a small sampling of the studies that have been conducted with the HOME. For a more extensive review, see Totsika and Sylva (2004).

Family Environment Scale–3rd Edition.   Another widely used measure is the Family Environment Scale–III (Moos & Moos, 1994), a 90-item true/false questionnaire with 10 subtests. It is available in four forms: Real Form, which measures perceptions about the family environment; Ideal Form, which measures perceptions about an ideal family; Expectations Form, which measures perceptions about what the family may be like in the future; and the Children's Version (only 30 items). The Real Form, Ideal Form, and Expectations Form are completed by the parent, and the Children's Version can be administered to children between the ages of 5 and 12. Like the HOME, the FES–III is a broad measure of family and home dynamics, and examines constructs such as family cohesion, conflict, organization, and expressiveness. It has been researched with many populations, such as children with special needs and parents with substance abuse problems (Mancini, 2001).

The FES–III generally has strong psychometrics. Test-retest reliability is acceptable, with correlations as high as .86 over a 4-month period (Moos & Moos, 1994). The FES–III has been criticized for its internal consistency, which ranges from .61–.78 (Roosa &

Beals,1990). Although this is lower than some other well-developed scales, Sanford, Bingham, and Zucker (1999) have judged this to be acceptable given that the FES–III aims for each construct to measure a broad array of behavior. The greatest strength of the FES–III is said to be its content validity, which is based on sound theory (Bagarozzi, 1984). Concurrent and predictive validity of the FES–III has been confirmed by many research studies. For example, relationships have been found among FES–III scores and the presence of major depression, conduct disorder, attention deficit/hyperactivity disorder, oppositional defiant disorder, post traumatic stress disorder, dysthymic disorder, and alcohol use (Halloran, Ross, & Carey, 2002). FES–III scores also predicted the likelihood of females developing eating disorders (Latzer, Hochdorf, Bachar, & Canetti, 2001).

Other Broad Measures.   Another broad measure is the Family Assessment Measure–III (Skinner, Steinhauer & Sitarenios, 2000), which assesses overall family functioning. One form can be completed for dynamics between each family member, which provides information about all relationship combinations in the home. Internal consistency coefficients range from .86–.94 for each scale (Spillane, 2001) and there is evidence of predictive validity. The Family Assessment Form (McCroskey & Nishimoto, 1991) is a 102-item rating scale that assesses numerous family factors, with special attention to identifying stressors. Reliability ranges from .70–.90, and moderate content and construct validity has been established (McCroskey & Nishimoto, 1991). It should be noted that there are no norms for this scale.

ASSESSMENT METHODS AND MEASURES FOR SPECIFIC DOMAINS

As discussed previously, there are several domains of importance to consider when assessing home and family dynamics. This section provides an overview of methods to assess aspects of these domains, supplemented by a listing of measures in Tables 8.1, 8.2, and 8.3. Criteria for inclusion were: (a) moderate to high reliability and validity, (b) general positive regard by researchers in the area, and/or (c) utility in assessing home and family dynamics. Although they are segregated according to domain, it should be noted that there is some overlap between constructs.

Demographics.   Typically, demographic data are gathered through an interview, which is an excellent method for conveying a sense of professional-parent partnership and gaining information (Cohen & Spenciner, 2003; Kalesnick, 1999). Family factors and stressors that may be asked about include significant losses or changes in family structure (e.g., death or divorce), changes in residence or SES, and psychological, psychiatric, and drug or alcohol problems of family members (McConaughy & Ritter, 2002). Demographic information can also be gathered by questionnaires, like those used in research studies (e.g., Feldman & Steptoe, 2004; Christie-Mizell, Steelman, & Stewart, 2003). In addition, Hollingshead's measure of socioeconomic status (Hollingshead & Redlich, 1958), which consists of three subscales—the Residential Scale, which measures quality of the home; the Occupational Scale, which measures value and status of occupation; and the Educational Scale, which measures level of education received—has been used extensively. The Family Resources Scale (Dunst & Leet, 1987), which assesses the resources (e.g., food, shelter, and financial resources) that are available to a family, is also applicable.

TABLE 8.1.
Description of Measures Assessing Family Relationships

Scale	Description	Notes
Family Relationships		
Family Adaptability and Cohesion Evaluation Scales-Fourth Edition (FACES–IV; Olson, Geisel, & Gorall, 1996)	24-item scale designed to measure how the family functions as a unit.	Moderate test-retest reliability (.65–.79). Convergent and discriminant validity established.
Family Relations Test (Bene & Anthony, 1957)	Projective measure for children as young as three; assesses relationships with family members	Standardized; no psychometrics established. Not recommended as diagnostic tool (Carlson, 1992).
Parent-Child Relationship Inventory (Gerard, 1994)	78-item rating scale assessing a number of relationship factors.	Internal consistency (.82). Test-retest reliability (.81).
Attachment		
Massie-Campbell Scale of Mother–Infant Attachment-Indicators During Stress (ADS; Massie & Campbell, 1984)	Observation system measuring aberrant mother–infant interactions for birth to 18 months.	Very strong inter-rater reliability (.83–.89)
AQS Home Observation (Waters, 1987)	Observer completes 90 items based on videotaped interaction between mothers and 1–5 year-old children.	Can provide much information, but needs a great deal of training to be completed correctly.
Childrearing Behaviors and Beliefs		
Parent Behavior Checklist (Fox, 1994)	100-item rating scale; measures parents' beliefs about child-rearing	Internal consistency (.82–.97), test-retest (.81–.98). Has Spanish version.
Parenting Satisfaction Scale (Guidubaldi & Cleminshaw, 1985)	Self-report; assesses attitude toward own and spouse's parenting skills.	Reliability .76–.93. Use caution with diverse populations (Katz, 2001).
Parent Behavior Inventory (Lovejoy et al., 1999)	Rating scale that measures supportive/hostile parenting skills.	Test-retest reliability (.69–.74); convergent validity with PSI.

Family Relationships.   Table 8.1 summarizes some of the available measures addressing family relationships. One well-known and widely used scale is the Family Adaptability and Cohesion Evaluation Scales–Fourth Edition (FACES; Olson et al., 1996), which assesses how a family functions as a unit. It is fairly brief and has moderate reliability and validity. Another useful scale is the Parent-Child Relationship Inventory (Gerard, 1994), which has higher reliability and validity, but takes longer to administer. A projective measure that has received attention is the Family Relations Test (Bene & Anthony, 1978). It is not standardized, which makes it inappropriate for diagnostic use, but it could be used to gather information that does not surface from rating scales. Attachment is typically measured through observation (see Table 8.1 for a description of two observation systems). Three measures that address child-rearing beliefs and behaviors are the Parent Behavior Checklist (Fox,

TABLE 8.2.
Description of Measures Assessing Family Strengths

Scale	Description	Notes
Intrafamilial Strengths		
Family Hardiness Index (McCubbin, McCubbin, & Thompson, 1987)	20-item rating scale which measures internal strengths of the family and resistance to stressors.	Very strong internal consistency (.92), criterion validity with Family Hardiness Index ($p < .0001$)
Family Functioning Style Scale (Trivette, Dunst, Deal, Hamby, & Sexton, 1994)	26 items measuring family's perception of their strengths such as coping, commitment to one another, and values.	Criterion validity with the Family Support Scale at the $p < .0001$ level. (Trivette, et al., 1994)
Family Strengths Inventory (Stinnett & DeFrain, 1985b)	13 items to measure family strengths. (e.g., time together and communication)	Not available
Cognitive Environment		
Home Environment Survey (Gottfried & Gottfried, 1994)	Assesses learning opportunities and parental involvement in education.	Strong predictive and construct validity. Inter-rater reliability (.61–.85)
Family Involvement Questionnaire (Fantuzzo, Tighe & Childs, 2000)	Assesses parental home and school-based involvement in education	High reliability (.85) with evidence of construct validity.
Extrafamilial Strengths		
Family Support Scale (Dunst, Jenkins, & Trivette, 1984)	18-item rating scale to assess degree of external family supports (e.g., extended family, social service agencies).	Adequately reliable and valid. Test-retest (.91). Caution with diagnosis (Bradley, 1993).

1994), the Parenting Satisfaction Scale (Guidubaldi & Cleminshaw, 1985) and the Parent Behavior Inventory (Lovejoy, Weis, O'Hare, & Rubin, 1999), which are reviewed in Table 8.1.

Strengths.   Dunst and Trivette, leaders in the field of family strengths, have developed a number of scales that are described in Table 8.2 (e.g., Trivette et al., 1994). A family's strengths can be divided into two categories: intrafamilial (those within the family; e.g., communication) and extrafamilial (those from outside the family; e.g., church, school). Cognitive measures can be placed in a category of their own due to the important role this specific aspect of environment can play in a child's success (e.g., Bradley et al., 2001). Table 8.2 provides information on suggested measures for assessing such strengths.

Stressors.   The Parenting Stress Index (Abidin, 1995) is a 120-item self-report measure with the specific purpose of identifying problems in parent-child interactions that may place the child at risk for adjustment. It can be administered to parents with children 12 years or younger, including preschoolers. A short form is also available. This is an extremely widely used and psychometrically sound measure. One of its many strengths is that it examines not only parent characteristics, but also child characteristics and demographic factors. A well-established measure for parental mental health is the Beck Depression Inven-

TABLE 8.3.
Description of Measures Assessing Family Stressors

Scale	Description	Notes
Parenting Stressors		
Parenting Stress Index (Abidin, 1995)	120-item parent self-report; identifies problems in parent-child interactions.	High internal consistency (.95). Strong test-retest reliability (.96).
Addiction Severity Index (McClellan et al., 1992)	Assesses parental addiction and substance abuse.	Strong construct validity. Other psychometric properties vary, but are continually being improved.
Beck Depression Inventory–II (Beck, Steer, & Brown, 1996)	Measures depression in adults and adolescents.	Reliability (.80). Discriminant validity (.92). Well normed.
Child Maltreatment		
Conflict Tactics Scale-Parent/ Child (Strauss, Hamby, Finkelhor, Moore, & Runyan, 1988)	Extension of the Conflict Tactic Scale–II to assess abuse and neglect.	Reliability is low to moderate; evidence of discriminant and construct validity.
Child Abuse Potential Inventory (Milner, 1986)	160-item rating scale to screen for abuse.	Includes a lie scale. Internal consistency (.92–.96). Test-retest reliability (.71–.91).
Checklist for Child Abuse Evaluation (Petty, 1988)	Informal checklist of factors that are commonly associated with child abuse	Not standardized, but helpful in guiding the observer/ assessor.
Other		
Family Needs Scale (Dunst, Trivette, & Deal, 1988)	Assesses six domains of family needs such as shelter and child care.	High internal consistency and validity.
Life Experiences Survey (Sarason, Johnson, & Siegel, 1978)	57 item rating scale which assesses life stressors.	Test-retest reliability (.64); Training needed to administer properly.

tory–II (Beck, Steer, & Brown, 1996). Child maltreatment can be assessed with the Conflict Tactics Scale–Parent/Child (Strauss, Hamby, Finkelhor, Moore, & Runyan, 1988), as well as other available measures. General stressors on the family should also be evaluated, and applicable measures are described in Table 8.3.

LIMITATIONS

Understanding family and home dynamics is essential for conducting comprehensive, ecologically valid assessments of preschool children, however, there are limitations that may impede a professional's ability to gain accurate and meaningful information. First, the reliability and validity of these assessment results could be affected in many ways. Because a parent's relationship with a child is personal and emotionally laden, parents may knowingly or unknowingly compromise the results of assessments by answering in socially desirable ways during interviews and rating scales or by behaving differently when observed. In addition, family and home dynamics is a very broad construct that is difficult to define and assess accurately. Mahoney, Spiker, and Boyce (1996) criticized existing established protocols assessing parent-child interactions for their questionable content, construct, and criterion validity, as many are based on qualities that have been assumed to be important yet are not empirically related, to outcomes. They also raised the issue that there are low correlations between measures purporting to assess the same constructs.

A more practical limitation involves the home setting and the role of professionals within that setting. Professionals may feel awkward, unsafe, or ill-prepared to interact with families within their homes. In addition, many service providers are from the dominant culture and lack sufficient training in family dynamics/systems and ethnic and cultural diversity (Hanson & Lynch, 1992), which may contribute to feelings of frustration or discomfort when encountering people with language and cultures unlike their own (Hanson & Lynch, 1990).

Similarly, families may not be comfortable having professionals in their homes and may question the need for intervention. Halpern (1993) raised the important issue about the tendency for professionals in American society to view multiply disadvantaged families (e.g., those in poverty, child with a disability) as needing expert intervention instead of relying on the experiences of the family and community. This perspective may be at odds with the family's needs and beliefs.

RECOMMENDATIONS FOR PRACTICE/FUTURE DIRECTIONS

We have argued for the importance of assessing family and home dynamics, a view that is consistent with current legislation and ideology in the field. Given the number of considerations that face professionals doing this work, it is imperative that training programs, as well as educational and service agencies, instill this value and train personnel to do this specialized work. Assessments should be performed with attention to the individual needs and values of families and should use a multiple method approach that includes interviews to develop rapport and obtain information, and psychometrically sound observation systems and rating scales. There is also a need to more clearly define important constructs in family and home dynamics and to develop corresponding measures that assess these constructs reliably and validly.

REFERENCES

Abidin, R. (1995). *Parenting Stress Index*. Odessa, FL: Psychological Assessment Resources.

Ainsworth, M. D. S., Blehar, M. C., Waters, E., & Wall, S. (1978). *Patterns of attachment: A psychological study of the strange situation*. Hillsdale, NJ: Lawrence Erlbaum Associates.

Ainsworth, M. D. S., & Bowlby, J. (1991). An ethological approach to personality development. *American Psychologist, 46*, 333–341.

Bagarozzi, D. (1984). Family measurement techniques. *The American Journal of Family Therapy, 12*, 59–62.

Bagnato, S. J., & Neisworth, J. T. (1991). *Assessment for early intervention: Best practices for professionals*. New York: Guilford Press.

Bank, L., & Burraston, B. (2001). Abusive home environments as predictors of poor adjustment during adolescence and adulthood. *Journal of Community Psychology, 29*, 195–217.

Banks, J. A. (1988). Ethnicity, class, cognitive, and motivational styles: Research and teaching implications. *Journal of Negro Education, 57,* 452–466.

Barnett, D. W., Lentz, F. E., Bauer, A. M., Macmann, G., Stollar, S., & Ehrhardt, K. E. (1997). Ecological foundations of early intervention: Planned activities and strategic sampling. *Journal of Special Education, 30,* 471–490.

Baumrind, D. (1980). New directions in socialization research. *American Psychologist, 35,* 639–652.

Beck, A. T., Steer, R. A., & Brown, G. K. (1996). *Manual for the Beck Depression Inventory* (2nd ed.). San Antonio, TX: The Psychological Corporation.

Bene, E., & Anthony, E. (1978). *Manual for Family Relations Test.* National Foundation for Educational Research in England and Wales, London.

Benzies, K., Harrison, M., Magill-Evans, J. (2004). Parenting stress, marital quality, and child behavior problems at age 7 years. *Public Health Nursing, 21,* 111–121.

Bradley, R. H. (1993). Assessment of the home environment. In J. Culbertson & D. Willis (Eds.), *Testing young children* (pp. 128–166). Austin, TX: PRO-ED.

Bradley, R. H., Caldwell, B. M., Rock, S. L., Ramey, C. T., Barnard, K. E., Gray, C., Hammond, M. A., Mitchell, S., Gottfried, A. W., Siegel, L., & Johnson, D. L. (1989). Home environment and cognitive development in the first three years of life: A collaborative study involving six sites and three ethnic groups in North America. *Developmental Psychology, 25,* 217–235.

Bradley, R., Corwyn, R., Burchinal, M., McAdoo, H., & Coll, C. (2001). The home environments of children in the United States part II: Relations with behavioral development through age thirteen. *Child Development, 72,* 1868–1886.

Bradley, R., Corwyn, R., & Whiteside-Mansel, L. (1996). Life at home: Same time, different places. An examination of the HOME Inventory in different cultures. *Early Development and Parenting, 5,* 251–269.

Bradley, R., Mundfrom, D., Casey, P., & Barrett, K. (1994). A factor analytic study of the infant-toddler and early childhood versions of the HOME inventory administered to White, Black, and Hispanic American parents of children born preterm. *Child Development, 65,* 880–888.

Bronfenbrenner, U. (1986). Ecology of the family as a context for human development: Research perspectives. *Developmental Psychology, 22,* 723–742.

Brook, J. S., Whiteman, M., Shapiro, J., & Choen, P. (1996). Effects of parent drug use and personality on toddler adjustment. *The Journal of Genetic Psychology, 157,* 19–35.

Brooks-Gunn, J., & Duncan, G. J. (1997). The effects of poverty on children. *The Future of Children, 7,* 55–71.

Burry, C. L. (2002). Working with potentially violent clients in their homes: What child welfare professionals need to know. *The Clinical Supervisor, 21,* 145–153.

Caldwell, B. M., & Bradley, R. H. (2001). *Home inventory and administration manual* (3rd ed.). University of Arkansas for Medical Sciences and University of Arkansas at Little Rock.

Carlson, C. (1992). Review of the Family Relations Test: Children's Version. In J. J. Kramwe & J. C. Conoley (Eds.). *The eleventh mental measurement yearbook.* Buros Institute: University of Nebraska Press.

Christie-Mizell, C., Steelman, L. C., & Stewart, J. (2003). Seeing their surroundings: The effects of neighborhood setting and race on maternal distress. *Social Science Research, 32,* 402–428.

Cohen, L. G., & Spenciner, L. J. (2003). *Assessment of children and youth with special needs* (2nd ed.). Boston: Pearson Education.

Cohen, S., & Wills, T. A. (1985). Stress, social support, and the buffering hypothesis, *Psychological Bulletin, 98,* 310–357.

Doll, B., & Lyon, M. A. (1998). Risk and resilience: Implications for the delivery of educational and mental health services in schools. *School Psychology Review, 27,* 348–363.

Dunst, C., Jenkins, V., & Trivette, C. (1984). Family Support Scale: Reliability and validity. *Journal of Individual, Family and Community Wellness, 1,* 45–52.

Dunst, C., & Leet, J. (1987). Measuring the adequacy of resources in households with young children. *Child Care Health and Development, 13*, 114–125.

Dunst, C., Trivette, C., & Deal, A. (1988). *Enabling and empowering families: Principles and guidelines for practice.* Cambridge, MA: Brookline Books.

Elicker, J., Englund, M., & Sroufe, L. A. (1992). Predicting peer competence and peer relationships in childhood from early parent-child relationships. In R. D. Parke & G. W. Ladd (Eds.), *Family-peer relationships: Modes of linkage* (pp. 77–106). Hillsdale, NJ: Lawrence Erlbaum Associates.

Entwisle, D. R., & Alexander, K. L. (1996). Family type and children's growth in reading and math over the primary grades. *Journal of Marriage and the Family, 58*, 341–355.

Fantuzzo, J., Tighe, E., & Childs, S. (2000). Family Involvement Questionnaire: A multivariate assessment of family participation in early childhood education, *Journal of Educational Psychology, 92*, 367–376.

Farver, J. M., Natera, L. X., & Frosch, D. L. (1999). Effects of community violence on inner-city preschoolers and their families. *Journal of Applied Developmental Psychology, 20*, 143–158.

Feldman, P., & Steptoe, A. (2004). How neighborhoods and physical functioning are related: The roles of neighborhood socioeconomic status, perceived neighborhood strain, and individual health risk factors. *Annals of Behavioral Medicine, 27*, 91–99.

Fewell, R. R. (2000). Assessment of young children with special needs: Foundations for tomorrow. *Topics in Early Childhood Special Education, 20*, 38–42.

Fox, R. A. (1994). *Parent Behavior Checklist.* Austin, TX: PRO-ED.

Gallagher, J. J. (2000). The beginnings of federal help for young children with disabilities. *Topics in Early Childhood Special Education, 20*, 3–6.

Gelfand, D. M., & Teti, D. M. (1990). The effects of maternal depression on children. *Clinical Psychology Review, 10*, 329–353.

Gerard, A. B. (1994). *Parent-Child Relationship Inventory (PCRI) Manual.* Los Angeles, CA: Western Psychological Services.

Gersten, J. C. (1992). Families in poverty. In M. E. Procidano & C. B. Fisher (Eds.), *Contemporary families: A handbook for school professionals* (pp. 137–158). New York: Teachers College Press.

Gringlas, M., & Weintraub, M. (1995). The more things change . . . single parenting revisited. *Journal of Family Issues, 16*, 29–52.

Guidubaldi, J., & Cleminshaw, H. (1985). The development of the Cleminshaw-Guidubaldi Parent Satisfaction Scale. *Journal of Clinical Child Psychology, 14*, 293–298.

Halloran, E., Ross, G., & Carey, M. (2002). The relationship of adolescent personality and family environment to psychiatric diagnosis. *Child Psychiatry and Human Development, 32*, 201–216.

Halpern, R. (1993). The societal context of home visiting and related services for families in poverty. *The Future of Children, 3*, 158–171.

Hanson, M. J., & Lynch, E. W. (1990). Honoring the cultural diversity of families when gathering data. *Topics in Early Childhood Special Education, 10*, 112–131.

Hanson, M. J., & Lynch, E. W. (1992). Family diversity: Implications for policy and practice. *Topics in Early Childhood Special Education, 12*, 283–306.

Hetherington, E. M. (1999). Should we stay together for the sake of the children? In E. M. Hetherington (Ed.), *Coping with divorce, single parenting, and remarriage* (pp. 93–116). Mahwah, NJ: Lawrence Erlbaum Associates.

Hollingshead, A. B., & Redlich, F. C. (1958). *Social class and mental illness.* New York: John Wiley & Sons.

Kalesnik, K. J. (1999). Family assessment. In E. V. Nuttall, I. Romero, & J. Kalesnik (Eds.), *Assessing and screening preschoolers: Psychological and educational dimensions* (2nd ed., pp. 112–125). Needham Heights, MA: Allyn and Bacon.

Kaplan, S.J., Pelcovitz, D., & Labruna, V. (1999). Child and adolescent abuse and neglect research: A review of the past 10 years. Part I: Physical and emotional abuse and neglect. *Journal of the American Academy of Child and Adolescent Psychiatry, 38*, 1214–1222.

Katz, I. (2001) Review of Parenting Satisfaction Scale. In B. S. Plake & J. C. Impara (Eds.). *The fourteenth mental measurement yearbook.* Buros Institute: University of Nebraska Press.

Kern, J., West, E., Grannemann, B., Greer, T. Snell, L., Cline, L., VanBeveren, T., Heartwell, S., Kleiber, B., & Trivedi, M. (2004). Reductions in stress and depressive symptoms in mothers of substance exposed infants participating in a psychosocial program. *Maternal and Child Health Journal, 8,* 127–136.

Klebanov, P. K., Brooks-Gunn, J., & Duncan, G. J. (1994). Does neighborhood and family poverty affect mothers' parenting, mental health, and social support? *Journal of Marriage and the Family, 56,* 441–455.

Latzer, Y., Hochdorf, Z., Bachar, E., & Canetti, L. (2002). Attachment style and family functioning as discriminating factors in eating disorders. *Contemporary Family Therapy: An International Journal, 24,* 581–599.

Lovejoy, C., Weis, R., O'Hare, E., & Rubin, E. (1999). Development and initial validation of the Parent Behavior Inventory. *Psychological Assessment, 11,* 534–545.

Mahoney, G., Spiker, D., & Boyce, G. (1996). Clinical assessments of parent-child interaction: Are professionals ready to implement this practice? *Topics in Early Childhood Special Education, 16,* 26–50.

Malinosky-Rummel, R., & Hansen, D. J. (1993). Long-term consequences of childhood physical abuse. *Psychological Bulletin, 114,* 68–79.

Mancini, J. (2001). Review of the Family Environment Scale [Third Edition Manual]. In B. S. Plake & J. C. Impara (Eds.). *The fourteenth mental measurements yearbook.* Buros Institute: University of Nebraska Press.

Martin, S. E., & Clements, M. L. (2002). Young children's responding to interparental conflict: Associations with marital aggression and child adjustment. *Journal of Child and Family Studies, 11,* 231–244.

Massie, H. N., & Campbell, B. K. (1984). The Massie-Campbell Scale of Mother Infant Attachment Indicators During Stress. In H. N. Massie, & J. Rosenthall (Eds.), *Childhood psychosis in the first four years of life* (pp. 253–282). NY: McGraw-Hill.

McBride, S. L. (1999). Family centered practices. *Young Children, 54,* 62–68.

McClellan, A. T., Kushner, H., Metzger, D., Peters, R., Smith, I., Grissom, G., Pettinati, H., & Argeriou, M., (1992). The fifth edition of the addiction severity index. *Journal of Substance Abuse Treatment, 9,* 199–213.

McConaughy, S. H., & Ritter, D. R. (2002). Best practices in multidimensional assessment of emotional or behavioral disorders. In A. Thomas & J. Grimes (Eds.), *Best practices in school psychology IV* (pp. 1303–1320). Washington, DC: National Association of School Psychologists.

McCroskey, J., & Nishimoto, R. (1991). Assessment in family support programs: Initial reliability and validity testing of the family assessment form. *Child Welfare, 70,* 19–33.

McCubbin, M., McCubbin, H., & Thompson, A. (1987). Family Hardiness Index. In H. I. McCubbin & A. I. Thompson (Eds.), *Family assessment inventories for research and practice* (pp. 125–130). Madison, WI: University of Wisconsin.

McLean, M. E., & Odom, S. L. (1996). Establishing recommended practices in early intervention/ early childhood special education. In S. L. Odom & M. E. McLean (Eds.), *Early intervention/ early childhood special education: Recommended practices* (pp. 1–22). Austin, TX: PRO-ED.

McLennan, J. D., & Kotelchuck, M. (2000). Parental prevention practices for young children in the context of maternal depression. *Pediatrics, 105,* 1090–1095.

McLoyd, V. C. (1998). Socioeconomic disadvantage and child development. *American Psychologist, 53,* 185–204.

McLoyd, V. C., Jayaratne, T. E., Ceballo, R., & Borquez, J. (1994). Unemployment and work interruption among African American single mothers: Effects on parenting and adolescent socioemotional functioning. *Child Development, 65,* 562–589.

Milner, J. S. (1986). *The Child Abuse Potential Inventory: Manual* (2nd ed.). Webster, NC: Psytec.

Molfese, V., Dilalla, L., & Bunce, D. (1997). Prediction of intelligence scores of 3- to 8-year-old children by home environment, socioeconomic status and biomedical risks. *Merrill-Palmer Quarterly, 43*, 219–234.

Molfese, V. J., & Molfese, D. L. (2002). Environmental and social influences on reading skills as indexed by brain and behavioral responses. *Annals of Dyslexia, 52*, 121–137.

Moos, R. H., & Moos, B. S. (1994). *Family Environment Scale manual* (3rd ed.). Palo Alto, CA: Consulting Psychologists Press.

Neisworth, J. T., & Bagnato, S. J. (1996). Assessment for early intervention: Emerging themes and practices. In S. L. Odom & M. E. McLean (Eds.), *Early intervention/early childhood special education: Recommended practices* (pp. 23–57). Austin, TX: PRO-ED.

NICD Early Child Care Research Network (2001). Before Head Start: Income and ethnicity, family characteristics, child care experiences, and child development. *Early Education and Development, 12*, 545–576.

Olson, D., Geisel, J., & Gorall, D. (1996). *Family Adaptability and Cohesion Evaluation Scales–IV.* St. Paul, MN: Family and Social Sciences, University of Minnesota.

Parke, R. D., O'Neil, R., Isley, S., Spitzer, S., Welsh, M., Wang, S., Flyr, M., Simpkins, S., Strand, C., & Morales, M. (1998). Family-peer relationships: Cognitive, emotional, and ecological determinants. In M. Lewis & C. Feiring (Eds.), *Families, risk, and competence* (pp. 89–112). Mahwah, NJ: Lawrence Erlbaum Associates.

Patterson, G. R. (1986). Performance models for antisocial boys. *American Psychologist, 41*, 432–444.

Patterson, S. M., & Albers, A. B. (2001). Effects of poverty and maternal depression on early child development. *Child Development, 72*, 1794–1813.

Petty, J. (1988). *Checklist for Child Abuse Evaluation.* Lutz, FL: Psychological Assessment Resources, Inc.

Roosa, M., & Beals, J. (1990). Measurement issues in family assessment: The case of the Family Environment Scale. *Family Process, 29*, 191–198.

Rousey, A., Wild, M., & Blacher, J. (2002). Stability of measures of the home environment for families of children with severe disabilities. *Research in Developmental Disabilities, 23*, 17–35.

Rutter, M. (1985). Resilience in the face of adversity: Protective factors and resistance to psychiatric disorder. *British Journal of Psychiatry, 147*, 598–611.

Sanford, K., Bingham, R., & Zucker, R. (1999). Validity issues with the Family Environment Scale: Psychometric resolution and research application with alcoholic families. *Psychometrics, 11*, 315–325.

Sarason, I., Johnson J., & Siegel, J. (1978). Assessing the impact of life change: Development of the Life Experiences Survey. *Journal of Consulting and Clinical Psychology, 46*, 932–946.

Schneider, B. H. (1993). *Children's social competence in context: The contributions of family, school, and culture.* New York: Pergamon Press.

Shulman, S. (1995). *Close relationships and socioemotional development. Human Development* (Vol. 7). Norwood, NJ: Ablex.

Skinner, H., Steinhauer, P., & Sitarenios, G. (2000). Family Assessment Measure (FAM) and process model of family functioning. *Journal of Family Therapy, 22*, 190–209.

Spillane, S. (2001). Review of the Family Assessment Measure Version III. In B. S. Plake & J. C. Impara (Eds.). *The fourteenth mental measurement yearbook.* Buros Institute: University of Nebraska Press.

Sroufe, L. A. (1988). The role of infant-caregiver attachment in development. In J. Belsky & T. Nezworski (Eds.), *Clinical implications of attachment* (pp. 18–88). Hillsdale, NJ: Lawrence Erlbaum Associates.

Stinnett, N., & DeFrain, J. (1985b). Family Strengths Inventory. In N. Stinnet & J. DeFrain (Eds.), *Secrets of strong families* (pp. 180–182). New York: Berkley Books.

Strauss, M., Hamby, S., Finkelhor, D., Moore, D., & Runyan, D. (1988). Identification of child maltreatment with the Parent-Child Conflict Tactics Scales: Development and psychometric data for a national sample of American parents. *Child Abuse and Neglect, 22*, 249–270.

Suchman, N. E., & Luthar, S. S. (2000). Maternal addiction, child maladjustment and socio-demographic risks: implications for parenting behaviors. *Addiction, 95*, 1417–28.

Totsika, V., & Sylva, K. (2004). The Home Observation for Measurement of the Environment Revisited. *Child and Adolescent Mental Health, 9,* 25–35.

Trivette, C., Dunst, C., Deal, A., Hamby, D., & Sexton, D. (1994). Assessing family strengths and capabilities. In C.J. Dunst, C.M. Trivette, & A.G. Deal (Eds.), *Supporting and strengthening families, Vol 1: Methods, strategies and practices* (pp. 132–138). Cambridge, MA: Brookline.

Vuchinich, S., Bank, L., & Patterson, G. R. (1992). Parenting, peers, and the stability of antisocial behavior in preadolescent boys. *Developmental Psychology, 28*, 510–521.

Waters, E. (1987). Attachment Behavior Q-Set (Revision 3.0). Unpublished instrument, State University of New York at Stony Brook, Department of Psychology.

White, K. S., Bruce, S. E., Farrell, A. D., & Kliewer, W. (1998). Impact of exposure to community violence on anxiety: A longitudinal study of family social support as a protective factor for urban children. *Journal of Child and Family Studies, 7*, 187–203.

Zimet, D. M., & Jacob, T. (2001). Influences of marital conflict on child adjustment: Review of theory and research. *Clinical Child and Family Psychology Review*, 4, 319–335.

9

Assessment of School and Classroom Environment

Sandra G. Gagnon
Appalachian State University

Pamela Kidder-Ashley
Appalachian State University

Amanda B. Nickerson
University at Albany, SUNY

The traditional method of looking for problems within the child has been met with discontent by many psychologists and educators involved in the assessment of preschool children. This general dissatisfaction with the medical model (Rubin & Ballow, 1971), combined with the increasing acceptance of the ecological perspective, which describes behaviors as arising from interactions between children and their environments (Algozzine, 1976), has prompted a change from a within-child approach to identifying problems and diagnosing disabilities to a social-ecological approach (Schroeder, Schroeder, & Landesman, 1987) in which children are assessed within their surrounding environments, and results are used to inform educational programming. The trend toward increased consideration of the social environment in clinical assessment has a long history, dating back to the 1960s (Wahler, House, & Stambaugh, 1976), though movement toward this approach has been slow. It is no longer considered best practice to conduct assessments of preschool children independent of their environments.

For children who attend day care or preschool programs, these settings provide important contextual frameworks from which to view the development of school-related skills. Though the reasons for evaluating classrooms and schools are readily apparent, these contextual aspects of preschoolers' development and functioning have not historically been included in assessments, nor focused on by trainers. This chapter will acquaint readers with a novel, contextually based approach to assessing children's learning environments that easily relates to the development of interventions. We will review a theory that is particularly relevant, yet often ignored, within the context of preschool assessment, describe indicators of quality in early childhood programs, and present an alternative conceptualization of the developmental domains typically characterizing preschool assessment. The reader also should gain information about effective, empirically based methods and instruments for conducting these assessments within the conceptual framework presented. Practical suggestions to assist evaluators and interventionists with the implementation of such assessments also will be provided.

INTRODUCTION TO THE CONCEPTUAL FRAMEWORK

The aforementioned approach to conceptualizing the assessment of school and classroom environments will be described next, with three major components receiving focus. First, the theoretical foundation of the approach will be presented, followed by dimensions of early childhood programs to include in assessments. The section will conclude with a reconceptualization of developmental domains for young children.

Theory.   In their discussion of the application of ecological assessment within the classroom, McLellan and Sanchez (1997) emphasize the importance of focusing on external rather than internal influences on children's functioning. Yet, traditional approaches to assessment tend to focus on identifying internal, or child-specific, influences. One theoretical model that merges these two perspectives is the "goodness-of-fit" model. First proposed by Thomas and Chess in the mid-1970s (Thomas & Chess, 1977), the goodness-of-fit model provides a useful framework for considering both external and internal influences on a child's functioning, with particular emphasis on how the two interact to produce child outcomes.

As originally conceptualized, the goodness-of-fit model focused on one particular aspect of internal child functioning—temperament—and how it interacts with environmental demands. Defined as "behavioral style," or "the characteristic way that the individual experiences and responds to the internal and external environment" (Carey, 1998; Thomas & Chess, 1977), temperament is an aspect of child development that is well known and supported in the literature as an important variable in child development. However, this construct is seldom considered within the context of formal early childhood assessment (Carey & McDevitt, 1995), despite its demonstrated relationship with various important child outcomes. For example, some aspects of parent- and teacher-rated temperament have demonstrated significant relationships with intelligence (Martin, 1988b; Martin & Holbrook, 1985), academic ability (Burchinal, Peisner-Feinburg, Pianta, & Howes, 2002; Lerner, Lerner, & Zabski, 1985), achievement (Martin & Holbrook, 1985; Pullis & Cadwell, 1982), classroom behaviors (Billman & McDevitt, 1980; Martin, Nagle, & Paget, 1983; Paget, Nagle, & Martin, 1984), and school adjustment (Carey, Fox, & McDevitt 1977; Garrison, Earls, & Kindlon, 1984). Persistence, distractibility, and adaptability are most often cited as significant temperamental traits in these relationships. Because evidence supports the relationships between children's innate styles of responding emotionally to the environment and a variety of school-related behaviors, it is strongly recommended that practitioners incorporate measures of temperament in their evaluations of young children and, according to Carey's (1998) recommendations, consider "maladaptive" temperamental traits to exist as extremes on the continuum of "normal variations of behavioral style," and thus not in and of themselves leading to dysfunction.

Although originally focused on temperament and its interaction with environmental characteristics and demands, the goodness-of-fit model can be broadened to incorporate other important child characteristics or individual differences. As such, it provides an excellent framework from which to approach the assessment of preschoolers' classroom environments and should contribute positively to assessments and resulting interventions (Carey, 1998).

According to the original goodness-of-fit model, when child temperament and environmental demands are well-matched, favorable child outcomes are produced. In contrast, when the structures and demands characterizing the environment are not well suited to a child's temperament, a "poor fit" results, characterized by problems in child development and outcomes. Carey explains that dysfunction often results from discordant relationships between temperamentally "difficult" children and environments that are incompatible with those temperaments. Specifically, a "poor fit," rather than temperamental traits alone, typically results in stress and problems in behavioral, social, and/or academic functioning. Thus, different children who are similar in their temperaments (or similar in other important characteristics, to apply the model more broadly) may experience a variety of outcomes, depending on the quality of the fit between child characteristics and environmental demands. When problems are viewed within this context, as opposed to the traditional medical model of diagnosing pathology within individual children, interventions can focus on modifying the fit rather than attempting to change individual characteristics of the child. To apply this model to the practice of preschool assessment, one must assess the goodness of fit between important individual child characteristics and the child's educational environment, which includes such variables as the physical environment, classroom structure/routine, classroom and school climate, and teacher involvement. Because of its historical importance in shaping the goodness-of-fit model, we have focused on temperament as an important individual child variable to evaluate within the context of a goodness-of-fit framework. There are, however, other individual difference variables that contribute to the quality of fit between children and their environments, such as intelligence/cognitive ability, culture/ethnicity, gender, socioeconomic status, and disability status (including ADHD, as seen below.)

In a broadened application of the model, Greene (1996) provides an excellent rationale for the use of a goodness-of-fit approach to assessing and intervening with children with Attention Deficit Hyperactivity Disorder (ADHD), emphasizing the importance of situation specificity in the assessment of ADHD-related behaviors, as contextual factors contribute much to their presentation. Rather than focusing on the effectiveness of individualized interventions, as has historically been the practice, we should consider important interactional and contextual factors, such as the degrees of compatibility, or goodness of fit, between students and teachers, teachers and prescribed treatments, and students and treatments. Greene's work, though specific to the assessment of children with ADHD, illustrates how a goodness-of-fit framework can be applied to a variety of childhood characteristics, problems, and disorders.

Dimensions of Program Quality.   High-quality preschool programs contribute significantly to children's development and long-term school performance (Schweinhart & Weikart, 1989). Preschoolers who attend high-quality preschools compare favorably to those who do not, with stronger performance on measures of cognitive and academic functioning and more positive social and behavioral outcomes, even through adolescence (Schweinhart & Weikart, 1989). With this information in mind, one recognizes the importance of including assessments of the preschool classroom and school environments in evaluations of individual children with disabilities.

Researchers in early childhood typically employ a framework of four broad components characterizing young children's care and learning environments (Aytch, Cryer, Biley,

& Selz, 1999). *Contextual* features describe the actual setting in which care takes place, which might be a child care facility or classroom in a public or private school. Because this variable is obvious and easy to assess, it will not be included in our subsequent discussion of program quality. *Global* aspects, which are positively associated with child outcomes, refer to a combination of broad qualities of classrooms, such as available materials, arrangement of space, and schedules (Aytch et al., 1999; Kontos, Burchinal, Howes, Wisseh, & Galinsky, 2002). *Structural* characteristics refer to the specific framework of the setting, including such features as group size, adult-child ratios, or teacher education, within which individual children's dynamic experiences, or *processes*, take place (Aytch et al., 1999). *Process* variables include such aspects as interactions with adults and peers and actual activities engaged in (Cryer, Tietze, Burchinal, Leal, & Palacios, 1999; Phillips & Howes, 1987). Aspects of these four dimensions have demonstrated relationships to important child outcomes and to one another, with structural and process characteristics standing out as the major variables investigated (Cryer, et al., 1999).

Child Outcomes Redefined.   In order to evaluate preschool environments, the desired child outcomes must be identified and operationalized. In other words, what are the goals of preschool educational programs concerning individual children? These goals should inform and guide curricular planning, program evaluation, and assessments of individual children within the program. Once these desired outcomes are determined, consideration and arrangement of environmental variables that promote their development should be undertaken. The major domains typically assessed with preschoolers include language, social, cognitive, motor, and adaptive skills (McConnell, Priest, Davis, & McEvoy, 2002). In addition to these well-known domains, an alternative, conceptually-based model of child competencies has been proposed and will be described briefly.

The practical application of the goodness-of-fit model is presented in a chapter by Schwartz, Garfinkle, and Davis (2002), whose proposed framework reflects both the need for high-quality programming and the achievement of individual child outcomes. The authors emphasize the importance of evaluating "the match between an individual child's needs and the corresponding supports available in that environment" (p. 456), while criticizing the use of traditional, norm-based, standardized tests because of their lack of contextual focus. In their investigation of outcomes necessary for success in inclusive preschool settings, Schwartz, Staub, Gallucci, and Peck (1995) delineated a framework that appears consistent with the trend toward more ecologically-based assessments and reflects the goodness-of-fit model. This framework "describes outcomes without the constraints imposed by traditional developmental and educational domains" (Schwartz et al., 2002, p. 458) and consists of three interrelated domains: *membership*, *relationships*, and *knowledge/ skills*. A brief description of each child outcome domain will be provided next; the reader is referred to the chapter for a more detailed explanation of these concepts.

According to the authors, *membership* is defined as the degree to which the individual child is accepted into and participates in groups, or the child's "sense of belonging" (Schwartz et al., 2002, p. 459) achieved through formal and informal activities such as participating in class meetings or being included in outdoor play activities. The concept of a child's membership is related to more traditional aspects of group social interaction, such as the child's initiation of activity and response to interactions. This domain is in contrast to *relationships*, the second child outcome domain described by Schwartz and colleagues. *Relationships* are defined as involving the child's interactions with individual peers and are considered to be more complex than the child's membership. The authors describe different categories of relationships, which capture the nature of the various relationships a child experiences with peers, such as play/companionship or helper/helpee. Keeping the goodness-of-fit perspective in mind, one should evaluate both membership and relationships in terms of how the temperaments of individual children fit within the environmental demands of the classroom. For example, in an evaluation of a child's difficulty with membership, as evidenced by rejection by his or her peer group, characteristics of the environment that might be contributing to a poor fit might include the physical arrangement of space and materials in the classroom, or the grouping of children during activities. Either of these variables can be altered to promote a good fit and, thus, improve the child's social competence. This approach is superior to a more traditional evaluation of a child with social skills problems, which might involve the use of norm-based rating scales and observations to determine the degree of clinical significance of the behaviors exhibited, as well as information regarding how the child's behaviors compare to same-age peers in the normative sample. The traditional approach emphasizes the individual child as the source of the problem and leads to a focus on changing internal traits of the child, which are often not alterable and, thus, are not appropriate targets for interventions.

The third and final domain represents the most traditional and familiar child outcome and is typically the easiest to quantify (Schwartz et al., 2002). *Knowledge/skills* involves the child's capacities that are typically assessed individually, such as cognitive, language, motor, and social skills. Though not usually assessed from a contextual perspective, knowledge and skills are affected by physical and social aspects of the classroom environment, as will be described in subsequent sections.

Schwartz and colleagues (2002) contend that all three child outcome domains should be considered within the context of individual assessments and educational planning for children with disabilities in order to provide a meaningful picture of a child's educational progress. Similarly, we contend that utilization of this outcome framework, as opposed to the traditional approach that emphasizes more specific, discrete skills or outcomes, should provide an expanded, more holistic perspective on children's development and progress within preschool classrooms.

PROPOSED MODEL FOR ASSESSING PRESCHOOL ENVIRONMENTS

Having presented information on the underlying theory, relevant quality indicators, and important developmental outcomes, we now propose a contextually based approach to the ecological assessment of preschool environments. Using goodness-of-fit theory as the core conceptual framework shifts the focus from looking for problems that lie within the child to analyzing the broad and specific aspects of the learning environment to discover which elements may be impeding the progress of individual children in particular developmental domains. We propose that broad and specific assessment methods and tools should be used to evaluate global, structural, and process variables that contribute to the development of skills in the areas of membership, relationships, and knowledge/skills.

The following section will describe *global* dimensions of the preschool environment, including curricular and physical aspects, available materials, and class schedules/routines. Contextual, or *structural*, aspects of the classroom also will be described, such as teacher education, adult-child ratios, group size, adult responsibilities, and parent involvement. Finally, the actual interactions, or *processes*, children engage in will be presented, such as student-teacher relationships and peer relationships. (Because the assessment of cognitive, developmental, and other specific skill areas is covered in other chapters of this text, those process aspects will not be included here.) Empirically based approaches and instruments used in the assessment of the previously described dimensions also will be presented. It should be noted that the limitations of this chapter preclude coverage of all variables within each dimension of the preschool environment. Our intent is to present information that will provide readers a strong foundation for the many varied aspects of the school and classroom environment that may be examined as they relate to the developmental progress of individual children with disabilities.

Global Dimensions

Curriculum.   Curriculum, as defined by the recent Joint Position Statement of the National Association for the Education of Young Children (NAEYC) and the National Association of Early Childhood Specialists in State Departments of Education (NAECS/SDE) (2003), is "a complex idea containing multiple components, such as goals, content, pedagogy, or instructional practices" that is affected by "many factors, including society's values, content standards, accountability systems, research findings, community expectations, culture and language, and individual children's characteristics" (p. 6). The early childhood literature contains some disagreement and conflict regarding the most appropriate curriculum for typically developing children and those with disabilities (Carta, Schwartz, & Atwater, 1991).

The NAEYC recommends the use of what some purport to be *Developmentally Appropriate Practice* (DAP; Bredekamp, 1987; Bredekamp & Copple, 1997; Sandall, McLean, & Smith, 2000), a constructivist approach involving student-initiated, hands-on activities (Huffman & Speer, 2000). DAP has demonstrated positive associations with cognitive functioning (Bryant, Burchinal, Lau, & Sparling, 1994), letter/word recognition and math reasoning skills (Huffman, & Speer, 2000), and school readiness (Bryant et al., 1994) in preschool and kindergarten children, as well as increased rates of high school graduation, fewer arrests, and higher monthly incomes in adults (Schweinhart & Weikart, 1993). Classrooms rated as lower in the use of DAP have reported low motivation as a negative child outcome (Stipek, Feiler, Daniels, & Milburn, 1995).

In contrast to the underlying philosophy of DAP are highly structured, didactic approaches to instruction, often referred to as *Developmentally Inappropriate Practice*s (DIP). DIP, though considered by many to be more appropriate for children from low-income and culturally diverse families (Gersten, Darch, & Gleason, 1988; Stipek & Byler, 1997), have demonstrated negative links with child development, such as future declines in social adjustment (Schweinhart, Weikart, & Larner, 1986). The Early Childhood Special Education (ECSE) literature emphasizes the positive outcomes resulting from direct instruction for typically developing children and those with disabilities (Adams & Englemann, 1996). Despite the potential confusion fostered by these conflicting approaches and their labels, all programs emphasize positive outcomes for children. The NAEYC and NAECS/SDE (2003) emphasize that programs implementing developmentally appropriate practice should evidence the following: active engagement, free play/exploration, evidence-based instructional strategies, sensitivity to language, culture, ethnic, and developmental differences, comprehensive and individualized curriculum that covers critical areas of development and is understood by teachers, families, and administrators.

Because the curriculum provides the foundation for specific aspects of the preschool classroom, it should be the first element to be examined in an assessment of the school and class environment. The curriculum provides a basis for the arrangement of the physical environment, which includes not only furniture and materials, but also schedules, transitions, and other non-tangible aspects. These global aspects of the classroom will be discussed next.

Physical Environment.   It is important to assess the physical environment, which includes not only the arrangement of furniture, equipment, and materials, but also non-tangible aspects of the classroom, such as schedules and transitions. Schwartz and colleagues (2002) posit that the physical dimensions of the classroom have the potential to promote or hinder development in each of the domains they describe: membership, relationships, and knowledge/skills. They describe, for example, how membership can be promoted by providing each student specific spaces, such as cubbies, that are labeled as their own, thus facilitating a sense of belonging. Another empirically based resource for organizing the physical environment to promote the development of preschool children with disabilities is presented by McEvoy and Fox (1991). In terms of the arrangement of furniture and materials, their recommendations include dividing the classroom into well-defined areas (Bailey & Wolery, 1992), with ample space in each area for the designated activities, and separating areas in which incompatible activities will take place. Specifically, it is recommended that areas with activities involving large movements and noise separate from more passive, quiet activities. Motor skills can be enhanced by having ample space for large movements (McEvoy & Fox, 1991).

Instructional materials also are important components of the physical environment that affect learning and behaviors. When evaluating the fit between an individual child and the school and class environment, examiners should observe the available materials, such as books, computers, and art supplies, to ensure that the student will be able to engage in activities that will facilitate learning. For example, the use of therapy balls as seats has been found to increase engagement in young children with autism (Schilling & Schwartz, 2004), thus providing increased potential for learning and development in terms of knowledge/skills. Of foremost importance, materials should be interesting and engaging enough to promote active exploration and play (NAEYC & NAECS/SDE, 2003) and should be sufficient in number so that students are able to engage in a variety of activities without having to wait for extremely long periods (McEvoy & Fox, 1991). It should be noted, however, that expressive language skills are promoted when children have to share (Hart & Risley, 1974). Thus, a balance must be struck in terms of the numbers and availability of materials. Frequently rotating materials also is advised as a method of increasing variety and engagement (Nordquist & Twardosz, 1990), as is allowing children to move among activities individually and autonomously (McEvoy & Brady, 1988). These aspects of the physical environment can particularly affect learning in the knowledge/skills domain.

The classroom environment, including both the physical arrangement and materials, also can promote the development of relationships (Schwartz et al., 2002) by facilitating peer interactions. The establishment of effective and appropriate peer relationships is typically included among the goals of early childhood programs, as they provide critical means through which young children's cognitive, communicative, and social skills are developed. Research indicates that having a limited number of materials requires children to share, thus promoting peer interactions (Montes & Risley, 1975). Small areas for activities (Brown, Fox, & Brady, 1987) and careful grouping of materials and activities promote interactions among classmates.

Peer interactions also can be facilitated by effective scheduling. Because social competence is such an important aspect of special education programs for preschoolers (Schwartz et al., 2002), it is important to evaluate how well the schedule provides time for activities involving social interactions. Play activities are instrumental in the development of social competence, as they promote student involvement and social cooperation (Johnson, Christie, & Yawkey, 1999). Through peer play, children are able to observe the skills and behaviors of others and gain a more objective view of their environment, thus increasing relationship competence (Musatti, 1993). Thus, free and structured play times should be included in the daily schedules of preschoolers with disabilities.

Additional support for the inclusion of play in classroom schedules is based on its crucial role in the development of cognitive and linguistic abilities, which are elements of the knowledge/skills domain. Better attention, memory, and language use have been reported during play, as have categorization, generalization, problem-solving and other higher-order skills (Johnson et al., 1999). Relationships also have been demonstrated between play and school-related skills, including reading and writing ability (Pellegrini, 1980; Wolfgang, 1974), story comprehension (Pellegrini & Galda, 1982), and early literacy (Pellegrini, Galda, Dresden, & Cox, 1991).

Another important consideration regarding scheduling is the degree to which it ensures that children are engaged in a variety of activities involving different materials (LeLaurin & Risley, 1972), both of which promote the development of knowledge/skills. For example, findings suggest that when children are engaged in creative activities, their interactions with objects and peers tend to be more complex (Kontos et al., 2002).

Several global dimensions of school and classroom environments for preschoolers that have significant implications for children's developing competencies have been presented. Next, two instruments that have been used in the assessment of preschool environmental quality will be reviewed.

One widely used broad measure of global and process quality is the *Early Childhood Environment Rating Scale, Revised Edition* (*ECERS–R*; Harms, Clifford, & Cryer, 1998), a well-established tool for use with children ages 2½ to 5 years. According to the ECERS–R manual, "environment" is defined as "those spatial, programmatic, and interpersonal features that directly affect the children and adults in an early childhood setting" (Harms et al., 1998, p. 1). A 7-point Likert format is used to quantify quality indicators for seven subscales (*Space and Furnishings, Personal Care Routines, Language-Reasoning, Activities, Interaction, Program Structure, and Parents and Staff*) and for the total scale.

Though research on the revised version is currently limited, the original ECERS has a long history of international use in a wide variety of settings and with culturally and developmentally diverse populations. The scale has been used successfully as a measure of classroom quality in a study of the effects of Head Start attendance on child cognitive and social development (Hubbs-Tait et al., 2002), as a measure of program quality to examine changes in preschoolers' play and verbal behaviors (Farran & Son-Yarbrough, 2001), to determine predictors of global program quality in child care programs (Buysse, Wesley, & Bryant, 1999), and to evaluate the effects of a community-based initiative designed to improve the quality of preschoolers' child care (Bryant, Maxwell, & Burchinal, 1999). The ECERS also has demonstrated cross-cultural sensitivity in studies of parents' perceptions of early childhood programs (Cryer, Tietze, & Wessels, 2002) and investigations of variations in structural features of classrooms and predictors of process quality (Cryer et al., 1999), and evaluations of reliability (Munton, Rowland, Mooney, & Lera, 1997) across several different countries.

Because the validity of the original ECERS as a measure of early childhood program quality has been well established, the ECERS–R manual focuses on the reliability of the revised scale. Inter-rater reliability and internal consistency are strong, and recent studies comparing the original and revised versions have revealed convergence and a similar two-factor solution (Sakia, Whitebook, Wishard, & Howes, 2003). Though further research with the revised version is needed, it promises to continue the original scale's reputation as a valid and reliable tool in the ecological assessment of young children's learning environments.

The *Assessment Profile for Early Childhood Programs: Research Version* (Abbott-Shim & Sibley, 1992) represents another promising tool for observing the composition and procedures of preschool classroom environments. Based on the guidelines for Developmentally Appropriate Practices (DAP; Bredekamp & Copple, 1997; Bredekamp, 1987)) set forth by the NAEYC, the scale is designed to determine the quantity and accessibility of various materials in the classroom and their respective contributions to learning and development (Huffman & Speer, 2000). Responses to 75 yes/no items yield scaled scores on each of five subscales: *learning environment, scheduling, curriculum, interacting, and individualizing*. The content validity of the Assessment Profile has been established by examining the consistency between the subscales and those on the ECERS (Harms & Clifford, 1980), as well as by expert review.

Research with the Assessment Profile, though limited in availability, attests to its potential usefulness in the evaluation of classroom environments. It has been used successfully as a measure of process quality in an investigation of the effects of DAP on at-risk children transitioning from Head Start to public school (Huffman & Speer, 2000), teaching quality in Head Start classrooms (Abbott-Shim, Lambert, & McCarty, 2000), quality of care in classrooms and centers serving infants, toddlers, and preschoolers (Scarr, Eisenberg, & Deater-Deckard, 1994), and differences in preschoolers' play behaviors across classroom and playground settings (Shim, 1997).

Other broad measures of program quality are listed and briefly described in Table 9.1. In keeping with the conceptual framework for this chapter, examiners should consider global aspects of programs in terms of their "fit" with children's individual difference variables. In other words, do the curricular, physical, and other goals and associated activities of the classroom appear to enhance development of membership, relationships, and knowledge/skills?

Structural Dimensions

Global dimensions of the classroom, described in the previous section, also contribute to structural features, such as adult-child ratios and group size (Abbott-Shim et al., 2000; Kontos & Fiene, 1987) and teacher involvement (Kontos et al., 2002). These variables have demonstrated positive relationships with program quality and child outcomes and are particularly important to consider since they tend to be modifiable, thus providing ecological targets for intervention. In other words, structural aspects of the environment can be changed to meet the needs of individual students in order to optimize the "fit."

One structural feature that is relatively easy to assess is teacher education, which appears in the literature in terms of both degree obtained and content area. Teacher education has demonstrated significant correlations with quality of care (Buysse et al., 1999; Cost, Quality, and Child Outcomes Study Team, 1995), as have professional experience and self-ratings of knowledge and skill (Buysse et al., 1999), such that higher-quality programs tend to employ teachers with more education and experience in early childhood education. Knowledge of teachers' training and experience should be considered when eval-

TABLE 9.1.

Measures of Global and Structural Dimensions

Scale	Description	Notes
Classroom Environment **Global Measures**		
Classroom Assessment Scoring System (CLASS) (La Paro, Pianta, & Stuhlman (2004)	Likert-based observational measure of classroom processes in prekindergarten through third grade; includes focus on student-teacher interactions	Nine scales; two-factor structure (Emotional Support, Instructional Support); good internal consistency for both factors
Early Childhood Classroom Observation Measure (ECCOM) (Stipek & Byler, 2004)	32-item Likert-based observational measure for classrooms serving 4–7 year-olds; assesses nature and quality of instruction, social climate, and management	High alpha values for all scales
Early Intervention Services Assessment Scale (EISAS) (Aytch, et al., 1999)	18-item self-report of structural aspects program quality; primary goal is evaluation of early intervention services	Under development
Structural Measures		
Caregiver Interaction Scale (CIS) (Arnett, 1989)	26-item observation instrument, evaluates quality and content of teacher's interactions with children, including emotional tone, discipline style, and responsiveness	Strong internal consistency and inter-rater reliability; moderate, significant correlations with ECERS and Assessment Profile
Howes' Adult Involvement Scale (Howes & Stewart, 1987)	Differentiates between securely and insecurely attached children	Good inter-rater reliability
Teaching Styles Rating Scale (TSRS) (McWilliam, Scarborough, Bagby, & Sweeney, 1998)	Likert-based observational measure of quality of interaction behaviors and emotional characteristics of early childhood teachers	Strong internal consistency (.89) See de Kruif, et al., 2000
Co-Teacher Relationship Scale (CRS)	Examines co-teachers' perceptions of similarity in philosophical beliefs, personal characteristics and traits, and professional style	

Instrument	Description	Psychometric Properties
Parent Checklist (Hemmeter, 2000)	Checklist for parents to use in evaluating quality of programs; based on DEC Recommended Practices in Early Intervention/Early Childhood Special Education (Sandall, McLean, & Smith, 2000); can be used for program selection or improvement	
Self-Assessment for Child Care Professionals (Buysse, Wesley, & Bryant, 1999)	38-item teacher/staff self-report of perceptions of knowledge, skills, and training needs in areas related to early childhood education and children with disabilities	Strong internal consistency across four sub-scales (range from .82–.98); significant correlations with ECERS
Teachers' Beliefs About Parents Scale (Feldman & Gerstein, 1988)	17-item teacher report; evaluates aspects of parent involvement in classroom activities and at home	Strong internal consistency (.95)
Family Involvement Questionnaire (Fantuzzo, Tighe, & Childs, 2000)	Assesses parental home and school-based involvement in education	High reliability (.85) with evidence of construct validity

uating the fit between a program and an individual child's learning needs. For example, if an examiner noted that a teacher (or other staff member) appeared not to have the requisite training to provide appropriate instruction for a child with special needs, the examiner could advocate for relevant staff development and/or in-service training. Additional research suggests that participation in quality improvement activities, such as training workshops, as part of a comprehensive, community-based program, is associated with improved program quality (Bryant et al., 1999).

The assignment of teacher and staff responsibilities also affects opportunities for learning, as demonstrated by LeLaurin and Risley (1977). They found that the "Zone" procedure, in which teachers are responsible for specific activity areas, was superior to the "Man-to-Man" strategy, which puts teachers in charge of different groups of students, in reducing instructional time lost during transitions. Teacher involvement also has demonstrated relationships with children's interactions with objects and peers (Kontos et al., 2002). Specific findings indicate that when teachers were involved, children's interactions with peers and objects were described as less complex. Thus, the nature of teacher activity within the classroom appears to be an important factor to include in assessments of classroom environments.

Given the family-centered focus of preschool programs for children with disabilities, parent involvement represents a particularly important dimension to assess. Findings suggest that parent involvement promotes the development of linguistic, social, motor, adaptive (Marcon, 1999), and academic skills (Miedel & Reynolds, 1999). In addition, parent involvement, as rated by teachers and/or parents, has demonstrated associations with adaptive functioning, mastery of basic skills, GPAs, reading achievement, retention, and initial special education placements and duration of such placements. Specifically, fewer retentions and special education placements and better school performance characterize children whose parents participate more frequently in classroom-related activities. Active participation, such as help with a class-wide activity, appears to be associated with more favorable outcomes than does passive participation, which might involve attendance at parent-teacher conferences. Recent research suggests that employed parents tend to be less involved in the classroom than nonworking parents and that higher quality classrooms are associated with higher numbers of parent volunteers (Castro, Bryant, Peisner-Feinberg, & Skinner, 2004). Given this information, assessments of school and classroom environments should include consideration of the emphasis on parent involvement.

In determining how to assess structural variables, it appears that traditional methods would be appropriate for most of those described. Teacher education, group size, adult-child ratio, and parent involvement all can be assessed by observations, records review, interviews, or questionnaires. While similar methods also could be utilized in assessing teacher interactions, instruments have been developed to provide a more objective view of this important structural variable. Examples of these measures can be found in Table 9.1.

Process Dimensions

Studies of process quality, which represents the actual activities and interactions children engage in, also reveal important findings, with teacher sensitivity and involvement significantly related to child outcomes. Specifically, students' relationships with teachers (Birch & Ladd, 1997; Pianta, 1999) and peers (Fantuzzo, Sekino, & Cohen, 2004) are positively associated with child outcomes (Birch & Ladd, 1996). Though much is known about the influential nature of these relationships, they are not typically included in assessments of young children. We contend that these relational variables contribute much to the understanding of child development and should be included in evaluations of school and classroom environments.

Interchanges between peers involve the active exchange of ideas and provide opportunities for discovery and learning within a context of social support (Damon, 1994). Through peer interactions, children acquire knowledge about the social world and develop cognitive processes that help them learn to use this socially mediated knowledge (Musatti, 1993). Findings indicate that social competence and popularity are positively related to the ability to discern and respond to the emotional reactions of peers (Denham, McKinley, Couchoud, & Holt, 1990), which are important aspects of relationships, as described by Schwartz and colleagues (2002). Measures of peer interactions are described in Table 9.2.

Pianta's (1999; 2001) influential work involving student-teacher relationships provides theoretical and empirical grounds for including this critical aspect of development in assessments of young children. As evidenced in the literature, positive relationships with significant adults can promote desirable outcomes and mitigate the effects of impoverished environments that put children at risk for school-related problems. Significant associations have been demonstrated between student-teacher relationships and the development of receptive language and reading skills (Burchinal et al., 2002); academic performance, affective responses and attitudes toward the school experience (Birch & Ladd, 1997); popularity, social interaction, and early school adjustment, including attitudes toward and avoidance of school; (Ladd, 1990; Ladd & Price, 1987); and academic behavior and achievement (Ladd, 1990). Thus, the relationships students have with their teachers have important associations with all three domains in Schwartz and colleagues' framework: membership, relationships, and knowledge/skills.

Evaluating the quality of the relationships between preschool children and their teachers is in accord with the goodness-of-fit perspective promoted in this chapter. Recognizing the need for a psychometrically sound instrument to assess these relationships, Pianta developed the *Student-Teacher Relationship Scale* (STRS; Pianta, 2001), a measure of teachers' perceptions of relational quality. Designed as a tool for detecting problematic relationships, the STRS has a complementary instrument to assist in the development and implementation of interventions, entitled *Students, Teachers, and Relationship Support* (STARS; Pianta & Hamre, 2001).

The STRS (Pianta, 2001) is a 28-item Likert scale developed for use with children in preschool through third grade. Three aspects of relational quality are assessed and represented by the subscales—Conflict, Closeness, and Dependency—along with a Total Scale. Test-rest reliability and internal consistency are good, as is the validity of the scale. Concurrent, predictive, and discriminant validity have been demonstrated in comparison studies with measures of classroom behavioral functioning (Birch & Ladd, 1998; Hightower et al., 1986), academic performance, work habits and discipline referrals (Hamre & Pianta, 2001), and special education referrals and retention status (Pianta, Steinberg, & Rollins, 1995). In sum, given its ease of administration and scoring (e.g., 5–10 minutes to complete) and sound psychometric properties, the STRS represents a unique and effective tool that fits well within the framework of a goodness-of-fit approach to preschool assessment.

Interactions between adults in the classroom also are important to program quality, as demonstrated in an examination by McCormick, Noonan, and Ogata (2001) of the collaborative quality of the relationships between co-teachers in inclusive preschool programs. These authors found positive associations between the quality of the co-teaching relationship, which included such traits as amenability to change, confidence, flexibility, professional style, and the social and communication dimensions of program quality. A measure of the co-teaching relationship is provided in Table 9.2.

TABLE 9.2.
Measures of Process Dimensions

Scale	Description	Notes
Engagement/Play		
Engagement Check II (McWilliam, 1999)	Observation measure of level of engagement, defined as attention to or active participation in classroom activities	See de Kruif, et al., 2000
Howes Object Play Scale (Howes & Stewart, 1987)	5-category coding system for observing the complexity of children's play with objects; may be used as an indicator of cognitive competence	Good inter-observer reliability (.86)
Relationships		
Howes Peer Play Scale–Second Edition (Howes & Matheson, 1992)	6-category coding system for observing the complexity of children's play with peers; may be used as an indicator of social competence	Good inter-observer reliability (.87)
Penn Interactive Peer Play Scale (PIPPS) (Fantuzzo, et al., 1998)	32-item teacher rating scale; describes play behaviors on three scales: Play Interaction, Play Disruption, Play Disconnection	Valid measure; developed for use with children attending urban Head Start centers; used in many studies; also has parallel parent measure
Social-Emotional/Temperament		
Adjustment Scales for Preschool Intervention (ASPI) (Lutz et al., 2002)	Teacher observation measure of emotional and behavioral development; includes 144 observable behaviors (both maladaptive and positive)	Internal consistency and concurrent validity established
Behavioral Style Questionnaire (McDevitt & Carey, 1978)	110-item rating scale for use with 3–7 year olds; measures nine temperamental traits identified in Thomas and Chess' work	
Temperament Assessment Battery for Children (TABC; Martin, 1988)	Likert-based rating scales; forms for teachers, parents, clinicians; 48 items across six scales representing dimensions of temperament	Good reliability and validity

APPLICATIONS FOR PROFESSIONAL PRACTICE

This chapter presents a relatively unique approach to the assessment of school and classroom environments for preschool. We have attempted to provide an expanded perspective on ecological assessment, in which not only the actual environment is evaluated, but also the fit between individual characteristics of the child and various dimensions of the learning environment. We endorse the framework developed by Schwartz and colleagues (2002), which reconceptualizes child outcomes in a way that is holistic and more meaningful than traditionally defined child competencies. Finally, we have incorporated the dimensions of quality typified by early childhood education and care researchers to outline various aspects of the school and classroom to be assessed. Though in contrast with more traditional approaches, we contend that, if educators and other professionals are truly interested in creating environments conducive to learning for all students, we must make the shift from a child-centered approach to one that credits the environment for its role in development.

The assessment of school and classroom environments for preschool children with disabilities is complex and multifaceted. In order to understand the nature and quality of the fit between young children and their learning environments, it is necessary to look beyond traditional measures of individual child characteristics and include assessments of various aspects of the actual classroom believed to influence child outcomes. Evaluating quality in early intervention programs is particularly challenging. A compelling explanation for the inherent difficulties encountered in evaluating such programs is provided by Aytch and colleagues (1999), who cite as challenges to methodologically sound assessments of quality, the wide-ranging services provided, the individualized nature of services, and the multiple goals involved in meeting the needs of children with disabilities and their families. Because interventions are designed within the context of both child and family needs, each child in a classroom receives services that are unique. Thus, global assessments of quality may not capture all aspects of a particular child's program. Therefore, although we believe it is important to evaluate overall program quality, such evaluations should be undertaken within the goodness-of-fit framework, such that the program's features are evaluated with respect to how well they match the needs of individual children.

For many professionals involved in the evaluation and provision of services to preschool children with disabilities, there is comfort in the traditional practice of looking for "within-child" problems to explain developmental difficulties and dysfunction, as opposed to looking for things that might be "wrong" in the child's learning environment. It is likely that a major paradigm shift will have to take place for practitioners to develop comfort and competency with the practice of entering a classroom and assessing the quality of the learning environment, particularly as it relates to an individual child. Take, for example, the practice of evaluating the relationship between students and their teachers; evaluators might feel uncomfortable suggesting to teachers that they may actually be playing a major role in sustaining the child's problems. Teachers are used to having evaluators assess children and determine "what is wrong with them" and not with their own behaviors. However, if professionals approach the assessment from the goodness-of-fit model, there need not be a focus on the "wrongness" of one individual's behaviors or actions; rather, the focus would be on evaluating and subsequently improving the "fit" between the learner and the classroom environment, with the goal of facilitating student success. This change in thinking is likely to be met with considerable resistance from teachers. The reader is referred to Zins, Kratochwill, and Elliott (1993) for information on such resistance and how to manage it.

Gaddis and Hatfield (1997) acknowledge these difficulties that may face examiners using ecologically-driven measures, as opposed to more child-focused instruments. In response, they recommend taking a broader, systems-level approach to the assessment and intervention in relation to the environment. One such example would be to conduct inservice presentations focused on increasing teachers' understanding of and sensitivity to individual differences in temperament.

Using a goodness-of-fit approach to the assessment of preschool environments necessarily leads to alternative interventions that focus more on changing the environment than on changing children. As a result, teachers may feel overwhelmed by the new roles they will have to play in the process of altering environmental variables. Evaluators and interventionists should be prepared to provide support to teachers in order to facilitate change.

REFERENCES

Abbott-Shim, M., Lambert, R., & McCarty, F. (2000). Structural model of Head Start classroom quality. *Early Childhood Research Quarterly, 15*, 115–134.

Abbott-Shim, M. S. & Sibley, A. N. (1992). *Assessment Profile for Early Childhood Programs: Research Version*. Atlanta: Quality Assist.

Abbott-Shim, M. S., Sibley, A. N., & Neel, J. (1992). *Research Manual, Assessment Profile for Early Childhood Programs*. Atlanta: Quality Assist.

Adams, G. L., & Engelmann, S. (1996). *Research in Direct Instruction: 25 Years Beyond DISTAR*. Seattle, WA: Educational Achievement Systems.

Algozzine, B. (1976). The disturbing child: What you see is what you get? *The Alberta Journal of Educational Research, 22*, 330–333.

Arnett, J. (1989). Caregivers in day-care centers: Does training matter? *Journal of Applied Developmental Psychology, 10*, 541–552.

Aytch, L. S., Cryer, D., Bailey, D. B., & Selz, L. (1999). Defining and assessing quality in early intervention programs for infants and toddlers with disabilities and their families: Challenges and unresolved issues. *Early Education and Development, 10*, 7–23.

Bailey, D. B. Jr., & Wolery, M. (1984). Teaching infants and preschoolers with handicaps. Columbus, OH: Charles E. Merrill Publishing.

Bailey, D. B. Jr., & Wolery, M. (1992). Teaching infants and preschoolers with disabilities (2nd ed). New York: Merrill.

Billman, J., & McDevitt, S. (1980). Convergence of parent and observer ratings of temperament with observations of peer interactions in nursery school. *Child Development, 51*, 395–400.

Birch, S., & Ladd, G. (1997). The teacher-child relationship and children's early school adjustment. *Journal of School Psychology, 35*, 61–79.

Birch, S., & Ladd, G. (1998). Children's interpersonal behaviors and the teacher-child relationship. *Developmental Psychology, 34*, 934–946.

Birch, S. H., & Ladd, G. W. (1996). Interpersonal relationships in the school environment and children's early school adjustment: The role of teachers and peers. In J. Juvonen & K. R. Wentzel (Eds.), *Social motivation: Understanding children's school adjustment*. New York: Cambridge University Press.

Bredekamp, S. (Ed.). (1987). *Developmentally appropriate practice in early childhood programs from birth through age 8*. Washington, DC: National Association for the Education of Young Children.

Bredekamp, S., & Copple, C. (Eds.). (1997). *Developmentally appropriate practice in early childhood programs from birth through age 8*. Revised Edition. Washington, DC: National Association for the Education of Young Children.

Brown, W. H., Fox, J. J., & Brady, M. P. (1987). The effects of spatial density on the socially directed behavior of three- and four-year-old children during freeplay: An investigation of a setting. *Education and Treatment of Children, 10*, 247–258.

Bryant, D. M., Burchinal, M., Lau, L. B., & Sparling, J. J. (1994). Family and classroom correlates of Head Start's developmental outcomes. *Early Childhood Research Quarterly, 9*, 289–309.

Bryant, D. M., Maxwell, K. L., & Burchinal, M. (1999). Effects of a community initiative on the quality of child care. *Early Childhood Research Quarterly, 14*, 449–464.

Burchinal, M. R., Peisner-Feinburg, E., Pianta, R., & Howes, C. (2002). Development of academic skills from preschool through second grade: Family and classroom predictors of developmental trajectories. *Journal of School Psychology, 40*, 415–436.

Buysse, V., Wesley, P. W., & Bryant, D. M. (1999). Quality of early childhood programs in inclusive and noninclusive settings. *Exceptional Children, 65*, 301–314.

Carey, W. B. (1998). Temperament and behavior problems in the classroom. *School Psychology Review, 27*, 522–534. Retrieved November 30, 2004, from PsycINFO/Academic Search Elite database.

Carey, W., Fox, M., & McDevitt, S. (1977). Temperament as a factor in early school adjustment. *Pediatrics, 60*, 621–624.

Carey, W. B., & McDevitt, S. C. (1995). Coping with children's temperament: A guide for professionals. New York: Basic.

Carta, J. J., Schwartz, I. S., & Atwater, J. B. (1991). Developmentally appropriate practice: Appraising its usefulness for young children with disabilities. *Topics in Early Childhood Special Education, 11*, 1–21.

Castro, D. C., Bryant, D. M., Peisner-Feinberg, E. S., & Skinner, M. L. (2004). Parent involvement in Head Start programs: The role of parent, teacher, and classroom characteristics. *Early Childhood Research Quarterly, 19*, 413–430.

Cost, Quality, and Child Outcomes Study Team. (1995). *Cost, quality, and child outcomes in child care centers public report*. Denver: University of Colorado-Denver Economics Department.

Cryer, D., Tietze, W., Burchinal, M., Leal, T., & Palacios, J. (1999). Predicting process quality from structural quality in preschool programs: A cross country comparison. *Early Childhood Research Quarterly, 14*, 339–361.

Cryer, D., Tietze, W., & Wessels, H. (2002). Parents' perceptions of their children's child care: A cross-national comparison. *Early Childhood Research Quarterly, 17*, 259–277.

Damon, W. (1994). Commentary. *Human Development, 37*, 140–142.

De Kruif, R. E. L., McWilliam, R. A., & Ridley, S. M. (2000). Classification of teachers' interaction behaviors in early childhood classrooms. *Early Childhood Research Quarterly, 15*, 247–268.

Denham, S. A., McKinley, M., Couchoud, E. A., & Holt, R. (1990). Emotional and behavioral predictors of preschool peer ratings. *Child Development, 61*, 1145–1512.

Fantuzzo, J., Sekino, Y., Cohen, H. L. (2004). An examination of the contributions of interactive peer play to salient classroom competencies for urban Head Start children. *Psychology in the Schools, 41*, 323–336.

Fantuzzo, J., Coolahan, K., Mendez, J., McDermott, P., & Sutton-Smith, B. (1998). Contextually-relevant validation of peer play constructs with African American Head Start children: Penn Interactive Peer Play Scale. *Early Childhood Research Quarterly, 13*, 411–431.

Farran, D. C., & Son-Yarbrough, W. (2001). Title I funded preschools as a developmental context for children's play and verbal behaviors. *Early Childhood Research Quarterly, 16*, 245–262.

Gaddis, L. R., & Hatfield, L. (1997). Characteristics of the learning environment: Students, teachers, and their interactions. In J. L. Swartz and W. E. Martin (Eds.), *Applied ecological psychology for schools within communities* (pp. 31–54). Mahwah, NJ: Lawrence Erlbaum Associates.

Garrison, W., Earls, F., & Kindlon, D. (1984). Temperament characteristics in the third year of life and behavioral adjustment at school entry. *Journal of Clinical Child Psychology, 13*, 298–303.

Gersten, R., Darch, C., & Gleason, M. (1988). Effectiveness of a direct instruction academic kindergarten for low-income students. *The Elementary School Journal, 89*, 227–240.

Greene, R. W. (1996). Students with Attention Deficit Hyperactivity Disorder and their teachers: Implications of a goodness-of-fit perspective. In T. H. Ollendick & R. J. Prinz (Eds.), *Advances in clinical psychology* (Vol. 18). New York: Plenum Press.

Hamre, B. K., & Pianta, R. C. (2001). Early teacher-child relationships and the trajectory of children's school outcomes through eighth grade. *Child Development, 72*, 625–638.

Harms, T., Clifford, R. M., & Cryer, D. (1998). *Early Childhood Environment Rating Scale–Revised Edition*. New York: Teachers College Press.

Harms, T., & Clifford, R. M. (1980). *Early Childhood Environment Rating Scale*. New York: Teachers College Press.

Hart, B., & Risley, T. R. (1974). Using preschool materials to modify the language of disadvantaged children. *Journal of Applied Behavior Analysis, 7*, 243–256.

Hemmeter, M. L. (2000). Parent checklist. In S. Sandall, M. E. McLean, & B. J. Smith, *DEC Recommended Practices in Early Intervention/Early Childhood Special Education* (pp. 117–120). Longmont, CO: Sopris West.

Hightower, A. C., Work, W. C., Cowen, E. L., Lotyczewski, B. S., Spinnell, A. P., Guare, J. C., & Rohrbeck, C. A. (1986). The Teacher-Child Rating Scale. A brief objective measure of elementary children's school problem behaviors and competencies. *School Psychology Review, 15*, 393–409.

Howes, C., & Matheson, C. (1992). Sequences in the development of competent play with peers: Social and social pretend play. *Developmental Psychology, 28*, 961–974.

Howes, C., & Stewart, L. K. (1987). Child's play with adults, toys, and peers: An examination of family and child-care influences. *Developmental Psychology, 23*, 423–430.

Hubbs-Tait, L., Culp, A. M., Culp, E. H., Starost, H. J., & Hare, C. (2002). Relation of Head Start attendance to children's cognitive and social outcomes: Moderation by family risk. *Early Childhood Research Quarterly, 17*, 539–558.

Huffman, L. R., & Speer, P. W. (2000). Academic performance among at-risk children: The role of developmentally appropriate practices. *Early Childhood Research Quarterly, 15*, 167–184. Retrieved December 28, 2004, from PsycINFO database.

Johnson, J. E., Christie, J. F., & Yawkey, T. D. (1999). *Play and early childhood development* (2nd ed.). New York: Longman.

Kontos, S., Burchinal, M., Howes, C., Wisseh, S., & Galinsky, E. (2002). An eco-behavioral approach to examining the contextual effects of early childhood classrooms. *Early Childhood Research Quarterly, 17*, 239–258.

Kontos, S., & Fiene, R. (1987). Child care quality, compliance wit regulations, and children's development: The Pennsylvania study. In D. Phillips (Ed.), *Quality in child care: What does research tell us?* (pp. 57–80). Washington, DC: National Association for the Education of Young Children.

Ladd, G. W. (1990). Having friends, keeping friends, making friends, and being liked by peers in the classroom: Predictors of children's early school adjustment? *Child Development, 61*, 1081–1100.

Ladd, G. W., & Price, J. M. (1987). Predicting children's social and school adjustment following the transition from preschool to kindergarten. *Child Development, 58*, 1168–1189.

Le Paro, K. M., Pianta, R. C., & Stuhlman, M. (1994). The Classroom Assessment Scoring System: Findings from the prekindergarten year. *The Elementary School Journal, 104*, 409–427.

LeLaurin, K., & Risley, T. R. (1972). The organization of day care environments: "Zone" to "man-to-man" staff assignments. *Journal of Applied Behavior Analysis, 5*, 225–232.

Lerner, J. V., Lerner, R. M., & Zabski, S. (1985). Temperament and elementary school children's actual and rated academic performance: A test of a "goodness-of-fit" model. *Journal of Child Psychology and Psychiatry, 26*, 125–136.

Lutz, M. N., Fantuzzo, J., & McDermott, P. (2002). Multidimensional assessment of emotional and behavioral adjustment problems of low-income preschool children: Development and initial validation. *Early Childhood Research Quarterly, 17*, 338–355.

Marcon, R. A. (1999). Positive relationships between parent school involvement and public school inner-city preschoolers' development and academic performance. *School Psychology Review, 28*, 395–412. Retrieved December 28, 2004, from PsycINFO database.

Martin, R. P. (1988a). *The Temperament Assessment Battery for Children*. Brandon, VT: Clinical Psychology Publishing.

Martin, R. P. (1988b). Child temperament and educational outcomes. In A. D. Pellegrini (Ed.), *Psychological bases for early education* (pp. 85–205). New York: John Wiley & Sons.

Martin, R. P., & Holbrook, J. (1985). Relationship of temperament characteristics to the academic achievement of first grade children. *Journal of Psychoeducational Assessment, 3*, 131–140.

Martin, R. P., Nagle, R., & Paget, K. (1983). Relationship between temperament and classroom behavior, teacher attitudes, and academic achievement. *Journal of Psychoeducational Assessment, 1*, 377–386.

McConnell, S. R., Priest, J. S., Davis, S. D., & McEvoy, M. A. (2002). Best practices in measuring growth and development for preschool children. In A. Thomas & J. Grimes (Eds.), *Best Practices in School Psychology* (4th ed., Vol. 2, pp. 1231–1246). Washington DC: National Association of School Psychologists.

McCormick, L., Noonan, J. J., & Ogata, V. (2001). Co-teacher relationship and program quality: Implications for preparing teachers for inclusive preschool settings. *Education and Training in Mental Retardation and Developmental Disabilities, 36*, 119–132.

McDevitt, S. C., & Carey, W. B. (1978). The measurement of temperament in 3- to 7-year old children. *Journal of Child Psychology and Psychiatry, 19*, 245–254.

McEvoy, M. A., & Brady, M. P. (1988). Contingent access to play materials as an academic motivator for autistic and behavior disordered children. *Education and Treatment of Children, 11*, 5–18.

McEvoy, M. A., & Fox, J. J. (1991). Organizing preschool environments: Suggestions for enhancing the development/learning of preschool children with handicaps. *Topics in Early Childhood Special Education, 11*, 18–28.

McLellan, M. J., & Sanchez, I. (1997). Principles and application of ecological assessment for teachers. In J. L. Swartz and W. E. Martin (Eds.), *Applied ecological psychology for schools within communities* (pp. 77–94). Mahwah, NJ: Lawrence Erlbaum Associates.

McWilliam, R. A. (1999). *Engagement Check II*. Chapel Hill, NC: Frank Porter Graham Child Development Center, University of North Carolina.

McWilliam, R. A., Scarborough, A. A., Bagby, J., & Sweeney, A. (1998). *Teaching Styles Rating Scale (TSRS)*. Chapel Hill, NC: Frank Porter Graham Child Development Center, University of North Carolina.

Miedel, W. T., & Reynolds, A. J. (1999). Parent involvement in early intervention for disadvantaged children: Does it matter? *Journal of School Psychology, 37*, 379–402. Retrieved December 28, 2004, from PsycINFO database.

Montes, F., & Risley, T. R. (1975). Evaluating traditional day care practice: An empirical approach. *Child Care Quarterly, 4*, 208–215.

Munton, A. G., Rowland, L., Mooney, A., & Lera, M. J. (1997). Using the Early Childhood Environment Rating Scale (ECERS) to evaluate the quality of nursery provision in England: Some data concerning reliability. *Educational Research, 39*, 99–104.

Musatti, T. (1993). Meaning between peers: The meaning of the peer. *Cognition and Instruction, 11*, 241–250.

National Association for the Education of Young Children (NAEYC). (2003). *Early childhood curriculum, assessment, and program evaluation: Building an effective, accountable system in programs for children birth through age 8*. Joint Position Statement of the NAEYC and National Association of Early Childhood Specialists in State Departments of Education (NAECS/SDE).

Nordquist, V. M., & Twardosz, S. (1990). Preventing behavior problems in early childhood special education classrooms through environmental organization. *Education and Treatment of Children, 13*, 274–287.

Paget, K., Nagle, R., & Martin, R. P. (1984). Interrelations between temperament characteristics and first-grade teacher-student interactions. *Journal of Abnormal Child Psychology, 12*, 547–560.

Pellegrini, A. (1980). The relationship between kindergartners' play and achievement in prereading, language, and writing. *Psychology in the Schools, 17*, 530–535.

Pellegrini, A. D., & Galda, L. (1982).The effects of thematic-fantasy play training on the development of children's story comprehension. *American Educational Research Journal, 19*, 443–452.

Pellegrini, A. D., Galda, L., Dresden, J., & Cox, S. (1991). A longitudinal study of the predictive relations among symbolic play, linguistic verbs, and early literacy. *Research in the Teaching of English, 25*, 219–235.

Phillips, D. A., & Howes, C. (1987). Indicators of quality in child care: Review of research. In D. A. Phillips (Ed.), *Quality in Child Care: What Does the Research Tell Us?* (pp. 1–19). Washington, DC: National Association for the Education of Young Children.

Pianta, R. C. (1999). *Enhancing relationships between children and teachers*. Washington, DC: American Psychological Association.

Pianta, R. C. (2001). *Student-Teacher Relationship Scale*. Lutz, FL: Psychological Assessment Resources.

Pianta, R. C., & Hamre, B. K. (2001). *Students, teachers, and relationship support consultant's manual*. Odessa, FL: Psychological Assessment Resources.

Pianta, R. C., Steinberg, M. S., & Rollins, K. (1995). The first two years of school: Teacher-child relationships and deflections in children's classroom adjustment. *Development and Psychopathology, 7*, 297–312.

Pullis, M., & Cadwell, J. (1982). The influence of children's temperament characteristics on teachers' decision strategies. *American Educational Research Journal, 19*, 165–181.

Rubin, R., & Balow, B. (1971). Learning and behavior disorders: A longitudinal study. *Exceptional Children, 36*, 293–299.

Sakia, L. M., Whitebook, M., Wishard, A., & Howes, C. (2003). Evaluating the Early Childhood Environment Rating Scale (ECERS): Assessing differences between the first and revised edition. *Early Childhood Research Quarterly, 18*, 427–445.

Sandall, S., McLean, M. E., & Smith, B. J. (2000). *DEC Recommended Practices in Early Intervention/Early Childhood Special Education*. Longmont, CO: Sopris West.

Scarr, S., Eisenberg, M., & Deater-Deckard, K. (1994). Measurement of quality in child care centers. *Early Child Research Quarterly, 9*, 131–151.

Schilling, D. L., & Schwartz, I. S. (2004). Alternative seating for young children with autism spectrum disorder: Effects on classroom behavior. *Journal of Autism and Developmental Disorders, 34*, 423–432

Schroeder, S. R., Schroeder, C. S., & Landesman, S. (1987). Psychological services in educational settings to persons with mental retardation. *American Psychologist, 42*, 805–808.

Schwartz, I. S. (2000). Standing on the shoulders of giants: Looking ahead to facilitating membership and relationships for children with disabilities. *Topics in Early Childhood Special Education, 20*, 123–128.

Schwartz, I. S., Garfinkle, A. N., & Davis, C. (2002). Arranging preschool environments to facilitate valued social and educational outcomes. In M. R. Shinn, H. M. Walker, & G. Stoner (Eds.), *Interventions for academic and behavior problems II: Preventive and remedial approaches* (pp. 455–468). Bethesda, MD: National Association of School Psychologists.

Schwartz, I. S., Staub, D., Gallucci, C., & Peck, C. A. (1995). Blending qualitative and behavior analytic research methods to evaluate outcomes in inclusive schools. *Journal of Behavioral Education, 5*, 93–106.

Schweinhart, L. J., & Weikart, D. P. (1993). Success by empowerment: The High/Scope Perry Preschool Study through age 27. *Young Children*, 54–58.

Schweinhart, L. J., & Weikart, D. P. (1989). The High/Scope Perry Preschool study: Implications for early childhood care and education. *Prevention in Human Services, 7*, 109–132.

Schweinhart, L. J., Weikart, D. P., & Larner, B. (1986). Consequences of three preschool curriculum models through age 15. *Early Childhood Research Quarterly, 1*, 15–45.

Shim, S. Y. (1997). Play behaviors and peer interactions of preschoolers in classroom and playground settings (Doctoral dissertation, Iowa State University, 1997). *Dissertation Abstracts International, 58*, 731.

Stipek, D. J., & Byler, P. (1997). Early childhood education teachers: Do they practice what they preach? *Early Childhood Research Quarterly, 12*, 305–325.

Stipek, D. J., & Byler, P. (2004). The Early Childhood Classroom Observation Measure. *Early Childhood Research Quarterly, 19*, 375–397.

Stipek, D., Feiler, R., Daniels, D., & Milburn, S. (1995). Effects of different instructional approaches on young children's achievement and motivation. *Child Development, 66*, 209–223.

Thomas, A., & Chess, S. (1977). *Temperament and development.* New York: Brunner/Mazel.

Walher, R. G., House, A. E., & Stambaugh II, E. E. (1976). *Ecological assessment of child problem behavior: A clinical package for home, school, and institutional settings.* Elmsford, New York: Pergamon Press.

Wolfgang, C. (1974). An exploration of the relationship between the cognitive area of reading and selected developmental aspects of children's play. *Psychology in the Schools, 11*, 338–343.

Zins, J. E., Kratochwill, T. R., & Elliott, S. N. (1993). Handbook of Consultation Services for Children: Applications in Educational and Clinical Settings. San Francisco: Jossey-Bass Publishers.

10

Adaptive Behavior Assessment for Preschool Children

Patti L. Harrison and Gina Raineri
The University of Alabama

Adaptive behavior, or children's ability to take care of themselves and get along with others, is an extremely important aspect of multi-dimensional assessment and interventions for preschool children. The purpose of this chapter is to explore the uses of adaptive behavior assessment for diagnosing possible disabilities and developmental problems of preschoolers and planning effective home, family, and school programs. The characteristics of adaptive behavior and the relevance of adaptive behavior assessment for preschool children are described. Norm-referenced adaptive behavior scales are reviewed, and important supplemental assessment techniques are summarized. The final section of the chapter provides a review of research related to adaptive behavior assessment of preschool children.

DEFINITION AND CHARACTERISTICS OF ADAPTIVE BEHAVIOR

The American Association on Mental Retardation (AAMR; 2002) defines adaptive behavior as "a collection of conceptual, social, and practical skills learned by people in order to function in their everyday lives" (p. 73) and states that deficits in adaptive skills, in addition to significant limitations in intellectual functioning, are essential requirements for a classification of mental retardation. Deficits in adaptive behavior are not limited to preschool children with mental retardation, but may also impact the functioning of children with developmental delays, emotional disturbances, learning disabilities, physical disabilities, sensory disabilities, or other disabilities and learning and behavior problems (Bucy, Smith, & Landau, 1999; Harrison & Oakland, 2003, Kamphaus & Frick, 2002). Traditionally, the definition of adaptive behavior has focused on both personal independence and social responsibility (Horn & Fuchs, 1987).

Adaptive behavior is a key component of classification of mental retardation in three separate systems, the *Diagnostic and Statistical Manual of Mental Disorders–Fourth Edition–Text Revision* (DSM–IV–TR; American Psychiatric Association, 2000), the American Association on Mental Retardation (AAMR; 2002), and the 1997 reauthorization of the

Individuals with Disabilities Education Act (IDEA; 2004). The DSM–IV–TR defines mental retardation as:

> . . . Significantly subaverage general intellectual functioning (Criterion A) that is accompanied by significant limitations in adaptive functioning in at least two of the following skill areas: communication, self care, home living, social/interpersonal skills, use of community resources, self direction, functional academics, work, leisure, health and safety, (Criterion B) and onset must occur before age 18 (Criterion C). (p. 41)

AAMR (2002), as noted above, defines mental retardation as "a disability characterized by significant limitations in intelligence and adaptive behavior as expressed in the conceptual, perceptual, and social domains. This disability originates before age 18" (p. 1). IDEA has a comparable definition and characterizes mental retardation with "significant subaverage intellectual functioning existing concurrently with deficits in adaptive behavior manifested during the developmental period that adversely affects a child's educational performance" (Department of Education, 1999, p. 12422).

Developmental Nature

Definitions of adaptive behavior emphasize the developmental nature of the construct and note that children's skills increase and become more complex as they grow older. The developmental relevance of adaptive skills is related to children's physical development and also to the demands and expectations that are encountered in new environments or situations (AAMR, 2002; Edwards, 1999). As children age, mature physically, and encounter different experiences, their adaptive behavior broadens to meet the demands of the new environments. Children acquire new adaptive skills, or refine and expand existing skills, to function in the new situations. Children's skills become more complex as their social and environmental demands become more abstract. The determination of appropriate adaptive behavior is typically based on social and cultural expectations about how an individual of a certain age should behave in a given situation (Demchak & Drinkwater, 1998). Thus, children's adaptive skills always must be examined in the context of a typical age peer. For instance, adaptive skills such as brushing teeth without assistance, pouring a glass of juice, or answering the telephone may be deemed appropriate for preschool and school-age children, while not expected of infants and toddlers. Ultimately, the decision of appropriate and typical behaviors for a given age is a reflection of the cultural standards and social norms within a community.

Researchers over the years have suggested that specific age groups or developmental periods are characterized by certain types of adaptive behavior. According to Grossman (1983), the infancy and early childhood periods emphasize sensorimotor, communication, self-help, and socialization skills. Later, childhood and adolescence are characterized by the acquisition of basic academic skills necessary for daily life activities, judgment and reasoning in the mastery of the environment, and social skills necessary for interacting with others. Vocational and social skills are required for older adolescents and adults. Similarly, Demchak and Drinkwater (1998) noted that children's skills in responding to the environment develop as they grow older.

Basic Dimensions

Definitions and measures of adaptive behavior typically include three major dimensions: conceptual skills, social skills, and practical skills (AAMR, 2002). Similar dimensions have been supported by a number of factor analytic studies as summarized in reviews by Reschly, Myers, and Hartel (2002) and Thompson, McGrew, and Bruininks (1992). In addition to the three broad domains of conceptual, social, and practical skills, AAMR (1992, 2002) and the DSM–IV–TR (2000) have identified more specific skill areas that have implications for assessment and interventions. These skill areas, and the broad dimension under which they are categorized, are identified by the AAMR (2002, p. 82) as the following:

- Specific skill areas in the conceptual domain:
    - Communication (e.g., expressive and receptive language skills)
    - Functional academics (e.g., basic reading, writing, math)
    - Self-direction (e.g., using a schedule, managing time)
    - Health and safety (e.g., eats only edibles, communicating sickness or injury, following safety rules)
- Specific skill areas in the social domain:
    - Social skills (e.g., interacting with others, cooperating, playing)
    - Leisure (e.g., playing with toys or games, watching television and videos)
- Specific skill areas in the practical domain:
    - Self-care (e.g., eating, toileting, dressing, hygiene)
    - Home living (e.g., clothing care, food preparation, housekeeping)
    - Community use (e.g., traveling in the community, using the library)
    - Health and safety (e.g., eating only edibles, communicating sickness or injury, following safety rules)
    - Work (e.g., job-related skills)

The areas emphasized during adaptive behavior assessment generally are influenced by the age of the child (Kamphaus & Frick, 2002). Self-care, communication, social skills, health and safety skills, and leisure skills are emphasized for younger children. Older children, adolescents, and adults add home living skills, community use skills, self-direction skills, functional academics, and work skills to their array of skills needed for daily functioning.

According to the AAMR (2002), individuals can have coexisting strengths and limitations in adaptive behavior skills. For example, a child may have strengths in self-care skills and a coexisting limitation in social behavior. This child may have other strengths or limitations within his or her adaptive behavior profile. The existence of strengths does not imply that interventions are not needed to address limitations. For this reason, the selection of an adaptive behavior instrument, as well as other supplemental methods of assessing adaptive skills, should ensure a comprehensive assessment of an individual child's adaptive behavior profile. This assessment should identify a child's strengths and limitations across all age-relevant adaptive behavior skill areas. Developing an understanding of a child's adaptive behavior profile is critical for determining needs and developing interventions.

Social and Cultural Influences

The construct of adaptive behavior is recognized as being dependent on the expectations of the social and cultural groups to which a person belongs. Undoubtedly, different cultures have different expectations for the behavior of children. Social and cultural norms and expectations determine what behaviors are considered adaptive skills (AAMR, 2002; Demchak & Drinkwater, 1998). These norms are specified by members of the community and are used to judge the adaptive skills of particular children.

The social, cultural, and ethnic contexts of individuals must be examined when assessing their adaptive behaviors (Tasse & Craig, 1999). The culture of the community, the ethnicity of the family and team members, the climate of the classroom, and the dynamics of the family are all important considerations when examining children's adaptive skills. As suggested by Leland (1983), it is perfectly acceptable for children to urinate in public in some countries. In other countries, this practice is unacceptable. There are also different expectations for children within the different subcultures of the same country. For example, different subcultures within the United States place different expectations on dress, social skills, leisure activities, and other variables related to adaptive behavior. Cultural expectations about age-appropriate behavior may also influence parental expectations for children's adaptive skills. Talia, a preschool child, may not be allowed to dress herself because her parents feel that preschool children cannot dress themselves properly. Talia's performance of this skill may be more a reflection of parent expectations than of her ability.

Considerations about preschool children's adaptive skills must recognize that adaptive behavior does not occur in a vacuum. Thus, assessment of adaptive behavior must also explore environmental, cultural, and family contexts that impact the behavior of children. Developing an understanding of the cultural, linguistic, and behavioral factors that impact children is necessary when assessing their adaptive behavior (AAMR, 2002). The emphasis on developing a contextual understanding of the individual's adaptive behavior provides information about the skills of the individual, as well as information about possible support systems and resources within the environment that can be utilized in the development and implementation of interventions (Tasse & Craig, 1999).

Situational Specificity

Children's adaptive behavior is very much influenced by the demands and expectations of the settings in which they are involved (Greenspan, 1999). Different situations demand different adaptive behaviors or skills. Jackson, a preschool child, may not perform the expected behavior of sharing toys with other classmates at school because he has no siblings or others that he is expected to share toys with on a regular basis at home. In Jackson's case, the adaptive skills required in the classroom may be quite different from those expected at home. Other examples of the adaptation process occur when children enter preschool and are expected to acquire the adaptive skills of taking turns or waiting in line. Children learn adaptive skills through their interactions with teachers and classmates in the new environment.

When children encounter these new expectations in ever-expanding settings and situations, their adaptive skills will increase and become more complex. Adaptation occurs through an interaction of situational demands, social intelligence, and biology (Greenspan, 1999). Children's development of adaptive skills is influenced by the expectations of the significant others and the situations in which they must interact with others. Assessment of children's adaptive behavior must take into account the situational specificity of different skills. Interventions to address limitations in children's adaptive skills may involve nothing more than providing a context for this new skill or allowing sufficient time for development of this skill within the new situation. Preschool children that have had no exposure to sharing or taking turns may develop these skills upon entering school as a process of their adaptation to the new environment with little need for an intense intervention.

Performance or Ability?

Adaptive behavior is defined as the *performance* of daily activities required for personal and social competence. Although an implicit assumption is that children must have the *ability* to perform daily activities, assessment of adaptive behavior stresses the observable performance of these activities. AAMR (2002) emphasizes the expression, or performance, of adaptive skills as opposed to the acquisition of skills. Adaptive behavior scales typically focus on what children *usually do,* rather than what they are capable of doing (Kamphaus & Frick, 2002), and adaptive behavior is considered to be deficient if children have a skill but do not routinely perform it (Demchak & Drinkwater, 1998). For example, Molly may be able to tie her shoes, but does not routinely do so, perhaps because she does not want to do so or prefers a parent to do it. An emphasis on performance, not ability, implies that the concept of adaptive behavior includes the *motivation* for performing activities. As reported by AAMR (2002), ". . . reasons for limitations in adaptive skills may include (a) not knowing how to perform the skill (acquisition deficit), (b) not knowing when to use the skills (performance deficit), and (c) other motivational factors that can affect the expression of skills (performance deficit)" (pp. 73–74).

The emphasis on performance of adaptive skills requires a method of assessment that measures what children do daily, rather than what they can do. Most adaptive behavior scales utilize a *third-party informant* approach, in which individuals familiar with children's daily activities are questioned about their performance. It is important to ensure that individuals rating children's adaptive behavior understand the distinction between performance and ability and rate children based on this understanding. Although adaptive behavior assessment focuses on performance rather than ability, knowledge of children's ability is useful for developing interventions. Identification of typical performance of adaptive skills is used to identify limitations, while knowledge about ability provides a basis for targeting the limitations. The limitations can be addressed as either acquisition deficits, performance deficits, or motivation deficits.

IMPORTANCE OF ADAPTIVE BEHAVIOR ASSESSMENT FOR PRESCHOOL CHILDREN

The ability to take care of oneself and get along with others represents important goals for everyone, regardless of age or disability. Adaptive behavior assessment has been emphasized for almost 50 years due to needs for nonbiased assessment and effective interventions for individuals with mental retardation. The developmental characteristics and the needs of preschool children are quite different from those of older individuals, and the assessment of adaptive behavior is of great importance during the preschool years. In this section of the chapter, the traditional importance of adaptive behavior assessment and the specific importance of adaptive behavior assessment for preschool children are summarized.

Traditional Importance

Adaptive behavior assessment has its roots in the field of mental retardation. Legislation and litigation has established the importance of adaptive behavior assessment in diagnosis, assessment, and intervention for individuals with mental retardation (AAMR, 2002, Nihira, 1999; Reschly, et al., 2002). One reason for the inclusion of adaptive behavior assessment when diagnosing an individual with mental retardation is to ensure that assessments are nonbiased and comprehensive. Several lawsuits beginning in the 1970s and continuing through present day (e.g., Larry P., PASE, Marshall, Lee v. Macon) focused on the use of intelligence test scores as the sole or primary criterion for placing children into special education programs for mental retardation. These lawsuits identified disproportionate placement of children from minority groups as a result of an over-emphasis on intelligence test scores and an inadequate consideration of adaptive behavior assessment results when making eligibility decisions. These lawsuits resulted in an emphasis on adaptive behavior assessment as one method for addressing disproportionate placement and for promoting nonbiased assessment of children from minority groups.

Special education legislation has also suggested the importance of adaptive behavior assessment in planning interventions. Federal laws such as the Education for all Handicapped Act in 1975, IDEA in 1991, and reauthorization of IDEA in 1997 emphasize that assessment of an individual should be nonbiased, comprehensive, *and* linked to interventions. The latest revision of IDEA in 2004 (Individuals with Disabilities Education Improvement Act, 2004) includes an increased focus on reducing disproportionate placement and overrepresentation of minority children in special education programs, along with a significant emphasis on implementing early intervention programs for all children, including those in groups that may be overrepresented.

During the last 50 years, agencies serving individuals with mental retardation and other developmental disabilities, including residential facilities, have increasingly focused on the importance of developing effective interventions for individuals with mental retardation and other disabilities that would enable them to live more independently (Nihira, 1999). A critical assumption of the AAMR (2002) definition of mental retardation is that with appropriate, individually tailored supports and interventions over a continued period of time, the life functioning of an individual will improve. Thus, interventions targeting the adaptive skills of individuals with disabilities such as mental retardation may facilitate increased levels of inclusion in general education programs and enhance involvement in the community. In order to develop interventions for adaptive skill areas, assessment must provide a complete picture of adaptive behavior strengths and limitations and must identify supports that are needed by individuals in order to live more independently.

Importance for Preschool Assessment

Reauthorizations of the Individuals with Disabilities Education Act in 1997 and 2004 provided guidelines for early educational services for preschool and school-age children with a disability. These reauthorizations expanded the definition of developmental delay to allow for the inclusion of children ages 3 years through 9 years in the category. The 1991 Individuals with Disabilities Education Act specified that developmental delay only included children ages 3 through 5 years. The more recent expansion through age 9 allows for more flexibility in classification, placement, and educational services for preschool and young school-age children. This flexibility in the new definition of developmental delay avoids labeling a child with a specific disability at a young age and may reduce the stigmatization that occurs with some special education classifications. It also promotes educators' examination of the needs of children and prevents an overemphasis on a specific disability classification. Furthermore, the recent revisions to the Individuals with Disabilities Education

Act passed in 2004 also include changes regarding transition, individualized education programs, over identification, student discipline, due processes and litigation, monitoring and compliance, and funding.

Other components of the Individuals with Disabilities Education Act outline the need for early intervention for children with disabilities. These interventions should address the needs of young children and their families. Major requirements of the laws also include assessment and intervention in all developmental areas (physical, cognitive, communication, social or emotional, and adaptive). Current legislation recognizes adaptive behavior as an integral part of preschool children's development and indicates that remediation of deficits in adaptive behavior represents an important goal for early intervention programs. Thus, adaptive behavior assessment is an important component of the flexible, multidimensional assessment process recommended for evaluating the development of preschool children.

Characteristics of the assessment process for preschool children include assessment of multiple domains, assessment from multiple sources, involvement of parents in the assessment, ecologically valid assessment, and assessment that leads to early intervention (National Association of School Psychologists, 1999). Adaptive behavior assessment contributes to the recommended process in a number of ways. Adaptive behavior measures typically assess activities in several areas and across multiple domains. For preschool children, assessment of adaptive behavior domains usually allows a sampling of behavior from a number of developmental areas.

Most adaptive behavior scales utilize one or more third-party informants (e.g., parent, teacher, caregiver) to describe children's adaptive behavior and promote assessment using multiple sources of information. Information from multiple sources increases the understanding of children, their environments, and interactions between the children and the environment. During adaptive behavior assessment of preschool children, parental involvement is imperative. Parents may provide information about children's behavior at home, such as their dressing and sleeping habits, which may not be observed at school (Sattler, 2002).

Preschool assessment must be ecologically valid, or sample behavior appropriate to the various environments (e.g., home, school, community) in which preschool children must function. Third-party adaptive behavior assessment is based on informants' observations of children's activities in the "real world," rather than being based on observations of children in an artificial, structured testing situation. In addition, informants can provide information about behavior in a variety of different environments and specific situations.

Adaptive behavior assessment can be directly integrated with interventions for preschool children, and interventions targeting specific areas can result in increases in adaptive behavior of the child. A critical assumption of the AAMR (2002) definition of mental retardation is that with appropriate supports and interventions, the adaptive skills of an individual can improve. Furthermore, deficits in adaptive behavior may be related to home, family, and school factors that are amenable to change.

SELECTED ADAPTIVE BEHAVIOR SCALES FOR USE WITH PRESCHOOL CHILDREN

There are many different instruments and techniques used to assess the adaptive behavior strengths and limitations of children. In this section of the chapter, several comprehensive adaptive behavior scales and related scales that can be used with preschool children are described.

Scales of Independent Behavior–Revised (SIB–R)

The SIB–R (Bruininks, Hill, Weatherman, & Woodcock, 1986) provides a comprehensive, norm-referenced assessment of adaptive behavior for infants through 80 years of age. It consists of four adaptive behavior skill clusters encompassing 14 subscales. The four adaptive behavior clusters (motor skills, social interaction and communication skills, personal living skills, and community living skills) are combined to form the Broad Independence Scale. The SIB–R also contains a problem behavior scale. The SIB–R can be administered to a parent or caregiver as an interview, or as a checklist to be completed by a person that has sufficient knowledge of the individual. An easel may be used during administration, and the informant is shown possible responses to items on the easel pages.

The SIB–R is most often administered in the Full Scale interview format. However, an Early Development Form is available, which is a particularly useful feature of the SIB–R to assess the adaptive functioning of preschoolers. This form can be used as a screener or as a separate assessment to measure adaptive behavior. The Early Development Form is used with children in infancy through age 6 years or with individuals that experience developmental levels below age 8. The scale includes 40 questions from the developmental areas of the Full Scale form that have relevance for young children and preschoolers.

The SIB–R yields a wide variety of derived scores, including age equivalents, percentile ranks, standard scores with a mean of 100 and standard deviation of 15, and normal curve equivalents. Samples of 2,182 individuals were used for standardization. The data for the samples were collected for individuals' ages 3 months to 90 years, and the samples were stratified according to gender, race, Hispanic origin, occupational status, occupational level, geographic region, and community type.

Internal consistency estimates were found using corrected split-half reliability coefficients. The median split-half reliability estimates for the cluster scores across all age levels on the SIB–R Full Scale Form range from .88 to .94. The Broad Independence score has a median corrected split-half reliability of .98 across all age levels on the Full Scale Form. The Early Development Form has a total internal consistency of .84.

Test-retest reliability estimates are provided for children without disabilities ages 6 through 13. The test-retest reliability estimates across the clusters range from .96 to .97 on the Full Scale Form. The Broad Independence score has a test-retest reliability estimate of .98. The Early Development Form has a test-retest reliability estimate of .97.

Inter-rater reliability correlations between mothers and fathers for children without disabilities (ages 6–13) are also reported. The estimates of inter-rater reliability for the clusters across all ages range from .88 to .93 on the Full Scale Form. The Broad Independence score inter-rater reliability estimate is .95 for this population. The inter-rater reliability correlation between teachers and teacher aides for children ages 2–5 on the Early Development Form is .91 for the Broad Independence score.

The SIB–R technical manual reports validity evidence including developmental progression of scores, differences between scores of individuals with disabilities and individuals without disabilities, and correlations with other adaptive behavior scales and intelligence tests.

Vineland Adaptive Behavior Scales

The Vineland Adaptive Behavior Scales (Sparrow, Balla, & Cicchetti, 1984a, 1984b, 1985), a revision of the Vineland Social Maturity Scale, consists of three versions that provide comprehensive information about adaptive behavior. The Survey Form is administered to parents and caregivers of infants, children through 18 years of age, and low functioning adults and provides a norm-referenced assessment of adaptive behavior. The primary purpose of the Expanded Form is to provide detailed information about specific deficits in adaptive behavior and a sequential guide for planning intervention programs. The Classroom Edition is administered to teachers of children ages 3 through 12 and provides a norm-referenced assessment of adaptive behavior in the classroom. The Vineland–II encompasses a wider age range on the Survey and Expanded Forms (ages birth to 77+ years) and the Teacher Rating form (ages 3 to 21 years). Updated norms and content are included.

All three versions of the Vineland measure adaptive behavior in four domains and 11 subdomains of adaptive behavior. The four domains (Communication, Daily Living Skills, Socialization, and Motor Skills) are combined to form a general measure of adaptive behavior, the Adaptive Behavior Composite. The Survey Form and Expanded Form include a maladaptive behavior domain. This domain is only administered to children ages 5 and older because many of the behaviors assessed by this domain (e.g., thumb sucking, bed wetting) are usually not considered maladaptive for preschool age children.

The Survey Form and Expanded Form are administered to parents and caregivers during a semi-structured interview. This type of interview is typically conducted by a trained professional, and its flexible nature allows clinicians to make valuable observations about parental concerns. The Classroom Edition is administered with a questionnaire completed by teachers.

The Survey Form was standardized with a sample of 3,000 individuals selected on the basis of sex, race, socioeconomic status, geographic region, and community size. The Expanded Form was not included in a national standardization, but an equating study allowed the generation of norms using Survey Form standardization data. The Classroom Edition was standardized with a sample of 2,984 children, also stratified according to sex, race, socioeconomic status, geographic region, and community size. Standard scores with a mean of 100 and standard deviation of 15, percentile ranks, stanines, and age equivalents are yielded by all three versions of the Vineland.

Internal consistency was supported using split-half reliability coefficients for each Vineland Form. The median split-half reliability estimates across all ages for the domains on the Survey Form range from .83 to .90. The median split-half reliability estimate across all age ranges for the Adaptive Behavior Composite on the Survey Form is .94. The internal consistency estimates reported for the Expanded Form are stepped-up estimates for split-half reliability coefficients from the Survey Form. The median stepped-up estimates of split-half reliability coefficients across all ages for the domains on the Expanded Form range from .91 to .95. The median stepped-up estimate of split-half reliability coefficient across all ages on the Expanded Form for the Adaptive Behavior Composite is .97. Internal consistency estimates for the Classroom Edition were calculated using coefficient alphas. The median internal consistency estimates across all ages for the domains on the Classroom Edition range from .80 to .95. The median internal consistency estimate across all ages for Adaptive Behavior Composite on the Classroom Edition is .98.

Test-retest reliability coefficients and inter-rater reliability estimates are available for the Survey Form. The test-retest reliability estimates across all ages range from .81 to .86 for the domains on the Survey Form. The Adaptive Behavior Composite test-retest reliability estimate is .88 for the Survey Form across all ages. Inter-rater reliability estimates across all ages range from .62 to .78 for the domains on the Survey Form. Inter-rater reliability across all age ranges is .74 for the Adaptive Behavior Composite on the Survey Form. The manuals for the three Vineland versions report validity data including factor analyses, developmental progression of scores, differences between scores of individuals with disabilities and individuals without disabilities, and correlations with other adaptive behavior scales and intelligence tests.

In addition, a measure for early childhood social-emotional development is titled the Vineland Social-Emotional Early Childhood Scale (SEEC; Sparrow, Balla, Cicchetti, 1998). The Vineland SEEC is administered to parents or caregivers of children ages birth through 5 years 11 months. The Vineland SEEC assesses a child's strengths and weaknesses in social and emotional behavior development. A social-emotional composite and three subscale scores (interpersonal relationships, play and leisure time, and coping skills) result from assessment with Vineland SEEC. Standard scores with a mean of 100 and standard deviation of 15, percentile ranks, stanines, and age equivalents are yielded by the Vineland SEEC.

Internal consistency for the Vineland SEEC was supported using split-half reliability coefficients. Median internal consistency estimates for the scales on the Vineland SEEC range from .80 to .87. The internal consistency for the composite score is .93. Test-retest reliability estimates for the scales range from .71 to .76, and the test-retest reliability estimate for the composite is .79.

AAMR Adaptive Behavior Scale-School, Second Edition (ABS-S: 2)

The ABS-S: 2 (Lambert, Nihira, & Leland, 1993) is a comprehensive norm-referenced instrument designed for children 3 through 18 years, 11 months of age. The ABS-S: 2 is divided into two parts. Part I explores adaptive behaviors and is used in assessment for diagnosis and intervention, and Part II examines maladaptive behavior. Nine adaptive behavior subdomains comprise Part I and are combined from three broad factors. The ABS-S: 2 can be administered by asking a parent, teacher, or other informant to complete a questionnaire booklet or by conducting an interview with the informant.

The ABS-S: 2 was standardized with 1,254 individuals without mental retardation and 2,074 individuals with mental retardation. Groups of individuals without mental retardation were stratified according to the following variables: age, gender, geographic region, domicile, ethnicity, parent education, instructional setting, and place of residence. The group of individuals with mental retardation was stratified on additional variables of IQ, other disabling conditions, and etiology. Percentile ranks can be obtained and factor scores are reported as standard scores with a mean of 100 and a standard deviation of 15.

Internal consistency was supported using coefficient alphas. The average internal consistency estimates for individuals without mental retardation for the Part I factors range from .88 to .93. Lambert et al. (1993) also report inter-scorer reliability estimates for the ABS-S: 2. Inter-scorer reliability estimates for the Part I factors range from .98 to .99. Test-retest corrected coefficients from the Adaptive Behavior Scale-Residential and Community: Second Edition (ABS-RC: 2) are cited by Lambert et al. (1993) to support the reliability of the ABS-S: 2 of individuals with mental retardation and individuals with emotional disturbance. Test-retest corrected coefficients range from .72 to .98 for the Part I factors.

Validity data reported in the manual consists of correlations with other adaptive behavior and intelligence scales, developmental analysis, comparison of children with disabilities and children without disabilities, and factor analyses.

Adaptive Behavior Assessment System–Second Edition (ABAS–II)

The ABAS–II (Harrison & Oakland, 2003) is a comprehensive measure of adaptive skills and consists of five versions completed by respondents familiar with the functioning and adaptive skills in the settings of the individual being assessed. The Parent/Primary Caregiver Form is administered to parents or caregivers of infants 0 to 5 years of age. The Parent Form is completed by parents or primary caregivers of individuals ages 5 to 21 years. The Teacher/Daycare Provider Form is used for children ages 2 to 5 and is completed by teachers, nurses, or other care providers involved in service settings of the child being assessed. The Teacher Form is completed by teachers of children ages 5 to 21. There is also an Adult Form for individuals ages 16 to 89, which may be completed by any third party informant in the setting of the person being assessed, or it may be completed by the persons themselves if the level of functioning allows.

The five forms available for the ABAS–II all measure adaptive behavior in the three domains (social, practical, and conceptual) listed in the AAMR (2002) definition of adaptive behavior and 10 specific adaptive skill areas. The three domains combine to produce a General Adaptive Composite.

The infant and preschool-age forms were standardized with national samples of 1,350 parents and 750 teachers, and the school-age forms were standardized with national samples of 1670 parents and 1690 teachers. Samples were stratified according to sex, race, educational level, and geographical region. Standard scores, percentile ranks, test-age equivalents, and confidence intervals are provided for the General Adaptive Composite and three domains.

Average internal consistency estimates for the Parent/Primary Caregiver Form (ages 0 to 5:11) range from .91 to .93 for the domains and is .97 for the General Adaptive Composite. The average internal consistency for the Parent Form (ages 5 to 21) ranges from .95 to .97 for the domains and is .98 for the General Adaptive Composite. Average internal consistency for the Teacher/Daycare Provider Form (ages 2:0 to 5:11) ranges from .94 to .96 for the domains, and is .98 for the General Adaptive Composite. Average internal consistency for the Teacher Form (ages 5 to 21) ranges from .97 to .98 for the domains and is .99 for the General Adaptive Composite.

Corrected test-retest reliability estimates for the Parent/Primary Caregiver Form (ages 0 to 5) across all ages range from .84 to .86 for the domains, and the reliability estimate is .88 for the General Adaptive Composite. The corrected test-retest estimates for the Parent Form (ages 5 to 21) across all ages range from .89 to .93 for the domains, and the test-retest correlation is .93 for the General Adaptive Composite. Corrected test-retest reliability estimates for the Teacher/Daycare Provider Form (ages 2 to 5:11) across all ages range from .88 to .90 for the domains, and the correlation is .91 for the General Adaptive Composite. Corrected test-retest estimates for the Teacher Form (ages 5 through 21) across all ages range from .94 to .96 for the domains, and test-retest reliability is .96 for the General Adaptive Composite.

Corrected inter-rater reliability estimates for the Parent/Primary Caregiver Form (ages 0 to 5) across all ages range from .72 to .86 for the domains, and the correlation is .82 for the General Adaptive Composite. Corrected inter-rater reliability estimates for the Parent Form (ages 5 to 21) across all ages range from .76 to .91 for the domains, and the estimate is .91 for the General Adaptive Composite. Corrected inter-rater reliability estimates for the Teacher/Daycare Provider Form (ages 2 to 5) across all ages range from .74 to .87 for the domains, and the correlation is .83 for the General Adaptive Composite. The corrected inter-rater reliability estimates for the Teacher Form (ages 5–18) across all ages range from .72 to .88 for the domains, and the estimate is .90 for the General Adaptive Composite.

Cross-form consistency estimates, or correlations between scores on the Teacher/Daycare Provider Form and the Parent/Primary Caregiver Form (ages 2 to 5) and between scores on the Teacher Forms and Parent Forms (ages 5 to 21), are provided. The corrected cross-form consistency correlations between the Teacher/Daycare Provider Form and the Parent/Primary Caregiver Form range from .58 to .69 for the domains, and the correlation is .68 for the General Adaptive Composite. The corrected cross-form consistency estimates for the Teacher Form and the Parent Form range from .63 to .79 for the domains, and the correlation is .70 for the General Adaptive Composite.

The ABAS–II manual provides validity data, which includes factor analysis, intercorrelations, and correlations of scores between behavior rating scales, intelligence scales and other adaptive behavior scales. Validity studies investigated differences of scores for individuals with and without disabilities.

Others

Several additional scales may contribute to the adaptive behavior assessment of preschool children. The Adaptive Behavior Inventory (ABI; Brown & Leigh, 1986) is administered as a questionnaire for teachers. It can be used for assessing the adaptive behavior of individuals' ages 3 through 17 years. The ABI measures academic skills, self-care skills, occupational skills, communication skills, and social skills.

The Inventory for Client and Agency Planning (ICAP; Bruininks et al., 1986) measures maladaptive and adaptive skills of infants through adults. The ICAP is a questionnaire that is completed by an individual that is familiar with the person being assessed. The domains included on the ICAP are as follows: community living skills, motor skills, personal living skills, and social and communication skills. The ICAP elicits additional information about the individual, including a general description, diagnostic status, needed assistance, functional limitations, residential placement, support services, daytime program, social involvement, and leisure activities.

The Adaptive Behavior Evaluation Scale, Revised Second Edition (ABES–R; McCarney, 1995) involves the completion of a rating scale by a teacher or parent. The instrument can be used with children in kindergarten through twelfth grade, with norms for children ages 5 through 18. The ABES–R contains 10 subscales measuring specific adaptive skill areas.

The Battelle Developmental Inventory, although not an adaptive behavior scale, can be useful because it measures several areas typically associated with adaptive behavior assessment. A new version of the Battelle Developmental Inventory, the Battelle Developmental Inventory–Second Edition (BDI–2; Newborg, 2004), is now available with new comprehensive norms and a more extensive range of items for all the domains. The BDI–2 is used with children from birth to age 8 and evaluates five domains of development (personal-social, adaptive, motor, communication, and cognitive), with each domain consisting of two or three subdomains. The five domains are combined to yield a total measure of development. Administration of the BDI–2 is flexible, as it can be administered as structured testing, as an observation, or as a parent/teacher interview.

Information obtained from instruments such as the Behavior Assessment System for Children–Second Edition (BASC–2; Reynolds & Kamphaus, 2004) and the Social Skills Rating System (SSRS; Gresham & Elliott, 1990) may provide supplemental information about the adaptive behavior of preschool children. The BASC–2 has preschool and school age clinical and adaptive scales for both parents and teachers to complete. The adaptive scales measure functioning in areas such as social skills, daily living skills, leadership, functional communication, and adaptability. The SSRS also includes both parent and teacher ratings for preschool and school age children. It measures the social skills of a child, as well as his or her externalizing, internalizing, and problem behaviors.

Clinical Assessment for Behavior (CAB; Bracken & Keith, 2004) is a behavior rating scale designed to assess adjustment, problem behaviors, and the strengths and weaknesses of individuals. The CAB has a parent rating scale for individuals ages 2 through 18 and a teacher scale for individuals ages 5 through 18. Clinical scales measure internalizing and externalizing problems, and adaptive scales measure social skills and competence. These scores are combined to create the CAB Behavioral Index. Some of the clinical and adaptive scales cluster behaviors associated with autism, mental retardation, anxiety, attention deficit and hyperactivity, and executive functioning. An extended parent version scale is also available which includes more items and two more scales than the other versions.

SUPPLEMENTAL TECHNIQUES FOR ADAPTIVE BEHAVIOR ASSESSMENT

The scales described in the previous section provide norm-referenced information about preschool children's adaptive behavior. Standardized procedures are an integral part of the assessment of preschool children, but fail to take into account a variety of factors necessary to obtain a complete picture of adaptive functioning. The informants used in a third-party assessment of adaptive behavior may present biased information or may not have the knowledge of a child's activities necessary for a valid assessment of adaptive behavior (AAMR, 2002). For example, teachers completing adaptive behavior rating scales are often forced to make estimations about children's behavior at home (Kamphaus & Frick, 2002). These estimates may not reflect knowledge of children's actual behavior, but may be based on teachers' perceptions. The ratings of general education teachers may differ significantly from those provided by special education teachers. The reference group of the person completing the instrument may result in a skewed picture of the adaptive behavior of an individual child. Adaptive behavior scales cannot sample children's adaptive skills in every possible situation encountered in daily life. Finally, standardized adaptive behavior scales measure behavior up to a given point in time. Like instruments that measure other constructs, such as intelligence and achievement, they neglect the rapid behavior and developmental changes that characterize preschool children (Telzrow, 1992).

It is important to take into account these limitations of standardized adaptive behavior rating scales when interpreting data and making decisions. Because standardized scales have a number of inherent limitations, supplemental assessment techniques should be utilized in comprehensive adaptive behavior assessment and can increase information about children's adaptive skill strengths and limitations. As is true with any type of assessment with preschool children, adaptive behavior assessment must depend as much on non-test-based assessment as it does on test-based assessment. Observations, interviewing, and continuous assessment techniques are described in this section of the chapter.

Naturalistic Observation Techniques

Behavioral observations of children's adaptive behavior in naturalistic settings provide opportunities for assessing behaviors in a variety of settings and situations (Knoff, Stollar,

Johnson, & Chenneville, 1999). Although standardized adaptive behavior scales yield a fund of information about children's activities, they are usually limited to behaviors that can be reliably and validly measured in a rating scale format. When the third-party informant method of assessment is used, there is a great reliance on respondents' memory of a wide variety of activities. Observations of children's adaptive behavior by psychologists, counselors, teachers, or other professionals allow professionals to see, first hand, children's responses to the situational demands in their environments.

Several topics discussed earlier in this chapter are relevant for structuring observations of children in a variety of situations. First, a characteristic of the construct of adaptive behavior is its situational specificity; children's adaptive behavior changes to meet the demands of different situations. Second, adaptive behavior scales, when used with parents, teachers, and other informants, can provide information about children's behavior in different settings, such as home and school. However, the response to an adaptive behavior scale by parents or teachers is often a generalized response; informants are required to indicate what children usually do across *all* situations in that environment. Observation of children's behavior in response to different situations is needed to allow a more comprehensive assessment of adaptive behavior.

There are many specific situations where children's adaptive behavior can be observed. For example, children can be observed on the playground interacting with younger versus older peers. They can be observed meeting new people and going to places they have never been before. Their interactions with parents and teachers can be compared. An astute observer should also assess the situation, in addition to assessing the child. For instance, what characteristics of a situation are preventing a child from exhibiting an adaptive behavior in that situation but not in another? What interactions seem to motivate the child and promote adaptive behavior? What interactions appear to threaten the child and impede adaptive behavior? How does adaptive behavior change as the child gains more experience with the situation?

Many children are evaluated with an adaptive behavior scale before entering preschool special education programs or other special programs. An important area to assess is children's reaction to the new program and changes in adaptive behavior that occur as a result of the program. Preschool or other early education and intervention programs may result in increases in adaptive behavior or, with some children, may extinguish previously acquired skills. Functional assessment may be used to examine responses to specific situational demands within the natural environment. This profile of the strengths and limitations can be used to develop relevant interventions for a preschool child. According to Downing and Perino (1992), functional-ecological assessment can be used as a formative evaluation that targets specific activities and environments and generates potential interventions. The use of functional assessment may provide additional information about the adaptive skills of children, the role of environmental variables in strengths and limitations, and target areas for intervention. It may also provide information about resources and supports that can be used during the intervention.

Interviews with Parents and Teachers

The third-party interview used with many adaptive behavior scales also presents a means of discussing, on an informal basis, issues which are related to adaptive behavior. Parent and teacher responses to interviews may assist in the development of a comprehensive assessment plan for children (Knoff et al., 1999). Interviews may suggest possible areas of strength and limitation in children's adaptive behavior profiles that should be thoroughly investigated. Interviews may also provide some insight into environmental factors or parenting and teaching styles that may impact adaptive behavior. Discussion with parents and teachers may provide details about parenting and teaching techniques that are being used with children. Deficits in children's adaptive behavior may be more of a function of teaching, parenting, or other environmental factors than delays in children's development. Interviews can often serve as a foundation for parent and teacher education and changing parenting and teaching to meet the needs of a particular child.

A second important function of interviews is to communicate results of assessment to parents and teachers. After the administration of an adaptive behavior scale, it is important to discuss the activities or behaviors of the child that parents and teacher find worrisome (Leland, 1983). Parents and teachers often have limited knowledge of normal child development, and they may be expecting more than a child of that age is capable of doing. For example, a parent of a 3-year-old child may be concerned that the child continues to wet the bed occasionally and will be relieved to know that this is typical of many 3-year-old children. In other cases, the worries of parents and teachers may be well founded and discussing their concerns may yield information that is important for planning interventions. Additionally, discussions should center on the implications of assessment results. In particular, parents and teachers should be involved in a discussion of types of support services available, possible interventions, and needs of children.

Continuous Assessment

Standardized and supplemental assessment procedures for preschool children must ensure that the comprehensive assessment provides a profile of the adaptive behavior strengths and limitations of a child. Information obtained during the assessment is then used to develop interventions and facilitate the needed supports in the environment. Another function of assessment is to monitor, evaluate, and modify interventions during their implementation. Continuous assessment of children's responses to interventions and supports should be conducted at several times during the implementation to examine the effectiveness of the particular intervention. If it is determined that the intervention needs modification, informal assessment may yield information about what types of changes may improve the intervention.

The role of continuous assessment of preschool children is imperative. A critical assumption of the AAMR (2002) definition of mental retardation is that with needed supports, an individual's adaptive skills will improve. Thus, the focus of assessment should extend beyond identifying strengths and limitations. It should also be used to evaluate programs and interventions. Modifications of interventions and programs can be developed from the information obtained using informal and formal assessment procedures. There should be continuous assessment of the intervention and program to ensure that supports being provided are effective at improving skill deficits.

USES OF ADAPTIVE BEHAVIOR ASSESSMENT

Information obtained from adaptive behavior assessment can be used for diagnosis and classification, eligibility decisions in special education programs and other agencies, intervention planning, and determining needed supports in the environment. Ysseldyke, Algozzine and Thurlow (2000) noted that assessment is important in decision making and planning the intervention process. A major function of adaptive behavior assessment is to provide information that leads to decisions about the nature, diagnosis, and classification of disabilities. A second use of adaptive behavior assessment is to acquire information that will assist in the determination of needed supports and the development of appropriate interventions for children with disabilities and other problems.

Diagnosis/Classification

Historically, adaptive behavior assessment has been used to diagnose and classify individuals with mental retardation. The AAMR (2002) definition of mental retardation requires that deficits in adaptive behavior, as well as in intellectual functioning, must be substantiated for a person to be classified as having mental retardation. Most states include adaptive behavior deficits in their definitions of mental retardation and require assessment of adaptive behavior to determine eligibility for special services for individuals with mental retardation (Denning, Chamberlain, & Polloway, 2000).

Adaptive behavior assessment can also be used for the identification of disabilities or problems other than mental retardation, because it is reasonable to expect that many disabilities and problems will involve limitations in personal and social functioning. Research reviewed by Harrison (1990) suggested that individuals with learning disabilities, emotional disturbances, and sensory impairments experienced deficits in adaptive behavior areas. Furthermore, she stressed that children with any type of disability or developmental problem can benefit from training and interventions in specific adaptive skill areas. Bucy et al. (1999) suggested that adaptive behavior assessment plays an important role in assessment of children with developmental disabilities and at-risk conditions.

Adaptive behavior scales have recently become more widely used in identifying children with disorders such as autism and developmental delay. Children with autism typically have delays in communication and socialization (Gillham, Carter, Volkmar, & Sparrow, 2000; Stone, Ousley, Hepburn, Hogan, & Brown, 1999). Gillham et al. (2000) noted that adaptive behavior scales often measure behaviors such as communication, social skills, and other developmental skills that are central in diagnosing autism in young children. Kamphaus and Frick (2002) suggested that adaptive behavior assessment for children with autism is useful for identifying needed skills and monitoring interventions.

Intervention Planning

All assessment of preschoolers must lead to appropriate intervention plans. Verhaaren and Conner (1981) wrote that the results of assessment have three major purposes. Assessment should lead to education, or the teaching of skills to children that enable them to achieve their potential. Assessment should lead to prevention, or keeping any further problems or disabilities from occurring. Finally, assessment should lead to correction, or the reduction of any disabilities.

The important links between assessment, intervention, and supports are stressed in the AAMR (2002) manual. AAMR's manual describes the expanded role of an assessment team as a multidisciplinary group that explores not only the strengths and limitations, but also identifies supports and services that can address the adaptive skill needs of individuals. Additionally, this assessment should be an ongoing, problem-solving process that meets the needs of individuals. AAMR suggests that the support plan developed from the comprehensive and continuous assessments of strengths and limitations should result in greater independence, improved relationships, more involvement in school and community events, greater contributions, and improved happiness for individuals

Adaptive skills training programs will be more effective when they occur in the environments where the children are expected to exhibit the skills. For example, all interventions for preschool children must involve parents, in addition to teachers and other professionals, because many activities, such as dressing and hygiene, occur more often at home. Other adaptive skills, such as eating and interpersonal skills, occur both at home and school. Doll (1953) reported that parental education was one of the primary uses of assessment with the Vineland Social Maturity Scale, the first major measure of adaptive behavior.

Training of adaptive behavior should be an ongoing process for children and not limited to structured training situations. Certain skills can be learned by children through direct teaching, but efforts should be made to foster generalization of the skills to daily activities. For example, using dolls or other toys to teach dressing skills should be accompanied by teaching that occurs when children are actually dressing themselves.

Langone and Burton (1987) suggested that adaptive skills training requires carefully designed task sequences. These task sequences should be hierarchically arranged, from the simplest component of an activity to the most difficult. Several adaptive behavior scales, including the ABS-SE: 2, Vineland Expanded Form, and Vineland SEEC, list activities in hierarchical sequences.

Cone (1987) listed a series of steps to be used for planning adaptive behavior intervention programs. The first step is to determine a long-range goal for the child, which, according to Cone, should be the behavior that is required for a specific situation, such as entry into the next less restrictive program. The second step is to determine the child's performance of that activity. Step 3 is to determine the skills needed by the child to achieve the long-range goal. The fourth step is to estimate the amount of time it will take for the child to achieve the long-range goal. The final steps are to establish annual goals, monthly goals, short-term goals, and immediate instructional objectives.

AAMR (2002) focuses on the supports needed for individuals with mental retardation. The model suggests that support areas, support functions, and personal outcomes are affected by the individual's personal capabilities and adaptive skills, risk and protective factors, and participation in different environments. In assessing skills and creating individual support plans for preschool children with any type of disability or learning and behavior problem, the following points appear to be particularly relevant: (a) Recognize appropriate support areas (human development, teaching and education, health and safety, behavioral, social, and protection and advocacy) that may be the most relevant areas for the young child; (b) Identify support activities according to the child's interests; (c) Identify settings in which the child prefers to enhance participation; (d) Determine the frequency and amount of support needed; (e) Emphasize the use of natural supports; (f) Determine the person or persons in charge of implicating supports; and (g) Create goals for personal outcomes appropriate for the child.

RESEARCH AND ADAPTIVE BEHAVIOR ASSESSMENT

Two areas of research have major implications for the use and interpretation of adaptive behavior assessment. First, because deficits in intelligence and adaptive behavior are key features of diagnosing mental retardation, much research has investigated the relationship between intelligence tests and adaptive behavior scales. Second, adaptive behavior scales have their primary use with individuals with disabilities such as mental retardation, autism, developmental delays, and others, and research has investigated adaptive behavior deficits for children with disabilities. Research relevant for adaptive behavior assessment of preschool children is summarized in the following sections.

Relationship between Adaptive Behavior and Intelligence

A common misconception is that adaptive behavior and cognitive functioning are equivalent (Coulter, 1980). Harrison (1990) suggested that correlations between adaptive behavior scales and intelligence test scores typically are in the moderate range for a number of reasons, including the following: (1) intelligence is conceptualized as a thought process, while adaptive behavior emphasizes everyday behavior; (2) intelligence scales measure maximum performance (potential), while adaptive behavior scales measure typical performance; and (3) intelligence scales assume a stability in scores, while adaptive behavior scales assume that performance can be modified. Research by Keith, Fehrmann, Harrison and Pottebaum (1987) provided support for the hypothesis that intelligence and adaptive behavior are two distinct, but related, constructs.

A number of studies have supported the moderate correlations between scores from intelligence tests and adaptive behavior scales. Manuals for recent adaptive behavior scales report generally low to moderate correlations between adaptive behavior scales and intelligence test scores.

Bruininks, Hill, Weatherman, and Woodcock (1986) reported high correlations between the SIB–R adaptive behavior clusters and Broad Independence Score and the Woodcock Johnson Revised (WJ–R) Broad Cognitive Ability scores. Correlations between SIB–R and WJ–R ranged from .27 to .34 for young children without disabilities and .63 to .80 for children without disabilities. Bruininks et al. reported higher correlations between earlier versions of the instruments (SIB and WJ) for children with disabilities. Goldstein, Smith, Waldrep, and Inderbitzen (1987) compared the Early Development and Short Forms of the SIB and the Survey Form of the Vineland with the Bayley Scales of Infant Development. Correlations were moderate between the adaptive behavior scales (Vineland and SIB) and moderate to high between the adaptive behavior scales and the mental and motor development scales on the Bayley Scales of Infant Development.

Sparrow et al. (1984b, 1985) reported low to moderate correlations between the Vineland Adaptive Behavior Scales and the Kaufman Assessment Battery for Children (K-ABC) and the Peabody Picture Vocabulary Test–Revised (PPVT–R) for samples of children that participated in the national standardization. Correlations between the Vineland Survey Form domains and Adaptive Behavior Composite and the K-ABC global scale standard scores ranged from .07 to .52. Correlations between the Vineland Survey Form and PPVT–R ranged from .12 to 37. Correlations between the domains and Adaptive Behavior Composite on the Vineland-Classroom Edition and the K-ABC global standard scores ranged from .23 to .64. Correlations between the Vineland- Classroom Edition and PPVT–R ranged from .20 to .45. The highest correlations were found between the communication domain of the Vineland and K-ABC. The Vineland authors also reported correlations between adaptive behavior and intelligence test scores for several samples of individuals with disabilities and reported correlations that are somewhat higher than those found for children in the national standardization.

Lambert et al. (1993) reported correlations between the ABS-S: 2 and various intelligence tests for individuals with mental retardation. Correlations were generally in the low to moderate range.

Harrison and Oakland (2003) reported correlations between the ABAS–II and several intelligence scales, such as the Wechsler Preschool and Primary Scale of Intelligence-Revised (WPPSI–II), the Wechsler Intelligence Scale for Children–Third Edition and Fourth Edition (WISC–III and WISC–IV). Correlations between the intelligence test scores and ABAS-II domains and composite were moderate for samples of children without disabilities. Correlations between the WPPSI–II Full Scale IQ scores and ABAS–II domains and composite ranged from .48 to .60 for the Parent/Primary Caregiver Form and .51 to .63 for the Teacher/Daycare Provider Form. Correlations between the ABAS–II Parent Form and the WISC–III Full Scale IQ ranged from .34 to .50, and correlations for the ABAS–II Teacher Form and the WISC–III Full Scale IQ ranged from .52 to 69. The ABAS–II Parent Form and the WISC–IV Full Scale IQ had correlations ranging from .28 to .49, and the ABAS–II Teacher Form and the WISC–IV Full Scale IQ had correlations ranging from .43 to .63. The ABAS–II authors also reported correlations between adaptive behavior and intelligence test scores for several clinical samples of individuals with disabilities and other problems and reported correlations that are somewhat higher than those found for children without disabilities.

Adaptive Behavior Scores of Young Children with Disabilities

Mental Retardation.   Children with mental retardation and associated disorders, such as Williams syndrome, Fragile X syndrome, and Down syndrome, often have deficits in adaptive functioning. Harrison and Oakland (2003) reported studies of individuals with mental retardation in the ABAS-II manual. Samples of preschool-age and school-age children with mild and moderate mental retardation were compared to matched control groups. Results indicated that children with mental retardation had significantly lower scores on the skill areas, domains, and the General Adaptive Composite of the ABAS–II. Harrison and Oakland (2003) reported similar results for children with Down syndrome and children with mental retardation (unspecified), when compared to matched control groups.

Dykens, Hodapp, and Evans (1994) conducted a study of 80 children with Down syndrome to determine adaptive skills, as measured by the Vineland, which were strengths and weaknesses for these individuals. They found that communication, relative to daily living and social skills, was a weakness. Receptive communication appeared to be a relative strength, compared to expressive communication.

Fragile X is a syndrome associated with mental retardation and is frequently a genetic cause of mental retardation. Many individuals with Fragile X are found to experience symptoms of autism and IQ scores in the range of mental retardation. Rogers, Wehner, and Hagerman (2001) found that samples of preschool-age male children with Fragile X syndrome had lower Vineland scores than samples of children with autism and other developmental disorders. Williams syndrome is another syndrome associated with mental retardation. Children with Williams syndrome ages 4 through 8 were examined by Mervis, Klien-Tasman, and Mastin (2001). The researchers reported that children with Williams syndrome had weaknesses in daily living skills and stronger adaptive skills in communication and social skills.

Autism.   Autism is a disorder characterized by delays in communication and social skills and often delays in other adaptive behavior skill areas. For this reason, it is important that children are identified early in order to promote developmental skills. It has been found that children with autism typically score lower on adaptive behavior scales than individuals with other disorders or with typical functioning, especially in the communication and socialization domains.

Stone et al. (1999) and Carpentieri and Morgan (1996) found that children with autism had lower scores on the Communication and Socialization domains than on other domains of the Vineland. Children with autism are often compared to children with Fragile X, as individuals with Fragile X often have symptoms of autism. Fisch, Simensen, and Schroer (2002) examined Vineland adaptive behavior scores and cognitive abilities in these two groups over an eight-year period and reported that children with autism had declines in adaptive behavior with age across all domains. Fisch et al. (2002) noted that children with autism have generally lower levels of adaptive functioning, socialization, and communication.

Other studies comparing children with autism to children with other disorders and typically developing children have shown similar results. Rodrigue, Morgan, and Geffken (1991) and Loveland and Kelley (1991) reported that, when compared to children with Down syndrome and typically developing children, children with autism showed greater deficits in social skills and lower scores and often more scattered scores on adaptive behavior measures. Paul et al., (2004) found that when comparing children with autism to children with Pervasive Developmental Disorder-Not Otherwise Specified of similar intellectual levels, children with autism exhibited lower scores in the socialization, daily living, and communication domains on the Vineland. They reported that the greatest deficit noted in children with autism was found in the expressive communication subdomain.

Harrison and Oakland (2003) summarized studies of preschool-aged children with autism and Pervasive Developmental Disorder-Not Otherwise Specified. They reported that children with these disorders scored significantly lower than matched controls on many skill areas, domains and the General Adaptive Composite on the ABAS–II than do children in the matched control group.

Other Disabilities.   Comparative studies have also been conducted with children with other disabilities, such as developmental delay, Attention Deficit Hyperactivity Disorder (ADHD), and emotional or behavioral problems. Bruininks et al. (1996) reported a comparative study of individuals with and without disabilities in the SIB–R manual. Individuals with moderate disabilities and developmental delay were compared with age-matched individuals without disabilities using the SIB–R Early Development Form. Adaptive behavior scores were significantly lower for children with disabilities than for children without disabilities.

Harrison and Oakland (2003) compared ABAS–II scores of children with developmental delay to those of matched controls. Children with developmental delays showed significant deficits across domains and on the General Adaptive Composite. However, the children did not have lower scores on all specific skill areas when compared to controls.

Harrison and Oakland (2003) compared ABAS–II scores of children with ADHD and matched controls. Results with the Teacher Form showed that children with ADHD had lower scores across skill areas, domains, and the General Adaptive Composite. However, for the Parent Form, children with ADHD had significantly lower scores on three skill areas (communication, functional academics, and self-direction), one domain (conceptual) and the General Adaptive Composite.

Sparrow et al. (1984b) and Harrison and Oakland (2003) reported adaptive behavior score comparisons for children with emotional disturbance. Sparrow et al. (1984b) found that average Vineland standard scores of a sample with emotional disturbance were lower than scores of the national standardized sample. The lowest area of performance for the group with emotional disturbance was the socialization domain. Harrison and Oakland (2003) had similar results for the ABAS–II.

Finally, Harrison and Oakland (2003) compared the ABAS–II scores of young children with motor and physical impairments with scores of matched controls. Children with motor impairments had lower scores on the Teacher/Day care Provider Form for most skill areas (excluding communication and self-direction), across all domains, and the General Adaptive Composite. For the Parent/Primary Caregiver Form, children with motor impairments had lower scores across all adaptive behaviors skill areas, domains, and the General Adaptive Composite.

CONCLUSION

The importance of adaptive behavior assessment in developing a comprehensive understanding of preschool children has become widely accepted. Standardized scales, combined with supplemental observations and interviews, provide important information about the strengths and limitations of children's adaptive behavior. Information about adaptive skills can be used to develop interventions and support services for needed areas. Adaptive behavior assessment also has a major role in the ongoing evaluation of the needs of preschool children and the progress of interventions.

Adaptive behavior assessment has become an integral part of early childhood diagnosis, classification, and intervention programs. Legislation has emphasized assessment and intervention of all developmental areas. In addition, the Individual with Disabilities Act of 1991 and its 1997 reauthorization have widened the scope of adaptive behavior beyond the field of mental retardation and support the use of the construct in assessment and intervention of children with other disabilities. The 1997 legislation expands the age limits for developmental delay, and the 2004 reauthorization of IDEA places increasing emphasis on early interventions and on identifying the needs of young children. The most important factors to address when examining adaptive behavior of preschool children are that the assessment must provide comprehensive information that enhances the understanding of the strengths and limitations of children and, ultimately, facilitates the development of interventions and support systems that address the needs of children.

REFERENCES

American Association on Mental Retardation. (1992). *Definitions, classifications, and systems of supports* (9th ed.). Washington, DC: Author.

American Association on Mental Retardation. (2002). *Mental retardation: Definition, classification, and systems of supports* (10th ed.). Washington, DC: Author.

American Psychiatric Association. (2000). *Diagnostic and Statistical Manual of Mental Disorders* (4th ed., text revision). Washington, DC: Author.

Bracken, B. A., & Keith, L. K. (2004). *Clinical Assessment of Behavior*. Lutz, FL: Psychological Assessment Resources.

Brown, L., & Leigh, J. E. (1986). *Adaptive Behavior Inventory*. Austin, TX: PRO-ED.

Bruininks, R. H., Woodcock, R. W., Weatherman, R. F., & Hill, B. K. (1996). Scales *of Independent Behavior, Revised*. Chicago, IL: Riverside.

Bruininks, R. H., Hill, B. K., Weatherman, R., & Woodcock, R. W. (1986). *Inventory for Client and Agency Planning*. Chicago, IL: Riverside.

Bucy, J. E., Smith, T., & Landau, S. (1999). Assessment of preschool children with developmental disabilities and at-risk conditions. In E. V. Nuttall, I. Romero, & Kalesnik, J. (Eds.). *Assessing and screening preschoolers* (2nd ed., pp. 318–339). Boston: Allyn & Bacon.

Carpentieri, S., & Morgan, S. B. (1996). Adaptive and intellectual functioning in autistic and nonautistic retarded children. *Journal of Autism and Developmental Disorders, 26*(6), 611–620.

Cone, J. D. (1987). Intervention planning using adaptive behavior instruments. *Journal of Special Education, 21*, 127–148.

Coulter, W. A. (1980). Adaptive behavior and professional disfavor: Controversies and trends for school psychologists. *School Psychology Review, 9*, 67–74.

Demchak, M. A., & Drinkwater, S. (1998). Assessing adaptive behavior. In B. Vance (Ed.), *Psychological assessment of children: Best practices for school and clinical settings* (2nd ed., pp. 297–319). New York: Wiley.

Denning, C. B., Chamberlain, J. A., & Polloway, E. A. (2000). An evaluation of state guidelines for mental retardation: Focus of definition and classification practices. *Education and Training in Mental Retardation and Development, 35*, 226–232.

Department of Education. (1999). Individuals with disabilities education act of 1997.

Doll, E. A. (1953). *Measurement of social competence.* Circle Pines, MN: American Guidance Service.

Downing, J., & Perino, D. M. (1992). Functional versus standardized assessment procedures: Implications for educational programming. *Mental Retardation, 30*, 289–295.

Dykens, E. M., Hodapp, R. M., & Evans, D. W. (1994). Profiles and development of adaptive behavior in children with Down syndrome. *American Journal on Mental Retardation, 98*(5), 580–587.

Edwards, C. P. (1999). Development in the preschool years: The typical path. In E. V. Nuttall, I. Romero, & Kalesnik, J. (Eds.), *Assessing and screening preschoolers* (2nd ed., pp. 9–24). Boston: Allyn & Bacon.

Fisch, G. S., Simensen, R. J., & Schroer, R. J. (2002). Longitudinal changes in cognitive and adaptive behavior scores in children and adolescents with the Fragile X mutation or autism. *Journal of Autism and Developmental Disorders, 32*(2), 107–114.

Gillham, J. E., Carter, A. S., Volkmar, F. R., & Sparrow, S. S. (2000). Toward a developmental operational definition of autism. *Journal of Autism and Developmental Disorders, 30*(4), 269–278.

Goldstein, D. J., Smith, K. B., Waldrep, E. L., & Inderbitzen, H. M. (1987). Comparison of the Woodcock Johnson scales of independent behavior and the Vineland Adaptive Behavior Scales in infant assessment. *Journal of Psychoeducational Assessment, 3*, 1–6.

Greenspan, S. (1999). A contextualize perspective on adaptive behavior. In R. L. Schalock (Ed.), *Adaptive behavior and its measurement* (pp. 61–80). Washington, DC: American Association on Mental Retardation.

Gresham, R. M., & Elliott, S. N. (1990). *Social Skills Rating System.* Circle Pines, MN: American Guidance Service.

Grossman, H. J. (1983). *Classification in mental retardation.* Washington, DC: American Association on Mental Deficiency.

Harrison, P. L. (1990). Mental retardation, adaptive behavior assessment, and giftedness. In A. S. Kaufman, *Assessing adolescent and adult intelligence* (pp. 533–585). Boston: Allyn & Bacon.

Harrison, P. L., & Oakland, T. (2003). *Adaptive Behavior Assessment System, Second Edition.* San Antonio, TX: The Psychological Corporation.

Horn, E., & Fuchs, D. (1987). Using adaptive behavior assessment and intervention: An overview. *Journal of Special Education, 21*, 11–26.

Individuals with Disabilities Education Improvement Act. (2004). Retrieved January 21, 2005, from http://edworkforce.house.gov/issues/108th/education/idea/conferencereport/confrept.htm

Kamphaus, R. W., & Frick, P. J. (2002). *Clinical assessment of child and adolescent personality and behavior* (2nd ed.). Boston: Allyn & Bacon.

Keith, T. A., Fehrmann, P. G., Harrison, P. L., & Pottebaum, S. M. (1987). The relationship between adaptive behavior and intelligence: Testing alternative explanations. *Journal of School Psychology, 25*, 31–43.

Knoff, H. M., Stollar, S. A., Johnson, J. J., & Chenneville, T. A. (1999). Assessment of social-emotional functioning and adaptive behavior. In E. V. Nuttall, I. Romero, & Kalesnik, J. (Eds.), *Assessing and screening preschoolers* (2nd ed., pp. 126–160). Boston: Allyn & Bacon.

Lambert, N., Nihira, K., & Leland, H. (1993). *Adaptive Behavior Scale-School Edition, second edition, examiner's manual*. Austin, TX: PRO-ED.

Langone, J., & Burton, T. A. (1987). Teaching adaptive behavior skills to moderately and severely handicapped individuals: Best practices for facilitating independent living. *Journal of Special Education, 21*, 149–166.

Leland, H. (1983). Assessment of adaptive behavior. In K. D. Paget, & B. A. Bracken (Eds.), *The psychoeducational assessment of preschool children* (pp. 191–206). New York: Grune & Stratton.

Loveland, K. A., & Kelley, M. L. (1991). Development of adaptive behavior in preschoolers with autism or Down syndrome. *American Journal on Mental Retardation, 96*(1), 13–20.

McCarney, S. B. (1995). *Adaptive Behavior Evaluation Scale, Revised Second Edition*. Columbia, MO: Hawthorne Educational Service.

Mervis, C. B., Klein-Tasman, B. P., & Mastin, M. E. (2001). Adaptive behavior of 4- through 8-year-old children with Williams syndrome. *American Journal on Mental Retardation, 106*(1), 82–93.

National Association of School Psychologists. (1999). Position statement on early childhood assessment. Retrieved on January 24, 2005, from http://nasponline.org/information/popaper_eca.html

Newborg, J. (2004). Battelle Developmental Inventory (2nd ed.). Chicago, IL: Riverside Publishing Company.

Nihira, K. (1999). Adaptive behavior: A historical overview. In R. L. Schalock (Ed.), *Adaptive behavior and its measurement* (pp. 7–14). Washington, DC: American Association on Mental Retardation.

Paul, R., Miles, S., Cicchetti, D., Sparrow, S., Klin, A., Volkmar, F., Coflin, M., & Booker, S. (2004). Adaptive behavior in autism and pervasive developmental disorder-not otherwise specified: Microanalysis of scores on the Vineland Adaptive Behavior Scales. *Journal of Autism and Developmental Disorders, 34*(2), 223–228.

Reschly, D. J., Myers, T. G., & Hartel, C. R. (Eds.). (2002). *Disability determination for mental retardation*. Washington, DC: National Academy Press.

Reynolds, C. R., & Kamphaus, R. W. (2004). *Behavior Assessment System for Children, Second Edition*. Circle Pines, MN: American Guidance Service.

Rogers, S. J., Wehner, E. A., & Hagerman, R. (2001). The behavioral phenotype in fragile X: Symptoms of autism in very young children with fragile X syndrome, idiopathic autism, and other developmental disorders. *Journal of Developmental and Behavioral Pediatrics, 22*(6), 409–418.

Rodrigue, J. R., Morgan, S. B., & Geffken, G. R. (1991). A comparative evaluation of adaptive behavior in children and adolescents with autism, Down syndrome, and normal development. *Journal of Autism and Developmental Disorders, 21*(2), 187–196.

Sattler, J. M. (2002). *Assessment of children: Behavioral and clinical applications*. San Diego, CA: Author.

Sparrow, S. S., Balla, D. A., & Cicchetti, D. V. (1984a). *Vineland Adaptive Behavior Scales, Expanded Form*. Circle Pines, MN: American Guidance Service.

Sparrow, S. S., Balla, D. A., & Cicchetti, D. V. (1984b). *Vineland Adaptive Behavior Scales, Survey Form*. Circle Pines, MN: American Guidance Service.

Sparrow, S. S., Balla, D. A., & Cicchetti, D. V. (1985). *Vineland Adaptive Behavior Scales, Classroom Edition*. Circle Pines, MN: American Guidance Service.

Sparrow, S. S., Balla, D. A., & Cicchetti, D. V. (1998). *Vineland Social-Emotional Early Childhood Scale*. Circle Pines, MN: American Guidance Service.

Stone, W. L., Ousley, O. Y., Hepburn, S. L., Hogan, K. L., & Brown, C. S. (1999). Patterns of adaptive behavior in very young children with autism. *American Journal on Mental Retardation, 104*(2), 187–199.

Tasse, M. J., & Craig, E. M. (1999). Critical issues in the cross-cultural assessment of adaptive behavior. In R. L. Schalock (Ed.), *Adaptive behavior and its measurement* (pp. 161–183). Washington, DC: American Association on Mental Retardation.

Telzrow, C. F. (1992). Young children with special educational needs. In T. R. Kratochwill, S. N. Elliott, & M. Gettinger (Eds.). *Preschool and early childhood treatment directions* (pp. 55–88). Hillsdale, NJ: Lawrence Erlbaum Associates.

Thompson, J. R., McGrew, K. S., & Bruininks, R. H. (1999). Adaptive and maladaptive behavior: Functional and structural characteristics. In R. L. Schalock (Ed.), *Adaptive behavior and its measurement* (pp. 15–42). Washington, DC: American Association on Mental Retardation.

Verhaaren, P., & Conner, F. P. (1981). Physical disabilities. In J. M. Kauffman & D. P. Hallahan (Eds.), *Handbook of Special Education*. Englewood Cliffs, NJ: Prentice-Hall.

Ysseldyke, J.E., Algozzine, B., & Thurlow, M. (2000). *Critical issues in special education* (3rd ed.). Boston, MA: Houghton Mifflin.

11

Play-Based Approaches
to Preschool Assessment

Michelle S. Athanasiou
University of Northern Colorado

As a major activity of childhood, play has been given considerable attention by professionals concerned with the diagnosis and treatment of young children. Although play was first used as a medium for assessing and treating emotional and behavioral difficulties, more recent attention has focused on the information play can provide about child development. This interest is based on the developmental nature of play and its correspondence to cognitive, social/emotional, language, and motor functioning.

This chapter is divided into two major sections. First, an overview of play development is presented, along with brief discussions of how play is related to development in other domains. The second section addresses play-based assessment. First, two models of play-based assessment are presented. Next, informal play observations are discussed, followed by a consideration of the strengths and limitations of a play-based approach to assessment.

OVERVIEW OF PLAY DEVELOPMENT

Play has proven difficult to define, because of the multitude of behaviors that can be considered play and because connotations of "play" are vague and often idiosyncratic (Johnson, Christie, & Yawkey, 1999). What has helped shape accepted definitions of play are discussions about the characteristics of play. Some commonly accepted play characteristics include the following:

1. *Play is intrinsically motivated*. It is not dependent on rewards or other external motivation; rather, it is engaged in for its own sake (Hughes, 1995; Johnson et al., 1999).
2. *Play is freely chosen*. Any coercion to engage in an activity may preclude it from being considered play (Hughes, 1995). Children themselves are more likely to consider an activity play if it is chosen (Johnson et al., 1999).

Michelle S. Athanasiou, Ph.D. is a Professor of School Psychology at the University of Northern Colorado. She received her M.A. degree from The University of Memphis and her Ph.D. from the University of Nebraska-Lincoln. Her teaching and research interests include early childhood assessment, intervention, and service delivery, and school-based consultation.

3. *Play is pleasurable*. It is something enjoyable that usually elicits positive affect (Hughes, 1995; Johnson et al., 1999).

4. *Play is nonliteral*. It involves an element of pretend or make-believe that takes precedence over external reality (Hughes, 1995; Johnson et al., 1999). It should be noted that some argue that earlier actions with objects that do not involve pretend are also play (e.g., Casby, 2003b).

5. *Play involves a "means-over-ends" orientation*. Play does not seem to serve an immediate purpose. Children at play are less concerned about the outcome of their behavior than the processes operating during play (Bjorklund & Pellegrini, 2002; Johnson et al., 1999).

6. *Play involves active engagement*. During play, children are more attentive to the play than most other stimuli (Hughes, 1995).

In addition to the characteristics of play discussed above, play can be considered a developmental phenomenon that follows a relatively set sequence. The following section contains a brief discussion about typical play development. Consistent with the focus of this text, the discussion highlights the development of play in early childhood, as opposed to advances in play skills made after this period. The following information pertains to how play development relates to concomitant cognitive development and the increasingly social nature of play. Although other aspects of play are certainly important (e.g., competition, object usage), a more comprehensive discussion of play development is beyond the scope of this chapter.

Cognitive Dimensions of Play Development

Advances in the sophistication of children's play follow concurrent advances in cognitive development. Piaget's (1962) model of play set the stage for contemporary play development theories (see Lowe, 1975; Sinclair, 1970; Uzgiris & Hunt, 1975, for example). Casby (2003b) reviewed theories of play development, and he aggregated them to build a framework of play development (Casby, 2003a). Casby (2003b) proposed the following stages of play which are discussed in this section: 1) sensorimotor-exploratory; 2) relational-nonfunctional; 3) functional-conventional; and 4) symbolic.

Sensorimotor-exploratory play emerges at approximately 2 to 4 months and extends to approximately 10 to 12 months. This type of play is characterized by the manipulation and inspection of objects, and it is associated with the secondary circular reactions substage of Piaget's sensorimotor period (i.e., actions with objects are repeated, with no regard for the conventional function of the object). For example, infants bang objects on tables in order to produce an effect (i.e., sound production).

Relational-nonfunctional play emerges around 5 to 10 months and is prevalent between 6 and 12 months. This type of play corresponds to the coordination of secondary circular reactions sensorimotor substage, and it involves infants acting on more than one object at a time, still in a way that disregards typical uses for the objects. It includes actions such as nesting, stacking, or pushing objects together.

During the period of functional-conventional play, young children begin to use objects in ways for which they are intended (e.g., stirring a spoon in a bowl, holding a brush to their hair). This type of play is sometimes referred to as presymbolic, and it represents the child's understanding of the functional use of the object, rather than an expression of pretense (McCune, 1995).

Symbolic play, which appears slowly beginning in the second year of life, requires the use of mental symbols to represent objects (Piaget, 1962). It is during this period that pretend or make-believe play begins. Casby (2003a) characterized the development of pretense as involving increasing sophistication in three components of symbolic play: agent, instrument, and scheme.

Development of the agent component involves the instigator of the pretend action moving from self to other. Initially, the child himself or herself is the instigator of play actions (e.g., the child pretends to comb her own hair). This is considered the *self-as-agent* stage. Later, in *passive-other-agent* symbolic play, the child uses a substitute agent, but it does not perform an action. For example, the child might hold a telephone to a doll's ear, but not have it speak (Casby, 2003a). Finally, in *active-other-agent* play, the substitute object is animate (e.g., having the teddy bear talk to the doll).

The instrument component deals with the objects used to enact the pretend. At first, these objects are real or very realistic (e.g., pretending to drink from an empty cup) (Bjorklund & Pellegrini, 2002). Object substitution becomes less dependent on functional or characteristic similarity as children develop, such that by age 3, children are able to substitute play objects that bear little resemblance to the real object. For example, a child can pretend a long stick is a horse for riding (McCune, 1995; Rubin & Pepler, 1982). Finally, children are able to pretend with imaginary objects that stand in for the real objects (e.g., pretending to hold a phone to their ear).

With regard to schemes, or actions that children perform, symbolic play proceeds from the simple to the complex. Play proceeds from single schemes (e.g., pretending to feed a doll) to multi-scheme combinations (e.g., feeding, rocking, and putting the doll to bed) by late in the second year of life. Additionally, the schemes themselves become more complex and involve more pre-planning. Initially, pretend play sequences appear to be prompted by and dependent upon present objects. A child who is playing with a doll and a cup may have the doll drink from the cup, for example. Later, young children begin to plan pretend activities in the absence of environmental props and subsequently gather the necessary materials to enact the planned pretend.

Social Dimensions of Play Development

According to Piaget, play becomes increasingly social throughout the preschool period. The ability to play with other children reflects the increasing social maturity of children. Nevertheless, Piaget's interest lay primarily in the cognitive aspects of play development. Mildred Parten (1932), by contrast, provided an early framework for play development specifically as a social entity. Based on observations of nursery school children ages 2 to 5, Parten proposed five stages of social play behaviors that were supposedly related to children's increasing social skills. In *solitary* play, children play alone with toys or engage in activities independent of other children, with no attempts at social interaction. This is purportedly followed by *onlooker* play, which involves children watching or otherwise showing an interest in the play of nearby children, but not attempting to join the play. *Parallel* play occurs when children near each other play with similar toys in similar ways, but mutual play does not occur. *Associative* play includes interaction among children through sharing materials, but the play is loosely organized, and the child's own play is of greater interest than that of others. Finally, *cooperative* play involves group activity that is goal oriented, and children work together to devise or elaborate upon a game or play theme.

According to Parten, as children's social skills increase, they display more of the later types of play and rely less on solitary and parallel play. Therefore, younger children would be expected to play alone or in tandem with other children, but as social interaction skills increase, children would then to engage in more associative and cooperative play.

Although widely cited as a useful framework, some writers have questioned Parten's typology. Howes and Matheson (1992) wrote that Parten's stages do not form a developmental sequence that reflects increases in social competence. Instead, they are more likely to appear as sequences in individual play episodes. Children may play alone, and as their social comfort increases in the play environment, they often progress to playing with others close by. Smith (1978) stated that not all children follow Parten's stages. Furthermore, children often rehearse play skills in solitary play before trying them out with others. Therefore, solitary play does not necessarily imply social immaturity. Howes and Matheson (1992) also developed and validated a typology for the development of social play skills. Unlike Parten's model, this scheme has more of a focus on pretend play skills with peers. According to this model, peer play begins with *parallel aware play*, which emerges at approximately 12 to 15 months and is defined as parallel play with eye contact (Howes, Unger, & Seidner, 1989). Next, *simple social play* emerges (15–20 months). This is defined as playing the same, or a similar activity, while engaging in social interaction with a peer. *Complementary and reciprocal social play* occurs at 13 to 23 months and includes demonstration of action-based role reversals in games (e.g., run and chase). *Cooperative social pretend play* (24–30 months) is the enactment of complementary pretend roles within social play (roles being clear by the actions of the children). During this stage, children play together in a pretend fashion without verbally communicating about their pretense (Howes, 1987). Finally, *complex social pretend play* (30–35 months) is described as social pretend play with metacommunication about the pretend aspects of the play (Howes & Matheson, 1992). For example, children engaging in complex social pretend direct each others' pretend play by giving each other instructions (e.g., "You be the mommy and I am the baby, and let's say I'm sick."). Because complex social pretend requires children to communicate about the pretense with a peer who is equal to themselves in terms of communicative sophistication, Howes and Matheson (1992) stated this type of play represents an intersection of cognitive, linguistic, and social aspects of development.

The Importance of Play: Relation to Other Developmental Domains

Play has been viewed as an all-encompassing activity which assists in all other areas of development (Casby, 2003b; Stagnitti, Unsworth, & Rodger, 2000). The following is a brief synopsis of the relation of play to cognitive, social/emotional, language, and motor development, in terms of how play enhances functioning in these domains and vice versa. For more extensive information, the reader is referred to Hughes (1995), Slade and Wolf (1994), and Johnson et al. (1999).

Cognitive Development

Play and its relation to cognitive characteristics have been studied extensively, probably in part because of the role of cognition in the development of play. Several aspects of cognitive development, as they are influenced by play, have been given significant attention. Play has been credited for increases in divergent thinking, because it provides practice with abstract thinking and imagination, as well opportunities to practice divergent strategies (Barnett, 1991; Russ, 2004). These findings were supported by Fisher (1992), who conducted a meta-analysis of 46 studies of the relation of play to development. Of all the variables investigated, Fisher found the largest effect sizes for divergent thinking and perspective taking. The effect of play on divergent thinking, along with the demonstrated relationship between play and insight, has led many to believe in the impact of play on creativity (Russ, 2004).

Others have found that symbolic play is related to problem-solving (Athey, 1984; Simon & Smith, 1983). The mechanism for this is unclear, however. Play may provide children with a flexible approach to their environment that they use in problem situations (Barnett, 1991). Play also has been linked to improvements in decentration (ability to consider more than one aspect of a situation or problem at a time) and reversibility, or recognition that reversing a process will bring about the original conditions from which the process began (Golomb & Cornelius, 1977; Sutton-Smith, 1967), although others have highlighted methodological problems with related research (Barnett, 1991). Other cognitive skills tied to play are hypothetical reasoning, understanding of basic concepts, classification, and measurement (Hughes, 1995; Johnson et al., 1999).

Social and Emotional Development

With regard to social development, it has been found that play with peers is related to advances in social skills. First, in pretend play, children are able to practice playing social roles other than that which in reality limit them. This allows children to develop concepts of different roles and the behaviors associated with them (Athey, 1984). Second, play with peers affords young children the opportunity to practice various social skills necessary for functioning in a social world, such as communication and empathy (Mendez & Fogle, 2002). A third aspect of play and social development relates to conflict and negotiation. During peer play, rules are established and followed. Not surprisingly, conflicts often ensue when one or more parties decide to change or ignore rules. Play provides children with practice at negotiating these conflicts (Lillard, 2002).

Recent research also has focused on the role of play in children's development of a theory of mind (Farrar & Maag, 2002; Lillard, 2002). A theory of mind is the awareness of one's own and others' psychological states. Through pretend play, it is posited, children learn that others have their own minds and perspectives (Johnson et al., 1999).

With regard to emotional functioning, play has long been recognized as an avenue for expressing emotional issues; this recognition is seen in the use of play as a therapeutic medium with children (Hughes, 1995). Pretend play makes it possible for children to express feelings and explore possible solutions to problems in a relatively safe atmosphere (Athey, 1984; de Lorimier, Doyle, & Tessier, 1995). This can be seen, for example, when children act out familiar domestic scenes in play. Relatedly, Parker and Gottman (1989) stated that the primary affective task of preschool children is to learn to regulate affect and behavior in arousing situations. During play, children are in a state of arousal. If they are unable to control their affect and behavior, they risk losing play partners. Prolonging play therefore serves to motivate children to learn affective regulation.

Language Development

Play is also related to the development of language. Especially as play becomes more social, it provides opportunities to practice and refine language skills. Researchers have found that advances in play and language follow parallel courses, especially at very young ages (e.g., McCune, 1995; Ogura, 1991). This parallel is not necessarily seen as causal, but rather the result of cognitive advances which allow for use of mental representation in both symbolic play and language (McCune, 1995).

Research also has highlighted the impact of play on early literacy development (Stagnitti et al., 2000). Pretend play, in particular, provides children with opportunities to utilize metacommunication about play, which has been found to be related to measures of emergent literacy, including story comprehension (Bergen & Mauer, 2000; Roskos & Christie, 2001; Rowe, 2000). Relatedly, play scenarios allow children to demonstrate their ideas about the functional uses of print, and pretending provides a context for teaching and learning literacy (Roskos & Christie, 2001).

Motor Development

Play influences motor development primarily through the repetition of motor sequences with objects used in play and the hands-on manipulation and exploration that occurs during play (Athey, 1984; NAECS/SDE, 2001). Early sensory exploration of objects helps develop and refine motor skills to permit later, more functional use of objects in play. Conversely, increases in motor skills permit more refined play with objects.

In summary, play in young children is a developmental phenomenon that follows a distinct sequence. Play begins as a sensorimotor activity before becoming more symbolic in nature. Socially, children's focus on play with peers increases with age. These social play episodes also increasingly involve pretend. Play is important for furthering development in other areas, and it is enhanced by increased development in other domains. As a major activity of childhood, the importance of play can not be overstated. Its significance has led to the recognition that play is an appropriate medium for assessing young children's functioning. Vygotsky (1967) stated that ". . . a child's greatest achievements are possible in play . . ." (p. 14), suggesting that assessment during play may elicit children's best efforts.

PLAY-BASED ASSESSMENT

The use of play as medium for assessing and treating children began early in the 20th century (O'Connor, 1991). At this time, psychoanalysts began interpreting children's play for the information it could provide about emotional functioning. Since that time, play has been used by therapists of many theoretical orientations in therapy with children (e.g., Landreth, 1991; O'Connor, 1991). Play-based assessment of developmental functioning, by contrast, has a relatively recent history. Begun as a method of gaining information primarily about infants and toddlers, strategies for assessment through observations of play have been in existence since the late 1970s and early 1980s (Lynch, 1996). Play-based assessment has been used across disciplines by those desiring a natural approach to assessing young children. Interest in play-based assessment increased more recently with the publication of Linder's (1993a) transdisciplinary play-based assessment model, which will be discussed in the next section.

Models of Play-Based Assessment

Play-based assessment is represented by a myriad of different procedures, instruments, and methods that differ on several dimensions. First, some models are primarily used in research related to play development, and at least one is intended for use by developmental specialists for assessment and program planning for young children (Linder, 1993a; in press). Other differences in the way assessment tools are set up also differentiate them (Fewell & Glick, 1993). For example, methods differ with regard to the amount of structure in the model. Structure refers to the degree to which directions and prompts given, toys provided, and so on, are used to prompt certain behaviors. Measures also differ on the amount of specificity of coding and scoring play behaviors. Some methods employ scoring based on behaviors seen with specific toys. Others allow more flexibility in the context in which behaviors are observed.

The following section describes two methods of play-based assessment that differ on several of the aforementioned dimensions. These two instruments were chosen to present an example of a clinical tool and a research tool that are widely cited in the literature. Other play measures are available, however most directly assess play, with varying levels of focus on how observed play relates to development in other domains (see Casby, 2003a; Lewis & Boucher, 1997; Stagnitti et al., 2000). It is important to note that play assessment is often an informal procedure during which play is seen as providing information about developmental skills. A brief discussion of informal observations of play is included here.

Transdisciplinary Play-Based Assessment

Transdisciplinary play-based assessment (TPBA; Linder, 1993a; in press) is an observational scale of development for use by early childhood assessment teams. The most widely used model of play-based assessment, this system includes the assessment of development in several domains for children ages birth to 6 years via unstructured play and parent reports of development. According to Linder (in press), TPBA can be used for diagnosis and eligibility determination, program planning, and quantitative and qualitative program evaluation. The current revision includes updated and expanded developmental content, more detailed strategies for facilitating the play of children and working with families, more focus on integrating family reports into assessment data, and strategies for improving resulting transdisciplinary reports (Linder, in press).

Developmental Content.   Like its predecessor, the TPBA–Revised measures development in the areas of sensorimotor, communication, cognitive, and emotional and social development, with each targeting several relevant subdomains. Note-taking forms, observation guidelines worksheets, and developmental age tables are provided for each domain to assist team members in organizing their findings and recording their observations. Observations guidelines in the TPBA–Revised are presented in question form to encourage team members to attend to qualitative aspects of the child's skills. New in the revision is the inclusion of procedures for screening vision and hearing. The vision screening, for example, includes several items relevant to a variety of vision problems, and it allows team members to use observations of the child at play to determine whether referral to a vision specialist is necessary. Also included in the revision is expanded content related to receptive language, as well as early literacy and math and science concepts (Linder, in press).

Teaming.   TPBA–Revised utilizes a transdisciplinary model of assessment. In this model, professionals on the team see the child together, information is shared across disciplines, and members contribute to disciplines other than their own. This model is different from a multidisciplinary model in which children are seen by several disciplines independent from one another, and from the interdisciplinary model, where disciplines see the child separately, but then meet to discuss the child's results and program recommendations. The team can include any number of professionals such as a psychologist, speech-language pathologist, occupational therapist and/or physical therapist, special educator, social worker, nurse or other health care provider, and a vision or hearing specialist. In addition to their discipline-specific roles, one member of the team serves as the play facilitator; this person actually interacts with the child during the assessment, providing encouragement for the child, modeling play behaviors, and providing structure. Another member is the family facilitator. This professional communicates with and advocates for the parents during all phases of the TPBA–Revised process. A third member is chosen to videotape the session, and the other professionals present observe play behaviors and record their observations.

In the TPBA–Revised model, parents are involved throughout the entire process, promoting solid parent-professional teamwork. Prior to the play assessment, parents complete checklists of their child's at-home behaviors. The TPBA–Revised (Linder, in press) includes a Child and Family History Questionnaire and a Family Assessment of Child Functioning scale. The latter has two components: a Daily Routines Rating Form and an All About Me Questionnaire. The Daily Routines Rating Form allows parents or caregivers to report on the routines followed at home, as well as their effectiveness and family's satisfaction or concern with them. The All About Me Questionnaire asks parents to rate their child's developmental skills. This allows team members to look systematically at the perspectives of caregivers and consider the child's demonstrated skills across contexts. During the assessment, parents talk to the family facilitator about how their child's demonstrated skills during the play session compare with what they see in other settings. At one point in the session, parents are asked play with their child, so the team can assess child-caregiver interactions. Finally, subsequent to the assessment, parents are involved in team discussions and program planning.

TPBA–Revised Process.   Prior to the assessment, the family facilitator meets with the caregivers to obtain the information described previously. This information is summarized by the facilitator and presented to the team. During this planning meeting, the team plans details of the play session, including team member roles, location, structure, materials needed, sequence, and any necessary adaptations.

Sessions can be conducted in any large room, with toys placed in distinct areas (e.g., block area, sand/water table area, etc.). A typical early childhood classroom is usually ideal, but assessments can also be conducted in homes, as long as necessary materials are available. The TPBA–Revised process is designed to be flexible enough to meet the needs of any child and family (Linder, in press). In general, however, the TPBA–Revised includes several periods of play. During unstructured play, for example, the child plays at will, with the play facilitator imitating, modeling, and expanding on the child's play. Structured play also is typically included and involves attempting to elicit play behaviors that the child did not spontaneously demonstrate. If possible, a peer is brought into the play session at some point, so that observations of child-child interaction can be made. Parents are also observed playing with the child in both unstructured and structured play situations. Usually at the end of the play session, a snack is given to allow for a screening of oral-motor difficulties, and observations of various adaptive skills (e.g., dressing, toileting) are made when appropriate.

No specific behaviors are required in this model; rather, observations of various aspects of cognitive, emotional and social, communication, and sensorimotor skills are made to allow the team to describe the child's abilities and difficulties, set intervention goals, and plan programs. As such, TPBA–Revised provides mostly qualitative information about the child. The TPBA–Revised does include a Developmental Summary form on which developmental age levels can be recorded and ratings can be made of the typicality of the child's skills in each domain (Linder, in press). These ratings include Above Average (i.e., 25% or more above age level and no qualitative concerns), Typical (i.e., within 24% of age level and no qualitative concerns), Watch (i.e., marginal performance that needs to be monitored), and Concern (25% or more below age level or a qualitative concern is present).

After the assessment is completed, the team analyzes the data collected. This might be done immediately after the session or after non-present team members have had an opportunity to review the videotape. This step includes interpreting domain-specific information gathered during the play session and integrating information provided by the family and other available information. This information is discussed with the family at a post-session meeting. At the meeting, professionals discuss their observations and ideas or hypotheses about the child's functioning, and they may use videotaped segments for illustration and clarification. Team observations are used to derive qualitative descriptions and quantitative ratings of the child's level of development. The TPBA–Revised Developmental Summary is completed at this stage as well. This summary allows the team to document the child's level of functioning (i.e., above average, typical, etc.), to note ipsative strengths and concerns for each domain, and to provide a judgment about the child's eligibility for special services. Recommendations for program planning are discussed and may be recorded for the family to take home with them. Finally, a formal report is written that addresses the details of assessment results, implications for intervention, and recommendations for services.

The TPBA model is the most comprehensive model of play-based assessment available, and the revision has increased its comprehensiveness. It allows for the assessment of several developmental domains, is based on a team approach to evaluation, and it gives specific and detailed guidelines for interpretation of child play behaviors. The model has intuitive appeal, due to these factors, as well as the child friendliness of the procedures. Although research on TPBA is limited, some published studies have investigated its psychometric integrity.

Friedli (1994) examined the reliability and validity of TPBA by conducting TPBA evaluations with 20 children between 3½ and 6 years of age (10 with and 10 without identified disabilities). With regard to reliability, Friedli found that ratings of play behaviors remained consistent across a 6-week period. Relatedly, summary sheet ratings for two independent observers of 10 taped TPBA administrations were statistically significant, suggesting inter-observer reliability. Content validity of the TPBA model was investigated by having 24 early childhood professionals rate the clarity, comprehensiveness, and relevance of the domains assessed in TPBA. The professionals viewed all areas as clear, comprehensive, and relevant (i.e., mean ratings for all areas exceeded 4.6 on a 7-point Likert scale). Concurrent validity was addressed by administering the Battelle Developmental Inventory to all participants, and comparing the degree to which the professionals reached the same decision about eligibility for special education services based on type of data. In addition, agreement on conclusions about ipsative strengths and weaknesses of subjects based on the two instruments was compared. Chi-square analyses supported similar findings between instruments, in terms of eligibility decisions and intra-individual comparisons. One major limitation regarding the first concurrent validity question (i.e., eligibility decision) was that the professionals conducting the assessment were not blind to subjects' disability classifications (identified or non-identified).

The Friedli (1994) study represents a good first attempt at investigating the psychometric properties of TPBA and implementing TPBA as specified in the manual. Nevertheless, the study had a small sample size. Other research has incorporated modifications to TPBA, typically for the purposes of standardizing observations and providing a numeric index of development for statistical analyses. Although these modifications have permitted more controlled research, the modifications make it difficult to compare findings across studies.

Kelly-Vance and colleagues have investigated the reliability and validity of play-based assessment using a standardized observation system largely based on the cognitive domain of the TPBA model (Kelly-Vance, Needelman, Troia, & Oliver, 1999; Kelly-Vance & Ryalls, 2005; Kelly-Vance, Ryalls, & Glover, 2002). Construct validity of play-based assessment was demonstrated by the finding that the complexity of play increases with age (Kelly-Vance et al., 2002). In addition, moderate test-retest reliability and acceptable inter-observer reliability were also demonstrated (Kelly-Vance & Ryalls, in press), supporting the findings of Friedli (1994).

One important question in this area is how results of play-based assessment compare with those derived from standardized instruments. Kelly-Vance et al. (1999) compared TPBA age equivalent scores (derived by comparing observed play behaviors with the developmental age tables provided in the TPBA manual) for 32 two-year-olds being seen at a NICU follow-up clinic to scores on the Bayley Scales of Infant Development–II. The researchers found a significant difference between scores from the two instruments, with the TPBA scores being higher than the Bayley scores. These results suggest that higher level skills might be elicited using a play-based assessment format. Although this finding only applies to skills measured in the cognitive domain, Calhoon (1997) found a similar pattern when comparing play-based and standardized measures of receptive and expressive language.

Additional research is needed to validate TPBA. It will likely remain difficult to compare findings across studies, given the modifications being made. Still, additional studies of reliability and validity, using larger samples of both typically developing and exceptional children, are needed.

Play Assessment Scale

The Play Assessment Scale (PAS; Fewell, 1992) is an experimental and observational measure of play development for use with children ages 2 to 36 months. It contains a series of 45 play items, sequenced in terms of developmental skills needed to perform the item. Observations of play skills are used to compute a "play age" for the assessed child. Eight toy sets corresponding to developmental levels are listed in the scale directions. Examiners choose several toy sets corresponding to the child's chronological age or presumed developmental level.

The assessment, which can be conducted in any comfortable environment that is spacious enough for floor play, consists of two conditions. In the first condition, observations are made of the child's spontaneous play behaviors. Specifically, the child is observed playing with the toys until no novel behaviors are produced (i.e., usually between 2 and 15 minutes). In the second, limits of play development are assessed by prompting the child to perform items. Prompts are gradually increased from verbal to motor to verbal plus motor.

Items on the scale include increasingly sophisticated behaviors ranging from visually tracking toys to simple functional behaviors directed toward the self (e.g., brushing hair) to symbolic pretend behaviors with a doll being the actor. Each item is scored as occurring during the first condition (spontaneous), the second condition (prompted), or neither. Only those behaviors observed during the spontaneous condition are counted toward the child's computed play age. Play ages are derived by counting numbers of behaviors credited be-tween a basal and ceiling, and converting raw scores to play ages on a conversion chart. Ob-servations of behaviors elicited during the prompted condition are used for qualitative de-scriptions of child development and emerging skills.

The PAS has several strengths as a play assessment method. First, it is a relatively easy scale to administer, provided the examiner is familiar with behaviors of interest. Sec-ond, the PAS has more evidence of validity than other play assessment scales. Studies cor-relating PAS scores to other developmental instruments have lent some support to the in-strument as a measure of development. The PAS has been found to correlate significantly with the Gessell Developmental Schedules, as well as non-standardized measures of com-munication, cognition, social functioning, and receptive, expressive, and nonverbal com-munication (Eisert & Lamorey, 1996; Fewell & Rich, 1987; Finn & Fewell, 1994). Weak-nesses of the PAS include play ages not being derived from a standardization sample, little parent involvement in the procedure, a limited age range for the scale (i.e., 2 to 36 months), and limited evidence of the scale's reliability.

Informal Observations of Play

In addition to formal play-based assessment measures, assessment based on play can also be conducted through informal or nonstructured play observations. In nonstructured ob-servations, as in formal instruments, clinicians observe children (or children and their par-ents) at play, and play behaviors form the basis of decisions about developmental level and/or treatment. Unlike more formal measures, however, the clinician has more freedom to struc-ture the observation setting in a way that is most comfortable for the family and clinician, and in a manner that is most likely to elicit behaviors of interest (Segal & Webber, 1996).

Several specific aspects of nonstructured play observations can be determined by the cli-nician. One important decision is where to conduct the observation. Observations may be conducted in a clinical setting, home setting, or child care/classroom setting. Malone, Stone-man, and Langone (1994) found that, particularly for children with disabilities, observations of independent play were superior to observations in a classroom with peers. Specifically, these authors found that the distractions in the classroom made it difficult for children to maintain sustained levels of play. Home settings are more likely to put the child at ease; however, toys may need to be transported to the home if they are not already available.

A related issue is materials that will be used. Segal and Webber (1996) stated that it is appropriate for the toys used to be determined by parents. If observations are conducted in the home, it is appropriate to use toys already in the home. Using toys familiar to the child may lead more quickly to play. Specifically, in novel situations children's behaviors are at first exploratory in nature (i.e., actions are more stereotyped and designed to learn about the objects; affect may be neutral to mildly negative, and intensity is higher than in play; Hughes, 1995; Johnson et al., 1999). If the intent is to assess play behaviors, it is important to ensure that children are more familiar with surroundings and/or materials. This can be done by conducting observations in the home or with the child's toys, or by allowing the child time to explore the environment prior to beginning observations. Time to get comfortable is not only important for nonstructured observations, but also for more formal procedures.

Another decision is whether to include parents in the play observations. Gowen, Johnson-Martin, Goldman, and Hussey (1992) found in a study of 40 children (20 with and 20 with-out identified disabilities) that mothers serving as play partners during play episodes served to increase the level of their children's play. Through suggesting and modeling, mothers encouraged play behaviors that were at or slightly higher than their current levels. In addition, play was facilitated for less mobile children by mothers bringing toys to and holding toys for their children. If independent or spontaneous play behaviors are the focus of the observation, it would be preferred to exclude parents for the same reasons. Observations of parent and child at play together can also provide important information about parent-child interactions (e.g., parent responsiveness, child compliance).

Benefits of Play-Based Assessment

Proponents of play-based assessment have discussed in depth the advantages of the approach. Primarily these advantages are related to what are believed by many researchers and professional organizations to constitute the tenets or standards for early childhood assessment. This section contains a discussion of advantages of play-based assessment and how these perceived benefits relate to early childhood assessment standards.

Flexibility

Play-based assessment generally includes a great deal of flexibility in its procedures (Fewell & Rich, 1987; Linder, in press). In TPBA for example, children are allowed to play while observations are being made. The specific behaviors required often are not predetermined. This flexibility is believed to be less stressful, less threatening, and to result in increased cooperation from young children (Linder, in press; Myers, McBride, & Peterson, 1996). Bagnato and Neisworth (1994) have stated that, in order for early childhood assessment procedures to be developmentally friendly, flexible administration procedures are necessary.

The flexibility in the administration of play-based procedures also means that every child is testable. With play-based assessment, observations of what a child does at play are the basis for decisions and service plans. According to Fewell and Rich (1987), play is related to several domains which are difficult to assess in children with severe impairments. Children with sensory impairments and limited cognitive skills have similar opportunities as typically developing children to display their skills in various developmental domains during play. Flexibility meets federal mandates that children should not be assessed using instruments that penalize them in one area because of a deficit in another (Finn & Fewell, 1994). Conversely, flexibility makes reliability and validity more difficult to investigate.

Links to Intervention

Researchers and professional groups have been adamant that early childhood assessment should provide information that not only provides for noncategorical eligibility determination (Bagnato, Neisworth, & Munson, 1993), but that is linked directly to intervention planning (Bagnato & Neisworth, 1996; McConnell, 2000; NASP, 1995). Information obtained from play-based assessments can be more readily translated into intervention recommendations and IFSP/IEP goals and objectives, possibly enhancing treatment validity (i.e., extent to which assessment information leads to valid treatments) (Bagnato & Neisworth, 1994; Kelly-Vance et al., 1999). TPBA, for example, includes a volume that focuses on transdisciplinary approaches to play-based interventions for young children (Linder, 1993b). Although these methods appear to put intervention planning at the forefront, claims of treatment validity are premature, as no empirical evidence is available to suggest that early childhood professionals in fact implement assessment-derived interventions, or that implementation of these interventions leads to improved functioning.

Relatedly, assessment should be useful for monitoring child progress once interventions have been implemented (Bagnato et al., 1993; McConnell, 2000). Because play-based assessment provides information that is linked to an intervention curriculum, and because practice effects are less of an issue with this type of assessment (i.e., TPBA has no specific items to remember), progress toward goals can be measured by intermittent assessment of this type, especially with the incorporation of quantitative ratings in the TPBA–Revised (Linder, in press).

Family Involvement

Another strength of play-based assessment is the ease with which parents can be brought into the assessment/intervention planning process. Both federal mandates and best practices dictate that assessment with young children needs to be family friendly, recognize the import of involving parents in the entire assessment process, and call for parent-professional teamwork (Bagnato & Neisworth, 1994; Bagnato et al., 1993). Play-based assessment is set up so that parents are easily made part of the team. TPBA–Revised in particular involves the parents at every phase of the assessment process, including having parents play with their child during the assessment and incorporating parent report information into observation-based data, so that important information about parent-child interaction can be obtained.

Ecological Focus

Play-based assessment is ecologically sensitive. Ecological assessments recognize the importance of various contexts in which children operate; play-based assessment can involve observations of children with parents and peers. In addition, they can be conducted in a child's home or classroom setting. Because of the flexibility of play-based approaches, ecological factors that might influence child responding (e.g., child-examiner variables, child-setting variables) are recognized and can be modified.

Teaming

Early childhood assessment should be conducted by several disciplines, and should involve team collaboration and consensus (Greenspan & Meisels, 1994; NASP, 1995). Play-based assessment easily adheres to these ideals. Fewell and Glick (1993) stated that because play is not the unique study of any particular discipline, it is a good medium for bringing together members from various areas. In addition, in the TPBA model, members of various disciplines gather their information based on the same set of child behaviors, which may lead to better team communication and collaboration (Linder, in press).

Social Validity

There is limited evidence of the social validity of play-based assessment. Social validity is the validation of work by consumers of that work (Wolf, 1978), and it provides an index of the acceptability of procedures, usually to professionals and parents, as well as the perceived importance of the information gained. One study to date has examined social validity of play-based assessment. Myers et al. (1996) compared parent and professional perceptions of transdisciplinary play-based assessment and multidisciplinary standardized assessment. The standardized assessments consisted of individual professionals separately administering discipline-specific standardized instruments (e.g., Bayley Scales of Infant Development–II; Receptive-Expressive Emergent Language–III). Results suggested that parents viewed the two types of evaluations equally as favorably. Professionals reported that play-based assessment produced more information about communication, social development, and motor skills than traditional assessment. Information produced about cognitive, sensory, and self-help skills was commensurate across groups. Also, school psychologists and speech-language pathologists viewed play-based assessments as better for ascertaining child strengths/weaknesses. In addition, play-based assessments were completed in a significantly shorter amount of time than standardized assessments for early childhood special education teachers. No significant differences in the amount of time spent in assessment for speech pathologists, school psychologists, occupational therapists, or physical therapists were found. Finally, with regard to utility of written reports, play-based reports were rated significantly higher than standardized reports for ease of obtaining an overview of the child's abilities, areas of concern, developmental areas covered in the report, absence of jargon, integration of cross-discipline information, and objectives being based on the child's strengths and weaknesses.

Other Strengths

There are several other strengths of play-based assessment. First, this type of assessment is natural to young children (Linder, in press). Because young children are at play much of their time, conducting assessments using play as the basis of information lessens artificiality in the assessment situation. Relatedly, this type of assessment elicits functional skills, or skills that are useful for everyday functioning. As such, when delays or gaps in development are found, skills to be targeted for intervention follow naturally (Bagnato & Neisworth, 1996). Third, in play-based assessment, information about development in various domains (e.g., cognition, motor, social, language) is gleaned through play. As such, it is not necessary to compartmentalize development according to domain; some claim this leads to a more holistic view of the child (Linder, in press; Wolery & Dyk, 1984). In addition, when play-based assessment is conducted as part of an interdisciplinary or transdisciplinary process, redundancy in testing is limited, such that information related to all disciplines is based on the same behavioral data (Linder, in press; Wolery & Dyk, 1984). Finally, rapport with children is more easily gained with a transdisciplinary play-based model of assessment. Specifically, only one professional directly interacts with the child in this model, making it easier for the child to feel comfortable. No empirical support for this claim is available, however.

In summary, play-based assessment has several characteristics that make it an attractive assessment approach. It is a flexible approach that elicits information from a naturally occurring behavior in a young child's repertoire. This flexibility allows for modifications so that, regardless of impairment severity, all children can be tested. Play-based assessment easily involves parents and is otherwise ecologically sensitive and functional. Play-based assessment encourages team cooperation and consensus, as members from all disciplines can be involved simultaneously in the assessment process. A holistic view of a child's functioning is encouraged by looking at development as an integrated, rather than compartmentalized, phenomenon. Finally, the approach attends to the importance of linking assessment to intervention, although data as to treatment validity are limited at present.

Limitations of Play-Based Assessment

Despite its many strengths and advantages, play-based assessment cannot be considered a panacea for early childhood assessment, due to several significant actual and potential limitations. Shortcomings include limited research on the reliability and validity of play-based measures along with unsupported claims about the strengths of the approach, state regulations that may preclude the use of play-based assessment in isolation as a method for determining service eligibility, some limitations to the amount of information that can be derived from play-based measures, and limited information about diversity issues with this type of assessment.

Reliability and Validity

With regard to reliability and validity concerns, it appears that play-based assessment has gained widespread use, despite limited information on the psychometric integrity of the method (Eisert & Lamorey, 1996; Myers et al., 1996). Proponents of this and other non-traditional assessment methods have argued that the paucity of research investigating traditional types of reliability and validity (e.g., inter-rater reliability; concurrent validity) is less important for early childhood developmental testing than for other types of assessment. Instead, according to these writers, information related to treatment validity and social validity of early childhood assessment measures is more important (Bagnato & Neisworth, 1994).

There are at least two issues that arise in response to claims that social and treatment validity are paramount with regard to play-based assessment. First, although treatment and social validity are undoubtedly important (as they are with any measure), it does not follow that they can be used to the exclusion of other types of reliability and validity. For example, it is important to ascertain empirically whether behaviors observed during play-based assessment represent the constructs supposed, that information obtained from play-based assessment correlates with development as measured by other methods, and that examiners would concur about the level of development observed. It is suggested that social and treatment validity be used in conjunction with more traditional reliability and validity measures, not instead of them (Bracken, 1994).

The fact that decisions or judgments are made by professionals in response to behaviors observed during play-based assessment make it characteristic of judgment-based assessment (Neisworth & Bagnato, 1988). In judgment-based assessment, professional perceptions of many individuals are collected and used to make evaluations of children's functioning (Fleischer, Begredan, Bagnato, & Ogonosky, 1990). Specifically, these measures involve collecting, structuring, and in some cases quantifying impressions (or judgments) of professionals. Although there are many positive aspects of judgment-based approaches, it is important to consider research on the limitations of human judgment. Reviews of related research suggest that humans, including professionals and experts, are very prone to error in their judgment, because of poor judgment habits and cognitive limitations (Faust, 1986; Tversky & Kahneman, 1974).

The second issue with some authors' claims that treatment and social validity can be used in place of other types of validity and reliability information is that, even if it were true that social and treatment validity were all the data needed to support the integrity of this method, we currently do not have sufficient evidence of either. As discussed, only one published empirical study addressing the social validity of play-based assessment is available. Although the Myers et al. (1996) study lends partial support for play-based assessment's social validity (i.e., parents were equally favorable of the play-based and multidisciplinary models; professionals preferred the play-based model), the study represents only a very first step in supporting claims of social validity.

Determining Eligibility

A second limitation of play-based assessment is that, depending on the specific measure used, the data produced may not be sufficient for eligibility determination. Linder's TPBA model, for example, produces mostly qualitative data about the presence or absence of developmental skills based on professional observations and judgments. Standard scores are not derived from the measure. In many states, clinical opinion apart from the quantitative determinants of relative functioning is insufficient for placement in special education, especially in the birth to age 3 population. Gross ratings of the typicality of development are included in the TPBA–Revised (Linder, in press). Whether these will suffice for eligibility determination remains to be seen.

Cultural Differences and Disability Influences

Information about cultural, gender, race, ethnicity, and age differences, as well as differences in play behaviors that are related to certain disabilities (e.g., sensory impairments), and how these affect performance on play-based measures, is needed for professionals to be sensitive to such differences so as not to unfairly penalize children. For example, cultural and socioeconomic differences may exist in the pretense of children, and these differences may appear as, but not reflect, differences in cognitive functioning or symbolic representational skills (see Johnson et al., 1999). Differences in sensorimotor and symbolic play that appear to be more related to a disability than developmental level have also been found for various disabilities (e.g., Casby, 1997; Rutherford & Rogers, 2003). Guidelines for interpretation of play-based approaches are needed in order to use these methods to fairly evaluate all children.

Other Limitations

Other potential limitations to play-based assessment were discussed by Segal and Webber (1996). These include expense, logistical concerns, and difficulty of clinicians remaining purely observers. In addition, some parents may find play-based observations intrusive, and sometimes play observations do not yield a sufficient amount of information, particularly if a child perseverates on one play action. Including some structure in the play assessment in the form of prompting for emerging behaviors, for example, may alleviate this concern.

Given the strengths and limitations of play-based assessment, it is suggested that the model can provide important information about practical and functional skills of young children, which can be easily translated into interventions. Nevertheless, additional research on the reliability and validity of this information is imperative. It is also suggested that these procedures be used in conjunction with more traditional forms of assessment. Combining multiple models accounts for the strengths and limitations of each, and will more likely provide all the information necessary for eligibility determination as well as program planning.

SUMMARY

A large body of research has demonstrated the significance of play for young children, most notably in terms of its correlations to and significance for promoting development in other domains of functioning. Additionally, play provides a window to children's skills and abilities. As such, play is an appropriate and logical medium through which to evaluate development. Several play-based assessment tools have been developed, and one comprehensive instrument has enjoyed widespread use. This model of assessment has intuitive appeal and satisfies most tenets of best practices with young children. Nevertheless, some weaknesses, especially the limited empirical support for the technique, have not been addressed satisfactorily. Hopefully, well-controlled studies of the psychometric properties and cultural fairness of this model will be forthcoming.

REFERENCES

Athey, I. (1984). Contributions of play to development. In T. D. Yawkey & A. D. Pellegrini (Eds.), *Child's play: Developmental and applied* (pp. 9–28). Hillsdale, NJ: Lawrence Erlbaum Associates.

Bagnato, S. J., & Neisworth, J. T. (1994). A national study of the social and treatment "invalidity" of intelligence testing for early intervention. *School Psychology Quarterly, 9*, 81–102.

Bagnato, S. J., & Neisworth, J. T. (1996). *Linking assessment and intervention: An authentic curriculum-based approach*. Baltimore: Brookes.

Bagnato, S. J., Neisworth, J. T., & Munson, S. M. (1993). Sensible strategies for assessment in early intervention. In D. M. Bryant & M. A. Graham (Eds.), *Implementing early intervention: From research to effective practice* (pp. 148–182). New York: Guilford Press.

Barnett, L. A. (1991). Developmental benefits of play for children. In B. L. Driver, P. J. Brown, & G. L. Peterson (Eds.), *Benefits of leisure* (pp. 215–247). State College, PA: Venture Publishing.

Bergen, D., & Mauer, D. (2000). Symbolic play, phonological awareness, and literacy at three age levels. In K. A. Roskos & J. F. Christie (Eds.), *Play and literacy in early childhood: Research from multiple perspectives* (pp. 45–62). Mahwah, NJ: Lawrence Erlbaum Associates.

Bjorklund, D. F., & Pellegrini, A. D. (2002). *The origins of human nature: Evolutionary developmental psychology*. Washington, DC: American Psychological Association.

Bracken, B. A. (1994). Advocating for effective preschool assessment practices: A comment on Bagnato and Neisworth. *School Psychology Quarterly, 9*, 103–108.

Calhoon, J. M. (1997). Comparison of assessment results between a formal standardized measure and a play-based format. *Infant-Toddler Intervention, 7*, 201–214.

Casby, M. W. (1997). Symbolic play of children with language impairment: A critical review. *Journal of Speech, Language, and Hearing Research, 40*, 468–479.

Casby, M. W. (2003a). Developmental assessment of play: A model for early intervention. *Communication Disorders Quarterly, 24*, 175–183.

Casby, M. W. (2003b). The development of play in infants, toddlers, and young children. *Communication Disorders Quarterly, 24*, 163–174.

de Lorimier, S., Doyle, A. B., & Tessier, O. (1995). Social coordination during pretend play: Comparisons with nonpretend play and effects on expressive content. *Merrill Palmer Quarterly, 41*, 497–516.

Eisert, D., & Lamorey, S. (1996). Play as a window on child development: The relationship between play and other developmental domains. *Early Education and Development, 7*, 221–235.

Farrar, M. J., & Maag, L. (2002). Early language development and the emergence of a theory of mind. *First Language, 22*, 197–213.

Faust, D. (1986). Research on human judgment and its application to clinical practice. *Professional Psychology: Research and Practice, 17*, 420–430.

Fein, G. G. (1981). Pretend play in childhood: An integrative review. *Child Development, 52*, 1095–1118.

Fewell, R. R. (1992). *Play assessment scale* (5th rev.). Unpublished document. Miami: University of Miami School of Medicine.

Fewell, R. R., & Glick, M. P. (1993). Observing play: An appropriate process for learning and assessment. *Infants and Young Children, 5*, 35–43.

Fewell, R. R., & Rich, J. S. (1987). Play assessment as a procedure for examining cognitive, communication, and social skills in multihandicapped children. *Journal of Psychoeducational Assessment, 2*, 107–118.

Finn, D. M., & Fewell, R. R. (1994, Jul–Aug). The use of play assessment to examine the development of communication skills in children who are deaf-blind. *Journal of Visual Impairment & Blindness*, 349–356.

Fisher, E. (1992). The impact of play on development: A meta-analysis. *Play & Culture, 5*, 159–181.

Fleischer, K. H., Belgredan, J. H., Bagnato, S. J., & Ogonosky, A. B. (1990). An overview of judgment-based assessment. *Topics in Early Childhood Special Education, 10*(3), 13–23.

Friedli, C. R. (1994). *Transdisciplinary Play-Based Assessment: A study of reliability and validity*. Unpublished doctoral dissertation, University of Colorado, Boulder, CO.

Golomb, C., & Cornelius, C. B. (1977). Symbolic play and its cognitive significance. *Developmental Psychology, 13*, 246–252.

Gowen, J. W., Johnson-Martin, N., Goldman, B. D., & Hussey, B. (1992). Object play and exploration in children with and without disabilities: A longitudinal study. *American Journal on Mental Retardation, 97*, 21–38.

Greenspan, S. I., & Meisels, S. (1994). Toward a new vision for the developmental assessment of infants and young children. *Zero to Three, 14*(6), 1–8.

Howes, C. (1987). Social competence with peers in young children: Developmental sequences. *Developmental Review, 7*, 252–272.

Howes, C., & Matheson, C. C. (1992). Sequences in the development of competent play with peers: Social and social pretend play. *Developmental Psychology, 28*, 961–974.

Howes, C., Unger, O., & Seidner, L. B. (1989). Social pretend play in toddlers: Parallels with social play and with solitary pretend. *Child Development, 60*, 77–84.

Hughes, F. P. (1995). *Children, play, and development* (2nd ed.). Boston, MA: Allyn and Bacon.

Johnson, J. E., Christie, J. F., & Yawkey, T. D. (1999). *Play and early childhood development* (2nd ed.). Boston, MA: Allyn & Bacon.

Kelly-Vance, L., Needelman, H., Troia, K., & Oliver, B. (1999). Early childhood assessment: A comparison of the Bayley Scales of Infant Development and Play-Based Assessment in two-year-old at-risk children. *Developmental Disabilities Bulletin, 27*, 1–15.

Kelly-Vance, L., & Ryalls, B. O. (2005). A systematic, reliable approach to play assessment in preschoolers. *School Psychology International, 26*(4), 398–412.

Kelly-Vance, L., Ryalls, B. O., & Glover, K. G. (2002). The use of play assessment to evaluate the cognitive skills of two- and three-year-old children. *School Psychology International, 23*, 169–185.

Landreth, G. L. (1991). *Play therapy: The art of the relationship*. Bristol, PA: Accelerated Development.

Lewis, V., & Boucher, J. (1997). *Test of Pretend Play*. London: Psychological Corporation.

Lillard, A. (2002). Pretend play and cognitive development. In U. Goswami (Ed.), *Blackwell handbook of childhood cognitive development* (pp. 189–205). Malden, MA: Blackwell Publishers.

Linder, T. W. (1993a). *Transdisciplinary play-based assessment: A functional approach to working with young children* (Rev. ed.). Baltimore: Brookes.

Linder, T. W. (1993b). *Transdisciplinary play-based intervention: Guidelines for developing a meaningful curriculum for young children*. Baltimore: Brookes.

Linder, T. W. (in press). *Transdisciplinary play-based assessment–Revised*.

Lowe, M. (1975). Trends in the development of representational play in infants from one to three years: An observational study. *Journal of Child Psychology and Psychiatry, 16*, 33–47.

Lynch, E. W. (1996). Assessing infants: Child and family issues and approaches. In M. J. Hanson (Ed.), *Atypical infant development* (2nd ed., pp. 115–146). Austin, TX: PRO-ED.

Malone, D. M., Stoneman, Z., & Langone, J. (1994). Contextual variation of correspondences among measures of play and developmental level of preschool children. *Journal of Early Intervention, 18*, 199–215.

McConnell, S. R. (2000). Assessment in early intervention and early childhood special education: Building on the past to project into our future. *Topics in Early Childhood Special Education, 20*, 43–48.

McCune, L. (1995). A normative study of representational play at the transition to language. *Developmental Psychology, 31*, 198–206.

Mendez, J. L., & Fogle, L. M. (2002). Parental reports of preschool children's social behavior: Relations among peer play, language competence, and problem behavior. *Journal of Psychoeducational Assessment, 20*, 370–385.

Myers, C. L., McBride, S. L., & Peterson, C. A. (1996). Transdisciplinary, play-based assessment in early childhood special education: An examination of social validity. *Topics in Early Childhood Special Education, 16*, 102–126.

National Association of Early Childhood Specialists in State Departments of Education (2001). *Recess and the importance of play. A position statement on young children and recess*. Author.

National Association of School Psychologists (1995). *Position statement on early childhood assessment*. Washington, DC: Author.

Neisworth, J. T., & Bagnato, S. J. (1988). Assessment in early childhood special education. In S. L. Odom & M. B. Karnes (Eds.), *Early intervention for infants and children with handicaps* (pp. 23–49). Baltimore: Brookes.

O'Connor, K. J. (1991). *The play therapy primer: An integration of theories and techniques*. New York: John Wiley and Sons.

Ogura, T. (1991). A longitudinal study of the relationship between early language development and play development. *Journal of Child Language, 18*, 273–294.

Parker, J. G., & Gottman, J. M. (1989). Social and emotional development in a relational context. In T. J. Berndt & G. Ladd (Eds.) *Peer relationships in child development*. New York: Wiley.

Parten, M. (1932). Social participation among preschool children. *Journal of Abnormal and Social Psychology, 27*, 243–269.

Piaget, J. (1962). *Play, dreams and imitation in childhood*. New York: W. W. Norton & Company.

Roskos, K., & Christie, J. (2001). Examining the play-literacy interface: A critical review and future directions. *Journal of Early Childhood Literacy, 1*, 59–89.

Rowe, D. W. (2000). Bringing books to life: The role of book-related dramatic play in young children's literacy learning. In K. A. Roskos & J. F. Christie (Eds.), *Play and literacy in early childhood: Research from multiple perspectives* (pp. 3–26). Mahwah, NJ: Lawrence Erlbaum Associates.

Rubin, K. H., & Pepler, D. J. (1982). Children's play: Piaget's views reconsidered. *Contemporary Educational Psychology, 7*, 289–299.

Russ, S. W. (2004). *Play in child development and therapy*. Mahwah, NJ: Lawrence Erlbaum Associates.

Rutherford, M. D., & Rogers, S. J. (2003). Cognitive underpinnings of pretend play in autism. *Journal of Autism and Developmental Disorders, 33*, 289–302.

Segal, M., & Webber, N. T. (1996). Nonstructured play observations: Guidelines, benefits, and caveats. In S. J. Meisels & E. Fenichel (Eds.), *New visions for the developmental assessment of infants and young children* (pp. 207–230). Washington, DC: Zero to Three.

Sinclair, H. (1970). The transition from sensorimotor behavior to symbolic activity. *Interchange, 1*, 119–125.

Simon, T., & Smith, P. (1983). The study of play and problem solving in preschool children: Have experimenter effects been responsible for previous results? British *Journal of Developmental Psychology, 1*, 289–297.

Slade, A., & Wolf, D. P. (1994). *Children at play: Clinical and developmental approaches to meaning and representation*. New York: Oxford University Press.

Smith, P. K. (1978). A longitudinal study of social participation in preschool children: Solitary and parallel play reexamined. *Developmental Psychology*, *14*, 517–523.

Stagnitti, K., Unsworth, C., & Rodger, S. (2000). Development of an assessment to identify play behaviours that discriminate between the play of typical preschoolers and preschoolers with pre-academic problems. *Canadian Journal of Occupational Therapy, 67*, 291–303.

Sutton-Smith, B. (1967). The role of play in cognitive development. *Young Children, 22*, 361–370.

Tversky, A., & Kahneman, D. (1974). Judgment under uncertainty: Heuristics and biases. *Science*, *185*, 1124–1131.

Uzgiris, I., & Hunt, J. McV. (1975). *Assessment in infancy: Ordinal scales of psychological development*. Urbana, IL: University of Illinois Press.

Vygotsky, L. S. (1967). Play and its role in the mental development of the child. *Soviet Psychology, 12*(6), 62–76.

Wolery, M., & Dyk, L. (1984). Arena assessment: Description and preliminary social validity data. *Journal for the Association of Persons with Severe Handicaps, 9*, 231–235.

Wolf, M. M. (1978). Social validity: The case for subjective measurement or how applied behavior analysis is finding its heart. *Journal of Applied Behavior Analysis, 11*, 203–214.

III

ASSESSMENT OF COGNITIVE ABILITIES

12

Cognitive Assessment with the Wechsler Preschool and Primary Scale of Intelligence–Third Edition

Diane Coalson
The Psychological Corporation

Jean Spruill
University of Alabama

The *Wechsler Preschool and Primary Scale of Intelligence–Third Edition* (WPPSI–III; Wechsler, 2002a) is an individually administered measure of cognitive ability for children ages 2 years 6 months through 7 years 3 months. It is the latest revision of the Wechsler intelligence scales designed for use with preschoolers and young children. The evolution of all Wechsler intelligence scales begins with the *Wechsler-Bellevue Intelligence Scale* (Wechsler, 1939). Rather than basing the structure of this adult intelligence scale on a particular theory, Wechsler developed and selected subtests based on his extensive clinical expertise and previous experience testing army recruits. The Wechsler-Bellevue subtests included measures of abstract reasoning, perceptual organization, verbal comprehension, quantitative reasoning, memory, and processing speed, all of which have been confirmed as important aspects of cognitive ability in contemporary theories and measures of intelligence (Carroll, 1993, 1997; Horn, 1991).

Subsequent versions of the Wechsler intelligence scales included downward extensions to children and preschoolers, periodic renorming, and revisions based on emerging trends in intelligence and cognitive developmental theory. The WPPSI–III is considerably different from its predecessor, the *Wechsler Preschool and Primary Scale of Intelligence–Revised* (WPPSI–R; Wechsler, 1989). Five subtests were dropped (Arithmetic, Sentences, Mazes, Animal Pegs, and Geometric Design) and seven new subtests were added (Receptive Vocabulary, Picture Naming, Word Reasoning, Matrix Reasoning, Picture Concepts, Coding, and Symbol Search) to enhance the measure of basic expressive and receptive vocabulary skills, as well as fluid reasoning and processing speed. The age range of the WPPSI–III was extended downward to age 2 years 6 months, and separate test batteries were created for younger and older children to reflect the rapid progression of cognitive development observed in early childhood. Evidence of improved reliability and validity is presented in the *WPPSI–III Technical and Interpretive Manual* (Wechsler, 2002b), including test-retest data by age and a number of validity studies aimed at examining the relationship between WPPSI–III performance and performance on other measures (e.g., cognitive ability, achievement, adaptive behavior, and memory) or special group membership (e.g., mental retardation, language disorders, autistic disorder). Published reviews describe the WPPSI–III as a thorough and welcome revision of an established measure of young children's intellectual ability (Hamilton & Burns, 2003; Lichtenberger & Kaufman, 2004).

STRUCTURE OF THE WPPSI–III

Assessment of cognitive ability in young children is complicated by the normally occurring age differences in successful achievement of developmental milestones. Siegler (1996) has demonstrated that children simultaneously show strategies and concepts characteristic of a variety of different developmental stages. The young child's cognitive development may therefore be viewed as a series of overlapping waves, in which one strategy or approach may predominate at a given point, but not to the exclusion of others. To accommodate the extensive cognitive development that occurs during early childhood, the WPPSI–III age range is split into two bands: 2 years 6 months to 3 years 11 months (2:6–3:11; referred to as the younger age band) and 4 years to 7 years 3 months (4:0–7:3; referred to as the older age band). (See the *WPPSI–III Technical and Interpretive Manual* [Wechsler, 2002b] for a detailed discussion of the theoretical and practical reasons for separating the age range.) Figure 12.1 depicts the organization of subtests within the WPPSI–III test structure for each age band.

The WPPSI–III has three types of subtests: core, supplemental, and optional. Core subtests are typically used to compute the Verbal IQ (VIQ), Performance IQ (PIQ), and the Full Scale IQ (FSIQ). Only four core subtests are administered to children in the younger age band, reducing the possible confounding effects of limited attention span and language development on performance. Children in the older age band are administered seven core subtests, including measures of verbal comprehension and expression (i.e., Vocabulary and Word Reasoning), perceptual reasoning (i.e. Block Design and Matrix Reasoning), and a measure of visual-motor processing speed (i.e., Coding).

Supplemental subtests provide a broader sampling of intellectual functioning than the core subtests alone and may be used as substitutes for core subtests when appropriate. Supplemental subtests also can be used to derive additional composite scores. Administration of the supplemental Picture Naming subtest to children in the younger age band allows for derivation of the General Language Composite (GLC), and administration of the supplemental Symbol Search subtest to children in the older age band allows for derivation of the Processing Speed Quotient (PSQ). Like the supplemental subtests, optional subtests provide additional measures of cognitive ability; however, optional subtests may not be used as substitutes for any core subtest. Administration of the optional Receptive Vocabulary and Picture Naming subtests to children in the older age band allows for derivation of the GLC and is recommended when the referral question includes concerns with language-related abilities (Lichtenberger & Kaufman, 2004).

The absence of memory subtests in the WPPSI–III should not be interpreted as suggesting that memory ability is not an important aspect of intelligence in young children. Memory ability is an important domain of cognitive functioning and is measured in versions of the Wechsler intelligence scales for older children and adults (i.e., the *Wechsler Intelligence Scale for Children–Fourth Edition* [WISC–IV; Wechsler, 2003a] and the *Wechsler*

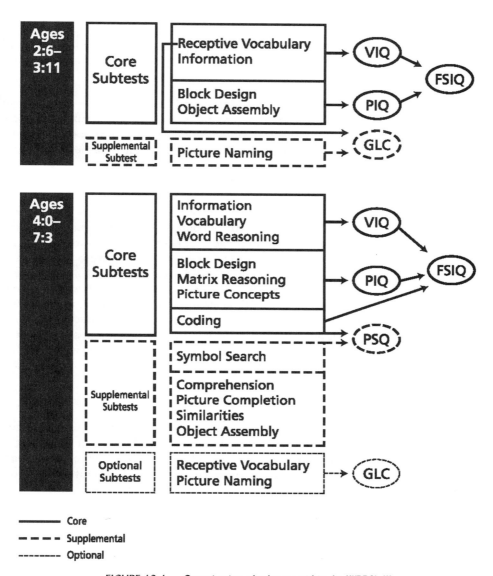

FIGURE 12.1.   Organization of subtests within the WPPSI–III.

Adult Intelligence Scale–Third Edition [Wechsler, 1997]) A comprehensive assessment of memory functioning requires an evaluation of several different aspects of memory, including immediate and delayed auditory memory, immediate and delayed visual memory, fluency, and working memory. The additional subtests required to accurately assess these abilities would greatly lengthen the WPPSI–III administration time and were not included in the WPPSI–III in lieu of the addition of processing speed measures, which are relatively brief in terms of administration time. If concerns exist regarding a child's memory functioning, a comprehensive measure of memory functioning should be considered as part of the assessment (e.g., *California Verbal Learning Test–Children's Version* [Delis, Kramer,

Kaplan, & Ober, 1994]; *Children's Memory Scale*, [Cohen, 1997]; *NEPSY: A Developmental Neuropsychological Assessment.* [Korkman, Kirk, & Kemp, 1998]).

Subtest Descriptions

The following section provides brief descriptions of the WPPSI–III subtests and the cognitive abilities they are designed to measure. For a more thorough review of subtest item content and rationale, the reader is referred to the *WPPSI–III Technical and Interpretive Manual* (Wechsler, 2002b), Lichtenberger and Kaufman (2004), and Sattler and Dumont (2004).

Information

Information is a core Verbal subtest for both age bands. All items require the child to demonstrate his or her knowledge of a broad range of general knowledge topics. The first six items are presented using pictures, and the child can point to a picture to indicate his or her response. Remaining items are presented as questions that are read aloud by the examiner (e.g., "How many eyes do you have?"), to which the child typically provides a verbal response. Scores on this subtest represent the child's ability to acquire, retain, and retrieve general factual knowledge, commonly referred to as fund of knowledge. Successful performance also requires auditory comprehension and verbal expression, and may be related to opportunities for learning in the home and school environment, as well as cultural influences (Lichtenberger & Kaufman, 2004; Sattler & Dumont, 2004).

Vocabulary

Vocabulary is a core Verbal subtest for the older age band and is not administered to children in the younger age band. The first five items are designed to extend the floor of the subtest, and include items from the Picture Naming subtest that require the child to name common objects. Remaining questions require the child to provide definitions for words presented aloud by the examiner (e.g., "What is a chair?"). Scores on this subtest represent a child's word knowledge, concept formation, and verbal comprehension. Successful performance also requires auditory comprehension, long-term memory, abstract thinking, and verbal expression (Lichtenberger & Kaufman, 2004; Sattler & Dumont, 2004).

Word Reasoning

Word Reasoning is a core Verbal subtest for the older age band and is not administered to children in the younger age band. A new subtest for the WPPSI–III, Word Reasoning is modeled after subtests such as the Word Context subtest of the *Delis-Kaplan Executive Function System* (Delis, Kaplan, & Kramer, 2001), the Riddles subtest of the Kaufman Assessment Battery for Children (Kaufman & Kaufman, 1983), and cloze tasks (e.g., tasks requiring the child to complete missing portions of a paragraph). Items on this subtest require the child to identify a common concept being described by a series of clues (e.g., the first clue may read, "This is something you ride," and the second clue may read, "This is something you ride with two wheels."). Successful performance on this subtest involves verbal comprehension, abstract reasoning ability, and the ability to integrate sequentially-presented information (Lichtenberger & Kaufman, 2004; Sattler & Dumont, 2004).

Comprehension

Comprehension is a supplemental Verbal subtest for the older age band, and is not administered to children in the younger age band. Items on this subtest are presented as questions that require the child to explain situations, activities, or events that are commonly experienced by most children (e.g., "Why do ambulances have sirens?"). Comprehension measures verbal concept formation, the ability to evaluate and utilize past experiences, and verbal expression. A child's responses to subtest items also provide the child with an opportunity to demonstrate knowledge of practical information, social standards of behavior, and common sense (Groth-Marnat, 1999; Lichtenberger & Kaufman, 2004; Sattler & Dumont, 2004).

Similarities

Similarities is a supplemental Verbal subtest in the older age band, and is not administered to children in the younger age band. Unlike the WPPSI–R, which included three different item types, the WPPSI–III version of this subtest includes a single item type: sentence completion (e.g., "Blue and green are both _____."). Scores on Similarities represent the child's verbal reasoning and concept formation, as well as auditory comprehension, categorization ability, verbal expression, and the ability to discriminate between essential and nonessential details (Cooper, 1995; Lichtenberger & Kaufman, 2004; Sattler & Dumont, 2004).

Receptive Vocabulary

Receptive Vocabulary is a core Verbal subtest for the younger age band and an optional Verbal subtest for the older age band. Items on this subtest require the child to look at a group of four pictures and point to the one that best depicts the word the examiner reads aloud. The stimulus words include nouns, verbs, and adjectives. Receptive Vocabulary is a new subtest for the WPPSI–III; however, similar measures have been used extensively as part of more comprehensive language measures (e.g., *Clinical Evaluation of Language Fundamentals–Fourth Edition* [Semel, Wiig, & Secord, 2003]), or as stand-alone measures (e.g., *Peabody Picture Vocabulary Test–Third Edition* [Dunn & Dunn, 1997]). Scores on Receptive Vocabulary represent the child's word knowledge and understanding of verbal concepts. Successful performance requires comprehension of verbal directives, auditory and visual discrimination, long-term memory, and the integration of visual and auditory input (Brownell, 2000b; Lichtenberger & Kaufman, 2004).

Picture Naming

Picture Naming is a supplemental Verbal subtest for the younger age band and an optional Verbal subtest for the older age band. It is a new subtest developed for the WPPSI–III, but similar measures have appeared on other measures (e.g., *Differential Ability Scales* [DAS; Elliott, 1990]; *Expressive One-Word Picture Vocabulary Test–Third Edition* [Brownell, 2000a]). For each item, the child names a displayed picture. Scores on Picture Naming represent a child's word knowledge, language development, word retrieval from long-term memory, and association of visual stimuli with language (Brownell, 2000a; Lichtenberger & Kaufman, 2004; Sattler & Dumont, 2004) Performance may also be influenced by home environment, exposure to language stimulation, and cultural factors.

Block Design

Block Design is a core Performance subtest for children in both age bands. Part A (Items 1–10) is primarily designed for the younger age band and utilizes one-color blocks, either red or white. No degree of rotation, even complete 180° reversals, is penalized in Part A. The familiar red and white two-color blocks are used on Part B (Items 11–20), and only pronounced rotations of 30° or more are penalized. All items require the child to view a constructed model or a picture and use blocks to re-create the design within a specified time limit. Scores on Block Design represent the child's ability to analyze and synthesize abstract visual stimuli. Successful performance also requires visual perception and discrimination, simultaneous processing, visual-motor coordination, learning, and the ability to separate figure and ground in visual stimuli (Groth-Marnat, 1999; Lichtenberger & Kaufman, 2004; Sattler & Dumont, 2004).

Matrix Reasoning

Matrix Reasoning is a core Performance subtest for children in the older age band and is not administered to children in the younger age band. This is a new subtest for the WPPSI–III, and is included to enhance the measure of fluid reasoning. Items require the child to view and evaluate an incomplete matrix and to choose the response that best completes the matrix. Matrix reasoning tasks appear on all current editions of the Wechsler intelligence scales and a number of other measures, and are generally considered to be good measures of fluid reasoning and general cognitive ability (Raven, Raven, & Court, 1998; Wechsler, 1997, 2002a, 2003b). Successful performance also requires visual-perceptual organization, spatial ability, and the ability to discriminate between essential and nonessential details (Lichtenberger & Kaufman, 2004; Sattler & Dumont, 2004).

Picture Concepts

Picture Concepts is a core Performance subtest for the older age band and is not administered to children in the younger age band. It is a new subtest and may be viewed as an analog of the Similarities subtest that does not require a verbal response. For each item, the child is presented with two or three rows of pictures and chooses one picture from each row to form a group with a common characteristic. Correct responses are often based on a common classification (e.g., animals or toys) or function (things you eat with, things you read). More difficult items place a greater emphasis on abstract reasoning ability than the initial items of this subtest, which can often be solved using concrete representations (e.g., color and size). Picture Concepts is designed to measure abstract, categorical reasoning ability (Wechsler, 2003b; Wechsler et al., 2004b). Successful performance may also require simultaneous processing, concentration, and flexibility (Lichtenberger & Kaufman, 2004).

Picture Completion

Picture Completion is a supplemental Performance subtest for the older age band and is not administered to children in the younger age band. Each item requires the child to look at a picture and identify the important missing part. All artwork for this subtest has been redrawn, enlarged, and colorized, and scoring criteria were revised to assist the examiner when scoring vague verbal responses. Successful performance on Picture Completion requires visual perception and organization, concentration, and visual recognition of essential details of objects (Cooper, 1995; Lichtenberger & Kaufman, 2004; Sattler & Dumont, 2004).

Object Assembly

Object Assembly is a core Performance subtest for the younger age band and a supplemental Performance subtest for the older age band. For each item, the child is allowed 90 seconds to fit the pieces of a puzzle together to form a meaningful whole. Scores in this subtest reflect the child's visual-perceptual organization, cognitive flexibility, visual-motor ability, and nonverbal reasoning ability. Successful performance may also involve the ability to integrate and synthesize part-whole relationships and to benefit from trial-and-error learning (Lichtenberger & Kaufman, 2004; Sattler & Dumont, 2004; Wechsler, 2002b).

Coding

The Coding subtest is a core Processing Speed subtest for the older age band and is not administered to children in the younger age band. For this subtest, the child is allowed 120 seconds and uses a key to draw specific symbols that correspond to simple geometric shapes. In addition to speed of mental processing, performance on Coding may be related to perceptual organization, visual scanning ability, visual-motor coordination, sequential processing, attention, and motivation (Lichtenberger & Kaufman, 2004; Sattler & Dumont, 2004; Wechsler, 2002b).

Symbol Search

Symbol Search is a supplemental Processing Speed subtest for the older age band and is not administered to children in the younger age band. For each item on this subtest, the child scans group of symbols and indicates whether the target symbol appears in the group. All children are allowed 120 seconds to complete as many items as possible. Successful performance requires speed of mental processing, short-term visual memory, visual-motor coordination, visual scanning ability, and concentration (Lichtenberger & Kaufman, 2004; Sattler & Dumont, 2004; Wechsler, 2002b).

Subtest and Composite Scores

There are two types of age-corrected standard scores provided by the WPPSI–III: scaled scores and composite scores. The subtest-scaled scores represent a child's performance relative to his or her same-age peers. They are scaled to a metric with a mean of 10 and a standard deviation of 3. Thus, a subtest scaled score of 10 reflects the average performance of a given age group. The WPPSI–III composite scores (i.e., the VIQ, PIQ, PSQ, FSIQ, and GLC) are standard scores based on various sums of subtest scaled scores, and are scaled to a metric with a mean of 100 and a standard deviation of 15. A score of 100 on any of the composites defines the average performance of children similar in age. About 68% of all children obtain composite scores between 85 and 115, about 98% score in the 70–130 range, and nearly all children (about 99.9%) obtain scores between 55 and 145 (3 SDs on either side of the mean).

For children in the younger age band, a total of four composite scores can be derived: the VIQ, PIQ, FSIQ, and GLC. Five composite scores are available for children in the older age band: the VIQ, PIQ, PSQ, FSIQ, and GLC. The VIQ is a measure of verbal comprehension and reasoning, acquired knowledge, and the ability to express thoughts using words. The PIQ is a measure of nonverbal (fluid) reasoning, spatial and perceptual processing, attention to detail, and visual-motor integration. The PSQ is a measure of the child's ability to rapidly scan and discriminate simple visual information. The FSIQ for the younger age band is based on the sum of scaled scores for the four subtests that contribute to the VIQ and PIQ. For the older age band, the FSIQ is based on the sum of scaled scores for the six subtests that contribute to the VIQ and PIQ, as well as the scaled score for the Coding subtest. The FSIQ is usually considered to be the most representative measure of global intellectual functioning.

The GLC is supplemental for the younger age band and optional for the older age band. For both age bands, the GLC is based on the sum of scaled scores for the Receptive Vocabulary and Picture Naming subtests. The score is designed primarily for children in the younger age band to provide a measure of basic receptive and expressive language development. However, the GLC can also be derived for children in the older age band that are experiencing substantial delays in language development. Low scores on the GLC may suggest the need for a thorough evaluation of language ability (Lichtenberger & Kaufman, 2004; Wechsler, 2002b).

RESEARCH WITH THE WPPSI–III

A comprehensive review of the literature did not reveal any published research using the WPPSI–III. This is not unexpected given the recent publication date. The research described in this section is a summary of studies that were conducted as part of the scale's standardization to provide initial evidence of validity. In addition to details of reliability and factor-analytic studies, the WPPSI–III Technical and Interpretive Manual provides details for a number of concurrent studies, including correlational studies with other measures and studies with special groups of children. Results of some of these preliminary reliability and validity studies are described briefly in the following sections. For more details about the studies, the reader is referred to chapters 4 (reliability studies) and 5 (validity studies) of the *WPPSI–III Technical and Interpretive Manual* (Wechsler, 2002b). Additional research is needed to replicate the findings and to provide a broader evidence base for the reliability, validity, and clinical utility of the WPPSI–III across different populations and settings.

Standardization

Standardization data were obtained from a stratified sample of 1,700 children in the following nine age groups: 2:6–2:11, 3:0–3:5, 3:6–3:11, 4:0–4:5, 4:6–4:11, 5:0–5:5, 5:6–5:11, 6:0–6:11, and 7:0–7:3. The sample was stratified (based on October 2000 U.S. census data) along the following variables: age, race, parent education level, and geographic region. For each age group, the sample included an equal numbers of boys and girls, and proportional representations of Whites, African Americans, Hispanics, Asians, and other racial/ethnic groups. Five levels of parent education were used as socioeconomic variables for stratification, and children from four geographic regions (i.e., Northeast, South, Midwest, and West) were proportionally represented. The WPPSI–III standardization sample has been described as excellent in critical reviews (Lichtenberger & Kaufman, 2004; Sattler & Dumont, 2004).

Reliability

The WPPSI–III has very good internal consistency reliability as well as test-retest stability. The FSIQ is the most reliable composite, with an average internal consistency reliability coefficient of .96 for the nine age groups. The reliability coefficients of the VIQ (.95), PIQ (.93), and GLC (.93) are excellent. The slightly lower PSQ reliability coefficient (.89) is based on test-retest reliabilities for the Coding and Symbol Search subtests. The average internal consistency estimates for the 14 subtests ranged from a low of .83 for Symbol Search to a high of .95 for Similarities.

Retest data were obtained from 157 children, with a mean testing interval ranging from 14 to 50 days. For the overall sample, the stability coefficients for the VIQ (.91), PSQ (.90), GLC (.91), and FSIQ (.92) are excellent, and the stability coefficient for the PIQ is good (.86). At the subtest level, the stability coefficients range from a high of .90 for Similarities to a low of .61 for Picture Concepts. The mean composite score gains at the second testing for the combined age bands are 2.8 points for the VIQ, 5.0 points for the PIQ, 6.2 points for the PSQ, 2.7 points for the GLC, and 5.2 points for the FSIQ. These results are consistent with those of other Wechsler intelligence scales, which indicate that the Verbal subtests show less retest gains than Performance (or Perceptual Reasoning) subtests (Wechsler, 1989, 1997, 2003a).

Validity

The validity of a test is often viewed as the most important aspect of test development and evaluation. As stated in the *Standards for Educational and Psychological Testing*, "evolving conceptualizations of . . . validity no longer speak of different types of validity but speak instead of lines of validity evidence, all in service of providing information relevant to a specific intended interpretation of test scores" (American Educational Research Association, 1999, p. 5).

The test developer is responsible for providing initial evidence of validity, and subsequent use of the scale often builds upon this evidence base. Test users are responsible for evaluating all lines of validity evidence to determine whether a test's use is supported for their particular purpose. The following section provides a brief summary of validity evidence for the WPPSI–III, with a focus on lines of evidence traditionally referred to as construct and criterion validity. The reader is referred to chapter 5 of the *WPPSI–III Technical and Interpretive Manual* (Wechsler, 2002b) for a thorough discussion of all lines of evidence, including evidence based on test content, response processes, internal structure, and relationships to other variables.

Exploratory Factor-Analyses

A series of exploratory factor analyses was conducted separately for each age band to examine the factor structure of the WPPSI–III. Results for the younger age band support a two-factor structure (Verbal and Performance factors). Results were generally consistent with the predicted factor structure for the older age band, with the exception of stable factor loadings for the Performance factor. Results for the three subgroups of the older age band indicated a variable pattern for the factor loadings of Performance subtests, "due perhaps to developmental trends in the differentiation of cognitive functions across these ages" (Wechsler, 2002b, p. 83). For children ages 4:0–4:11, Picture Concepts exhibited loadings on the Verbal (.33) and Processing Speed (.34) factors and Matrix Reasoning had its highest loading (.39) on the Processing Speed factor. For children ages 5:0–5:11, Matrix Reasoning and Picture Concepts subtests exhibited their highest loadings on the Performance factor, but Matrix Reasoning continued to exhibit a weaker loading on the Processing Speed factor. For children ages 6:0–7:3, Matrix Reasoning had its highest loading on the Performance factor, but Picture Concepts had its highest loading on the Verbal factor.

Results from the exploratory factor analyses provide strong support of the scale's two-factor structure for the younger age band (Sattler & Dumont, 2004). Evidence in support of the three-factor structure for the older age band is relatively strong for the Verbal and Processing Speed factors, but less clear for subtests on the Performance factor, especially Picture Concepts (Lichtenberger & Kaufman, 2004; Wechsler, 2002b). Additional research is needed to further examine the cognitive processes and problem-solving strategies utilized on this subtest and to determine whether these processes and strategies vary with the developmental level of the child.

Studies With Other Measures of Cognitive Ability

The relationship between test scores and external variables can provide additional evidence of validity. This is often provided by studies that examine the relationship between test scores and scores on measures that are designed to measure the same or similar construct. For this purpose, several studies were conducted in which children were administered the WPPSI–III and another measure of cognitive ability. For all of these studies, the WPPSI–III and the other measure were administered in counterbalanced order with retest intervals of less than 60 days. For more details about the studies reported here the reader is referred to the *WPPSI–III Technical and Interpretive Manual* (Wechsler, 2002b). For more about the study comparing the WPPSI–III with the WISC–IV, the reader is referred to the *WISC–IV Technical and Interpretive Manual* (Wechsler, 2003b) *or the WISC–IV Integrated Technical and Interpretive Manual* (Wechsler et al., 2004b).

Correlations With the WPPSI–R

The differences between mean composite scores on the WPPSI–III and WPPSI–R are small (.4 points for the VIQ, 3.1 points for the PIQ, and 1.2 points for the FSIQ), and only the difference between the PIQs is significant. Mean composite scores on the WPPSI–R are higher than those on the WPPSI–III, consistent with, but slightly smaller than expected, according to the Flynn effect (Flynn, 1987, 1998). As described previously, substantial differences exist in the subtest composition of composite scores for the WPPSI–III and WPPSI–R, and differences between the scores must be interpreted in light of these differences. The corrected correlation coefficients for the two instruments are .86, .70, and .85 for VIQ, PIQ, and FSIQ, respectively and are consistent with the previous research (Wechsler, 1989). The magnitude of these correlations suggests that the WPPSI–III and WPPSI–R measure similar constructs.

Correlations With the WISC–IV

The WPPSI–III and WISC–IV have similar factor structures for children ages 6:0–7:3, and the differences between mean composite scores are very small (.3 points for the VIQ/Verbal Comprehension Index comparison, .6 points for the PIQ/Perceptual Reasoning Index comparison, 1.3 points for the PSQ/Processing Speed Index comparison, and .2 points for the FSIQ comparison). The corrected correlation coefficients for composite scores on the two instruments range from .69 (for the PSQ/PSI correlation) to .89 (for the FSIQ correlation). Like the WPPSI–III/WPPSI–R study, the magnitude of correlations and consistency of mean composite scores suggest that the WPPSI–III and WISC–IV measure similar constructs (Wechsler, 2003b; Wechsler et al., 2004b).

The WPPSI–III and the WISC–IV were standardized at approximately the same time and either test can be administered to children age 6:0–7:3. Because of the greater breadth of coverage of the WISC–IV than the WPPSI–III (10 core subtests versus 7 core subtests, 4 composite scores versus 3 composite scores), the WISC–IV will provide more information about the child's intellectual functioning than the WPPSI–III. However, it should be noted that the differences between the mean composite scores ranged from .3 to 1.3—hardly a meaningful difference.

Correlations With the Bayley Scales of Infant Development–Second Edition (BSID–II)

The WPPSI–III mean composite scores range from 101.8 (for the VIQ and FSIQ) to 102.9 (for the GLC). The mean BSID–II Mental and Motor standard scores are 102.7 and 104.2, respectively. All of the WPPSI–III composites have higher correlations with scores on the BSID–II Mental scale (.61 to .80) than with scores on the Motor scale (.33 to .48). The WPPSI–III FSIQ shares its largest correlation ($r = .80$) with the BSID–II Mental scale composite. Results are consistent with the previous research examining the relationship between scores on the WPPSI–R and BSID–II (Bayley, 1993).

Either the BSID–II and WPPSI–III can be administered to children ages 2:6–3:6. The advantage of the BSID–II is the lower floor, which may be helpful for children suspected of mental retardation or developmental delay. For children of average or above ability, the WPPSI–III is the preferred instrument.

Correlations With the Differential Abilities Scale (DAS)

The DAS (Elliott, 1990) is an individually administered cognitive ability instrument for children ages 2:6–17:11. The differences between mean composite scores on the WPPSI–III and DAS are 1.5 points for the WPPSI–III VIQ/DAS Verbal composite comparison, 3.8 points for the WPPSI–III PIQ/DAS Nonverbal composite comparison, and 1.6 for the FSIQ/General Conceptual Ability (GCA) composite comparison. The difference between the WPPSI–III PIQ and the DAS Nonverbal Reasoning composite is statistically significant ($t = 3.17, p < .01$), but produces a small effect size ($d' = .26$). The correlation between the WPPSI–III VIQ and the DAS Verbal composite is .78, and the correlation between the WPPSI–III PIQ and the DAS Nonverbal Reasoning composite is .76. The correlation between the WPPSI–III FSIQ and the DAS GCA is .87. These results indicate that the WPPSI–III and the DAS are measuring similar constructs, and are consistent with those reported previously for the DAS and WPPSI-R (Elliott, 1990).

Studies With Measures of Achievement and Memory

Because measures of intellectual ability are often used in conjunction with measures of achievement as part of a psychoeducational evaluation, a linking study was conducted to examine the relationship between scores on the WPPSI–III and scores on the *Wechsler Individual Achievement Test–Second Edition* (WIAT–II; Harcourt Assessment, Inc., 2001). An additional study was conducted to examine the relationship between scores on the WPPSI–III and scores on a comprehensive measure of memory (i.e., the CMS).

Correlations With the WIAT–II

The WPPSI–III and the WIAT–II were administered to 208 children ages 4:0–7:3. All mean WPPSI–III composites were approximately 100 and all of the WIAT–II composites are within 1.4 points of 100. The lowest correlation was observed for the WPPSI–III PSQ/WIAT–II Reading composite ($r = .31$) and the highest correlation was observed for the WPPSI–III FSIQ/WIAT–II Total Achievement composite ($r = .78$). Of the WPPSI–III composites, the PSQ exhibited the lowest correlation to the Total Achievement composite ($r = .36$). The VIQ shared its highest correlations with Total Achievement ($r = .77$) and Oral Language ($r = .72$) and least correlations with the Mathematics composite ($r = .56$). The PIQ and PSQ correlated most highly with the Mathematics composite ($r = .60$ and $r = .55$, respectively). This pattern of correlations provides evidence of convergent and discriminant relationships between the WPPSI–III and WIAT–II composite scores. Overall, the correlations between the WPPSI–III and WIAT–II are similar to those reported between the WISC–IV and WIAT–II (Wechsler, 2003b; Wechsler et al., 2004b). These results support the construct validity of the WPPSI–III, replicate findings from earlier research, and demonstrate that the WPPSI–III composite scores relate differentially to specific domains of achievement.

Correlations with the CMS

The WPPSI–III and the CMS were administered to 40 children ages 5:0–7:3. The WPPSI–III mean composite scores ranged from 99.0 (VIQ) to 102.3 (PSQ) and the CMS index scores ranged from 93.2 (Learning) to 103.4 (Attention/Concentration). The highest correlation was observed between the WPPSI–III FSIQ and the CMS Attention/Concentration Index ($r = .79$). The lowest correlation was observed between the WPPSI–III PSQ and the CMS Visual Delayed Index ($r = .07$). With the exception of the PSQ, the WPPSI–III composites shared their highest correlations with the CMS Attention/Concentration Index, suggesting that these aspects of memory are more closely related to general intelligence than the aspects of memory represented by the other CMS Index scores. The current results are consistent with the previous results examining the relationship between WPPSI–R and CMS performance (Cohen, 1997).

Studies With Special Groups of Children

The WPPSI–III scores are often used as part of a comprehensive assessment to classify children for diagnostic or psychoeducational purposes; therefore, evidence of the scale's clinical utility for such purposes is critical. As with any single measure of intellectual or cognitive ability, the WPPSI–III scores should never be used in isolation for diagnostic or classification decisions. As Wechsler (1991) noted, "Psychological assessment is a clinical activity that employs test scores, but only as one of the sources from which an astute clinician develops a well-integrated and comprehensive psychological portrait of the adult or child examined" (p. iii).

Ten matched control group studies were conducted as part of the WPPSI–III standardization to demonstrate that the WPPSI–III produces valid estimates of intellectual ability for children in the following special groups: Intellectually Gifted, Mental Retardation, Developmental Delay, Developmental Risk Factors, Autistic Disorder, Expressive Language Disorder, Mixed Receptive-Expressive Language Disorder, Limited English Proficiency (now referred to as English Language Learners), Attention-Deficit/Hyperactivity Disorder, and Motor Impairment. The results of six of these special group studies are summarized in this section. Control groups for the summarized studies were matched on sex, race, parent education level, and geographic region. Results of the four remaining special group studies (Developmental Delay, Developmental Risk Factors, Limited English Proficiency, and Motor Impairment) and additional details (e.g., descriptions of the inclusion criteria and sample demographics) of all special group studies appear in the *WPPSI–III Technical and Interpretive Manual* (Wechsler, 2002b).

Children Identified as Intellectually Gifted

The term *gifted* is used to describe children who demonstrate exceptionally high performance in intellectual functioning, creative and productive thinking, leadership, performing or visual arts, and/or other specific ability areas (Marland, 1972; Sparrow & Gurland, 1998). The primary purpose of identifying gifted children is educational planning; thus, the assessment of intelligence or cognitive ability is often employed in these evaluations. Children with IQs of 130 or above (98th percentile) are typically identified as gifted. States vary in their criteria for the assessment of giftedness, some allowing group measures of intelligence, but the best instrument available for identifying children with superior intellectual abilities is an individually administered, well-standardized, multidimensional test of intelligence (Sattler, 2002). Previous research indicates that some gifted children may show unusually large discrepancies between their VIQ and PIQ scores (Sparrow & Gurland, 1998; Wechsler, 1991, 1997), and that some gifted children do not perform as well on timed subtests which contribute to the PSQ as they do on subtests contributing to the VIQ or PIQ (Sparrow & Gurland, 1998).

In a study of 70 children who previously had been identified as intellectually gifted (i.e., had scores ≥ 130 on an individually administered standardized measure of intelligence), the WPPSI–III mean composite scores ranged from 113 (PSQ) to 126 (FSIQ). It is not unusual in such studies for samples of intellectually gifted children to obtain lower general cognitive ability scores (e.g., FSIQ scores) than those originally used to identify the sample as gifted. For example, children in the WPPSI–R gifted sample were included in the study if they could provide evidence of IQ scores of 130 or above, yet the mean WPPSI–R FSIQ for these children was only 122 (Wechsler, 1989). Similar results were found for the *Stanford-Binet Intelligence Scales–Fourth Edition* (Thorndike, Hagen, & Sattler, 1986), the WISC–III (Wechsler, 1991), the WISC–IV (Wechsler, 2003b; Wechsler et al., 2004b), and the *Stanford-Binet Intelligence Scales–Fifth Edition* (Roid, 2003).

All mean composite scores were significantly higher for the intellectually gifted group than the matched control group, and large effect sizes were noted for differences on the VIQ, PIQ, and FSIQ. Consistent with previous research, the group mean PSQ differences were not as great as differences produced for the other composites. Based on these findings, what should the practitioner do if the VIQ and PIQ are both in the gifted range but the FSIQ is not? If a child who is otherwise gifted scores below average on the Coding subtest, his or her FSIQ may not fall in the gifted range. In such cases, the examiner should interpret the FSIQ in light of the child's Coding performance, and may choose to place more emphasis on the VIQ or PIQ for gifted identification. In the authors' opinion, it makes much more sense to provide gifted learning experiences for these children rather than apply strict adherence to a cutoff score that is based on such variable performance. It is also interesting to note that the reliability coefficients of the supplemental subtests for the intellectually gifted group are somewhat lower that those of the core subtests, suggesting that special care should be taken when interpreting composites that are based on scores from substituted subtests (Wechsler, 2002b). As with any classification or diagnosis, scores on an intelligence test should never be the only determinate of giftedness.

Children With Mental Retardation

Identification of mental retardation requires demonstration of significant limitations in both intellectual functioning and adaptive behavior (American Psychiatric Association, 2000). The most accurate diagnosis derives from multiple data sources, including assessment of the individual's functioning at home, in school, and in the community. In the normal distribution of IQ scores, about 2.2% of children obtain scores at least 2 SDs below the mean IQ of 100. However, because the diagnosis of mental retardation takes into account adaptive functioning, the prevalence of diagnoses of mental retardation varies from study to study, ranging from 2.5% to 3.0% of the general population (Harrison, 1990). Furthermore, both the *Diagnostic and Statistical Manual of Mental Disorders,* Fourth Edition, Text Revision (*DSM–IV–TR*; American Psychiatric Association, 2000) and the newly revised American Association of Mental Retardation (AAMR; 2002) criteria emphasize the need to consider a scale's standard error of measurement in interpreting scores, thus reemphasizing the need for multiple criteria and careful clinical judgment in identifying children with mental retardation.

The WPPSI–III was administered to a total of 59 noninstitutionalized children diagnosed with mental retardation (IQ scores on a standardized measure of cognitive ability that were 2–4 SDs below the mean). For the 40 children in the mild severity subgroup, the WPPSI–III composite scores ranged from 62.1 (FSIQ) to 69.5 (GLC), and all were significantly lower than the matched control group's corresponding means. The composite score means for 19 children with moderate mental retardation were even lower, ranging from 53.1 (FSIQ) to 58.3 (PSQ). The variability in the performance at both levels of severity of mental retardation was less than the population standard deviation of 15—a finding that has been found in several studies (e.g., Slate, 1995; Spruill, 1991).

The results for both levels of severity are generally consistent with previous reports by Atkinson (1992), Craft and Kronenberger (1979), and Spruill (1991) for adult participants, and by Wechsler (1991, 2003) for children. Because of the rapid progression of developmental change in children, practitioners should be cautious in the classification of mental retardation and its levels of severity for children under 5 years of age. When a child shows evidence of significant delay in intellectual and adaptive functioning, a diagnosis of Developmental Delay should be considered (Sattler, 2001, 2002). Many changes taking place in the developmental period could result in temporary reductions in both intellectual and adaptive functioning, and a diagnosis of mental retardation implies a permanent impairment in ability.

Cautions for Interpreting an Extremely High or Low FSIQ

Note that the FSIQ range is 45–155 for children in the younger age band and 45–160 for children in the older age band. Therefore, the WPPSI–III is not an appropriate instrument for assessing the intelligence of children who are extremely low functioning or extremely high functioning. The assessment of intelligence in the extremely low range is further complicated because a raw score of 0 on a subtest can yield a scaled score greater than 0 (e.g., a child age 4 years 2 months obtains a scaled score of 2 on Receptive Vocabulary even when unable to pass a single item). Thus, it is possible to obtain an estimate of the FSIQ even when a child obtains scores of 0 on all contributing subtests. For this reason, the WPPSI–III test developers provide guidelines regarding the invalidation of composite scores when raw scores of 0 are obtained on a subtest. If these guidelines are applied, the lowest possible FSIQ for a child age 2 years 6 months is 48. If the guidelines for the older age band are followed, the lowest possible FSIQ (without proration) for a child age 4 years 0 months is 50. These examples illustrate the need to examine the floors of each subtest that contribute to a specific composite score (e.g., VIQ, PIQ, and FSIQ). Similar scrutiny of the subtest ceiling is warranted when assessing children of extremely high ability.

Children With Autistic Disorder

Previous research with children diagnosed with Autistic Disorder suggests that their general intellectual functioning is lower than that of nondelayed children, particularly on tasks requiring expressive verbal ability (Wechsler, 1991, 2003). Numerous studies have found that the typical profile for children with a diagnosis of Autistic Disorder is characterized by a VIQ that is significantly lower than the PIQ (e.g., Bishop, 1997; Green, Fein, Joy, & Waterhouse, 1995; Miller & Ozonoff, 2000; Siegel, Minshew, & Goldstein, 1996). The WPPSI–III was administered to a group of 21 children who were identified with Autistic Disorder according to *DSM–IV–TR* criteria. Children were excluded from this study if they had existing general cognitive ability scores of less than 60. When compared to a matched control group, children in the Autistic Disorder group scored significantly lower on all composites, with large effect sizes noted for all but the PIQ difference, which produced a moderate effect size. The mean VIQ for the Autistic Disorder group (70.6) was the lowest mean composite score obtained by this special group (mean PIQ = 88.2, mean PSQ = 82.5, mean FSIQ = 76.6, and mean GLC = 84.7). Children with Autistic Disorder have IQs that cover the entire spectrum, and may also be diagnosed as learning disabled, gifted, developmentally delayed, or mentally retarded. For more information about intelligence and children with Autistic Disorder, the reader is referred to Lovecky (2004).

Children With Expressive Language Disorder

Children with Expressive Language Disorder (ELD) have substantially lower scores on measures of expressive language development than scores obtained on measures of nonverbal intelligence and receptive language development (American Psychiatric Association, 2000). The WPPSI–III was administered to 23 children diagnosed with ELD according to *DSM–IV–TR* criteria (totally nonverbal children were excluded from the study). When compared to the matched control group, the mean FSIQ and VIQ differences were significant, with the VIQ difference producing the largest effect size ($d' = .72$). No significant group mean differences were noted for the PIQ, PSQ, or the GLC.

At the subtest level, significant group mean differences with moderate to large effect sizes were noted for all Verbal subtests except Receptive Vocabulary, on which the group performance did not differ significantly. At first look, the lack of a significant group mean difference for the GLC may seem counterintuitive; however, the GLC includes a measure of receptive vocabulary ability, which is relatively intact in children with ELD as compared to their expressive abilities. In addition, research indicates that children with ELD may have typical vocabularies relative to their peers at school entry, but they may continue to experience more difficulty than their peers in more complex tasks that require verbal reasoning, drawing conclusions, and sequential reasoning (e.g., Phelps, 1998).

Children With Mixed Receptive-Expressive Language Disorder

Children diagnosed with Mixed Receptive-Expressive Language Disorder (RELD) obtain substantially lower scores on measures of receptive and expressive language ability than scores on nonverbal measures of intelligence (American Psychiatric Association, 2000). Research indicates that children with RELD tend to have general deficits in cognitive functioning (e.g., Beitchman, Wilson, Brownlie, Walters, & Lancee, 1996; Doll & Boren, 1993; Rose, Lincoln, & Allen, 1992; Wechsler, 1989, 1991) and lower processing speed than children without language disorders (e.g., Bishop, 1992; Doll & Boren, 1993).

The WPPSI–III was administered to 27 children diagnosed with RELD according to *DSM–IV–TR* criteria (totally nonverbal children were excluded from the study). Consistent with prior research, children in the RELD group appeared to have global deficits in intellectual functioning as evidenced in their significantly lower scores than the matched control group for all composites. Large effect sizes were produced by all group mean differences except the PIQ difference, which produced a moderate effect size.

Children With Attention Deficit Hyperactivity Disorder

One of the most frequent referrals for a psychoeducational evaluation is for children suspected of having Attention Deficit Hyperactivity Disorder (ADHD). ADHD is a neurodevelopmental disorder that is characterized by chronic inattention problems. Symptoms of hyperactivity may be present, but are not required for a diagnosis of ADHD (American Psychiatric Association, 2000). In general, traditional IQ scores are not useful in discriminating children or adults with ADHD from a non-clinical population. However, some research suggests that children with ADHD may perform worse on measures of processing speed than on measures of verbal or perceptual—organizational ability (e.g., Pennington & Ozonoff, 1996; Prifitera & Dersh, 1992; Wechsler, 2003b; Wechsler et al., 2004b; Wilcutt et al., 2001)

The WPPSI–III was administered to 41 children diagnosed with ADHD according to *DSM–IV–TR* criteria (American Psychiatric Association, 2000) who also had clinically significant parent ratings on the *Brown Attention-Deficit Disorder Scales for Children and Adolescents* (Brown, 2001). As expected, no significant group mean differences were found between the ADHD and matched control groups on the VIQ, PIQ, or FSIQ. Contrary to predictions based on previous research, no significant group mean difference was noted for the PSQ. Previous research had found that lower processing speed scores were more prevalent in the inattentive subtype of ADHD; thus, it is possible that the inclusion of children with symptoms of hyperactive or impulsive behavior masked group differences among the subtypes of ADHD (e.g., Wilcutt et al., 2001). In addition, approximately half of the children in the ADHD group were taking medications for this condition at the time of testing. Research with separate samples of children with ADHD with and without hyperactivity is needed, as well as investigations comparing the performance of medicated and nonmedicated children with ADHD.

INTERPRETATION OF THE WPPSI–III

Several resources are available to assist the practitioner with the interpretation of WPPSI–III scores (e.g., Lichtenberger & Kaufman, 2004; Sattler & Dumont, 2004; Wechsler, 2002b). However, results from the WPPSI–III should never be used in isolation and should be interpreted in light of the child's historical background (e.g., medical and psychosocial history), behavioral observations during the assessment, results of previous evaluations, and the referral question. Rather than reviewing the basic steps of WPPSI–III score interpretation, the authors chose to include a case study as an example of how the WPPSI–III scores may be used for interpretive purposes. This interpretive report is based on a composite of actual cases drawn from clinical practice, and is adapted from a case study that appeared in the *Wechsler Preschool and Primary Scale of Intelligence–Third Edition: Canadian* (Wechsler, 2004a). All identifying information has been changed to ensure confidentiality.

CASE STUDY

Psychoeducational Evaluation

Identifying Information

Child: Susanna Wright
Parent(s): Susan and Alan Wright
Examiner: Jacque Simkins, Ph.D.

Date of Testing: June 7, 2005
Date of Birth: September 9, 2000
Age at Testing: 4 yrs. 8 mo. 28 days

Reason for Referral

Susanna was referred for a psychological assessment by her parents to assist with planning for her transition to kindergarten. In January of 2003, Susanna was referred to a speech-language pathologist for parental concerns regarding speech delays. Her speech and language evaluation indicated that Susanna's receptive and expressive language abilities were poorly developed for her age (2½ years), scoring at the 16th and 10th percentiles respectively. Susanna has been attending a speech and language therapy program since that time.

Tests Administered

Wechsler Preschool and Primary Scale of Intelligence–Third Edition (WPPSI–III)
Adaptive Behavior Assessment System–Second Edition (ABAS–II)
Preschool Language Scale–Fourth Edition (PLS–4; Zimmerman, Steiner, & Pond, 2002)

Additional Sources of Information

Parent interview
Review of previous speech-language evaluation
Developmental questionnaire

Relevant History

Susanna lives with both biological parents and her two older sisters, ages 7 and 9. Although no learning or communication disorders have been formally identified in Susanna's immediate family members, Susanna's mother withdrew from school in tenth grade because of the difficulties that she experienced meeting the reading and writing expectations of her high school classes. Susanna's mother has not worked outside of the home since her eldest daughter's birth, and Susanna has never attended day care or preschool.

Susanna's mother reported that she gave birth to Susanna after a full-term pregnancy with no complications. She indicated that she did not consume alcohol or drugs while pregnant; however, she smoked 10–15 cigarettes a day during her pregnancy. Susanna weighed 6 pounds, 4 ounces at birth. She was described as a challenging baby who was colicky and irritable, with feeding and sleeping difficulties. Susanna has struggled with chronic ear infections since infancy. Her hearing and vision were assessed approximately 2 years previous to the date of testing, and no difficulties were identified at that time. No other significant injuries, illnesses, or accidents were described by her mother.

Susanna reportedly reached her motor milestones in a timely fashion, but she was much slower to develop language skills. For example, she did not say her first words until age 2½, and she did not begin to speak in simple phrases until close to her fourth birthday. Recently, Susanna has become better able to communicate her own thoughts and wishes (e.g., "Look at the doggie!" or "Watch TV?"). However, her sentences continue to be quite short, and she often becomes frustrated when others do not understand what she is trying to say. Mr. and Mrs. Wright expressed continued concern with respect to Susanna's language development, noting that she appears to lag behind her peers despite progress in speech and language therapy. In contrast to her limited linguistic skills, Susanna's parents reported her to be very talented in the areas of art and construction. They noted that she loves to make puzzles, play with modeling clay, and draw. The Wrights indicated that Susanna is much more creative and artistic than either of her sisters was at that same age. Susanna's parents did not express any concerns with respect to emotional difficulties, such as depression, anxiety, or withdrawal.

Susanna is scheduled to enter kindergarten in September 2005. Her parents are concerned that it may be a difficult adjustment for Susanna, as she has not attended pre-school or other settings where multiple children are present. Susanna's mother believes that it will be difficult for Susanna to share the teacher's attention with other children and that it will be challenging for her to sit still and listen during structured activities.

Test Results

Susanna obtained a Full Scale IQ of 87 on the WPPSI–III, placing her in the 19th percentile when compared with her same-age peers in the U.S. population. The 95% confidence interval of her Full Scale IQ is 82–92, which corresponds to the Low Average to Average range of overall intellectual functioning; however, Susanna's Full Scale IQ may not provide the best estimation of her overall cognitive abilities, due to the large discrepancies between her performance on those tasks that require a verbal response (Verbal subtests) and those that do not (Performance and Processing Speed subtests).

Verbal subtests measure verbal comprehension skills, including the ability to think with words, to process and express verbal information, and to apply verbal skills to problem solving. Susanna obtained a Verbal IQ of 72, placing her in the 3rd percentile relative

TABLE 12.1.
WPPSI-III

Composite Scale	Sum of Scaled Scores	Composite Score	Percentile Rank	95% Confidence Interval
Full	58	87	19	82–92
Verbal	14	72	3	67–80
Performance	35	110	75	103–116
Processing Speed	20	100	50	91–109
General Language	17	91	27	84–99
Verbal Subtest	Raw Score	Scaled Score	Percentile Rank	
Information	12	5	5	
Vocabulary	5	4	2	
Word Reasoning	2	5	5	
Comprehension	2	6	9	
Similarities	3	7	16	
Performance Subtest				
Block Design	22	10	50	
Matrix Reasoning	15	13	84	
Picture Concepts	13	12	75	
Processing Speed Subtest				
Symbol Search	9	11	63	
Coding	9	9	37	
General Language Subtest				
Receptive Vocabulary	21	9	37	
Picture Naming	16	8	25	

to her same age peers. The 95% confidence interval of her Verbal IQ is 67–80, which falls in the Extremely Low to Borderline range of functioning. Susanna's performance on the Verbal subtests was characterized by brief, often one word, responses. She rarely offered additional elaboration after query, which was especially evident on those subtests requiring a more lengthy response for full credit, such as Vocabulary and Comprehension.

Subtests on the General Language scale required Susanna to identify which of four pictures matched a vocabulary word spoken aloud by the examiner, and to name pictures with a single word. Susanna's General Language Composite (GLC) of 91 falls in the 27th percentile relative to her same-age peers. The 95% confidence interval of the score is 84–99, placing her in the Low Average to Average range of functioning. Comparison of Susanna's GLC and Verbal IQ suggests that she has greater difficulty with tasks that require verbal elaboration of language concepts and/or a more complex understanding of language than those tasks that require brief verbal responses or understanding of basic concepts and words. Susanna performed significantly better on a categorical reasoning task that used verbal stimuli and required no verbal response (Picture Concepts) than she did on a categorical reasoning task that used verbal stimuli and required a verbal response (Similarities). The difference between Susanna's performances on these subtests occurs in less than

8% of her peers and provides additional evidence that her verbal reasoning abilities are more limited than her visual-spatial reasoning abilities.

Performance subtests measure perceptual organizational skills, including the abilities to think in visual images, to manipulate visual materials, and to reason without using words. Unlike her relatively low Verbal IQ, Susanna's Performance IQ of 110 falls in the 75th percentile. The 95% confidence interval of her Performance IQ is 103–116 and is in the Average to High Average range of functioning. The 38-point difference observed between Susanna's Verbal IQ and Performance IQ is significant and very unusual, occurring in less than 0.4% of peers with similar levels of overall cognitive functioning. Susanna performed well on tasks requiring visual-spatial organization, constructional skills, and attention to visual detail. Her nonverbal reasoning skills represent an area of personal strength.

Processing Speed subtests measure visual-motor processing speed, including the ability to quickly and correctly scan and discriminate visual information. Although not as high as her Performance IQ score, Susanna's Processing Speed Quotient (PSQ) of 100 is at the 50th percentile, with a 95% confidence interval of 91–109 falling within the Average range of functioning. The 28-point difference between Susanna's scores on the Verbal and Processing Speed scales is significant and unusual, occurring in less than 3.5% of peers with similar levels of overall cognitive functioning.

Susanna's adaptive behavior skills were assessed using the ABAS–II Parent/Primary Caregiver Form that was completed by Mrs. Wright. Results on the ABAS–II indicate that Susanna obtained a General Adaptive composite (GAC) score of 88, which corresponds to the 21st percentile when compared with her same age peers. The 95% confidence interval of her GAC score is 83–93, which falls in the Below Average to Average range of overall adaptive functioning. A significant strength was observed in an area measuring basic fine and gross motor skills, and a significant weakness was observed in an area measuring social skills. In general, her adaptive behavior is consistent with her cognitive abilities. Because some variability was observed within the three areas of adaptive behavior, Susanna's GAC score may not provide the best representation of her overall adaptive behavior abilities as represented by the GAC.

The Conceptual domain measures communication and adaptive skills, including the ability to use speech and language necessary for communication and the ability to produce pre-academic skills necessary for achievement and independent functioning. Susanna obtained a Conceptual Domain composite score of 71, placing her in the 3rd percentile when compared with her same-age peers. The 95% confidence interval of her Conceptual Domain composite score is 64–78, which falls in the Extremely Low to Borderline range of adaptive functioning. Susanna's scores in the Conceptual Domain skill areas indicate Below Average adaptive behavior in receptive and expressive language abilities, counting skills, and self-direction skills. According to Mrs. Wright's report, Susanna has limited abil-

TABLE 12.2.
ABAS–II

Composite	Sum of Scaled Scores	Composite Score	Percentile Rank	95% Confidence Interval
General Adaptive	84	88	21	83–93
Conceptual	18	71	3	64–78
Social	12	74	4	65–83
Practical	44	105	63	98–112

ities in letter recognition, vocabulary, and listening skills, and difficulty in following directions and completing tasks.

The Social domain measures interpersonal and social competence skills, including the ability to interact socially and engage in recreational activities. Susanna obtained a Social Domain composite score of 74, placing her in the 4th percentile when compared with her same age peers. The 95% confidence interval of her Social Domain composite score is 65–83, which falls in the Extremely Low to Borderline range of functioning. Within the Social domain, Susanna's scores indicate particular difficulties with interpersonal relationship skills. Her scores in this specific area occur in only 2% to 5% of peers with similar levels of social adaptive functioning. In addition, Susanna's Social Domain scores indicated Extremely Low adaptive functioning in following rules and engaging in play activities with others.

The Practical domain measures independent living skills and social competence skills, including the ability to function appropriately in the community, home, and/or school, as well as the ability to perform basic skills required in personal care. Susanna obtained a Practical Domain composite score of 105, placing her in the 63rd percentile when compared with her same age peers. The 95% confidence interval of her Practical Domain composite score is 98–112, which falls in the Average to Above Average range of functioning. Susanna's scores in the Practical Domain skill areas indicate Average abilities in eating, toileting, and dressing skills.

The 34-point difference observed between Susanna's Conceptual and Practical composite scores is significant and very unusual, occurring in only 1.2% of children below the age of five. The 31-point difference observed between Susanna's Social and Practical composite scores is significant and very unusual, occurring in only 0.5% of children below the age of 5. At the composite-score level, Susanna's ABAS–II scores are consistent with the discrepancy between her Verbal and Performance IQ scores on the WPPSI–III. That is, her composite score in the Practical domain suggests a relative strength in this area in contrast to her scores in the Conceptual and Social domains, which are more reliant on verbal ability.

Susanna's receptive and expressive language skills were assessed using the PLS–4. Results indicate that Susanna obtained a Total Language score of 81, which corresponds to the 10th percentile when compared with her same age peers. The 95% confidence interval of her Total Language score is 73–89, indicating that we can be 95% sure that her true score falls within this range. However, Susanna's Total Language score may not provide the best representation of her overall receptive and expressive language abilities, due to the large and unusual discrepancy between Susanna's performance on those tasks that require auditory comprehension and those that require expressive comprehension.

The Auditory Comprehension subtests measure receptive language skills, including Susanna's understanding of basic language concepts (e.g., quantity, size, time, and spatial position) and her ability to understand expanded sentences with pronouns and adjectives.

TABLE 12.3.
PLS–4

Composite	Raw Score	Standard Score	Percentile Rank	95% Confidence Interval
Total Language	165	81	10	73–89
Auditory Comprehension	52	96	39	87–105
Expressive Communication	40	69	2	61–77

Susanna obtained an Auditory Comprehension score of 96, which corresponds to the 39th percentile when compared with her same age peers. The 95% confidence interval of her Auditory Comprehension score is 87–105.

The Expressive Communication subtests measure expressive language skills, including Susanna's ability to respond to where and why questions, name categories, repeat sentences, and use adjectives and verb tenses appropriately. Susanna obtained an Expressive Communication score of 69, which corresponds to the 2nd percentile when compared with her same age peers. The 95% confidence interval of her Expressive Communication score is 61–77. The difference between Susanna's Auditory Comprehension and Expressive Communication scores is significant and unusual, occurring in less than 5% of her peers. This difference is also consistent with her WPPSI–III results, which also suggest that Susanna has substantially more difficulty with those tasks that place greater demands on expressive language ability than receptive language ability.

RECOMMENDATIONS AND INTERVENTIONS

Because the results of this assessment suggested a possible expressive language disorder, it was recommended that a comprehensive evaluation of Susanna's speech and language skills be performed upon her entry into kindergarten to identify more specific areas for intervention. In addition, it was recommended that Susanna's hearing be re-evaluated to ensure that her chronic ear infections have not resulted in significant hearing loss since the time of her previous evaluation.

A meeting was held to help plan for Susanna's transition into kindergarten. Individuals in attendance included Susanna's parents, this psychologist, her speech-language pathologist, and the school team from her kindergarten. Strategies were identified to facilitate Susanna's development in the areas of academic learning, communication, and socialization. It was decided that Susanna should continue to receive regular speech and language therapy after entering kindergarten. In addition, it was agreed that Susanna would benefit from the support of a teacher's aide within her classroom. The teacher's aide should be available to provide frequent checks for comprehension, to assist Susanna in sustaining her attention during focused learning activities, and to facilitate and model appropriate conversational skills. In addition, the teacher's aide should assist in using Susanna's strong nonverbal skills (e.g., supplementing verbal instructions with pictures and opportunities for "hands-on" experience) and in encouraging Susanna to talk about things that she had enjoyed creating, such as modeling clay constructions or her drawings.

Prior to entering kindergarten, Susanna should participate in the 6-week summer preschool program to provide her with the opportunity to meet and interact with some of the students who are enrolled in her kindergarten class. Additionally, this program will expose Susanna to structured learning activities, communication among peers, and expectations for classroom behavior (e.g., the need to share the teacher's attention with other students).

It was noted that Susanna's development in the areas of communication and attention will need to be monitored over the next several years. Because Susanna's language difficulties place her at increased risk for learning challenges, the school personnel indicated that they would monitor the development of her reading and writing skills as she progressed through kindergarten and the early school years. It was recommended that a psychologist reassess Susanna after she completes the first grade.

REFERENCES

American Association of Mental Retardation. (2002). *Mental retardation: Definition, classification, and system of supports* (10th ed.). Washington, DC: Author.

American Educational Research Association. (1999). *Standards for educational and psychological testing*. Washington, DC: Author.

American Psychiatric Association. (2000). *Diagnostic and statistical manual of mental disorders*, Fourth edition, Text revision. Washington, DC: Author.

Atkinson, L. (1992). Mental retardation and WAIS–R scatter analysis. *Journal of Intellectual Disability Research, 36*, 443–448.

Bayley, N. (1993). *Bayley Scales of Infant Development* (2nd ed.). San Antonio, TX: Harcourt Assessment.

Beitchman, J. H., Wilson, B., Brownlie, E. B., Walters, H., & Lancee, W. (1996). Longterm consistency in speech/language profiles: I. Developmental and academic outcomes. *Journal of the American Academy of Child and Adolescent Psychiatry, 35*(6), 804–814.

Bishop, D. V. (1992). The underlying nature of specific language impairment. *Journal of Child Psychology & Psychiatry & Allied Disciplines, 33*(1), 3–66.

Bishop, D. V. (1997). Cognitive neuropsychology and developmental disorders: Uncomfortable bedfellows. *The Quarterly Journal of Experimental Psychology: Human Experimental Psychology, 50A*(4), 899–923.

Brown, T. E. (2001). *Brown Attention-Deficit Disorder Scales for Children and Adolescents*. San Antonio, TX: Harcourt Assessment.

Brownell, R. (Ed.) (2000a). *Expressive One-Word Picture Vocabulary Test* (3rd ed.). Novato, CA: Academic Therapy Press.

Brownell, R. (Ed.) (2000b). *Receptive One-Word Picture Vocabulary Test* (2nd ed.). Novato, CA: Academic Therapy Press.

Carroll, J. B. (1993). *Human cognitive abilities: A survey of factor-analytic studies*. Cambridge, England: Cambridge University Press.

Carroll, J. B. (1997). The three-stratum theory of cognitive abilities. In D. P. Flanagan, J. L. Genshaft, & P. L. Harrison (Eds.), *Contemporary intellectual assessment: Theories, tests, and issues* (pp. 122–130). New York: Guilford Press.

Cohen, M. (1997). *Children's Memory Scale*. San Antonio, TX: Harcourt Assessment.

Cooper, S. (1995). *The clinical use and interpretation of the Wechsler Intelligence Scale for Children–Third Edition*. Springfield, IL: Charles C. Thomas.

Craft, N. P., & Kronenberger, E. J. (1979). Comparability of WISC–R and WAIS IQ scores in educable mentally handicapped adolescents. *Psychology in Schools, 16*(4), 502–504.

Delis, D. C., Kaplan, E., & Kramer, J. H. (2001). *Delis–Kaplan Executive Function System*. San Antonio, TX: Harcourt Assessment.

Delis, D. C., Kramer, J. H., Kaplan, E., & Ober, B. A. (1994). *California Verbal Learning Test–Children's Version*. San Antonio, TX: Harcourt Assessment.

Doll, B., & Boren, R. (1993). Performance of severely language-impaired students on the WISC–III, language scales, and academic achievement measures. In B. A. Bracken & R. S. McCallum (Eds.), *Journal of Psychoeducational assessment, WISC–III Monograph, 11*, (pp. 77–86). Brandon, VT: Clinical Psychology Publishing.

Dunn, L., & Dunn, L. (1997) *Peabody Picture Vocabulary Test* (3rd ed.). Circle Pines, MN: American Guidance Service.

Elliott, C. D. (1990). *Differential Ability Scales*. San Antonio, TX: Harcourt Assessment.

Flynn, J. R. (1987). Massive IQ gains in 14 nations: What IQ tests really measure. *Psychological Bulletin 101*, 171–191.

Flynn, J. R. (1998). IQ gains over time: Toward finding the causes. In U. Neisser (Ed.), *The rising curve: Long-term gains in IQ and related measures* (pp. 25–66). Washington D. C.: American Psychological Association.

Green, L., Fein, D., Joy, S., & Waterhouse, L. (1995). Cognitive functioning in autism: An overview. In E. Schopler, & G. B. Mesibov (Eds.), *Learning and cognition in autism* (pp. 13–31). New York: Plenum.

Groth-Marnat, G. (1999). *Handbook of psychological assessment* (3rd ed.). New York: John Wiley & Sons.

Hamilton, W., & Burns, T. G. (2003). Wechsler, D., WPPSI–III: Wechsler preschool and primary scale of intelligence (3rd ed.), The Psychological Corporation., San Antonio, TX, 2002. *Applied Neuropsychology, 10*(3), 188–190.

Harcourt Assessment, Inc. (2001). *Wechsler Individual Achievement Test* (2nd ed.). San Antonio, TX: Author.

Harrison, P. L. (1990). Mental retardation, adaptive behavior assessment, and giftedness. In A. S. Kaufman (Ed.), *Assessing adolescent and adult intelligence* (pp. 533–585). Boston: Allyn & Bacon.

Horn, J. L. (1991). Measurement of intellectual capabilities: A review of theory. In K. S. McGrew, J. K. Werder, & R. W. Woodcock, *WJ–R technical manual* (pp. 197–232). Itasca, IL: Riverside.

Kaufman, A. S., & Kaufman, N. L. (1983). *Kaufman Assessment Battery for Children (K-ABC)*. Circle Pines, MN: American Guidance Service.

Korkman, M., Kirk, U., & Kemp, S. (1998). *NEPSY: A developmental neuropsychological assessment*. San Antonio, TX: Harcourt Assessment, Inc.

Lichtenberger, E. O., & Kaufman A. S. (2004). *Essentials of WPPSI–III assessment*. New York: Wiley.

Lovecky, D. V. (2004). *Different Minds: Gifted children with AD/HD, Asperger syndrome and other learning deficits*. London: Jessica Kingsley Publishers.

Marland, S. P. (1972). *Education of the gifted and talented*. [Report to Congress]. Washington, DC: U.S. Government Printing Office.

Miller, J. N., & Ozonoff, S. (2000). The external validity of Asperger disorder lack of evidence from the domain of neuropsychology. *Journal of Abnormal Psychology, 109*(2), 227–238.

Pennington, B. P., & Ozonoff, S. (1996). Executive functions and developmental psychopathology. *Journal of Child Psychology and Psychiatry, 37*(1), 51–87.

Phelps, L. (1998). Utility of the WISC–III for children with language impairments. In A. Prifitera & D. Saklofske (Eds.), *WISC–III clinical use and interpretation: Scientist-practitioner perspectives* (pp. 157–173). San Diego: Academic Press.

Prifitera, A., & Dersh, J. (1992). Base rates of the WISC–III diagnostic subtest patterns among normal, learning-disabled, and ADHD samples. *Journal of Psychoeducational Assessment (WISC–III Monograph), 11*, 43–55.

Raven, J., Raven, J. C., & Court, J. H. (1998). *Manual for Raven's Progressive Matrices and Vocabulary Scales*. Oxford, United Kingdom: Oxford Psychologists Press.

Roid, G. H. (2003). *Stanford-Binet Intelligence Scales* (5th ed.). Chicago: Riverside.

Rose, J. C., Lincoln, A. J., & Allen, M. H. (1992). Ability profiles of developmental language disordered and learning disabled children: A comparative analysis. *Developmental Neuropsychology, 8*(4), 413–426.

Sattler, J. M. (2001). *Assessment of children: Cognitive applications* (4th ed.). San Diego, CA: Author.

Sattler, J. M. (2002). *Assessment of children: Behavioral and clinical application* (4th ed.). San Diego, CA: Author.

Sattler, J. M, & Dumont, R. (2004). *Assessment of children: WISC–IV and WPPSI–III supplement*. San Diego, CA: Author.

Semel, E., Wiig, E. H., & Secord, W. A. (2003). *Clinical Evaluation of Language Fundamentals* (4th ed.). San Antonio, TX: Harcourt Assessment.

Siegel, D. J., Minshew, N. J., & Goldstein, G. (1996). Wechsler IQ profiles in diagnosis of high-functioning autism. *Journal of Autism & Developmental Disorders, 26*(4), 389–406.

Siegler, R. S. (1996). Unidimensional thinking, multidimensional thinking, and characteristic tendencies of thought. In A. J. Sameroff & M. M. Haith (Eds.), *The five to seven year shift: The age of reason and responsibility* (pp. 63–84). Chicago, IL: The University of Chicago Press.

Slate, J. R. (1995). Discrepancies between IQ and index scores for a clinical sample of students: Useful diagnostic indicators? *Psychology in the Schools*, *32*, 103–108.

Sparrow, S., & Gurland, S. T. (1998). Assessment of gifted children with the WISC–III. In A. Prifitera & D. H. Saklofske, (Eds.), *WISC–III clinical use and interpretation: Scientist-practitioner perspectives* (pp. 59–72). San Diego: Academic Press.

Spruill, J. (1991). A comparison of the Wechsler Adult Intelligence Scale–Revised with the Stanford-Binet Intelligence Scale (Fourth Edition) for mentally retarded adults. *Psychological Assessment: A Journal of Consulting and Clinical Psychology, 3*(1), 1–3.

Thorndike, R. L., Hagen, E. P., & Sattler, J. M. (1986). *Stanford-Binet Intelligence Scale* (4th ed.). Chicago: Riverside.

Wechsler, D. (1939). *Wechsler-Bellevue Intelligence Scale*. New York: Harcourt Assessment.

Wechsler, D. (1989). *Wechsler Preschool and Primary Scale of Intelligence–Revised*. San Antonio, TX: Harcourt Assessment.

Wechsler, D. (1991). *Wechsler Intelligence Scale for Children* (3rd ed.). San Antonio, TX: Harcourt Assessment.

Wechsler, D. (1997). *Wechsler Adult Intelligence Scale* (3rd ed.). San Antonio, TX: Harcourt Assessment.

Wechsler, D. (2002a). *Wechsler Preschool and Primary Scale of Intelligence* (3rd ed.). San Antonio, TX: Harcourt Assessment.

Wechsler, D. (2002b). *WPPSI–III technical and interpretive manual*. San Antonio, TX: Harcourt Assessment.

Wechsler, D. (2003a). *Wechsler Intelligence Scale for Children* (4th ed.). San Antonio, TX: Harcourt Assessment.

Wechsler, D (2003b). *WISC–IV technical and interpretive manual*. San Antonio, TX: Harcourt Assessment.

Wechsler, D. (2004a). *Wechsler Preschool and Primary Scale of Intelligence* (3rd ed.): *Canadian*. Toronto, Canada: Harcourt Assessment.

Wechsler, D., Kaplan, E., Fein, D., Kramer, J., Morris, R., Delis, D., & Maerlender, A. (2004b). *WISC–IV Integrated technical and interpretive manual*. San Antonio, TX: Harcourt Assessment.

Wilcutt, E. G., Pennington, B. F., Boada, R., Ogline, R., Tunick, R. A., & Chhabildas, N. A. (2001). A comparison of the cognitive deficits in reading disability and attention deficit/hyperactivity disorder. *Journal of Abnormal Psychology, 110*(1), 157–172.

Zimmerman, I. A., Steiner, V. G., & Pond, R. E. (2002). *Preschool Language Scale* (4th ed.). San Antonio, TX: Harcourt Assessment.

13

Best Practices in the Use of the Stanford-Binet Intelligence Scales, Fifth Edition (SB5) with Preschoolers[†]

Vincent C. Alfonso
Fordham University

Dawn P. Flanagan
St. John's University

The Stanford-Binet (SB) intelligence scales have the longest history of any intelligence test and perhaps the most articles written about it (Becker, 2003). The original Binet was developed by Alfred Binet and Theodore Simon in 1905. It was published as a measure of general intellectual functioning and used by the French government to assist in the diagnosis and placement of children with mental retardation. Although a few revisions of Binet's original scale were constructed by researchers in the Untied States, it was not until 1916 that a full revision and extension was published by Lewis Terman of Stanford University (Becker, 2003; Roid & Barram, 2004).

In 1937, Maud Merrill joined Terman in developing and publishing the next edition of the Binet intelligence test, which had two forms: Form L and Form M. This version, called the *New Revised Stanford-Binet Tests of Intelligence*, was standardized on more than 3,000 individuals between the ages of 1½ and 18 years and assessed general intellectual functioning via multiple items (e.g., copying shapes, counting, repeating digits) just as previous versions (Becker, 2003; Roid & Barram, 2004). Even though Terman died in 1956, he was instrumental in revising the 1937 version of the test with Merrill, who then published this third edition in 1960: the *Stanford-Binet Intelligence Scale, Third Edition* (Terman & Merrill, 1960). This edition included the deviation IQ, instead of the intelligence quotient that was used on previous editions, and combined Forms L and M to produce Form L-M, which was used in several future editions. In 1973, the next edition of the SB was published. Although the test content of this edition did not change, it was renormed under the leadership of Robert L. Thorndike of Columbia University. With no content changes, however, the name of the test remained the same.

[†]For an electronic copy of the interpretive worksheets referenced in this chapter, please email the first author at alfonso@fordham.edu.

Thirteen years later, the fourth edition of the SB was published (Stanford-Binet Intelligence Scale: Fourth Edition [SB: IV]; Thorndike, Hagen, & Sattler, 1986). This edition surprised many examiners because its design and structure were vastly different from previous versions of the SB. For example, the SB: IV was the first version of the test to include subtests and factors together with an estimate of overall general intellectual functioning. In addition, a *point-scale* format replaced the age-level format, and a *routing test* was included to assist examiners in determining the start point for all subtests (Thorndike et al., 1986). These features were designed to make testing more efficient and "to provide a variety of content to keep examinees involved in the testing experience and to allow for the introduction of developmentally distinct items across levels" (Becker, 2003, p. 3). For an excellent, comprehensive review of the history of the various SB scales, including structure, content, and theoretical foundation, see Becker (2003).

The fifth and most current edition of the SB represents a blending of the child-friendly content and manipulatives that made the earlier versions so popular, especially for evaluating preschoolers, and the differentiation among IQs and theoretical cognitive factors that made the SB: IV state of the art at the time of its publication.

DESCRIPTION AND EVALUATION OF THE STANFORD-BINET INTELLIGENCE SCALES, FIFTH EDITION

The Stanford-Binet Intelligence Scales, Fifth Edition (SB5; Roid, 2003a) is an individually administered intelligence battery that is appropriate for use with individuals between the ages of 2 and 85+ years. The SB5 was published by Riverside Publishing in 2003, approximately 17 years after the publication of the SB: IV. The SB5 is composed of 10 subtests, five nonverbal (NV) and five verbal (V). The NV subtests combine to yield a NVIQ, the V subtests combine to yield the VIQ, and all 10 subtests combine to yield a FSIQ. Two of the 10 subtests are *routing* subtests—one for the nonverbal domain and one for the verbal domain. The routing subtests assist examiners in determining where to begin the administration of the remaining eight subtests. An abbreviated IQ (i.e., ABIQ) may be obtained by combining the scaled scores earned on the routing subtests. In addition to IQs, the SB5 subtests are organized into five separate CHC factors, including Fluid Reasoning, Knowledge, Quantitative Reasoning, Visual-Spatial Processing, and Working Memory. Each factor is composed of one NV and one V subtest.

The SB5 subtests have a mean of 10 and standard deviation of 3; the composites (i.e., IQs and factors) have a mean of 100 and a standard deviation of 15. The reported range of standard scores for the FSIQ is 40–160 (Roid, 2003b). Derived scores that are available to assist in test interpretation include standard scores, percentiles, change-sensitive scores, and age equivalents. Administration time for the SB5 is 45–75 minutes, depending on the age and ability of the individual. This chapter provides a comprehensive description and evaluation of the SB5, particularly for the preschool population (i.e., ages 2–5 years). An alternative interpretive method is also provided to assist examiners in deriving meaning from the performance of very young children.

Key Features of the SB5

The SB5 contains many features that make it especially appropriate and useful for assessing the intellectual functioning of preschoolers. First, it includes multiple toys, child-friendly stimuli, and innovative activities (e.g., block span) that are engaging for young children. Although these features were enjoyed by SB L-M users, they were almost completely eliminated from the SB: IV, which was a major criticism of this edition (e.g., Alfonso & Flanagan, 1999). Second, the inclusion of four IQs and five factors provides examiners with the flexibility to select the type of scores that provide the most reliable and valid estimates of a child's cognitive capabilities. Additionally, by measuring each CHC broad ability via one NV and one V subtest, an examiner may find it easier to discern whether a lack of English language proficiency adversely affects performance on this battery as compared to others. For example, if NVIQ > VIQ for a child who is an English Language Learner (ELL), then it may be likely that a lack of proficiency in English led to a spuriously low VIQ. This hypothesis should be tested, however, prior to concluding that the finding of NVIQ > VIQ represents a real difference (Roid, 2003d).

Third, although not particular to preschoolers, changing the subtest mean and standard deviation from 50 and 8 (SB: IV) to 10 and 3 (SB5), respectively, is a welcomed change because it allows examiners to make comparisons across batteries more readily. Likewise, the standard deviation for the IQs and factors is now 15 instead of 16 (SB: IV) and, therefore, consistent with most composite scores found on other intelligence batteries. Fourth, the inclusion of two routing subtests (one nonverbal and one verbal) and the ABIQ provides examiners with the flexibility to screen and monitor young children's intellectual functioning in an efficient manner. Fifth, the *Stanford-Binet Intelligence Scales Interpretive Manual: Expanded Guide to the Interpretation of SB5 Test Results* (Roid, 2003d) includes a reliable and valid method for the calculation of FSIQs as low as 10 and as high as 225. This feature is especially useful in assessing young children with moderate to severe mental retardation, as well as those who are exceptionally gifted, respectively. Sixth, the inclusion of change-sensitive scores allows examiners to determine if young children have made progress over time despite either no change in standard score performance or lower standard score performance. This feature allows examiners to describe a young child's intellectual development in positive terms despite the fact that associated standard scores may not reveal growth and development. Change-sensitive scores may prove particularly useful for the purpose of monitoring response to intervention.

Theory and Structure of the SB5

The SB5, like many other newly revised intelligence batteries (e.g., Kaufman Assessment Battery for Children–Second Edition [KABC–II]; Kaufman & Kaufman, 2004; Woodcock-Johnson III Tests of Cognitive Abilities [WJ III COG]; Woodcock, McGrew, & Mather, 2001) was developed based on CHC theory. The CHC theory is the most comprehensive and empirically supported psychometric theory of the structure of cognitive and academic abilities to date. It represents the integrated works of Raymond Cattell, John Horn, and John Carroll (Flanagan, McGrew, & Ortiz, 2000; McGrew, 2005). Because it has an impressive body of empirical support in the research literature (e.g., developmental, neurocognitive, outcome-criterion; Horn & Blankson, 2005) it is used extensively as the foundation for selecting, organizing, and interpreting tests of intelligence and cognitive abilities (see Alfonso, Flanagan, & Radwan, 2005).

The CHC structure of the SB5 is depicted in Figure 13.1. This structure is similar to that of current intelligence batteries in that it is hierarchical in nature. Figure 13.1 shows that general intellectual ability or "g" is located at the apex of the model underlying the SB5, which encompasses several second-order factors that correspond to CHC broad cognitive abilities. Each factor of the SB5 is composed of one nonverbal and one verbal subtest designed to assess specific aspects of the broad ability. For example, Figure 13.1

General Ability

CHC
Factors

Subtests

IQs

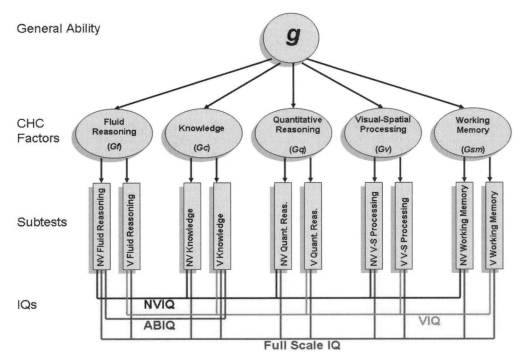

FIGURE 13.1.   CHC structure of the SB5.

shows that the *Gc* factor (i.e., Knowledge) is composed of the Nonverbal Knowledge subtest (which measures mainly KO and LS at preschool levels, see Table 13.1) and the Verbal Knowledge subtest (which measures mainly KO and VL at the preschool levels, see
Table 13.1). In addition, Figure 13.1 shows that the nonverbal subtests yield a NVIQ and
the verbal subtests yield a VIQ. Table 13.1 contains descriptions of the SB5 subtests as
well as our own CHC classifications of the subtests at the broad and narrow ability levels.

Because our CHC broad and narrow ability classifications of SB5 subtests differ at
times from the test's author, Gale Roid, Table 13.2 provides our classifications alongside
Roid's classifications, as well as a rationale for each disparity. In general, when our classifications differ from Roid's, it is because the activities that are presented at early levels of
the SB5 (i.e., levels appropriate for preschoolers) differ from activities corresponding with
higher levels. Because the activities within a subtest change across the levels of the subtest,
there are instances in which a given subtest measures a different ability for a preschool
child than it does for a high school student, for example. In short, the structure presented
in Figure 13.1 is most likely not representative of the structure of the SB5 for very young
children. Although there is a need to test this assumption empirically, we believe the structure of the SB5 is different for preschoolers as compared to older samples simply because
many of the activities administered to preschoolers appear to measure different abilities
than those underlying activities more typically administered to older children. This assumption is also shared by Gale Roid, the author of the SB5 (April 1, 2005, personal communication). Figure 13.2 includes an alternative factor structure of the SB5 that we believe
may be more reflective of the preschool population.

TABLE 13.1.
SB5 Subtest Descriptions and CHC Broad and Narrow Ability
Classifications for Preschoolers

Subtest	Description of Subtest	Alfonso and Flanagan's CHC Broad and Narrow Ability Classification (SB5 Levels)
1. Nonverbal Fluid Reasoning	The child is required to hand the examiner an object that matches the target object from an array of several objects, choose an object from five possible response options that completes a row of a pattern of objects, and to identify from several response options the missing shape/design that completes a matrix.	Gv – visual discrimination Gf – RG beginning at approximately age 7 (No levels because this is the nonverbal routing subtest that uses a point-scale format)
2. Nonverbal Knowledge	At levels 2–3 the child is required to perform everyday actions stated by the examiner or demonstrate physically how common objects are typically used. At level 4 the child is required to identify verbally and by pointing to what is silly or impossible about a picture presented on a stimulus page.	Gc – KO, LS (Levels 2–3) Gf – RG (Level 4)
3. Nonverbal Quantitative Reasoning	At levels 2–3 the child is required to demonstrate his/her understanding of quantitative concepts such as "bigger" and "more" (e.g., point to the bigger car). At levels 3–4 the child is also required to solve addition problems and recognize numbers presented on a stimulus page.	Gq – KM (Levels 2–4) Gc – VL (Levels 2–3)
4. Nonverbal Visual-Spatial Processing	At levels 1–2 the child is required to complete a form board that contains several common shapes. At levels 3–4 the child is required to construct designs of common objects (e.g., car) under specified time limits, using plastic puzzle pieces that are presented on a stimulus page.	Gv – SR (Levels 1–2) Gv – SR, CS (Levels 3–4)
5. Nonverbal Working Memory	At level 1 the child is required to find an object (e.g., ball) placed under one of two or three inverted cups in view of the child. At levels 2–4 the child is required to tap blocks in a specified order stated by the examiner after the examiner has tapped the blocks.	Gv – MV (Levels 1–4) Gsm – MS (Level 2) Gsm – MW (Levels 3–4)
6. Verbal Fluid Reasoning	At level 2 the child views an illustration/picture presented on a stimulus page and is required to describe what is happening in the picture. At level 3 the child is presented with 30 randomly	Gc – OP (Level 2) Gf – I (Level 3) Gf – RG (Level 4)

(continued)

TABLE 13.1.

(*Continued*)

Subtest	Description of Subtest	Alfonso and Flanagan's CHC Broad and Narrow Ability Classification (SB5 Levels)
6. Verbal Fluid Reasoning (*continued*)	dispersed chips on a table. Each chip has a picture of a common object (e.g., book, pen, key). The child is required to create as many groups of three chips as possible so that the three chips share at least one common characteristic. At level 4 the child is required to state verbally what is silly or impossible about a sentence stated by the examiner.	
7. Verbal Knowledge	The child is required to demonstrate knowledge of body parts by pointing to body parts on him/herself (e.g., eyes) and on a picture card of a boy or girl (e.g., hands). In addition, the child is required to name common objects or things, describe with a one or two-word response what is happening in a picture, and define words presented orally by the examiner.	Gc – KO, VL (No levels because this is the verbal routing subtest that uses a point-scale format)
8. Verbal Quantitative Reasoning	At levels 2–4 the child is required to count using toys (e.g., blocks) and other objects (e.g., counting rods), name numbers, and to solve basic addition and subtraction problems presented verbally by the examiner and visually on a stimulus page. At level 4 the child is required to solve mathematical word problems presented orally by the examiner and visually on a stimulus page.	Gq – A3, (Levels 2–4) Gf – RQ (Level 4)
9. Verbal Visual-Spatial Processing	At levels 2–4 the child is required to place a block on a specified part of a picture of a common object (e.g., building) or scene (e.g., children on a playground) found on a stimulus page.	Gc – VL, KO (Levels 2–4)[a]
10. Verbal Working Memory	At levels 2–4 the child is required to repeat verbatim sentences of varying length presented orally by the examiner. At level 4 the child is required to recall in order the last word in a series of questions asked by the examiner (after all questions have been asked and answered).	Gsm – MS (Levels 2–4) Gc – LD (Levels 2–4) Gsm – MW (Level 4)

Note: The broad and narrow ability classifications in this table were provided by the present authors.
[a]The Verbal Visual-Spatial Processing subtest does not directly measure aspects of *Gv* until levels 5 and 6.

TABLE 13.2.
Differences between Alfonso and Flanagan's and Roid's Subtest Classifications

SB5 Subtest	Roid's CHC Classifications	Alfonso and Flanagan's CHC Classifications (SB5 Levels)	Rationale for Differences
Nonverbal Fluid Reasoning	Gf – I, RG Gv – MV	Gv – visual discrimination Gf – RG beginning at approximately age 7 (No levels because this is the nonverbal routing subtest that uses a point-scale format)	The initial items on this subtest involve visual discrimination where a child has to match a target object with the same object in an array. Items involving completing an object series and matrices involve deductive reasoning (RG) rather than inductive reasoning (I). We do not believe visual memory (MV) is involved in this subtest.
Nonverbal Knowledge	Gc – KO, OP	Gc – KO, LS (Levels 2–3) Gf – RG (Level 4)	Listening ability (LS) is involved in the items that require the child to demonstrate how to do something such as knocking on a door. Oral production and fluency (OP) refers to more expressive language than is required on this subtest. Deductive reasoning (RG) is involved in items that require the child to state and point to what is silly or impossible about a picture.
Nonverbal Quantitative Reasoning	Gq – KM Gf – RQ	Gq – KM (Levels 2–4) Gc – VL (Levels 2–3)	We do not believe that the items given to preschoolers measure quantitative reasoning (RQ), a higher level cognitive ability. At levels 2–3 the child is required to demonstrate his/her understanding of quantitative concepts or lexical knowledge (VL).
Nonverbal Visual-Spatial Processing	Gv – SR, CS	Gv – SR (Levels 1–2) Gv – SR, CS (Levels 3–4)	Closure speed (CS) is not involved until levels 3–4 when the child has to assemble puzzle pieces to resemble a common object.
Nonverbal Working Memory	Gv – MV, PI, MW	Gv – MV (Levels 1–4) Gsm – MS (Level 2) Gsm – MW (Levels 3–4)	We do not believe that this subtest involves serial perceptual integration (PI) and that at level 2 only memory span (MS) is involved

(continued)

TABLE 13.2.

(*Continued*)

SB5 Subtest	Roid's CHC Classifications	Alfonso and Flanagan's CHC Classifications (SB5 Levels)	Rationale for Differences
Nonverbal Working Memory (*continued*)			because the child repeats a block tapping sequence in the same order as the examiner. Working memory (MW) is not involved until level 3 when the child has to sort and transform information to tap blocks in a sequence.
Verbal Fluid Reasoning	Gf – I, RG Gc – OP Gv – MV	Gc – OP (Level 2) Gf – I (Level 3) Gf – RG (Level 4)	We believe that oral production and fluency (OP) is involved only at level 2 when the child has to describe a picture in detail. It is not until level 3 that inductive reasoning (I) is involved on this subtest when a child has to sort chips according to a category. At level 4 deductive reasoning (RG) is involved when the child has to indicate what is silly or impossible about a statement read by the examiner. Visual memory (MV) is not involved on this subtest.
Verbal Knowledge	Gc – VL, LD	Gc–KO, VL (No levels because this is the verbal routing subtest that uses a point-scale format)	General information (KO) is involved in initial items of this subtest when a child has to point to body parts, name common objects, and state a common activity. We do not believe language development (LD) is involved in defining words.
Verbal Quantitative Reasoning	Gf – RQ Gq – KM	Gq – A3, (Levels 2–4) GK – RQ, (Level 4)	Math achievement (A3) is involved with levels 2–4 when the child has to count, name numbers, and to solve basic addition and subtraction problems. Quantitative reasoning (RQ) is not involved until level 4 when the child has to solve complex math problems.

(*continued*)

TABLE 13.2.

(*Continued*)

SB5 Subtest	Roid's CHC Classifications	Alfonso and Flanagan's CHC Classifications (SB5 Levels)	Rationale for Differences
Verbal Visual-Spatial Processing	Gv – VZ	Gc – VL, KO (Levels 2–4)	The items at levels 2–4 require the child to place a block on a specified part of a picture of a common object or scene (VL) found on a stimulus page. The items also involve general information (KO) because the child is shown pictures of common objects. No visualization (VZ) is involved.
Verbal Working Memory	Gc – LD Gsm – MW	Gsm – MS (Levels 2–4) Gc – LD (Levels 3–4) Gsm – MW (Level 4)	Memory span (MS) is involved at levels 2–4 because the child has to repeat verbatim sentences of varying length presented orally by the examiner. Working memory (MW) is not involved until level 4 when the child has to recall in order the last word in a series of questions asked by the examiner (after all questions have been asked and answered).

The organization of the SB5 differs from most intelligence batteries in that it includes functional levels and testlets in addition to subtests, factors, and IQs. *Levels of testing* apply to all of the SB5 subtests except the two routing subtests. There are six levels in the nonverbal domain (Levels 1–6) and five levels in the verbal domain (Levels 2–6). Each level of testing has four testlets (except nonverbal Level 1, which has two). *Testlets* are groupings of 3–6 items in a common range of difficulty as determined by item response theory or Rasch modeling. Groups of 5 or 6 testlets, arranged in order (or level) of increasing difficulty, combine to form a subtest. The SB5 subtests have very specific basal and ceiling rules that enable examiners to know when to advance, or drop back, a level. The use of routing subtests, levels of testing, and testlets allows examiners to assess individuals with greater flexibility and efficiency as compared to most other intelligence batteries. Notwithstanding, because the activities that make up testlets often change within a subtest, the ability measured by a subtest may change as a function of age. In sum, based on our classifications of the SB5 subtests for preschoolers (Table 1) and our rationale for these classifications (Table 2), we believe the SB5 measures four, rather than five, CHC abilities (see Figure 13.2) at the preschool age range (viz., ages 2–5 years).

General Ability

CHC
Factors

Subtests

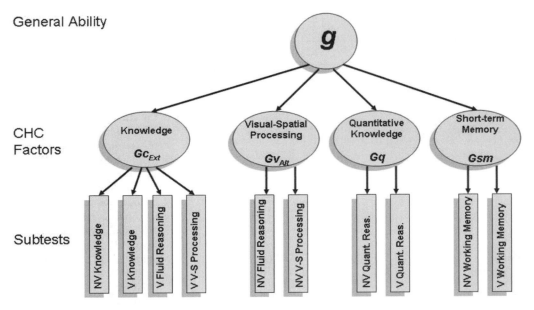

FIGURE 13.2.   Alternative factor structure of the SB5.

Administration and Scoring of the SB5

Administration and scoring of the SB5 is actually straightforward, although it may not seem so when first learning the test. All SB5 subtests are contained in three item books. These item books include all the information necessary to administer the subtests, including directions to the examiner and materials needed. The item books also include scoring criteria. The structure of the item books corresponds directly to the layout of the test record. As such, it is important for examiners to follow the standard administration procedures unless extenuating circumstances suggest otherwise. The test record contains basal and ceiling rules, scoring methods for each subtest and testlet, as well as tables for determining where to begin each subtest based on performance on the routing subtests.

The examiner begins with Item Book 1 which contains the two routing subtests—Nonverbal Fluid Reasoning and Verbal Knowledge. A child's raw score performance on each of these subtests indicates the level at which the examiner should begin all subsequent nonverbal and verbal subtests, respectively. If an examiner believes that the routing test performance is not accurate for a particular child (i.e., either overestimates or underestimates performance), then the examiner may start the child at a lower or higher level to ensure that the child meets with success and that the testing is efficient. After the routing subtests are administered, the examiner turns to Item Book 2. This book contains the remaining nonverbal subtests, including Nonverbal Knowledge, Nonverbal Quantitative Reasoning, Nonverbal Visual-Spatial Processing, and Nonverbal Working Memory. Each subtest in this book begins at the same level indicated by either the routing subtest or the examiner's best estimate of where testing should begin. Once the child has reached a ceiling level of functioning on the nonverbal subtests found in Item Book 2, the examiner proceeds to Item Book 3. This book contains the remaining verbal subtests, including Verbal Fluid Reasoning, Verbal Quantitative Reasoning, Verbal Visual-Spatial Processing, and Verbal Working

Memory. Once the child has reached a ceiling level of functioning on the verbal subtests found in Item Book 3, testing is completed. Thus, administration of the SB5 is complete after the examiner administers all relevant testlets from Item Books 1, 2, and 3.

Standardization Characteristics of the SB5

The standardization sample of the SB5 included 1,400 children between the ages of 2–5 years. The sample closely approximated the U.S. population (2001 Census data) on the following variables: gender, geographic region, race/ethnicity, and socioeconomic level (i.e., years of education completed, or parent's educational attainment). The norm tables of the SB5 are divided into two-month age blocks for children between the ages of 2–0 and 5–11.

Psychometric Characteristics of SB5 Subtests for Preschoolers

Several psychometric characteristics are important to consider prior to selecting an intelligence battery to use with preschool children. The characteristics we believe are most important include test reliability, *g* loadings, floors, and item gradients. Typically, one or more of these characteristics is necessary to consider prior to selecting tests for use with preschoolers and/or interpreting the test performance of young children. The nature of the referral can guide decisions related to which technical characteristics ought to be considered in the test selection and interpretation process. For example, if a three-year-old child is referred because of suspected developmental delay, then the *floor* of a test is one important psychometric characteristic to consider before selecting the instrument for use. Tests with poor floors can *overestimate* ability in very young children and in low functioning children and will not provide much information about a child's capabilities. Each psychometric characteristic listed above is defined briefly here. Table 13.3 provides an evaluation of these test characteristics for the SB5 subtests that are administered to preschoolers. Space limitations preclude an in-depth discussion of these characteristics. The reader is referred to Alfonso and Flanagan (1999), Bracken and Walker (1997), Bracken (1987), Flanagan and Alfonso (1995), and McGrew and Flanagan (1998) for extensive coverage of issues related to the technical qualities of intelligence tests.

Reliability.   The reliability of a particular test is important to consider because it affects interpretation of the test results. Reliability is defined as the degree to which test scores are free from errors of measurement (AERA, APA, & NCME, 1999). Reliability guides decisions concerning the range of scores likely to occur as the result of irrelevant chance factors (i.e., standard error of measurement). In its broadest sense, test reliability indicates the extent to which individual differences are attributed to true differences in the characteristics under investigation or chance errors (Urbina, 2004). Table 13.3 shows that the SB5 subtests generally have *Medium* (.80–.89) to *High* (.90 or greater) reliability at the preschool age range. Oddly, the Nonverbal Knowledge and Nonverbal Quantitative Reasoning subtests have Medium to High reliability at ages 2–4 and *Low* reliability (i.e., less than .80) at age 5. Test-retest reliability is *Medium* to *High* for half of the SB5 subtests at the preschool age range. Overall, the SB5 subtests have excellent reliability at early ages as compared to other intelligence batteries with norms for preschoolers.

g-loadings.   *g* loading characteristics are also important to consider in the test interpretation process. Intelligence tests are interpreted often as reflecting a *general* mental

TABLE 13.3.
Psychometric Characteristics of SB5 Subtests for Preschoolers

| Subtest Name | Reliability | | g loading | Test floor[a] | Item Gradients Evaluation (Age in Years) |
	Internal Consistency Evaluation (Age in years)	Test-Retest			
NONVERBAL (NV) DOMAIN					
Nonverbal Fluid Reasoning (Nonverbal Routing Test)	Medium (2–4) High (5)	Low	Medium	3.6	Fair (2) Good (3 to 5)
Nonverbal Knowledge	Low (5) Medium (4) High (2–3)	Medium	High	2.10	Fair (2) Good (3 to 5)
Nonverbal Quantitative Reasoning	Low (5) Medium (2,4) High (3)	Medium	High	3.8	Fair (2) Good (3 to 5)
Nonverbal Visual-Spatial Processing	Medium (2, 4–5) High (3)	Low	Medium	2.6	Fair (2 to 4) Good (5)
Nonverbal Working Memory	Medium (2, 4) High (3, 5)	Low	High	3.0	Fair (2 to 3) Good (4 to 5)
VERBAL (V) DOMAIN					
Verbal Fluid Reasoning	Medium (2) High (3–5)	Medium	High	4.6	Poor (2 to 3) Good (4 to 5)
Verbal Knowledge (Verbal Routing Test)	Medium (3–5) High (2)	High	High	2.0	Good (2 to 5)
Verbal Quantitative Reasoning	Medium (2–5)	Low	High	4.0	Poor (2 to 4) Fair (5)
Verbal Visual-Spatial Processing	Low (3) Medium (2, 4–5)	Low	High	3.6	Poor (2) Good (3 to 5)
Verbal Working Memory	Medium (2–5)	High	High	3.6	Poor (2) Good (3 to 5)

[a]The years and months found in the test floor column indicate the age at which the subtest begins to have an adequate floor. For example, the Nonverbal Knowledge subtest has an adequate floor beginning at age 2.10 (i.e., 2 years, 10 months).

ability called *g* (Carroll, 1993; Jensen, 1998; Keith, 2005; Urbina, 2004). Despite the numerous theoretical arguments that surround the concept and meaningfulness of *g*, an appreciation of a subtest's relationship to a general intelligence factor is considered useful in interpretation (Kaufman, 1979, 1990). *g* loadings provide information that is needed to anticipate those tests within an intelligence battery that are likely to vary from the remainder of the test profile (Kaufman, 1979). Tests that are expected to be at a similar level of performance as most of the other tests in the battery (and the global or full scale score) are those that have *High g* factor loadings. In contrast, tests that are expected to vary from the other tests within an intelligence battery are those that have *Low g* factor loadings.

Thus, a test with a low factor loading that differs from most other tests in the battery may not represent a diagnostically or clinically significant finding. Knowledge of each test's loading on the general factor (*g*) within an intelligence battery is important because it can help practitioners identify unusual test variations. Table 13.3 shows that the majority of SB5 subtests have *High g* loadings. None of the subtests has a *Low g* loading. In general, the SB5 subtests are highly *g* saturated.

Test Floors.   Because test floors have been identified as one of the poorest technical qualities of preschool intelligence tests (e.g., Flanagan & Alfonso, 1995), this characteristic ought to be evaluated during the test selection process. Intelligence batteries with *Adequate* floors will yield scores that discriminate effectively among several levels of functioning at the lower extreme of the cognitive ability continuum. Tests with *Inadequate* floors cannot adequately distinguish between individuals functioning in the average, below average, and lower extreme ranges of ability or between various levels of mental retardation (e.g., mild, moderate) because they contain an insufficient number of easy items (Bracken, 1987). An intelligence battery that does not have adequate floors will provide little (if any) information about what a young child *can do*. Therefore, tests with inadequate floors should not be used for diagnostic, classification, or placement decisions, especially with individuals who are suspected of developmental delay (Bracken, 1987; Flanagan & Alfonso, 1995; McGrew & Flanagan, 1998). Table 13.3 reports the ages at which the SB5 subtests have *Adequate* floors. This table shows that three subtests have adequate floors at age 2, and nearly all subtests have adequate floors at age 3 years, 6 months. In general, the SB5 subtests have better floors than those comprising other intelligence batteries with norms for preschoolers.

Item Gradients.   The information gained from examining the item gradients of a test compliments information related to the floor of the test. That is, the extent to which a test effectively differentiates among various ability levels at the low end of the cognitive ability continuum (e.g., average, below average, lower extreme) can be determined by examining test floors, whereas the extent to which a test effectively differentiates *within* various ability levels (e.g., within the below average range) along the entire scale of the test can be determined by examining item gradients. In other words, item gradients are sensitive to *fine gradations* in ability across the scale of the test. Item gradient refers to the density of items across a test's latent trait scale. A test with good item gradient characteristics has items that are approximately equally spaced in difficulty along the entire scale of the test, and the distance between items is small enough to allow for reliable discrimination between individuals on the latent trait measured by the test (Flanagan, Genshaft, & Mascolo, 2000). Item gradient information is concerned with the extent to which changes in a single raw score point on a test result in excessively large changes in ability scores (or standard scores; Bracken, 1987). With the exception of age 2, most SB5 subtests have *Fair* to *Good* item gradients.

Qualitative Characteristics of the SB5 Subtests for Preschoolers

Qualitative test characteristics provide non-technical information about tests that can enrich and inform the test selection and interpretation process. The qualitative test characteristics reviewed here include degree of cultural loading inherent in the test, degree of linguistic demand necessary to perform the test, background/environmental factors, and individual/situational factors. As was true of psychometric characteristics, the nature of the referral can guide decisions related to which qualitative characteristics ought to be considered in test use and interpretation. The qualitative characteristics listed previously are defined briefly here. For a more detailed and expansive discussion of these and other qualitative characteristics of intelligence tests, the reader is referred to Alfonso and Flanagan (1999), Bracken (1997), Ford and Dahinten (2005), and McGrew and Flanagan (1998).

Degree of Cultural Loading and Linguistic Demand. According to Flanagan and Ortiz (2001) and Ortiz and Ochoa (2005), assessment of the intellectual capabilities of culturally and linguistically diverse populations is one of the most difficult tasks facing psychologists today. An overrepresentation of individuals from diverse populations in special education and other remedial programs has resulted because of a failure to accurately distinguish normal, culturally based variation in behavior, first and second language acquisition, acculturation, and cognitive development from true disabilities. Systematic and appropriate evaluation methods should be incorporated in the assessment of culturally and linguistically diverse populations in order to circumvent the negative effects on learning, social, and psychological development that often result from improper educational placement (Ortiz & Ochoa, 2005; Rhodes, Ochoa, & Ortiz, 2005). Flanagan and Ortiz (2001) evaluated the degree to which cultural and linguistic factors influence test performance on the major intelligence batteries. Their methods were applied here to classify the degree to which performance on the SB5 subtests are influenced by culture and language. Table 13.4 provides the cultural loading and linguistic demand classifications of the SB5 subtests for preschoolers.

As may be seen in Table 13.4, the degree to which the SB5 subtests require specific knowledge of and experience with mainstream U.S. culture ranges from *Low* to *High*, with an approximately equal number of subtests in each category. Classification of tests along the cultural dimension was based on logical analyses of task demands following criteria related to process, content, and nature of expected response. Tests that were more process dominant (versus product dominant), included abstract or novel stimuli (versus culture-specific stimuli), and required simple, less culturally bound communicative responding, such as pointing, were thought to yield scores that are less influenced by an individual's level of exposure to mainstream U.S. culture (Ortiz & Ochoa, 2005; Valdés & Figueroa, 1994).

Our classification of tests along the linguistic dimension was based on factors related to test administration and responding. First, tests were evaluated according to the degree to which they involved expressive language on behalf of the examiner in order to be administered correctly. Some tests have relatively long instructions (e.g., Nonverbal Working Memory), whereas others have relatively short instructions or minimal language (e.g., Nonverbal Visual-Spatial Processing). Second, tests were evaluated according to the level of English language proficiency required of the examinee in order to understand the examiner's instructions and offer an appropriate response. Responses for some tests require considerable expressive language skills (e.g., the Wechsler Comprehension subtest) while others may be accomplished without uttering a word (e.g., Nonverbal Fluid Reasoning). Thus, our classifications of subtests as having either *High*, *Medium*, or *Low* linguistic demand were based on a consideration of language requirements for both the examiner and examinee. These classifications are listed in Table 13.4.

Background/Environmental and Individual/Situational Variables. Two additional broad categories of variables that are important to consider when interpreting an individual's perfor-

TABLE 13.4.

Culture, Language, Background/Environmental, and Individual/Situational Factors Influencing Performance on SB5 Subtests

Subtest Name	Cultural Loading	Linguistic Demand	Background/environmental	Individual/situational
NONVERBAL (NV) DOMAIN				
Nonverbal Fluid Reasoning (Nonverbal Routing Test)	Low	Moderate to High	Vision difficulties	Reflectivity vs. impulsivity Field dependence vs. independence Planning
Nonverbal Knowledge	High	High	Language stimulation Alertness to the environment Cultural opportunities and experiences Educational opportunities and experiences	
Nonverbal Quantitative Reasoning	Moderate	High	Math difficulties Educational opportunities and experiences	Concentration Reflectivity vs. impulsivity
Nonverbal Visual-Spatial Processing	Low	High	Vision difficulties	Visual-motor coordination Reflectivity vs. impulsivity Field dependence vs. independence
Nonverbal Working Memory	Low	High	Vision difficulties	Attention span/Distractibility Concentration Verbal rehearsal Visual elaboration Reflectivity vs. impulsivity Field dependence vs. independence
VERBAL (V) DOMAIN				
Verbal Fluid Reasoning	High	High	Language stimulation Alertness to the environment Cultural opportunities and experiences Educational opportunities and experiences	

Verbal Knowledge (Verbal Routing Test)	High	High	Language stimulation Intellectual curiosity Cultural opportunities and experiences Educational opportunities and experiences	Concentration Reflectivity vs. impulsivity
Verbal Quantitative Reasoning	Moderate	High	Math difficulties Educational opportunities and experiences	Attention span/Distractibility Concentration
Verbal Visual-Spatial Processing	Moderate to High	High	Language stimulation Cultural opportunities and experiences Educational opportunities and experiences Vision difficulties	Reflectivity vs. impulsivity
Verbal Working Memory	Moderate	High	Hearing difficulties Language stimulation	Attention span/Distractibility Concentration Verbal rehearsal Visual elaboration

mance on preschool intelligence tests include background/environmental and individual/ situational variables. These two sets of variables (or non-cognitive factors) inform the interpretive process by focusing and placing an individual's test performance within an appropriate context. Background/environmental variables (e.g., language stimulation, educational opportunities and experiences) typically have a distal (i.e., far or remote) influence on an examinee's test performance because they do not directly operate during the testing session, but rather, may have contributed to the development of the traits that are measured by a test (McGrew & Flanagan, 1998). For example, the meaning of a very low auditory processing test score would be different for a child with a history of inner ear infections as compared to a child without such a history. In the case of the child with chronic ear infections, a practitioner may reason that such difficulties may have hindered the development of auditory processing abilities. Thus, prior development or certain environmental factors may affect the development of the ability being assessed (Flanagan et al., 2000).

Conversely, individual/situational variables (e.g., attention span, distractibility, color blindness) are intrinsic to the examinee and can have a proximal (i.e., near or immediate) influence on test performance (either in a positive or negative direction) during the testing session (McGrew & Flanagan, 1998). For instance, highly distractible behavior during testing may influence performance negatively, leading to spuriously low scores. That is, when a child exhibits highly distractible behavior during the administration of a particular test, the reliable variance associated with the test is reduced, with the result being a tautological increase in error variance. Thus, non-cognitive factors (in this case, distractibility) must play a significant role in interpreting test performance.

Knowledge of both the background/environmental and individual/situational variables that may have either distal or proximal influences on an individual's test performance is necessary for appropriate interpretation. Table 13.4 lists the background/environmental and individual/situational variables that may influence performance on the SB5 subtests for preschoolers. These variables were selected based on an extensive review of the literature and logically derived criteria for inclusion specified by McGrew and Flanagan (1998). The interested reader is referred to these authors for more details.

In summary, having access to qualitative characteristics of the SB5 subtests will provide examiners with important information, above and beyond the psychometric domain, that will enhance their ability to make informed interpretations. While knowledge of the background/environmental and individual/situational variables is integral to understanding the test performance of any child, knowledge of the degree of cultural loading and linguistic demand of cognitive ability tests seems particularly relevant for multicultural/multilingual populations. Due to the more subjective nature of the qualitative characteristics of tests (as compared to the psychometric characteristics), it is recommended that the information included in Table 13.4 be used in conjunction with other relevant information to inform interpretation.

ALTERNATIVE APPROACH TO INTERPRETING THE SB5: APPLYING A THEORY-BASED METHOD DEVELOPED BY FLANAGAN AND KAUFMAN

The *Stanford-Binet Intelligence Scales Interpretive Manual: Expanded Guide to the Interpretation of SB5 Test Results* (Roid, 2003d) provides a detailed approach to interpretation. Although this approach encompasses the test performance of preschoolers, it is not specific to this population. As already mentioned, many SB5 subtests measure different abilities in preschoolers as compared to older children (see Table 13.2). Therefore, in order to provide practitioners with a psychometrically and theoretically defensible approach to interpreting the SB5 performance of preschoolers, we applied a new interpretive system to the SB5 here that was developed recently by Flanagan and Kaufman (2004).

In general, the Flanagan-Kaufman method links ipsative interpretive methods with normative interpretive methods, rather than focusing exclusively on either one or the other. The rationale for applying this new method of interpretation to the SB5 is threefold. First, the method presented here deemphasizes subtest-level interpretation and ensures that CHC constructs are interpreted only when they represent *unitary* abilities. Second, the method uses the characteristics of the normal probability curve in conjunction with base rate data to evaluate the clinical meaningfulness of score variability. Third, because the factor structure of the SB5 is very likely not the same in a preschool sample as compared to school age and adult samples (Gale Roid, personal communication, April 1,2005), this interpretive method incorporates clinical clusters that are more in line with ability constructs inherent to the preschool population (Flanagan et al., 2000; Ford & Dahinten, 2005). Table 13.8 presents the "Scaled Score to Clinical Cluster Conversion Tables" for the new combinations of SB5 subtests that we have incorporated into the interpretive system presented here. Finally, it is important to note that this interpretive approach also includes an alternative categorical system for describing standard scores.

Traditional descriptive category systems consider Average functioning to be 90–109 and include categories such as Low Average (80–89) and Superior (120–129). A traditional category system is included in the SB5 *Examiner's Manual* (Roid, 2003c), and those descriptive labels appear frequently in case reports. Kaufman and Kaufman (2004) and Flanagan and Kaufman (2004) offer an alternative categorical system. Their categories are based on the distance, in standard deviation (*SD*) units, from the mean (see Table 13.5). The Average Range is, therefore, represented by a standard score range of 85–115, which corresponds to $100 \pm 1SD$. Although any existing categorical system may be used to classify a person's overall intellectual functioning on the SB5, Flanagan and Kaufman (2004) recommend a *normative descriptive system*, particularly because it is "commonly used by neuropsychologists and is becoming more widespread among clinical and school psychologists" (p. 123). The following section describes a new step-by-step approach to interpreting the SB5 performance of preschoolers. Each step is illustrated using the test results from a child, Mark, age 4, who was evaluated using the SB5. Mark's SB5 performance is reported in Table 13.6.

TABLE 13.5.
Alternative Descriptive System for SB5

Standard Score Range	Alternative Description of Performance[1]
131+	Upper Extreme/Normative Strength
116 to 130	Above Average/Normative Strength
85 to 115	Average Range/Normal Limits
70 to 84	Below Average/Normative Weakness
≤69	Lower Extreme/Normative Weakness

[1]This classification system is preferred by the authors and is identical to the system used by Kaufman and Kaufman (2004) for the KABC–II and Flanagan and Kaufman (2004) for the WISC–IV.

TABLE 13.6.
SB5 Performance of Mark, age 4 years, 2 months

Factor/IQ Subtest	Scaled Score	Standard Score	Confidence Interval (95%)	Percentile Rank
FR		88	81–97	21
Nonverbal Fluid Reasoning	6			
Verbal Fluid Reasoning	10			
K		108	99–115	70
Nonverbal Knowledge	11			
Verbal Knowledge	12			
QR		94	86–102	34
Nonverbal Quantitative Reasoning	8			
Verbal Quantitative Reasoning	10			
V-SP		82	75–91	12
Nonverbal Visual-Spatial Processing	5			
Verbal Visual-Spatial Processing	9			
WM		89	82–98	23
Nonverbal Working Memory	6			
Verbal Working Memory	10			
NV		82	77–89	12
V		101	95–107	53
FS		91	90–98	27
AB		94	87–103	34

Required Interpretive Steps: Analyze the FSIQ, NVIQ, VIQ, and Factor Profile When the 10 SB5 Subtests are Administered.

Step 1: Determine Whether the FSIQ is the Best Estimate of Overall Intellectual Ability.

Calculate the difference between the child's SB5 NVIQ and VIQ. Answer the following question: *Is the size of the standard score difference greater than one standard deviation (>15)?*[1]

- If yes, then the variation in the IQs that compose the FSIQ is considered too great for the purpose of summarizing global ability in a single score (i.e., FSIQ).
- If no, then the FSIQ may be interpreted as a reliable and valid estimate of a child's global intellectual ability.

The difference between Mark's NVIQ of 82 and his VIQ of 101 is 19 standard score points. The magnitude of Mark's NVIQ-VIQ difference is greater than 15 points, indicating that

---

[1]NVIQ-VIQ differences that exceed one standard deviation are considered uncommon in the SB5 standardization sample of children ages 2–9 years. An uncommon difference is one that occurs in less than 10% of the standardization sample. This information was derived from Table B.2 on page 170 of the *SB5 Technical Manual* (Roid, 2003c). Note that a NVQ-VIQ standard score difference of 9 points is statistically significant ($p < .05$) for children ages 2–9 years in the SB5 standardization sample.

his FSIQ is not the best estimate of his overall intellectual ability. The next step will determine whether Mark's intellectual capabilities are best understood by the separate NV and V IQs.

Step 2: Determine Whether the NVIQ and VIQ Are Interpretable

2a. To determine whether the NVIQ is interpretable, subtract the lowest nonverbal subtest scaled score from the highest nonverbal subtest scaled score. Answer the following question: *Is the size of the difference greater than 7 scaled score points?*[2]

- If yes, then the variation among the subtests that compose the NVIQ is too great for the purpose of summarizing intelligence as measured by tasks requiring limited language demands.
- If no, then the NVIQ may be interpreted as a reliable and valid estimate of a child's intellectual ability as measured by tasks requiring limited language demands.

2b. To determine whether the VIQ is interpretable, subtract the lowest verbal scaled score from the highest verbal scaled score. Answer the following question: *Is the size of the difference greater than 7 scaled score points?*[2]

- If yes, then the variation among the subtests that compose the VIQ is too great for the purpose of summarizing intellectual ability as measured by receptive and expressive language (i.e., VIQ).
- If no, then the VIQ may be interpreted as a reliable and valid estimate of a child's intellectual ability as measured by tasks requiring receptive and expressive language.

For Mark's SB5 performance, the variation of scaled scores within the NV and V domains was not statistically significant, indicating that Mark's intelligence may be best described through separate NV and V IQs. The reader is referred to Table 1.1 in the *Stanford-Binet Intelligence Scales Interpretive Manual: Expanded Guide to the Interpretation of SB5 Test Results* (Roid, 2003d, p. 5) for a description of the cognitive skills and abilities that are measured by the subtests that compose the NV and V IQs. Because a number of broad cognitive abilities (or factors) are assessed using subtests that are either primarily nonverbal (NVIQ) or verbal (VIQ) in nature, examining Mark's performance on the separate broad abilities that are measured through both nonverbal and verbal means may yield additional useful information. Step 3 therefore examines performance on the 5 factors comprising the SB5.

Step 3: Determine Whether Each of the Five Factors Is Unitary, and Thus Interpretable

When the variability between subtest scaled scores within a factor is unusually large, then the factor does not provide a good estimate of the ability it is intended to measure and,

---

[2]A range of 8 or more scaled score points is considered uncommon in the SB5 standardization sample of children ages 2–9 years. This information was derived from Table B.5 on page 173 of the *SB5 Technical Manual* (Roid, 2003c).

therefore, is not interpretable. In other words, when a substantial difference between the scaled scores composing a factor is found, the factor cannot be interpreted as representing a unitary ability.

3a. Determine whether the size of the difference between subtest scaled scores within the Fluid Reasoning (FR) Factor is too large. Calculate the difference between the FR subtest scaled scores. Answer the following question: *Is the size of the difference greater than one standard deviation* (>3)[3].
- If yes, then the difference is too large (4 points or greater) and the FR Factor cannot be interpreted as representing a unitary ability.
- If no, then the ability presumed to underlie the FR Factor is unitary and may be interpreted.

3b. Follow the same procedure as in "3a" to determine the interpretability of the Knowledge Factor.

3c. Follow the same procedure as in "3a" to determine the interpretability of the Quantitative Reasoning Factor.

3d. Follow the same procedure as in "3a" to determine the interpretability of the Visual-Spatial Processing Factor.

3e. Follow the same procedure as in "3a" to determine the interpretability of the Working Memory Factor.

As may be seen in Mark's performance, the variation within the FR, V-SP, and WM Factors was too large, suggesting that his performance in the broad ability domains of *Gf*, *Gv*, and *Gsm*, respectively, cannot be summarized in a single score. In contrast, Mark's K and QR Factors can be reliably and validly interpreted as adequate estimates of his *Gc* and *Gq* abilities, respectively. Because the majority of factors were nonunitary, it is worthwhile to examine the scaled scores within factors to determine whether any patterns are evident. For example, Mark performed higher on the verbal subtests within each factor as compared to the nonverbal subtest (see Table 13.6). This pattern, coupled with the fact that 3 of 5 factors are noninterpretable for Mark, suggest that his intellectual capabilities may be best described by his obtained NV and V IQs as stated in Step 2. Nevertheless, it appears worthwhile to further examine Mark's profile, particularly as it applies to understanding his most salient strengths and weaknesses.

Step 4: Determine Normative Strengths and Normative Weaknesses in the Factor Profile

Only unitary factors identified in the previous step are included in this analysis. For example, in the case of Mark, only the K and QR Factors are included in this analysis. To determine *Normative Strengths* and *Normative Weaknesses* in a child's factor profile, review the exact value of the interpretable factors. If the factor standard score is greater than 115, then the ability measured by the factor is a *Normative Strength*. If the factor standard

---

[3]According to Table B.4 in the *SB5 Technical Manual* (2003c), the difference required for statistical significance ($p < .05$) between any two subtests is 3 when rounded to the nearest whole number (p. 172).

score is less than 85, then the ability measured by the factor is a *Normative Weakness*. If the factor standard score is between 85 and 115 (inclusive), then the ability measured by the factor is within the *Average Range*. Mark's K and QR Factors of 108 and 94, respectively, fall within the Average Range. Next, it is informative to know whether these factors represent either personal strengths or personal weaknesses for Mark, as such information is particularly useful in educational planning and intervention.

Step 5: Determine Personal Strengths and Personal Weaknesses in the Factor Profile

The Normative Strengths and Normative Weaknesses identified in Step 4 indicate a child's abilities relative to other children of about the same age. In contrast, Personal Strengths and Personal Weaknesses refer to factors that differ significantly from the person's *own* factor mean. To determine personal strengths and weaknesses, follow the instructions below.

5a. Compute the mean of the child's factor standard scores and round to the nearest whole number. Note that all factors (interpretable and noninterpretable) are included in the computation of the mean for practical reasons. Excluding any factor would result in the need for numerous tables for determining both statistical significance and uncommon factor variation (i.e., mean factors based on 2, 3, 4, and 5 factor combinations). Mark's mean factor standard score is 92.2 or 92.

5b. Subtract the mean of all factor standard scores from each *interpretable* factor standard score. Use the critical value of 9 which is based on analyses suggested by Longman (2004). In order to be considered statistically significant, the difference must be equal to or greater than 9.[4] Use the following criteria for identifying personal strengths and weaknesses:

   i.   If the difference is significant and the Interpretable Factor is higher than the mean, then the factor is a *Personal Strength* for the child.

   ii. If the difference is significant and the Interpretable Factor is lower than the mean, then the factor is a *Personal Weakness* for the child.

   Only two of Mark's factors (K and QR) were found to be interpretable when Step 3 was conducted. Therefore, these 2 factors were considered for interpretation for this step. One of his difference scores was large enough to be significant at the .05 level (i.e., his K Factor of 108 denotes a PS). Because Mark demonstrated a personal strength, it is necessary to go next to 5c. If Mark did not demonstrate any personal strengths or weaknesses, then the examiner would advance to Step 6.

5c. Determine whether Personal Strengths and/or Personal Weaknesses are uncommon using the <10% base rate criterion. Because statistical significance means only that an observed difference is "real" (i.e., not due to chance), it is necessary to determine whether the difference is also unusually large or uncommon. Differences among factors that occur infrequently in the standardization sample may be valuable in making diagnoses and generating educational recommendations when corroborated by other data. A critical value of 15 (estimated from appropriate formulas by Longman,

---

[4]The critical value of 9 also represents the average standard score difference required for statistical significance ($p < .05$) using the SB5 standardization data for children ages 2–5 years (Roid, 2005).

2004) is necessary to determine whether the magnitude of the differences between a child's interpretable factors and the mean of all factors is uncommon (i.e., occurs less than 10% of the time) in the standardization sample[5]. If the magnitude of the observed differences between an interpretable factor and the mean of all factors is equal to or greater than 15, then the difference is uncommon; otherwise, the difference is not uncommon. Mark's difference score of 16 for his K Factor exceeds the critical value of 15 for a 10% base rate, and is, therefore, uncommon.

5d. Identify "Key Assets" and "High Priority Concerns" in the child's profile using the following criteria to identify personal strengths and weaknesses that are of greatest importance, diagnostically and educationally.

    i.   Significant Personal Strengths that are also uncommon and greater than 115 are labeled *Key Assets*.

    ii.   Significant Personal Weaknesses that are also uncommon and less than 85 are labeled *High Priority Concerns*.

An inspection of Mark's profile did not demonstrate any Key Assets or High Priority Concerns. At this point in the test interpretation process, it is necessary to integrate the results of Steps 3–5 and determine whether or not there exists sufficient information to draw valuable and useful conclusions from the data. This represents the focus and purpose of Step 6.

Step 6. Interpret Fluctuations in the Child's Factor Profile

As Flanagan and Kaufman (2004) stated, "Interpreting the child's profile provides reliable and useful information for making diagnostic and educational decisions. Because many of the descriptions that are used to classify Indexes or Factors (e.g., High Priority Concern, Key Asset) are new to the examiner and other professionals and laypersons who read psychological reports, you should include a paragraph in (or appendix to) your report that defines these terms" (p. 145). Table 13.7 provides a description of all the terms that are used to classify factors.

A review of the results of Steps 3–5 of the interpretive system shows that most of the factors are not interpretable. In addition, previous steps revealed 1) the V subtest scaled scores within each factor are higher than the NV subtest scaled scores; and, 2) the VIQ > NVIQ. Taken together, these data suggest that the separate NV and V IQs may be the best way to summarize Mark's intellectual capabilities. However, before concluding that Mark expresses his intelligence significantly better when tasks are verbal versus nonverbal in nature, it seems worthwhile to proceed to Step 7 and calculate the clinical clusters that are more representative of the differentiation of cognitive abilities among preschoolers.

Step 7. Calculating Clinical Clusters

Figure 13.2 depicted the four CHC cognitive factors most likely to be present in the SB5 sample of preschool children. This step allows for the calculation of two of those factors,

---

[5]The critical value of 15 also represents the average standard score difference considered uncommon (i.e., base rate 10%) in the SB5 standardization data for children ages 2–5 years (Roid, 2005).

TABLE 13.7.
Terms Used to Describe Fluctuations in a Child's SB5 Factor Profile

Term (Abbreviation)	Definition
Factor	A standard score with a mean of 100 and a standard deviation of 15.
Normative Strength (NS)	A Factor that is above 115
Normative Weakness (NW)	A Factor that is below 85.
Normal Limits (NL)	A Factor that is 85–115 (inclusive).
Personal Strength (PS)	A Factor that is significantly higher than the child's own mean Factor, using the .05 level of significance.
Personal Weakness (PW)	A Factor that is significantly lower than the child's own mean Factor, using the .05 level of significance.
Uncommon Personal Strengths (PS/Uncommon)	A Personal Strength that is not only statistically significant but that is also substantially different from the child's own mean. That is, the size of the difference between the Factor and the child's mean of all five Factors is unusually large, occurring less than 10% of the time in the SB5 standardization sample.
Uncommon Personal Weaknesses (PW/Uncommon)	A Personal Weakness that is not only statistically significant but that is also substantially different from the child's own mean. That is, the size of the difference between the Factor and the child's mean of all five Factors is unusually large, occurring less than 10% of the time in the SB5 standardization sample.
Key Asset (KA)	A Factor that is an Uncommon Personal Strength and a Normative Strength.
High Priority Concern (HPC)	A Factor that is an Uncommon Personal Weakness and a Normative Weakness.

namely Gc_{EXT} (NVK + VK + VFR + V V-SP) and Gv_{ALT} (NVFR+NV V-SP). To determine whether the Crystallized Intelligence Clinical Cluster–Extended (Gc_{EXT}) is unitary, it is necessary to compute the difference between the highest scaled score and the lowest scaled score from the four subtests that comprise this clinical cluster. If the difference for the Gc_{EXT} subtest scaled score is greater than 5 points, the clinical cluster is not unitary and, therefore, cannot be interpreted. If the difference is 5 points or less, the clinical cluster is considered unitary and can be interpreted. The difference between Mark's highest Gc_{EXT} scaled score of 12 and lowest scaled score of 9 is 3, indicating a nonsignificant difference. Therefore, Mark's Gc_{EXT} is considered unitary and can be interpreted as a reliable and valid estimate of his Gc ability.

To determine whether the Visual Processing Clinical Cluster–Alternative (Gv_{ALT}) is unitary, it is necessary to compute the difference between the scaled scores that comprise this clinical cluster. If the difference for the Gv_{ALT} subtest scaled scores is greater than 3 points, the clinical cluster is not unitary and, therefore, cannot be interpreted. If the difference is 3 points or less, the clinical cluster is considered unitary and can be interpreted. In Mark's case, the Gv_{ALT} is interpretable.

To calculate the Gc_{EXT} and Gv_{ALT} Clinical Clusters, the sum of the scaled scores comprising each cluster is converted to a deviation quotient (i.e., clinical cluster) having a mean of 100 and a standard deviation of 15. Tables for converting the Gc_{EXT} and Gv_{ALT} sums of scaled scores to clinical clusters are provided in Tables 13.8 and 13.9, respectively. Using Table 13.8, the Gc_{EXT} sum of scaled scores (42) yields a Gc_{EXT} Clinical Cluster of 103. Using Table 13.9, the Gv_{ALT} sum of scaled scores (11) yields a Gv_{ALT} Clinical Cluster of 73. Based on the additional information obtained from the clinical clusters, it appears that Mark's pattern of better performance on verbal versus nonverbal tasks (viz., VIQ > NVIQ) is attributable to a deficit in the processing of visual information. As such, Mark's performance on the Verbal Fluid Reasoning subtest is likely a more reliable estimate of Gf than his Fluid Reasoning Factor standard score. Likewise, his Verbal Working

TABLE 13.8.
Scaled Score to Clinical Cluster Conversion Tables for Children Ages 2–5 years

Crystallized Intelligence Extended Clinical Cluster (Gc_{Ext}) Equivalent of Sums of Scaled Scores for Nonverbal Knowledge, Verbal Knowledge, Nonverbal Fluid Reasoning, and Nonverbal Visual-Spatial Processing

Sum of Scaled Scores	Gc_{Ext} Clinical Cluster Score	95% CI Lower	95% CI Higher	Percentile Rank
4	44	37	51	0.01
5	45	38	52	0.01
6	47	40	54	0.02
7	48	41	55	0.03
8	50	43	57	0.05
9	51	44	58	0.06
10	53	46	60	0.09
11	55	48	62	0.16
12	56	49	63	0.16
13	58	51	65	0.25
14	59	52	66	0.30
15	61	54	68	0.49
16	62	55	69	1
17	64	57	71	1
18	66	59	73	1
19	67	60	74	1
20	69	62	76	2
21	70	63	77	2
22	72	65	79	3
23	73	66	80	3
24	75	68	82	5
25	77	70	84	6
26	78	71	85	7
27	80	73	87	9
28	81	74	88	11
29	83	76	90	13
30	84	77	91	14
31	86	79	93	17
32	88	81	95	21
33	89	82	96	23

TABLE 13.8.

(*Continued*)

Sum of Scaled Scores	Gc_{Ext} Clinical Cluster Score	95% CI Lower	95% CI Higher	Percentile Rank
34	91	84	98	27
35	92	85	99	29
36	94	87	101	35
37	96	89	103	40
38	97	90	104	43
39	99	92	106	48
40	100	93	107	50
41	102	95	109	55
42	103	96	110	57
43	105	98	112	65
44	107	100	114	67
45	108	101	115	69
46	110	103	117	75
47	111	104	118	77
48	113	106	120	81
49	114	107	121	83
50	116	109	123	86
51	118	111	125	88
52	119	112	126	89
53	121	114	128	92
54	122	115	129	92
55	124	117	131	95
56	125	118	132	95
57	127	120	134	97
58	129	122	136	97
59	130	123	137	98
60	132	125	139	98
61	133	126	140	99
62	135	128	142	99
63	136	129	143	99
64	138	131	145	99
65	140	133	147	99.64
66	141	134	148	99.70
67	143	136	150	99.80
68	144	137	151	99.84
69	146	139	153	99.89
70	147	140	154	99.93
71	149	142	156	99.94
72	151	144	158	99.96
73	152	145	159	99.97
74	154	147	161	99.99
75	155	148	162	99.99
76	157	150	164	99.99
77	158	151	165	99.99
78	160	153	167	99.99

Note: The reliability of Gc_{Ext} = .94, SEM = 3.35.

TABLE 13.9.
Visual Processing Clinical Cluster – Alternative (Gv$_{ALT}$) Equivalent
of Sums of Scaled Scores for Nonverbal Fluid Reasoning + Nonverbal
Visual-Spatial Processing

Sum of Scaled Scores	Gv$_{ALT}$ Clinical Cluster Score	95% CI Lower	95% CI Higher	Percentile Rank
2	46	37	55	0.01
3	49	40	58	0.04
4	52	43	61	0.07
5	55	46	64	0.16
6	58	49	67	0.25
7	61	52	70	0.49
8	64	55	73	1
9	67	58	76	1
10	70	61	79	2
11	73	64	82	3
12	76	67	85	3
13	79	70	88	8
14	82	73	91	12
15	85	76	94	16
16	88	79	97	21
17	91	82	100	27
18	94	85	103	35
19	97	88	106	43
20	100	91	109	50
21	103	94	112	57
22	106	97	115	65
23	109	100	118	73
24	112	103	121	79
25	115	106	124	84
26	118	109	127	88
27	121	112	130	92
28	124	115	133	95
29	127	118	136	97
30	130	121	139	98
31	133	124	142	99
32	136	127	145	99
33	139	130	148	99.57
34	142	133	151	99.75
35	145	136	154	99.87
36	148	139	157	99.93
37	151	142	160	99.96
38	154	145	163	99.99
39	157	148	166	99.99
40	160	151	169	99.99

Note: The reliability of Gv$_{ALT}$ = .90, SEM = 4.7.

Memory subtest performance is likely a more reliable estimate of his memory span ability than his Working Memory Factor standard score. Overall, these data suggest that Mark has a Gv deficit and that his capabilities in other CHC domains are best estimated through verbal rather than through nonverbal means.

CONCLUSIONS

The SB5 is a substantial improvement over its predecessor, particularly with respect to its utility for assessing the cognitive capabilities of young children ages 2–5 years. In particular, it contains many child-friendly features that make it an especially useful tool for assessing the intellectual capabilities of preschoolers. As compared to other currently available intelligence tests that have norms for preschoolers, the SB5 is superior with respect to both psychometric and qualitative characteristics. Because the five-factor structure purported to underlie the SB5 *total* standardization sample is unlikely to emerge as the best explanation of the structure of cognitive abilities in the SB5 *preschool* standardization sample, we proposed an alternative, more plausible, factor structure for the preschool age range (2–5 years). As a result, we provided an interpretive system that integrates information from both the published five-factor model and our alternative four-factor model. The information presented in this chapter will prove useful in guiding practitioners in the use and interpretation of the SB5 for preschool children.

ACKNOWLEDGEMENT

Our appreciation is extended to Agnieszka Dynda for her review of earlier drafts of this manuscript and her excellent editorial assistance.

REFERENCES

Alfonso, V. C., & Flanagan, D. P. (1999). Assessment of cognitive functioning in preschoolers. In E. V. Nuttall, I. Romero, & J. Kalesnik (Eds.), *Assessing and screening preschoolers* (2nd ed., pp. 186–217). New York: Allyn & Bacon.

Alfonso, V. C., Flanagan, D. P., & Radwan, S. (2005). The impact of the Cattell-Horn Carroll theory on the assessment of cognitive abilities. In D. P. Flanagan & P. L. Harrison (Eds.) *Contemporary intellectual assessment: Theories, tests, and issues* (2nd ed., pp. 185–202). New York: Guilford.

American Educational Research Association, American Psychological Association, & National Council on Measurement in Education (1999). *Standards for educational and psychological testing.* Washington, DC: American Educational Research Association.

Becker, K. A. (2003). *History of the Stanford-Binet Intelligence Scales: Content and psychometrics.* (Stanford-Binet Intelligence Scales, Fifth Edition Assessment Service Bulletin No. 1). Itasca, Il: Riverside Publishing.

Bracken, B. A. (1987). Limitations of preschool instruments and standards for minimal levels of technical adequacy. *Journal of Psychoeducational Assessment, 4*, 313–326.

Bracken, B. A., & Walker, K. C. (1997). The utility of intelligence tests for preschool children. In D. P. Flanagan, J. L. Genshaft, & P. L. Harrison (Eds.), *Contemporary intellectual assessment: Theories, tests, and issues* (pp. 484–505). New York: Guilford.

Carroll, J. B. (1993). *Human cognitive abilities: A survey of factor-analytic studies*. Cambridge, England: Cambridge University Press.

Flanagan, D. P., & Alfonso, V. C. (1995). A critical review of the technical characteristics of new and recently revised intelligence tests for preschool children. *Journal of Psychoeducational Assessment, 13*, 66–90.

Flanagan, D. P., Genshaft, J. L., & Mascolo, J. L. (2000). A conceptual framework for interpreting preschool intelligence tests. In B. A. Bracken (Ed.), *The psychoeducational assessment of preschool children* (3rd ed., pp. 428–473). Boston: Allyn & Bacon.

Flanagan, D. P., & Kaufman, A. S. (2004). *Essentials of WISC-IV assessment*. New York: Wiley.

Flanagan, D. P., McGrew, K. S., & Ortiz, S. O. (2000). *The Wechsler intelligence scales and Gf-Gc theory: A contemporary approach to interpretation*. Needham Heights, MA: Allyn & Bacon.

Flanagan, D. P., & Ortiz, S. O. (2001). *Essentials of cross-battery assessment*. New York: Wiley.

Ford, L., & Dahinten, S. (2005). Use of intelligence tests in the assessment of preschoolers. In D. P. Flanagan & P. L. Harrison (Eds.), *Contemporary intellectual assessment: Theories, tests, and issues* (2nd ed., pp. 487–503). New York: Guilford.

Horn, J. L., & Blankson, N. (2005). Foundations for better understanding of cognitive abilities. In D. P. Flanagan & P. L. Harrison (Eds.), *Contemporary intellectual assessment: Theories, tests, and issues* (2nd ed., pp. 41–68). New York: Guilford.

Jensen, A. R. (1998). *The g factor: The science of mental ability*. Westport, CT: Praeger.

Kaufman, A. S. (1979). *Intelligent testing with the WISC–R*. New York: Wiley.

Kaufman, A. S. (1990). *Assessing adolescent and adult intelligence*. Needham, Heights, MA: Allyn & Bacon.

Kaufman, A. S., & Kaufman, N. L. (2004). *Kaufman Assessment Battery for Children, Second Edition*. Circle Pines, MN: AGS Publishing.

Keith, T. Z. (2005). Using confirmatory factor analysis to aid in understanding the constructs measured by intelligence tests. In D. P. Flanagan & P. L. Harrison (Eds.), *Contemporary intellectual assessment: Theories, tests, and issues* (2nd ed., pp. 581–614). New York: Guilford.

Longman, R. S. (2004). Values for comparison of WAIS–III index scores with overall means. *Psychological Assessment, 16*, 323–325.

McGrew, K. S. (2005). The Cattell-Horn-Carroll theory of cognitive abilities: Past, present, and future. In D. P. Flanagan & P. L. Harrison (Eds.), *Contemporary intellectual assessment: Theories, tests, and issues* (2nd ed., pp. 136–181). New York: Guilford.

McGrew, K. S., & Flanagan, D. P. (1998). *The intelligence test desk reference (ITDR): Gf-Gc cross-battery assessment*. Boston: Allyn and Bacon.

Ortiz, S. O., & Ochoa, S. H. (2005). Advances in cognitive assessment of culturally and linguistically diverse individuals. In D. P. Flanagan & P. L. Harrison (Eds.), *Contemporary intellectual assessment: Theories, tests, and issues* (2nd ed., pp. 234–250). New York: Guilford.

Rhodes, R. L., Ochoa, S. H., & Ortiz, S. O. (Eds.). (2005). *Assessing culturally and linguistically diverse students: A practical guide*. New York: Guilford Press.

Roid, G. (2003a). *Stanford-Binet Intelligence Scales, Fifth Edition*. Itasca, Il: Riverside Publishing.

Roid, G. (2003b). *Stanford-Binet Intelligence Scales, Fifth Edition examiner's manual*. Itasca, Il: Riverside Publishing.

Roid, G. (2003c). *Stanford-Binet Intelligence Scales, Fifth Edition technical manual*. Itasca, Il: Riverside Publishing.

Roid, G. (2003d). *Stanford-Binet Intelligence Scales interpretive manual: Expanded guide to the interpretation of SB5 test results*. Itasca, Il: Riverside Publishing.

Roid, G. (2005). *Interpretation of SB5/Early SB5 factor index scores: Contrasting each factor index score with the mean of an individual's profile of factor index scores*. Retrieved June 3, 2006, from http://riverpub.com/products/sb5/pdf/fse_590.5pdf

Roid, G., & Barram, R. A. (2004). *Essentials of Stanford-Binet Intelligence Scales (SB5) assessment*. New York: Wiley.

Terman, L. M., & Merrill, M. A. (1960). *Stanford-Binet Intelligence Scale: Manual for the Third Revision Form L-M.* Boston: Houghton Mifflin.

Thorndike, R. L., Hagen, E. P., & Sattler, J. M. (1986). *Standford-Binet Intelligence Scale–Fourth Edition.* Chicago, IL: Riverside Publishing.

Urbina, S. (2004). *Essentials of psychological testing.* New York: Wiley.

Valdes, G., & Figueroa, R. A. (1994). *Bilingualism and testing: A special case of bias.* Norwood, NJ: Ablex.

Woodcock, R. W., McGrew, K. S., & Mather N. (2001). *Woodcock-Johnson III Tests of Cognitive Abilities.* Itasca, IL: Riverside Publishing.

14

The Assessment of Preschool Children with the Kaufman Assessment Battery for Children–Second Edition (KABC–II)

Elizabeth O. Lichtenberger
Alliant International University, San Diego, CA

Alan S. Kaufman
Yale University, School of Medicine

The original Kaufman Assessment Battery for Children (K–ABC; Kaufman & Kaufman, 1983) was a popular instrument for assessing the cognitive abilities of children beginning at age 2½ years and extending to age 12½ (Lichtenberger & Kaufman, 2000). Like its predecessor, the Kaufman Assessment Battery for Children–Second Edition (KABC–II; Kaufman & Kaufman, 2004a) was developed to make it appropriate for use with preschoolers. The KABC–II is a measure of processing and cognitive abilities of children and adolescents between the ages of 3 years 0 months and 18 years 11 months. For preschoolers, the KABC–II offers two levels: one for children age 3 and one for ages 4–6. The composition of the KABC–II scales varies depending on the age level of the child and the interpretive approach that the clinician chooses to take. These scales and the KABC–II's interpretive approaches are described in the sections that follow.

This chapter highlights the use of the KABC–II with preschoolers and can be used to guide clinical assessment practice. An overview of the theory underlying the KABC–II is provided along with a review of the structure of the KABC–II and its psychometric properties. Throughout this chapter, we highlight the features of the KABC–II that are particularly useful for assessing preschoolers. This chapter concludes with a brief description of how to interpret the KABC–II, and the interpretive process is exemplified with a clinical case report of a 4-year-old assessed with the KABC–II. In general, for this chapter, preschool is defined as ages 3 to 5 years. For those readers that are unfamiliar with the KABC–II, we recommend two excellent sources: the KABC–II Manual (Kaufman & Kaufman, 2004a), which provides administration and scoring guidelines and pertinent psychometric and interpretive data; and Essentials of KABC–II Assessment (Kaufman, Lichtenberger,

Fletcher-Janzen, & Kaufman, 2005), which provides detailed information on administration and scoring, as well as in-depth information on interpretation and clinical applications, as exemplified in four comprehensive case reports.

KABC–II THEORY

The original K-ABC, published in 1983 was rooted in neuropsychological theories—Sperry's (1968) cerebral specialization approach and the Luria-Das successive-simultaneous processing dichotomy. Both the Sperry and Luria-Das models are characterized by a dual-processing approach that has been well supported by a large body of cognitive and neuropsychological research (Das, Kirby, & Jarman, 1979; Neisser, 1967). The structure of the K-ABC included an overall estimate of cognitive ability, the Mental Processing Composite (MPC), and two global scales: Sequential and Simultaneous. The K-ABC also yielded a separate Achievement Composite and a Nonverbal Scale.

In its second edition, the K-ABC underwent major revision, structurally and conceptually. The original K-ABC's theoretical foundation in Luria's (1966) sequential-simultaneous processing theory and cerebral specialization theory was modified and supplemented in the second edition. The most significant modification from the original K-ABC's theoretical foundation is that the KABC–II is firmly grounded in two separate theories: (1) Luria's (1970) three Blocks or functional systems, and (2) Cattell-Horn-Carroll (CHC) theory (Carroll, 1997; Flanagan, McGrew, & Ortiz, 2000; McGrew, 2005). This dual theoretical foundation gives examiners more flexibility both in the choice of administration (i.e., selecting which theoretical model is most appropriate for each child assessed) and in interpretation. To create the dual theoretical basis, 10 new subtests were created and eight old ones were removed, while eight original K-ABC subtests were retained.

A critical component of the KABC–II is measurement of high-level, complex intelligent behavior. Conceptually, Luria's theory encapsulates that complexity with the integration of the three functional systems or blocks: Block 1 involves arousal and attention, Block 2 involves the use of one's senses to analyze, code, and store information, and Block 3 involves applying executive functions for formulating plans and programming behavior (Luria, 1970). Kaufman et al. (2005) explain this integration further:

> Luria's theory emphasizes the integration of the incoming stimuli and the responsibility of Block 2 to make connections with Block 3. Thus, the KABC–II includes subtests that require synthesis of auditory and visual stimuli (e.g., Word Order, Atlantis, Rebus Learning, and Rover). To capture the linkage between Blocks 2 and 3, the KABC–II includes measures of simultaneous processing that require not just the analysis, coding, and storage of incoming stimuli, but also demand executive functioning and problem solving for success (e.g., Rover, Conceptual Thinking) (p. 8).

The second foundation of the KABC–II, CHC theory, has been well articulated elsewhere (e.g., Flanagan, McGrew, & Ortiz, 2000; Flanagan & Ortiz, 2001; McGrew, 2005; McGrew, Woodcock, & Ford, 2005). Generally, CHC theory is psychometrically driven and rests on a large body of research. When applied to the KABC–II at the preschool level, four of the CHC broad abilities are measured: Long-Term Storage and Retrieval (Glr), Short-Term Memory (Gsm), Visual Processing (Gv), and Crystallized ability (Gc). Table 14.1 depicts how the Luria and CHC theories fit together in the KABC–II, as it describes how each of the KABC–II's scales is conceptualized by the two theories.

TABLE 14.1.
Luria and CHC Conceptualizations of KABC–II Scales
Administered to Preschoolers

Name of KABC–II Scale	Luria Conceptualization	CHC Conceptualization
Learning/Glr	**Learning Ability** Reflects an integration of the processes associated with all three of Luria's Blocks, placing a premium on the attention-concentration processes that are in the domain of Block 1, but also requiring Block 2 coding processes and Block 3 strategy generation to learn and retain the new information with efficiency. Sequential and simultaneous processing are associated primarily with Luria's Block 2, and pertain to either a step-by-step (sequential) or holistic (simultaneous) processing of information.	**Long-Term Storage & Retrieval (Glr)** Storing and efficiently retrieving newly-learned, or previously learned, information
Sequential/Gsm	**Sequential Processing** Measures the kind of coding function that Luria labeled "successive," and involves arranging input in sequential or serial order to solve a problem, where each idea is linearly and temporally related to the preceding one.	**Short-Term Memory (Gsm)** Taking in and holding information, and then using it within a few seconds
Simultaneous/Gv	**Simultaneous Processing** Measures the second type, or simultaneous, coding function associated with Block 2. For its tasks, the input has to be integrated and synthesized simultaneously (holistically), usually spatially, to produce the appropriate solution. As mentioned earlier, the KABC-II measure of simultaneous processing deliberately blends Luria's Block 2 and Block 3 to enhance the complexity of the simultaneous syntheses that are required	**Visual Processing (Gv)** Perceiving, storing, manipulating, and thinking with visual patterns
Knowledge/Gc	*(This scale is not included in the Luria model)*	**Crystallized Ability (Gc)** Demonstrating the breadth and depth of knowledge acquired from one's culture

Note: Table adapted from Kaufman, Lichtenberger, Fletcher-Janzen, and Kaufman (2005, p. 14). Knowledge/Gc is included in the CHC system for the computation of the FCI, but it is *excluded* from the Luria system for the computation of the Mental Processing Index (MPI). Only the MPI and FCI are offered for 3-year-olds. The KABC–II yields a fifth scale, Planning/*Gf*, for children ages 7–18.

TWO THEORETICAL MODELS AND TWO GLOBAL SCORES

The KABC–II yields a separate global score for each of its two theoretical models. The Luria model yields a global score that measures general mental processing ability, called the Mental Processing Index (MPI). From the perspective of CHC theory, the global score is called the Fluid-Crystallized Index (FCI). The key difference between these two global scores is that the MPI (Luria's theory) excludes measures of acquired knowledge, whereas the FCI includes measures of acquired knowledge, referred to as crystallized ability (Gc) by CHC theory. Only one of these two global scores is computed for any given child. Prior to testing a child on the KABC–II, examiners choose the interpretive system (i.e., Luria or CHC) based primarily on information about the child's background and the reasons for referral. Deciding which interpretive system to use dictates which global score is reported and whether or not measures of acquired knowledge are administered as part of the Core battery (see Table 14.2).

Kaufman and Kaufman (2004a) state that, "The CHC model should generally be the model of choice, except in cases where the examiner believes that including measures of acquired knowledge/crystallized ability would compromise the validity of the Fluid-Crystallized Index (FCI). In those cases, the Luria global score (MPI) is preferred" (pp. 4–5). Table 14.3 summarizes when examiners are advised to administer either the FCI or the MPI.

KABC–II STRUCTURE

The KABC–II offers two batteries for preschool age children, one for age 3 and another for children ages 4–6. At age 3, the KABC–II yields one scale, a global measure of ability, composed of either five subtests (the MPI) or seven subtests (the FCI). For ages 4–6, the KABC–II yields the MPI and FCI along with a profile of scores on four additional separate scales. These scales are named to reflect the KABC–II's dual theoretical foundation (i.e., Luria/CHC): Sequential/Gsm, Simultaneous/Gv, Learning/Glr, and Knowledge/Gc. The CHC model includes the Knowledge/Gc scale; the Luria model does not. A Nonverbal scale is also available for all ages to serve as a global score for children who cannot be

TABLE 14.2.
Select One of Two Theoretical Models Prior to KABC–II Administration

Theoretical Foundation	Measurement of Acquired Knowledge	Global Score
Luria Theory	Excludes measure of acquired knowledge	Mental Processing Index
CHC Theory	Includes measure of acquired knowledge	Fluid Crystallized Index

Note. From *Essentials of KABC–II Assessment* (p. 2), by A. S. Kaufman, E. O. Lichtenberger E. Fletcher-Janzen, and N. L. Kaufman, 2005, New York: Wiley. Copyright © 2005 by Wiley. Reprinted with permission.

TABLE 14.3.
When to Administer the FCI or MPI

CHC Model is Preferred (FCI)	Luria Model is Preferred (MPI)
• In the majority of cases • If a child has (or is suspected of having) a disability in reading, written expression, or mathematics. • If a child has mental retardation • If a child has attention deficit hyperactivity disorder • If a child has an emotional or behavioral disturbance • If a child may be gifted	• If a child is from a bilingual background • If a child's nonmainstream cultural background may have affected his or her knowledge acquisition and verbal development • If a child has known or suspected language disorders (expressive, receptive, or mixed) • If a child has known or suspected autism • If the examiner has a firm commitment to the Luria processing approach and believes that acquired knowledge should be excluded from any cognitive score.

Note. Examiners must select either the Luria or CHC model before testing the child or adolescent. The global score that the examiner decides to interpret should be based on referral and background factors. Both Luria and CHC theories are equally important as foundations of the KABC-II. Neither is deemed as theoretically superior to the other. From *Essentials of KABC–II Assessment* (p. 3), by A. S. Kaufman, E. O. Lichtenberger E. Fletcher-Janzen, and N. L. Kaufman, 2005, New York: Wiley. Copyright © 2005 by Wiley. Reprinted with permission.

validly assessed by either the MPI or FCI (e.g., children who are hearing impaired or have Limited English Proficiency).

The subtests that compose each scale are outlined and briefly described in Table 14.4. In this table, only the subtests for ages 3, 4, and 5 years are featured. The age 6 level offers the same scales as ages 4 and 5, but includes some additional subtests. Because the focus of this chapter is on preschool children, these additional subtests are excluded from Table 14.2. Interested readers should consult other sources (Kaufman & Kaufman, 2004a; Kaufman et al., 2005) for a full description of the age 6 level, as well as thorough treatment of the level for ages 7–18 years. The latter level, for older children and adolescents, more fully conforms to the breadth of both the Luria and CHC theories. This school-age level includes an additional scale, labeled Planning/Gf, that measures the planning functions associated with Luria's Block 3 as well as fluid reasoning (Gf), an integral component of CHC theory. These abilities are measured to some extent for preschool children by the Simultaneous/Gv subtests of Conceptual Thinking and Pattern Reasoning (see Table 14.4). However, developmentally, these high-level abilities do not emerge as a separate factor of cognitive and processing ability until age 7.

KABC–II SCORING PROCEDURES

On the KABC–II, subtest raw scores are converted to subtest scaled scores with a mean of 10 and SD of 3. These scaled scores are then summed and converted to index standard scores with a mean of 100 and SD of 15. Unlike most tests of cognitive ability, the KABC–II's descriptive categories are delineated by the test's standard deviation. That is, index standard scores that are ±1 SD (85–115) are designated "Average," those between −1 and −2 SD (70–84) are "Below Average," and scores less than 2 SD from the mean are considered to be in the "Lower Extreme." The analogous categorizations for scores above

TABLE 14.4.
Subtests That Compose the KABC–II Scales for Ages 3–5

Scale and Subtests	Age at which subtest is administered			Description
	3	4	5	
Sequential/Gsm Subtests				
Word Order	Core	Core	Core	The child touches a series of silhouettes of common objects in the same order as the examiner said the names of the objects; more difficult items include an interference task (color naming) between the stimulus and response.
Number Recall	Supplementary	Core	Core	The child repeats a series of numbers in the same sequence as the examiner said them, with series ranging in length from 2 to 9 numbers; the numbers are single digits, except that 10 is used instead of 7 to ensure that all numbers are one syllable.
Hand Movements	—[a]	Supplementary[a]	Supplementary[a]	The child copies the examiner's precise sequence of taps on the table with the fist, palm, or side of the hand.
Simultaneous/Gv Subtests				
Triangles	Core	Core	Core	For most items, the child assembles several identical rubber triangles (blue on one side, yellow on the other) to match a picture of an abstract design; for easier items, the child assembles a different set of colorful plastic shapes to match a model constructed by the examiner.
Conceptual Thinking	Core[a]	Core[a]	Core[a]	The child views a set of 4 or 5 pictures and the child identifies the one picture that does not belong with the others; some items present meaningful stimuli and others use abstract stimuli.
Face Recognition	Core[a]	Core[a]	Supplementary[a]	The child attends closely to photographs of one or two faces that are exposed briefly, and then selects the correct face or faces, shown in a different pose, from a group photograph
Gestalt Closure	Supplementary	Supplementary	Supplementary	The child mentally "fills in the gaps" in a partially completed "inkblot" drawing and names (or describes) the object or action depicted in the drawing.

			Description
Block Counting	—	—	Supplementary	The child counts the exact number of blocks in various pictures of stacks of blocks; the stacks are configured such that one or more blocks is hidden or partially hidden from view.
Pattern Reasoning	—	—	Core[a]	The child is shown a series of stimuli that form a logical, linear pattern, but one stimulus is missing; the child completes the pattern by selecting the correct stimulus from an array of 4 to 6 options at the bottom of the page (most stimuli are abstract, geometric shapes, but some easy items use meaningful).

Learning/Glr Subtests

			Description
Atlantis	Core	Core	Core	The examiner teaches the child the nonsense names for fanciful pictures of fish, plants, and shells; the child demonstrates learning by pointing to each picture (out of an array of pictures) when it is named.
Atlantis–Delayed	—	—	Supplementary	The child demonstrates delayed recall of paired associations learned about 15-25 minutes earlier during Atlantis by pointing to the picture of the fish, plant, or shell that is named by the examiner.
Rebus	Core	Core	Core	The examiner teaches the child the word or concept associated with each particular rebus (drawing) and the child then "reads" aloud phrases and sentences composed of these rebuses.
Rebus–Delayed	—	—	Supplementary[a]	The child demonstrates delayed recall of paired associations learned about 15-25 minutes earlier during Rebus by "reading" phrases and sentences composed of those same rebuses

Knowledge/Gc Subtests

			Description
Riddles	Core	Core	Core	The examiner provides several characteristics of a concrete or abstract verbal concept and the child has to point to it (early items) or name it (later items).
Expressive Vocabulary	Core	Core	Core	The child provides the name of a pictured object.
Verbal Knowledge	Supplementary	Supplementary	Supplementary	The child selects from an array of 6 pictures the one that corresponds to a vocabulary word or answers a general information question

Note. Adapted from Table 1.2 of KABC–II Manual (Kaufman & Kaufman, 2004a). At Age 3 the KABC-II yields only a global standard score, either the Mental Processing Index (MPI), Fluid-Crytallized Index (FCI), or the Nonverbal Index (NVI). However, at ages 4-5 four separate scales are available. Knowledge/Gc subtests are only administered if giving the CHC model.

[a]Subtests also included on the Nonverbal Index.

the mean are "Above Average" (scores of 116–130) and "Upper Extreme" (for scores +131). Confidence intervals and percentile ranks are other scoring metrics available to aid interpretation of the KABC–II profile.

FEATURES OF THE KABC–II FOR PRESCHOOLERS

Developmentally Appropriate Materials

While administering the KABC–II, one can see the game-like nature of the tasks, which are quite enjoyable for preschoolers (and to examiners who administer them). The KABC–II was designed to attract the interest of preschoolers by using colorful and true-to-life materials. Tests such as Atlantis, Face Recognition, Expressive Vocabulary, and Conceptual Thinking use either full color artwork or photographs. These features are helpful in maintaining rapport with a young child and facilitate a valid administration. Although the KABC–II is clearly tailored to the preschool level, some clinicians feel that it could benefit from having even more objects to manipulate to further interest young children. The Triangles subtest is a good example of such a manipulative task, but other manipulative tasks (like Rover and Story Completion) are only suitable for ages 6 and above

The child's developmental level at each of the age ranges tested with the KABC–II preschool battery was taken into account in its development. A thorough item analysis helped to tailor the battery to make each of the items developmentally appropriate. Because the items are so well selected for the child's developmental level, this tailoring of the tasks prevents the frustration that often occurs when too many difficult items are presented and also prevents boredom when too many easy items are administered.

Sensitivity to Attention Span

The attention span of a very young child can be notably short. In light of this, the KABC–II shows an awareness of developmental changes in attention span as children get older. The length of time to administer the KABC–II increases as the age of the child and the child's attention span increases. Thus, instead of requiring all preschoolers to take the same number of subtests, the number of KABC–II subtests that makes up the core battery a child equals 5–7 for age 3 and increases to 7–9 for ages 4–5. At ages 6 and above, the Core battery comprises 8–10 subtests. Administration times for the core battery average about 25–35 minutes for 3-year-olds, 30–45 minutes for 4-year-olds, and 35–50 minutes for 5-year-olds. At each age level, administering the CHC model takes about 10–15 minutes longer than the Luria model (i.e., the shorter end of the time ranges are for the Luria model and the longer times are for the CHC model). Generally, examiners will find that a child's attention is easy to maintain because the KABC–II materials are attractive and appealing to young children.

Clear Instructions

The KABC–II authors took great care to ensure that young children are able to understand the test instructions. If the child doesn't understand the test directions, that child's obtained score is not likely to be a valid indicator of the child's ability on that test. Creating understandable directions for the preschool child was accomplished by removing potentially difficult verbal concepts from the examiner's instructions. Such concepts as "middle" and "after," which Boehm (1971) found to be difficult for young disadvantaged children, appeared commonly in the directions spoken by the examiner when administering various standardized preschool instruments that were available in the late 1970s (Kaufman, 1978). The original K-ABC specifically avoided difficult concepts in the directions spoken by the examiner to the child, and the KABC–II likewise was developed to minimize basic concepts in test directions.

Sample and Teaching Items

In addition to carefully selecting the verbiage in the directions, the KABC–II provides other mechanisms to ensure that each child understands the task prior to obtaining a score on a task. Sample and teaching items give children fair opportunity to adequately learn a task during administration. If a child responds incorrectly on a sample item or a teaching item, examiners demonstrate the correct response, give a second trial, and teach the task, if necessary. All subtests, except the Knowledge/Gc subtests and the Delayed Recall subtests, include teaching items. The specific teaching instructions are conveniently printed on the pages of the easel.

Instructions for teaching the task are clearly articulated in the easel, but sometimes a child may still not understand a task after the teaching is complete. This lack of understanding is evident if a child fails a second trial. In such a situation, the administration rules allow examiners to use their own words to restate the directions, or describe the task more generally using additional examples, easy words, or gestures. If necessary, a different language may be used to communicate the directions to the child (e.g., ASL, Spanish, Vietnamese) or the directions may be written for the child to read.

Out of Level Norms for Gifted or Very Low-Functioning Children

Preschool children ages 4 to 5 who are very low functioning may benefit from the administration of a battery designed for children of a younger chronological age. For example, if a 5-year-old is very low functioning, the 5-year-old battery may be too frustrating (and may not have an adequate floor), but the core battery for 4- or 3-year-olds may be at an appropriate level of difficulty. At the opposite end of the spectrum, very high-functioning children ages 3 to 6 may benefit from the administration of a battery designed for chronologically older children. For example, a high-functioning 3-year-old may be bored during administration of the 3-year-old battery (and may not achieve a ceiling), but will be appropriately challenged by the battery for children ages 4–5. For these reasons, the KABC–II provides the opportunity for "out-of-level" testing.

The decision to do out-of-level testing must be made with caution. The KABC–II core batteries were designed to be appropriate for most children in the specific age groups. In general, for an average child, an out-of-level subtest will usually not have an adequate floor or ceiling. Thus, examiners must have a strong expectation that a child will perform below average when administering a core battery that is below the child's chronological age or that a child will perform above average when administering a core battery that is above the child's chronological age.

The out-of-level battery yields scores based on norms for the child's own age group. For example, if a 3-year-old is administered the age 4 out-of-level battery, then the scores are based on how other 3-year-olds performed on those same subtests. The battery administered determines the scores that are possible: if a 3-year-old battery is administered, then only the FCI or MPI can be calculated, but if a 4-year-old battery is administered then the full profile of indexes is yielded.

Adequate Floor

One of the goals in developing the KABC–II was to strengthen the subtest floors for low functioning children. This goal was achieved by developing an adequate number of easy items for each subtest. As Table 14.5 shows, the global scales (MPI, FCI, and NVI) yield standard scores as low as 40–41 for all preschool age children. The four separate KABC–II scales for ages 4–5 yield standard scores of more than 3 *SD* below the mean (with floors ranging from standard scores of 40–50). Table 14.6 shows the subtest scaled scores that correspond to raw scores of zero for ages 3:0 to 5:11. Most core subtests for preschoolers have floors as low as scaled scores of 1 to 3, with Conceptual Thinking as the main exception, yielding minimum scaled scores of 3–5 from raw scores of 0.

Nonverbal Scale

The KABC–II's Nonverbal Scale is useful for the evaluation of young children with communication difficulties. The Nonverbal Scale is composed of subtests that may be administered in pantomime and responded to motorically, to permit the valid, reliable assessment of children without demanding strong linguistic or English skills. The Nonverbal Scale can be administered for the evaluation of hearing-impaired and severely speech-impaired preschoolers. It is also very useful in the assessment of children who have limited English proficiency.

PSYCHOMETRIC PROPERTIES

Reliability

The internal consistency of a test evaluates the degree to which a score represents a homogeneous ability or trait. The KABC–II Manual (Kaufman & Kaufman, 2004a) presents comprehensive information on reliability and validity. Table 14.7 reviews the internal consistency and test-retest data for the preschool age range. The average internal consistency coefficients for ages 3–5 are .93 for the MPI and .96 for the FCI. The four separate scales have internal reliability coefficients ranging from .90 to 91. Values for individual subtests ranged from .66 for the supplementary Hand Movements subtest to .93 on Rebus. The me-

TABLE 14.5.
Floors of KABC–II Scales: Lowest Possible Global Standard Scores

Age	MPI	FCI	NVI	Sequential/ Gsm	Simultaneous/ Gv	Learning/ Glr	Knowledge/ Gc
3:0–3:11	40	40	40	—	—	—	—
4:0–4:11	41	40	40	49	40	48	50
5:0–5:11	40	40	40	49	40	48	50

Note. Data are from Table D.2 of the *KABC–II Manual* (Kaufman & Kaufman, 2004a).

TABLE 14.6.
Subtest Scaled Scores that Correspond to Raw Scores of Zero for Ages 3:0 to 5:11

Age	Atlantis	Conceptual Thinking	Face Recognition	Story Completion	Number Recall	Gestalt Closure	Rover	Atlantis Delayed	Expressive Vocabulary	Verbal Knowledge	Rebus	Triangles	Block Counting	Word Order	Pattern Reasoning	Hand Movements	Rebus Delayed	Riddles
3:0–3:2	2	5	3	—	5	3	—	—	3	5	6	2	—	3	—	6	—	4
3:3–3:5	2	5	3	—	5	3	—	—	3	4	5	2	—	3	—	6	—	3
3:6–3:8	2	5	3	—	4	2	—	—	2	3	3	2	—	2	—	4	—	2
3:9–3:11	1	5	2	—	4	2	—	—	2	3	5	1	—	2	—	3	—	2
4:0–4:2	1	4	2	—	3	1	—	—	1	2	4	1	—	1	—	3	—	1
4:3–4:5	1	4	2	—	3	1	—	—	1	2	4	1	—	1	—	3	—	1
4:6–4:8	1	3	2	—	3	1	—	—	1	1	3	1	—	1	—	3	—	1
4:9–4:11	1	3	2	—	2	1	—	—	1	1	2	1	—	1	—	2	—	1
5:0–5:2	1	2	2	6	2	1	6	2	1	1	2	1	4	1	3	2	6	1
5:3–5:5	1	2	2	5	1	1	5	2	1	1	1	1	3	1	2	2	5	1
5:6–5:8	1	2	2	5	1	1	5	2	1	1	1	1	2	1	2	2	4	1
5:9–5:11	1	2	1	5	2	1	4	2	1	1	1	1	2	1	1	2	3	1

Note. Data are from Table D.1 of the *KABC–II Manual* (Kaufman & Kaufman, 2004a).

■ Dark gray shading indicates subtests that are *Out of Level* at that age.

□ Light gray shading indicates subtests that are *Supplementary* at that age.

307

TABLE 14.7.
KABC–II Internal-Consistency Reliability and Test-Retest Stability for Ages 3–5

Scale or Subtest	Internal Consistency Reliability[a]	Test-Retest Reliability[b]
Sequential/Gsm	**.91**	**.79**
Number Recall	.85	.69
Word Order	.87	.72
Hand Movements	.66	.50
Simultaneous/Gv	**.91**	**.74**
Block Counting	.91	—
Conceptual Thinking	.80	.55
Face Recognition	.75	.56
Triangles	.84	.79
Gestalt Closure	.75	.70
Pattern Reasoning	.88	—
Learning/Glr	**.90**	**.79**
Atlantis	.81	.73
Rebus	.93	.70
Delayed Recall	.81	—
Knowledge/Gc	**.91**	**.93**
Expressive Vocabulary	.85	.86
Riddles	.85	.80
Verbal Knowledge	.84	.81
MPI	**.93**	**.86**
FCI	**.96**	**.90**
NVI	**.88**	**.72**

Note: Data are adapted from Tables 8.1 and 8.3 of the KABC-II Manual (Kaufman & Kaufman, 2004a). Scale reliabilities are shown in bold. Reliability and stability coefficients for Sequential/Gsm, Simultaneous/Gv, Learning/Glr, and Knowledge/Gc are based only on data for ages 4 and 5 (these scales are not included for age 3). Similarly, mean values shown for some subtests are based only on the ages at which those subtests are administered (e.g., the values for Rebus are based only on ages 4 and 5, and the values for Pattern Reasoning are based only on age 5).

[a]Reliabilities for scales and global scales were computed using the formula provided by Nunnally (1978, p. 248).

[b]All test-retest reliability coefficients were corrected for the variability of the sample, based on the standard deviation obtained on the first testing, using the variability correction of Cohen, et al. (2003. p. 58).

dian internal consistency value for the individual subtests was .85 for ages 3–5. The values for the global and separate scales are excellent, and the values for the subtests are good.

As shown in Table 14.7, the KABC–II is a stable instrument for preschoolers, as evidenced by the average adjusted test-retest coefficients of .86 and .90 for the MPI and FCI, respectively (the NVI is less stable with a correlation of .72). Across the separate scales for the preschoolers, the stability values of Simultaneous/Gv (.74), Learning/Glr (.79), Sequential/Gsm (.79), and Knowledge/Gc (.93) also denote adequate stability. Practice effects are most notable for the Simultaneous/Gv and Learning/Glr scales, but are relatively small (5–6 points). The Sequential/Gsm and Knowledge/Gc scales have minimal 2- to 4-point practice effects (See Table 14.8).

TABLE 14.8.
Practice Effects for the KABC–II Global Scales for Ages 3–5

Scale	Gain From 1st to 2nd Testing
Sequential/Gsm[a]	2.2
Simultaneous/Gv[a]	5.0
Learning/Glr[a]	5.9
Knowledge/Gc[a]	3.9
MPI	5.9
FCI	5.3
NVI	4.8

Note: Data are from *KABC–II Technical Manual* (Table 8.3). Intervals ranged from 12 to 56 days with a mean of 27 days.

[a]Ages 4–5 only.

Validity

Results of confirmatory factor analyses (CFA) across age levels support the construct validity of the KABC–II (Kaufman & Kaufman, 2004a). At age 3, a single factor model is the basis for the KABC–II (although CFA did yield a distinction between the Sequential/Gsm subtests and the rest of the battery). At age 4, the Conceptual Thinking subtest loaded substantially on both Knowledge/Gc and Simultaneous/Gv. This dual-loading led to a nonsignificant distinction between Knowledge/Gc and Simultaneous/Gv. Despite the findings of the CFA, the final battery separates Knowledge/Gc and Simultaneous/Gv into distinct scales on the basis of the distinct content in each of the scales. The other two factors measured at age 4, Sequential/Gsm and Learning/Glr, were well supported and distinct. At ages 5–6 (which were analyzed as a single group), all four separate scales corresponded to separate and distinct factors in the CFA.

The main CFA statistics for evaluating how well a test's data fit a theoretical model are the comparative fit index (CFI) and the root mean square error of approximation (RMSEA). According to Hu and Bentler (1999), CFI values should be greater than .95 and RMSEA values should be less than .06 to provide evidence of good fit. When all KABC–II subtests (core and supplementary) were evaluated by CFA, the following values were yielded for age 4 (CFI = .999 and RMSEA = .027) and for ages 5–6 (CFI = .995 and RMSEA = .047) (Kaufman & Kaufman, 2004a, Figure 8.1). Overall results of the CFA for preschool children are very strongly supportive of the theory-based scale structure of the KABC–II.

The validity of the KABC–II for use with preschoolers was further supported by correlations with other measures of preschool cognitive ability. The KABC–II exhibits some overlap with other measures of cognitive ability, yet also contributes something new. The relationship between the KABC–II and the Wechsler Preschool and Primary Scale of Intelligence–Third Edition (WPPSI–III; The Psychological Corporation, 2002) was detailed in a study of 36 children ages 3–4 and 39 children ages 5–6 (Kaufman & Kaufman, 2004a, Tables 8.19 and 8.20). At ages 3–4, the WPPSI–III Full Scale IQ correlated .76 and .81 with the KABC–II MPI and FCI, respectively. These relationships were of similar magnitude for children ages 5–6 (.80–.81). The strongest correlations between the various scales of the two tests were found on the General Language Composite and Verbal IQ when compared to the KABC–II Knowledge/Gc index (rs ranged from .75 for ages 5–6 to .89 for ages 3–4).

Correlations were also reported between the KABC–II and the original K-ABC for 74 children ages 3–5 years (Kaufman & Kaufman, 2004a, Table 8.15). The FCI correlated .72 with the K–ABC Mental Processing Composite (MPC) and .74 with the Achievement Index. For the MPI, the corresponding values were .65 and .57. For this preschool sample, the KABC–II Sequential/Gsm Index correlated .76 with K–ABC Sequential Processing standard score; the Simultaneous/Gv Index correlated .62 with K–ABC Simultaneous Processing standard score; and the Knowledge/Gc Index correlated .74 with the K-ABC Achievement standard score.

Correlations between the KABC–II and the key criterion of academic achievement, as measured by the Kaufman Test of Educational Achievement–Second Edition (KTEA–II, Kaufman & Kaufman, 2004b) indicated a moderately strong relationship between ability and achievement at the preschool level. For ages 4–6 through Kindergarten, average adjusted correlations between the KTEA–II Comprehensive Achievement Composite and KABC–II MPI and FCI were .72 and .74, respectively. The individual KABC–II scales all correlated moderately highly with the KTEA–II Comprehensive Achievement Composite: Sequential/Gsm (.58), Simultaneous (.65), Learning/Glr (.53), and Knowledge/Gc (.61; Kaufman & Kaufman, 2004b). Interestingly, at the preschool and kindergarten level, the Knowledge/Gc scale did not correlate more strongly with achievement than the other scales. However, this finding may reflect the fact that at the youngest ages children have not had as much academic experience, so their cognitive processing is as important in predicting their scores on tests such as the KTEA–II as their academic knowledge.

All of the data from the CFA and the correlational studies reported in the manual provide excellent support of the validity of the KABC–II scales for preschool children.

INTERPRETATION

An in-depth discussion of KABC–II interpretation is not possible in this limited space, so a brief overview of the interpretive process is provided here. The interested reader can find more detail in the test's manual as well as in the following text: Essentials of KABC–II Assessment (Kaufman et al., 2005). The focus in KABC–II interpretation was designed to be on the scale indexes rather than the subtests. The main goal of KABC–II interpretation is to identify and understand the child's strong and weak areas of cognitive functioning and mental processing, from both normative (age-based) perspective and ipsative (person-based) perspectives. The KABC–II scales are interpreted from the vantage point of the two theories on which the KABC–II is based: the CHC theory of cognitive abilities and Luria's neuropsychological theory. A brief description of the KABC–II scales from a CHC and Luria perspective was provided earlier in Table 14.1.

Interpretation of the KABC–II at age 3 involves only evaluating global scores (MPI or FCI). At ages 4–5, interpretation also includes both normative and ipsative analyses of the child's scale profile. An optional portion of the interpretive process for KABC–II assessments involves conducting planned clinical comparisons that go beyond the global score and the scale index profile to try to uncover additional potentially meaningful hypotheses about the child's functioning. Some of the optional steps involve utilizing data from the supplementary subtests and combining subtests into alternate groupings of clinically relevant clusters. All of the optional steps are intended primarily to generate hypotheses to be verified with other data.

Although the interpretive approach for the KABC–II has been modified from that of the K–ABC, one key component remains the same: it is crucial to find multiple sources of data to support hypotheses that are based on a pattern of index or clinical composite scores. Table 14.9 briefly outlines the interpretive steps presented in the KABC–II Manual and by Kaufman et al. (2005).

CLINICAL CASE REPORT

The case report of Javier H., age 4, that follows, demonstrates the use of the KABC–II in a comprehensive assessment. Pertinent information has been changed to protect the confidentiality of the client and the family.

Reason for Evaluation

Javier H. is a 4-year-old boy who attends preschool. This evaluation was initiated at the recommendation of his preschool teacher because of her concerns regarding Javier's poor eye contact, his difficulty attending to a task, and his repetitive speech. His parents are also concerned about his difficulty understanding directions and his sporadic ability to respond appropriately to questions. Javier has been previously diagnosed with expressive and receptive language delays. Mr. and Ms. H. requested this evaluation in order to determine

TABLE 14.9.
Summary of KABC–II Interpretive Steps

ESSENTIAL STEPS

Step 1. Interpret the **global scale index**, whether the FCI (CHC model), MPI (Luria model), or Nonverbal Index (NVI) (ages 3–18)

Step 2. Interpret the child's profile of scale indexes to **identify strengths and weaknesses**, both personal (relative to the child's overall ability) and normative (compared to children about the same age) (ages 4–18)

OPTIONAL STEPS

Step 3. Planned Scale Comparisons
   Step 3A: **Initial Learning** vs. **Delayed Recall**—Learning/*Glr* (Initial) vs. Delayed Recall (ages 5–18)
   Step 3B: **Learning** vs. **Acquired Knowledge**—Learning/*Glr* vs. Knowledge/*Gc* (ages 4–18)

Step 4. Supplementary Subtest Analysis

Step 5. Planned Clinical Comparisons
   Step 5A: **Nonverbal** Ability (NVI) vs. **Verbal** Ability (ages 3–18)
   Step 5B: **Problem-Solving** Ability vs. **Memory & Learning** (ages 3–18)
   Step 5C: Visual Perception of **Meaningful** Stimuli vs. **Abstract** Stimuli (ages 4–18)
   Step 5D: **Verbal** Response vs. **Pointing** Response (ages 4–18)
   Step 5E: Little or **No Motor** Response vs. **Gross-Motor** Response (ages 4–18)

Step 6. Generate Hypotheses to Explain Fluctuations in Two Circumstances:
   Step 6A: Scales that Are **Not Interpretable** (ages 4–18)
   Step 6B: **Supplementary Subtests** that Are Inconsistent with Pertinent Core Subtests (ages 3–18)

Note: Adapted from Kaufman et al. (2005).

if Javier has some underlying developmental disorder or cognitive dysfunction that may be contributing to these problems, aside from language factors. This assessment will therefore evaluate Javier's neuropsychological status, as well as assess his adaptive behavior and any developmental delays.

Background Information

Developmental History and Health. According to Ms. H., Javier is the product of a normal pregnancy; however, she reported experiencing a significant amount of stress during her pregnancy due to the passing away of her mother, as well as some uncertainty at work. Ms. H. went into labor at 28 weeks and Javier was born 12 weeks premature, weighing 2 lb. 2 oz. He remained in the hospital for 10 weeks; he was on a ventilator and oxygen for some-time, and he had some blood transfusions. However, no major complications were apparent. No further health problems were reported as an infant or toddler. His parents described Javier as an easy infant and toddler who ate and slept well. Javier reached his motor mile-stones a little late, but overall within normal limits. His language milestones were initially reached on time; however, he was late in combining words into phrases and sentences, which his parents indicated may be partly due to the fact that he has been cared for by a Brazilian nanny, who spoke Portuguese to him. Javier is reported to be bilingual.

Since birth, a developmental pediatrician has tracked Javier's health and develop-ment. His pediatrician has reported some delays with expressive and receptive language, but she did not report any other concerns. Javier's gross and fine motor skills are reported to be intact overall, and his vision and hearing were reported to be within normal limits. At the time of this evaluation, Javier was on no medications.

Academic History. Javier's mother returned to work when he was 5 months old, and he stayed at home with his nanny until he started preschool at the age of 2 years. During his first year at school, aside from some separation anxiety, he adjusted well. The only problems noted by his teachers were his delays in language and some problems remaining seated with the group. This year, however, he has had more difficulties. He has significant difficulty participating appropriately in circle time, he is very inattentive, and he tends to blurt out irrelevant responses. He also repeats phrases over and over again, which appear to be unrelated to the task at hand, although his parents believe that these phrases are rel-evant to something that has happened in the past, but not to the immediate situation. He is echolalic but his parents indicated that this is most apparent when he is imitating and modeling his parents, rather than merely repeating their words. This is also noticeable when Javier is very excited or is anticipating an event. Mr. and Ms. H. noted that Javier's repetitive speech may reflect some discomfort in a group setting and some anxiety.

Javier's teachers have also complained about his poor eye contact, and this is noticeable at home. His mother noted that when Javier initiates conversation, he is able to make good eye contact. However, his eye contact is poor if he does not want to follow instructions or if he does not know how to respond to a question. His mother indicated that she believes that his poor eye contact may also be related to his inattention and his high level of distractibility.

Javier displays a fixation about cars, and he apparently knows almost every model of car and can point them out. He has an excellent memory for obscure details, yet he does not always focus on the big picture and is instead somewhat distracted by irrelevant details. Javier has some notable language delays, and he has received speech pathology services for the past 5 months. These sessions are conducted twice a week and include some sessions with a peer in order to work on Javier's social interaction skills. Javier apparently enjoys these sessions and is cooperative and responsive. In an interview with Javier's speech pathologist, she indicated that he had made some improvement in terms of his expressive language skills, but his receptive language skills were significantly impaired. She noted particular concerns about his poor eye contact and his high level of distractibility. She further noted that he does much better in a small group rather than in a large setting.

Behavioral Observations

Javier presented as a very sweet, friendly, and outgoing young boy. He was happy to remain with the examiner in her office while his parents waited in the waiting room, and no separation anxiety was evident. On the second day of testing, Javier was very excited to return to the office, and he greeted the examiner appropriately by saying, "Hello Dr. Lurie," and at the end of the morning he said, "Thanks for playing games." In contrast to observations of Javier at school, he was noted to be very verbal throughout the testing and he made good eye contact on most occasions. He responded appropriately to the examiner's questions, followed most simple directions, and even initiated conversation with the examiner. However, at times he was noted to be echolalic. This was most evident when Javier did not appear to understand the nature of the task presented, and that those times he would mimic the question "what doesn't belong, doesn't belong, doesn't belong" rather than respond appropriately. When he did understand a task, he was able to verbalize his answer, although he did demonstrate some poor articulation and at times he spoke in a sing-song voice. He also added details to his responses, such as "this is a nice person," "he is crying," or "the boy is opening his mouth" on a Face Recognition task. Javier was able to sing most of the ABC song, although he wasn't able to respond to a question about how old he is. He could also not be encouraged to count for the examiner. However, he was able to name numerous shapes and colors and respond appropriately when he was asked about these by the examiner.

Javier was noted to have some significant difficulty paying attention. This was evident throughout the assessment, but was most noticeable on the second day of testing. He required frequent repetition and redirection by the examiner, and he was extremely fidgety. Many times, directions had to be rephrased and repeated on numerous occasions before Javier would attempt a task. Javier also appeared to be distracted by his own internal thoughts. For example, he constantly referred to the car wash, although this was not part of the stimulus material. He also spoke constantly about cars, and he became very excited when he saw a car in the stimulus material.

Despite his difficulties, Javier was cooperative and persevered with the testing. He enjoyed playing with the toys in the office, stapling paper with a stapler, and looking through a car magazine. However, he had no problem transitioning from play to a structured task, and he did not display any oppositionality when the toys were put away. He was able to ask the examiner when he needed to use the restroom, although he whispered his request. During the first day of testing, Javier worked well with the examiner on a one-on-one basis for about an hour (with breaks) before indicating that "I am done," and at that time he clearly was unable to continue with any structured assessment. On the second day of testing, Javier had more difficulty remaining attentive and could only focus for a few minutes on a task. He would state, "I am done," and refuse to attempt any further items. He could not be encouraged to complete some tasks due to his limited attention span.

On the basis of these behavior observations, this assessment appears to be a valid measure of Javier's current neuropsychological functioning.

Assessment Procedures

> Clinical interviews with Mr. and Ms. H., Javier's teacher, his developmental pedia-
> trician, and speech pathologist
>
> Kaufman Assessment Battery for Children–Second Edition (KABC–II)
>
> A Developmental Neuropsychological Assessment (NEPSY)
>
> Achenbach Child Behavior Checklist/1.5–5 (CBCL) & Teacher Report Form
>
> Conners' Parent Rating Scale–Revised: Long Version
>
> Conners' Teacher Rating Scale–Revised: Long Version
>
> Gilliam Asperger's Disorder Scale (GADS)
>
> Adaptive Behavior Assessment System–Second Edition (ABAS–II): Teacher/Daycare
> Provider Form and Parent Form
>
> (Javier's psychometric summary is presented in Table 14.10.)

Test Results

Intellectual Functioning. In order to assess Javier's intellectual ability, he was administered the Kaufman Assessment Battery for Children, Second Addition (KABC–II) which
is an individually administered test of a child's intellectual ability and cognitive strengths
and weaknesses. The KABC–II is based on a double theoretical foundation, Luria's neuro-

TABLE 14.10.
Psychometric Summary of Javier H.

Kaufman Assessment Battery for Children—Second Edition (KABC-II): Luria Model				
Scale or Subtest	Standard Score	90% Confid. Interval	Percentile Rank	Descriptive Category
Sequential/*Gsm*	**83**	**77–91**	**13**	**Below Average**
Word Order	9		37	
Number Recall	5		5	
Simultaneous/*Gv*	**93**	**84–102**	**32**	**Average**
Conceptual Thinking	9		37	
Face Recognition	9		37	
Triangles	8		25	
Learning/*Glr*	**111**	**102–118**	**77**	**Average**
Rebus	13		84	
Atlantis	11		63	
Knowledge/*Gc*	**90**	**83–97**	**25**	**Average**
Expressive Vocabulary	*10*		*50*	
Verbal Knowledge	*11*		*63*	
Riddles	*6*		*9*	
Mental Processing Index (MPI)	**94**	**88–100**	**34**	**Average**

Note. Supplementary subtests are shown in italics. The Knowledge/Gc scale is supplementary in the
Luria model, and is therefore not included in the calculation of the MPI.

A Developmental Neuropsychological Assessment (NEPSY)

Attention/Executive	Standard Score	Percentile Rank
Visual Attention	10	50
Statue	6	9
Language		
Body Part Naming	10	50
Phonological Processing	8	25
Comprehension of Inst.	7	16
Verbal Fluency	8	25
Oromotor Sequences	—	26–75
Sensorimotor		
Imitating Hand Positions	9	37
Visuomotor Precision	6	9
Manual Motor Sequences	—	26–75
Visuospatial		
Design Copying	8	25
Block Construction	6	9
Memory		
Narrative Memory	9	37
Sentence Repetition	4	2

Adaptive Behavior Assessment System–Second Edition (ABAS–II)

Composite	Composite Score		Percentile Rank		Confidence Interval		Qualitative Description	
	Teacher Rating	Parent Rating	Teacher Rating	Parent Rating	Teacher Rating	Parent Rating	Teacher Rating	Parent Rating
GAC	85	98	16	45	82–88	94–102	Below Average	Average
Conceptual	80	97	9	42	75–85	90–104	Below Average	Average
Social	73	96	4	39	67–79	88–104	Borderline	Average
Practical	92	101	30	53	86–98	94–108	Average	Average

ABAS–II Skills Areas	Scaled Score		Percentile Rank	
	Teacher Rating	Parent Rating	Teacher Rating	Parent Rating
Communication	5	10	5	50
Community Use	—	12		75
Functional Pre-Aca	10	9	50	37
School Living	6	—	9	—
Home Living	—	10		50
Health/Safety	8	10	25	50
Leisure	5	10	5	50
Self-Care	12	9	75	37
Self-Direction	6	10	9	50
Social	6	9	9	37
Motor	12	8	75	25

Gilliam Asperger's Disorder Scale (GADS)

Subscale	Scaled Score		Percentile Rank		Probability of Asperger's Disorder	
	Teacher Rating	Parent Rating	Teacher Rating	Parent Rating	Teacher Rating	Parent Rating
Social Interaction	10	1	50	<1		
Restricted Patterns of Behavior	10	4	50	2		
Cognitive Patterns	9	5	37	5		
Pragmatic Skills	9	2	37	<1		
Asperger's Disorder	**97**	**53**	**58**	**<1**	**High/ Probable**	**Low/Not Probable**

psychological model and the Cattell-Horn-Carroll (CHC) psychometric theory. For 4-year-olds, the KABC–II yields four scales, each given a label that reflects both theoretical models: Sequential/Gsm, Simultaneous/Gv, Learning/Glr, and Knowledge/Gc. (From the perspective of CHC theory, Gsm = short-term memory; Gv = visual processing; Glr = long-term storage & retrieval; and Gc = crystallized ability.)

Examiners are given the option of selecting either the Luria model or the CHC model of the KABC–II, based on the child's background and the reason for referral. (Knowledge/Gc is excluded from the Luria model because measures of language ability and acquired knowledge may not provide fair assessment of some children's cognitive abilities (e.g., those from bilingual or non-mainstream backgrounds or those with language disorders). Based on Javier's previously diagnosed expressive and receptive language difficulties, the Luria KABC–II model was administered. However, Javier was additionally administered the Knowledge/Gc scale as a supplement that did not factor into his overall global score. This model yields the Mental Processing Index (MPI) as the global measure of general cognitive ability.

Javier earned a KABC–II MPI of 94, ranking him at the 34th percentile and classifying his overall cognitive ability as falling within the Average Range. The chances are 90% that his "true" MPI is between 88 and 100. He displayed considerable variability in his standard scores on the three theory-based scales that compose the MPI with Indexes ranging from 111 on Learning/Glr to 83 on Sequential/Gsm. This wide variation in Indexes renders his MPI meaningless as an estimate of global ability and is nothing more than the mid-point of diverse abilities. However, unlike the MPI, all three of Javier's Scale Indexes were found to be interpretable, as he performed consistently on the tasks that compose each separate scale. Javier was administered the Knowledge/Gc scale as a supplement to the MPI, and this Index was also found to be interpretable because he performed consistently on the tasks involved in the scale.

Javier demonstrated a well-developed ability to learn new information when working on problems that require him to learn new pairs of visual and auditory stimuli (some meaningful and some not). This skill was evident in Javier's performance on the Learning/Glr scale (index = 111; 77th percentile). Relative to his own Average level of ability, his performance on this scale was significantly higher on the Learning/Glr Index (a difference that size occurred less than 10% of the time in a group of same-age peers). The types of tasks that measured this skill include learning nonsense names for pictures of fish, plants, and shells, and learning the words that are paired with abstract symbols. Although he became extremely inattentive as these tasks progressed, he continued to guess at his responses and persevered with the tasks. Overall, his ability in this area is indicative of intact capability to store information in long-term memory and retrieve this information in an efficient manner.

In contrast to this relatively well-developed long-term memory ability, was Javier's Below Average ability to process information in a serial or temporal order and to hold information in immediate awareness. His performance on the Sequential/Gsm index (standard score = 83; 13th percentile) was significantly lower than his Average level of ability across all the indexes, and may reflect some difficulties with Javier's attentional ability, as well as his short-term auditory memory. For example, he was very inattentive and distractible on a subtest that required him to repeat a series of numbers in the same sequence as the examiner said them. On another short-term memory task assessing his ability to touch a series of silhouettes in the same order as the examiner said their names, although he appeared to listen carefully to the names as stated by the examiner, he often did not make any response, or only responded to the last name said.

Javier's visual processing of information and non-verbal reasoning were within the Average range of ability compared to other children his age. He performed consistently on all tasks in this domain, earning a Simultaneous/Gv index of 93 (32nd percentile). His greatest difficulty (still in the Average range) was on a measure of spatial visualization in which he was required to assemble several shapes together to match a model made by the examiner (25th percentile) which reflects his skill with the spatial management of visual stimuli. However, overall his non-verbal reasoning ability appears intact.

Despite Javier's previously diagnosed language difficulties, he scored in the Average range on supplementary tests of Expressive Vocabulary (50th percentile) and on a test of Verbal Knowledge (63rd percentile). He was able to select from an array of pictures that correspond to a general information question. Although his articulation was poor, he gave appropriate descriptions of many of these scenes (although this was not required by the examiner). He had more difficulty when required to name a verbal concept as described by the examiner (9th percentile). He tended to repeat the examiner's question rather than name a concept; this was a pattern noted whenever Javier had difficulty understanding task requirements. Overall, his results in this area were indicative of slightly variable language abilities, and which were summarized by his Knowledge/Gc index of 90 (25th percentile).

Attention and Executive Functions.   Javier's performances were inconsistent on subtests of attention on the NEPSY, and ranged from Average to Borderline. He displayed Average performance on a test of selective visual attention (50th percentile). This subtest of the NEPSY assessed his ability to attend to a visual stimulus and locate target pictures quickly in an array. Javier had to be strongly encouraged to keep working on this task, and he was somewhat resistant to completing it. He tended to color over and over the target picture, rather than search for more targets, and despite his intact performance overall, he did demonstrate some significant inattention and had to be redirected by the examiner on numerous occasions. Javier's motor inhibition was Borderline as evidenced by his performance on a subtest assessing self-regulation and inhibition (9th percentile). This task measured his ability to sustain a position over a 75-second interval despite distractions. Javier displayed difficulty inhibiting the impulse to respond to auditory distraction on this task, and his motor persistence was impaired.

Further measures of Javier's attentional functioning were obtained by having his parents and teachers complete the Conners = Rating Scale–Revised. On this scale, Javier's teachers identified him as both inattentive and impulsive, and indicated that he meets the diagnostic criteria for ADHD, Combined Type. They expressed concerns regarding his failure to finish what he starts, his difficulty remaining seated, his inability to listen to what is said to him, his high distractibility, his poor sustained attention, and his fidgetiness. They also described him as having a low frustration tolerance, a very short attention span, and a significant amount of restlessness. On the Conners = Rating Scales–Revised, Mr. H. reported Javier as being moderately inattentive and having some concentration problems. His profile was borderline for ADHD. The profile generated by Ms. H.'s responses to the Conners = was almost identical to that of Mr. H., although Ms. H. expressed more concerns regarding Javier's attentional abilities. Her report identified Javier as having ADHD, Combined Type.

Language.   Javier's receptive and expressive language skills on the NEPSY were within the Low Average to Average ranges. He scored in the Average range on a measure of naming ability, a basic component of expressive language (50th percentile) and on a measure of oromotor coordination (26–75th percentile). His performances were Low Average on measures of phonological processing (25th percentile), on a subtest assessing his comprehension of verbal instructions of increasing complexity (16th percentile), and on a subtest assessing his ability to generate words in semantic categories (25th percentile). He demonstrated a high level of distractibility and inattention on these tasks, had to be redirected constantly, and required a great deal of prompting to respond appropriately.

Sensorimotor.   Javier demonstrated Average sensorimotor abilities on a subtest requiring him to imitate hand and finger positions (37th percentile) and on a subtest requiring him to learn and automatize a series of rhythmic movements (26–75th percentile). However, Javier displayed significant difficulty on a task requiring him to remain inside a curved track while drawing a line between these tracks (9th percentile). Although he completed this task quickly, he made a significant number of errors and had great difficulty remaining inside the lines. This reflects a high level of impulsivity and a lack of planning. These difficulties often co-occur with the attentional problems discussed above.

Visuospatial.   Javier's performance was Low Average on a task requiring him to copy two-dimensional geometric figures of increasing complexity (25th percentile). Surprisingly enough, he was able to copy a circle and a square, but he was unable to draw a simple vertical or horizontal line. He struggled on a subtest requiring him to reproduce three-dimensional block constructions from models (9th percentile), reflecting some difficulty integrating his visuospatial skills with motor activity. Directional confusion was evidenced by Javier's numerous rotations of blocks, reflecting some difficulty understanding and visualizing spatial relations. This difficulty with spatial visualization has been noted above on the KABC–II.

Memory.   Although Javier appeared to have a great deal of difficulty focusing to the details of a story read to him on a test of Narrative Memory, he performed in the Average range, and he was able to spontaneously recall three details from the text, which was within normal limits for his age (37th percentile). His verbal memory span and short-term memory were significantly more impaired on a Sentence Repetition task (2nd percentile) and he was only able to repeat one sentence as stated by the examiner. He was extremely distracted on this task and could not be encouraged to sit in his chair and listen to the sentences.

This reflects not only a poor attention span, but most likely a great deal of difficulty focusing on auditory information, which is related to his poor receptive language processing.

Adaptive Behavior and Developmental Functioning.   Both Mr. and Ms. H.'s responses to the CBCL were not indicative of any concerns regarding Javier's current level of emotional reactivity, anxiety, depression, somatic complaints, or aggressive behaviors. They did note some problems in terms of his tendency to be withdrawn, but this was within normal limits. The profile generated by Ms. H.'s responses was indicative of a moderate level of inattention, but once again this was within normal limits. However, Ms. H.'s responses indicated the possibility that Javier meets the diagnostic criteria for Pervasive Developmental problems, characterized by avoidance of eye contact, difficulty when things are out of place, disturbed by changes in routine, speech problems, and a refusal to answer when others talk to him. In contrast, the profile generated by Mr. H.'s responses was not indicative of any Pervasive Developmental problems. The profile generated by Javier's teachers = responses to the C-TRF was significantly different to that of his parents, and suggested some notable problems in the areas of emotional reactivity, anxiety and depression, withdrawn behaviors, somatic complaints, and aggressive behaviors. Of particular importance was the Attention Problems scale which was well within the clinically significant range. These teachers expressed concerns regarding Javier's affective problems, and indicated that he most likely meets the diagnostic criteria for Pervasive Developmental problems as well as ADHD. As discussed above, on the Conners', Javier's teachers reported a significant number of concerns, primarily in the areas of inattention, anxiety, and social adjustment. Their responses met the criteria for ADHD, Combined Type.

Javier's parents were asked to complete the Gilliam Asperger's Disorder Scale (GADS). They identified him as performing normally in all areas, and their descriptions of him did not meet the criteria for Asperger's Disorder. In contrast, when Javier's teachers were asked to complete the GADS, they expressed significant concern regarding Javier's social interaction, his restricted patterns of behavior, his cognitive patterns, and his pragmatic skills. On the GADS, they identified Javier as having a high probability of Asperger's Disorder. However, it should be noted that many of the areas that they identified as being a concern may be attributed to significant language delays and significant attentional difficulties, rather than a Pervasive Developmental Disorder.

Javier's teachers and parents completed the ABAS–II in order to obtain a measure of Javier's adaptive behaviors. Adaptive skills are practical everyday skills required to function and meet environmental demands, including effectively taking care of oneself and interacting with other people. The categories of adaptive behaviors assessed by the ABAS–II include Conceptual (communication and academic skills), Social (interpersonal and social competence skills), and Practical (independent living and daily living skills). Javier's teachers rated him as having Average Practical skills, at the 30th percentile (such as picking up and throwing away trash, putting on a coat when the weather is cold, using the bathroom, and using scissors). They noted more difficulty with his Conceptual skills (9th percentile), reflecting significant difficulty in the areas of communication and self-direction. Even further concern was noted in the area of Social skills (4th percentile), such as seeking friendship from others in his age group, participating in simple games, and pretend-playing with his peers. His overall adaptive functioning was rated by his teachers as falling within the Below Average range (16th percentile). Javier's parents rated Javier as having Average adaptive behaviors in all areas, with behaviors ranging from the 39th to 53rd percentiles. They did not identify him as having any adaptive impairments.

Summary and Diagnostic Impressions

Javier is a 4-year-old boy who was referred for an evaluation of his neuropsychological status. Javier was born 12-weeks premature, although no early problems were noted. However, his preschool teachers have expressed great concern about his difficulty focusing in the group, his inability to complete a task, and his problems following directions. He has previously been diagnosed with delays in his expressive and receptive language. During the evaluation, Javier was friendly and cooperative. Although he is reported to have great difficulty making appropriate eye contact and verbalizing in his classroom, his communications were appropriate during the testing, and he was able to make eye contact on most occasions. However, he demonstrated significant inattentiveness and impulsivity, and he had to be constantly redirected to the task at hand.

The results of this assessment indicate that Javier's abilities are variable, ranging from Below Average to Average, with greater difficulty on tasks that rely heavily on intact attention and receptive language functioning and stronger skills in the area of long-term memory and learning. Variability was noted in all areas of neuropsychological functioning, reflecting both uneven cognitive development as well as notable inattention. On measures of adaptive functioning, Javier was rated as having some areas of impairment by his teachers, although his parents described his adaptive behaviors as falling within normal limits. His teachers constantly rated him as meeting the criteria for Pervasive Developmental problems, and although his parents did not rate him as having Asperger's Disorder on the GADS, the profile generated by his mother on the CBCL was indicative of some Pervasive Developmental problems. Both his parents and teachers indicated significant concerns about his attentional functioning, and he was rated by his mother and teachers on the Conners' as having ADHD, Combined Type.

From a diagnostic point of view, it is clear that Javier displays significant variability in both his expressive and, particularly, his receptive language skills. He is also clearly extremely inattentive, and this significantly impacts his day-to-day functioning. However, it is unclear to what extent problems with prematurity may account for these delays and how his speech delays are impacted by his attentional functioning. Therefore, although Javier appears to meet the diagnostic criteria for Attention-Deficit/Hyperactivity Disorder-Combined Type, it would be hasty to diagnose him with this disorder at this time. In addition, he clearly demonstrates some traits of Pervasive Developmental Disorder (PDD), although he does not appear to meet the criteria for PDD-NOS at this time. Javier's language issues and possible other developmental delays may be confounding his attentional problems, as he has difficulty and frustration communicating and he may therefore be responding to this frustration. It is anticipated that many of Javier's difficulties may decrease once he is placed in a more appropriate academic setting, or appropriate modifications to his current academic environment are made. However, it is strongly recommended that his progress be monitored on an ongoing basis and that he be reassessed within the next 2 years to determine his level of attentional functioning, as well as any ongoing traits of PDD that may be impacting his development.

Recommendations

On the basis of these diagnostic concerns, the following recommendations are made:

1.   It is strongly recommended that Mr. and Ms. H. contact The Preschool Language Development Program in order to determine whether their language-intensive preschool

would be an appropriate placement for Javier. The goal of this program is to promote language skills and social and cognitive development.

2.   If Mr. and Ms. H. choose to keep Javier at his current educational placement, they may consider hiring a Shadow to assist him in his daily activities. Due to his significant language delays and attentional impairment, Javier's teachers do not have the resources to meet his needs without ongoing, daily assistance. The H.s may contact the department of developmental disabilities to assist them in finding an appropriate person, or alternatively the staff at his preschool may have contact with someone who has had prior experience in their school. It is strongly recommended that Javier be involved in a language-intensive program in the afternoons after school and that he receive daily speech therapy in the school setting if possible. It is also recommended that Javier repeat his current year at preschool since he is not ready to move into his pre-K year. Next year, Javier should be enrolled in a 5-day program, and ongoing daily language therapy should be continued.

3.   Until appropriate educational decisions have been made for Javier, his teachers will be faced with the ongoing challenge of meeting his needs in the classroom. It is essential that Javier be provided with both visual and oral instruction whenever possible. Nonverbal input and visual reinforcement such as gestures, drawings, and modeling are essential. He will often need to have instructions repeated. Ensure that Javier is paying attention before speaking to him and encourage Javier to ask for such repetition if he initially has difficulty understanding. His repetition of questions when he is unsure of how to respond may be behaviorally managed by teaching him other ways to respond when he is uncertain and rewarding him when he uses the new techniques. When giving directions, make frequent eye contact and stop at various points to ensure that Javier understands. It may be useful to discuss task requirements with Javier to ensure that he has an accurate interpretation of what is expected of him. Make sure that Javier feels comfortable to ask for clarification and repetition of instructions. All new information should be presented in shorter increments in a multi-sensory format (charts, graphs, videotapes etc.). He would also benefit from new information being presented in a meaningful context so that he is able to relate it to his everyday life and, hopefully, better focus on it.

Within the classroom seating arrangements, surround Javier with model students who will set an example for him and perhaps socialize at appropriate times. Javier will benefit from preferential seating close to the teachers, where they can monitor him and provide him with ongoing feedback. Whenever possible, minimize distractions in his seating area. Javier's teachers may decide to discuss his attentional difficulties with him in appropriate terms, and agree on a signal to use when he is not paying attention, such as squeezing his hand gently, or tapping his back. He could be offered reinforcement for returning to the task at hand when provided with this non-verbal signal.

Javier should be provided with clear expectations and rules for behavior in class. To the extent possible, he should be encouraged to self-monitor his responses in the classroom and, when necessary, Javier should be provided with a "break" from the classroom environment and no penalties should be imposed at those times. As discussed above, Javier would benefit from frequent teacher feedback and redirection, and nonverbal cues may be useful to get his attention.

If his teachers do not think it will be disruptive to other classmates, Javier may be provided with a reward for focusing attentively for a certain period of tim (e.g., throughout Circletime). In fact, Javier's teachers may decide that this is an appropriate technique to use with all class members. He could be given a token for each time period appropriately completed, with the agreement that when he has a certain number of tokens, he will obtain his reward. This could be worked out between his parents and teachers, and together they could encourage Javier to strive towards reaching this goal on a daily basis.

4.   Medication to control symptoms of ADHD may be an appropriate recommendation at a later date.

5.   Retesting at a later date is strongly recommended, as mentioned above.

Michelle Lurie, Psy.D.
Clinical Psychologist

CONCLUSIONS

Many improvements were made to the original edition of the K-ABC that have made the KABC–II a strong instrument for the assessment of preschoolers. For example, there are better floors for younger children, better ceilings for gifted children, a well-developed nonverbal scale for children with linguistic difficulties (or differences), more subtests that require reasoning, and fewer subtests focusing solely on memory. The theoretical and evidence base for the KABC–II is very strong, which is useful in interpretation. The KABC–II has excellent reliability, validity, and factor analytic properties as well as a large-well stratified normative base. Like the original K-ABC, the KABC–II consistently produces lower global score differences between ethnic groups than many other tests of intelligence.

The original K-ABC was widely accepted as a measure of preschool intelligence (Lichtenberger & Kaufman, 2000). Although the KABC–II is still in its infancy, it is reasonable to assume that it, too, will be accepted as a useful measure in assessing preschoolers. There are not yet research articles available using the KABC–II, but the prepublication data available in the manual show promise for better understanding the cognitive abilities of preschoolers. Thus, the strong qualities of the KABC–II indicate that it can be used effectively as a tool in a comprehensive preschool assessment battery, including measures of academic and language ability, for creating a thorough understanding of a young child's abilities.

REFERENCES

Boehm, A. E. (1971). *Manual for the Boehm Test of Basic Concepts*. San Antonio, TX: Psychological Corporation.

Carroll, J. B. (1997). The three-stratum theory of cognitive abilities. In D. P. Flanagan, J. L. Genshaft, & P. L. Harrison (Eds). *Contemporary intellectual assessment: Theories, tests, and issues* (pp. 122–130). New York: Guilford.

Cohen, J., Cohen, P., West, S. G., & Aiken, L. S. (2003). *Applied multiple regression/correlation analysis for the behavioral sciences*. Mahwah, NJ: Lawrence Erlbaum Associates.

Das, J. P., Kirby, J. R., & Jarman, R. F. (1979). *Simultaneous and successive cognitive processes*. New York: Academic Press.

Flanagan, D. P., McGrew, K. S., & Ortiz, S. O. (2000). *The Wechsler intelligence scales and Gf-Gc theory: A contemporary approach to interpretation*. Boston: Allyn & Bacon.

Flanagan, D. P., & Ortiz, S. O. (2001). *Essentials of cross-battery assessment*. New York: Wiley.

Hu, L., & Bentler, P. M. (1999). Cutoff criteria for fit indexes in covariance structure analysis: Conventional criteria versus new alternatives. *Structural Equation Modeling, 6*, 1–55.

Kaufman, A. S. (1978). The importance of basic concepts in the individual assessment of preschool children. *Journal of School Psychology, 16,* 207–211.

Kaufman, A. S., & Kaufman, N. L. (1983). *Kaufman Assessment Battery for Children Manual.* Circle Pines, MN: AGS.

Kaufman, A. S., & Kaufman, N. L. (2004a). *Kaufman Assessment Battery for Children, Second Edition Manual.* Circle Pines, MN: AGS.

Kaufman, A. S., & Kaufman, N. L. (2004b). *Kaufman Test of Educational Achievement, Second Edition Manual.* Circle Pines, MN: AGS.

Kaufman, A. S., Lichtenberger, E. O., Fletcher-Janzen, E., & Kaufman, N. L. (2005). *Essentials of KABC–II assessment.* New York: Wiley.

Lichtenberger, E. O., & Kaufman, A. S. (2000). The assessment of preschool children with the Kaufman Assessment Battery for Children. In B. A. Bracken (Ed.). *The psychoeducational assessment of preschool children* (pp. 103–123). Needham, MA: Allyn & Bacon.

Lichtenberger, E. O. & Kaufman, A. S. (2004). *Essentials of WPPSI–III assessment.* New York: Wiley.

Luria, A. R. (1966). *Human brain: An introduction to neuropsychology.* New York: Basic Books.

Luria, A. R. (1970). The functional organization of the brain. *Scientific American, 222,* 66–78.

McGrew, K. S. (2005). The Cattell-Horn-Carroll theory of cognitive abilities: Past, present, and future. In D. P. Flanagan & P. L. Harrison (Eds.), *Contemporary intellectual assessment: Theories, tests, and issues* (2nd ed., pp. 136–181). New York: Guilford.

McGrew, K. S., Woodcock, R., & Ford, L. (2005). The Woodcock-Johnson Battery, Third Edition. In A. S. Kaufman & E. O. Lichtenberger, *Assessing adolescent and adult intelligence* (3rd ed., pp. 561–628). New York: Wiley.

Neisser, U. (1967). *Cognitive psychology.* New York: Appleton-Century-Crofts.

Nunnally, J. C. (1978). *Psychometric theory* (2nd ed.). New York: McGraw-Hill.

Saye, K. B. (2003). Preschool intellectual assessment. In C. R. Reynolds & R. W. Kamphaus (Eds.), *Handbook of psychological and educational assessment of children–second edition* (pp. 187–203). New York: Guilford Press.

Sperry, R. W. (1968). Hemisphere deconnection and unity in conscious awareness. *American Psychologist, 23,* 723–733.

The Psychological Corporation (2002). *WPPSI–III technical and interpretive manual.* San Antonio, TX: Author.

15

Infant and Toddler Cognitive Assessment

Sharon Bradley-Johnson and C. Merle Johnson
Central Michigan University

HISTORY OF INFANT AND TODDLER ASSESSMENT

A hundred years ago in France, Binet and Simon (1905) published the first intelligence test designed to discriminate between school children making adequate academic progress and those needing additional help to succeed. The 30-item test included several tasks for children under age 2. Wyly (1997) noted that because of inclusion of these items, some consider this the first measure of mental development for infants. The reason for including items for such young children was to ensure that some tasks would be appropriate for school-age children who were cognitively impaired. Examples of tasks for children under age 2 included an awareness of food item requiring discrimination between a piece of chocolate and a piece of wood, and a visual coordination item requiring following a lighted match. However, when Terman (1916) revised the test for use in the United States, he eliminated the items for children under 2 years of age.

Major advances in the assessment of infants and toddlers occurred in the 1920s and 1930s as a result of pioneering work by Arnold Gesell and Nancy Bayley. Their work served as the basis for development of many items on today's measures of mental ability for infants and toddlers. Over a period of about 40 years, Gesell, a pediatrician, in collaboration with colleagues at the Yale Clinic for Child Development, attempted to chart the mental growth of normally developing young children. The Gesell Developmental Schedules were based on this work that involved observation of children in their natural environments as well as supplemental information provided by caregivers. The schedules provided a systematic method of assessment, including a normative approach resulting in age scores for the domains of physical and cognitive development. Although revised several times over the years by Gesell and others, the schedules continue to have limitations in terms of standardization, reliability and validity. Nonetheless, the schedules provided extensive, age-based descriptions of normal infant and toddler development.

Unlike Gesell, Nancy Bayley's work centered on theoretical and clinical questions, such as the relationship between infants' early skill development and their later performance (Hynd & Semrud-Clikeman, 1993). Bayley participated in the Berkley Growth Study of children from birth through age 3 and used this information with Gesell's schedules to develop items for a mental and a motor scale first published in 1933. She continued to improve the scale that became the most frequently used measure of mental development for infants and toddlers. The scale was revised in 1969, 1993, and 2006. Most of the original items on the mental scale were retained, some were modified, and several new items added. Although Bayley's scale was clearly the most well-standardized measure of mental development for the youngest children, Bayley and others found that the results were not useful in predicting infants' later intellectual performance, but for children beyond the age of 2 prediction improved (Bayley, 1933; Fagan & Singer, 1983; Sternberg, Grigorenko, & Bundy, 2001; Wyly, 1997).

More recent developments have focused on alternative assessment methods involving specific abilities such as sensorimotor skills. Several scales use Piaget's description of the sensorimotor period as a framework, including the Ordinal Scales of Psychological Development (Uzgiris & Hunt, 1975), the Albert Einstein Scales of Sensorimotor Development (Escolona & Corman, 1966), and the Observation of Behavior in Socially and Ecologically Relevant and Valid Environments scale (Dunst & McWilliam, 1988). These scales represent a change from a normative to a qualitative view of young children's mental development. Items on these scales are sequential in nature and thus, become progressively more complex.

Another alternative involves an information-processing paradigm. Interest in this approach was spurred by the significant, but modest ability of traditional measures of infant cognitive development to predict later intellectual performance (Colombo, Shaddy, Richman, Maikranz, & Blaga, 2004). Several information processing models have been proposed using different types of responses including looking, smiling, changes in heart rate, sucking, and eye widening. These measures appear to be culture free and do not require use of the hands or vocal responses, which can be advantageous when assessing infants with developmental delays.

One information-processing model involves habituation/dishabituation. Habituation is a decrease in responding as a function of repeated presentation of a stimulus; dishabituation occurs when responding recovers as a result of a change in the stimulus or the presentation of a novel stimulus. The assumption with habituation is that infants have encoded the initial stimulus, and with dishabituation they have discriminated the change from the initial stimulus. Although habituation/dishabituation can be assessed through different modalities, visual stimuli are most often used. Research shows that individual differences in infant habituation are modestly correlated with later childhood intelligence (see reviews by Bornstein & Sigman, 1986; Colombo, 1993; McCall & Carringer, 1997; Rose, 1989). A recent meta-analysis of 38 samples from 25 studies (Kavsek, 2004) found an average correlation between infant habituation/dishabituation and later cognitive performance of .37. A related model emphasizes visual recognition memory. One method of measurement for this model uses habituation and dishabituation. Another uses a paired comparison, where two identical patterns are presented followed by presentation of one of the stimuli paired with a novel pattern. Attention is measured by duration of looking at the novel pattern. As infants mature they process visual stimuli more efficiently (Wyly, 1997). Also, Colombo, Shaddy, and Richman (2000) noted looking time and preference for novelty are sensitive in reflecting different clinical disorders.

The paired-comparison model is used in the Fagan Test of Infant Intelligence (FTII; Fagan & Detterman, 1992). Results for the predictive ability of this test are mixed. For example, FTII results obtained at 5 and 7 months did not predict Bayley Mental Scale (1969) results at 12 months, but did correlate at .21 with the Bayley at 2 years and at .25 with the Stanford-Binet at 3 years (Thompson, Fagan, & Fulkner, 1991). However, similar to Di-Lalla et al. (1990), Tasbihsazan, Nettelbeck, and Kirby (2003) recently found mostly nonsignificant, and sometimes negative, correlations with both the Bayley Mental Scale (1993) one year later and Stanford-Binet–IV results at age 3. Tasbihsazan et al. (2003) found one exception; at the FTII 52-week assessment results significantly correlated with the Bayley (1993) given at 24 months ($r = .49$), but not with the Stanford-Binet–IV. Although Thompson et al. (1991) reported reasonable internal consistency for the FTII, others (Andersson, 1996; Jacobson et al., 1992, Tasbihsazan et al., 2003) found poor internal consistency ($-.46$ to .28). Stability results over 2–13 weeks also have been low, e.g. Tasbihsazan et al. (2003) found correlations ranging from $-.17$ to .29. Further, Benasich and Bejar (1992) questioned the representativeness of the FTII norm sample. Thus, further studies are needed to clarify reliability and predictive validity results for this test.

Although different information processing models may have potential for predicting children's later performance, particularly for children with developmental disabilities, more research is necessary before these approaches can be used routinely in practice. For example, results of habituation tasks are affected by fluctuations in infants' attention evidenced by poor internal consistency and test-retest reliability. Even for high-risk infants, Brian, Landry, Szatmari, Niccols, and Bryson (2003) found test-retest coefficients on a habituation task ranging from .49 to .59 for one stimulus and nonsignificant results for another, suggesting that the type of stimulus affects performance. Concern also exists regarding whether the criterion typically used for habituation indicates that all infants have habituated. Thomas and Gilmore (2004) proposed a model-based nonlinear regression framework that may help equate infants on levels of habituation and improve reliability as well as long-term predictions. Kavsek (2004) found that predictive validity is better for infants at risk if dishabituation measures are used, whereas habituation measures seem to predict future performance better for nonclinical samples. Columbo et al. (2004) examined habituation, novelty preference, and infant heart rate results longitudinally. They found that look duration may reflect different aspects of cognition at different ages as shown by non-monatonically linear results. Their data demonstrate the need for further research on the developmental course of habituation. These issues suggest that more studies are needed before such approaches are understood well enough to be used diagnostically.

In addition to these alternative approaches and revision of traditional measures, federal legislation (P.L. 99-457, Education of the Handicapped Act Amendments of 1986) focused attention on the needs of the youngest children and expanded the scope of assessment to include more comprehensive and interdisciplinary methods for children with disabilities and their families. The rationale for this emphasis is that family assessment and support for early intervention may prevent many developmental disabilities. Further, current theories and tests suggest that separating infant and toddlers' abilities into cognitive, motor, communication, and social areas is impossible because these areas are inextricably related (Bagnato & Neisworth, 1991; McCune, Kalamanson, Fleck, Glazewski, & Sillari, 1990). Comprehensive cognitive measures necessarily require some social, motor, and communication skills. Hence, useful assessments include input from different tests and different perspectives with results integrated through inter- or trans-disciplinary work (Bagnato & Neisworth, 1991; Wyly, 1997).

COMPLICATING FACTORS AND HELPFUL STRATEGIES

In many ways assessing infants and toddlers is more difficult than assessing older children. Fortunately there are strategies that can lessen or eliminate many of these problems.

Changing States

One difficulty is that infants' levels of arousal change quite frequently. For example, infants can quickly change from an alert, attentive state to one where the infant is drowsy, fussy, and averse to stimulation. This limits the time available for obtaining a child's best performance. Planning ahead for the assessment is key to addressing this factor.

To take advantage of infants' active, alert states, examiners must be very familiar with the administration and scoring of the tests so that they can be administered as efficiently as possible. Even for examiners very familiar with a test, it helps if just before testing they scan items that are likely to be used. New examiners, or seasoned examiners using a new test, should practice several times before using the test for diagnosis. Also, prior to testing, test materials to be used should be grouped together and placed where they can be reached quickly.

Scheduling the assessment when an infant is typically alert is important. Nap times and times immediately following a feeding should be avoided. If upon arrival a baby appears alert and attentive, beginning the testing as soon as possible may avoid missing an active-alert state. So that testing shortly after arrival is possible, when arranging the appointment explain to the parents the purpose of the assessment, what they can expect, and answer their questions. Let them know that during testing you will have to focus primarily on the child, but afterward you will be able to discuss results with them. Also indicate that to get a good sample of the child's skills; you will be presenting some tasks that will be too difficult for the child. By discussing this information beforehand parents will be prepared if you need to begin testing shortly after they arrive. Finally, infants tire easily and several short sessions may be more effective than one longer session. Several sessions may provide a better sample of a child's typical performance.

Attention Difficulties

Another complicating factor is that the attention span of infants and toddlers is short and young children are easily distracted by both internal and external stimuli. Several strategies can enhance their attending and reduce distraction. One strategy is to carry out testing in a familiar setting where a child is likely to be relaxed and comfortable, i.e., in the child's home or classroom. Testing young children in an unfamiliar, quiet testing room can be anxiety provoking for them. Even though their familiar environment may be noisy with other activities occurring, the noises and activities are familiar to the child. We find that testing in noisy daycare environments is very distracting to us, but not problematic for most children, especially toddlers.

Another strategy to facilitate attending is use of a fast pace for presenting items; this usually makes the activities more exciting. Fast pacing is one of the most powerful techniques to ensure attending (Engelmann & Colvin, 1983). Examiners should rush themselves, but not the children. To do this requires thorough knowledge of the tests. Pacing, however, must be adapted to match the child's behavior. Focusing intently on children's responsiveness to items is essential so as to recognize children's signals indicating when they are ready to continue and when they want to slow down or stop an activity. Recognition of these signals requires intense concentration on children's facial expressions, body language, and vocalizations. The aim is to develop a synchrony where the examiner and child are responding to each other within a few seconds. Timing is critical. The ability to obtain this synchrony typically develops as examiners gain experience working with young children.

For shy or withdrawn children, a slower, calmer, more relaxed presentation will be necessary, along with sensitivity to children's signals. Another exception to fast pacing involves modeling tasks that children are asked to imitate, such as building with blocks. For many children very slow modeling is more effective than a fast-paced presentation.

Another strategy to enhance attending is to use highly salient toys during testing. In addition to test materials, having some attractive, age-appropriate toys available to follow less interesting items is helpful. Except for the item being administered, test kits should be out of sight or covered to lessen distractions. On most tests the order of presentation of items can be altered to accommodate children's interest and keep them engaged. For example, if a child is unlikely to be interested in two upcoming tasks, intersperse an interesting task between them.

Mobility

Infants typically are positioned for testing on a parent's lap or in a highchair or infant seat. Examiners should sit at the child's level so they can make direct eye contact easily. For toddlers, a child-size table and chairs are needed for the child and examiner (Bagnato & Neisworth, 1991), or the toddler can be seated on the parent's lap. If an examiner is not seated at the child's level this may intimidate a child, interfere with observing the child's signals, and disrupt attending.

Rather than sit in a chair, toddlers prefer to toddle or walk about, making standardized testing difficult or impossible. Use of fast pacing, highly salient toys, and being responsive to the child's signals, help with this problem. A child-size chair (preferably one with arms), a highchair with a tray, or seating the child on the parent's lap at a table also helps. Testing a toddler seated on the floor may work initially, but rarely will a toddler remain in one spot for long!

Establishing Rapport

With the youngest children, if building rapport lasts more than several minutes, examiners may miss times when the children are most alert and ready to participate. If infants and toddlers are presented with a highly salient toy and given a few minutes to investigate the object, they usually will be intrigued and ready to proceed with testing. This is true even for those fearful of strangers. For fearful children, having the parent hand the child the toy may be more effective. Thus, the presentation of interesting toys, and responsiveness to children's verbal and nonverbal signals, typically are more important than extensive rapport building.

Noncompliance

As Culbertson and Willis (1993) noted, it is normal for a toddler "to be more negative and to assert his or her will with persistence" and to "insist on playing with test materials in an idiosyncratic way rather than following the examiner's instructions" (p. 5). Such behavior is challenging for examiners. Often toddlers are unwilling to give up an interesting test item and say that the toy is "Mine!" when asked to change tasks. To enlist their cooperation Culbertson and Willis suggested that examiners present new materials before removing materials for the previous item. Allowing a child to play with the previous materials until you present new ones puts novelty on your side. We find it helpful to say, "Look!" and present the new item quickly with a surprised expression. This approach avoids leaving children unoccupied between items.

Certain test items will not be interesting for some infants and toddlers. In this case response momentum (Nevin, 1992) can be quite effective. This procedure involves presenting several trials of a task the child enjoys (i.e., to get momentum in responding) and then quickly slipping in a trial for the item that was not interesting. This last trial should be followed quickly by a trial or two of the more interesting task and then, perhaps another trial on the task that was not interesting. Following standardized testing procedures is necessary, but flexibility in using them is important with infants and critical with toddlers.

Adults' Presence

At least one adult, usually the parent, is present during testing of young children. Their presence can make it difficult to focus intently on the child and administer tests efficiently because parents also require attention. Some anxious parents interfere by prompting the child, and some demand considerable attention themselves. There is no strategy we know of to make it easy to attend to a child and the parent at the same time. However, considering that the parent's presence can be a advantage may make this situation less stressful.

With guidance from the examiner, on several tests parents can assist by administering a few items, especially for children who are fearful or withdrawn. Also, parents' presence provides a sample of the parent-child interaction, information that can be helpful when considering whether the parent will be able to assist with intervention. The greatest advantage in having parents present, however, is the opportunity it provides to enhance parents' feelings of competence by modeling appropriate ways of interacting with the child, skills a child has learned and those that are appropriate to teach next, and teaching procedures to be used. Thus, assessment can function as intervention (Bradley-Johnson, 1982; Parker & Zuckerman, 1990). Parents typically are very observant when their child is tested and modeling is one of the most effective techniques for parent education (Parker & Zuckerman, 1990).

To ensure that assessment enhances parents' feelings of competence, examiners must communicate effectively. Jargon should be avoided (Sattler, 2001); this is essential and cannot be overemphasized. Parker and Zuckerman (1990) suggested that the following methods can enhance parents' confidence in helping with their child's instruction and convey to them that they are a valuable resource for their child. First, demonstrate an interest in the parents as individuals, i.e., acknowledge them as more than the child's parents. Ask about their child's development, request that they administer some test items (e.g. "To get the baby's best performance, would you try this with him"), and comment on positive things they have done for the child (e.g., "Thank you for coming for Tamara's appointment today"). Other helpful approaches include encouraging parents to ask questions, asking whether they think the child's test performance was typical, acknowledging their observations of the child, and asking what parts of the assessment were helpful to them. Feedback from parents regarding what was helpful can improve examiners' communication skills and assessment methods. The information also may indicate how much information the parents understood. Any comments suggesting that the parents missed important points or misinterpreted something can then be clarified. Finally, if parents will be asked to assist with intervention, some recommendations should be discussed and modeled during the assessment. Having parents try recommendations, and tactfully providing feedback, may improve their instructional methods. A rationale for each recommendation should be given because the educational relevance of some recommendations may not be obvious to parents. For example, when suggesting that parents imitate their baby's vocal sounds, explain that imitating these sounds can increase the frequency of sounds the baby makes, sounds that are important prespeech skills.

TO CORRECT OR NOT TO CORRECT?

Whether or not to correct the age of infants and toddlers for prematurity is not clear from the literature. Questions about the validity of standard gestational age assessment methods (Dipietro & Allen, 1991) cloud the issue. Consequently, it may not be possible to accurately determine whether some children are premature or how premature some children are.

Many studies have examined correcting test scores for prematurity. Siegel (1983), for example, found that through the first year, corrected scores were better predictors of performance at ages 3 and 5 years, but from 12 months on uncorrected scores usually correlated better with performance at 3 and 5 years. Barrera, Rosenbaum, and Cunningham (1987) compared full-term and high-birth weight preterm infants and observed that performance of preterm infants was lower at 4 and 8 months than that of full-term infants, but no difference was noted between the groups by 12 months. However, they found that lower birth weight preterm infants (less than 1,500 grams) performed less well than full-term infants even through 16 months of age. Blasco's (1989) review of research suggested that half a correction was appropriate after 4 months and no correction was needed after 18–24 months, depending on prematurity. Likewise, Roid and Sampers (2004) found that no correction was necessary after 24 months. Because results differ regarding the degree of correction needed, and the upper age level for which correction is necessary, additional studies are required to clarify these issues.

Based on these studies, in general, full correction for prematurity seems appropriate through 11 months, and no correction seems necessary from 24 months on, except perhaps for infants with very low birth weight. From 12 to 24 months, the need for correction is unclear. Calculation of both corrected and uncorrected scores for some children seems warranted, so that both results can be used in decision making. However, if a manual for a norm-referenced test has instructions for correcting for prematurity, these instructions must be followed to obtain valid results. Methods of adjusting age vary with different tests.

REVIEWS OF ASSESSMENT OPTIONS

In any assessment, information from direct testing should be augmented by information obtained from reviewing medical and school records, interviewing parents and professionals familiar with the children, and systematically observing children in their natural environments. This information is critically important for infants and toddlers. Further, because of the limited number of measures for these children and concerns about current measures, more than one test should be used. Also, because of the interdependent nature of cognitive, motor, social, adaptive, and communication skills, an inter- or trans-disciplinary approach is necessary to diagnose problems, formulate instructional plans, and evaluate the effectiveness of instruction.

Following is a detailed review of cognitive measures for children from birth to age 2. Comprehensive norm-referenced measures are emphasized, however, examples of the many options available for screening are included also. Several tests assess areas besides cognitive development, but because of the focus of this chapter, only the cognitive sections are reviewed.

To evaluate reliability, the criteria suggested by Salvia and Ysseldyke (2004a) of .80 for screening measures and .90 for measures used to make important educational decisions were employed. Bracken's (1987) criteria were used for evaluating floors and item gradients. He suggested that adequate floors discriminate levels of performance up to at least two standard deviations below the mean; for adequate item gradients he suggested that each raw score point should be equal to or less than one third of a standard deviation. If these criteria for floors and item gradients are not met, tests will not be sensitive to varying levels of performance.

Screening Measures

Screening tests are designed to determine which children need more comprehensive assessment. We reviewed two of the many screening tests as examples. To be of use, screening tests should be easy to administer and score, relatively inexpensive, and include information obtained from directly observing or testing a child as well as input from the child's caregivers. Technical adequacy is important, particularly information indicating whether test results correctly identify children. In other words, knowing the percent of false positives (percent of children identified as delayed who were found to have no developmental problems in the more comprehensive assessment) and percent of false negatives (percent with developmental delays who were not identified by the screening measure) helps evaluate the usefulness of a test.

Denver–II

The Denver–II (Frankenburg et al., 1996) consists of 125 items, divided into four domains: personal-social, fine motor-adaptive, language, and gross motor. In the manual the test is described as a "general developmental screening test" (p. 16) for children from 1 month to 6 years. However, Frankenburg (2002) emphasized its use as "a growth chart of development" and de-emphasized its use as a test. This is one of the most popular screening measures, particularly for medical clinics (Wyly, 1997). Most items are scored through direct testing, but parent input can be used for 40 items. The child's performance is described as normal, questionable, abnormal, or untestable. Children in the abnormal category are referred for additional assessment. Administration time is approximately 10–20 minutes. Materials include a training manual, technical manual, videotapes, test forms, and a small test kit.

Although the norms are based on a large sample of 2,096 children, with more than 1,000 children from 0–13 months, and more than 300 from 13–24 months, a representative, national sample was not obtained. In terms of geographic distribution 49.5% were from Denver, Colorado and 50.4% from counties outside of Denver. Boys made up about half the sample, but compared with U.S. Census data, there were too few children from rural areas, too many Hispanic-Americans, and too few children with parents with more than a twelfth grade education.

Reliability and validity data are limited. Reliability was examined for only 107 of the 125 items. For inter-rater reliability data indicate $k \geq .75$. Test-retest was examined with a 7–10 day interval and for 63 items $k \geq .75$ and for 44 items $k < .75$. No large validity study has been conducted with the Denver–II (Wyly, 1997). However, when the Denver–II was compared with the Bayley Scales of Infant Development–Second Edition, results yielded similar classifications (Bayley, 1993). Unfortunately, data on percent of false positives and false negatives are lacking.

Developmental Assessment of Young Children

The Developmental Assessment of Young Children (DAYC; Voress & Maddox, 1998) is for children from birth through 5 years, 11 months. This battery consists of five subtests: Cognitive, Communication, Social-Emotional, Physical Development, and Adaptive Behavior. The 78-item Cognitive subtest covers skills such as attention, memory, and discrimination and requires about 10–20 minutes to administer. Items can be scored based on observation of the child, direct testing, or by interviewing caregivers. Subtest results can be described as standard scores ($M = 100$, $SD = 15$), percentiles, or age equivalents. Materials consist of the examiner's manual and a scoring form.

The norm sample of 1,269 children included 191 from birth to age 1 and 250 from age 1–2. Demographic characteristics of the sample were similar to1996 U.S.Census data in terms of geographic distribution, gender, race, residence, ethnicity, and parents' income and educational background; 7% had disabilities. Thus, a nationally representative sample was obtained.

Internal consistency coefficients for the Cognitive subtest from birth–23 months range from .91–.97. Coefficients for subgroups (boys, girls, European American, African American, Hispanic, at-risk, and disabled) range from .98–.99. Two test-retest reliability studies each used a 15-day retest interval and children from 15–39 months. One correlation was .98, the other .99. These coefficients exceed the minimum of .80 for acceptable reliability for screening measures.

In terms of content validity, item format was based on a review of the literature, and 20 tests for young children were reviewed to assist in item development. Conventional item analysis was used to select the final items. For criterion-related validity, Cognitive subtest results were compared with the Screen of the Battelle Developmental Inventory (Newborg, Stock, Wnek, Guidubaldi, & Svinicki, 1988) for ages 2–58 months, and with the Gesell (Knobloch, Stevens, & Malone, 1987) for 3–58 months. Correlations were .61 and .51 respectively. In terms of construct validity scores increase with age, discriminate between a normal group of children and one at-risk as well as a group with identified disabilities. Correlations of the Cognitive subtest and the other DAYC subtests range from .84–.94. Unfortunately no information is available for the Cognitive subtest or the overall DAYC results in terms of false positive or false negatives.

Comprehensive Measures

Battelle Developmental Inventory-Second Edition

The Battelle Developmental Inventory–Second Edition (BDI–2; Newborg, 2005) retains the multidisciplinary emphasis of the original BDI (Newborg, Stock, Wnek, Guidibaldi, & Svinicki, 1987) in covering five domains: Adaptive, Personal-Social, Communication, Motor, and Cognitive, and now includes 13 subdomains. The age range, from birth through 7 years, remains as well as inclusion of a Screening Test. The content has been updated considerably to reflect current research. For children under age 2 the Cognitive Domain consists of two subdomains: Attention and Memory as well as Perception and Concepts.

Materials include the examiner's manual, an Item Test Book for each domain, Record Forms, Student Workbooks, Presentation Cards, a Stimulus Book, a plastic Puzzle/Strips Sheet, many toys (some of which were made specifically for the BDI-2), and a carrying case. Additional materials are needed for the Screening Test. The entire inventory can be administered in about 1 hour for children under age 2. A few items are timed.

Domain results are described as quotients ($M = 100$, $SD = 15$), subdomain results as scaled scores ($M = 10$, $SD = 3$). Both results also can be described as percentiles or age equivalents. The Cognitive Domain is said to assess "abilities most commonly thought of as 'mental' or 'intellectual'" (p. 19). The 30-item Attention and Memory subdomain (AM) for birth to age 6 taps abilities that involve attending to visual and auditory stimuli and re-trieving "information when given relevant clues to do so." The 40-item Perception and Concepts subdomain (PC) is for birth through age 7; for infants sensorimotor skills are assessed, some of which are of a social nature.

All instructions for administering and scoring the BDI–2 appear on the protocol and are clearly written and easy to follow. Items may be scored by direct testing, observation, or in-formation obtained from interviews. Which methods can be used to score a particular item are indicated on the protocol, e.g., for some items either of two methods or both may be used.

Standardization.   Data for norms were collected over 14 months from 2002–2003 for 2,500 children, with 125 participants for each 3-month interval from birth through 23 months.

For children under age 2 the sample was similar to U.S. Census data in terms of gen-der, race, ethnicity, urban/rural residence, and geographic distribution. This was true even for data presented for three variables simultaneously (e.g., age, race, and region). Children receiving special education services for more than 50% of the day, and those with special medical or educational services were excluded from the norm sample. Norm tables are pre-sented in 1-month intervals for subdomains through 23 months; a single norm table is used for domain scores from birth through 23 months. The BDI–2 has a large, representative norm sample with the exception of the exclusion of children with disabilities, including those with cognitive delays.

Reliability.   Internal consistency coefficients for the Cognitive Domain for birth–23 months range from .83–.94; for the AM Subdomain .90–.95, and for the PC Subdomain .58–.84.

No test-retest reliability data for the Cognitive Domain or its subdomains are presented for children under age 2. Thus, stability of results for infants and toddlers is unknown.

Data describing agreement for scoring items from protocols are presented. However, no data are presented for inter-scorer reliability in terms of having two examiners present during testing with each independently scoring a child's responses.

Validity.   Items are based on an extensive review of the literature, and many re-searchers, experts in assessment, and examiners reviewed the items. Item analysis and numerous model-data-fit statistics from the Rasch model were used to evaluate items.

Criterion-related validity for the Cognitive Domain with samples including children under age 2 was examined by comparing BDI–2 results with those of the BDI; the corre-lation was .64. BDI–2 results also were compared with those of the Bayley Scales of Infant Development-Second Edition (BSID–II: Bayley, 1993) resulting in a correlation of .61.

For children under age 2 discriminate validity studies for the Cognitive Domain indicate that those with developmental delays and those who were premature had mean scores more than one standard deviation below the mean. Those with a speech/language delay had a mean of 85.

In terms of construct validity, raw scores increase with age, and domains and subdomains correlate at a reasonable level. Differential item functioning and review by experts were used to evaluate item bias. Biased items were deleted.

No predictive validity studies are yet available on this version of the test. Until such data are available, caution is warranted in interpreting results.

Floors, Item Gradients, and Norm Table Cut-Offs.   Floors for the Cognitive Domain and both subdomains are adequate, except for the Attention and Memory subdomain where an adequate floor begins at 1 month rather than birth. Item gradients seem adequate except under 6 months of age for raw scores of 4 or lower on the subdomains. No problems were found in cut-off scores for adjacent norm tables for subdomains. No problems were noted for the Cognitive Domain results because only 1 table is used for the entire age range from birth–23 months. However, for cut-off scores between the Domain Quotient table for birth–23 months and the adjacent table that begins at 24 months, substantial changes were evident. If the same sum of scaled scores were entered in the table for a child 23 months, 30 days and in the table for 24 months, 0 days, quotients that differ by 6 to 35 standard score points are evident. This problem occurs for the sum of scaled scores from 12 through 38. For example, a sum of scaled scores of 20 yields a DQ of 100 at 23 months and a DQ of 82 at 24 months; a sum of scaled scores of 35 yields a DQ of 143 at 23 months and a DQ of 109 at 24 months.

Concerns.   Whether BDI–2 results are intended for diagnostic purposes is unclear. According to the manual, the inventory "may be used to identify and describe developmental delay. . . It is not intended as an instrument for diagnosing specific disabilities, such as mental retardation. . . . However it is appropriate for a multidisciplinary assessment team to use results from the BDI–2 as they determine the nature and extent of a child's disability" (p. 13). Identifying developmental delay and "determining the nature of a child's disability" could include diagnosing mental retardation. The manual also states that "Professionals who use the scores in determining eligibility for services must be cognizant of federal, state, and local eligibility criteria for early childhood services" (p. 10). Determining eligibility for services often requires specific diagnosis. The Cognitive Domain is said to assess intellectual abilities (p. 19), and information in the manual indicates that "a teacher could administer the Cognitive Domain" (p. 27). State regulations and position statements from professional organizations should be considered if results are used for diagnosis or to qualify a child for special services to ensure that a teacher has adequate training and credentialing to use the results for these purposes.

The inventory is said to be ideal for developing individualized educational programs, but considering the test's age range and the number of items for the combination of the cognitive subdomains, this assertion is questionable for infants and toddlers. BDI–2 results may, however, suggest general areas to assess further with a more comprehensive measure.

The BDI–2 has several timed items. Such items pose problems for some children with motor problems, may interfere with observing the child, and make administration and scoring more difficult.

For many items options are given for obtaining information for scoring (observation, direct testing, or from interviews). However, no data are presented in the manual to suggest that the same results will be obtained through the different assessment methods. For example, would an item be scored the same if the information were obtained from a caregiver interview and from direct testing of a child? The different assessment options may affect the validity of the results.

Summary.   The BDI–2 is a substantial improvement over the BDI in terms of the content of items and the inventory's technical adequacy. A large, representative norm sample was obtained, but no children at risk for, or with delayed development, were included.

Internal consistency for the Cognitive Domain is quite good, but no test-retest reliability data are provided for children under age 2, leaving examiners uncertain of the inventory's stability for infants and toddlers. No interscorer reliability data are presented based on the scoring of two examiners being present during testing and who independently scored protocols.

A considerable amount of information is presented to support the validity of the Cognitive Domain. For infants and toddlers, BDI–2 results correlate moderately with the BDI and BSID–2. Discriminate validity data for various clinical groups support use of the inventory. Items found to be biased were eliminated. However, predictive validity evidence is lacking. Floors are adequate; item gradients are generally adequate, except for the lowest scores for infants less than 6 months old. Cut-off scores for adjacent norm tables for subdomains are not problematic. However, for the Cognitive Domain large standard score changes are evident if a child's age changes by 1 day for many scores for 23 versus 24 months.

The intended use of Cognitive Domain results is unclear from the description in the manual. Considering the age range (birth–7 years, 11 months) for the inventory, as in the BDI, the number of items for children under age 2 is limited for the purpose of planning instruction.

A strength of the BDI–2 is the format which makes it suitable for a multi-disciplinary approach. Many attractive toys for young children are included to enhance children's motivation. Additional studies of the inventory's stability as well as interscorer reliability for the youngest children would be valuable.

Bayley Scales of Infant and Toddler Development–Third Edition

The most well known measure of cognitive development for infants and young children is the Bayley Scales of Infant and Toddler Development–Third Edition (Bayley–III; Bayley, 2006). The test is for children from 1–42 months of age and includes five domains: Cognitive, Language, Motor, Social-Emotional, and Adaptive. A Behavior Observation Inventory completed by the examiner and caregiver describes children's behavior during the assessment and at home.

The 91 items on the Cognitive Domain assess a variety of skills including memory, exploratory behavior, and sensorimotor development. Twenty-one items (23%) are timed. On this edition of the Bayley scales no vocalization is required on any of the cognitive items, a strength of the test because it can be used with children who cannot or will not vocalize during testing, or those whose speech cannot be understood. According to the Administration Manual, the test ". . . is not designed to be used as a measure of intelligence or to predict academic achievement" (p. 7), instead it is described as assessing "developmental functioning" (p.1).

Materials include an Administration Manual, a Technical Manual, a Stimulus Book, Record Form, a Social-Emotional and Adaptive Behavior Questionnaire, a Caregiver

Report used to interpret results to caregivers, a Scoring Assistant with PDA administration and the accompanying User's Guide, and a large kit of toys. The toys are of interest to young children and facilitate their involvement in the tasks. The test kit has wheels to make it easier to transport. Facial tissue, five small coins, food pellets, index cards, safety scissors, standard stairs, a stopwatch, and unlined white paper are to be provided by examiners. Optional training materials are purchased separately. These materials include a Fundamental Administration Videotape describing basic information on administration and scoring, and an Enhanced Administration and Scoring Resource DVD describing administration in more detail, including items that are difficult to score. For children less than 12 months of age, administration takes about 50 minutes for the entire test, and about 90 minutes are required for older children.

Results for the Cognitive domain are described as either a scaled score ($M = 10$, $SD = 3$) or as a Composite score ($M = 100$, $SD = 15$). Other options for describing results of this domain include percentiles, age equivalents, and growth scores (used to describe development over time ($M = 500$, $SD = 100$).

Abbreviated directions for administering and scoring items are printed on the Record Form. However, the Bayley–III should not be given until an examiner is familiar with the directions as described in the Administration Manual. To obtain valid results, these longer and more detailed directions are required. How a child should be positioned varies with the item administered; 11 different positions are used on the test. The position needed for each item is described in the Administration Manual, but not on the Record Form. Each item is scored 1 or 0. Because of the complex directions, even after administering the test a number of times, examiners would do well to periodically review directions in the Administration Manual or those on the Enhanced Administration and Scoring DVD to prevent examiner drift and ensure accurate administration of the test.

Standardization. Data for norms were collected from January through October of 2004. The sample of 1,700 children included 100 for each age group. The children's demographic characteristics in terms of sex, geographic region, race/ethnicity, and parents' education were very similar to the U.S. Census data, even when stratified on several variables simultaneously. Urban-rural residence was not addressed. Children with atypical development were not included in the original norm sample, however, a "representative proportion" of these children who participated in validity studies (about 10% of the overall sample) were later added to the norm sample. Unfortunately the percentages of children with various behavioral, mental, or physical disabilities was not described.

Reliability. The 12 coefficients describing internal consistency for children under age 2 range from .79 − .93; five of the 12 coefficients are .90 or higher.

Test-retest reliability was evaluated with a mean retest interval of 6 days (range 2–15 days). The sample consisted of 197 children from four age groups. For the Cognitive domain three age groups were included for children under 24 months of age. For the 2–4 month age group the correlation corrected for restricted range was .71, for the 9–13 month group the corrected correlation was .77, and for the 19–26 month group the corrected correlation was .86. Further, the conventional retest interval is 2 weeks and the shorter the interval, the higher the estimate of reliability (Salvia & Ysseldyke, 2004a). We think that the exceptionally rapid rate of development at these young ages may justify a somewhat shorter retest interval. However, a retest interval as short as 2 days for some children seems short, even for infants. Because all correlations for the Cognitive Domain for children under age

2 are less than .90 even over relatively short time periods, results should be very cautiously interpreted.

Although interscorer reliability data were reported for the second edition of the test, and these data are reported for the Adaptive Behavior Scale for the Bayley–III, no interscorer reliability data are reported for the Bayley–III Cognitive Domain.

Validity.   Based on information obtained from experts who reviewed the second edition of the (Bayley, 1993), and a review of the literature, items on the Cognitive Domain no longer require vocal responses, a number of items, administration procedures, and materials were updated, some previous items were eliminated, and several new items were added. Also, a number of administration procedures, materials, and items were updated, some items were eliminated, and several new items were added. These revisions make the test more appealing to children and make the test somewhat easier to administer and score. Unfortunately, 22 of the 91 items are still timed.

In terms of construct validity, intercorrelation of the Cognitive Domain results with the language and motor domains resulted in correlations ranging from .39 to .51. Confirmatory factor analysis indicated that the best fit for the scales was a 3-factor model: Motor, Language, and Cognitive.

For children under age 2, concurrent validity was addressed only by comparing Bayley–III results for the Cognitive Domain with the Mental, Motor, and Behavior Rating Scale results from the second edition of the test (Bayley, 1993). The correlations were .60, .40, and .38, respectively.

Several studies to evaluate the criterion-related validity of the Bayley–III Cognitive Domain included children less than 2 years of age. Comparison with results from the Preschool Language Scale–Fourth Edition (PLS–4; Zimmerman, Steiner, & Pond, 2002) resulted in a correlation of .57 for the PLS-4 Total Language Composite, .50 for the Auditory Comprehension Subscale, and .59 for the Expressive Communication Subscale. Comparison of the Bayley–III Cognitive Domain results with the Peabody Developmental Motor Scales–Second Edition (PDMS–II; Folio & Fewell, 2000) resulted in a correlation of .45 for Total Motor, .36 for Fine Motor, and .42 for Gross Motor. Correlations with the various PDMS–II subtests ranged from −.02 to .45. Comparison of the Cognitive Domain results with those of the Adaptive Behavior Assessment System–Second Edition (ABAS–II; Harrison & Oakland, 2003) resulted in the following correlations with the ABAS–II Composites: General Adaptive .36, Conceptual .49, Social .23, and Practical .22.

To examine the clinical utility of the Bayley–III a number of studies were carried out with nine special populations whose performance was compared with that of a matched group from the norm sample. These populations included children diagnosed with Down syndrome, Pervasive Developmental Disorder, Cerebral Palsy, Specific Language Impairment, at risk for developmental delay, asphyxiation at birth, prenatal alcohol exposure, small for gestational age, and premature or low-birth weight. On the Cognitive Domain children from the special populations scored significantly lower than their matched control for all comparisons except the small for gestational-age group and the premature group.

Potential item bias was examined by having several groups of experts review the items by evaluating the performance of African American and Hispanic children during the tryout phase of test development and during collection of the norms using the Mantel-Haenszel bias analysis. Results from these analyses were not presented in the manual.

No predictive validity data are yet available for the Bayley–III. Studies indicate that the previous version had very limited predictive validity for infants and toddlers, even for those with delayed development (e.g., Fagan & Singer, 1983; Sternberg, Grigorenko, & Bundy, 2001; Wyly, 1997). As with the BDI-2, caution in interpreting results is warranted until such data are available to evaluate the test's predictive ability.

Floors, Item Gradients, and Norm Table Cut-off Points.   Adequate floors for the Bayley–III Cognitive domain begin at 16 days of age and item gradients are adequate. The cut-off points for adjacent norm tables result in very little change when a child's age changes by one day. This is a strength of the test and one that is difficult to achieve for the youngest children.

Concerns.   Consideration of a child's performance on the various Bayley–III domains and subdomains may provide general information for planning instruction, however, the item sample is too limited to use for the purpose of determining which skills need instruction. In addition, the educational relevance of some cognitive items is questionable. For example, completing pegboards or puzzles within a time limit does not appear to be prerequisite to later cognitive or academic performance and evidence to support the predictive validity of such skills is lacking.

Norm-referenced scores go as low as 55. If lower scores were available the test would be more useful with children who are lower functioning.

Considering the distractability and limited attention span of infants and toddlers, the timed items on the Bayley–III can be problematic. On the prior edition of the test, Chandlee, Heathfield, Salganik, Damokosh, and Radcliffe (2002) found that children could pass or fail some items because of a split-second discrimination, and examiner errors in timing could affect the resulting scores. Also, attending to a stopwatch competes with observing the child. For some children with motor problems timed items would be inappropriate. Further, Gyurke, Lynch, Lagasse, and Lipsitt (1992) concluded that timing items on the Bayley (1969) added little unique information about infants' performance.

Summary.   A very large, nationally representative sample make up the norm group for the Bayley–III, and children with atypical development were added to this sample. The only demographic data missing are for urban-rural residence. Toys for the test are attractive and the tasks playful, making it easy to engage children. This edition is easier to administer and score than previous editions and the kit is easier to transport. However, examiners should periodically review directions in the Administration Manual to ensure accurate administration because important details appear only in the manual. The fact that no vocal response is required on the Cognitive Domain is a considerable improvement as well.

Reliability data are a concern. Internal consistency results are mixed. Test-retest reliability is too low, even over short time periods, and interscorer reliability data are lacking.

In terms of validity the Bayley–III Cognitive Domain items have been improved considerably. Results correlate moderately with the previous version of the test and low to moderate correlations were found with measures of language, of motor skills, and of adaptive behavior. Efforts were made to eliminate biased items, but these results were not described. Studies with clinical groups of young children indicate that most receive lower scores on the Bayley–III than a matched group from the norm sample. Obtaining good predictive validity for the youngest children on previous versions of the Bayley scales has been difficult, but predictive validity data are needed if results for the Cognitive Domain are used for diagnostic purposes. The test's floors and item gradients are both acceptable.

Cognitive Domain results provide only very general information for instructional purposes because the item sample is limited, 22% of the items are timed, and some the items are of questionable educational relevance. If the test is ". . . not designed to be used as a measure of intelligence or to predict academic achievement." (p. 7), it is not clear what aspects of cognition are being measured.

Nancy Bayley's scale was a remarkable pioneering effort that clearly advanced the assessment of mental development for the youngest children. Each edition of the scale has been an improvement and this edition is a substantial improvement. However, caution is still needed in interpreting results because of limitations with the reliability and validity of the scale.

Cognitive Abilities Scale–Second Edition

The first edition of the Cognitive Abilities Scale (CAS; Bradley-Johnson, 1987) was designed for 2- and 3-year-old children; the second (CAS–2; Bradley-Johnson & Johnson, 2001) extends the age range from 3 months through 3 years. The CAS–2 consists of two forms: an Infant Form for 3–23 months, and a Preschool Form for 2- and 3-year-olds.

The 79-item Infant Form has three sections: Exploration of Objects, Communication with Others, and Initiation and Imitation. Exploration of Objects consists of 25 items addressing methods of exploring the environment using different modalities. The 25 items on the Communication with Others section cover both receptive and expressive skills. The Initiation and Imitation section consists of 29 items. Willingness to initiate activities with objects and to imitate others' behaviors are covered on this section.

Materials include an examiner's manual, a Record Booklet, and numerous toys contained in an attache case. Administration time ranges from about 20–25 minutes. No items are timed.

A General Cognitive Quotient (GCQ; $M = 100$, $SD = 15$) can be used to describe overall performance on all test items. There are no subtest scores. However, for children who cannot or will not vocalize or talk and those whose speech cannot be understood, results can be described as a Nonvocal Cognitive Quotient (NCQ: $M = 100$; $SD = 15$). The NCQ is based on performance on the nonvocal items. Either result can be described as a percentile or age equivalent also.

A unique aspect of the test is that each item is presented three times in succession to address the inconsistent nature of infants and toddlers' responding, and ensure an adequate sample of skills for instructional planning. To assist in selecting skills for instruction, the age at which at least 75% of the norm sample demonstrated each skill three times is indicated on the Record Book. To ease administration, all directions for administering and scoring the test appear in the Record Book.

Standardization. The CAS-2 was normed on 1,106 children from October 1997 through August 1999. The number of children per age level ranges from 248 through 305. The children's demographic characteristics are similar to those reported by the U.S. Bureau of the Census (1997) in terms of race, geographic region, gender, race, ethnicity, parents' educational background, and urban/rural residence. Children with disabilities were included in the sample (1% had been diagnosed as mentally impaired and 5% had other disabilities). Demographic characteristics also appear to be representative for different ages. Norm tables are presented in 1-month intervals through 12 months and 2-month intervals through 23 months.

Reliability. Internal consistency data are presented in 3-month intervals. GCQ coefficients are .90 or higher, except at 21–23 months where the coefficient is .88. The GCQ internal consistency is adequate for making individual decisions across all but one age interval, and NCQ results are less reliable (Salvia & Ysseldyke, 2004b). Three NCQ coefficients reached at least .90, and four range from .84–.89. Thus, items appear to be closely related.

Stability reliability data are presented for each age level. For infants from 3–11 months a 1-week retest interval was used; the GCQ correlation was .81, the NCQ correlation .79. Because these correlations are less than .90, results for these ages should be interpreted cautiously. However, for children from 12–23 months a 2-week retest interval was used; the GCQ correlation was .90, the NCQ .93. Results for ages 12–23 months appear to be very stable.

Interscorer reliability was evaluated with 79 children from 3 months through 3 years old. Correlations are presented by age level. For 3–11 months the GCQ correlation was .94, and the NCQ .93. For 12–23 months the GCQ correlation was .95, and the NCQ .93. These data suggest good interscorer reliability.

Validity. For content validity, several considerations underlie the development of CAS–2 items. First, items are based on research suggesting that the skills tested are relevant to cognitive development for young children. The content validity of each item is addressed in the manual. Second, the test is playful and many engaging toys are included to enhance participation. Third, because timing of items adds little unique information (Gyurke et al., 1992), interferes with observing a child, and inaccurate timing can impact results (Chandlee et al., 2002), no items are timed. Finally, items are grouped into three sections for the purpose of organizing the information to aid in planning instruction. Item analysis also was used to select items that discriminate well.

For construct validity, scores on the Infant Form of the CAS–2 are shown to increase with age. Results indicate that the means for both genders as well as for European American, African American, and Hispanic American children fall within the average range. Also, mean scores for children with physical impairments fall within the average range, whereas results for children identified as mentally impaired fell within the below average range. A comparison of the CAS–2 GCQ with the Receptive-Expressive Emergent Language Test–Fourth Edition (REEL–4) for 6–18 month olds found correlations of .59 for Receptive Language, .38 for Expressive Language, and .48 for the Language Ability Composite (Bzoch, League, & Brown, 2003).

Criterion-related validity was addressed by comparing results for the Infant Form with those of the BSID–II. The correlation for the CAS-2 GCQ was .66, and for the NCQ .62.

Logistic regression was used to evaluate bias. Only one item was found to be of concern. An examination of this item indicated that it did not warrant elimination; thus, it was retained.

One study (Johnson & Bradley-Johnson, 2002) examined the predictive ability of the CAS–2 Infant Form. Children were given the CAS–2 Infant Form when they were less than 24 months old. They were retested on average 22.9 months later (*SD* = 1.5) on the CAS–2 Preschool Form when they were either 2 or 3 years old. The CAS–2 Infant and Preschool Forms have no overlapping items, use different formats for testing skills, and each has separate technical adequacy data. The two forms could be separate tests, but are published together under the same name. Thus, these results can be considered construct stability or predictive validity. The correlation for children under 12 months was .28 (.46 when corrected for restricted range), and for children from 12–23 months was .65 (.76 when corrected for restricted range). Anastasi and Urbina (1997) noted that for cognitive assessment of young children, "Negligible correlations may be found over intervals even as short as three months, and correlations with performance on the same or different scales at the age of two years and beyond are usually insignificant" (p. 329). Correlations is this study were significant over a 2-year period. Results for 12–23 months were particularly strong. For infants under 12 months results were lower, but tend to support the stability of the construct even for the youngest infants.

Floors, Item Gradients, and Norm Table Cut-off Points.   Floors and item gradients for both the GCQ and NCQ are adequate. Lidz (2003) raised the issue of changes in scores as a result of cut-off points in adjacent CAS-2 norm tables. In some cases, because of cut-off points in norm tables, quotients change up to 10 points if a child's age changes by one day. Although substantial, this is 2/3 of a standard deviation.

Concerns.   Although age equivalents are provided, GCQ and NCQ results do not go below 55. If lower quotients were available the test would be more useful for children who are lower-functioning.

Both Meikamp (2003) and Goldman (2003) suggested that further predictive validity evidence should be added. Subsequent to publication of the CAS–2, one predictive validity study (Johnson & Bradley-Johnson, 2002) described above has been published on the Infant Form, but additional studies are needed.

Summary.   A large, nationally representative sample made up the CAS–2 norm group, including children with identified cognitive impairments and developmental delays. Because the toys are highly salient and the tasks are playful, it is easy to engage infants and toddlers.

Internal consistency and interscorer results are good and presented by age level, but data for the NCQ are lower than for the GCQ. Data for stability also are presented by age level and are strong for 12–23 months, but less than .90 for 3–11 months. Consequently, results for children 3–11 months should be interpreted with this concern in mind.

The CAS–2 correlates well with the BSID–II. Data suggest that items are not biased for various subgroups of children. Results also correlate moderately with the REEL–4, a measure of early language development. The predictive ability of the test over about a 2-year period was very good for children 12–23 months of age, but not as strong for children under 12 months. Based on test-retest reliability and construct stability for children less than 12 months of age, CAS–2 results should be interpreted cautiously for these ages. For children 12–23 months, both the reliability and validity are strong. However, additional predictive validity studies are needed.

CAS–2 floors and items gradients are acceptable. The fact that cutoff points for adjacent norm tables sometimes may result in substantial changes in quotients is important to note.

The Nonvocal Cognitive Quotient option is an advantage for use with children who are unable to, or who will not vocalize, and those whose speech cannot be understood. The lack of timed items and having all directions for administering the test on the Record Book ease administration and free examiners to attend to a child's responses. Goldman (2003) concluded that directions are clear and straightforward and that the test is not complicated to learn to administer. However, Meikamp (2003) noted that considerable familiarization with CAS–2 materials is essential before use. Heeding suggestions from critiques of the CAS has made this version more user-friendly (Meikamp, 2003)

In addition to providing norm-referenced results, because each item is assessed three times, and items are based on research suggesting their importance for cognitive development, CAS–2 results can link assessment to instruction (HaileMariam, 2004). Salvia and Ysseldyke (2004b) concluded that the test seems useful for identifying cognitive strengths and weaknesses and targeting areas for intervention. In sum, Meikamp (2003) concluded that the CAS–2 can be used with "reasonable confidence."

Merrill-Palmer-Revised

The Merrill-Palmer–Revised (M-P–R; Roid & Sampers, 2004), is an update of the classic Merrill-Palmer Scale developed by Stutsman in 1931. The original scale began at 18 months; the current version is for children from 1 month through 6 years, 6 months. The M-P–R includes a Cognitive Battery, a Gross Motor Scale, and parent-report scales describing a child's social-emotional development, social-emotional temperament, expressive language, self-help/adaptive behavior, as well as scales completed by the examiner describing a child's expressive language and social-emotional problem indicators, and other supplementary scales. The Cognitive Battery consists of three scales: Cognitive, Fine Motor, and Receptive Language. The Receptive Language scale is not used until a child is at least 13 months old.

The entire Cognitive Battery includes 49 subtests, each consisting of 1–14 items. For the 18 subtests for children from 1–23 months, 5 have timed items. The Cognitive Scale is said to assess fluid reasoning and crystallized ability. Skills in manipulating materials and speed in correctly assembling materials are tapped by the Fine Motor Scale. The Receptive Language Scale assesses "the ability to understand, and follow, spoken directions and give nonverbal responses" (p. 5).

Materials include the examiner's manual, protocols, rating scales, an easel book (for children about 2–6 and older), a storage box for test forms, many toys, and a rolling case for transporting materials. Administration of the Cognitive Battery requires 30–40 minutes.

A Developmental Index (DI) is a summary score to describe overall performance on the three scales of the Cognitive Battery. Results can be described as standard scores ($M = 100$, $SD = 15$), percentiles, age equivalents, or as Rasch Growth Scores. Rasch Growth Scores are based on item response theory scaling and can demonstrate small improvements in performance that may not be evident with normed scores. Growth Scores are criterion referenced because achievement is compared to a child's prior performance on the M-P–R on a standard set of tasks. This information may be particularly useful for children who are very low functioning and who typically make slow progress. These scores also can help determine which tasks are too difficult, too easy, or at about an appropriate difficulty level for a child, information that may assist in planning instruction by defining strengths and difficulties.

From birth to 24 months the M-P–R does not require vocal expression by the child. Thus, the test can be used with those who cannot or will not vocalize during testing and with children whose speech is not understandable. If only the Cognitive and Fine Motor Domains are used, the test would be mostly nonverbal, requiring that the child understand only the words used in brief directions. When only these two domains are used a DI cannot be obtained. Materials needed for each item and shortened directions for administering the test appear on the record form. Instructions spoken to the child appear in both English and Spanish.

Standardization.   According to the manual, development of the M-P–R took place over 6 years, but the years of data collection are not indicated. Thus, the age of the norms is unclear. A sample of 1,068 children participated, with 195 for 1–12 months and 161 for 13–24 months. For children under age 2, the sample was similar to the 2000 U.S. Census data for gender, parent education, and racial/ethnic background for European Americans, Asian Americans, Native Americans, and Hispanic Americans. Based on numbers in one table, the percentage of parents with a high school education or GED in the sample is 24.1%, but the percentage reported in the table is 4.1%. Only 7.2% of children 1–12 months were African-American (14.9% in the census). Geographic distribution was representative except that for 1–12 months where only 6.7% were from the North East (17.8% in the census), and for 13–24 months 34.2% were from the West (23.6% in the census). "Highly significant" differences were found on the M-P-R when performance was examined for community size, with children in small towns and rural areas performing the highest. Although the data for urban/rural residence were used in that analysis, percentages for urban and rural children in the norm sample are not provided. The rationale for not including these data appears to be that "Most individually-administered tests published in recent years have not included community size" (p. 121). Children with physical, mental, or emotional impairments, who were premature, suffered severe birth trauma, or had other biological risk factors, who did not comprehend English adequately, or who did not live with either or both parents were excluded from the sample. One exception was a group of children whose primary language was Spanish. Norm tables are presented in 1-month intervals through 12 months and 2-month intervals through 24 months.

Reliability.   Internal consistency coefficients for the DI and each Cognitive Battery domain for children 1–24 months are high ranging from .90–.98.

Test-retest reliability for the Cognitive Battery was examined with 41 children from 3–70 months (12 were 0–12 months, 6 were 13–24 months) with a retest interval of approximately 3 weeks. Data were collapsed across age levels. Correlations were .89 for the DI, .87 for Cognitive, .90 for Receptive Language, and .90 for Fine Motor. Because data were collapsed, the stability of M-P–R results for a 1-year-old, for example, are unknown. The information presented is inadequate for evaluating the test's stability.

Growth Scale test information curves are presented for the DI and all but the Cognitive Scale. The curves indicate that test data are the least reliable for very young children; the DI curve is quite low for young children. Why an information curve is not presented for the Cognitive Scale is not addressed. No data are provided on interscorer reliability.

Validity.   In terms of content validity, the Uzgiris and Hunt (1975) exploratory play model and Carroll's (1993) model of cognitive abilities form the theoretical basis for most test items. When developing the scale the authors reviewed research on infant cognition, used item-response theory analysis and scaling verification, and incorporated input from content experts who reviewed the items, including those from various ethnic groups. As in the original version, many engaging toys are included, and hands-on activities are emphasized to encourage participation. Materials have been updated considerably and many were added for children under 18 months.

To evaluate the Cognitive Battery's criterion-related validity for children less than 2, results were compared with the BSID–II Mental Scale. For 24 infants 1–39 months old, correlations were .92 for the DI, .76 for Cognitive, .86 for Fine Motor, and .92 for Receptive Language. Thus, results of these tests appear to be closely related.

Discriminate validity was addressed by comparing results for the norm sample with those of several clinical groups. Data from three studies involved children under age 2. The mean standard score on the Cognitive Domain for children with a severe cognitive delay or mental retardation was 49.6, for children who were deaf or hard-of-hearing 92.5, and for those with a motor delay 76.5.

The accuracy of the M-P–R in predicting classification status for cognitive delay was very good when a cut point of 70 was used. In terms of construct validity, raw scores increase with age, and factor analysis supported combining the Cognitive, Fine Motor, and Receptive Language scales under the DI because they had high factor loadings on a single factor.

To evaluate possible item bias, differential item functioning was used. According to the manual, most problem items were eliminated; but results for these analyses were not presented. No long-term predictive validity data were available.

Floors, Item Gradients, and Norm Table Cut-offs.   The floors are adequate and standard scores go much lower than on other tests, at some ages as low as 10. Item gradient violations occur for raw scores of 4 or less for the DI (1–9 months) and the Cognitive Scale (1–10 months). For the Fine Motor Scale violations occur for most raw scores of 12 or less (1–23 months), and for Receptive Language for raw scores of 3 or less (13–23 months). However, most violations occur only with very low raw scores. In some cases, because of cut-off points in norm tables, standard scores change up to 7 or 8 points if a child's age changes by one day. Although substantial, this is 1/2 of a standard deviation.

Concerns.   Abbreviated instructions appear on the record book to aid administration. However, to obtain valid results the detailed information on administration and scoring in the manual is required. Descriptions in the manual are complicated and lengthy, sometimes requiring nearly half a page for one item. Many practice administrations using the manual appear necessary before one could administer and score items correctly using only information in the record book. Because of the complicated instructions, even experienced examiners would seem to benefit from reviewing information in the manual periodically to avoid examiner drift. For example, one scoring instruction states that if it is necessary to test backward to another subtest to obtain a basal, and if a basal is obtained in the middle of that subtest, the subtest should be completed. All items administered and completed correctly are to be counted, even if they are beyond the 10 basal points, and even if they appear after the 12 errors for the ceiling.

Considering the complexity of administering and scoring, it is curious that no data are presented on interscorer reliability. How consistently this test can be administered and scored by different examiners remains to be studied.

Examples are provided in the manual (p. 82) to clarify use of the Growth Scale. However, the number given for one figure is incorrect, the item numbers for several examples are not shown in the figures as suggested, and the growth scale locations noted do not correspond to those used in the figures. This information is more confusing than helpful.

Children who were premature, had an impairment, a biological risk factor, did not understand English adequately, or were not living with at least one parent were excluded from the norm sample. A major concern is that if these groups of children who were likely to receive low scores were excluded from the norms, how were standard scores ($M = 100$) as low as 10 obtained? Rather than basing these scores on data for children who were low functioning, the low scores must be based on extensive extrapolation, raising questions about their accuracy.

Although the test does not have as many timed items as the BSID–II, there are several. Timed items are inappropriate for some children with motor problems and, as noted previously, timing interferes with observing the child and complicates test administration and scoring.

Summary. The M–P–R is a long-overdue revision of the original test, a considerable improvement, and the revision extends the norms down to 1-month. The M–P–R retains the emphasis on hands-on activities as well as many up-dated versions of the original materials that are interesting for young children.

Unfortunately the years of data collection for the norms are not presented. For children 1–12 months the sample does not appear representative for African-Americans or for those from the Northeast, nor for 13–24 months for children from the West. Urban/rural residence was not described, although the authors found that children in the sample from rural areas scored significantly higher on the test. No children with risk factors were included in the sample.

The test does not require vocalization for children under age 2, making it one of the few tests appropriate for young children who cannot or will not vocalize or talk during testing or whose speech cannot be understood. Also, if only the Cognitive and Fine Motor Scales are administered, very little receptive language is required.

Internal consistency data are strong. Because test-retest data are collapsed across ages 3–70 months, evaluation of stability for a particular age level is not possible. Thus, examiners cannot be confident in the stability of M–P–R results. Results from Growth Scale test information curves suggest reliability is weak for young children, and information for the Cognitive Scale was omitted without an explanation.

Substantial information is provided to support content validity and the tasks are engaging for young children. Results for the Cognitive Battery correlate well with the BSID–II.

Studies with clinical groups indicate that children with various risk factors receive lower scores than the norm sample. Support is provided for combining the three domains under the Developmental Index. Efforts were made to eliminate biased items. However, no long-term predictive validity data are available.

M-P–R floors are acceptable. Some problems exist with item gradients for low raw scores. Cut-off points in adjacent norm tables result in relatively minimal changes in standard scores, about 7–8 points.

The timed items can be problematic for some children and for examiners. To ensure valid results, the lengthy, complicated directions for the M–P–R require considerable practice and perhaps occasional review by experienced examiners. Errors in the manual for some examples for interpreting results need correction. Because of the complicated nature of the administration and scoring directions, the lack of interscorer reliability data is particularly troublesome.

The M–P–R has a number of unique strengths, but unfortunately there are problems with the norm sample, reliability, and the basis for standard scores that go well below 50. Criterion-referenced Growth Scores can indicate small performance gains, help determine strengths and difficulties, and provide more sensitive results than norm-referenced scores. The revision is clearly an improvement and hopefully the concerns noted can be addressed in future revisions.

Mullen Scales of Early Learning

The Mullen Scales of Early Learning (MSEL; Mullen, 1995) are designed for children from birth through 68 months and are a combination and revision of the Infant MSEL (Mullen, 1989) and the Preschool MSEL (Mullen, 1992). The scale is based primarily on the author's information processing model and includes five scales: Gross Motor, Visual Reception, Fine Motor, Receptive Language, and Expressive Language.

General intelligence is said to be assessed by an Early Learning Composite, consisting of all but the Gross Motor Scale. This composite is made up of 124 untimed items. The Visual Reception Scale assesses visual discrimination, memory, and fine motor skills. The Fine Motor Scale addresses visual discrimination and memory with an emphasis on fine motor planning and control. The Receptive Language Scale covers "understanding of verbal directions, auditory-spatial and auditory-quantitative concepts, and general information" (manual, p. 11). The Expressive Language Scale assesses "spontaneous utterances, specific vocal or verbal responses to tasks, and high-level concept formation" (manual, p. 11).

Materials include the examiner's manual, an administration manual, a stimulus book, a toy kit, and a protocol. The toys are attractive to children, and the case is well designed and easy to carry. A few items listed in the manual must be provided by the examiner, e.g., paper, coins, and a small bench. Administration time for infants and toddlers is about 15–30 minutes.

Results for each of the scales can be described as T scores ($M = 50$, $SD = 10$), percentiles, or age equivalents. Results for the Early Learning Composite (ELC) can be described as a standard score ($M = 100$, $SD = 15$) or a percentile. Items are scored primarily by administering items to a child, but some may be scored based on interviewing parents, and parents may assist in administering several items.

Standardization.   Data for the norms were collected on 1,849 children from 1981–1986 and 1987–1989. Norms for 1–14 months are grouped in 2-month intervals and for 15–68 months in 6-month intervals. The number of children per age group ranged from 84 to 156. Demographic characteristics were similar to 1990 U.S. Census data in terms of gender, father's occupation, race/ethnicity, and urban-rural residence. However, the sample was not geographically representative because 40% were from the Northeast, 25% from the South, 20% from the West, and 15% from what was termed the North/South Central region. The Northeast was over represented, and the North/South Central and South were under represented. No participants from the North/South Central region from birth–14 months were included. The demographic characteristics are described by age also. No children with physical or mental impairments were part of the norm sample.

Reliability.   Internal consistency coefficients for birth to age 2 for the ELC range from .87–.94, with 8 of 10 reaching at least .90. Coefficients for the four ELC scales range from .53–.92, with most being less than .80.

Stability reliability data are presented for ages 1–24 months only for the separate scales, with a retest interval of approximately 1–2 weeks ($MD = 7$ days). Correlations for the four ELC scales range from .82–.85; data are not presented by age level. Correlations for these ELC scales for this age range are very high for interscorer reliability, ranging from .91–.98.

Validity.   Evidence in support of the theory on which the test is based is referenced to the manual for the earlier version of the MSEL. This evidence is not research based.

Construct validity data suggest that scores increase with age and that the scales are moderately intercorrelated. Factor analysis suggests one factor in support of the ELC as an overall performance measure.

Concurrent validity was examined with 6–15 month olds by comparing results for the ELC and its four scales to the MDI of the BSID (Bayley, 1969). The correlation for the ELC was .70; correlations with the four scales range from .53–.59. The Receptive and

Expressive Language Scales also were compared with the Auditory Comprehension and Verbal Ability scales on the Preschool Language Assessment (Zimmerman, Steiner, Evatt, & Pond, 1979) for children 15–59 months old. Correlations ranged from .72–.85. The MSEL Fine Motor Scale was compared with the Peabody Fine Motor Scale (Folio & Fewell, 1983) for 6–36 months. Correlations ranged from .65–.82 across age levels. Why more recent versions of these tests were not used is unclear. No predictive validity information is provided for the current edition for infants and toddlers, nor is there evidence indicating that items were examined for possible item bias.

Floors, Item Gradients, and Norm Table Cut-off Points.   Floors and item gradients for the ELC appear adequate. However, cut-off points for adjacent norm tables are an issue. If a child's age falls at a cut-off point in the norm tables, T scores can change up to 13 points in some cases. Eight T-score points are roughly equivalent to 15 points for a quotient.

Concerns.   The norms for the MSEL need updating. Like other norm-referenced measures for young children, the test's norms do not go below a T score of 20, which is comparable to a standard score of 55. Thus, the test is not likely to be very helpful in assessing the lowest functioning children.

The MSEL does not have an overall nonvocal score. The Visual Reception, Receptive Language, and Fine Motor Scales, however, do not require verbal expression.

In the manual the scale is described as useful for planning instruction, and stages of development for the areas assessed are described to help plan instruction. Unfortunately, empirical data are not provided to support the stages or the theory on which the test is based. Many studies have shown that instruction focused on perceptual skills has not been helpful in terms of achievement. For example, see the meta-analysis of Kavale and Forness (1987).

Summary.   The norms for the MSEL appear representative for children above 14 months, except for geographic distribution, but the norms need to be updated. No children with disabilities were included in the norm sample and no nonvocal score is available.

Overall results for internal consistency, interscorer reliability, and support for a single factor described by the ELC were good. Stability data are not provided by age level and no data were provided for the ELC.

Evidence for concurrent, content, and construct validity for the current version is very limited, and item bias analysis and predictive validity data are lacking. For the purpose of instructional planning, the item sample is too small. Problems with cut-off points for adjacent norm tables should be considered when interpreting results.

The fact that the MSEL has no timed items is a strength of the test. Toys in the test kit are attractive and the tasks are interesting for young children. Many of the concerns noted for the test could be addressed when the MSEL is updated.

Tables 1 through 3 summarize information on technical adequacy for the five tests.

SUMMARY

A number of diverse approaches to cognitive assessment of infants and toddlers have evolved over the past 100 years, approaches that have become more sophisticated, comprehensive, and useful. Yet, today there are relatively few options for the youngest children and more research is needed to address the many remaining questions.

TABLE 15.1.

Representativeness of Norm Samples for Tests for Children Under Age 2

			Tests		
Characteristics	*BDI–2*	*Bayley–III*	*CAS–2*	*M–P–R*	*MSEL*
Age range	Birth–95 months	1–42 months	3–47 months	1–78 months	Birth–68 months
Years of sampling	2002–03	2004	1997–99	Years not given	1981–89
Geographic Dist.	Yes	Yes	Yes	No	No
Race/Ethnicity	Yes	Yes	Yes	Yes, except for African-Americans	Yes
Gender	Yes	Yes	Yes	Yes	Yes
SES	Yes	Yes	Yes	Yes	Yes
Urban/Rural	Yes	No data presented	Yes	No data presented	Yes
Children with Disabilities	No	Yes, 10%	Yes, 6%	No	No
N/age levels used in manuals	600 (1–12 months) 600 (13–24 months)	800 (1–10 months) 400 (11–22.5 months)	248 (3–11 months) 288 (12–23 months)	195 (1–12 months) 161 (13–24 months)	504 (1–12 months) 358 (13–26 months)

BDI-2: Battelle Developmental Inventory–Second Edition; Bayley-III: Bayley Scales of Infant & Toddler Development–Third Edition; CAS–2: Cognitive Abilities Scale–Second Edition; M-P–R: Merrill-Palmer Scales–Revised; MSEL: Mullen Scales of Early Learning

TABLE 15.2.
Reliability of Test for Children Under Age 2

Construct	Tests				
	BDI-2	*Bayley-III*	*CAS-2*	*M-P-R*	*MSEL*
Internal Consistency	Cog Domain .83–.94 Subdomains .58–.95	Cog Domain .79–.93	GCQ .88–.96 NCQ .84–.91	D I .97–.98 Scales .90–.96	ELC .87–.94 Scales .53–.92
Test-retest (interval)	No data presented.	2–4 mos=.71 9–13 mos=.77 19–26 mos=.86 (2–15 days, *Md*=6 days)	3–11 mos=.81 GCQ, .79 NCQ (1 week) 12–23 mos=.90 GCQ, .93 NCQ (2 weeks)	3–70 mos.=.89 DI, .87 Cog, .90 Rec Lang . Lang, .90 Fine Motor (3 weeks)	1–24 mos.=.82–.85 (1–2 weeks, *Md*=7 days)
Interscorer	No data with two examiners present during testing.	No data presented.	3–11 mos GCQ=.94, NCQ=.93; 12–23 mos. GCQ=.95, NCQ=.93	No data presented.	ELC scales: 0–6 mos .91–.97, 7–12 mos .94–.97; 13–24 mos .93–.98

BDI–2: Battelle Developmental Inventory–Second Edition; Bayley–III: Bayley Scales of Infant & Toddler Development–Third Edition; CAS–2: Cognitive Abilities Scale–Second Edition; M–P–R: Merrill-Palmer Scales–Revised; MSEL: Mullen Scales of Early Learning.

TABLE 15.3.
Validity of Tests for Children Under Age 2

Construct	Tests				
	BDI–2	Bayley–III	CAS–2	M-P-R	MSEL
Content	Expert review, item analysis, model-data-fit statistics, based on prior version	Expert review, based on prior version and research	Based on research, item analysis	Expert review, based on prior version, item response theory analysis	Based on author's theory and prior version
Construct	Scores increase with age, domains intercorrelate	Scores correlate with PLS–4, PDMS–II, and ABAS–II	Scores increase with age, correlates with REEL–4	Scores increase with age, factor analysis supports DI composite	Scores increase with age, correlates with PLA, scales intercorrelate
Discriminate	Scores lower for clinical groups	Scores lower for clinical groups	Scores lower for cognitively impaired	Scores lower for clinical groups	Scores lower for clinical groups
Concurrent	BDI & BSID–II	BSID–II	BSID–II	BSID–II	BSID (1969)
Predictive	None	None	To CAS–2 Preschool: 3–11 mos .46 corrected; 12–23 mos .76 corrected (2-year interval)	None	None

BDI–2: Battelle Developmental Inventory-Second Edition; Bayley–III: Bayley Scales of Infant & Toddler Development–Third Edition; CAS–2: Cognitive Abilities–Second Edition; M-P-R: Merrill-Palmer Scales–Revised; MSEL: Mullen Scale of Early Learning

Because cognitive skills are necessarily related to motor, language, social, and adaptive skills, inter- or trans-disciplinary assessment efforts are essential. Methods to address many of the unique challenges infants and toddlers pose for examiners were presented, as well as descriptions of methods to ensure that assessment functions as intervention with caregivers. Issues regarding correcting ages for prematurity also were discussed.

An alternative to traditional assessment involves information processing. Typically habituation/dishabituation and novelty preference are used with this approach, measures that seem to be culture free, do not require vocal responses, and involve minimal motor skills. The Fagan Test of Infant Intelligence uses this approach. Studies suggest that this type of assessment discriminates well between infants with developmental delays and those without. However, mixed reliability and validity results, concerns about the criterion for habituation, and questions regarding which functions are measured longitudinally, illustrate the need for more research before this approach is used routinely for diagnosis.

Screening measures for young children, such as the Denver–II and DAYC, have improved considerably. Data on false positive and false negative classifications are particularly important for these tests, but such data are often inadequate or missing. This situation leaves examiners uncertain of a screening test's ability to accurately indicate who needs more comprehensive assessment. Additional research on the predictive accuracy of screening measures would be beneficial.

The five comprehensive, norm-referenced cognitive measures for infants and toddlers (BDI–2, Bayley–III, CAS–2, M-P–R, and MSEL) were examined. Each has strengths and limitations that require consideration to ensure the appropriateness of tests for each child. All five are revised editions, and more technically adequate than their predecessors. All use interesting play activities and toys that should peak children's interest.

One concern for some tests is that timed items seem of questionable relevance considering the limited attention span of infants and toddlers. The Bayley–III has a number of timed items, and the M-P–R and BDI–2 have a few. Timed items complicate scoring, interfere with observing a child's performance, and depress scores for some children with motor problems. Further, they seem to add little unique information regarding the performance of young children.

The Bayley–III, CAS–2 and M-P–R are appropriate for children who cannot or will not vocalize, or whose speech cannot be understood. Results that do not require vocalization or speech from a child can be obtained with these measures; the M-P–R requires less receptive language than the Bayley–III and the CAS–2.

With regard to standardization, norms for the MSEL are dated. The Bayley–III has the largest sample, and norm samples for the BDI–2, Bayley–III, and CAS–2 appear to be nationally representative. However, Salvia and Ysseldyke (2004a) noted that "... it is essential to test the full range of intellectual ability" when developing norms and "failure to consider individuals with mental retardation in standardization procedures introduces systematic bias into test norms" (p. 111). Without these children the mean is likely to be higher and the standard deviation lower than if these children had been included. Unfortunately, all tests except the Bayley–III and the CAS–2 excluded these children from their norms. Results for clinical samples are described in each of the other four test manuals, but these data are not included in the norms. Often these tests are used to diagnose cognitive impairment, but because the norms do not include children at risk or those with cognitive impairments, the norms may be biased. Furthermore, low scores in norm tables must be estimates (i.e., extrapolated scores) because children likely to receive low scores were excluded. If test authors choose to exclude certain groups from the norms, a rationale for the exclusion of each group should be provided. Also, if the test is to be used to identify cognitive delays, because children with, or at risk for, delayed development were not in the norm sample, reliability and validity data should be provided for these groups to demonstrate the appropriateness of the test for them. Unfortunately, none of the tests that excluded these children from their norms provide this information.

The internal consistency of all five tests is similar and reasonably good, but stability reliability is a concern. Test-retest reliability for the M-P–R cannot be determined for a particular age because data are collapsed across age levels. For children under age 2 data for the Bayley–III are too low to be technically adequate. Reliability for the CAS–2 GCQ and NCQ is satisfactory for 12–23 months, but less than .90 for 3–11 months. No stability data are provided for the BDI–2 or MSEL ELC for children under age 2. Obtaining adequate reliability for infants less than 12 months is particularly difficult and results should be interpreted in light of this problem. When test authors fail to provide adequate test-retest data, examiners cannot be confident that results will hold up even over relatively short time periods. Because decisions are rarely made about children on the day of testing, this is a concern. Instead, planning meetings typically occur several weeks later. Thus, a 2- or 3-week retest interval would be helpful. However, because of the rapid growth rate and inconsistent responding of children under 1 year, a 1-week retest interval may be justified. To be useful for examiners, correlations should be provided for each 1-year interval rather than collapsing data across several ages, especially for the youngest children. Good interscorer reliability is reported for most tests. Interscorer reliability for the BDI–2 is based on scoring protocols only. No data are provided for the Bayley–III and the M-P-R, which is a concern because the tests' directions are relatively complicated.

Substantial information is presented for all of the tests in support of their validity. Unfortunately, however, predictive validity evidence is lacking for four, and limited data are presented for the CAS–2. All five tests need further research in this critical area. Floors and item gradients for all five are adequate except for item gradients for the lowest scores for the BDI–2 and M-P-R. The adequacy of floors and item gradients is somewhat surprising considering how difficult it is to develop age-appropriate items for the youngest children.

For four tests standard scores do not go below 55, limiting their use with children who are very low functioning. Standard scores on the Bayley–III, the BDI–2, and CAS–2 go to 55, and on the MSEL to a T-score of 20 (equivalent to a quotient of 55). Although M-P–R standard scores go as low as 10 for some ages, these low scores must be based on extensive extrapolation because children at-risk or with cognitive delays were excluded from the norms.

Because development from birth to age 2 is so rapid, norm tables for these ages have smaller age intervals (1–3 months) than tests for older children. Despite small intervals, some cut-off points for adjacent norm tables can result in substantial changes in standard scores if a child's age changes by 1 day. These score changes are more problematic for some tests than others. The Bayley–II has the least amount of change and the M-P–R changes only a moderate amount (7–8 points). Thus, when interpreting results, or comparing results from different tests for the same child, cut-off points in norm tables should be reviewed. Also, examiners should consider this potential problem when selecting tests and scheduling appointments. If a child's age falls near the middle of an age interval in a norm table rather than at the extremes, results are more likely to be accurate. Score changes as a result of cut-off points in adjacent norm tables introduce error and probably affected results for predictive validity studies involving infants and toddlers. The effect of this problem warrants consideration in future predictive validity research.

Predictive validity studies for norm-referenced tests for children under age 2 typically show that the tests are not good at predicting later intellectual performance (Bayley, 1933; Fagan & Singer, 1983; Sternberg, Grigorenko, & Bundy, 2001). However, considering issues such as cut-off points in norm tables, the degree of extrapolation in determining standard scores, and the representativeness of norm samples, this problem is not surprising. Excluding children with physical, cognitive, or emotional impairments as well as those with biological risk factors from norm samples may potentially impact results of predictive validity studies also. For example, if these children are excluded from the norms of a test for young children, but were included in the norms for the criterion measure used several years later, this introduces error that is likely to depress the correlation. The reliability and predictive validity of norm-referenced tests for the youngest children may be improved substantially if basic psychometric issues are more carefully addressed in future test development.

Despite the importance of predictive validity, no such data are available for the BDI–2, Bayley–III, M-P–R, or MSEL. Although previous editions of the Bayley scales were reasonably good at predicting later cognitive performance for age 2 or older, the predictive ability was poor for younger children. Data for the CAS–2 indicate that the construct remains stable over a 2-year period for children assessed between 12–23 months, but is lower (.46 corrected) for infants under 12 months of age. Additional predictive validity data are needed for all five tests, particularly data gathered over a 4–5 year period when children are of school age.

In terms of using test results for planning instruction, the CAS–2 is the only test that assesses each skill three times. Thus, other tests often provide a relatively limited sample of performance. Considering the inconsistent nature of infant and toddlers' responding, obtaining an adequate sample of performance is important. CAS–2 results provide a better sample, even for children who are very low functioning for whom a norm-referenced score cannot be obtained. Growth Scores for the M-P–R can be used to determine the difficulty level of the various tasks on the test. This information may help determine strengths and difficulties to aid instructional planning, as well as assist in monitoring gains in performance. Because the scores are criterion-referenced they may be more sensitive to small gains in performance than norm-referenced results.

All norm-referenced results must be interpreted in light of information from medical and school records, interviews with caregivers, results from criterion-referenced and informal measures, and systematic observation of children in their natural environments. At no age is this issue more important than for infants and toddlers. Useful norm-referenced results describing cognitive development of infants and toddlers can be obtained if careful consideration is given to various aspects of technical adequacy of tests as well as the complicating factors that are necessarily involved in testing these children. Hopefully future revisions and new tests will be based on representative norm samples, avoid excessive extrapolation, decrease or eliminate timed items, lessen problems with cut-off points in norm tables, and provide comprehensive data on stability reliability and predictive validity.

REFERENCES

Andersson, H. W. (1996). The Fagan Test of Infant Intelligence: Predictive validity in a random sample. *Psychological Reports, 78,* 1015–1026.

Anastasi, A., & Urbina, S. (1997). *Psychological testing* (7th ed.). Upper Saddle River, NJ: Prentice-Hall.

Bagnato, S. J., & Neiswirth, J. T. (1991). *Assessment for early intervention.* New York: Guilford Press.

Barrera, M. E., Rosenbaum, P. L., & Cunningham, C. E. (1987). Corrected and uncorrected Bayley scores: Longitudinal developmental patterns in low and high birth weight preterm infants. *Infant Behavior and Development, 10,* 337–346.

Bayley, N. (1933). Mental growth during the first three years. *Genetic Psychology Monographs, 14,* 1–92.

Bayley, N. (1969). *Bayley Scales of Infant Development.* New York: Psychological Corp.

Bayley, N. (1993). *Bayley Scales of Infant Development-Second Edition.* San Antonio, TX: Psychological Corp.

Benasich, A. A., & Bejar, I.I. (1992). The Fagan Test of Infant Intelligence: A critical review. *Journal of Applied Developmental Psychology, 12,* 153–171.

Binet, A., & Simon, T. (1905). Methodes noubelles pour le diagnostic du niveau intellectual des anormaux. *L'anne Psychologique, 11,* 191–244.

Blasco, P. A. (1989). Preterm birth: To correct or not to correct. *Developmental Medicine and Child Neurology, 31,* 816–826.

Bornstein, M. H., & Sigman, M. D. (1986). Continuity in mental development from infancy. *Child Development, 57,* 251–274.

Bracken, B. A. (1987). Limitations of preschool instruments and standards for minimal levels of technical adequacy. *Journal of Psychoeducational Assessment, 4,* 313–326.

Bradley-Johnson, S. (1982). Assessment as intervention. *Infant Mental Health Journal, 3,* 293–297.

Bradley-Johnson, S. (1987). *Cognitive Abilities Scale.* Austin, TX: PRO-ED.

Bradley-Johnson, S., & Johnson, C. M. (2001). *Cognitive Abilities Scale-Second Edition.* Austin, TX: PRO-ED.

Brian, J. A., Landry, R., Szatmari, P., Niccols, S., & Bryson, S. (2003). Habituation in high-risk infants: Reliability and patterns of responding. *Infant and Child Development, 12,* 387–394.

Bzoch, K. R., League, R., & Brown, V. L. (2003). *Receptive-Expressive Emergent Language Test.* Austin, TX: PRO-ED.

Carroll, J. B. (1993). *Human cognitive abilities: A survey of factor-analytic studies.* Cambridge: Cambridge.

Chandlee, J., Heathfield, L. T., Salganik, M., Damokosh, A., & Radcliffe, J. (2002). Are we consistent in administering and scoring the Bayley Scales of Infant Development-II? *Journal of Psychoeducational Assessment, 20,* 183–200.

Colombo, J. (1993). *Infant cognition: Predicting later intellectual functioning.* Newbury Park, CA: Sage.

Columbo, J., Shaddy, D., & Richman, W. A. (2000). Cognition, development, and exceptional talent in infancy. In R. C. Friedman, & B. M. Shore (Eds.), *Talents unfolding: Cognition and development* (pp. 123–147). Washington, DC: American Psychological Association.

Columbo, J., Shaddy, D., Richman, W., Maikranz, J., & Blaga, O. (2004). The developmental course of habituation in infancy and preschool outcome. *Infancy, 5,* 1–38.

Culbertson, J. L., & Willis, D. J. (1993). Introduction to testing young children. In J. L. Culbertson & D.J. Willis (Eds.) *Testing young children* (pp. 1–10). Austin, TX: PRO-ED.

DiPietro, J. A., & Allen, M. C. (1991). Estimation of gestational age: Implications for developmental research. *Child Development, 62,* 1184–1199.

Dunst, C., & McWilliam, R. A. (1988). Cognitive assessment of multiply handicapped young children. In T. D. Wachs & R. Sheehan (Eds.). *Assessment of developmentally disabled children* (pp. 213–238). New York: Plenum Press.

Engelmann, S., & Colvin, G. (1983). *Generalized compliance training.* Austin, TX: PRO-ED.

Escalona, S., & Corman, H. (1966). *Albert Einstein Scales of Sensorimotor Development.* Albert Einstein College of Medicine, Department of Psychiatry, New York.

Fagan, J. F., & Detterman, D. K. (1992). The Fagan Test of Infant Intelligence: A technical summay. *Journal of Applied Developmental Psychology, 13,* 173–193.

Fagan, J. F., & Singer, L. T. (1983). Infant recognition memory as a measure of intelligence. *Advances in Infancy Research, 2*, 31–78.

Flanagan, D. P., & Alfonso, V. C. (1995). A critical review of the technical characteristics of new and recently revised intelligence tests for preschool children. *Journal of Psychoeducational Assessment, 13*, 66–90.

Folio, M. R., & Fewell, R. R. (1983). *Peabody Developmental Motor Scales and Activity Cards.* Chicago: Riverside Publishing.

Folio, M. R., & Fewell, R. R. (2000). Peabody Developmental Motor Scales-Second Edition. Austin, TX: PRO-ED.

Frankenberg, W. K. (2002). Developmental surveillance and screening of infants and young children. *Pediatrics, 109*, 144–145.

Frankenberg, W. K., Dodds, J., Archer, P., Bresnick, B., Maschka, P., Edelman, N., & Shapiro, H. (1990). *Denver II Technical Manual.* Denver, CO: Denver Developmental Materials.

Frankenberg, W. K., Dodds, J., Archer, P., Bresnick, B., Maschka, P., Edelman, N., & Shapiro, H. (1996). *Denver II Technical Manual.* Denver, CO: Denver Developmental Materials.

Goldman, B. A. (2003). Review of the Cognitive Abilities Scale-Second Ed. In B. S. Blake, J. C. Impara, & R. A. Spies (Eds.), *The fifteenth mental measurements yearbook.* Lincoln, NE: The Buros Institute of Mental Measurements.

Gyurke, J. S., Lynch, S. J., Lagasse, L., & Lipsitt, L.P. (1992). Speeded items: What do they tell us about an infant's performance? In C. Rovee-Collier & L. P. Lipsitt (Eds.), *Advances in infancy research* (Vol. 7, pp. 215–225). Norwood, NJ: Ablex.

HaileMariam, A. (2004). Review of the Cognitive Abilities Scale-Second Edition. *Journal of School Psychology, 42*, 171–176.

Harrison, P. L., & Oakland, T. (2003). *Adaptive Behavior Assessment System-Sedond Edition.* San Antonio, TX: Harcourt Assessment, Inc.

Hynd, G. W., & Semrud-Clikeman, M. (1993). Developmental considerations in cognitive assessment of young children. In J. L. Culbertson & D. J. Willis (Eds.), *Testing young children: A reference guide for developmental, psychoeducational, and psychosocial assessments* (pp. 11–26). Austin, TX: PRO-ED.

Jacobson, S. W., Jacobson, J. L., O'Neill, J. M., Padgett, RlJ., Frankowski, J. J., & Bihun, J. T. (1992). Visual expectation and dimensions of infant information processing. *Child Development, 63*, 711–724.

Johnson, C. M., & Bradley-Johnson, S. (2002). Construct stability of the Cognitive Abilities Scale-Second Edition for infants and toddlers. *Journal of Psychoeducational Assessment, 20*, 144–151.

Kavale, K. A., & Forness, S. R. (1987). Substance over style: Assessing the efficacy of modality testing and teaching. *Exceptional Children, 54*, 228–239.

Kavsek, M. (2004). Predicting later IQ from infant visual habituation and dishabituation: A meta-analysis. *Applied Developmental Psychology, 25*, 369–393.

Knobloch, H., Stevens, F., & Malone, A. F. (1987). *Manual of developmental diagnosis: The administration and interpretation of the Revised Gesell and Amatruda Developmental and Neurologic Examination.* Houston, TX: Developmental Evaluation Materials.

Lidz, C. S. (2003). *Early childhood assessment.* Hoboken, NJ: John Wiley & Sons.

McCall, R. B., & Carriger, M. S. (1997). A meta-analysis of infant habituation and recognition memory performance as predictors of later IQ. *Child Development, 64*, 57–79.

McCune, L., Kalamanson, G., Fleck, M. B., Glazewski, B., & Sillari, J. (1990). An interdisciplinary model of infant assessment. In S. J. Meisels & J. P. Shonkoff (Eds.) *Handbook of early childhood intervention* (pp. 219–245). Cambridge: Cambridge.

Meikamp, J. (2003). Review of the Cognitive Abilities Scale-Second Edition. In B. S. Blake, J. C. Impara, & R. A. Spies (Eds.), *The fifteenth mental measurements yearbook.* Lincoln, NE: The Buros Institute of Mental Measurements.

Mullen, E. M. (1989). *Infant Mullen Scales of Early Learning.* Cranston, RI: T.O.T.A.L. Child.

Mullen, E. M. (1992). *Preschool Mullen Scales of Early Learning.* Cranston, RI: T.O.T.A.L. Child.

Mullen, E. M. (1995). *Mullen Scales of Early Learning.* Circle Pines, MN: American Guidance.

Neisworth, J. T., & Bagnato, S. J. (1996). Assessment for early intervention: Emerging themes. In S. Odom & M. McLean (Eds.), *Early intervention/early childhood special education: Recommended practices* (pp. 23–57). Austin, TX: PRO-ED.

Nellis, L., & Gridley, B. E. (1994). Review of the Bayley Scales of Infant Development–Second Edition. *Journal of School Psychology, 32,* 201–209.

Nevin, J. A. (1992). An integrative model for the study of behavioral momentum. *Journal of the Experimental Analysis of Behavior, 39,* 49–59.

Newborg, J., Stock, J. R., Wnek, L., Guidibaldi, J. E., & Svinicki, J. (1987). *Battelle Developmental Inventory.* Allen, TX: DLM.

Newborg, J., Stock, J. R., Wnek, I., Guidibaldi, J., & Svinicki, J. (1988). *Battelle Developmental Inventory Screening Test.* Chicago, IL: Riverside.

Newborg, J. (2005). *Battelle Developmental Inventory-Second Edition.* Itasca, IL: Riverside.

Parker, S. J., & Zuckerman, B. S. (1990). Therapeutic aspects of the assessment process. In S. J. Meisels & J. P. Shonkoff (Eds.) *Handbook of early childhood intervention* (pp. 350–369). Cambridge: Cambridge.

Roid, G. H., & Sampers, J. L. (2004). *Merrill-Palmer-Revised: Scales of Development.* Wood Dale, IL: Stoelting.

Rose, S. A. (1989). Measuring infnat intelligence: New perspectives. In M. H. Bornstein & N. A. Krasnegor (Eds.), *Stability and continuity in mental development: Behavioral and biological perspectives* (pp. 171–188). Hillsdale, NJ: Lawrence Erlbaum Associates.

Salvia, J., & Ysseldyke, J. A. (2004a). *Assessment* (9th ed.). Boston, MA: Houghton Mifflin.

Salvia, J., & Ysseldyke, J. A. (2004b). *Assessment* (New Test Reviews). http://college.hmco/education/salvia/assessment/9e/students/reviews/cas_2.html.

Sattler, J. M. (2001). *Assessment of children (*4th ed.). San Diego, CA: J. M. Sattler Publisher.

Schock, H.H., & Buck, K. (1995). Review of Bayley Scales of Infant Development-Second Edition. *Child Assessment News, 5(2),* 1, 12.

Siegal, L. S. (1983). Correction for prematurity and its consequences for the assessment of the very low birth weight infant. *Child Development, 54,* 1176–1188.

Sternberg, R. J., Grigorenko, E. L., & Bundy, D. A. (2001). The predictive value of IQ. *Merrill-Palmer Quarterly, 47,* 1–41.

Stutsman, R. (1931). *Merrill-Palmer Scales of Mental Development.* Chicago, IL: Stoelting.

Tasbihsazan, R., Nettelbeck, T., & Kirby, N. (2003). Predictive validity of the Fagan Test of Infant Intelligence. *British Journal of Developmental Psychology, 21,* 585–597.

Terman, L. M. (1916). *The measurement of intelligence.* Boston, MA: Houghton Mifflin.

Thomas, H., & Gilmore, R. O. (2004). Habituation assessment in infancy. *Psychological Methods, 9,* 70–92.

Thompson, L. A., Fagan, J. F., & Fulker, D. W. (1991). Longitudinal prediction of specific cognitive abilities from infant novelty preference. *Child Development, 62,* 530–538.

Uzgiris, I., & Hunt, J. McV. (1975). *Assessment in Infancy: Ordinal Scales of Psychological Development.* Urbana, IL: University of Illinois Press.

Voress, J. K., & Maddox, T. (1998). *Developmental Assessment of Young Children.* Austin, TX: PRO-ED.

Wyly, M. V. (1997). *Infant assessment.* Boulder, CO: Westview Press.

Zimmerman, I. L., Steiner, V. G., Evatt, R. L., & Pond, R. E. (1979). *Preschool Language Assessment.* Columbus, OH: Charles E. Merrill.

Zimmerman, I. L., Steiner, V. G., & Pond, R. E. (2002). *Preschool Language Scale-Fourth Edition.* San Antonio, TX: The Psychological Corp.

IV

ASSESSMENT OF SPECIFIC ABILITIES

16

Assessment of Communication, Language, and Speech: Questions of "What to Do Next?"

Nickola Wolf Nelson
Western Michigan University

Candis Warner
Private Practice, Portage, MI

First words, along with first steps, are universal harbingers of typical development, awaited and celebrated. When they are slow to appear, parents and others begin to worry. By the preschool years, if children cannot express themselves intelligibly and understand most of what is said to them, or if they appear uninterested in communicating, or if they perseverate on certain topics, more red flags are raised. Delays and difficulties in such areas trigger concerns about communication, language, and speech development, and about development in general. In fact, it is difficult to imagine a developmental difficulty that does not find some expression through problems of speech, language, or communication.

Sophie, Jack, and Connor have been referred to their local school district for assessment. At age 3 years 5 months, Sophie is a highly motivated communicator who is beginning to experience frustration when people cannot understand her. She uses a complicated system of gestures and sophisticated facial expressions to assist her spoken communication attempts. Sophie seems to comprehend the language expected of a three-year-old, and her use of nonverbal communication is exceptional. She works hard to engage adults in her communication and expects them to share her attention and interpret her utterances. However, she sometimes employs an exaggerated pout and a stern face when her efforts to communicate are not reciprocated or when she is not understood. Sophie's parents note that she is sometimes an exhausting communicative partner, but they enjoy her high need to interact with them. They are pleased with her tenacious, high-spirited nature, but concerned that she will lose her outgoing personality if she continues to experience difficulty communicating.

Jack has perfect articulation. At age 3 years 5 months, Jack also uses complex sentences, and he is beginning to "read" snatches of print, such as videotape labels and warnings. Jack can operate the most complex computer software and can repeat the dialogue from several "Thomas the Train" videos. However, when asked about a book featuring a dog, just read to him, he responds with a long utterance about Star Wars. He repeated the alphabet at 15 months of age and subsequently spent long hours lining up his lettered blocks in the correct order. He seems to be a sensitive, kind child, but his refusal to wear any clothing with buttons and his picky eating habits make care giving difficult. Jack's parents report that he talks incessantly, but communicating with him is difficult. He seems to enjoy one-to-one communication with adults, but only when he chooses the topic, and he rarely stays on the same topic for more than two conversational turns, unless it is one of his favorites. Jack withdraws from group activities with peers and situations in which he is expected to respond to questions. Jack seems attached to his parents. He runs to greet them when they return home, and he takes them by the hand when he wants something, but they wish he were more interactive with them and with other children.

Connor, age 4, rarely initiates conversations, but he does respond to direct questions. He uses short, one- or two-word utterances, omits all forms of the verb "to be," substitutes "me" for "I," and has a limited expressive vocabulary for his age. He correctly points to pictured items when asked, but has difficulty naming the pictures. He follows orally presented directions well and is eager to participate in all planned activities in preschool. Connor positions himself in the middle of the group, but never chooses to be a leader. He often quietly plays beside another mild mannered child at school who does not expect Connor to speak to him. Most of the communication between the two is conducted with gestures and noises. Connor's parents express concern that other peers will not accept him. They also are concerned that his immature speech and language skills will cause others to underestimate his abilities to learn.

All three children have normal hearing and are from middle class families in which English is the only language spoken. The team psychologist has found all three to have nonverbal cognitive abilities within normal limits. Although each has been diagnosed with language impairment, the three children reveal quite different assessment profiles.

In this chapter, we present a framework for guiding the assessment of communication, language, and speech development in the preschool years, including the acquisition of basic concepts. This framework is set within the context of children's other developing systems and internal and external supports. Although assessment for Sophie, Jack, and Connor does not require accommodation for cultural-linguistic differences or socio-economic challenges, the increasingly diverse demographics of the United States suggest that second language learning or socioeconomic influences will need to be considered more frequently now and in the future (National Clearinghouse for English Language Acquisition, 2005). In a study of 240 children being raised in poverty in the United Kingdom, Locke, Ginsborg, and Peers (2002) found more than half to be language delayed in their first year of preschool, with language skills lower than cognitive abilities.

Language-learning difficulties also may co-occur with hearing impairment or any other developmental disability. Communication problems are a key feature of autism spectrum disorders. Diverse circumstances justify flexible practices for supporting parents and early childhood educators to address problems and concerns proactively. In this framework, assessment is seen not as a static effort to measure and label, but as a dynamic precursor to answering the question, "What to do next?"

COMMUNICATION, LANGUAGE, AND SPEECH—RELATED BUT DISTINCT ABILITIES

Assessment activities should illuminate children's relative strengths and needs across communication, language, and speech systems (see Table 16.1 for definitions). Our case stud-

TABLE 16.1.
Definitions of Communication, Language, and Speech

Communication	Communication is the broadest term, meaning essentially "getting an intended message across to another." Messages can be communicated through language (spoken or written), but communication also can occur through gestures, facial expression, and other forms of nonverbal communication. Many animal species communicate but do not have language. Communication is always possible, even if speech-language abilities are profoundly impaired. For infants or individuals with severe disabilities, communication "intentions" may need to be inferred by communication partners.
Language	Language is the term for symbolic communication. Members of a linguistic community use orderly combinations of phonemes (or print), words, sentences, and discourse to express and comprehend unique meanings. All peoples of the world speak equally complex spoken languages, but not all languages have a written form. To "know" a language means to be able to integrate five linguistic subsystems for comprehending and formulating messages: • **Phonology** is the sound system of language. • **Morphology** is the system of smallest meaningful units, including word roots, derivational morphemes, and inflectional grammatical morphemes, such as -ed and -ing. • **Syntax** is the grammatical system for combining words into sentences, and combining sentence into more complex ones. • **Semantics** is the meaning system of language. • **Pragmatics** is the system for using language in contextually and socially appropriate ways
Speech	Speech is the term for one modality in which language may be produced. Speech production is a complex motor act, directed by the brain. It requires: • **Respiratory** support to provide the airstream • **Vocal tract** and **articulators,** to shape the airstream into phonological patterns by manipulating voicing with the larynx, and articulatory/resonatory shapes, transitions, and sequences with the teeth, tongue, jaw, and soft palate.

ies illustrate how these related but independent systems may be relatively spared or impaired. Disconnections across systems reduce the resources that children have for all other forms of learning. At the same time, reciprocal relationships can be exploited in the intervention process. Identification of learning strengths in assessment helps interdisciplinary teams know what to do next when designing intervention.

Sophie's pattern appears to represent primarily a problem of speech development, accompanied by delayed acquisition of the phonological system of language, but with relative strengths in other aspects of language and communication. Her expressive syntax may be marginally affected as well, particularly verb tense and plural endings, but it is difficult to tell because the language she produces is only partially intelligible, even to those who know her well, and she leaves final consonants off many words. Although Sophie has difficulty pronouncing words, she is apparently using meaningful ones to formulate sentences with a variety of syntactic structures. Another important note about Sophie's language is that she understands age-appropriate linguistically encoded messages, an observation that was confirmed in assessment tasks using few nonverbal cues to meaning. In the area of communication, Sophie has exceptional strengths, using gestures and other communicative strategies to get her message across. She is an active communicator (Fey, 1986), both initiating and responding in communicative exchanges and completing multiple communicative circles with her parents (Greenspan, 1992). Her high use of gestural communication is a positive prognostic indicator (Thal & Tobias, 1992). Therapy will capitalize on these communication strengths while Sophie receives specialized attention to learn the articulatory skills to speak clearly and to develop phonological awareness that she can use when learning to read (e.g., Kamhi & Catts, 1989; Stanovich, 1985).

Jack shows a different pattern of relationship among the three elements, communication, language, and speech. For him, communication is the major concern. Not only his verbal interactions, but also his communicative gestures are atypical. For example, Jack rarely uses distal gestures, such as pointing, to guide his parents' attention or to accompany the requests he makes by pulling them by the hand toward desired objects. Jack's perceptual-motor grasp of the surface features of both speech and written language are exceptional. When assessment probes beneath the surface, however, not only is Jack's understanding of how to communicate with others impaired, but his difficulty in comprehending the conceptual aspects of language also becomes apparent. Jack is a verbal noncommunicator (Fey, 1986). He chatters, but has marked difficulty completing communicative circles (i.e., responding to communication acts initiated by others; Greenspan, 1992) and participating in play. In addition, Jack's symptoms of early reading without comprehension might be described as "hyperlexia," but the label does not fully convey Jack's difficulties with broader aspects of language and communication. Jack's unusual social interactions reflect his difficulties in learning linguistic rules and communicative expectations for participating in meaning making. The team has decided that Jack's pattern of communication, along with his insistence on sameness and unusual responses to sensory input, supports a diagnosis of autism spectrum disorder.

Like Sophie, Connor has relative strengths in functional communication. Connor's difficulties are concentrated in the area of language, involving delays in comprehension to some extent, but most clearly language expression. Connor shows his relative strength in the area of communication by completing communicative circles (Greenspan, 1992), but he rarely initiates them. Thus, the team describes Connor as a passive communicator (Fey, 1986) and plans intervention activities involving play that will encourage him to make more active communication bids. Connor has fewer strategies than Sophie for compensating communicatively for his limited speech-language skills. Formal testing with the Bracken Basic Concept Scale (Bracken, 1998) has shown Connor to have relative strengths for comprehending conceptual vocabulary. This strength will be used to encourage him to elaborate his sentence production in intervention (e.g., *Which horse do you want, Connor, the big one or the little one?* [before drawing toy figures from a bag, to prevent a pointing response]; *Shall we make the farmer's tractor go fast or slow?*). Several factors, including long pauses before producing known vocabulary, a preponderance of inexact words such as *stuff* and *thing*, and a low frequency of different words, suggest a pattern of word finding difficulties for Connor. More than just phonology seems to be involved. By comparison, Sophie, who also lacks the speech capabilities to be understood, seems to retrieve words easily and to have the linguistic capabilities to formulate them into sentences. Along with word retrieval, Connor's problems are focused in syntactic formulation and working memory. For him, the risks in school when it comes to reading and writing are comprehensive, in that he is likely to have difficulty with reading decoding and comprehension when he reads, and with spelling words and formulating sentences and discourse when he writes. Getting Connor's oral language going now will serve an important role in secondary prevention of educational problems in the future.

SCREENING AND REFERRAL AS ENTREES TO ASSESSMENT

Children with suspected speech-language and communication disorders may come to the attention of diagnostic teams through a variety of pathways. Sophie, Jack, and Connor all were brought to the local school district's Child Find team for assessment when their parents and pediatricians became concerned about their children's development.

Other children with risks for speech-language and communication delays are identified through individual screening activities, such as provided by health care professionals at well baby visits, or through group screening in situations such as Head Start or prekindergarten programs. Most of the commonly used developmental screening devices include items designed specifically to assess speech and language development. Some are listed in Table 16.2.

Care must be taken to ensure that any screening procedure is cultural-linguistically appropriate; otherwise over- or under-referral may result (Brachlow, Jordan, & Tervo, 2001). Some researchers have suggested, however, that early identification of children at risk may lead to the provision of preventive services for children with lower skills, even if they are found not to have disabilities. For example, Glascoe (2001) reported that although some screening tests yield false-positive results, particularly for children from lower socioeconomic groups, children who fail "falsely" also are likely to perform significantly lower on other comprehensive assessment measures and to benefit from enriched language learning experiences designed to prepare them better for school.

CLARIFYING ASSESSMENT PURPOSES

Assessment teams, including parents as well as professionals, work best when guided by a shared purpose. As established throughout this book, developmental assessments are conducted not in the abstract, but in the contexts of families, cultures, and preschool experiences by teams of individuals (both family members and professionals) who are wondering what to do next. Diagnostic assessment purposes differ from purposes associated with intervention, and the two purposes often rely on different strategies and tools.

Diagnostic Purposes of Assessment

A number of questions are raised in the process of diagnosis, including: (a) Does this child have a disorder involving speech-language-communication development? (b) If so, what is its nature? (c) Does it fit a particular diagnostic category? (d) Is there value to the child and family in seeking a particular diagnostic label? (e) Does the child need specialized services to foster communication development? (f) Even if no disorder is found, are services needed nevertheless to enhance language and communication abilities?

For Sophie, Jack, and Connor, assessment results confirmed parental and physician concerns regarding the children's communication development. Each child was found to have

TABLE 16.2.

Screening Tools that Include Items for Assessing Speech-Language and Communication Skills

Test Name & Authors	Age Span	Description	Publisher
Ages and Stages Questionnaire (ASQ) Bricker, D., Squires, J., Mounts, L., Potter, L., Nickel, R., & Farrell, J. (2004)	4 mos. to 5 years	A "Parent Completed, Child-Monitoring System," which identifies children who have, or are at risk for, developmental delays. Actively involves parents and family members in assessment, intervention, and evaluation.	Paul H. Brookes Baltimore, MD
Developmental Indicators for the Assessment of Learning—Revised (DIAL-R). Mardell-Czudnowski, C. & Goldenberg, D. S. (1990)	2 to 6 years	A preschool and prekindergarten screening instrument that screens children in three development skill areas (motor, concepts, and language) in 20 to 30 minutes. Includes statistical data from three norming groups (1990 census, caucasian, and minority.) Results can be compared with cut-off scores at ± 1, ± 1.5, or ± 2 SD.	AGS Circle Pines, MN
Denver Developmental Screening Test II Frankenburg, W., Dodds, J., Archer, P., Bresnick, B., Maskchka, P., Edelman, M., & Shapiro, J. (1990)	0 to 6 years	Takes 20 minutes to administer. Reported to have less class and race bias, validity and sensitivity than previous version, but poorer specificity (i.e., more false positives). Includes a 10-minute parent checklist.	Denver Developmental Material, Denver, CO
Early Screening Profiles (ESP). Harrison, P., Kaufman, A., Kaufman, N., Bruininks, R., Rynders, J., Ilmer, S., Sparrow, S., & Cicchetti, D. (1990)	2 to 7 years	Comprehensive screening instrument. Yields screening indexes or standard scores in three areas:cognitive/language, motor, and self-help social. Identifies at-risk or gifted children.	AGS Circle Pines, MN

Fluharty Preschool Speech and Language Screening Test–Second Edition (FLUHARTY–2) Fluharty, N. B. (2000)	3-0 through 6-11 years	Designed to identify preschool children who need a complete speech and language evaluation, this screening test contains five subtests: Articulation, Repeating Sentences, Responding to Directives and Answering Questions, and Describing Actions and Sequencing Events. A Teacher Questionnaire provides opportunity for collaboration when assessing children in school populations	AGS Circle Pines, MN
Hawaii Early Learning Profile (HELP). Parks, S. (1992)	0 to 3 years	Criterion-reference charts are provided for 685 skills in 40 conceptual strands. of cognitive, language, gross motor, fine motor, social, and self-help. A sequenced checklist can be used to select objectives.	VORT Corporation Palo Alto, CA
Kaufman Survey of Early Academic and Language Skills (K-SEALS). Kaufman, A. S. & Kaufman, N. L. (1993)	3;0 to 6;11 years	Nationally normed measure that assesses children's expressive and receptive language skills, preacademic skills, and articulation.	AGS Circle Pines, MN

367

speech-language-communicative abilities that fell outside of the range of typical development, and each was found to need intervention services to address his or her specific needs.

Intervention Purposes of Assessment

Beyond purposes related to diagnosis and eligibility, assessment purposes address multiple questions about what to do next in intervention. Key assessment questions related to intervention decisions include: (a) Which goal areas should be targeted to yield the most positive results? (b) What baseline levels and abilities can be measured within those goal areas? (c) What does outcome assessment suggest about how well the intervention is working? (d) What transition points are on the horizon, such as kindergarten? (e) Do the child's needs continue to justify services from a speech-language pathologist and other special needs professionals?

Ongoing assessment needs for Sophie, Jack, and Connor are quite different. Assessment for Sophie involves gathering a complete inventory of her phoneme production capabilities and the immature phonological processes (e.g., fronting of all consonants, final consonant deletion, and syllable reduplication) that are limiting her abilities to produce intelligible words. This will also involve setting up a monitoring system to update the inventory on a regular basis. Assessment activities for Jack and Connor need to concentrate on their understanding of the concepts of language, as well as its forms, and its social, as well as its private, uses. Their abilities to interact with other children, and increases in social bids and responsiveness will be documented. As Connor develops a more extensive vocabulary, his word finding abilities, expressive syntax, and inflectional morphology (word endings, such as *-ing*, *-ed*, and plurals) will be monitored as well. All three children will be involved in emergent literacy experiences, and their phonological awareness, book interaction skills, and comprehension will be monitored.

DEFINITIONS OF LANGUAGE DISORDER

Several authoritative sources, including the *Diagnostic and Statistical Manual of Mental Disorder, fourth edition* (DSM–IV; American Psychiatric Association, 1994) and the *International Code of Diseases* (ICD–10; World Health Organization, 1992), require two primary diagnostic criteria for language impairments: (a) scoring significantly low on standardized language testing, and (b) being perceived by others as having a problem. Other definitions describe language parameters that are affected. Taking this approach, the American Speech-Language-Hearing Association (1982) defines *language disorder* as:

> impairment or deviant development of comprehension and/or use of a spoken, written, and/or other symbol system. The disorder may involve (1) the form of language (phonologic, morphologic, and syntactic systems), (2) the content of language (semantic system), and/or (3) the function of language in communication (pragmatic system) in any combination. (p. 949)

This definition addresses the form, content, and use of language, but like many other definitions, it is not explicit about how to determine "any disruption in the learning or use" (Lahey, 1988, p. 21), or "deficits in comprehension, production, and/or use of language" (Bashir, 1989, p. 181). Hence, most definitions by themselves do not operationalize criteria for diagnosing language disorder for a specific child. Policies at local, state, and federal levels that do establish operational definitions are often contradictory and controversial.

Generally, in order to diagnose an impairment or disorder of language development, a speech-language pathologist (SLP) must find a child's language performance on more than one formal measure to be significantly lower than the performance of an appropriate comparison group of children similar to them in age, socioeconomic status, and cultural linguistic history (Nelson, 1998). Problems arise, however, for operationalizing the process in that children in comparison groups often are not comparable in terms of background experiences; thus, many children from minority groups, different cultures, or families living in poverty receive biased assessments in spite of policies intended to avoid bias.

Another issue is whether diagnosis of language disorder should hinge on finding language scores significantly below scores on measures of general (or nonverbal) cognitive ability. If the goal is for early identification of all children who need specialized services to foster language development and help prepare them for school, children with low cognitive abilities, who are known to be particularly at risk, should be the first to be identified and served, not the last, as dictated by many current policies. A growing body of research with young children with developmental language disorders (Cole, Dale, & Mills, 1990; Cole, Dale, & Mills, 1992; Cole & Harris, 1992; Cole, Mills, & Kelley, 1994; Fey, Long, & Cleave, 1994), as well as related research with students with learning disabilities (e.g., Francis, Fletcher, Shaywitz, Shaywitz, & Rourke, 1996; Francis et al., 2005), has led to removal of the requirement for discrepancy formulas for identifying learning disability with the reauthorization of IDEA 2004. This shift indicates a turning of the tide on ill-advised (in the authors' opinion) cognitive-linguistic discrepancy policies, but effective alternatives are yet to be widely defined or accepted.

TECHNIQUES OF LANGUAGE ASSESSMENT

A range of approaches can be used to identify language disorders among preschool-age children, including norm-referenced assessments, questionnaires, and language samples. No single assessment procedure is sufficient to diagnose language disorder. Multiple techniques, including formal and informal measures, parent report, and dynamic assessment techniques, all are needed (Dockrell, 2001).

Formal Assessment Procedures

Formal assessments use structured activities to yield specifically defined information for comparison with normative or criterion referenced data. The choice of instrument influences the stimuli administered and establishes "correct" responses. Table 16.3 lists commonly used preschool-level formal language assessment tools.

Informal Assessment Procedures

Informal assessments involve less-structured observations of behaviors within meaningful, contextualized activities (e.g., conversations, dramatic play, storytelling, nonverbal interactions). Such child-centered interactions can vary with the preferences of the child and allow a wider range of acceptable responses. The term *informal* does not mean casual,

TABLE 16.3.

Formal Tests for Assessing the Language-Speech and Communication Skills of Toddlers and Preschoolers

Test Name & Authors	Age Span	Description	Publisher
Bankson Language Test (2nd ed.) (BLT–2) Bankson, N. W. (1990)	3 to 8 years	Assesses semantic knowledge, morphological/syntactic rules, and pragmatics. Test results may be reported as standard scores or percentile ranks. Standardized on 1200 children in 19 states.	Pro-Ed, Inc. Austin, TX
Bankson-Bernthal Test of Phonology (BBTOP) Bankson, N. W. & Bernthal, J. E. (1990)	3 to 9 years	Can be administered in 15 to 20 minutes to assess articulation and phonological processes using: a whole word accuracy analysis; a traditional consonant articulation analysis; and a phonological process analysis.	Pro-Ed, Inc. Austin, TX
Boehm Test of Basic Concepts–3 Preschool (BTBC–P; 3rd ed.) Boehm, A. E. (2001)	3 to 5.11 years	Measures concepts relevant to preschool and early childhood curriculum, with each concept tested twice to assess understanding across contexts. Standardized on a national sample. Includes curriculum-based test summary, observation and intervention planning tool, a parent report form, and suggestions for modifying and adapting administration directions and testing materials.	Harcourt Assessment, Inc. San Antonio, TX
Bracken Basic Concept Scale— Revised (BBCS–R) Bracken, B. A. (1998)	2.6 to 8 years	Assesses receptive knowledge of basic concepts. Results can be analyzed for norm-referenced, criterion-referenced, or curriculum-based assessment. A Spanish record form is available for criterion-referenced use. Deficiencies in concept acquisition can be addressed with the Bracken Concept Development Program (BCDP).	Harcourt San Antonio, TX
Clinical Assessment of Language Comprehension Miller, J. F., & Paul, R. (1995)	8 mos. to 10 years	Informal assessment for children who are very young or difficult to test. Designed to supplement formal measures. Response types include pointing, object manipulation, conversation, and behavioral compliance.	Paul H. Brookes Baltimore, MD

Test	Age	Description	Publisher
Clinical Evaluation of Language Fundamentals-Preschool (2nd ed.; CELF Preschool–2) Wiig, E. H., Secord, W. A., & Semel, E. (2004)	3 to 6 years	The CELF-Preschool–2 includes subtests for assessing language abilities of preschool age children who will be in academic-oriented settings.	Harcourt San Antonio, TX
Communication and Symbolic Behavior Scales Developmental Profile (CSBS DP) Wetherby, A. M., & Prizant, B. M. (2002)	9 mos. to 2 years	Data from a Caregiver Questionnaire and play observations are tallied on a Record Form of 22 scales and 7 clusters. Scoring yields percentile ranks or standard scores by chronological age (8–24 months) or language stage (prelinguistic, early one-word, late one-word, multiword). The scoring process takes about 60–75 minutes.	Paul H. Brookes Baltimore, MD
Comprehensive Receptive and Expressive Vocabulary Test (CREVT). Wallace, G. & Hammill, D. D. (1994)	4 to 18 years	Assesses receptive and expressive oral vocabulary strengths and weaknesses. Identifies students significantly below their peers in oral abilities. Scores from this tests are correlated with scores from the TOLD:P–2, PPVT–R, EOWPVT–R, and the CELF.	Pro-Ed, Inc. Austin, TX
Diagnostic Evaluation of Language Variance (DELV-Criterion Referenced Test, and DELV-Screening Test) Seymour, H. N., Roeper, T. W., & de Villiers, J. (2003)	4 to 12 years: Language variation status; 4 to 9 years: Diagnostic risk status	DELV is an individually administered comprehensive speech and language test, which includes items specifically designed to neutralize the effect of variations from Mainstream American English (MAE) on a child's test performance in order to assess a child's true language abilities. This test integrates pragmatics with syntax, semantics, and phonology.	Harcourt Assessment, Inc. San Antonio, TX
Dynamic Assessment and Intervention: Improving Children's Narrative Abilities Miller, L., Gillam, R. B., & Peña, E. D. (2000)	Preschool through elementary years	Intended as a practical guide for evaluating children's narrative abilities and providing intervention using dynamic assessment and mediated learning.	Pro-Ed, Inc. Austin, TX

(continued)

TABLE 16.3.
(Continued)

Test Name & Authors	Age Span	Description	Publisher
Early Language Milestone Scale (2nd ed.) (ELM Scale–2). Coplan, J. (1993)	0 to 36 mos.	Designed to assess auditory expressive, auditory receptive, and visual skills. Can be scored as pass/fail or with a point system. Yields percentile and standard score equivalents.	Pro-Ed, Inc. Austin, TX
Expressive One Word Picture Vocabulary Test–Revised (EOWPVT–R). Gardner, M. (1990)	2 to 12 years	Assesses expressive vocabulary in children. (Can be administered with ROWPVT).	Pro-Ed, Inc. Austin, TX
Functional Emotional Assessment Scale for Infancy and Early Childhood (FEAS) Greenspan, S. I. (1992)	0 to 48 months	Uses a free-play situation for observing children's abilities to attend and interact with parents and includes a rating scale for emotional development based on the levels of communication.	International Universities Press, Madison, CT
Goldman-Fristoe Test of Articulation (GFTA). Goldman, R., & Fristoe, M. (1986)	2 to 16+ years	Measures articulation of sounds-in-words, sounds-in-sentences, and stimulability. Yields percentile ranks for the sounds-in-words and stimulability subtests.	AGS Circle Pines, MN
Hodson Assessment of Phonological Patterns-Third Edition (HAPP–3) Hodson, B. (2004)	3 to 8 years	Can be administered in less than 30 minutes. Results can be compared with normative data, and phonological processes can be categorized to aid in intervention planning.	Pro-Ed, Inc. Austin, TX

MacArthur-Bates Communicative Development Inventories (CDI). Fenson, L., Dale, P. S., Resnick, J. S., Thal, D., Bates, E., Hartung, J. P., Pethick, S., & Reilly, J. S. (2003)	1 to 3 years	Uses a parental checklist format to assess first signs of understanding, comprehension of early phrases, and starting to talk. Vocabulary checklist (for both understanding and saying) includes lists of words in categories. Early gestures, play, pretending, and imitating behaviors are also probed. The Words and Sentences CDI probes sentences and grammar, including morphological endings and varied expressions of two-word meanings. Can be used with older children at early stages.	Paul H. Brookes Baltimore, MD
Oral and Written Language Scales (OWLS). Carrow-Woolfolk, E. (1995, 1996)	3 to 21 years	Intended as a quick measure of receptive and expressive language through comprehensive examination of semantic, syntactic, pragmatic, and supralinguistic aspects of language.	AGS Circle Pines, MN
Oral-Motor/Feeding Rating Scale. Jelm, J. M. (1990)	All ages	Observational scale for combined assessment and intervention purposes. Summarizes oral-motor and feeding functioning in eight areas: breast feeding, bottle feeding, spoon feeding, cup drinking, biting (soft cookie), biting (hard cookie), chewing, and straw drinking.	Harcourt Assessment, Inc. San Antonio, TX
Peabody Picture Vocabulary Test (3rd ed.), PPVT–III Dunn, L. M., Dunn, L. M., & Williams, K. T. (1997).	2 to 90 years	Uses a picture-pointing task to assess receptive vocabulary.	AGS Circle Pines, MN
Preschool Language Assessment Instrument (PLAI–2) Blank, M., Rose, S., & Berlin, L. (2003)	3 to 5.11 years	Assesses abilities needed to meet the demand of classroom discourse. Normed on a sample of 463 children residing in 16 states, PLAI–2 indicates how effectively a child integrates cognitive, linguistic and pragmatic components.	AGS Circle Pines, MN

(continued)

TABLE 16.3.
(*Continued*)

Test Name & Authors	Age Span	Description	Publisher
Preschool Language Scale, Fourth Edition (PLS–4) English Edition Preschool Language Scale, Fourth Edition (PLS–4) Spanish Edition Zimmerman, I. L., Steiner, V. G., & Pond, R. E. (2002)	0 to 6.11 years	Assesses comprehensive language skills for comparison with norms for children birth through 6 years, based on a larger, more diverse sample of approximately 1,500 children, including children with disabilities, and 39.1% ethnic minorities.	Harcourt Assessment, Inc. San Antonio, TX
Receptive-Expressive Emergent Language Scale, 3rd ed. (REEL–3) Bzoch, K., & League, R. (2003)	0 to 3 years	Designed in the U.K., uses parent interview to help public health nurses, pediatricians, and educators identify children with language development problems.	Pro-Ed, Inc. Austin, TX
Rossetti Infant-Toddler Language Scale Rosetti, L. (1990)	0 to 3 years	Criterion-referenced assessment scale that covers developmental domains: interaction and attachment, gestures, play, language comprehension, language expression. Includes 3 to 7 items in each area at each 3-month interval.	East Moline, IL: LinguiSystems
Structured Photographic Expressive Language Test-Preschool (2nd ed.) (SPELT–P2) Werner, E., & Kresheck, J. D. (2004)	3 to 5.11 years	Presents photographs and uses structured questions to elicit early developing morphological and syntactic forms. Can be administered in 10–15 minutes. Scoring may be modified for speakers of AAVE dialect.	Sandwich, IL: Janelle Publications
Test for Auditory Comprehension of Language (3rd ed.) (TACL–3) Carrow-Woolfolk, E. (1999)	3 to 10 years	Uses picture pointing to assess comprehension of word classes and relations, grammatical morphemes, elaborated sentence constructions. Standard scores, percentiles, age equivalents.	Pro-Ed, Inc. Austin, TX

Test	Age Range	Description	Publisher
Test of Early Language Development, 3rd ed. (TELD–3) Hresko, W. P., Reid, D. K., & Hammill, D. D. (1999)	2 to 8 years	Measures receptive and expressive language form and content. Includes expanded diagnostic profile, extended age range, and 2 alternative forms.	Pro-Ed, Inc. Austin, TX
Test of Early Reading Ability, 3rd ed. (TERA–3) Reid, D. K., Hresko, W. P., & Hammill, D. D. (2001)	3.6 to 8.6 years	Measures emergent and early reading abilities: knowledge of contextual meaning, alphabet, and conventions. Standard scores with a mean of 100 and SD of 15.	Pro-Ed, Inc. Austin, TX
Test of Early Written Language, 2nd ed. (TEWL–2) Hresko, W. P. (1996)	3 to 10.11 years	Measures emergent written language and yields standard scores and percentiles.	Pro-Ed, Inc. Austin, TX
Transdisciplinary Play-Based Assessment (revised ed.) (TPBA) Linder, T. W. (1993)	6 months to 6 years	Criterion referenced informal assessment in 4 domains: social-emotional, cognitive, language and communication, sensori-motor.	Paul H. Brookes Baltimore, MD

however. In fact, Notari-Syverson and Losardo (1996) preferred the term *nonformal assessment* to represent the structure and purpose of the ongoing information collection process.

Informal methods have advantages for choosing "what to do next" when selecting intervention content or strategies (Dockrell, 2001). They also can be adjusted more easily to accommodate cultural-linguistic differences and make it easier to integrate assessment and intervention (Crais & Roberts, 1991; Schraeder, Quinn, Stockman, & Miller, 1999). Formal procedures yield limited samples that may be sufficient for deciding whether special services are justified but insufficient for selecting specific forms, content, or functions to target in intervention.

Parent Report Measures

Parent report is an assessment tool commonly used in the earliest stages of development. Parent report tools save time and increase the ecological and socio-cultural validity of procedures conducted in natural contexts, which are more likely than brief samples to capture children's full range of life experiences (Bates, Bretherton, & Snyder, 1988). Parents must understand this role, however, and want to take a formal part in the assessment process (Crais, 1995). Dale (1996) indicated that parent report is most accurate when parents are asked to recognize rather than recall sample behaviors, and when assessment is limited to current, emergent behaviors, rather than retrospective memories.

Tools for parent report include vocabulary checklists that parents use to check off the words their infants and toddlers comprehend or produce (Fenson et al., 2003; Rescorla, 1989; Rossetti, 1990). Studies of concurrent validity of parent report instruments such as the MacArthur-Bates Communication Development Inventory (CDI; Fenson et al., 2003) have shown that expressive vocabulary can be monitored by parents until about 2 years 6 months to 3 years, after which it becomes too large (Dale, 1996; Miller, Sedey, & Miolo, 1995). Charman, Drew, Baird, and Baird (2003) also found that the children with autism spectrum disorders showed atypical results on the CDI. In particular, they showed delayed comprehension of words relative to word production and delayed early gestures for sharing reference relative to production of generally later gestures involving use of objects.

Dynamic Assessment

Dynamic assessment is an interactive approach to the assessment process based on direct intervention. In contrast to static assessment, dynamic assessment is an interactive process that deliberately fosters change and assesses ability based on how easy change is to facilitate (Lidz, 1991; Pena, 1996). Dynamic assessment has advantages over traditional, static testing in yielding predictive and prescriptive information (Lidz, 1991), making it particularly helpful in deciding what to do next in intervention.

Dynamic assessment also is useful when a child's cultural linguistic experiences differ from those of children in standardization samples. By providing a set of known language-learning experiences and assessing the child's response, examiners can gain a better perspective on who might have a language-learning disorder. For example, Peña, Iglesias, and Lidz (2001) assessed 79 children (3.8 to 4.8 years) from culturally and linguistically diverse backgrounds and found that they could differentiate typically developing from low ability children by dynamic assessment using response to mediated learning experiences (MLE). Jacobs (2001) also reported on improved ability to identify potential language impairment among preschool children from culturally and linguistically diverse backgrounds when a dynamic assessment component was added.

Language Sampling Techniques

Spontaneous language samples afford the richest opportunities to observe a preschool child's integrated communicative, speech, and language skills within relatively naturalistic communicative interactions. Language samples can be used to answer the questions of "what to do next" at the time of diagnosis, baseline assessment, or progress reporting (Fey, 1986; Miller, 1981; Roberts & Crais, 1989). In one survey, Kemp and Klee (1997) found that 85% of speech-language pathologists used language sample analysis, most frequently for diagnostic purposes, but also for screening and to measure intervention outcomes.

Language sampling procedures are implemented in several stages. Most clinicians start by tape recording a sample of their own interaction with the child or of the child interacting with a peer or parent. They transcribe the sample as soon as possible to accurately reflect the child's utterances. Next, many perform a general analysis of language form, content, and use. Analysis results provide evidence of features most in need of intervention, either because they should have developed earlier or should be appearing more frequently. For example, the clinician might count the number of times a child initiates or completes a communicative turn within a specified time frame. These data can serve as baseline data for documenting progress and deciding "what to do next."

A child's apparent communicative skill or lack thereof may be related directly to the time, context, tools, and strategies of the language sampling experience. No standard language sampling procedure has been proven to be most effective for all children. With all children, but especially with younger children or children from cultures different from the examiner's culture, a familiar sampling context and trusted conversational partner is more likely to provide better verbal interaction. Some children respond to specific toys, games, or story telling with zest and enthusiastic verbalizations; whereas others, depending on their culture or past experiences, find the same objects or activities frightening, uninteresting, or over stimulating. For those children who have experienced abuse or unpleasantness in their lives, the sight of some objects may even stimulate withdrawal. For example, one preschool girl put her head down on the table and refused to speak again in the session when a family of dolls was brought into the assessment. Her foster mother reported later that the dolls were similar to the ones used by the psychologist when the child first described being sexually abused.

A child must experience a sense of warmth and feel calm and connected to achieve the full engagement, shared attention, and verbal exchanges necessary for a good language sample. First, the adult must physically get down to the child's eye level—for a preschooler that is likely on the floor—and follow the child's lead playing or exploring the environment. Adults should try to capture the child's emotional tone as well (Greenspan, 1992). A child who feels understood and connected is more likely to stay engaged and to demonstrate his or her communicative abilities. In an assessment process, time constraints may tempt adults to try to get the child to match their own pace and emotional tone for expedient test results. This temptation must be avoided so as not to compromise the language sampling process.

Direct questioning, especially *yes* and *no* questions, should be avoided unless questions occur naturally. Small figures of people, animals, or television and storybook characters often provide children with ideas for representational play and rich language interaction. Such objects can be springboards for narrative discourse and interactive symbolic play, as can wordless picture books. Stockman (1996) used racecars and interactions with books to gather language samples from African American preschool children. Manipulative materials, such as play dough or art supplies, can be problematic, however, because children may become so involved in manipulating the objects they cease talking. Although materials are important in gathering a rich language sample, they provide only the props for shared attention and interaction. It is the adult's ability to provide a warm, responsive context that is the key to eliciting optimal two-way communication exchanges.

Play-Based Assessment

In typical development, communication abilities and semantic concepts tend to develop in parallel with play (Paul, 1995). Informal play scale observational tools are available (e.g., Carpenter, 1987; McCune, 1995; Westby, 1988), but relatively formal tools have been designed as well. Transdisciplinary Play-Based Assessment (Linder, 1993) is one that involves a single play facilitator and group of observing professionals. It uses play interaction contexts to assess four domains: social-emotional, cognitive, language and communication, and sensorimotor. The outcome is a criterion-referenced analysis of developmental level, learning style, interactions patterns, and other behaviors relevant to intervention planning.

Another relatively formal tool, the Communication and Symbolic Behaviors Scales Developmental Profile (CSBS; Wetherby & Prizant, 2002), uses direct sampling of interactive verbal and nonverbal play behaviors and a caregiver questionnaire. It is designed for children with functional communication between 6 and 24 months (with chronological ages from 6 months to 6 years), including those suspected of having autism (Wetherby, Prizant, & Hutchinson, 1998). The observation procedure uses communicative temptations, such as wind-up toys, balloons, and bubbles. Four areas—communicative function, communicative means, reciprocity, and social affective signaling—are each rated on scales of 1 to 5. Results can be compared with normative data.

The outcomes of play-based assessments generally include recommendations for symbolic and social interaction abilities to target in intervention. Play-based assessments have the advantage of exploring intervention contexts and materials, as well as language targets.

ASSESSING SPEECH-LANGUAGE AND COMMUNICATION FOR INFANTS AND TODDLERS

Preparation for preschool language assessment requires an appreciation for the developmental advances of the infant and toddler years. Whenever a child's communicative development is in question, a thorough audiometric examination by an audiologist is warranted. Assessment also should involve multiple opportunities to observe communication functions and discourse structures, receptive and expressive language abilities, and speech production at the syllable and word level (Wetherby, Yonclas, & Bryan, 1989). Prognosis is considered to be poorer if particular parameters, such as gestural communication or failure to establish joint attention, are involved, or if more parameters of language are affected.

Assessing Communicative Functions for Infants and Toddlers

Early communication between infants and caregivers begins as two-way, presymbolic exchanges. These lay the groundwork for later conversations. The child's earliest communicative functions are termed protoimperatives or protodeclaratives (Bates, 1976). Protoimperatives include conventional gestures to request objects or express rejection. Protodeclaratives function to draw attention by showing or pointing.

As toddlers develop, a wide range of "discourse functions" (Chapman, 1981) emerges, indicating that the child recognizes basic conversational expectations and can incorporate them into a communicative repertoire. Assessment should address the range, frequency, and means (nonverbal as well as verbal) of communicative functions (Paul, 1995). If a child shows few examples of nonverbal communication and does not complete circles of communication (Greenspan, 1992), the child may not yet recognize the value of communication. Discourse functions for toddlers include: (a) requests for information about their world, (b) acknowledgments of previous messages conveyed to them, and (c) answers to requests for information. Failure to produce a full range of early intentions, particularly comments (Paul & Shiffer, 1991), may indicate a risk for future communicative development (Wetherby & Prutting, 1984). Assessment of the range of functions can be completed informally, keeping a tally of the child's communicative intentions over time and in different contexts. The answer to the "what to do next" question for a child not using a full range of communicative intentions would include recommendations to increase both range of functions and the contexts in which they appear.

The frequency with which a child makes expressive communicative attempts also should be assessed. To assess communicative act frequency, speech-language pathologists tally the number of times a child initiates communication in a set period of time. The expectation is for 18-month-olds to produce approximately two intentional communication moves per minute. This increases to an expectation for more than five examples per minute by 24 months of age (Paul & Shiffer, 1991; Wetherby, Cain, Yonclas, & Walker, 1988). Even those children with limited speech production should communicate nonverbally at the expected rates. A child who does not initiate interactions in play with his parents or with examiners at these frequencies may have a problem with the expression of communicative intention. The answer to the "what to do next" question for such a child would include dynamic assessment activities and recommendations about how to persuade the child to engage adults in actions and to share attention with others.

Assessing the means by which communicative intentions are expressed is important, as well. Young children should decrease their reliance on presymbolic, nonverbal vocalizations and gestures and increase their use of verbal symbols during the toddler stage. Gestures are typically combined with vocalizations that sound increasingly like words from 12 to 18 months of age. From 18 to 24 months, conventional words or word combinations are used with increasing frequency to express a range of communicative intentions (Chapman, 1981). An assessment of the toddler's primary means of communication can help determine "what to do next" in intervention.

A well-developed gestural system is important in the development of overall communicative skills; however, if a child's communication is limited to gestures, a speech-language pathologist may need to assist the family and child to develop strategies for emphasizing the functionality of vocalizations and words and for assisting the child to acquire a broader range of spoken language possibilities. When speech production capabilities seem to be unusually limited, the assessment should consider whether limitations of speech motor control, as described subsequently, might provide a partial explanation.

Assessing Comprehension for Infants and Toddlers

Understanding the meaning of words is a benchmark indicator of the beginnings of language. Comprehension of a first word usually occurs about three months ahead of the production of a first word. Comprehension of 50 different words usually occurs about five months before 50 different words can be produced (Benedict, 1979). Most 18- to 24-month-old children comprehend probably only two or three words out of each sentence they hear (Chapman, 1978), but they can use nonverbal and contextual cues to respond appropriately to longer utterances. Parents and others thus can overestimate toddlers' language comprehension abilities.

The first question to be asked in an assessment of receptive language is, "Does the toddler with emerging language understand words without nonlinguistic cues?" Few formal tests of receptive language exist for toddlers that are useful for attaining specific information about comprehension of words and sentences. Standardized tests of receptive language such as the Peabody Picture Vocabulary Test–III (Dunn, Dunn, & Williams, 1997) only assess understanding of single word vocabulary. Because toddlers often understand a unique set of vocabulary words peculiar to their individual families, standardized tools for children with emerging language may be problematic. The MacArthur-Bates CDI (Fenson et al., 2003) parent-report checklists, however, would be appropriate for this purpose. Low receptive vocabulary abilities, inconsistent responses, or idiosyncratic meanings all could signal language disorder. For example, Jack, described at the beginning of this chapter, pointed correctly when asked, *Where is the computer?* but he did not respond to *Show me the doggie* or *Where is puppy?* while looking at a picture book. When asked, *Where is dolly?* he pointed to a toy dog because Dolly happened to be the name of his family's Collie. Parents can help identify explanations for such idiosyncratic vocabulary associations.

Miller and Paul (1995) described informal comprehension assessment activities for toddlers with emerging language. They suggested asking children to identify a variety of nouns and verbs at random intervals. Comprehension of single words without the support of nonlinguistic cues is taken to indicate performance expected at the 12-to 18-month level in normally developing children (Chapman, 1978). Expectations are for the child to demonstrate linguistic comprehension of three to five nouns and three to five verbs at the 12-to 18-month level. Expectations for the 18- to 24-month level are for the child to understand two-word instructions. Miller and Paul suggested using unusual combinations of action verb + object noun combinations, such as *Hug the shoe* or *Push the baby*, to assess whether the child is not just doing what usually is done with the object.

Following success on a majority of the 18- to 24-month items, toddlers are asked to process agent + action + object instructions typical for children in the 24- to 36-month-old age range. Children are asked to perform probable and improbable actions with agents and objects, such as to show: *The mommy feeds the baby* and *The baby feeds the mommy*. Miller and Paul (1995) provided a worksheet for charting results to such informal comprehension probes.

If toddlers succeed at the 24- to 36-month level, formal assessment measures might be administered. Possibilities include the PPVT–III (Dunn, Dunn, & Williams, 1997), the Preschool Language Scale–4th edition (Zimmerman, Steiner, & Pond, 2002), the Test for Auditory Comprehension of Language–Revised (TACL–R) (Carrow-Woolfolk, 1985), or the Test of Early Language Development (TELD) (Hresko, Reid, & Hammill, 1991). Other formal assessment instruments are listed and described in Table 16.3.

When poor comprehension is observed in a variety of contexts over time, the "what to do next" question results in recommendations to enhance language input and adult scaffolding to help the child discover meaning through child-centered activities. In such cases, it is particularly critical to assess the child's communication strengths and interests to develop a complete picture the team can use to plan intervention.

Assessing Communicative Expression for Infants and Toddlers

Before they say their first word, typically developing children have been expressing themselves for at least a year through nonverbal gestures, facial expressions, and vocalizations. During the second and third years of life, they become more verbal, as well as increase the range of intentions they express. When toddlers are referred for evaluation, it is likely that they are late in using words to communicate and have fewer resources for acquiring them. The MacArthur-Bates Communicative Development Inventories (CDI; Fenson, et al., 2003) are appropriate at this stage to judge early vocabulary use and preverbal indicators, such as gestures, play, pretending, and imitating. Parents are asked to check off specific forms of language they have observed their children comprehending or producing.

The accepted norm for age of acquisition of first words is 12 to 18 months. Although this well-known developmental milestone is important, the rate of acquisition of additional words is also a factor. At 18 months, 84% of children produce a wide variety of words; by 24 months, most produce more than 150 words; and by 30 months, the expectation is more than 450 words (Stoel-Gammon, 1991). This explosion includes words that represent a variety of semantic categories, for example, not only agents and actions, but also recurrence (e.g., *more*) and disappearance (e.g., *all gone*).

Theorists often cite perceptual and cognitive underpinnings for early development. Quinn and his colleagues (e.g., Quinn & Eimas, 1997; Quinn, Adams, Kennedy, Shettler, & Wasnik, 2003) have shown that infants are capable of forming spatial concepts even during prelinguistic stages of development from 7 to 10 months. Casasola (2005) showed early connections between concepts and words, by demonstrating that 18-month-olds who are beginning to comprehend words could benefit from hearing the word *on* in association with the concept of how one object can support another. The implication is that children acquire concepts first, making it easier to map words onto them. Greenspan and Shanker (2004) theorized as well that critical emotional interactions early in life are responsible for the development of symbol formation, language, and intelligence.

The transition from single-word production to two-word phrases occurs for most middle-class toddlers by 18 months of age. The mean length of utterance (MLU) at 24 months is between 1.5 and 2.4 morphemes (Miller, 1981). An MLU of 1.5 generally indicates an equal number of one- and two-word utterances, although a few three-word utterances may be sprinkled in, as well. An MLU of 2.4 indicates a higher proportion of three-word utterances and perhaps some four-word utterances. Although MLU has long been used as a measure of language development, a review of the research (Eisenberg, Fersko, & Lundgren, 2001) has revealed problems both in terms of validity and reliability. Eisenberg and her colleagues concluded that MLU may be an appropriate measure for younger children or those whose MLU is low; but language disorder cannot be ruled out for children with higher MLU. Hadley (1999) suggested counting *unique syntactic types* (UST) (defined as two or more words that could fit into the phrase structure of a grammatically complete utterance) as a measure of syntactic ability at early stages of development.

Assessing Speech Production for Infants and Toddlers

Analysis of a recorded speech sample of toddlers can help to answer the "what to do next" question about speech development. Parents can help by gathering video or audio recordings of their toddler's verbalizations at times when they are most likely to be talkative, such as during morning play, or at bedtime.

The expectation for speech production is that toddlers should be able to produce at least some words that are clear enough for unfamiliar adults to understand. By two years, the "typical" child can match the consonant phonemes of adult words with at least 70% accuracy (Stoel-Gammon, 1987). Although phonological difficulties are not generally included in the criteria for a diagnosis of SLI, young children with SLI often demonstrate phoneme production similar to younger children (Paul & Jennings, 1992; Rescorla & Ratner, 1996). That is, the phonological systems of children with SLI appear to be delayed and less systematic in development.

Ruling out Difficulty with Hearing

When speech production skills are delayed, a critical question is whether the child can hear. Even a mild impairment in only the high frequencies can impede the acquisition of speech and language (Northern & Downs, 1984). Intermittent hearing loss due to fluid in the middle ear can also cause difficulty in learning to perceive and produce all of the sounds of language (Gravel & Wallace, 1995; Klein, Chase, Teele, Menyuk, & Rosner, 1988). As with infants and toddlers, audiologists should be involved in the assessment of hearing.

Oral Motor Assessment

Another possible explanation for slow speech development is impairment of the oral motor mechanism structure and function. Oral motor examinations can be challenging with toddlers, who are notorious for resistance to procedures around their faces. Bright young children with oral motor difficulties also may be keenly aware that they are not able to speak as well as others, and may be particularly reticent to imitate speech or oral motor movements. Even after weeks of developing a good relationship with a toddler, a request for oral motor imitation may be met with a firm "no." Thus, clinicians must be unusually creative in setting a relaxed, playful tone, and they must be quick. Play with a penlight, modeling a playful look into a mirror, or performing amateur sleight of hand to find a small block or coin behind the ear before looking for one in the mouth may convince the child to allow quick examination of the oral cavity.

In the oral-motor examination, speech-language pathologists look for normal eruption and alignment of teeth, intact hard and soft palates, elevation and retraction of the soft palate when the child vocalizes, and a symmetrical and mobile tongue. The child may or may not permit the clinician to use a tongue blade to hold the tongue down for a better look at the posterior oral cavity and to check for normal muscle tone. Some young children are more likely to do so if first allowed to peek into the examiner's mouth. If a child's speech is hypernasal, the clinician looks for evidence of a submucous cleft. This is sometimes signaled by an area at the juncture of the hard and soft palates that is gray, rather than pink, or the presence of a bifid uvula (split in the little piece of skin that dangles from the soft palate).

Speech-Motor Control

When speech motor control problems are suspected, activities are designed to draw contrasts between reflexive and voluntary movements and between speech and nonspeech movements. *Dysarthria* is the term for the speech distortions associated with cerebral palsy and other forms of direct neuromotor impairment. It is diagnosed when articulatory difficulties are associated with general weakness or incoordination of reflexive neural-motor control affecting eating or respiratory behavior as well as speech. Drooling often accompanies dysarthria.

Oral-motor apraxia differs in that it is a motor programming problem that only appears during voluntary movement attempts, not during reflexive breathing, chewing, and swallowing. Thus, the child cannot coordinate movements of the tongue, lips, jaw, and teeth for voluntary acts such as blowing, kissing, or speech production, but can eat without major difficulty. Developmental apraxia of speech (DAS) is often, but not always, linked to oral-motor apraxia. Toddlers with autism spectrum disorders may be more likely to demonstrate oral motor apraxia, speech apraxia, or both.

Formal instruments such as the Preschool Oral Motor Examination (Sheppard, 1987) or the Pre-Speech Assessment Scale (Morris, 1982) involve direct clinical assessment of oral motor behaviors for infants and young children. They can help identify causal physical factors for late developing speech for toddlers with emerging language.

SUMMARY

To summarize, by 24 months, the vast majority of children are competent in producing correct phonemes, communicate frequently, have large vocabularies, and are combining words into sentences. However, assessment at this stage is still difficult because normal development varies considerably. Some children who are slow in early speech-language development do catch up. The question of "what to do next" is not easily answered when assessment reveals slow speech-language development for toddlers. The goal is to identify all and only those children who truly need intervention and who are unlikely to reach typical milestones without it.

ASSESSING THE LANGUAGE OF PRESCHOOLERS

Children in the preschool stage of language development are primed for acquiring the grammatical code. This is the stage during which children combine words into complete sentences and understand and express ideas about a wide variety of concepts. During this period, children learn to vary their language to fit specific contexts and use comprehension strategies that are more linguistic than nonlinguistic. They also become more adept at producing all the phonemes of their language and speaking with a reasonable degree of fluency.

Several comprehensive language assessment tools designed for preschoolers are listed in Table 16.3. Previous reviewers have criticized many formal assessment tools for their psychometric flaws (McCauley & Swisher, 1984; Plante & Vance, 1994) and failure to report the test's sensitivity in identifying *all* the children with potential language disorders, as well as specificity in identifying *only* the children with actual language disorders. Table 16.3 includes many newer editions that have presumably responded to such criticisms, but such modifications should not be assumed. Examiners are urged to read manuals carefully and to use the data from formal tests with a degree of caution.

Assessing Communication Functions in the Preschool Years

During the preschool years, children gain increasing ability to vary language use in different conversational contexts. Compared with their abilities between 2 to 4 years of age, children in the age range from 4 to 8 become more capable of: (a) getting attention specifically and effectively, (b) taking into account the listener's prior knowledge, (c) being sensitive to the effects of interruption and formulating polite indirect requests, (d) supplying reasons when attempting to persuade peers to comply with requests, and (e) using obligation, justification, or bribery, as well as urgency, when their requests are not met (Ervin-Tripp & Gordon, 1986).

It is difficult to assess pragmatic functions with a formal test because the essence of pragmatic use is the ability to modify how one says things to achieve varied communicative purposes in natural contexts (e.g., requesting actions or objects indirectly, making descriptive comments or evaluative statements to an unfamiliar partner). The ability to interpret social meanings by using nonverbal communicative cues such as prosodic tone, facial expression, and body posture, as well as the words spoken, is also an important target of pragmatic assessment. Such abilities are best observed in naturalistic contexts. Therefore, spontaneous language samples gathered in social interactions with peers, particularly during symbolic and creative play, may provide the richest opportunities to judge a child's repertoire of communicative acts.

Concern is noted particularly when a child is observed to have an imbalance of assertive and responsive communicative acts. Fey (1986) suggested coding assertive forms, including requests, comments, statements, and disagreements initiated by the child, and comparing them with the proportion of responsive forms the child produces in response to questions or statements. There are no hard-and-fast rules for identifying patterns, but a pattern of balanced assertive and responsive acts indicates an *active conversationalist*; a pattern with many assertive and few responsive acts indicates a *verbal noncommunicator*; a pattern with few assertive and many responsive acts indicates a *passive conversationalist*; and a pattern with few assertive and few responsive acts indicates an *inactive communicator* (Fey, 1986).

Assessing Language Comprehension in the Preschool Years

Preschoolers, like toddlers, may employ a variety of cognitive and nonlinguistic strategies to respond to commands and requests (Edmonston & Thane, 1992). English-speaking children rely on canonical word order to identify the subject in passive sentences at age 4. Thus, when asked to use stuffed animals to show, *The pig is kissed by the dog*, four-year-olds are likely to have the pig do the kissing, although they would not make this mistake for nonreversible passives such as, *The present was opened by the boy*. By age 5, most children can use syntactic strategies to comprehend passive syntax, even when canonical order is violated, as in, *The mother was fed by the baby*.

Formal tests of language comprehension (e.g., Test of Auditory Comprehension of Language–Revised, TACL–R, Carrow-Woolfolk, 1985) often test understanding of particular lexical and syntactic relationships by asking the child to point to a correct picture from several choices. When Plante and Vance (1994) assessed the properties of several comprehension measures, they found that the SPELT–II (Werner & Kresheck, 1983) had the best specificity and sensitivity for identifying specific language impairment.

Children with comprehension deficits may have difficulty understanding nonverbal, as well as verbal, concepts and relationships. Children with specific language impairments, however, may be able to rely on nonverbal means to appear to comprehend more language than they actually do. Informal assessment can be used to sort out such factors by playing with the child and looking for opportunities to probe for understanding of varied lexical items and syntactic relationships. For example, the examiner looking for comprehension of prepositions might say, *I think the baby's bottle is under the chair*, or *Let's put the cookies in the refrigerator*. Such probes should be presented without gestural cues, and direct commands or questions should be avoided. The context of playfulness is especially important when attempting to assess the comprehension abilities of children who have been sensitized to the demands of testing and who refuse to cooperate with more formal measures. Probes should also present some less plausible content so the child cannot rely on early nonlinguistic strategies, such as requests to put cookies in the refrigerator instead of the oven. To assess whether a child has moved beyond the order-of-mention strategy, a probe might be: *Before you feed the baby, let's give her a bath; What do we need for that?* A correct response would provide positive evidence of linguistic comprehension, but an incorrect response or no response might indicate only that the preschooler was determined to take a different pathway in play. In such cases, additional probes are needed, perhaps further into an interactive play sequence.

Assessing Concept Development in the Preschool Years

An inventory of conceptual vocabulary comprehension and expression also can be gathered. Bracken (1984) defined a basic concept as a "word, in its most elementary sense, that is a label for one of the basic colors, comparatives, directions, materials, positions, quantities, relationships, sequences, shapes, sizes, social or emotional states and characteristics, textures, and time" (p. 7). According to this definition, a word chosen to assess knowledge of a basic concept should be the most simple one. For example, the word *cold* would be considered a basic concept, whereas *frigid* or *chilly* would not.

Basic concepts are involved whenever a child makes relational judgments among objects, persons, or situations, or in relation to some standard (Boehm, 2001). Although children have a fairly complete mastery of most basic concept terms by age 5 or 6 years, some concepts are not fully understood until age 8 or 9. The language of directions is particularly rich in the language of basic concepts, and children who are delayed in the acquisition of basic concepts and related vocabulary are at a disadvantage in instructional and assessment contexts, as well as in social situations. Preschoolers who do not understand basic concepts of *first* and *last*, for example, are likely to experience difficulty with the common preschool activity of "lining up," or with completing tasks in orderly sequence.

The acquisition of basic concepts, although reflected in the ability to use "conceptual vocabulary" in language comprehension and expression, goes beyond the use of a set of vocabulary. As noted previously, Greenspan and Shanker (2004) emphasized connections between concept development and social-emotional factors. They theorized that concepts associated with emotional reciprocity were essential to acquiring the ability to empathize, form a theory of mind, think abstractly, and solve problems with others. This suggests the need for a broad interpretation of concept development when deciding "what to do next" in assessment and intervention.

Formal tests of basic concepts include the Boehm Test of Basic Concepts–Preschool Version (BTBC–PV; Boehm, 2001) and the Bracken Basic Concept Scale–Revised (BBCS–R; Bracken, 1998). The BTBC–PV assesses preschoolers' ability to understand 26 relational concepts thought to be important for successful entry into school. The BBCS–R can be used with children from 2 years 6 months to 7 years 11 months to assesses comprehension of 308 verbal concepts in 11 categories: colors, letters, numbers/counting, sizes, comparisons, shapes, direction/position, self-/social awareness, texture/material, quantity, and time/sequence. The BBCS–R includes a checklist for concepts "not mastered" (i.e., probably not understood), "transitional" (i.e., understood in some situations), or "mastered" (i.e., understood in most situations).

Assessing Language Expression in the Preschool Years

Most formal and informal language assessment procedures for preschoolers depend heavily on the observation of expressive language abilities. Among typically developing children, communication abilities and speech production skills advance at a remarkable pace.

Word knowledge development from ages 2 to 7 years is particularly rapid. The body of research suggests that children between 18 months and 6 years add an average of five word roots per day, allowing them to comprehend around 14,000 words by the time they are 6 years old (Crais, 1990). In fact, vocabulary acquisition is one aspect of language development that continues across the life span. As young as age 3 to 4 years, children can use contextual cues to "fast map" information about novel words into semantic memory with only one exposure (Carey & Bartlett, 1978). The fact that children can recognize new words as they encounter them provides additional evidence of an amazing auditory discrimination system that is tuned at birth to discriminate the sounds of speech (Eimas, 1975). When children are slow at learning words in spite of adequate opportunity, the integrity of the language learning system may be suspect.

The growing sophistication of syntactic abilities during the preschool years allows children to formulate and comprehend an infinite variety of sentences to communicate intricate descriptions; convey complex logical, temporal, or causative relationships; or to perform many other complex communicative functions. Although language specialists now recognize that language acquisition continues through the school-age years, development of grammatical knowledge during the preschool years is astounding in its breadth and speed.

The primacy of grammatical acquisition during this stage also makes it an important indicator for discriminating atypical language development. This may be one reason the SPELT–II (Werner & Kresheck, 1983) performed best in the study by Plante and Vance (1994) when compared with tests of language comprehension and multi-task assessment. Spontaneous language sampling techniques also are essential for observing acquisition of the syntactic rules for formulating increasingly lengthy sentences and the lexicon and semantic strategies for conveying increasingly abstract meanings.

Language sampling techniques are used prominently during the preschool years to assess language expression. Transcribed samples are analyzed for length and complexity of utterances. Mean length of utterance (MLU) is computed by counting the number of morphemes (words and word endings, such as plurals, possessives, and tense markers) in a sample of 100 or more utterances, then dividing this total by the number of utterances. The resulting MLU in morphemes is compared with data for expected ranges associated with normal development using sources such as Brown (1973) or Miller (1981). Examiners are reminded to be cautious, however, when interpreting MLU data as having normative implications (Eisenberg, Fersko, & Lundgren, 2001).

It is also helpful to look for the productive use of certain morphemes that have an expected order of emergence, starting with the inflectional rule for adding -*ing*, the early production of *in* and *on*, and the regular plural -*s*, and moving to inflected auxiliary and main verb forms of *to be*, as well as possessive and past tense endings (Brown, 1973; De Villiers & De Villiers, 1973). The typically developing child goes through a period of over generalizing rules for adding bound morphemes at this point, and that is a good sign. In other words, when a child "regularizes" the use of plural and past-tense endings (e.g., *feets* and *goed*), the clinician can conclude that the child is attending to the regularities of language. In typical development, the irregular forms may appear early as unanalyzed forms, but then disappear temporarily. Most children do not figure out the full set of irregular forms until well into their elementary school years. Adults may even struggle with irregular forms of a few infrequently used words.

On the other hand, persistence of immature forms of irregularly inflected words, such as *me/I* pronoun confusion persisting into kindergarten, can signal cause for concern (Leonard, 1980). In fact, persistent difficulty with finite verb morphology (i.e., correct production of the regular past, -*ed*, present third person singular, -*s*, and copula and auxiliary forms of *is*, *are*, and *am*) is a better indicator of specific language impairment among 3- to 5-year-olds than problems with MLU or lexical diversity (Goffman & Leonard, 2000).

Some techniques for assessing the acquisition of particular grammatical forms and sentence structures are hybrids between formal and informal procedures. Developmental Sentence Scoring (Lee, 1974), in particular, has been used over several decades now because it can capture a set of indicators with a single score, which can be compared with normative data. Such tools provide clinicians with a means for assessing quantitatively how a child is doing relative to standard English learning peers and also describing qualitatively which structures a child is or is not using when obligated by linguistic context.

Cultural Linguistic Diversity

A caution for using grammatical assessment checklists and similar tools is that they are particularly biased against children learning a dialect or language other than standard English. A child's grammatical performance always should be analyzed with reference to the linguistic community in which the child is immersed. Children learning English as a second language may use a mixture of forms from their first language (L_1), at the same time they are beginning to incorporate the rules of English (L_2). A child's language should be evaluated in the system in which the child is most fluent and comfortable, especially for purposes of determining disorder.

Particular care should also be taken when a child is learning a dialectal variant of standard English. For example, children learning African American Vernacular English (AAVE; also called Ebonics or Black English Vernacular) often use different rules for forming some sentence structures, such as questions (*What that is? Where you work? Do he still have it?*), complex sentences (*I aks him, do he want some more; Why he's in there cause baby scared the dog*), and negatives (*Can't nobody make me; He not a baby*). Verb inflections may differ for main verb and auxiliaries, such as forms of *to be* (*That boy my friend; The girl singin'*). Children using later developing AAE forms also have options for conveying temporal relations not available in standard English, such as the invariant be (*He be my friend*) and the remote past aspect (*I been wanted this*).

Several systems have been described for analyzing language samples of children learning AAVE. Nelson (1998) presented a Black English Sentence Scoring (BESS) system whose validity had been assessed by Hyter (1984). BESS is used in concert with DSS (Lee, 1974) to credit AAVE features that would be penalized with DSS. Washington and Craig (1994) listed 17 AAVE forms that signal dialectal difference. Stockman (1996) suggested a "minimal competency core" (MCC) to be used for criterion reference, looking for developmental evidence in four areas of language development expected for 33- to 36-month-olds— a phonological feature core, a pragmatic functions core, a semantic relations core, and a morphosyntactic core. This tool has the advantage of assessing more areas of language development than syntax and morphology and having adequate specificity (Schraeder, Quinn, Stockman, & Miller, 1999). Seymour, Roeper, and de Villiers (2003) developed a formal test and screening test, *Diagnostic Evaluation of Language Variance* (DELV-Criterion Referenced

Test, and DELV-Screening Test) using current linguistic theory to assess both language variation and language risk status among children learning AAVE.

Late Talkers and Ongoing Difficulties

Late talking toddlers diagnosed with specific language impairment involving expressive language (SLI-E) at age 2 years represent a discrete diagnostic group. Such children are at high risk for continuing difficulty with phonological and language skills through their preschool years, but not invariably so. Thus, they present a particular challenge to examiners. Roberts, Rescorla, Giroux, and Stevens (1998) found that children with SLI-E at age 2 had significantly fewer vocalizations than typically developing children, but there was no difference in frequency of vocalization at age 3. For many, however, there continued to be differences in other areas of articulation and language development, including lower overall intelligibility and MLU. Because the development of a productive phonetic inventory and grammatical skills continue to pose problems for toddlers with SLI as they move into later stages of development, comprehensive assessment may help determine "what to do next" in intervention.

Paul (1996) concluded from her review of the literature that 50% of late talkers do "catch up." She recommended a "watch and see" (not *wait* and see) policy of reassessment every 3 to 6 months for 2- to 3-year-olds, and every 6 to 12 months for 3- to 5-year-olds before diagnosing disorder and providing formal intervention services. Based on a similar review of the literature, Kelly (1998) concluded, in contrast, that the heterogeneity of the group and the difficulty of predicting who will and will not "catch up" indicate a need for referral for speech-language assessment and consultation, if not intervention.

Roulstone, Peters, Glogowska, and Enderby (2003) followed a group of 69 children for 12 months who were identified as having speech and language delay prior to 3.5 years. The children received no direct intervention during this time. Although general improvements were noted, variations were relatively wide. After one year, two-thirds of the children still met criteria for speech and language delay. Webster, Majnemer, Platt, and Shevell (2004) documented persistence of early language impairment for 36 of the 43 children (84%) they followed from preschool into elementary school. Negative trends for cognitive abilities also were observed. That is, the language impairment was specific to language at the preschool level (i.e., cognitive scores were within normal limits), but by elementary school, 57% of the children demonstrated cognitive scores more than one standard deviation below the mean. Only 10% of the group had both normal language and cognitive skills at follow-up, although the researchers could identify no factors at intake that predicted which outcome would appear. La Paro, Justice, Skibbe, and Pianta (2004) studied a large national database and used sophisticated statistical methods to look for predictors of persistent preschool language impairment. They found that maternal sensitivity and maternal depression both contributed significantly to persistent difficulty.

Narratives

In addition to assessing the child's expressive language at the sentence level, larger units of discourse should be considered. Preschoolers should be developing skill for telling and retelling events with an emerging narrative organizational structure. Those with higher levels of language competence generate stories that demonstrate better chronological sequencing, organization, and numbers of information units (Fiorentino & Howe, 2004).

Applebee's (1978) scheme for describing developing narrative ability indicated that children learn to maintain a central focus while chaining together a set of events using both temporal and logical links. Hedberg and Westby (1993) adapted this system along with story grammar analysis (Stein & Glenn, 1979) to describe a sequence of story development: (1) *isolated description*, with little relationship among elements, (2) *action sequence*, with temporal links, (3) *reactive sequence,* with cause and effect, (5) *abbreviated episode,* with an implied goal for addressing a central problem, (6) *complete episode*, with planning to achieve the goal, and (7) *complex (or embedded) episode*, in which the main character overcomes obstacles while implementing the plan. McCabe and Rollins (1994) recommended high point analysis, based on stories children told after hearing a story with a "high point" (i.e., problem, such as a bee sting) modeled by the clinician. Most preschoolers do not advance beyond the level of reactive sequence, which shows cause-effect, or abbreviated episode, which includes a problem but not true planning or resolution. Examiners also should note that even when children can produce more mature narratives under optimal conditions, most children move up and down the narrative maturity scales, depending on the context. That is, a child typically does not master a higher level of narrative maturity and then abandon all earlier levels. Miller, Gillam, and Peña (2000) have developed a narrative assessment and intervention system that uses techniques of dynamic assessment.

Narrative discourse analysis is generally better at answering questions about "what to do next" in intervention than answering diagnostic questions about whether or not the child has a language disorder. Actively playing with children as they develop stories and encouraging children to tell more complex stories are good ways to support development across lexical, syntactic, and discourse systems.

Assessing Speech Production in the Preschool Years

Improved speech production control and phonological knowledge combine to result in children's words becoming clearer and easier to understand during their preschool years. If a child is not speaking clearly enough to be understood by most adults by age 3, a formal articulation test and assessment of the child's use of immature phonological processes is warranted. Several frequently used tools for doing so are summarized in Table 16.3.

By age 7 years, most children produce all of the speech sounds of their language clearly and are able to blend them smoothly to produce clearly intelligible words and sentences with only minor dysfluencies. Children who persist in substituting /w/ for /r/ or /l/, or who produce /s/ with the tongue between the teeth as a lisp, may be identified as needing speech therapy, but not until the second or third grade unless other communicative symptoms justify the need. An exception would be if a child had difficulties with all of these phonemes and had marginal intelligibility as a result, or if a child had concurrent language problems.

Assessing Phonological Awareness and Emergent Literacy in the Preschool Years

When a child's phonological system for representing the speech sounds of language is limited, the child is particularly at risk for developing sound awareness abilities, one of the key indicators of preparation to read (Blachman, 1994; Kamhi & Catts, 1989). Examiners should assess whether the child has productive use of the phonological rules for articulating words in sentences with relative completeness (if not full correctness), based on expectation that preschool children's articulatory abilities and syllable and rime awareness (rime is the part after the onset, from the first vowel to the end of the word) develop earlier than their phoneme awareness (Carroll, Snowling, Hulme, & Stevenson, 2003; Lonigan, Burgess, Anthony, & Barker, 1998). Comprehensive assessment of emergent literacy abilities in the preschool years should assess not only phonological sensitivity, but vocabulary and print knowledge as well (Dickinson, Anastasopoulos, McCabe, Peisner-Feinberg, & Poe, 2003).

When a child is in kindergarten, first, or second grade, the assessment should extend to the child's awareness of phonemes in the contexts of rhyming, segmenting, and combining sounds in isolated words or nonsense words. The ability to connect sounds to print in both reading and writing modes might also be considered when assessing how the child is able to use speech capabilities to support the acquisition of written language, along with general language ability (Dickinson et al., 2003).

SUMMARY

This chapter presents assessment of speech-language and communication abilities in preschool-age children within a framework aimed at addressing the question "what to do next" for diagnostic or intervention purposes. Parents' concerns about their children's language and communication development always should be taken seriously. Screening tools, parent questionnaires, and informal observations may lead to a decision to complete a full speech-language assessment, or it may result in a recommendation for consultation about how to foster normal development and monitor ongoing development. The preschool years are both an exciting time and an essential time to be laying the communication and language foundations for social interaction, self-regulation, and academic preparation. Children who are demonstrating signs of difficulty may be affected to different degrees in the areas of communication, language, and speech. Within language, they may have relative strengths and needs related to language phonology, morphology, syntax, semantics, and pragmatics. Comprehensive assessment involves interdisciplinary input and a combination of formal and informal methods to describe the child's functioning in multiple areas. The outcome is information that diagnostic and intervention teams can use to make informed decisions regarding what to do next to promote the child's development and social and academic success.

REFERENCES

American Psychiatric Association. (1994). *Diagnostic and statistical manual of mental disorders* (4th ed.). Washington, DC: American Psychiatric Association.

American Speech-Language-Hearing Association. (1982). Committee on Language, Speech and Hearing Services in the Schools. Definitions: Communicative disorders and variations. *American Speech-Language-Hearing Association, 24*, 949–950.

Applebee, A. N. (1978). *The child's concept of story*. Chicago, IL: University of Chicago Press.

Bashir, A. S. (1989). Language intervention and the curriculum. *Seminars in Speech and Language, 10*(3), 181–191.

Bates, E. (1976). *Language in context: Studies in the acquisition of pragmatics*. New York: Academic Press.

Bates, E., Bretherton, E., & Snyder, L. (1988). *From first words to grammar: Individual differences and dissociable mechanisms*. New York: Cambridge University Press.

Benedict, H. (1979). Early lexical development: Comprehension and production. *Journal of Child Language, 6*, 183–200.

Blachman, B. A. (1994). Early literacy acquisition: The role of phonological awareness. In G. P. Wallach & K. G. Butler (Eds.), *Language learning disabilities in school-age children and adolescents* (pp. 253–274). Boston: Allyn & Bacon.

Boehm, A. (2001). *Boehm Test of Basic Concepts–Preschool Version*. San Antonio, TX: Harcourt Assessment.

Brachlow, A., Jordan, A. E., & Tervo, R. (2001). Developmental screenings in rural settings: A comparison of the child development review and the Denver II Developmental Screening Test. *Journal of Rural Health, 17*(3), 156–159.

Bracken, B. A. (1984). *Bracken Basic Concept Scale*. San Antonio, TX: The Psychological Corporation.

Bracken, B. A. (1998). *Bracken Basic Concept Scale–Revised* (BBCS–R). San Antonio, TX: Harcourt Assessment.

Brown, R. (1973). *A first language*. Cambridge, MA: Harvard University Press.

Carey, S., & Bartlett, E. (1978). Acquiring a single new word. *Papers and Reports in Child Language Development, 15*, 17–29.

Carpenter, R. (1987). Play Scale. In L. Olswang, C. Stoel-Gammon, T. Coggins, and R. Carpenter (Eds.), *Assessing prelinguistic and early behaviors in developmentally young children* (pp. 44–77). Seattle: University of Washington Press.

Carroll, J. M., Snowling, M. J., Hulme, C., & Stevenson, J. (2003). The development of phonological awareness in preschool children. *Developmental Psychology, 39*, 913–923.

Carrow-Woolfolk, E. (1985). *Test for Auditory Comprehension of Language–Revised* (TACL–R). Austin, TX: PRO-ED.

Casasola, M. (2005). Can language do the driving? The effect of linguistic input on infants' categorization of support spatial relations. *Developmental Psychology, 41*(1), 183–192.

Chapman, R. (1978). Comprehension strategies in children. In J. Kavanagh & P. Strange (Eds.), *Language and speech in the laboratory, school and clinic*. Cambridge: MIT Press.

Chapman, R. (1981). Exploring children's communicative intents. In J. Miller (Ed.), *Assessing language production in children* (pp. 111–138). Baltimore: University Park Press.

Charman, T., Drew, A., Baird, C., & Baird, G. (2003) Measuring early language development in preschool children with autism spectrum disorder using the MacArthur Communicative Development Inventory (Infant Form). *Journal of Child Language, 30*(1), 213–236.

Cole, K. N., Dale, P. S., & Mills, P. E. (1990). Defining language delay in young children by cognitive referencing: Are we saying more than we know? *Applied Psycholinguistics, 11*, 291–302.

Cole, K. N., Dale, P. S., & Mills, P. E. (1992). Stability of the intelligence quotient-language quotient relation: Is discrepancy modeling based on a myth? *American Journal on Mental Retardation, 97*, 131–143.

Cole, K. N., & Harris, S. R. (1992). Instability of the intelligence quotient-motor quotient relationship. *Developmental Medicine and Child Neurology, 34*, 633–641.

Cole, K. N., Mills, P. E., & Kelley, D. (1994). Agreement of assessment profiles used in cognitive referencing. *Language, Speech, and Hearing Services in Schools, 25*, 25–31.

Crais, E. R. (1990). World knowledge to word knowledge. World knowledge and language: Development and disorders. *Topics in Language Disorders, 10*(3), 45–62.

Crais, E. R. (1995). Expanding the repertoire of tools and techniques for assessing the communication skills of infants and toddlers. *American Journal of Speech-Language Pathology, 4*(3), 47–59.

Crais, E., & Roberts, J. (1991). Decision making in assessment and early intervention planning. *Language, Speech and Hearing Services in Schools, 22*, 19–30.

Dale, P. S. (1996). Parent report assessment of language and communication. In K. N. Cole, P. S. Dale, & D. J. Thal (Eds.), *Assessment of communication and language* (pp. 161–182). Baltimore: Paul H. Brookes.

De Villiers, J., & De Villiers, P. (1973). A cross-sectional study of the development of grammatical morphemes in child speech. *Journal of Psycholinguistic Research, 2*, 267–268.

Dickinson, D. K., Anastasopoulos, L., McCabe, A., Peisner-Feinberg, E. S., & Poe, M. D. (2003). The comprehensive language approach to early literacy: The interrelationships among vocabulary, phonological sensitivity, and print knowledge among preschool-aged children. *Journal of Educational Psychology, 95*(3), 465–481.

Dockrell, J. E. (2001). Assessing language skills in preschool children. *Child Psychology and Psychiatry Review, 6*(2), 74–85.

Dunn, L., Dunn, L., & Williams, K. T. (1997). *Peabody Picture Vocabulary Test–3rd edition*. Circle Pines, MN: American Guidance Service.

Edmonston, N. K., & Thane, N. L. (1992). Children's use of comprehension strategies in response to relational words: Implications for assessment. *American Journal of Speech-Language Pathology, 1*(2), 30–35.

Eimas, P. D. (1975). Developmental studies in speech perception. In L. B. Cohen & P. Salapatek (Eds.), *Infant perception: From sensation to cognition* (Vol. 2, pp. 193–231). New York: Academic Press.

Eisenberg, S. L., Fersko, T. M., & Lundgren, C. (2001). The use of MLU for identifying language impairment in preschool children: A review. *American Journal of Speech-Language Pathology, 10*(4), 323–342.

Ervin-Tripp, S., & Gordon, D. (1986). The development of requests. In R. L. Schiefelbusch (Ed.), *Language competence: Assessment and intervention* (pp. 61–95). Austin, TX: Pro-Ed.

Fenson, L., Dale, P. S., Resnick, J. S., Thal, D., Bates, E., Hartung, J. P., Pethick, D., & Reilly, J. S. (2003). *MacArthur-Bates Communicative Development Inventories (CDI)*. Baltimore, MD: Paul H. Brookes.

Fey, M. E. (1986). *Language intervention with young children*. San Diego, CA: College-Hill (now available from Pro-Ed., Austin, TX).

Fey, M. E., Long, S. H., & Cleave, P. L. (1994). Reconsideration of IQ criteria in the definition of specific language impairments. In R. V. Watkins & M. L. Rice (Eds.), *Specific language impairments in children*. Baltimore: Paul H. Brookes.

Fiorentino, L., & Howe, N. (2004). Language competence, narrative ability, and school readiness in low-income preschool children. *Canadian Journal of Behavioural Science, 36*(4), 280–294.

Francis, D. J., Fletcher, J. M., Shaywitz, B. A., Shaywitz, S. E., & Rourke, B. P. (1996). Defining learning and language disabilities: Conceptual and psychometric issues with the use of IQ tests. *Language, Speech, and Hearing Services in the Schools, 27*, 132–143.

Francis, D. J., Fletcher, J. M., Stuebing, K. K., Lyon, G. R., Shaywitz, B. A., & Shaywitz, S. E. (2005). Psychometric approaches to the identification of LD: IQ and achievement scores are not sufficient. *Journal of Learning Disabilities, 38*(2), 98–108.

Glascoe, F. P. (2001). Are overreferrals on developmental screening tests really a problem? *Archives of Pediatric and Adolescent Medicine, 155*(1), 54–59.

Goffman, L., & Leonard, J. (2000). Growth of language skills in preschool children with specific language impairment: Implications for assessment and intervention. *American Journal of Speech-Language Pathology, 9*(2), 151–161.

Gravel, J. S., & Wallace, I. (1995). Early otitis media, auditory abilities, and educational risk. *American Journal of Speech-Language Pathology, 4*(3), 89–94.

Greenspan S. (1992). *Infancy and early development*. Madison, CT: International Universities Press.

Greenspan, S., & Shanker, S. G. (2004). *The first idea: How symbols, language, and intelligence evolve from our early primate ancestors to modern humans*. Cambridge, MA: Da Capo Press.

Hadley, P. A. (1999). Validating a rate-based measure of early grammatical abilities: Unique syntactic types. *American Journal of Speech-Language Pathology, 8*, 261–272.

Hedberg, N. L., & Westby, C. E. (1993). Analyzing storytelling skills: Theory to practice. Tucson, AZ: Communication Skills Builders.

Hresko, W. P., Reid, D.K., & Hammill, D. D. (1991). *The Test of Early Language Development*, 2nd ed. (TELD–2). Austin, TX: PRO-ED.

Hyter, Y. (1984). *Reliability and validity of the Black English Sentence Scoring system*. Unpublished master's thesis, Western Michigan University, Kalamazoo.

Jacobs, E. (2001). The effects of adding dynamic assessment components to a computerized language screening test. *Communication Disorders Quarterly, 22*(4), 217–226.

Kamhi, A. G., & Catts, H. (1989). *Reading disabilities: A developmental language perspective.* Austin, TX: PRO-ED.

Kelly, D. J. (1998). A clinical synthesis of the "late talker" literature: Implications for service delivery. *Language, Speech, and Hearing Services in Schools 29*, 76–84.

Kemp, K., & Klee, T. (1997). Clinical language sampling practices: Results of a survey of speech-language pathologists in the United States. *Child Language Teaching and Therapy, 13*, 161–176.

Klein, J., Chase, C., Teele, D., Menyuk, P., & Rosner, B. (1988). Otitis media and the development of speech, language, and cognitive abilities at seven years of age. In D. Lim, C. Bluestone, J. Klein, & J. Nelson (Eds.), *Recent advances in otitis media* (pp. 396–400). Toronto: B.C. Decker.

La Paro, K. M., Justice, L., Skibbe, L. E., & Pianta, R. C. (2004). Relations among maternal, child, and demographic factors and the persistence of preschool language impairment. *American Journal of Speech-Language Pathology, 13*(4), 291–303.

Lahey, M. (1988). *Language disorders and language development.* New York: Macmillan.

Lee, L. L. (1974). *Developmental sentence analysis.* Evanston, IL: Northwestern University Press.

Leonard, L. B. (1980). The speech of language-disabled children. *Bulletin of the Orton Society (now Annuals of Dyslexia), 30*, 141–152.

Lidz, C. S. (1991). *Practitioner's guide to dynamic assessment.* New York: Guilford Press.

Linder, T. W. (1993). Transdisciplinary play-based assessment: A functional approach to working with young children (rev. ed.) Baltimore: Paul H. Brookes.

Locke, A., Ginsborg, J., & Peers, I. (2002). Development and disadvantage: Implications for the early years and beyond. *International Journal of Language and Communication Disorders, 37*(1), 3–15.

Lonigan, C. J., Burgess, S. R., Anthony, J. L., & Barker, T. A. (1998). Development of phonological sensitivity in 2- to 5-year-old children. *Journal of Educational Psychology, 90*, 294–311.

McCabe, A., & Rollins, P. R. (1994). Assessment of preschool narrative skills. *American Journal of Speech-Language Pathology, 3*(1), 45–56.

McCauley, R., & Swisher, L. (1984). Use and misuse of norm-referenced tests in clinical assessment: A hypothetical case. *Journal of Speech and Hearing Disorders, 49*, 338–348.

McCune, L. (1995). A normative study of representational play at the transition to language. *Developmental Psychology, 31*(2), 206.

Miller, J. F. (1981). *Assessing language production in children: Experimental procedures.* Austin, TX: PRO-ED.

Miller, J. F., & Paul, R. (1995). *The clinical assessment of language comprehension.* Baltimore: Paul H. Brookes.

Miller, J. F., Sedey, A. L., & Miolo, G. (1995). Validity of parent report measures of vocabulary development for children with Down syndrome. *Journal of Speech and Hearing Research, 38*, 1037–1044.

Miller, L., Gillam, R. B., & Peña, E. D. (2000). *Dynamic assessment and intervention: Improving children's narrative abilities.* Austin, TX: PRO-ED.

Morris, S. (1982). *Pre-speech Assessment Scale.* Clifton, NJ: J.A. Preston.

National Clearinghouse for English Language Acquisition. 2005. How has the English Language Learner (ELL) population changed in recent years? Accessed March 2, 2005, from http://www.ncela.gwu.edu/expert/faq/08leps.htm

Nelson, N. (1998). *Childhood language disorders in context: Infancy through adolescence.* Boston: Allyn and Bacon.

Northern, J. L., & Downs, M. P. (1984). *Hearing in children* (3rd ed.). Baltimore: Williams and Wilkins.

Notari-Syverson, A., & Losardo, A. (1996). Assessing children's language in meaningful contexts. In Cole, K. N., Dale, P. S., & Thal, D. J. (Eds.), *Assessment of communication and language* (pp. 257–279). Baltimore: Paul H. Brookes.

Paul, R. (1995). *Language disorders from infancy through adolescence*. St. Louis: Mosby-Year Book.

Paul, R. (1996). Clinical implications of the natural history of slow expressive language development. *American Journal of Speech-Language Pathology, 5*(2), 5–21.

Paul, R., & Jennings, P. (1992). Phonological behaviors in toddlers with slow expressive language development. *Journal of Speech and Hearing Research, 35*, 99–107.

Paul, R., & Shiffer, M. (1991). Communicative initiations in normal and late-talking toddlers. *Applied Psycholinguistics, 12*(4), 419–431.

Peña, E. D., (1996). Dynamic Assessment: The model and its language applications. In K. N. Cole, P. S. Dale, & D. J. Thal (Eds.), *Assessment of communication and language* (pp. 281–307). Baltimore: Paul H. Brookes.

Peña, E., Iglesias, A., & Lidz, C. S. (2001). Reducing test bias through dynamic assessment of children's word learning ability. *American Journal of Speech-Language Pathology, 10*(2), 138–154.

Plante, E., & Vance, R. (1994). Selection of preschool language tests: A data-based approach. *Language, Speech, and Hearing Services in Schools, 25*, 15–25.

Roulstone, S., Peters, T. J., Glogowska, M., & Enderby, P. (2003). A 12-month follow-up of preschool children investigating the natural history of speech and language delay. *Child: Care, Health & Development, 29*(4), 245–255.

Quinn, P. C., Adams, A., Kennedy, E., Shettler, L., Wasnik, A. (2003). Development of an abstract category representation for the spatial relation *between* in 6- to 10-month-old infants. *Developmental Psychology, 39*(1), 151–163.

Quinn, P. C., & Eimas, P. D. (1997). A reexamination of the perceptual-to-conceptual shift in mental representation. *Review of General Psychology, 1*, 271–287.

Rescorla, L. (1989). The Language Development Survey: A screening tool for delayed language in toddlers. *Journal of Speech and Hearing Disorders, 54*, 587–599.

Rescorla L., & Ratner, N. B. (1996). Phonetic profiles of toddlers with specific expressive language impairment (SLI-E). *Journal of Speech and Hearing Research, 39*, 153–165.

Roberts, J. E., & Crais, E. R. (1989). Assessing communication skills. In D. G. Bailey, Jr. & M. Wolery (Eds.), *Assessing infants and preschoolers with handicaps* (pp. 339–389). Columbus, OH: Merrill.

Roberts, J., Rescorla, L., Giroux, J., & Stevens, L. (1998). Phonological skills of children with specific expressive language impairment (SLI-E): Outcome at age 3. *Journal of Speech-Language-Hearing Research, 4*, 374–384.

Rossetti, L. (1990). *The Rossetti Infant-Toddler Language Scale*. East Moline, IL: LinguiSystems.

Schraeder, T., Quinn, M., Stockman, I. J., & Miller, J. (1999). Authentic assessment as an approach to preschool speech-language screening. *American Journal of Speech-Language Pathology, 8*, 195–200.

Seymour, H. N., Roeper, T. W., & de Villiers, J. (2003). *Diagnostic Evaluation of Language Variance* (DELV-Criterion Referenced Test, and DELV-Screening Test). San Antonio, TX: Harcourt Assessment.

Sheppard, J. (1987). Assessment of oral motor behaviors in cerebral palsy. In E. D. Mysak (Ed.), *Seminars in Speech and Language* (pp. 57–70). New York: Thieme-Stratton.

Stanovich, K. E. (1985). Explaining the variance in reading ability in terms of psychological processes: What have we learned? *Annals of Dyslexia, 35*, 67–96.

Stein, N., & Glenn, C. (1979). An analysis of story comprehension in elementary school children. In R. Freedle (Ed.), *New directions in discourse processing* (Vol. 2, pp. 53–120). Norwood, NJ: Ablex.

Stockman, I. J. (1996). The promises and pitfalls of language sample analysis as an assessment tool for linguistic minority children. *Language, Speech, and Hearing Services in Schools, 27*, 355–366.

Stoel-Gammon, C. (1987). Phonological skills of two-year olds. *Language, Speech, and Hearing Services in Schools, 18*, 323–329.

Stoel-Gammon, C. (1991). Normal and disordered phonology in two-year-olds. *Topics in Language Disorders, 11*(4), 21–32.

Thal, D., & Tobias, S. (1992). Communicative gestures in children with delayed onset of oral expressive vocabulary. *Journal of Speech and Hearing Research, 35*, 1281–1289.

Washington, J. A., & Craig, H. K. (1994). Dialectal forms during discourse of poor, urban, African American preschoolers. *Journal of Speech and Hearing Research, 37*, 816–823.

Webster, R. I., Majnemer, A., Platt, R. W., & Shevell, M. I. (2004). The predictive value of a preschool diagnosis of developmental language impairment. *Neurology, 63*, 2327–2331.

Werner, E., & Kresheck, J. D. (1983). *Structured Photographic Expressive Language Test–II.* Sandwich, IL: Janelle Publications.

Westby, C. E. (1988). Children's play: Reflections of social competence. *Seminars in Speech and Hearing. 9*, 1–14.

Wetherby, A. M., Cain, D., Yonclas, D., & Walker, V. (1988). Analysis of intentional communication of normal children from the prelinguistic to the multi-word stage. *Journal of Speech and Hearing Research, 31*, 240–252.

Wetherby, A. M., & Prizant, B. M. (2002). *Communication and Symbolic Behavior Scales–Developmental Profile (CSBS-DP).* Baltimore: Paul H. Brookes.

Wetherby, A. M., Prizant, B. M., & Hutchinson, T. A. (1998). Communicative, social/affective, and symbolic profiles of young children with autism and pervasive developmental disorders. *American Journal of Speech-Language Pathology, 7*(2), 79–91.

Wetherby, A. M., & Prutting, C. (1984). Profiles of communicative and cognitive-social abilities in autistic children. *Journal of Speech and Hearing Research, 27*, 364–377.

Wetherby, A. M., Yonclas, D., & Bryan, A. (1989). Communication profiles of preschool children with handicaps: Implications for early identification. *Journal of Speech and Hearing Disorders, 54*, 148–158.

World Health Organization. (1992). *International code of diseases, ed. 10.* New York: World Health Organization.

Zimmerman, I. L., Steiner, V. G., & Pond, R. E. (2002). Preschool Language Scale, Fourth Edition (PLS–4).

17

Assessment of Gross Motor Development

Harriet G. Williams and Eva V. Monsma
University of South Carolina

Motor development can be defined as the gradual acquisition of control and/or use of the large and small muscle masses of the body (neuromuscular coordination). Motor development is also often referred to as "perceptual-motor development" and/or "physical or motor coordination" in part because both the brain/nervous system and the muscles interact in intricate ways to allow the child to move the body skillfully in manipulating objects and exploring the physical world around him/her. Motor development is known to be an important dimension of child development and is a universally recognized means for assessing the overall rate and level of development of the child during the early months and years after birth (Butcher & Eaton, 1989; Dewey, Kaplan, Crawford & Wilson, 2002; Gesell, 1973; Illingworth, 1975). The years from 2 to 6 are considered the "golden years" of motor development (Hayes, 1994; Williams, 1983). During this period, most children acquire a basic repertoire of manipulative and locomotor skills, develop goal-directed motor behaviors, and learn to put together two or three movement sequences to accomplish specific end goals (Bruininks, 1978; Piaget, 1963; Sporns & Edelman, 1993). All of these behavioral achievements are forerunners of important aspects of adult functioning and are contingent upon the child's acquiring an adequate base of motor development. The early years of motor development set the foundation for neuromuscular coordination that will be used by the individual throughout life to deal with a multitude of mental, social, emotional, and recreational dimensions of living.

The learning process in the early years is a physically active one, which often centers around play, physical activity, and the use of a variety of motor skills (Butcher & Eaton, 1989; Keough & Sudgen, 1990; Martin, 2002). Most children have a natural tendency to seek stimulation and to learn about themselves and their environment. They spend hours upon hours actively exploring and examining both their bodies and the physical environment that surrounds them. Such activities necessarily involve and rely upon the use of fundamental motor skills. Adequate motor development is important in optimizing this early concrete and sensorimotor-based learning. A process instrumental in the child's progress from early primitive levels of thinking to those of higher abstraction is that of the symbolization of objects and events and the relationship between the two (Piaget, 1963). Physical activity provides the basis for carrying out important symbolic activities such as imitation (use of the body to represent objects and events), symbolic play (use of objects to represent other objects), and modeling, drawing, and cutting (construction of objects in two and three dimensions). Motor development and the physical activity associated with it, thus, are integral to promoting selected aspects of the early, active learning process.

A major function of the human nervous system is the coordinated control of movement. Evidence is clear that the acquisition of coordinated movements is inextricably linked to the development of the brain and that perception and action are intricately interrelated both early and throughout life (Sporns & Edelman, 1993). Coordinated motor responses enable the young child to explore his or her environment and to sample and process a variety of different sensory stimuli. This promotes brain development and perceptual function. Thus, movement appears to be crucial to the optimum development of perceptual development and to the development of fundamental concepts such as unity, boundedness, persistence of objects, construction of spatial maps of the environment, and so on (Spelke, 1990; Sporns & Edelman, 1993). It is a widely held belief that motor development may, in part, determine the nature and sequence in which certain perceptual and cognitive abilities unfold. If a child is unable to engage in a motor behavior that is prerequisite to the acquisition or practice of certain perceptual or cognitive abilities, that lack of motor competence may block or interfere with the natural emergence of those abilities (Bushnell & Boudreau, 1993).

Motor development also is linked during the early years to general psychological health, to social and emotional adjustment, and to educational achievement (Cantell, Smyth, & Ahonen, 1994; Henderson, Knight, Losse, & Jongmans, 1990; Losquadro-Little & Yorke, 2003; Piek & Dyck, In Press). Underachievement in school, lack of concentration, low self-esteem, poor social competence, and behavioral problems have all been linked to or associated with deficits in motor development in early and later years of childhood (Bauman, Loffler, Curie, Schmid & von Aster, 2004; Dewey et al., 2002; Geuze & Borger, 1993; Lyytinen & Ahonen, 1989; Rose & Larkin, 2002). For example, there is a greater incidence of difficulty in making appropriate social and emotional adjustments to both play and learning situations in children whose motor skills are less well developed than those of other children of similar chronological age. Lack of physical or motor skill often prevents children from joining in group games and other sports that encourage social interaction and personal growth.

Successful motor development is important not only in early development but also has important implications for development in adolescence (Cantell et al., 1994; Skinner & Piek, 2001) For example, Cantell et al. (1994), in a 10-year follow-up study, reported that, when compared to a group of age-matched peers, children who exhibited motor development problems at age 5 were still significantly poorer in performance of physical and motor skills at age 15. These children, now adolescents, also had less social interaction with peers, participated less often in team games, and had lower academic ambitions and future goals than other children. Losse et al. (1991) also reported that in addition to continuing motor problems at age 16, children with motor difficulties early in life (6 years) also had a variety of educational, social, and emotional problems. The inability to perforrn basic motor skills, thus, can have long-term negative effects on the individual; the potential implications for adult behavior, although not well studied, seem clear.

Motor development delays frequently accompany a number of potentially serious health conditions such as childhood obesity, etc. (Graf et al., 2004; Okely, Booth & Chey 2004) and are often associated with lack of integrity of neurological functioning (e.g., prematurity, mental subnormality, emotional disturbances, cerebral palsy, etc.). These are all conditions that may require medical and/or other special professional attention, and motor development needs or difficulties accompanying these conditions need to be identified early. Recent evidence suggests that some 57% of children born prematurely and who showed some minor neurological impairment early in life continue to show deficits in motor functions (balance, gross motor coordination, etc.), as well as in other school-related behaviors far into the preschool years (Lane, Attanasio, & Huselid, 1994; Losch & Damman, 2004). Assessment of motor development in these cases may be integral to help circumvent potential problems that may accompany school-related stresses.

Most tests of mental development in infants and young children include a large number of items that essentially are neuromuscular coordination or motor development tasks (Bayley, 1965; Cratty, 1972). Gesell (1973) grouped such items into a separate "motor category" in his developmental schedules. Pediatric neurologists often use, as a part of their assessment of the neurological status of the young child, items that directly involve neuromuscular coordination (e.g., evaluation of muscle tone, posture, gait, balance, alternating movements of the limbs, etc.). In general, a child whose motor development is considerably poorer than that observed in children of similar chronological age is more likely than others to exhibit soft and/or hard neurological signs, an indication that systems that provide support for the growth and refinement of neuromuscular coordination are not functioning appropriately (Capute & Accardo, 1996; Paine & Oppe, 1966; Precht, 1977; Precht & Beintema, 1964; Touwen, 1976). Still, many children do not show classical neurological signs and their difficulties cannot be linked to any identifiable neurological disease; yet they exhibit significant difficulty performing tasks that require coordination (e.g., writing, catching a ball, riding a bicycle). Several terms have been used to describe this condition; these include *developmental agnosia* and *apraxia* (Gubbay, 1975), *developmental dyspraxia* (Denckla, 1984), and most recently, *developmental coordination disorder* (DSM–IV, 1993). Most simply refer to this condition as the "clumsy child syndrome." The motor problems of these children are of concern not only because they are stressful to the children themselves, but also because they are often associated with higher incidences of learning difficulties, school failure, and psychological problems (Losse et al., 1991). For these reasons, assessment of gross motor development in the preschool-age child is an essential component in planning and providing for optimal conditions for growth and development during one of the most significant periods in the life of the child.

Gross motor development may be defined simply as the acquisition of control and use of the large muscle masses of the body. The preschool years are characterized by the appearance and mastery of a number of gross motor skills also known as "the fundamental motor skills." These fundamental motor skills include body projection (locomotor skills), body manipulation (nonlocomotor actions), and object control or ball handling skills. Body projection or locomotor skills include running, jumping, hopping, skipping, galloping, leaping, and sliding (e.g., Gallahue & Ozmun, 2002; Ulrich 2002; Williams, 1983). These skills all focus on the use of the large muscle masses of the body in moving the total body horizontally through space. Body manipulation skills, on the other hand, are concerned with moving the body and/or body parts within a well-defined, small area of space, and include stretching, curling, twisting, rolling, bending, and balancing skills. Universally recognized object control skills include throwing, catching, striking, kicking, and ball bouncing (Roberton & Halverson, 1984). Gross motor development includes both the adaptive or functional changes that take place in these motor skill behaviors across time, as well as the processes or factors that underlie or promote these changes (e.g., growth, development, experience, environmental issues, etc.)

A simple description of some proposed steps in motor skill development can help us to understand the complexity of the processes and factors involved in this aspect of the child's development. The following discussion describes some broad categories or steps involved in motor skill development (Burton & Miller, 1998). Generally, the child first develops or acquires the foundational processes necessary for the development of motor skills. The child then acquires the so-called motor development milestones; this is followed by the development of fundamental gross motor skills. Ultimately these skills and/or behaviors are manifested in a variety of specialized movement skills typical of the older child and young adult.

Motor Skill Foundations.   This aspect of motor skill development includes those factors and processes that are important to the development and performance of all motor skills. These factors include, among others, gender, body size and composition, cardiovascular endurance, flexibility/range of motion, muscular strength, neurological integrity, adequate sensory system function, perception, cognition, etc. These are all underlying factors that contribute to the pattern of gross motor development and play a critical role in what the nature of that pattern will be.

Early Motor Development.   The term *milestone* is often used to describe early motor skill development and highlights the significance of the impact that the motor skills acquired during this early period of development have on the social, perceptual, and cognitive development of the infant and young child. These milestones include the locomotor and object control skills that appear before the child achieves an easy upright stance and locomotion; they include rolling, crawling, creeping, sitting, standing, walking, object manipulation, etc. The onset of walking, which occurs, on average, at 12–13 months, is the last of the early motor development milestones. Lags or issues in the appearance of these milestones often signal potential difficulty with continued development and/or acquisition of the fundamental motor skills.

Fundamental Motor Skills.   These gross motor skills are ones that are universally observed in the development of the young child during the period from 2 to 7 years of age. They appear in a fairly orderly sequence during this developmental period and include the locomotor and object control skills described previously. Balance skills also undergo rapid development during this period.

Functional Motor Skills.   Functional motor skills are skills performed in natural and/or meaningful contexts and make up the primary activities that we perform on a daily basis. These movement skills are manifested in the form of specific sports skills and/or other specialized, complex movement behaviors. Various combinations of one or more of the earlier motor skills are integrated in a variety of ways and manifested in a wide variety of behaviors such as "shooting a free throw," "serving in tennis," "getting into and out of a car," "performing surgery," "driving a car," etc. Ultimately it is critical that an individual's motor skills become an integrated and spontaneous part of his/her educational, professional, recreational, and overall life activities. The pathway to this level is nurtured during the preschool period.

WHY SHOULD WE ASSESS GROSS MOTOR DEVELOPMENT?

The development and assessment of the young child's use of the large muscle masses of the body is the primary focus of this chapter. Not all of the skills included under the heading of fundamental motor skills will be addressed. Rather, major attention will be given to the locomotor skills of running, jumping, galloping, hopping, and skipping, and to the object control skills of throwing, kicking, catching, and striking. Balance and postural control are also mentioned.

Because motor skill development is a critical dimension of the overall development of the young child, it is important to have information about the present level of motor skill development of the child to establish a baseline against which to monitor the growth and development of the child. In this respect, assessment of gross motor development is integral to screening out and/or identifying those children who may not be developing or progressing as expected, e.g., those children who are or may be at risk for future problems. In general, screening or preliminary assessment of gross motor development is necessary for identifying the nature and extent of children's needs, in determining if additional diagnostic testing is needed, in deciding if and what type of enrichment may be appropriate for promoting optimum development, and in predicting potential neurodevelopmental outcomes at a later age. In the school setting, outcomes of motor development assessment are especially important for planning for and developing appropriate instructional strategies so that appropriate experiences for individual children can be implemented. It is also important to provide assessment information on the child's gross motor skills to parents and other concerned individuals, particularly those who are or may be involved in providing for adequate follow-up support for the child with special needs. Results or outcomes of any evaluation of gross motor development should identify strengths and weaknesses and highlight those skills that are lagging or deficient along with the nature and extent of the deficit.

THE DEVELOPMENT OF GROSS MOTOR SKILLS: AN OVERVIEW

The general sequence in which locomotor, object control, and balance skills develop is shown in Figure 17.1. Although locomotor skills tend to develop slightly in advance of object control skills, there is considerable overlap in the development of these skills. Balance is an important element in the mastery of both locomotor and ball handling skills (Williams, 1983). All of the fundamental motor skills develop during the preschool years and have

Balance	Locomotor Skills	Object Control Skills
Feet Shoulder Width	Run	Throw
↓	↓	↓
Feet Together	Jump	Kick
↓	↓	↓
Feet in Semi-Tandem	Gallop	Catch
↓	↓	↓
Feet in Tandem	Hop	Strike
↓	↓	↓
One-Foot-Eyes Open	Skip	Ball Bounce

FIGURE 17.1.   General Sequence of Development of Gross Motor Skills

many of the characteristics of mature patterns. Typically, balance progresses from balancing with the feet shoulder width apart to balancing with the feet together, with the feet in semi-tandem and tandem positions, and finally to balancing on one foot with the eyes open. Balance with eyes closed develops later. Children typically run, jump, and gallop in that order; most children gallop by age 3. The hop and skip tend to be the last of the locomotor skills to appear. Most children skip by age 6. Although there is considerable overlap in the development of object control skills, the typical order of mastery is throw, kick, catch, strike, ball bounce.

The preschool years are a period of rapid and important changes in the development of large muscle or gross motor coordination. Developmental sequences, often referred to as steps or stages, help identify the qualitative changes that occur as children acquire or master gross motor skills. General progressions or changes in and developmental characteristics of selected locomotor and object control skills are given in Tables 17.1 and 17.2, respectively. The information in these tables provides a brief overview and succinct summary of recognized changes in the development of these skills. Selected aspects of developmental changes in the skills included in the tables are discussed below. Balance is also described. Most aspects of the following discussion of motor skill development are generally supported by a number of authors and scientists including Branta, 1992; Espenschade and Eckert, 1980; Gallahue and Ozmun, 2002; Haywood and Getchell, 2005; Keough and Sudgen, 1990; Payne and Issacs, 2002; Wickstrom, 1977; Williams, 1983, Williams and Breihan, 2001, etc.

Running.   In general the early running pattern resembles a fast walk. The base of support is wide (feet are shoulder-width apart) and there is little or no use of the arms. The feet tend to toe-out, and the child receives the body's weight on a flat foot (foot control is still developing). As control and coordination increase, the base of support narrows (feet are placed one in front of the other), rhythmical arm/foot opposition is integrated into the run, and the body weight is received on the heel and rolled to the toe (slow-paced running). Quantitatively, the length of stride steadily increases as does speed and versatility of the running pattern; the child starts, stops, turns, and runs at a variety of speeds and in multiple directions. The running action is ultimately used skillfully in games and sports.

Jumping.   Jumping proceeds developmentally from a one-foot step-down from a low object to a skillful execution of a standing broad (long) jump that covers a distance of approximately 44 inches. In the beginning, the arms are used very little, if at all. When they are used, they are used ineffectively (the arms may be moved, but not in conjunction with the legs). Skillful jumping is manifested most clearly in the smooth coordination of arm and leg movements. In early jumping patterns, leg movements are characterized by incomplete flexion and extension. That is, the young or inexperienced jumper fails to assume a semi-crouched position in preparing to jump, fails to fully extend the body at take-off, and also often lands "stiff legged." That is, in landing they fail to flex to absorb the momentum of the body as it comes into contact with the ground. The accomplished 6-year-old jumper assumes a flexed (semi-crouched) position prior to jumping and fully extends the ankles, knees, and hips at take-off and flexes (most obviously at the knees) in landing. Last but not least, young jumpers tend to lose balance and take steps or fall on landing. The skillful jumper flexes (most obviously at the knees) to absorb the momentum of the body and rarely loses balance. Quantitatively, the distance of the jump (vertical, running broad, or standing broad) increases in a nonlinear fashion.

TABLE 17.1.
General Developmental Characteristics and Progressions in Gross Motor Development: Locomotor Skills in the Preschool Years

Locomotor/body Projection Skills

Walking and Running

General Progressions
Children walk before they run.
Children walk or run a straight path before a circular or curved one.
Children walk or run a straight path before they walk or run around obstacles.

Early vs Later Characteristics
The early run resembles a fast walk; it is a series of hurried steps with a wide base of support and no period of suspension.
Later the run involves a period of suspension; the base of support is narrower, the feet are placed one in front of the other.
Initially the weight is received on a flat foot;
Later the weight is received on the heel and shifted to the ball of the foot (slow pace)
In a faster run, the weight is often received on the ball of the foot.
Initially the child runs with short strides (there is minimal flexion/extension of the legs); they also run at a slow pace;
Later the child runs with longer strides (there is greater flexion/extension of the legs) and they run at a faster rate.
Initially, the arms are used minimally if at all and often are out for balance;
Later the arms move smoothly in opposition to the legs.
With practice the running action becomes more automatic; the child can start, stop, and turn easily; running is incorporated readily into games and other activities.

Jumping

General Progressions
Children exhibit a series of 'bunny hops' before they perform a true standing broad jump.
Children jump down from an object before they jump up onto or over an object.
Children execute jumps from lower heights before higher heights.
When jumping down from obstacles, children progress from aided jumping, to jumping alone with a one foot step down, to jumping alone with a simultaneous two-foot propulsion.
Children pass through the same progression described above at each height from which a jump is attempted.

Early vs Later Characteristics
Initially the jump covers short distances (there is minimal flexion/extension of the legs);
Later the jump covers longer and longer distances (there is more complete flexion/extension of the legs).
Initially the arms are not used or are used awkwardly;
Later the arms initiate the jumping action and are coordinated with the action of the legs.
Initially balance is often lost upon landing;
Later the child maintains balance on landing.

Galloping

General Progressions
Children gallop before they hop or skip.
Children gallop with the preferred foot leading before they gallop with the opposite foot in the lead.
Children usually gallop in rudimentary form by age 3.

(*continued*)

TABLE 17.1.
(*Continued*)

Early vs Later Characteristics

Initially children gallop with the body in a sideways position (a sliding action);
Later children gallop with the body facing forward.
Initially the arms are not used;
Later the two arms are used together (bilaterally) to support the leg action.
Early on, children execute 3–4 cycles of the gallop and then lose the pattern;
Later they gallop through a 50' distance without losing the pattern.

Hopping

General Progressions

Children 'hop' on both feet prior to developing a true hopping action on one foot.
Children hop in place before they perform a moving hop.
Children hop first on the foot on the preferred side;
Later they hop on the foot on the opposite side.
Children usually hop by age 3–4 years and complete 3–5 hops on the preferred side.

Early vs Later Characteristics

Initially the path of the hop is erratic;
Later the child hops in a straight path.
Initially there is minimal suspension in the hop (minimal flexion/extension of the legs);
Later there is good suspension in the hop (flexion/extension of the legs are more complete).
Initially the weight is received on the whole/flat foot;
Later the weight is received on the ball of the foot.
Initially the arms flail or are used awkwardly;
Later the arms are used together in a bilateral action and are coordinated with the leg action.

Skipping

General Progressions

Skipping is usually the last locomotor skill to appear.
Children may not skip until 6 years or later.
Skipping consists of a step and a hop on alternating sides.
Skipping progresses from a shuffle step to a skip on one side to a skip on alternating sides.

Early vs Later Characteristics

Initially the child may execute 2–3 cycles of the skipping pattern and then begin to gallop;
Later the skipping action is maintained for 50+ feet without loss of the pattern.
Initially the arms are not used; later they move in opposition to the legs.

Stair Climbing

Marking time (both feet placed on rung or step before next step is attempted) precedes alternation of feet in climbing.
Use of alternating feet appears first in ascending steps and later in descending stairs.
Children typically ascend a set of stairs before they descend.
Initially children develop proficiency in climbing a short flight of stairs or a ladder with rungs close together;
Later they gain proficiency in climbing a longer flight of stairs or a ladder with rungs farther apart.
Children alternate feet to climb short flights of stairs but still mark time on longer flights of stairs.

TABLE 17.2.
Some Developmental Changes in Gross Motor Development:
Object Control Skills in the Preschool Years

Ball-Handling/Object Control Skills

Throwing

General Progressions
Children throw a smaller ball farther than a large one.
Children develop a better throwing pattern if they throw forcefully.
Throwing at a target develops later than throwing for distance.
Targets should be large and at close distances initially; later they can be smaller in size and farther away.
There is a progression toward shorter periods of acceleration; that is, the necessary joint actions occur in shorter periods of time, thus creating increased force of the throw.

Early vs Later Characteristics
Initially the ball is held in the palm of the hand;
Later the ball is held in the tips of the fingers.
Initially the action is largely arm action in the vertical plane;
Later the whole body is involved in initiating the throwing action;
Still later arm action involves lateral and medial rotation of the shoulder and elbow extension.
Initially there is no trunk rotation;
Later there is block trunk rotation; still later there is differentiated trunk rotation.
Initially there is no shift of weight;
Later the weight is shifted onto the foot on the same side as the throwing arm; still later the weight is shifted onto the foot opposite the throwing arm.

Kicking

General Progressions
Children kick stationary balls successfully before they kick rolling balls.
Large, light balls are contacted more easily than smaller, heavier balls.
Children kick a rolling ball with greater success if it is rolled slowly and directly toward him/her.
Children progress from kicking stationary balls to kicking balls rolled to him/her and then to kicking balls rolled to the right and left.

Early vs Later Characteristics
Initially the leg action stops at ball contact;
Later the child kicks through the ball.
Initially the leg is swung forward only;
Later the child swings the leg backward and then forward and through the ball.
Initially ball contact is often inconsistent; it may be with the toes, the top of the foot/leg, or with the side of the foot;
Later contact is more consistent and appropriate for different types of kicks.
Initially the arms are not involved in the kicking action:
later the arm opposite the kicking leg swings forward and upward as the ball is contacted.

Catching

General Progressions
The child intercepts (stops) a rolling ball before they catch or intercept a bounced or aerial ball.
Bounced balls are caught more easily than aerial balls.
Balls bounced or tossed from shorter distances are easier to catch than balls bounced or tossed from greater distances.
Children successfully intercept a large ball before they successfully intercept a small ball.

(continued)

TABLE 17.2.

(*Continued*)

Early vs Later Characteristics

Initially children use the hands/arms as a single unit;

Later they trap the ball against the body; occasionally children contact the ball and then immediately drop it;

Still later they contact and control the ball with the hands/fingers.

Children revert to using the hands and arms as a single unit when they initially attempt to intercept a small ball; at the same time they easily coordinate the use of hands and fingers in catching a larger ball.

Initially children fixate and track the oncoming ball minimally or with little consistency and do not judge the speed or direction of a moving ball accurately and consistently; they often do not get to the ball in time to intercept or catch it.

Later they track the ball more effectively and judge the speed and direction of the moving ball more accurately and consistently; they are more likely to get to the ball in time to make effective contact.

Initially children may show an 'avoidance reaction' to the oncoming ball; they close the eyes and/or turn the head away as the ball approaches; with increasing skill and confidence, this reaction disappears.

Striking

General Progressions

Children initially use a one-arm striking pattern and gradually develop a two-arm striking pattern.

Children are successful in hitting a stationary ball before a moving ball.

Children are more successful using a large, light bat/implement than a small, heavy bat/implement.

Early vs Later Characteristics

Initially the bat is held against the shoulder;

Later the bat is held out away from the body.

Initially the child faces the oncoming ball;

Later they stand with the side of the body toward the ball.

Initially the arm action is a vertical chopping action;

Later the action is in the horizontal plane.

Initially the arm action stops at ball contact;

Later the child swings the implement through the ball.

Initially there is no shift of weight;

Later children step onto the foot on the same side as the preferred hand;

Still later they shift weight onto the foot on the side opposite the preferred hand.

The weight shift initiates the striking action in a kind of 'step and swing' pattern.

Ball Bouncing

General Progressions

Children attempt a two-hand bounce before a one-hand bounce.

Children bounce a smaller ball (one that fits the hand) before a larger ball.

Children perform a series of "bounces-and-catches" before they perform a continuous bounce.

Children bounce a ball in a stationary position before they bounce a ball while moving.

Early vs Later Characteristics

Initially children bounce a ball with whole body action;

Later they use the arm/hand independently of body action.

Initially children 'slap' at the ball with a flat/whole hand;

Later they use the fingers/wrist to bounce the ball.

Galloping.   The skill of galloping usually appears around the age of 3. Initially, children "gallop" with the body in a sideways position; this is often referred to as a "sliding" action. This is followed by a true gallop action in which the body faces forward and the leg action is in the sagittal plane. It is not uncommon for children to complete 2–3 cycles of the gallop action and then lose the pattern. Later, the child gallops a 50′ distance without a loss or disruption of the gallop action. Early in development, the arms are frequently not involved in the action or they flail awkwardly. Later, the arms move in a bilateral action to assist the action of the legs. The gallop typically appears on the dominant side first; later, the child executes the gallop with the foot on the nondominant side leading.

Hopping.   Early hopping patterns are characterized by little or no elevation of the body (the child doesn't get very high off the ground, if at all), little or no arm usage, limited use of the nonsupport leg, and landing on a "whole" or "flat foot." Early hopping patterns are often jerky, staccato, and arrhythmic. Gradually the arms and nonsupport leg are used to add to force production, and, thus, to the elevation of the body; the nonsupport leg actually "pumps" (flexes and extends rapidly) to aid in the forward momentum of the hopping action. Last, but not least, the body weight is received on the ball of the foot. The hopping action becomes smoother with practice, and the child advances from being unable to execute a hop, to hopping in place, to carrying out a short series of coordinated hopping movements, to hopping a 25-foot distance skillfully in approximately 5 seconds. The versatility of the hopping pattern also increases; the child can hop backward and sideward and alternate hops between right and left feet.

Skipping.   The early skip is a shuffle step. The shuffle step is followed by a one-sided skip; the final step in skipping is a step-hop on alternate sides of the body (a true skip). Early skipping patterns are characterized by a lack of use of the arms, a toeing out of the feet, and a lack of ability to maintain a continuous skipping sequence. Skillful skipping involves smooth and consistent arm/leg opposition (the arms move in opposition to the legs). The toes point forward and the body's weight is received on the ball of the foot. Mastery of a continuous skipping action is seen in the growing capacity of the child to skip longer distances in less time. The more skillful 6-year-old skipper can cover a distance of 25 feet in approximately 4 seconds.

Throwing.   The earliest beginning of a throwing pattern is simply the release of an object from the hand. The early over arm throwing pattern consists largely of flexion and extension of the trunk and arm (elbow). There is little or no weight shift or trunk rotation. Gradually, a shift of weight and trunk rotation appear and help to increase the force or velocity of the throw. The weight shift is first seen as a shift of weight forward onto the foot on the same side as the throwing arm; later, the skillful thrower steps onto the foot opposite the throwing arm. Trunk rotation first occurs in block form, that is the lower and upper trunk, e.g., pelvis and spine rotate together as a single unit. Later, trunk rotation is differentiated (the lower trunk or pelvis rotates first, followed by upper trunk or spinal rotation). Quantitatively, developmental changes are seen primarily in increases in the distance and velocity of the throw. Increases in both distance and velocity during development are nonlinear in nature.

Kicking.   Kicking is the least studied of gross motor object control skills. Available data suggest that early kicking pattern consists of a single forward action of the kicking leg; the child stands close to the ball and simply pushes or punches the ball forward from a stationary position. Typically the leg action stops at ball contact with a step backward to maintain balance. Later, the child swings the kicking leg backward and then forward and through the ball (full range of motion). At this time there is evidence of arm-leg opposition. Another important step in kicking is seen in the child's ability to execute a moving approach to the ball; this is often accompanied by a forward or side step and a hop after ball contact is made. An important step in the developmental process is evident in the child's successful kicking of rolling balls and the capacity to time the kicking action to the speed and direction of the oncoming ball. Proficient kickers also often exhibit a leap before kicking the ball.

Catching.   Early and/or immature catching patterns are characterized by lack of skillful use of the arms, hands, and fingers. Initially, the arms and hands are held stiffly in front of the body with the elbows extended. The ball often rebounds off the outstretched arms. Later, the arms are held at the sides with the hands relaxed and cupped. The arms, hands, and fingers of more accomplished catchers are positioned according to the flight of the oncoming object. The fingers and hands are pointed toward the ball. For balls above the waist, the fingers and hands point upward; for balls below the waist, the fingers and hands point downward. When ball contact is made, the fingers close around the ball. Young or inefficient catchers rarely display this fingertip control in making contact with the ball and often trap, touch and drop, or fail to make contact with the ball. Another aspect of the child's early catching response is a fear reaction in which the child turns the head, closes the eyes, and fails to track the ball as it comes toward him or her. This reaction disappears as skill and confidence increase; the child watches the ball intently as it approaches. The major characteristic of the highly proficient catcher is his or her ability to adjust the total movement of the body to receive balls bounced or thrown at different speeds and from varying distances and directions. Young catchers are unable to do this. Quantitatively, the number of successful catches (balls skillfully contacted with hands and fingers) slowly increases. Changes in catching skills have not been quantified to any great extent in children of preschool age.

Striking.   The development of striking skills is an important part of early gross motor development. Although there is little normative or descriptive data available on developmental changes in striking skill in young children, the little that is available suggests that striking patterns proceed from one-arm attempts at contacting stationary objects to skillful two-arm striking patterns made in an effort to contact objects moving at different speeds and in different directions. Initially, the striking movement is a vertical chopping motion; later, it becomes a sidearm motion executed in the horizontal plane (the swing is flat). Early in the development of the striking pattern (as in throwing), the trunk rotates as a single unit; later, differentiated or two-part trunk rotation occurs. Another important developmental change in striking is the appearance of a definite shift of weight onto the forward (opposite) foot prior to initiation of the swing. The child also gradually changes from standing in a position facing the oncoming ball to one in which the body is perpendicular to the ball (e.g. the side of the body is placed toward the ball). Quantitatively, with advancing development the bat is swung with greater force (the range and timing of the movement of the body are improved), and the ball is projected with increasingly greater velocity.

Balance.   Early balance development is manifested in the child's ability to maintain equilibrium in a variety of positions (e.g., on all fours, on the knees, in a standing position). This is followed by attempts to stand, to walk, and to navigate around objects in the environment. Once some success is achieved in these behaviors, the child will attempt to walk on narrow objects (e.g., balance beams, rails, lines) and shows some beginning ability to maintain balance on one foot. By 6 years of age, most children can balance for fairly long periods of time on the preferred foot with the eyes open (Mean = 22 sec). Balancing on the nonpreferred foot is more difficult (Mean = 14 sec), and balancing with the eyes closed is just beginning to be mastered (Mean = 7 sec). Most children can, at this age, walk a balance beam (2½ inches wide) in a controlled heel-toe manner in 23 seconds.

It is important to note that although the early versus later changes described for each skill can be loosely associated with chronological age, the relationship between these changes and chronological age per se is at best a tenuous one. One of the most dramatic characteristics of gross motor development in the preschool child is its great variability (Keogh & Sudgen, 1990). Some children fall nicely into a rather traditional "change with age" association, but many do not. Thus, ages have been intentionally de-emphasized in the discussion of developmental changes in gross motor skills in this chapter. The reader also should be aware that the changes described for individual skills are not mutually exclusive; children typically display changes in more than one skill at any given time (Roberton & Langendorfer, 1980).

Gender Differences.   Figure 17.2 shows the age in months of the emergence of several gross motor skills and the approximate age at which 60% of boys and girls performed these skills proficiently (Seefeldt & Haubenstricker, 1982). The numbers in the figure refer to the changes or *stages* that have identified characteristics and are part of the process of mastering or showing proficiency in the skill (1 = beginning or early characteristics of skill performance; 4 = proficiency and/or more mature characteristics). Observed gender differences indicate that boys acquire proficiency before girls in running, jumping, throwing, kicking, and striking. Gender differences in running and jumping are minimal (6–8 months); differences are greater for kicking and striking (12–16 months). Interestingly, differences are even more evident in throwing; boys tend to demonstrate proficiency at about 69 months, while girls show proficiency at about 102 months, some 33 months later. In contrast, girls have an advantage over boys in hopping, skipping, and catching and demonstrate proficiency some 6–10 months before boys (Seefeldt & Haubenstricker, 1982). Garcia (1994) and Greendorfer and Ewing (1981) also document gender differences in the development of fundamental motor skills.

It is important to note that in addition to gender differences, there is also considerable variability in the timing of the changes that occur in motor skill development for all children. For example, both girls and boys show some arm-foot opposition and heel-toe contact in running at about 3 years of age (Stage 3). However boys show full proficiency (Stage 4) in running just 10 months later, while girls do not exhibit proficiency until some 20 months later. Although some developmentalists have attributed differences between boys and girls to physical differences, it is generally the case that boys and girls do not differ substantially in physical size or muscular strength prior to puberty. Thus, cultural differences associated with opportunities for practice and encouragement may play a greater role in skill development than once was thought to be the case (Thomas & French, 1985).

ASSESSMENT OF GROSS MOTOR DEVELOPMENT

In deciding how to approach the assessment of gross motor development, it is important to consider a number of factors that may affect the child's motor skill performance. A

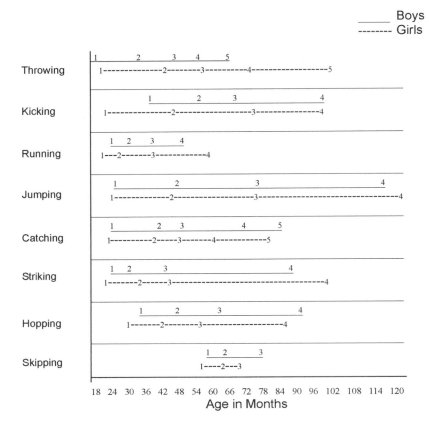

FIGURE 17.2.   Age in months at which 60% of boys and girls exhibit selected characteristics of fundamental motor skills.*

*Adapted from Seefeldt & Haubenstricker, 1982; numbers refer to the presence of selected characteristics in motor skill performances at different points in the developmental process.

contemporary approach to understanding motor performance is referred to as *dynamical systems*. We will describe this systems approach using the work of Newell (1986) who identifies three major factors that need to be considered in evaluating motor skill development. These factors include characteristics of the individual performing the skill (referred to as individual constraints), the nature and demands of the task itself or task constraints, and the environment or context in which the skill is performed (environmental constraints). *Individual constraints* refer to the physical characteristics of the child or what are known as *structural* and *functional* factors. Structural factors include such things as height, weight, strength, limb length, hand size, gender, etc. *Functional constraints* refer to the mental characteristics of the child and include such things as the child's level of cognitive function, their perceptual abilities, motivation, self-confidence, etc. How do individual characteristics affect children's motor skill performance? Briefly, for example, with regard to structural constraints, if a child has a lower center of gravity (due to shorter relative leg length), he/she may have a slight advantage in maintaining or performing balance tasks. Still, physical characteristics of young children do not vary greatly and thus often are not a major factor in skill development (Malina, Bouchard & Bar-Or, 2004). Functional constraints affect motor skill acquisition and performance in other ways. For example, a child who has developed control of one-foot balance is likely to be more confident, motivated, and successful in hopping simply because they have developed one of the important preliminary skills—one foot balance. This promotes interest and self-confidence.

Task constraints refer to the demands of the skill or task to be performed and include the rules for performing the task, the choice of equipment, etc. It is important to consider the properties or requirements of the task and how they relate to the characteristics of the child. By considering both, the teacher or examiner can better determine what equipment to select and how to structure a task so that the child demonstrates his/her true level of development. For example, if a child is having difficulty catching a small ball, because of small hands and/or limited eye-hand coordination, the teacher/examiner might use a larger ball and/or toss the ball from a closer distance. This would match individual characteristics more closely to task requirements, help to maximize success, and give a truer picture of the child's developmental level. Descriptions of early versus later accomplishments given in Tables 17.1 and 17.2 provide some simple examples of matching task requirements to individual characteristics.

The environment in which the skill is performed and/or assessed is also important to consider. These are the so-called *environmental constraints*; they include characteristics of both the physical and socio-cultural environments. Physical environmental constraints include such things as the surface on which the skill is performed (gym floor versus grass versus pavement, etc.), time of day, nature of the space available, etc. Socio-cultural environmental constraints refer to social and/or cultural factors that impact development and/or performance of motor skills. These include such things as the opportunity for socialization, as well as the freedom to select to participate or not participate in certain activities and experiences, etc.

It is also important to consider how individual, task, and environmental constraints interact to give rise to the motor skill performance observed. For example, a growth spurt that results in increased height can affect the performance of a number of motor skills. Jumping is a good example. Children usually grow taller before their muscular strength changes enough to accommodate the change in height (e.g., longer and heavier limbs, etc). This increase in height relative to muscular strength can affect both the distance jumped and the way in which the jumping action is carried out. At this time the child may look less skillful than he/she has previously. Usually once muscular development catches up to the changes in height, most children exhibit dramatic gains in the jumping action and jump longer distances and look more skillful and coordinated.

The interaction of these factors and how they affect motor skill development and performance is particularly relevant to pre-school children because of the dynamic, fast-paced changes that take place in growth and development and the variety of environmental experiences children undergo during this period. Although identifying an individual's motor development relative to normative data is an inherent feature of assessment, it is important that teachers and parents be aware that individual performances may differ from a stated norm and still be age and/or developmentally appropriate. Knowing something about the various constraints that affect motor skill development and performance can help teachers to interpret more effectively a child's motor performance data and develop appropriate experiences to promote skill development (Haywood & Getchell, 2004).

Process versus Product Assessment.   Gross motor development is most effectively evaluated by considering both process and product characteristics of the child's movement (Ulrich, 2002; Williams, 1983). *Process characteristics* address qualitative aspects of movement and have to do with how a child moves the body in performing a motor task. Thus, evaluation of process characteristics is concerned with assessing the form or quality of the movement itself (e.g., observing how the body is positioned, which limbs are moved, how they move, etc.). *Product characteristics*, in contrast, have to do with the end product or outcome of the movement and usually are more quantitative in nature. Evaluation of product characteristics of movement answer such questions as: How far did the child run? How high did he jump? How fast did she move? Techniques used for assessing gross motor development often incorporate measures of both process and product aspects of movement performance. Most motor development scales or tests available for use with younger children tend to emphasize process characteristics; tests for older children tend to emphasize product measures. Both types of information are needed at all ages if a complete and comprehensive assessment of the motor development of the child is to be made. An example of a simple checklist that includes both process and product characteristic items can be found in Cratty's Perceptual-Motor Behaviors Checklist (Cratty, 1972; see Table 17.3). Examples of items that emphasize process characteristics are: "can walk rhythmically at an even pace" (2 to 3 years), "can step off low objects, one foot ahead of the other" (2 to 3 years), and "walks and runs with arm action coordinated with leg action" (4 to 4½ years). Items that are more product-oriented include: "can walk a 2-inch-wide line for 10 feet" (2 to 3 years), "can jump 8 inches or higher" (5 to 5½ years), and "can run 50 feet in 5 seconds" (6 to 6½ years). The following sections address (1) screening for gross motor development problems, (2) process assessment of motor development, and (3) product assessment of gross motor development.

TABLE 17.3.
Process and Product Assessment Examples:
Cratty's Perceptual-Motor Behaviors Checklist

2–3 Years
Can walk rhythmically at an even pace **(process)**
Can step off low object, one foot ahead of the other **(process)**
Can walk a line on the ground (2 in wide/10 ft long) **(product)**

4–4½ Years
Can broad jump with both feet together and clear the ground **(process)**
Can walk and run with arm action coordinated with leg action **(process)**
Can walk a circular line a short distance **(product)**
Can hop 2 or 3 times on one foot without precision **(product)**

5–5½ Years
Can high jump with simultaneous two-foot take-off and landing **(process)**
Can high jump over a bar 8 inches high **(product)**
Can run 30 yds in just over 8 sec **(product)**
Balances on one foot: girls 6–8 sec, boys 4–6 sec **(product)**

Source: From B. J. Cratty. *Perceptual and Motor Development in Infants and Young Children.* Copyright 1986 by Allyn & Bacon.

Screening for Gross Motor Development Problems.   Screening for potential motor development needs can be easily accomplished by (1) having basic knowledge about the characteristics of typical motor development, (2) being aware of some signs and symptoms of potential delays or slowness in motor development, and (3) using a checklist designed to guide the observer in things to look for in the child's movements. Basic information about typical characteristics and accomplishments in gross motor development in young children is provided in the previous section on Gross Motor Skill Development: An Overview. Regardless of the approach used in screening the young child's gross motor development, there are some general indicators of potential slowness in motor development that may be helpful to teachers and parents alike and that will help make the initial screening process more complete and informative. Many of these behaviors are included and described in different ways in various screening tools.

Some Signs of Potential Delays in Gross Motor Development.   What are some of the signs that may indicate slowness or the possibility of a delay in the young child's gross motor development (Williams, 2001a)? Some of the more universally recognized signs to look for in observing the child's motor development are described next. Whether or not these signs are good indicators of potential problems in the child's gross motor development depend on a variety of factors including the age, gender, physical characteristics, and previous experience of the child. Even more important, many of these same characteristics are a natural and integral part of the process of achieving proficiency in various gross motor skills.

1. Is there **EXCESS TENSION** in the hands, face, or body?
    - Does the tongue protrude when the child performs the task?
    - Are the hands fisted as they run, jump, hop, etc.?
    - Are the fingers extended and stiff or contorted?
2. Is there **EXTRANEOUS MOVEMENT** of parts of the body not involved in the task?
    - Do the arms flail as the child runs, hops, or skips?
    - Does the head move from side to side or up and down?
3. Does the child have **DIFFICULTY BALANCING?**
    - Does the child trip and/or fall easily and often?
    - Does the child have difficulty jumping over an obstacle and landing?
    - Does the child touch the foot down or lose balance frequently when hopping?
4. Are the **FEET** used **AWKWARDLY?**
    - Do the feet toe in or out when the child runs, etc.
    - Does the child run flat-footed?
    - Does the child have difficulty placing the feet when walking on a line or beam?
5. Are the **ARMS/HANDS** used **AWKWARDLY?**
    - Are the arms held stiffly and not used?
    - Are the arms moved awkwardly or jerkily?
6. Are **EYE MOVEMENT PATTERNS** immature?
    - Does the child have difficulty fixating and tracking moving objects?
    - Does the child look away from or close the eyes as a ball approaches?

Screening Tools.   There are a few tools and techniques that have been developed for screening fundamental motor skills in young children. Four common approaches (two formal, two informal) are described below. All involve checklists of various lengths and content; one is designed for use by parents, but is also useful in the preschool setting.

The Movement ABC Checklist.   The Movement Assessment Battery for Children Checklist (Henderson & Sudgen, 1992) is a universally recognized tool for screening motor development in young preschool and school-age children. Although the checklist can be used flexibly by teachers, parents and other professionals working with children, it is designed primarily for use by teachers. The Checklist should be completed over a period of 1–2 weeks as the child is observed in different settings including the classroom and the playground. The checklist consists of four major parts; the child is observed in each of the following types of conditions:

1. When the child is stationary and the environment is stable or unchanging; a typical observation for this condition is (a) can the child stand on one leg in a stable position? or (b) does the child have good posture in sitting or standing?;

2. When the child is moving and the environment is unchanging; some examples of observations to be made here include (a) can the child hop on one or both feet?, (b) can the child jump across or over obstacles (blocks, ropes, etc.)?, and (c) can the child run to kick a large stationary ball?;

3. When the child is stationary and the environment is changing; some observations to be made here include (a) can the child catch a large, approaching ball using two hands?, (b) can the child keep time to a musical beat by clapping hands or tapping the foot?, and (c) can the child kick a rolling ball using the foot rather than the shin?; and

4. When the child is moving and the environment is changing; observations to be made here include (a) can the child participate in chasing games?, (b) can the child run to catch a moving ball?, (c) can the child run to hit a moving ball using a bat or racket?, and (d) can the child use the skills of kicking, catching, throwing to participate in a game?

Each set of conditions becomes increasingly more difficult or complex so that tasks in Condition 4 are more demanding and require more skill than those in previous conditions. In observing the child, the teacher/parent rates each task/skill on a scale of 0–3; zero indicates the child performs the task "very well" and 3 indicates that the child does not/cannot perform the task (e.g., is "not close"). Higher scores indicate slower or greater deficits in gross motor development. Scores are totaled and some data are provided for older children for cut-off performance levels at the lowest 5th and 15th percentiles. The Checklist can be used flexibly to help identify potential needs in specific motor skills based on observations of performances on different tasks. Normative data for the checklist are based on 1,200 children from 4 to 12 years of age; the sample in the age range from 4 to 6 years was 493 children. Boys and girls of different ethnic origins and from diverse regions of the United States were included.

Denver Developmental Screening Test.   The Denver test (Frankenburg & Dodds, 1967; Frankenburg, Dodds, Archer, Bresnick, & Shapiro, 1990) is one of the most universally recognized and widely used standardized procedures for screening/assessing gross and fine motor development in young children. It includes 32 simple gross motor tasks that are essentially product measures. Items are scored pass/fail; performances on each item are classified as "normal," "suspect," or "delayed." The items in this battery are helpful to the educator and clinician in that they provide information about whether certain common gross

TABLE 17.4.
Selected Gross Motor Items: Denver Development Screening Test

Item	Age*
Walks backward	21 mo
Walks up steps	22 mo
Kicks ball forward	2 yrs
Throws ball overhand	2½ yrs
Jumps in place	3 yrs
Pedals tricycle	3 yrs
Performs broad jump	3½ yrs
Balances on 1 foot for 1 sec	3½ yrs
Balances on 1 foot for 5 sec 2 of 3 times	4½ yrs
Hops on 1 foot	4½ yrs
Performs heel-toe walk 2 of 3 times	5 yrs
Catches bounced ball 2 of 3 times	5½ yrs
Balances on 1 foot for 10 sec 2 of 3 times	5½ yrs
Performs backward heel-toe walk 2 of 3 times	6 yrs

Source: Adapted from "The Denver Developmental Screening Test," W. K. Frankenburg and J. B. Dodds, 1967, Journal of Pediatrics, 71, p. 181.

* Age at which 90 percent of children pass individual items.

motor skills are within the behavioral repertoire of a child at a given age. They do not, however, provide information about why a given motor skill is not a part of the child's set of behavioral skills. This tool is most properly used as part of a more comprehensive and ongoing assessment of motor development. The Denver Developmental Screening Test can be very useful in outlining the general nature and/or level of motor skill development in children from birth to 6 years. Standards for passing items are described in simple language and are based on normative data from 1,036 children. Examples of gross motor items included in the test and the age at which 90% of children pass these items are given in Table 17.4. A prescreening developmental questionnaire is available for parents to help them determine if their child may need further assessment.

Williams' Preschool Motor Development Check List. Williams' checklist (Williams, 2001c) is an informal screening tool that asks questions about the movement or process characteristics of motor skill performance in children 3 to 6 years of age. This checklist focuses on basic motor development immaturities in six important gross motor skills; it includes four locomotor skills (running, jumping, hopping, skipping) and two ball-handling or object control skills (throwing, catching). Williams' checklist uses a question format and provides some simple guidelines for determining the presence or absence of developmental needs in each skill area. Information provided by this checklist can indicate whether the child has isolated motor control problems (e.g., difficulty hopping, but not in skipping, jumping, or running), more general locomotor skill difficulties (e.g., immaturities in the movements involved in several locomotor skills) and/or ball-handling problems (e.g., poor or deficient skills in throwing and catching). Data from the checklist provide an overview of the nature and extent of the child's gross motor skill development and thus is helpful in deciding whether or not additional assessment or diagnosis is needed or appropriate. Information from the checklist is detailed enough that beginning enrichment programs and instructional strategies can be planned. The checklist was developed from published research as well as from data on clinical observations of motor development characteristics of some 300 preschool age children with and without gross motor development needs. It can be used in both clinical and educational settings. The checklist items and score sheet are given in Table 17.5 and guidelines for interpreting the information gathered are given in Table 17.6.

Motor Development Checklist for Parents.   The Motor Development Checklist for Parents (Williams, 2001b) was developed to help parents recognize potential motor development needs in their preschool child. It consists of 12 questions which are answered *yes* or *no*. If the response to the majority of the questions (6 or more) is *yes*, the parent is encouraged to pursue further, more detailed evaluation of the child's gross motor development. The checklist is based on clinical and educational observations of some 200 preschool children and is meant to be used only as an informal guideline for parents who suspect that their child's motor development may not be progressing normally. The checklist includes the following questions:

1.   Does the child avoid physical activity and play with other children?
2.   Does the child often stumble over objects?
3.   Does the child have difficulty balancing?
4.   Does the child seem clumsy in running, jumping or galloping?
5.   Does the child have difficulty tracking a ball?
6.   Does the child seem awkward in throwing or catching balls?
7.   Does the child seem to fatigue or tire easily?
8.   Does the child have difficulty using crayons and/or pencils?
9.   Does the child have difficulty cutting out shapes?
10.   Does the child have poor attention or is easily distracted?
11.   Does the child routinely spill or drop things?
12.   Does the child move frequently and/or act impulsively?

Process Assessment of Gross Motor Development.   A popular, useful, and highly recommended approach to the assessment of gross motor development in young children focuses on observing and evaluating process characteristics of movement skills. This involves assessing the quality, form, and/or action sequence of the movement involved in performing fundamental motor skills. This approach focuses on how the child moves his or her body to perform a given motor skill. Process evaluation instruments are often informal in nature and rely on the skill and experience of the observer. They are rarely based on large standardization populations. Despite this, the process approach to motor skill assessment is widely recognized and endorsed. The process approach to the assessment of gross motor skill in young children is frequently used in clinical settings to examine children's movement problems as process measures provide critical information about and insight into the nature of the child's movement problems as well as possible factors that may be contributing to the

TABLE 17.5.
Williams Preschool Motor Development Checklist

Directions: Carefully observe the child perform each skill several times and if possible in different settings. Ask the following questions about the 'way' the child performs each motor skill. Try to answer 'yes' or 'no' to each question.

Running
1. Does the child have difficulty starting, stopping or making quick turns?
2. Does the child run using a flat foot; is the weight received on the whole foot?
3. Does the child run with the toes pointing outward?
4. Do the arms move back and forth across the body?

Jumping
1. Does the child fail to assume a crouched or flexed position in preparing to jump?
2. Does the child fail to extend the hips, knees, ankles in initiating the jump?
3. Does the child fail to use a two-footed take-off and landing?
4. Are the arms not used or used awkwardly in jumping?
5. Does the child land stiff legged, e.g., with hips/knees extended?
6. Does the child lose balance on landing?

Hopping
1. Does the child hop two or three steps and lose control?
2. Are the hopping movements staccato and/or stiff and arrhythmic?
3. Are the hands and fingers stiff, extended and/or tense?
4. Do the arms flail?
5. Is there no period of suspension, e.g., does the child fail to get up off on the ground?

Skipping
1. Does the child skip 2–3 cycles and then lose the pattern?
2. Does the child skip on one foot and walk or step with the other?
3. Does the child skip using a flatfoot?
4. Is there little or no arm-foot opposition?

Throwing
1. Is the arm moved primarily in the vertical or anteroposterior plane?
2. Is the ball held in the palm of the hand?
3. Does the child throw without any transfer of weight?
4. Does the child throw by stepping onto the same foot as the throwing arm?
5. Is there little or no trunk rotation?
6. Does the child fail to follow-through after ball release?

Catching
1. Does the child prepare to catch with the arms extended in front of the body?
2. Does the child use the arms, hands and body to 'trap' the ball?
3. Does the child turn the head away from the ball as they contact it?
4. Does the ball bounce off the outstretched arms?
5. Does the child only catch balls bounced from close distances (5 ft or less)?
6. Does the child fail to watch or track the ball?

Source: Williams' Preschool Motor Development Checklist, by H. Williams. Revised 2001. The Perceptual-Motor Development Laboratory Protocols-Revised, University of South Carolina-Columbia.

TABLE 17.6.
Interpretation of *Williams' Preschool Motor Development Checklist*

Skill	Guidelines
Running	If three of the four questions are answered yes, there may be a developmental lag in running.
Running	If four of the six questions are answered yes, there may be a development lag in jumping.
Hopping	If four of the five questions are answered yes, there may be a developmental lag in hopping.
Skipping	If the child is 5 to 6 years old and the answer to all five questions is yes, there may be a developmental lag in skipping.
Throwing	If a child is 4 or 5 years old and the answer to five of the six questions is yes, there may be a developmental lag in throwing.
Catching	If the child is 3 years old, and the answer to questions 2, 3, 4, and 5 is yes, keep a watchful eye on this aspect of motor development. If the child is 5 years old, and the answer to any question is yes, there may be a developmental lag in catching.

Source: *Williams' Preschool Motor Development Checklist*; H. Williams, 2001, The Perceptual-Motor Development Laboratory Protocols–Revised, University of South Carolina-Columbia

problems observed. Most of these instruments require some understanding of the developmental characteristics associated with the acquisition of motor skills in young children, as well as some experience in observing children's movement behavior in play or other naturalistic environments. Most process assessment techniques consist of a series of descriptive statements designed to identify important aspects of the child's movement performance. The interpretation of the information from these instruments is usually straightforward, but may vary from one instrument to another. Several of the most common instruments are discussed next.

Ulrich Test of Gross Motor Development.   The Ulrich Test of Gross Motor Development (Ulrich, 2002) is one of the most widely recognized and used motor skills process assessment tools. It is an excellent example of a battery that focuses solely on assessing process characteristics of children's gross motor skills that is both norm and criterion referenced. Importantly it is one of a very few standardized tests that use a quantitative approach to evaluating process aspects of gross motor skill development in young children. Data are provided on children between the ages of 3 and 10 years. The battery has a multidimensional purpose; it is designed to identify children who would benefit from special services or enrichment, to assist in the development of appropriate instructional programming strategies, to assess the progress of individual children, and/or to evaluate the effectiveness of specially designed gross motor development programs. It also has the potential, because of its quantitative approach, to be an excellent research tool for individuals interested in the scientific study of motor skill acquisition in young children.

Two areas of gross motor development are evaluated: locomotion (body projection) and object control (ball handling). Locomotor skills that are evaluated include running, hopping, leaping, jumping, and sliding. Object control skills include two-hand striking, stationary ball bouncing, catching, kicking, throwing, and an underhand roll. Each skill is scored according to the presence or absence of selected movement process characteristics.

TABLE 17.7.
Locomotor and Object Control Examples from Ulrich's Test
of Gross Motor Development

Skill	Description	Skill Characteristics (PC)*/**
Locomotor		
Run	Child runs through a 50' distance	Arms move in opposition (5)
		Lands on heel or toe (3)
Jump	Child jumps as far as possible	Knees flexed/arms extended behind (6)
		Takes off/lands on two feet (3)
		Arms extend fully above head (9)
Hop	Child hops 3 times on each foot	Foot of nonsupport behind body (6)
		Nonsupport legs swings in pendular fashion (7)
		Arms bent at elbows; swing forward to produce force (7)
		Able to hop 3 times on right/left feet (5)
Object Control		
Throw	Child throws ball against wall-20'	Hips/shoulders rotate so that non throwing side faces wall (9)
		Transfers weight onto foot opposite throwing arm (8)
		Follow-through beyond ball release (7)
Catch	Child catches ball tossed-15'	Hands in front of body to prepare (5)
		Ball caught with hands/fingers (8)
Bounce	Child bounces ball 4 consecutive times without moving feet	Contacts ball, 1 hand, hip height (8)
		Pushes ball with fingers (7)
		Ball contacts floor in front of foot on side of hand used for bouncing (6)

*Performance characteristics modified from original.
**Age at which 70+% of children exhibit the process characteristic.

An example of the specific locomotor and object control skill process characteristics are described in Table 17.7. If the process characteristic is present, a score of 1 is given; if it is absent, a score of 0 is given. Scores are summed for each skill and can be converted into percentile ranks (recommended for parental use) or standard scores (recommended for educational or clinical program planning). A scale is provided for arranging individual subtest standard scores into seven steps, ranging from very poor to very superior performance. Standard scores for each of the areas of locomotion and object control can be summed to arrive at a Gross Motor Development Quotient. This quotient provides an estimate of the child's overall gross motor development and is interpreted in the same way (very poor to very superior) as individual subtest standard scores. Raw scores can also be directly converted into *age equivalents*. These values provide a possible indication of the developmental age of the individual child. Caution should be exerted in using age equivalents in interpreting children's levels of motor development as development is age-related not age-specific. Normative data for the battery are based on some 1200 children from a variety of racial backgrounds from eight states; data on 332 children ages 3–5 years are included. A careful analysis of reliability and validity issues also is provided.

TABLE 17.8.
Examples of Process Characteristics of Selected Object Control Skills:
Motor Control Process Checklists

Object Control Skills	(Circle the number if the characteristics present)*			
Overarm Throw				
1. Trunk is rotated backward; weight is shifted to back foot	1	2	3	4
2. Throwing arm is moved backward with rotation occurring at the shoulder joint	1	2	3	4
3. Step is taken toward the intended target on the foot opposite the throwing arm	1	2	3	4
4. Body weight is shifted forward: the arm lags behind, the elbow leads	1	2	3	4
5. Arm begins moving in the horizontal plane	1	2	3	4
6. Medial rotation of the shoulder and elbow extension occur; the elbow is close to complete extension at the time of release	1	2	3	4
7. Wrist is flexed rapidly just before ball is released	1	2	3	4
8. On the follow-through the body and arm continue to rotate or move forward	1	2	3	4
Kick				
1. A preliminary step is taken on the support leg and toward the ball	1	2	3	4
2. The kicking leg swings backward and then forward with flexion at the knee	1	2	3	4
3. Body is inclined slightly backward	1	2	3	4
4. As the upper leg becomes perpendicular to the floor, lower leg extends (at knee)	1	2	3	4
5. The kicking leg extends and makes contact with the ball	1	2	3	4
6. Contact is made with the toes or instep	1	2	3	4
7. The ankle is slightly flexed	1	2	3	4
8. The opposite arm swings forward/upward in the follow-through	1	2	3	4
9. Trunk becomes slightly more vertical after contact	1	2	3	4
Catch				
1. Arms move to a position in front of the body	1	2	3	4
2. Hands are juxtaposed, the palms of the hands facing each other	1	2	3	4
3. Hands turn to accommodate the high or low trajectory of ball	1	2	3	4
4. Hands and fingers are "loose" but slightly cupped and pointed in direction of the oncoming ball	1	2	3	4
5. Eyes pick up and follow the flight of the ball until ball contact is made	1	2	3	4
6. Initially, the ball contact is made with both hands simultaneously	1	2	3	4
7. Adjustments in the elbow and shoulder joint positions are made to accommodate changes in the flight of the ball	1	2	3	4
8. Fingers close immediately around the ball and the arms "give" to absorb momentum of ball	1	2	3	4
One-Arm Strike				
1. Feet are positioned approximately shoulder width apart	1	2	3	4
2. Trunk is rotated backward and the weight is shifted onto the back foot	1	2	3	4
3. Lead elbow is held up and out from the body with bat off the shoulder	1	2	3	4
4. Eyes follow the flight of the ball until just before contact	1	2	3	4
5. Body weight is shifted forward onto the opposite foot in the direction of the intended hit	1	2	3	4
6. Hips and trunk rotate in the direction of intended hit; hips lead	1	2	3	4
7. Arms move forward independent of hips	1	2	3	4

* To be considered a consistent process characteristic, the characteristic should be present on 3 of 4 trials.

Motor Control Process Checklists. In the recently revised Motor Control Process Check-lists, Williams and Breihan (2001) have attempted to create a standardized approach to the assessment of process characteristics of movement control in young children. The 16 check-lists in the battery describe, in simple language, movement characteristics of selected gross and fine motor skills and are based on data from 350 children ages 4, 6, and 8 years. The statements in each checklist are descriptions of the actions required for mastery of the skill. Typically, full mastery of most of the tasks included in this battery is not expected until sometime after 6 years of age. Ten of the gross motor skill checklists are presented in Table 17.8. Each checklist consists of 4–8 statements about important process characteristics to look for in the movement behavior of the child during task performance. The statements in these checklists are more detailed than those discussed earlier and allow the evaluator to as-sess more precisely the nature and quality of the child's movement, as well as to determine whether or not a motor skill problem is present. The child performs each skill at least four times, preferably in a naturalistic setting. While the child moves, the evaluator circles the numbers of those statements that typify or characterize the movement behavior of the child. The general rule of thumb is that the child should display a given process characteristic 75% of the time if that characteristic is to be considered typical of his or her movement behavior. In addition, if the child does not exhibit three or more of the process characteristics that 70% of children the same age display, he or she might be experiencing some motor devel-opment delays. This child should be considered for additional monitoring of their motor de-velopment; some thought should also be given to providing enrichment activities to support the child's development in the area(s) of delay. Percentages of children 3–6 years of age ex-hibiting selected process characteristics are shown in Tables 17.9 and 17.10.

Product Assessment of Gross Motor Skill. The most common approach to the evaluation of motor development is the use of product assessment techniques. Normative data for such test batteries usually are given in standard scores, percentiles, or some other quanti-tative form derived from means, standard deviations, and/or standard errors. Normative data generally are used for comparing individual children to standards typical for children of comparable chronological ages. There are no comprehensive, published test batteries of this type for very young children (2- to 3-year-olds); several are available for assessing 4, 5, and 6-year-old children. Several of the more widely used product-oriented motor per-formance test batteries are reviewed here; all are formal, standardized measures of motor development.

Movement Assessment Battery for Children. The Movement Assessment Battery for Chil-dren is one of the more recent, most comprehensive, and widely-used test batteries for as-sessing motor development in children. It is generally referred to as the Movement ABC (Henderson & Sudgen, 1992; Schoemaker, Smits-Englesman, & Jongmans, 2003) and was designed to provide both process and product information about children's motor develop-ment. It consists of an objective *test*, which includes both a product and process component and a *checklist* (described earlier). The objective test is appropriate for use in arriving at a more detailed description of motor development needs. The test component of the Movement ABC is divided into different age bands; the youngest age band spans the years from 4 to 6. Each age band consists of eight tasks. Tasks in each age band are categorized as follows: manual dexterity (fine motor tasks), ball skills, and static and dynamic balance. The latter three categories assess gross motor development. For each task there is a quan-titative or product score (e.g., time in balance, number of steps, etc.) and a series of process

TABLE 17.9.
Percentages of 3–6 year olds Exhibiting Selected Process Characteristics:
Locomotor Skills

Run

60–68% of 3 year olds
70–74% of 4 year olds
73–78% of 5 year olds
80–85% of 6 year olds exhibit some or all of the following characteristics:
- Arms and legs move in opposition
- Brief period of suspension
- Weight is received on either heel or toes of foot
- Head is up/facing forward

Jump

16–30% of 3 year olds
32–40% of 4 year olds
44–50% of 5 year olds
50–80% of 6 year olds exhibit some or all of the following characteristics:
- Flexes, e.g., assumes a crouched position
- Extends legs at take-off
- Uses 2-foot take-off/landing
- Arms are coordinated with legs
- Maintains balance on landing

Gallop

10–30% of 3 year olds
23–66% of 4 year olds
32–89% of 5 year olds
49–81% of 6 year olds exhibit some or all of the following characteristics:
- Steps (or leaps) with lead foot; follows with step on trail foot
- Brief period of suspension
- Arms pump/lifted to waist at take-off
- Continually leads with same foot

Hop

10–49% of 3 year olds
36–61% of 4 year olds
50–85% of 5 year olds
62–90% of 6 year olds exhibit some or all of the following characteristics:
- Arms pump to produce force
- Weight received on ball of foot
- Hips/knees flex on landing
- Performs 3 consecutive hops/preferred foot

Skip

6–20% of 3 year olds
8–42% of 4 year olds
50–63% of 5 year olds
68–86% of 6 year olds exhibit some or all of the following characteristics:
- Arms/legs move in opposition
- Performs a step-hop on alternating sides
- Brief period of suspension

TABLE 17.10.
Percentages of 3–6 year olds Exhibiting Selected Process Characteristics:
Object Control Skills

Throw

11–20% of 3 year olds
29–42% of 4 year olds
33–56% of 5 year olds
52–65% of 6 year olds exhibit some or all of the following characteristics:
• Whole trunk rotates backward and forward
• Weight is shifted onto the foot opposite the throwing arm
• Ball is held in the fingertips
• Side is toward the target

Kick

16–50% of 3 year olds
20–68% of 4 year olds
28–84% of 5 year olds
54–89% of 6 year olds exhibit some or all of the following characteristics:
• Takes preliminary step to ball
• Kicking leg extends to make contact
• Kicks through the ball
• Contact is with instep or toe of preferred foot

Stationary Catch

5–33% of 3 year olds
14–62% of 4 year olds
51–84% of 5 year olds
35–90% of 6 year olds exhibit some or all of the following characteristics:
• Arms are flexed at elbows and in front of the body
• Eyes fixate and track ball to contact
• Ball is caught with hands/fingers

Two Arm Strike

26–40% of 3 year olds
32–56% of 4 year olds
38–65% of 5 year olds
52–68% of 6 year olds exhibit some or all of the following characteristics:
• Feet are parallel and shoulder width apart
• Side of body is toward the target
• Hips/trunk/shoulders rotate during swing
• Swing is horizontal
• Weight is shifted onto opposite foot

characteristics to be checked. Some selected examples of process characteristics for each of the gross motor tasks are given in Table 17.4. The process characteristics listed in the table are, for the most part, paraphrased and do not represent the verbatim wording found in the battery. Demonstration of and practice on all tasks is required; after practice, children are given 1 or more trials to perform the task. The number of trials varies from task to task and range from 2–10. Tasks in the age band for 4, 5, and 6 year olds include:

1. putting coins through a slot in a box
2. threading beads
3. drawing a single continuous line within a boundary
4. catching a bean bag tossed from 6′
5. rolling a ball into a goal 6′ away
6. one-leg balance
7. jumping over a cord knee high
8. walking 15 steps on a line with the heels raised.

Directions for administering and scoring each item are provided in simple, straightforward language. Means and standard deviations are given for total impairment scores by age and by gender. Cut-off scores for the 5th and 15th percentiles are provided. Scores below the 5th percentile are indicative of a definite motor development lag, while scores between the 5th and 15th percentiles suggest borderline motor development difficulties. Sample case studies are described in detail. Normative data for both the test and checklist components are based on 1,200 children from 4 to 12 years of age; the sample in the age range from 4 to 6 years was 493 children. Boys and girls of different ethnic origins and from diverse regions of the United States were included. The battery has been used throughout the world for assessing motor skill development in children.

Peabody Developmental Motor Scales–II.   A very widely used tool for assessing motor development in young children is the Peabody Developmental Motor Scales (Folio & Fewell, 2000). The scales were designed to evaluate gross and fine motor skills in children both with and without disabilities from birth to 6 years. The Gross Motor Scale consists of a total of 170 items, 10 items at each of 17 age levels. Items are grouped at 6-month intervals beginning at 2 years. The areas of gross motor development that are considered include reflexes (in children up to 1 year of age), balance/nonlocomotor behaviors, locomotor skills, and object manipulation skills. The gross motor development scale requires approximately 30 minutes to administer and is straightforward in administration, scoring, and interpretation. All items are scored 0 (the child cannot or does not perform the task), 1, or 2 (the child performs the task according to the differential criteria listed). Basal and ceiling ages are determined, and raw scores can be converted into percentile ranks, standard scores, and a gross and fine motor quotient. Normative data on 2,003 children (85.1% Caucasian) from a wide variety of geographical locations (northeastern, northern, central, southern and western United States) are provided. Of the total number of children in the standardization sample, there were at least 92 2-year-olds, 103 3-year-olds, 50 4-year-olds, and 55 5 year olds. Examples of each of the skill areas and the criteria for passing (for 4-year-olds) are described in Table 17.11. The Peabody Motor Activities Program is available for use by teachers.

Bruininks-Oseretsky Test of Motor Proficiency.   The Bruininks-Oseretsky Test (Bruininks, 1978) is designed for use with children 4½ through 14½ years of age. It consists of eight subtests (46 separate items) that provide a broad index of the child's proficiency in both gross and fine motor skills. A short form of the test (14 items) provides a brief overview of the child's general motor proficiency. Four of the subtests measure gross motor skills; these include running speed and agility, balance, bilateral coordination, and upper limb coordination. Selected items used to assess these four aspects of gross motor development are described in Table 17.12. Raw scores on gross motor items are converted to point scores that

TABLE 17.11.
Examples of Items from the Peabody Gross Motor Scale (4-year olds)

Skill Area	Item	Criterion for Passing
Balance (Stationary)	Walks a 4-in balance beam	Completes 4 steps without support
	Stands on tiptoes with hands	Maintains position for 8 sec with good stability over head
Locomotor	Jumps up with hands overhead	Jumps 3 ft beyond normal reach as high as possible
	Jumps down from 32 in	Jumps without support, leading with one foot
	Jumps forward as far as possible	Jumps forward 16 in on one foot
		Jumps forward 12 in on opposite foot
	Rolls forward (somersault)	Rolls forward over head without turning head 15 degrees to either side
Object Manipulation	Throws ball	Throws ball 10 ft on 1 of 2 trials

are then converted to standard scores. The standard scores are summed to give a gross motor composite; this is converted into a composite standard score. The standard score is used to determine a percentile rank for the individual child. Some age-equivalent data are provided, and norms are established at 6-month intervals. The standardization sample was based on 68 children for the 4 year 6 month to 5 year 5 month range and 82 children for the 5 year 6 month to 6 year 5 month range. The test is currently undergoing revision.

Cashin Test of Motor Development. The Cashin Test (Cashin, 2001) was designed for use with 4- and 5-year-olds and its database is approximately 1,000 children. This test assesses five different gross motor skills: static balance, dynamic balance, agility, over arm throw, and catch. General task descriptions, testing procedures, and a sample of normative data are given in Table 17.13. The Cashin Test was developed with ease of administration and minimal space requirements as important considerations. On average, a child can complete the entire test in 20 minutes. Since the test includes product measures of some skills and process assessment of others, some minimal training or experience in observing process characteristics of the over arm throw and catching skills in young children is necessary to use the battery successfully. Young children often have difficulty understanding exactly what to do on the agility task, and several practice trials may be needed if an accurate assessment of the child's agility is to be made. The normative data available provide a rough standard for assessing the level of motor development of individual children. Three categories of development are identified: *average, accelerated, and developmental lag.* The score(s) corresponding to these levels of motor development are based on group means and standard deviations (average level of development is within 1 +/− standard deviations; accelerated development is at least 2 standard deviations above the mean; developmental lag is at least 2 standard deviations below the mean). Important female-male differences are also noted in Table 17.13.

McCarthy Scales of Children's Abilities. Another example of a product approach to the evaluation of young children's motor development is the McCarthy Scales of Children's Abilities. This test battery was designed to help fulfill the need for a single instrument to

TABLE 17.12.
Items from Gross Motor Skills Subtest:
Bruininks-Oseretsky Test of Motor Proficiency

Running Speed/Agility (Time to nearest .2 sec)
Child runs a distance of 15 yds, picks up a block, runs back across the start line

Balance (Time or number of steps)
Child stands on preferred leg on floor; holds for 10 sec
Child stands on preferred leg on balance beam; holds for 10 sec
Child stands on preferred leg on balance beam with eyes closed
Child walks line on floor with normal stride for 6 steps
Child walks forward on balance beam in normal stride for 6 steps
Child walks forward in heel-toe fashion on line on floor for 6 steps
Child walks forward in heel-toe fashion on balance beam for 6 steps
Child walks forward on balance beam and steps over a stick held at knee height; hands on hips

Bilateral Coordination (Completes 10 cycles in 90 sec)
Child taps feet alternately while making circles with index fingers
Child simultaneously taps foot and index finger on one side of body and then the other
Child simultaneously taps right foot & left index finger and the left foot and right index finger
Child jumps in place with leg and arm on opposite sides of body and alternates sides
Child jumps as high as possible and touches heels (while in the air)

Upper Limb Coordination (Number in 5 attempts)
Child bounces tennis ball on floor and catches with both hands
Child uses preferred hand and bounces tennis ball on floor and catches it
Child catches tennis ball tossed from 10 ft using two hands
Child catches tennis ball tossed from 10 ft with preferred hand
Child throws ball overarm at target 4 feet away
Child attempts to touch a ball swung horizontally in front of them with the index finger

Source: Adapted from *Bruininks-Oseretsky Test of Motor Proficiency:* Examiner's manual, by Robert H. Bruininks, 1978, Circle Pines, MN: American Guidance Service, Inc.

evaluate strengths and weaknesses of young children's abilities (McCarthy, 1972). The McCarthy scales involve systematic observation of a variety of cognitive and motor behaviors that are subdivided into six scales. The Motor Development Scale assesses gross and fine motor skills through the following subtests: Leg Coordination, Arm Coordination, Imitative Action, Draw-A-Design, and Draw-A-Child. The latter two tasks are fine motor tasks and are included in the Perceptual-Performance and General Cognitive Scales. Leg Coordination is examined using the following tasks: walk backward, walk on tiptoes, walk on a straight line, stand on one foot, and skip. Arm Coordination involves three tasks: bouncing a ball, catching a bean bag, and throwing a bean bag at a target. Four tasks are included in the Imitative Action sequence: crossing feet at the ankles, folding hands, twiddling thumbs, and sighting through a tube. In the Draw-A-Design task, the child is asked to reproduce various geometric designs including a circle, vertical and horizontal lines, a parallelogram, and so on. In the Draw-A-Child task, the child is asked to draw a picture of a boy or girl according to the gender of the child. During performance of the motor items, observations concerning hand usage and eye preferences also are made. For each of the scales, including the Motor Scale, the child's raw scores are converted into T-scores based

TABLE 17.13.
Cashin Test of Motor Development

Task*	Scoring	Age/sex	Average	Accelerated	Lag
Agility	1 practice trial	4 M/F	9.5–10.2	Below 9.0	Above 11.0
(Obstacle	Average of 3	5 M	8.1–8.6	Below 7.9	Above 9.0
Course)		5 F	9.0–10.2	Below 8.5	Above 11.0
Static	1 practice trail	4 M	13.7–16.9	Above 19.0	Below 12.0
Balance	Average of 3	4 F	17.6–21.1	Above 23.0	Below 15.0
	30 sec max	5 M/F	20.3–22.5	Above 24.0	Below 19.0
Dynamic	3 trials/av steps	4 M	5.8–7.9	Above 9.0	Below 4.7
Balance	2 trips of 10 steps	4 F	11.9–14.2	Above 15.0	Below 10.7
	2 errors per trip	5 M/F	13.2–14.8	Above 16.0	Below 12.0
Throwing	2 trials/10 throws	4 M	55–59	Above 59	Below 53
	Total points	4 F	45–48	Above 49	Below 43
	5 pts per trial	5 M	56–58	Above 59	Below 55
		5 F	46–49	Above 51	Below 45
Catch	2 trials/12 tosses	4 M/F	30–32	Above 33	Below 29
	Av pts/2 trials	5 M	34–36	Above 37	Below 30
	5 pts per toss	5 F	34–35	Above 36	Below 30

Agility: On signal go, child follows the laid out path. **Static Balance:** Child places hands on hips and foot of choice against the inside of support leg just below the knee. **Dynamic Balance:** Child places hands on hips and steps onto beam 2-inches wide and walks 10 steps (heel-toe), stops, returns to end of beam and repeats task. **Throwing:** child stands behind a line 12 ft from a wall and throws ball, overarm, as hard as possible against the wall; a rating scale is used to determine points. **Catching:** Child stands on an 'x' 13 ft from the examiner and attempts to catch an 8½ inch playground ball; 4 tosses to child, 4 tosses to child's right and 4 tosses to child's left are given in random order in each of the 2 trials; a rating scale is used to determine points.

on the child's chronological age. Percentile ranks are also presented for purposes of interpretation. The scales are based on normative data gathered on 1,032 children ages 2½ through 8½ years.

The Vulpe Assessment Battery. The Vulpe Assessment Battery (Vulpe, 1994) was developed by physical and occupational therapists to assess a wide variety of behaviors using a clinical approach. Among the areas of behavior that are evaluated are gross and fine motor development, language, cognitive processes, adaptive behaviors, and activites of daily living. The test, which is a product-oriented assessment tool, also includes tests of muscle strength, motor planning, reflex development, and balance. These are useful tools for conducting a comprehensive analysis of the young child's gross motor development. With regard to specific gross motor skill development, significant individual motor development achievements are identified for different ages beginning at 1 month and extending to 8 years of age. Skills are organized in an age-based sequence, and criteria for assessing mastery of each skill at each age are provided. The gross motor skills assessed by the Vulpe include sitting, kneeling, standing, walking, stair climbing, running, jumping, kicking, throwing, and balancing. A number of different tasks (usually 1–3) are used to assess each motor skill; performance is judged on a number of dimensions ranging from whether the child requires physical or verbal assistance to perform the tasks to whether the child can perform the skill alone and/or can transfer the skill to a different task or environmental context. Overall, the test is most useful as a source of information about age-related motor development and other behavioral achievements in young children. There is a direct link between scoring and an accompanying curriculum.

Gross Motor Function Measure (GMFM).   The GMFM (Russell, Rosenbaum, Avery & Lane, 2002) is a clinical assessment tool designed to evaluate change in gross motor function in children with cerebral palsy, but can also be used to evaluate motor development in children with Down syndrome or with other children whose skills are at or below those typically observed in 5-year-olds. The original test consists of 88 items; a more recent version consists of a subset of 66 items. The tasks included span a range of skills from lying and rolling through walking, running, and jumping skills; the 88-item battery takes approximately 45–60 minutes to administer. Data are on children from 5 months to 16 years. A 4-point scale is used to evaluate each item; detailed standards for scoring are provided. The GMFM–88 scores can be summed to determine raw scores and percentile scores for the child's overall performance. There is a GMFM self-instructional CD ROM that can be used for training and experience prior to administering the test.

Multidomain Tests.   Zittel (1994) reviews important considerations in selecting an instrument for assessing gross motor development in preschool children with special needs. This work provides an excellent overview of several test batteries that could be used with preschoolers with special motor development needs. Other multidomain tests of potential interest include the I CAN Preprimary Motor and Play Skills (Wessel, 1980), Battelle Developmental Inventory–II (2004), Brigance Diagnostic Inventory of Early Development (Brigance, 1991), Miller Assessment for Preschoolers (Miller, 1988), and Developmental Indicators for the Assessment of Learning–Revised (Mardell-Czudnowski & Goldenberg, 1998). These are all multidomain tests and, thus, do not focus primarily on assessment of gross motor development.

USE OF ASSESSMENT RESULTS

Because we know that children who experience lags in motor development are more likely than their peers to display difficulties in adapting to both school and play environments, information about the level and nature of motor skill development is of major importance to the parent, the teacher, the school psychologist, and the family physician. It may be easy to note that a child moves awkwardly; however, it is another matter to describe or determine more precisely what was missing from or contributed to the lack of skillful performance. Poor or underdeveloped motor skills may be the product of a complex set of factors that include not only poor coordination and control, but also lack of appropriate spatial/body awareness, underdeveloped sensory function, lack of self-confidence, fear of failure, etc. Thus, a scientifically sound and insightful description and diagnosis of gross motor development should be based on information from formal and informal product and process assessments of the child's gross motor behaviors along with outcomes of a variety of other developmental measures. With regard to motor development, formal measures of gross motor development are needed to support, clarify, and extend observations of motor behavior made with informal instruments. Formal product measures of motor development are valuable because they provide a frame of reference for interpreting the current status of the child's motor development. It is important to note, however, that it is imprudent and unfair to act as though figures or descriptions in a table or on a chart are an irrefutable indication of whether or not a child is normal or typical.

Process information is used to elaborate on the product frame of reference. Process information is especially important because it considers directly how the body is moved and attempts to identify what is missing from or contributing to the child's lack of adequate motor control. Process assessment techniques are particularly important for gaining insight into how the child attempts to solve the problem of performing a motor task. This type of information is integral to an accurate description and/or ultimate diagnosis of the level of gross motor development because lags in motor development can be as much a function of the young child's understanding of the what and how of a task as they are of the child's ability to perform the task. The most significant, direct, and immediate uses that can be made of information from gross motor development screening and evaluation include the following:

1. *Planning and evaluating effective gross motor curricula for young children.* To individualize early sensory and motor learning experiences for young children, professionals need to be able to group or identify children according to motor development levels. When specific aspects of the gross motor behavior of the child are known, basic tasks can be modified in a variety of ways to encourage individual refinement of and success in motor skill performance at the child's present level of development, as well as to promote growth toward higher levels of skill mastery.

2. *Early identification of motor dysfunctions.* Motor dysfunctions can impede the child's physical, mental, social, and emotional development. Information about gross motor development can be valuable to the teacher of the young child for maximizing early learning potential and for educational counseling. Such information is vital when making decisions about whether the child possesses the basic skills needed to succeed in simple classroom activities. The child who devotes a major share of his or her energy to assuming and maintaining basic postures or to controlling movements of the body will have much less energy to devote to other important activities that are integral to optimal development. Data about the child's level of gross motor development are important in determining when and/or if a child should enter school, or whether he or she should be placed in a developmental enrichment environment.

3. *Design of individual programs of enrichment activities.* Motor skill deficiencies often accompany and contribute to other learning, behavior, and attention problems of the young child. When this is the case, some attention almost always is required to improve the motor capacities of the child before other learning and behavior problems can be effectively addressed. If, on the other hand, the young child has learning, memory, and/or attentional problems but no accompanying motor development difficulties, gross motor activities may be used in creative ways to help stimulate improvement in other dimensions of development.

Results of gross motor skill screening and evaluation of the preschool child are most useful as a part of a comprehensive, multidimensional assessment of the young child. At a minimum, information about the child's fine motor control or eye-hand coordination (e.g., cutting, peg manipulation, pencil or crayon usage), simple perceptual skills (e.g., identification of colors, color matching, visual, verbal, and tactile-kinesthetic discrimination of shapes and sizes, as well as figure ground perception), and general characteristics of cognitive function ought to accompany the child's motor development record. It is only when information from gross motor development testing is used or viewed in conjunction with information about these other aspects of sensory and motor development that appropriate prognostic statements and remediation techniques for gross motor and other dimensions of development can be established or prescribed.

If the child has gross motor deficiencies only (e.g., no accompanying deficits in other sensory and motor behaviors), it is more likely that the motor development problems observed are temporary and simply reflect an uneven growth process that will self-correct with time. If, on the other hand, gross motor deficits are accompanied by fine motor and/or other sensory-perceptual or cognitive difficulties, there may be underlying neurological problems. In this case, referral to a pediatric neurologist and/or other appropriate medical personnel for further evaluation is appropriate. The motor system (including the control of eye muscles) is more likely than other systems to show deficits when something has gone awry with basic central and/or peripheral neurophysiological processes. At a behavioral level, information-gathering behaviors (e.g., the way children use their eyes to pick up information from the environment) and information-interpretation skills (e.g., figure-ground perception) can contribute significantly to the lack of refined fine and gross motor skills. Gross motor deficits are often, at least in part, a reflection of inadequate support skills in visual perception. Therefore, remediation and enrichment programs for children with both gross motor and simple perceptual deficits need to focus on improving support behaviors as well as the movement behaviors themselves. Professionals working in educational settings with preschool children should use the following guide to gross motor development:

- Screen all children in gross motor development prior to or early in their entry into the preschool program.
- For initial screening, use a simple motor development screening tool such as the Denver Developmental Screening test or the Williams Preschool Checklist.
- Observe the children in naturalistic play settings.
- Use this information to determine which children need closer observation.
- Use a formal instrument to screen more carefully the children identified as potentially having gross motor process and product deficiencies.
- Examiners who must choose one measure over another should be sure to include some evaluation of the process characteristics of the child's motor skill performance.
- Children with questionable abilities should be referred to a motor development specialist, physical education teacher, or school psychologist for a more formal and comprehensive evaluation that includes a broad base of developmental information.
- Based on the total developmental profile, develop and implement appropriate instructional strategies and experiences to promote the motor development of the young child.
- When in doubt about the child's motor development difficulties, talk to or refer the child to the appropriate personnel within or outside the school setting.
- Remember that scores, percentiles, and other outcomes do not always tell the whole story about the child's overall motor development status and/or needs.

REFERENCES

American Psychiatric Association. (1993). *Diagnostic and Statistical Manual of Mental Disorders* (4th ed.). Washington, DC: Author.

Battelle Developmental Inventory, 2nd Edition (BDI–2). (2004). Itasca, IL: Riverside Publishing.

Baumann, C. Loffler, C., Curie, A., Schmid, E., & von Aster, M. (2004). Motor skills and psychiatric disturbances in children. *Psychiatric Prax, 31*(8), 395–9.

Bayley, N. (1965). Comparisons of mental and motor test scores for ages 1–15 months by sex, birth order, race, geographical location and education of parents. *Child Development, 36*, 379–411.

Branta, C. (1992). Motoric and fitness assessment of young children. In C. Hendricks (Ed.) *Young children on the grow: Health, activity and education in the preschool setting (Teacher Education Monograph: No.13)*. Washington, DC: ERIC Clearinghouse on Teacher Education.

Brigance, A. (1991). *Brigance Diagnostic Inventory of Early Development, Revised Edition* (BDIED–R). North Billerica, MA: Curriculum Associates.

Bruininks, R. (1978). *Bruininks-Oseretsky Test of Motor Proficiency. Examiner's Manual*. Circle Pines, MN: American Guidance Service.

Bushnell, E., & Boudreau, J. (1993). Motor development and the mind: The potential role of motor abilities as a determinant of aspects of perceptual development. *Child Development, 64*, 1005–1021.

Burton, A., & Miller, D. (1998). *Movement Skill Assessment*. Champaign, IL: Human Kinetics.

Butcher, J., & Eaton, W. (1989). Gross and fine motor proficiency in preschoolers: Relationships with free play behavior and activity level. *Journal of Human Movement Studies, 16*, 27–36.

Cantell, M., Smyth, M., & Ahonen, T. (1994). Clumsiness in adolescence: Educational, motor and social outcomes of motor delay detected at 5 years. *Adapted Physical Activity Quarterly, 11*(2), 115–129.

Capute, A., & Accardo, P. (1996). *Developmental Disabilities in Infant and Child: Neurodevelopmental Diagnosis and Treatment. Section III–Fundamentals of Pediatric Developmental Assessment* (pp. 263–424). Baltimore: Paul H. Brookes.

Cashin, G. (2001). *The Cashin Test of Motor Development*. In H. Williams, *The Perceptual-Motor Development Laboratory Protocols–Revised*. Columbia, SC: University of South Carolina.

Cratty, B. J. (1972). *Physical expressions of intelligence*. Englewood Cliffs, NJ: Prentice-Hall.

Denckla, M. (1984). Developmental dyspraxia. The clumsy child. In M. D. Levine, & P. Satz (Eds.), *Middle childhood: development and dysfunction*. Boston: University Park Press.

Dewey D., Kaplan B., Crawford S., & Wilson B. (2002). Developmental coordination disorder: Associated problems in attention, learning, and psychosocial adjustment. *Human Movement Science, 21*, 905–918.

Espenschade, A., & Eckert, H. (1980). *Motor development*. Columbus, OH: Merrill.

Folio, M., & Fewell, R. (2000). *Peabody Developmental Motor Scales (PMDS–2)*. Austin, TX: PRO-ED.

Frankenburg, W. K., & Dodds, J. B. (1967). The Denver Developmental Screening Test. *Journal of Pediatrics, 71*, 181.

Frankenburg, W., Dodds, J., Archer, P., Bresnick, B., & Shapiro, H. (1990). *The Denver II Revision and restandardization of the DDST*. Denver: Denver Developmental Materials.

Gallahue, D., & Ozmun, J. (2002). *Understanding motor development with Power Web: Health and Human Performance*. Boston: McGraw-Hill.

Garcia, C. (1994). Gender differences in young children's interactions when learning fundamental motor skills. *Research Quarterly for Exercise and Sport, 65*, 213–225.

Gesell, A. (1973). *The first five years of life: A guide to the study of the preschool child*. New York: Harper & Row.

Geuze, R., & Borger, H. (1993). Children who are clumsy: Five years later. *Adapted Physical Activity Quarterly, 10*, 10–21.

Graf, C., Koch, B., Kretschmann-Kandel, E., Galkowski, G., Christ, H., Coburger, S., et al. (2004). Correlation between BMI, leisure habits and motor abilities in childhood (CHILT-Project). *International Journal of Obesity, 28*, 22–26.

Greendorfer, S., & Ewing, M. (1981). Race and gender differences in children's socialization into sport. *Research Quarterly for Exercise and Sport, 52,* 301–310.

Gubbay, S. (1975). *The clumsy child: A study of developmental apraxic and agnosic ataxia.* London: W. B. Saunders.

Hayes, A. (1994). *Normal and impaired motor development: theory into practice.* London: Chapman & Hall Publishers.

Haywood, K., & Getchell, N. (2004). *Lifespan motor development, 4th Edition.* Champaign, IL: Human Kinetics.

Henderson, S., Knight, E., Losse, A., & Jongmans, M. (1990). The clumsy child in school: Are we doing enough? *British Journal of Physical Education,* 22(2) (Suppl. 9), 2–8.

Henderson, S., & Sudgen, D. (1992). *Movement Assessment Battery for Children,* London: Psychological Corporation.

Illingworth, R. S. (1975). *The development of the infant and young child: Normal and abnormal.* Edinburgh: Livingstone.

Keogh, J., & Sudgen, D. (1990). *Problems in movement skill development.* Columbia, SC: University of South Carolina Press.

Lane, S., Attanasio, C., & Huselid, R. (1994). (See citation: 1993) Prediction of preschool sensory and motor performance by 18 month neurologic scores among children born prematurely. *American Journal of Occupational Therapy,* 48(5), 391–396.

Losch, H., & Dammann, O. (2004). Impact of motor skills on cognitive test results in very-low birthweight children. *Journal of Child Neurology,* 19(5), 318–322.

Losquadro-Little, N., & Yorke, L. (2003). *Why motor skills matter: Improving your child's physical development to enhance learning and self-esteem.* Boston: McGraw-Hill.

Losse, A., Henderson, S., Elliman, D., Hall, D., Knight, E., & Jongmans, M. (1991). Clumsiness in children: Do they grow out of it? A 10-year follow-up study. *Developmental Medicine and Child Neurology, 33,* 55–68.

Lyytinen, H., & Ahonen, N. (1989). Motor precursors of learning disabilities. In D. J. Bakker & D. J. Vander Vlugt (Eds.), *Learning disabilities: Vol. 1, Neuropsychological correlates* (pp. 35–43). Amsterdam: Swets & Zeitlinger.

Malina, R., Bouchard, C., & Bar-Or, O. (2004). *Growth, maturation, and physical activity, 2nd Edition.* Champaign, IL: Human Kinetics.

Mardell-Czudnowski, C., & Goldenberg, D. (1998). *Development Indicators for the Assessment of Learning–Third Edition.* Circle Pines, MN: American Guidance Services.

Martin, S. (2002). *Functional movement: Development across the lifespan.* Philadelphia: W.B. Saunders.

McCarthy, D. (1972). *McCarthy Scales of Children's Abilities.* New York: Psychological Corporation.

Miller, L. (1988). *Miller Assessment for Preschoolers: Manual Revision.* San Antonio, TX: Harcourt Brace Jovanovich.

Newell, K. (1986). Constraints on the development of coordination. In M. Wade & H. Whiting (Eds). *Motor development in children: Aspects of coordination and control* (pp. 341–361). Amsterdam: Martin Nijhoff.

Okely, A., Booth, M., & Chey, T. (2004). Relationship between body composition and fundamental movement skills among children and adolescents. *Research Quarterly for Exercise and Sport,* 75(3), 238–247.

Paine, R. S., & Oppe, T. E. (1966). *Neurological examination of children.* Philadelphia: Lippincott.

Payne, G., & Isaacs, L. (2002). *Human motor development.* New York: McGraw-Hill.

Piaget, J. (1963). *The origins of intelligence in children.* New York: Norton.

Piek J., & Dyck, M. (In press). Sensory-motor deficits in children with Developmental Coordination Disorder, Attention Deficit Hyperactivity Disorder and Autistic Disorder. *Human Movement Science.*

Precht, H. (1977). Assessment and significance of behavioral states. In S. R. Berenberg (Ed.). *Brain-fetal and infant-current research on normal and abnormal development* (pp. 79–90). The Hague: Nijoff.

Precht, H., & Beintema, D. (1964). *The neurological examination of the full term newborn infant.* London: Heinemann.

Roberton, M., & Halverson, L. (1984). *Developing children: Their changing movements.* Philadelphia: Lea & Febiger.

Roberton, M., & Langendorfer, S. (1980). Testing motor development sequences across 9–14 years. In N. C. Nadeau, et al. (Eds.). *Psychology of motor behavior and sport* (pp. 269–279). Champaign, IL: Human Kinetic Press.

Rose, E., & Larkin, D. (2002). Perceived competence, discrepancy scores, and global self-worth. *Adapted Physical Activity, 19*(2), 316–327.

Russell, D., Rosenbaum, P., Avery, L., & Lane, M. (2002). *The Gross Motor Function Measures User's Manual.* Clinics in Developmental Medicine No. 159.

Schoemaker, M., Smits-Engelsman, B., Jongmans, J. (2003). Psychometric properties of the movement assessment battery for children-checklist as a screening instrument for children with a developmental co-ordination disorder. *British Journal of Educational Psychology, 73*(3), 425–41.

Seefeldt, V., & Haubenstricker, J. (1982). Patterns, phases, or stages: An analytical model for the study of developmental movements. In J. Kelso & J. Clark (Eds), *The development of movement control and coordination* (pp. 309–318). New York: John Wiley & Sons.

Skinner, R., & Piek, J. (2001). Psychosocial implications of poor motor coordination in children and adolescents. *Human Movement Science, 20*, 73–94.

Spelke, E. (1990). Origins of visual knowledge. In D. D. Osherson, S. M. Kosslyln, & J. M. Hollerback (Eds.), *Visual cognition and action* (Vol. 2, pp. 90–127). Cambridge, MA: MIT Press.

Sporns, O., & Edelman, G. (1993). Solving Bernstein's problem: A proposal for the development of coordinated movement by selection. *Child Development, 64*, 960–981.

Thomas, J., & French, K. (1985). Gender differences across age in motor performance: A meta-analysis. *Psychological Bulletin, 98*, 260–282.

Touwen, B. (1976). *Neurological development in infancy.* Philadelphia: J. B. Lippincott.

Ulrich, D. (2002). *Test of Gross Motor Development.* Austin, TX: PRO-ED.

Vulpe, S. G. (1994). *Vulpe Assessment Battery–Revised Edition (VAB–R).* East Aurora, NY: Slosson Educational Publications.

Wessel, J. (1980). *I CAN Pre-Primary Motor* Play Skills. East Lansing, MI: Field Service Unit in Physical Education and Recreation for the Handicapped.

Wickstrom, R. (1977). *Fundamental motor patterns.* Philadelphia: Lea & Febiger.

Williams, H. (1983). *Perceptual and motor development in young children.* Englewood Cliffs, NJ: Prentice-Hall.

Williams, H. (2001a). *Signs of potential delay in gross motor development.* In H. Williams, *The Perceptual-Motor Development Laboratory Protocols–Revised.* Columbia, SC: University of South Carolina.

Williams, H. (2001b). *The motor development checklist for parents.* In H. Williams, *The Perceptual-Motor Development Laboratory Protocols–Revised.* Columbia, SC: University of South Carolina.

Williams, H. (2001c). *Williams' Preschool Motor Development Checklist.* In H. Williams, *The Perceptual-Motor Development Laboratory Protocols–Revised.* Columbia, SC: University of South Carolina.

Williams, H., & Breihan, S. (2001). Motor Control Tasks for Young Children. In H. Williams, *The Perceptual-Motor Development Laboratory Protocols–Revised.* Columbia, SC: University of South Carolina.

Zittel, L. (1994). Gross motor assessment of preschool children with special needs: Instrument selection considerations. *Adapted Physical Activity Quarterly, 11*, 245–260.

18

Neuropsychological Assessment of the Preschool Child: Expansion of the Field

Stephen R. Hooper
University of North Carolina, School of Medicine

Andrew Molnar, Jennifer Beswick, and Jill Jacobi-Vessels
University of Louisville

The examination of brain-behavior relationships in the preschool child is a fledgling area; moreover, the assessment of these relationships is quite challenging to the psychologist working with this population. These concerns were raised with the previous editions of this text (Hooper, 1991, 2000), and they continue to remain accurate to the present. Despite these overriding concerns, exciting advances have slowly trickled forth within the domain of the neuropsychological assessment of the preschool child (Aylward, 1997; Espy, 1997; Korkman, Kirk, & Kemp, 1998). These advances have included the emergence of more tools to measure various aspects of cognitive functioning, the development of a contemporary formal battery to assess neurocognitive functioning, and evolution of newer models for higher-order cognition (e.g., executive functions).

Legislative mandates also have fueled these advances. Primary among these mandates was the passage of Public Law (P.L.) 99-457 about 20 years ago (U.S. Department of Education, 1986) explicitly focusing on the needs of preschool children with special needs; the 1991 reauthorization of funds for special education programs such as the Individuals with Disabilities Education Act (IDEA), which made services for the 3-to 5-year-old population mandatory for states rather than optional (U.S. Department of Education, 1997); and the 1997 amendments to IDEA (P.L. 105-17) which further extended the funding of preschool services (Hooper & Umansky, 2004), with an effort to address ages birth to 5. The most recent version of this legislation, the Individuals with Disabilities Education Improvement Act (P.L. 108-446), was signed into law on December 3, 2004 (U.S. Department of Education, 2004). This reauthorization of IDEA included changes that affect the kind of assessments that should be conducted and how eligibility for services for preschoolers should be determined.

For example, parents, teachers, or the Local Education Agency (LEA) may make requests for children's evaluations. Once a request has been made, the evaluation must be completed within 60 days, unless the state has already established a timeline for completion (Individuals with Disabilities, 2004). The authority to make the determination of whether the child has a disability lies with the team of qualified professionals—including the child's parent. The parent may provide their own observations or information from previous evaluations. Re-evaluations may be made no more than once per year and at least every 3 years, unless the parent and the LEA agree upon a change in frequency (Individuals with Disabilities, 2004).

In addition, P.L. 108-446 requires "the use of a variety of assessment tools that must be technically sound and used for purposes for which they are valid and reliable." These multiple assessments are used to gather relevant information on the functional, developmental, and academic status of children. Trained and knowledgeable personnel must conduct these assessments, and this is particularly necessary for neuropsychological assessments. The use of student screening, conducted by a teacher or specialist, is not considered to be a sufficient evaluation to determine eligibility for special education services. In addition, a review of existing data, including evaluations and information provided by the parent, teacher observations, and classroom or state assessments must be made (Individuals with Disabilities, 2004). Another interesting facet to this revision of IDEA is the notion that processes to determine if a child responds to scientific, research-based intervention may be used as part of the evaluation procedures (Individuals with Disabilities, 2004). The relationship between the integrity of specific neuropsychological functions and response-to-treatment should prove useful for both clinical and research venues over the next decade.

One challenge to the utilization of neuropsychological assessment with this population is the special emphasis being placed on the importance of measures that reduce the over-identification of minority and limited English proficient children as having special needs (Individuals with Disabilities, 2004). Assessments must be conducted so as to avoid racial or cultural discrimination. Administration of evaluations must be performed in the language and form "most likely to yield accurate information on what the child knows and can do academically, developmentally, and functionally, unless it is not feasible to so provide or administer," and these demands clearly will challenge neuropsychological assessment strategies at this time (Rhodes, Kayser, & Hess, 2000).

The increased focus on the assessment and treatment needs of preschool children with a variety of developmental needs is no accident, as children with a wide array of acquired and neurodevelopmental problems are now populating inclusive preschool classes and/or requiring special preschool services across the country. In part, improvements in medical care have contributed to lessening the mortality among sick or injured infants and toddlers; however, we are learning that the decrease in mortality likely has contributed to an increase in morbidity. It is this latter supposition that has contributed to increased research and clinical efforts addressing the assessment and treatment needs of preschool children with exceptionalities. For example, such efforts have examined the neurocognitive functioning of low birth weight preschoolers (Sommerfelt, Markestad, & Ellertsen, 1998), the effects of various drugs on preschool development (Walsh, Kastner, & Harmon, 1995), traumatic brain injury outcomes during the preschool years (Wetherington & Hooper, in press; Wrightson, McGinn, & Gronwall, 1995), attention problems (Mahone et al., 2002), and assessment-treatment linkages for learning (Aunola, Leskinene, Lerkkanen, & Nurmi, 2004; Espy & Cwik, 2004; Korkman & Peltomaa, 1993; Lyytinen et al., 2004). Further, the need to develop appropriate educational programs highlights the concurrent need for detailed profiles of abilities, and neuropsychological assessment strategies can provide one vehicle for addressing this need.

Given the steady growth of interest in this assessment domain as applied to preschool children, this chapter presents an overview of the current status of the neuropsychological assessment of the preschool child with an eye toward expansion that has occurred since the last edition approximately 5 years ago. As with the previous edition, the focus for this chapter is largely on the preschool years proper, that is, the ages 3 through 5 years. The utility of neuropsychological testing for this population is elucidated and, subsequently, followed by a discussion of the various neuropsychological assessment strategies available. This discussion spans formal batteries as well as flexible/informal batteries with significant discussion on the available tools that can assist in the appraisal of specific neuropsychological constructs. The chapter concludes with a brief discussion of some broader issues associated with neuropsychological testing of preschool children.

UTILITY OF A NEUROPSYCHOLOGICAL APPROACH

There are numerous complexities related to the neuropsychological assessment of children. Some of these complexities include test selection, interpretation issues, assessment-treatment linkages, and crucial developmental factors that also contribute to behavior and learning. These concerns are magnified further when a neuropsychological perspective is applied to children less than the age of 6 years. Approximately 20 years ago, Aylward (1988) described this latter area as a "no man's land" with respect to its current level of development, particularly for children from birth to 2 years of age. This area has advanced since that time, and it certainly has expanded in its interest and importance.

Despite these concerns, a number of investigators have asserted the utility of employing a neuropsychological approach with preschoolers (Aylward, 1988; Deysach, 1986; Hartlage & Telzrow, 1986; Hooper, 1988; Korkman et al., 1998; Molfese & Price, 2002; Rey-Casserly, 1999; Wilson, 1992), with recent evidence indicating its importance for establishing early intervention programs (Aunola et al., 2004; Espy & Cwik, 2004; Korkman & Peltomaa, 1993; Lyytinen et al., 2004). Consistent with the use of neuropsychological methods with school-age children and adults, a neuropsychological approach for the preschool child can yield a wealth of information pertaining to diagnostic profile description, prognosis, and various treatment factors. More generally, a neuropsychological perspective should serve to advance our understanding of brain-behavior relationships in the preschool population and facilitate examination of young children with special needs.

Diagnostic Profile Description

Historically, the primary role of a neuropsychological approach in diagnosis was to determine the presence of neurological deficits or dysfunction. Assessment procedures were designed to detect and localize brain lesions that would contribute to the discrimination between typically developing children and those with brain impairment. Prior to the mid-1970s, neuropsychological assessment strategies were appealing because of their noninvasive nature in lesion specification; however, the accuracy of these strategies remains in question, particularly in the preschool population. Further, given the recent advances of other neurodiagnostic methods, such as Magnetic Resonance Imaging (MRI), quantitative electroencephalography (QEEG), and Functional Magnetic Resonance Imaging (fMRI), the need to diagnose brain impairment solely with neuropsychological methods has been lessened. Difficulties with neuropsychological diagnosis have been compounded by the lack of an adequate nosology for various kinds of neurologically based disorders. This is especially true for young children where even working psychiatric nomenclature (i.e., Diagnostic and Statistical Manual-IV-TR, American Psychiatric Association, 2000) is ill-fitted for this population.

Despite these challenges, neuropsychological diagnosis has not been abandoned completely, but its role has changed. In this regard, about 25 years ago Behr and Gallagher (1981) proposed that professionals use a more flexible definition of what constitutes special needs in the preschool population. They suggested that the definition should describe not only the extent of developmental variation, but also the type of variation. Consistent with this formulation, neuropsychological diagnosis is concerned with the detailed and comprehensive description of a child's profile of strengths and weaknesses. This profile may provide clues reflecting the effects of a brain lesion or neurodevelopmental anomaly on subsequent learning and behavior. It also may lend much needed information to increasing our understanding of brain-behavior relationships during this developmental period. Further, the emphasis on profile description has forced clinicians to address the ecological validity of a set of neuropsychological findings (e.g., what is being affected in the child's day-to-day life and what might be affected later). In this regard, clinicians have begun to apply their findings to the preschool classroom setting, the preschooler's adaptive behavior and learning needs, and parent-child and teacher-child interactions. This latter application is critical in that it can help bring the family into the treatment equation as required by federal law and contemporary family-center practice (Stoneman & Rugg, 2004).

Neuropsychological testing also offers a unique diagnostic complement to other educational and neurological procedures by providing specific descriptions of the neurocognitive manifestation of brain impairment. This will apply to preschool children with acquired brain injuries and related neurological disorders, systemic illnesses, psychiatric disorders, or neurodevelopmental disorders, and requires a keen understanding of the particular environmental demands on a child over time (e.g., the shifting preschool requirements for learning). For example, one of the most common neurosurgical interventions in childhood involves the insertion of a shunt for the treatment of hydrocephalus. Children who have been treated—even successfully—have demonstrated cognitive deficits ranging from inattention and impulsivity to more specific problems with memory and visual-motor skills (Dennis et al., 2004; Fletcher et al., 2004). Such findings also have been demonstrated for a variety of other medical disorders in the preschool years, such as low birth weight (Vicari, Caravale, Carlesimo, Casadei, & Allemand, 2004) and prenatal cocaine exposure (Morrow et al., 2004), to mention but a few. The neuropsychological assessment of a preschool child with such difficulties requires not only a comprehensive appraisal of a wide range of abilities, but careful and systematic monitoring of the child's developing skills, particularly as the child moves from the demands of preschool to those of more formal schooling.

The diagnostic utility of preschool neuropsychological assessment also is relevant to children in the nonmedical domain in that approximately 10% of preschool children are estimated to experience learning and behavioral difficulties secondary to minor neurological disorders, with neglect and maltreatment being of increasing concern (Pears & Fisher, 2005). Neurobehavioral connections also might be more clear with preschoolers because of the relatively minimal influences of factors such as feelings of failure, labeling, expectancy artifacts, and social-emotional concerns (Ellison, 1983). Although these factors can manifest in preschool children, in older children these psychosocial variables typically play a larger role in a child's overall functioning, thus blurring possible neurobehavioral linkages. A comprehensive neuropsychological assessment will contribute to obtaining a detailed description of a child's specific strengths and weaknesses and, consequently, to the early identification and treatment of neurocognitive difficulties. It also might begin to elucidate risk factors associated with certain developmental outcomes, and sets the stage for making prognosis and treatment suggestions.

Prognosis

Obtaining a detailed description of a child's neurocognitive functioning is only part of the process for understanding a preschooler's difficulties. Unless the child is inflicted with a degenerative neurological process that is progressing rapidly, it is extremely difficult to predict a particular behavioral outcome. Previous (Satz, Taylor, Friel, & Fletcher, 1978; Spreen & Haaf, 1986; Stevenson & Newman, 1986) and more contemporary (Geary, Hamson, & Hoard, 2000; Jordan, Kaplan, & Hanich, 2002; Molfese, Modglin, & Molfese, 2003; Molfese, Molfese, & Modglin, 2001) longitudinal efforts in the areas of learning disability, language disorders (Molfese & Molfese, 1997; Puolakanaho, Poikkeus, Ahonen, Tolvanen, & Lyytinen, 2004), infant hemispherectomy (Dennis, 1985a, 1985b), and traumatic brain injury (Ewing-Cobbs, Prasad, Landry, Kramer, & DeLeon, 2004) have begun to provide some clues as to prognostic issues during the preschool years.

An important role for preschool neuropsychological assessment is the monitoring of a child's acquisition and/or reacquisition of function after brain injury. There is a complex array of factors that interact to influence the recovery patterns and developmental progress of children who experience early brain insults (Chelune & Edwards, 1981; Ewing-Cobbs et al., 2004), and knowledge with respect to the impact of specific neuropathological processes on a child's prognosis is only beginning to surface. Further, deficits involving "silent" brain regions might not become apparent until challenged during later developmental stages (Hooper, 1988; Rourke, Bakker, Fisk, & Strang, 1983), thus making the need for detailed, comprehensive, and ongoing systematic neuropsychological assessment crucial to issues of prognosis.

To illustrate these concerns, a variety of studies have demonstrated the importance of identifying preschool children at risk for learning (Aunola et al., 2004; Espy & Cwik, 2004; Korkman & Peltomaa, 1993; Lyytinen et al., 2004; Molfese, Beswick, Molnar, & Jacobi-Vessels, 2006; Molfese, Molfese, Modglin, Walker, & Neamon, 2004) and behavior problems (Hooper, Roberts, Zeisel, & Poe, 2003). For example, Espy et al. (In press) found that children manifesting early executive function deficits later reflected problems in the early development of their math skills, while Molfese et al. (2006) reported that name writing may be an early, strong predictor of later writing difficulties. Using longitudinal methodology, Hooper et al. (2003) found that core language functions in the preschool years were highly related to behavior problems in the early elementary school years, with increasing association between preschool language functions and later behaviors being noted with advancing age. These findings are highly consistent with findings reported nearly 30 years ago with respect to early predictors of later reading problems (Satz et al., 1978); meta-analysis data by Horn and Packard (1985) who found behavioral measures, language tasks, and IQ in the preschool years to be the best single predictors of reading achievement in grades 1 and 3; and a comprehensive review by Tramontana, Hooper, and Selzer (1988) who found effective predictors to span cognitive, verbal, and perceptual/perceptual-motor areas of functioning. These investigators also noted the complexities involved in accurately identifying specific predictor-criterion relationships, and called for more detailed questions in describing prognostic relationships in the learning patterns of preschool children.

Treatment Issues

The neuropsychological assessment of the preschool child perhaps has its greatest potential impact in contributing to the development of treatment programs, the monitoring of the
intervention process and suggesting adjustments based on follow-up findings, and the minimizing of educational and emotional difficulties associated with brain impairment and dysfunction. These contributions are particularly relevant for the preschooler who has the benefit of participating in early intervention programs under current federal and state
mandates. Neuropsychorugical assessment can play a formative role in developing a treatment program tailored to the needs of a child with a particular exceptionality. The detailed
strengths and weaknesses generated via a neuropsychological assessment can provide the
foundation for an aggressive treatment program. Although little is known about actual
assessment-treatment linkages for the preschool child, treatment options tend to be guided
by theoretical orientation, clinical experiences, and the availability of therapeutic resources.
More generally, however, evidence does exist to support the benefits of early intervention
for children at environmental risk (Ramey & Ramey, 1994), at biological risk (Blair,
Ramey, & Hardin, 1995), and at educational risk (e.g., Korkman & Peltomaa, 1993), and
a comprehensive neuropsychological assessment could aide in guiding this process.

Once an individualized treatment program is established, it becomes important for
the progress of the child to be monitored closely. This is important not only from charting
rates of progress, but also from the standpoint of providing needed adjustments in the
treatment program. The monitoring of a child's progress is crucial to determining the effectiveness of the neurosurgical, pharmacological, educational, and/or cognitive-behav-
ioral intervention strategies. Over 30 years ago, Craft, Shaw, and Cartlidge (1972)
demonstrated the importance of monitoring developmental progress with respect to treatment planning by documenting that even infants with mild brain injury who were described as "fully recovered" continued to manifest cognitive, behavioral, and sensorimotor deficits several years following their injuries. Similarly, Aylward, Gustafson, Verhulst,
and Colliver (1987) noted that diagnoses of motor functioning in infants were more stable
over time, whereas cognitive functioning status was more likely to change. Bagnato and
Dickerson-Mayes (1986) also demonstrated the importance of monitoring developmental
progress with respect to treatment planning in brain-injured infants and preschoolers following approximately a 3.5-month inpatient rehabilitation. These gains were noted to occur across all developmental domains, with gains ranging from 77% in gross motor functions to 93% in cognition.

NEUROPSYCHOLOGICAL ASSESSMENT PROCEDURES

A number of preschool neuropsychological assessment procedures were available at the last
edition of this text about 5 years ago, and this momentum has continued to the present. Most
of the procedures parallel assessment models utilized with adults and school-age children
and, generally, tend to cover a broad array of cognitive and motor functions. This section discusses the neuropsychological assessment strategies available for the preschool child. At present, there are two formal batteries that are available for use with preschool children, and a
third that has emerged. The discussion of these formal batteries is followed by a presentation
of informal or flexible approaches. The informal, or flexible, approaches typically are driven
by a specific set of constructs, either clinically or empirically derived, and are operationalized
by specific available tools purportedly measuring these domains. Included here is an over-

view of how some of the intellectual and developmental tests can facilitate the development of these batteries, and examples of specific tools for each neurocognitive construct.

Formal Neuropsychological Batteries

Given the dearth of appropriate neuropsychological batteries for the preschool child, neuropsychologists have had to depend upon their knowledge of brain-behavior relationships and neurodevelopmental theory in constructing assessment methodologies. In the last edition of this text, there were only two formal neuropsychological batteries that could be applied to the preschool population: the Reitan-Indiana Neuropsychological Battery (Reitan, 1969) and the NEPSY (Korkman et al., 1998). In addition, a third battery has surfaced in France, and this battery appears to have merit as well.

Reitan-Indiana Neuropsychological Battery

This battery is a downward extension of the classic Halstead-Reitan Neuropsychological Battery for Children and was designed for children ages 5 through 8 years. The tasks and accompanying directions were simplified and shortened from the parent Halstead-Reitan Neuropsychological Battery in an effort to adjust for the developmental differences suspected between older and younger children. As with the versions of the battery for older children and adults, these tasks typically are administered in conjunction with intellectual, academic/preacademic, lateral dominance, and social-behavioral measures. Traditional components of the Reitan-Indiana Battery include modified versions of the Category Test, and Tactual Performance Test, and an electric version of the Finger Tapping Test. The allied procedures of Strength of Grip, Sensory-Perceptual Examination, and Tactile Form Recognition also typically are administered. The Aphasia Screening Test and Finger-Tip Number Writing from the Sensory-Perceptual Examination were modified slightly for the younger population. In addition, several new tests were developed for inclusion in the battery. These included the Marching Test, Color Form Test, Progressive Figures Test, Matching Pictures Test, Target Test, and the Individual Performance Tests (i.e., Matching Figures, Matching Vs, Concentric Square, and Star). Collectively, these tasks purportedly assess gross motor coordination, selective attention, cognitive flexibility, visual perception, visual memory, fine-motor speed, and abstract reasoning.

Taken together, the Reitan-Indiana tasks purport to assess a broad range of functions including gross and fine-motor skills, sensory-perceptual abilities across visual, auditory, and tactile modalities, abstract thinking and problem solving, language, cognitive flexibility, and memory. Findings are interpreted in terms of four methods of inference that include: level of performance, pattern of performance, pathognomonic signs, and right-left differences on sensory and motor tasks (Selz & Reitan, 1979). These four levels of inference are important in that they contribute to distinguishing neuropsychological procedures from more traditional psychological and developmental assessment approaches, particularly with the preschool-age band, and can be generalized to other neuropsychological assessment procedures.

Level of performance refers to the comparison of a child's scores to an appropriate reference group. As an example, findings from this method will indicate whether a child's performance is normal or abnormal. *Pattern of performance* provides insights into the child's relative strengths and weaknesses across various functions. This method of inference also might provide clues with respect to intervention strategies for a particular child. *Pathognomonic signs* refer to symptoms or behaviors that are distinctively characteristic of a particular disease or disorder (e.g., brain impairment/dysfunction). The investigation of neuro-

psychological data for pathognomonic signs is especially relevant to the preschool child because their significance is dependent upon the developmental appropriateness of a particular behavior for a given age. For example, visual-spatial reversals in a 3- or 4-year-old
child's written output would not be pathognomonic, but their appearance in an 11- or 12-
year-old likely suggest pathology. Obviously, knowledge of normal developmental parameters is necessary for employing this method of inference with preschool children. The final method of inference regarding brain functioning is *left-right differences*. With this
inference, performance differentials in the sensory and motor domains on the two sides of
the body are examined. Although slight left-right differences are expected—even in preschool children, with the dominant side typically being stronger, more efficient, better coordinated, and accurate—lateralized sensory and/or motor deficits are considered to be
among the most significant neurobehavioral indicators of brain involvement in adults and
children (Rourke, 1983).

Despite the relative popularity of the Reitan procedures, the Reitan-Indiana was designed only to address the latter stages of the preschool years, and, consequently, its use with
younger preschool children is not appropriate. Although the same could be stated for other
batteries with normative data beginning at age 5 years (e.g., Cognitive Assessment System),
there has been some application of the Reitan-Indiana tasks to kindergarten children (Satz
et al., 1978; Teeter, 1985; Townes, Turpin, Martin, & Goldstein, 1980), as well as to
preschoolers ages 2, 3, and 4 (Reitan & Davison, 1974). The application of these assessment
procedures and the four methods of inference to children younger than age 5 years, however,
will require continued study, with the overall use of this battery by preschool practitioners
probably being relatively infrequent (Butler, Retzloff, & Vanderploeg, 1991).

NEPSY: A Developmental Neuropsychological Assessment

The NEPSY (*NE* for neuro, *PSY* for psychology) arguably represents one of the first
well-normed and well-standardized neuropsychological batteries for children ages 3–0
through age 12 (Korkman et al., 1998). Across this age range the NEPSY permits a closer
examination of abilities tapping five major domains: Attention/Executive Functions, Language, Sensorimotor Functions, Visuospatial Processing, and Memory and Learning. Within
each of these domains there are a variety of subtests that can be examined via quantitative
as well as qualitative strategies. There is great flexibility in administration wherein the entire
battery can be administered, a core set of tasks can be employed, or a specific domain and/or
specific subtests can be used. It is important to recognize that these domains are not true factors but, rather, conceptually constructed domains of neuropsychological functioning that are
inter-related. Standard scores are generated for the subtests and domains, and qualitative
analyses allow for more idiosyncratic examination of a child's performance. The NEPSY is
grounded in neurodevelopmental theory as presented by Luria (1980) and, as such, allows
for evaluation of simple as well as complex functions within each domain. In addition, the
NEPSY was developed on children with neurodevelopmental (e.g., learning disabilities) and
acquired disorders (e.g., traumatic brain injuries), and thus may prove more useful in delineating profiles of abilities in both groups. Published versions of the NEPSY also have been
produced in Finland, France, and Sweden, and it has been adapted for use in Israel.

For the preschool child ages 3 to 4, the NEPSY provides a core number of subtests as
well as an expanded version. Within the Attention/Executive Function Domain there are
two core subtests, Visual Attention and Statue, which tap selective visual attention and
motor persistence. In the Language Domain there are three core subtests, Body Part
Naming, Phonological Processing, and Comprehension of Instructions. These subtests tap

expressive and receptive capabilities, with a particular focus on developmentally emergent phonological processing abilities—functions critical to the emergence of basic literacy skills. Two additional subtests can be administered within the language domain, Verbal Fluency and Oromotor Sequences, which tap verbal speed and oral-motor coordination. Within the Sensorimotor Domain there are two core subtests, Imitating Hand Positions and Visuomotor Precision. These subtests measure motor praxis, graphomotor speed, and dexterity. One additional subtest can be administered to this age group, Manual Motor Sequences, which taps motor planning and motor sequencing. The Visuospatial Domain comprises two subtests for preschoolers, Design Copying and Block Construction, subtests that measure visuoconstructive abilities and visual-spatial functioning. Finally, the Memory and Learning Domain includes two subtests for this age range, Narrative Memory and Sentence Repetition, both tapping short-term verbal recall. Examiners can administer the core subtests and then, if any type of problem or concern is raised, administer additional selected subtests. Qualitative observations also can be recorded on each subtest (e.g., motor tremors, motor overflow, perseverations, misarticulations, etc.), and compared to the normative group with respect to the pathognomonic aspects of the behavior. The entire 14 subtests can be administered in about 1 hour, depending on the status of the preschooler, while the core battery can be completed in less than 1 hour.

In addition to providing a well-standardized, well-normed set of procedures, the NEPSY demonstrated adequate reliability, although the Attention/Executive Functions Domain was somewhat lower ($r = .70$). The validity of the tasks also appears to be satisfactory. In fact, the NEPSY compares favorably to many intellectual and achievement tasks, and its application to children with a variety of disorders appears promising. Despite these positive features, the utility of the NEPSY with preschool children remains to be demonstrated with few, if any, published studies being available to date.

Battery for Rapid Evaluation of Cognitive Functions (BREV)

One final battery deserves mention: The Battery for Rapid Evaluation of Cognitive Functions (Batterie Rapide d'Evaluation des Fonctions Cognitives; BREV). Although developed in France, its conceptualization should facilitate ongoing expansion in the area of preschool neuropsychological assessment. The BREV was designed as a clinical assessment for acquired and developmental cognitive dysfunction in children 4 to 8 years of age. The BREV includes 17 subtests assessing higher-order cognitive functions (oral language, nonverbal abilities, attention and memory, educational achievement) across 10 age groups (Billard, 2002). The BREV has begun to show good capabilities to document development changes in specific cognitive functions as well as to distinguish between children with and without neurodevelopmental problems. The BREV was administered in France to 500 normal male and female preschool and school-age Ss ages 4–8 years to assess linguistic and nonverbal functions, memory, and school achievement; it was also administered to 202 male and female children with different types of epilepsy in the same age range to measure the specificity and sensitivity of the BREV (Billard, 2002). The reference battery used as a benchmark for the BREV included the WPPSI–R, a French battery for oral language, the Rey-Osterrieth Complex Figure (copy and recall conditions), verbal and visuospatial memory from the McCarthy scale subtests, and educational achievement. Results showed that every function evaluated with the BREV was significantly correlated with the reference battery testing a similar function. Specificity and sensitivity of the BREV verbal and nonverbal scores were correlated with those of the Wechsler scale in more than 75% of children. Temporal reliability was tested in a retest for 70 children, and these scores correlated significantly with initial values. It is concluded that the BREV is a reliable battery with carefully established normative values appropriate for preschool and young school-age children. While application to English-speaking children remains a challenge at this time, the BREV presents as an emergent potential neuropsychological battery for assessment of the preschool child (Billard, 2002).

Informal/Flexible Neuropsychological Batteries

Despite these recent advances in neuropsychological batteries for preschool children, the informal or flexible batteries likely enjoy more widespread use (Butler et al., 1991). Conceptually, Rey-Casserly (1999) provided an initial approach for the neuropsychological assessment of preschool children that fits nicely with an informal or flexible battery approach. Advocating for use of a broad-based assessment approach, Rey-Casserly proposed a tripartite model for conducting preschool neuropsychological assessment that included clinical history, clinical observations in the clinical setting and natural environment, and test performance designed to extract both quantitative and qualitative data. In addition, Lezak (2004) offered recommendations for the construction of informal test batteries. Lezak suggested that the construction of an informal battery should provide for the examination of a broad range of input and output functions. The actual procedures selected for inclusion should be developmentally appropriate, have satisfactorily normative data, and serve to provide for a certain degree of redundancy. The battery also should be practical in relation to the fundamental purpose(s) of the neuropsychological examination. Informal batteries also should have the capacity to address the qualitative (i.e., how a child performs or approaches a task) and quantitative (i.e., level and pattern of performance) aspects of a child's functioning. With these guidelines in mind, several clinical and empirical preschool neuropsychological assessment models have emerged over the past several years that have described specific constructs important to this developmental time period. These models are listed in Table 18.1.

As can be seen from the models presented in Table 18.1, there is considerable overlap between the clinical models with respect to the neuropsychological constructs tested. Generally, these models attempt to assess language, motor skills, sensory-perceptual abilities, memory, higher-order problem solving, and preacademic skills, thus providing a comprehensive examination of brain functions. The clinical models presented by Deysach (1986) and Wilson (1986, 1992) are noteworthy in their attempts to provide a systematic examination of a broad range of functions in a hierarchical fashion (i.e., systematically measuring simple to more complex functions). Deysach (1986) stated that it is useful to assess simple as well as more complex functions across both input and output modalities. Similarly, Wilson (1986, 1992) presented a flexible, hypothesis-testing model utilizing a branching technique. Using her model, an initial assessment strategy is employed to assess higher-order, more complex cognitive processes. Depending on how the child performs on this initial testing procedure, additional assessment strategies are selected based on identified areas of weakness or concern in an effort to examine the child's difficulties in a more comprehensive manner. This "branching" or hypothesis testing approach requires the examiner to be a keen observer and to be sensitive to qualitative and quantitative aspects of a preschool child's performance.

In contrast to the clinical models, empirical models hold great potential for delineating specific neuropsychological constructs relevant to the preschool child. Utilizing a battery of neurocognitive tasks, Jansky (1970) provided one of the first studies uncovering specific un-

TABLE 18.1.
Proposed Neuropsychological Assessment Constructs for the Preschool Child

Model	Neuropsychological Constructs
Clinical Models	
Aylward (1988)	Basic neurological functions
	Receptive functions
	Expressive functions
	Processing
	Mental activity
Deysach (1986)	Gross motor
	Fine motor
	Sensory-perceptual
	Verbal
	Short-term memory
	Abstraction/Concept formation
Hartlage & Telzrow (1986)	Cognitive ability
	Basic language
	Preacademic
	Motor
	Sensory
	Social
	Adaptive
Wilson (1986)	Language
	Auditory integration
	Auditory cognition
	Auditory short-term memory
	Retrieval
	Visual
	Visual-spatial
	Visual cognition
	Visual short-term memory
	Motor
	Fine-motor
	Gross motor
Hooper (2000)	Motor
	Tactile-Perception
	Attention
	Language
	Visual Processing
	Memory
	Executive Functions
Empirical Models	
Jansky (1970)	Visual-motor
	Oral language
	Pattern matching
	Pattern memory
Silver & Hagin (1972)	Auditory association
	Visual-neurological
	Psychiatric impairment
	Chronological age
	General intelligence
Satz et al. (1978)	Socioeconomic status
	Conceptual-verbal
	Sensorimotor-perceptual

derlying neuropsychological constructs of the preschooler. In her factor analysis of these tasks, Jansky identified factors measuring oral language, memory, visual-motor abilities, and abstract thinking. All of these factors, particularly oral language, were found to be significantly predictive of second grade reading skills.

Silver and Hagin (1972) found five factors in their preschool assessment battery. These factors were slightly different than those obtained by Jansky (1970) and included factors measuring auditory association, visual-neurological functioning, higher-order problem solving, and interestingly, chronological age and psychiatric impairment. These factors accounted for approximately 61% of the entire battery, with the auditory association and visual-neurological factors being most predictive of later reading problems.

The final empirical study generating neuropsychological constructs relevant to the preschool child was conducted by Satz et al. (1978). Satz et al. conducted a factor analysis of 16 variables obtained from a large kindergarten population that resulted in three factors accounting for approximately 68% of the variance. These factors spanned sensorimotor-perceptual skills, verbal conceptual abilities, and verbal-cultural variables. These investigators found their factors, especially the sensorimotor-perceptual factor, to be predictive of later reading problems. They also found the predictive relationship to vary according to developmental parameters, thus placing differential importance upon different factors for particular developmental periods.

Constructing an Informal/Flexible Battery

When constructing a flexible battery for neuropsychological assessment of a preschool child, it becomes important to recognize that other data sources should be considered. For example, Rey-Casserly's (1999) tripartite model for conducting neuropsychological assessments of preschool children should serve as an important guide for a thorough assessment. Further, it should be noted that the development of the neuropsychological constructs associated with the empirical models emanated from examination of a specific population of children—that is, children at risk for learning disabilities. Consequently, their generalizability to neuropsychological assessment of other neurologically impaired populations (e.g., preschool traumatic brain injury) remains to be seen. Taken together, however, the models described earlier provide evidence for constructs tapping motor, sensory, language, visual processing, memory, and abstract thinking/concept formation. An examination of these models reveals that only two of them (Deysach, 1986; Wilson, 1992) attempt to examine functions in a hierarchical fashion (i.e., simple to more complex), only one of the models addressed some aspect of executive functions (i.e., Deysach, 1986), and none of them specifically described attentional components. The importance of these latter domains highlights the need for a more comprehensive examination of underlying constructs within the preschool years (e.g., Gnys & Willis, 1991; Welsh, Pennington, & Grossier, 1991), particularly with respect to developmental continuity into the school-age years and their overall utility with respect to diagnosis and treatment. Nonetheless, the clinical and empirical models provide the conceptual foundation for developing an informal neuropsychological assessment battery for the preschool child.

In constructing a flexible battery, the specific constructs employed should be selected in an effort to obtain a broad-based assessment of abilities as suggested by Lezak (2004). The test selection will be limited only by their availability and the knowledge of the examiner. In this regard, Table 18.2 provides a set of proposed constructs by Hooper (2000) based on a combination of the models presented to date and representative procedures

TABLE 18.2.
Sample Procedures for Key Neuropsychological Constructs
in an Informal Battery

Neuropsychological Construct	Representative Measure
Motor	Finger Oscillation (Electric)
	Peabody Developmental Motor Scale-2
Tactile-Perceptual	Finger Localization
	Tactile Form Recognition
	Dean-Woodcock Sensory-Motor Battery
Attention	ACPT-P
	K-CPT
Language	Expressive One Word Picture Vocabulary Test
	Peabody Picture Vocabulary Test–Third Edition
	CELF-P
	PLS-4
Visual Processing	VMI
	WRAVMA
	Test of Visual-Perceptual Skills
Memory	Subtests from selected intellectual batteries
	Children's Test of Nonword Repetition
Executive Functions	Espy Executive Function Battery
	Trails-P
	BRIEF-P

that could be used in constructing an informal preschool neuropsychological battery. In general, it is suggested that the psychologist employ one of the major intellectual batteries (e.g., WPPSI–III, KABC–II, SB–V) as the core of the neuropsychological assessment, in tandem with specific measures of cognition, measures of preacademic skills, and social-behavioral functioning as needed (Hooper, 2000). Depending on the psychometric qualities of the instrument selected, specific components of this tool could be used to provide measurement for a specific construct. Additional neuropsychological procedures should be selected according to (1) the needs of the child, (2) the specific referral questions, (3) the general philosophical approach of the examiner (e.g., is a branching assessment strategy being employed?), and (4) how they complement the core intellectual battery. Further, it will be important for the examiner to focus on observing the qualitative aspects of a child's spared and impaired abilities and, if appropriate, to gain information that will facilitate interpretation of the data using Reitan's four levels of inference. A hierarchical progression of tasks within a construct, ranging from simple to complex, will assist in identifying specific areas of concern. It also may be important, depending on the needs of the examiner, for the instruments selected to have adequate normative data for the preschool child so that all scores can be converted into a common metric for comparative purposes (e.g., T-Scores). This also could facilitate developmental surveillance and related tracking of cognitive and behavioral changes over time. The following sections provide description of a number of specific examples of measures in accordance with targeted neuropsychological constructs. Beginning with selected intellectual and developmental batteries, these descriptions are not meant to be exhaustive, but, rather, they should illustrate the range of tools that are currently available to the child neuropsychologist.

Intellectual Batteries

Pending the availability and ultimate usefulness of the formal neuropsychological assessment batteries for preschoolers, child psychologists and neuropsychologists have depended upon many of the more traditional intellectual test batteries as the core of informal neuropsychological assessment strategies (Butler et al., 1991; Sellers & Nadler, 1992). The past several years have witnessed significant gains in the intellectual and developmental assessment of infants, toddlers, and preschoolers. These advances have occurred not only in the form of more available procedures, but with these procedures being more child-friendly, psychometrically strong, and multidimensional in scope. This latter feature is of particular importance for constructing an informal neuropsychological battery, especially given the relatively limited cognitive stamina presented by preschool children. Further, while some of the currently available tests clearly have potential use in preschool neuropsychological assessment, their age range extends downward only to age 5 years. For example, the Cognitive Assessment System (Naglieri & Das, 1997), which is built upon a strong theoretical foundation, generates scores on Planning, Attention, Simultaneous, and Sequential Processing; however, it only extends downward to age 5 years, and many referred children will be bouncing off of the floor of the tasks, thus limiting its usefulness for the preschool years.

In this regard, many of the available developmental and intellectual batteries are presented in detail in this text, with the WPPSI–3 (Coalson & Spruill, Chapter 12), Stanford-Binet V (Alfonso & Flanagan, Chapter 13), K-ABC–II (Lichtenberger & Kaufman, Chapter 14), being of special importance to the construction of a neuropsychological battery for preschool children. Similarly, many of the key developmental measures are presented in Chapter 15 (Bradley-Johnson & Johnson). Of importance to the field is the Bayley Scales of Infant and Toddler Development, Third Edition (Bayley–III; Bayley, 2005). This revision of the Bayley provides (finally) for the formal capability of this test to measure developmental status in a multidimensional fashion. These five developmental domains include: cognition, language, motor, adaptive behavior, and social-emotional skills. In addition, a sixth scale, the Behavior Rating Scale, is an optional component of the assessment to evaluate children's behavior during the administration of the battery. The Bayley–III should provide a nice option for use in preschool neuropsychological assessments, particularly with preschoolers with significant developmental impairment.

In general, the psychometric integrity and multidimensional nature of these tools clearly will serve the needs of the preschool neuropsychologist well in their construction of a comprehensive battery of tasks. In particular, the theoretical foundations of the K-ABC–II, which take advantage of the Luria and Cattell-Horn Carroll models of cognitive functioning, and the newly revised Stanford-Binet V, which takes advantage of the Cattell-Horn-Carroll model as well, should prove especially useful in developing an informal neuropsychological battery. Details pertaining to each of these contemporary intellectual batteries can be found in their respective chapters in this text.

In addition to the above batteries, another battery that deserves mention with respect to its potential utility in preschool neuropsychological testing is the Leiter International Performance Scale (Leiter–R). The Leiter has been around since the early 1930s, and has provided clinicians and researchers with a nonverbal measure of cognitive abilities. The current revision of the Leiter continues in that mode, being applicable to individuals ages 2 through 20 years, but the test is now based on item-response theory, factor analysis, and Rasch scaling. The Leiter–R consists of 20 subtests organized into four domains: Reasoning, Visualization, Memory, and Attention. Included within these domains are subtests tapping visual figure-ground, visual discrimination, visual sequencing, short-term and delayed visual memory and learning, nonverbal working memory, visual recognition memory, and sustained attention. Standard scores are provided along with age and grade equivalents that are directly tied to developmental growth curves. Reliability and validity of the test are satisfactory, and its application to children with a wide range of developmental disabilities and acquired problems appears promising. The factors of this battery appear to remain intact for preschool-age children, and they should assist in providing detailed cognitive descriptions of preschool children having a wide range of exceptionalities and levels of function.

A more contemporary measure, The Reynolds Intellectual Assessment Scales (RIAS; Reynolds & Kamphaus, 2003), provides a measure of verbal abilities, nonverbal abilities, and memory functions from ages 3 to 94 years. The RIAS includes a two-subtest Verbal Intelligence Index (VIX), a two-subtest Nonverbal Intelligence Index (NIX), and a Composite Intelligence Index (CIX). The CIX assesses overall general intelligence, including the ability to reason, solve problems, and learn. The VIX assesses verbal intelligence by measuring verbal problem solving and verbal reasoning where acquired knowledge and skills are important. The NIX assesses nonverbal intelligence by measuring reasoning and spatial ability using novel situations and stimuli that are predominantly nonverbal. In addition, a Composite Memory Index (CMX) is derived from the two supplementary memory subtests: Verbal Memory and Nonverbal Memory. The Verbal Memory subtest provides a basic, overall measure of short-term memory skills (e.g., working memory, short-term memory, learning) and measures recall in the verbal domain. The Nonverbal Memory subtest measures the ability to recall pictorial stimuli in both concrete and abstract dimensions. The RIAS provides a thorough assessment of the client's current level of intellectual functioning and also allows the examiner to evaluate the relationship between the client's memory and cognitive skills. Finally, the RIAS also provides for a brief intellectual screener: the Reynolds Intellectual Screening Test (RIST). The RIST consists of two RIAS subtests, Guess What (one of the two verbal subtests), and Odd-Item Out (one of the two nonverbal subtests). This brief screening measure takes only 10 minutes to administer and helps to quickly identify individuals who need a more comprehensive intellectual assessment and who may or may not need intellectual re-evaluation. This may be particularly beneficial for preschool children who present assessment challenges.

A final battery worth mentioning from the perspective of preschool neuropsychological assessment is the Woodcock-Johnson III Tests of Cognitive Abilities (WJ–III COG; Woodcock, McGrew, & Mather, 2001). The WJ–III COG is one part of a co-normed battery that includes tests of achievement and tests of cognition for individuals ages 2 through 90. The WJ–III COG consists of a standard battery of 10 tests and an extended battery of 10 tests which were designed around the Cattell-Horn-Carroll model of intellectual functioning. The WJ–III COG contains a variety of subtests that can be used in the preschool years including: Memory for Names, Visual Closure, Rapid Picture Naming, Memory for Sentences, General Information, Retrieval Fluency, Picture Recognition, and Memory for Words. Taken together, these tasks tap verbal and visual memory, cognitive efficiency, and visual closure. For the preschool group, moderate correlations were demonstrated between the WJ–III and the Wechsler Preschool and Primary Scale of Intelligence–Revised ($r = .66$ to .73), and the Differential Ability Scales ($r = .57$ to .67).

Measures-by-Construct

Motor.   There are a variety of tools available to measure different aspects of motor functioning during the preschool years. One example is the Peabody Developmental Motor Scales–Second Edition (PDMS–2; Folio & Fewell, 2000). The PDMS–2 provides for a thorough assessment of both fine and gross motor functioning for children birth through age 5 years. The PDMS–2 comprises six subtests: Reflexes (birth through 11 months), which measure primary reflexes which should be integrated into the nervous system by 11 months of age; Stationary, which measures a child's ability to sustain control of his or her body within its center of gravity and retain equilibrium; Locomotion, which measures a child's ability to move from one place to another (e.g., crawling, walking, running, hopping, jumping forward); Object Manipulation, which measures a child's ability to manipulate balls (e.g., catching, throwing, kicking). Grasping, which measures a child's ability to use his or her hands; and Visual-Motor Integration, which measures a child's ability to use his or her visual-perceptual skills to perform complex eye-hand coordination tasks (e.g., reaching for and grasping an object, building with blocks, copying designs). These subtests combine to form three major composite scores: Fine Motor Quotient, Gross Motor Quotient, and a Total Motor Quotient. This revision also now links to an intervention program, The Peabody Motor Activities Program (PMAP), and provides direction for intervention. An overview of additional motor measures is provided in Chapter 17 (Williams & Monsma).

Sensory.   The assessment of sensory-perceptual functions in the preschool child has been a challenging one. In this regard, the Dean-Woodcock Neuropsychological Battery (Dean & Woodcock, 2003) is a welcome addition to the armamentarium of the neuropsychologist. This battery is relatively novel in that it can be used for the preschool population and nicely complements other measures in a comprehensive neuropsychological assessment. This battery provides a standardized assessment of sensory and motor functioning—domains that are typically less standardized in the field of neuropsychology. This battery of tasks measures both cortical and subcortical functions, and can be used for children as young as 4 years of age. There are three major parts to this battery: Structured Interview, Mental Status Exam, and Sensory-Motor Battery. During the Structured Interview, clinicians ask questions to determine an individual's medical and family background. The Mental Status Exam includes as assessment of psychiatric signs and symptoms—covering most major disorders found in the DSM–IV—as well as clinical impressions. The Sensory-Motor Battery consists of 18 subtests designed to measure simple and complex sensory and motor functioning. Its application to preschoolers is promising, if not necessary; however, its clinical utility remains to be seen.

Attention.   Efforts to develop tests of attention have proliferated over the past decade, with more recent efforts being driven by theoretical models of attention (Laicardi, Artistico, Passa, & Ferrante, 2000). The continuous performance test (CPT) paradigm has been used in research in an attempt to differentiate clinical populations from normal controls. Specifically, the CPT has most notably been used in Attention Deficit Hyperactivity Disorder (ADHD) research because of the required attention needed on the part of the participant to complete the assessment (Epstein et al., 2003), but its extension downward to the preschool years represents a significant advance in preschool neuropsychological assessment. One CPT task that is available for preschoolers is the Conners' Kiddie Continuous Performance Test (K-CPT; Conners, 2001). The K-CPT was developed for children 4–5 years of age. Like its parent tool, the Conners' Continuous Performance Test II (CPT–II; Conners, 2000), the K-CPT measures participants' response times, number of omission and commission errors, and the change in the speed and consistency as related to reaction time (Conners, 2000). In contrast, the K-CPT uses pictures of objects instead of letters to account for the variability in preschoolers' letter knowledge and requires only 7.5 minutes (as opposed to 14 minutes for the older child version) to complete.

Given earlier findings by Baker, Taylor, and Leyva (1995), suggesting differential performance of children on visual versus auditory attention tasks, Mahone, Pillion, & Hiemenz (2001) developed the Auditory Continuous Performance Test for Preschoolers (ACPT–P). This assessment employs a computerized Go-No-Go paradigm and has been used for children as young as 36 months of age. Results suggest that with increasing age, children's performance improves such that the 6-year-olds performed better than both the 3- and 4-year olds, and the 4-year-olds performed better than the 3-year-olds. In addition, Mahone et al. (2001) found that the ACPT–P scores were significantly correlated with data on the Conners' Parent-Rating Scale–Revised, and both the mean response latency and variability scores significantly correlated with motor persistence, praxis, graphomotor, and listening vocabulary. More recently, Mahone, Pillion, Hoffman, Hiemenz, and Denckla (2005) used the ACPT–P to classify children with ADHD from normal controls. It was found that children with ADHD performed worse on the ACPT–P compared to the controls on the number of omissions, mean reaction time, and variability, and on measures of motor persistence.

Language.   As noted in the Assessment of Communication and Language Chapter (Nelson & Warner), there is a growing number of tasks available for assessment in the preschool language domain. One battery, the Preschool Language Scale, Fourth Edition (PLS–4; Zimmerman, Steiner, & Pond, 2002), specifically assesses the expressive and receptive language abilities of children from birth–71 months of age (Zimmerman et al., 2002). The PLS–4 provides standard scores, percentiles, and language-age equivalent scores in both auditory comprehension (receptive) and expressive linguistic abilities (Carter, Briggs-Gowan, & Davis, 2004). The PLS–4 has made worthy improvements over the PLS–3 in that first, the assessment accounts for interaction, attention, vocal, and gestural behaviors in children from birth to 35 months of age. Second, more items have been included to assess children's phonological awareness as a predictor of school achievement at 5- and 6-years of age. Third, the PLS–4 now acknowledges the ability to detect language proficiency across dialects (e.g. African American English, Southern English, Appalachian, and Spanish and Asian influenced English), such that the child who speaks a variation of Standard American English will not be penalized but, rather, his/her score will be calculated according to the appropriate norms for that particular dialect (Carter et al., 2004; Zimmerman et al., 2002).

Similarly, the Clinical Evaluation of Language Fundamentals–Preschool (CELF–Preschool; Wiig, Secord, & Semel, 1992) measures a broad range of expressive and receptive language skills in preschool and early elementary-aged children ages 3 to 6 years of age. It is useful in the diagnosis and early identification of language dysfunction in preschool children. The CELF–P comprises six subtests measuring various aspects of receptive and expressive language. These subtests combine to form 3 summary scores: Expressive, Receptive, Total Language. The CELF–P can be employed in whole or in part to assist in the assessment of various language functions, and should provide a nice addition to the development of a flexible neuropsychological battery.

The Test of Early Language Development (TELD–3; Hresko, Reid & Hammill, 1999) provides another test of language functioning that is appropriate for children ages 2 through 7 years of age. Its extension downward to age 2 provides for a good floor for working with preschool neuropsychological referrals. The current version of the TELD comprises two subtests, Receptive Language and Expressive Language, and yields an overall Spoken Language score. The psychometric properties of the TELD–3 are adequate, and the tool relates well to other standardized language assessments. Items were included if they evidenced little or no bias relative to gender, disability, racial, socioeconomic, or ethnic groups. Standard scores are provided, and this should permit comparison to other measures comprising a flexible neuropsychological battery.

Two other tasks, the Expressive Vocabulary Test (EVT; Williams, 1997) and the Peabody Picture Vocabulary Test–III (Dunn & Dunn, 1997), require mentioning with respect to their inclusion in a flexible preschool neuropsychological battery. The EVT is an individually administered, norm-referenced assessment of expressive vocabulary and word retrieval for children and adults ages 2 to 90 years of age. The EVT includes a total of 190 items (in addition to four examples) and there are two primary tasks that participants complete during the assessment: 1) labeling items, in which the examiner points to a picture and the examinee responds with a one-word response (noun, verb, or adjective), and 2) synonym items, in which an examiner presents a picture and stimulus word and the examinee follows with a one-word response (noun, verb, or adjective). Williams (1997) emphasized that while the EVT only measures one component of language (i.e., expressive naming), the assessment is still a valuable tool because having or not having expressive vocabulary capabilities can serve as an indicator of those children with overall poor expressive vocabulary development and may signify larger language-based learning problems.

The PPVT–III serves as a receptive vocabulary counterpart to the EVT. This classic untimed test is intended for use in assessing subjects who are 2–6 through 90+ years of age who use standard English as their first language (Dunn & Dunn, 1997). Children are presented with four black-and-white illustrations on a page. The task is to select the picture that best represents the examiner's spoken word stimulus. The assessment consists of 204 possible test items grouped into increasingly more difficult sets of 12. Sets that are too easy or too hard for the examinee are not presented. Two parallel forms of the PPVT–III are available, which makes it attractive as a way to track change in both clinical and research venues. The assessment is also easily adaptable for use with children with special needs as it is not necessary for a child to speak or point. A signal for "yes" or "no" as the examiner points to each of the four pictures can be sufficient (Dunn & Dunn, 1997), and may be critical for even a shy or reticent preschooler. Like the EVT, poor performance on the PPVT–III may indicate larger language-based learning problems.

Visual Processing.   The Beery-Buktenica Developmental Test of Visual-Motor Integration (5th Edition; Beery, Buktenica, & Beery, 2003) is a well-known tool to most psychologists, occupational therapists, and other preschool evaluators. This test, now in its fifth edition, addresses visual perception, graphomotor control, and visual-motor integration across a wide age range. By extending downward to age 2 years, it provides a convenient tool to begin to address the visual-motor needs of preschool children. Black ink drawings are presented to the child, and he/she is asked to copy the figure as accurately as possible. The items are arranged in order of difficulty, so each item is incrementally more difficult. There is a short form for children ages 2 through 8 years of age, and supplemental scores for visual perception and motor coordination are available.

The Wide Range Assessment of Visual Motor Ability (WRAVMA; Adams & Sheslow, 1995) provides a more comprehensive assessment of visual-motor abilities. The WRAVMA was designed for individuals age 3 through 17, and thus is nicely appropriate for use in the preschool years. It was constructed to provide a reliable, accurate evaluation of the following domains: Visuo-Motor (integration) skills using the drawing test; Visuo-Spatial skills using the matching test; and Fine Motor Skills using the pegboard test. Similar to the supplemental procedures for the VMI, these three tests can be administered individually or in combination.

The Test of Visual Perceptual Skills–Revised (TVPS–R; Gardener, 1996) was designed as a non-motor assessment of visual-perceptual skills for children ages 4 through 13 years. The most recent revision provides updated normative data, new items, and clearer standardized procedures. The items of the TVPS–R span seven key visual-perceptual domains: Visual Discrimination, Visual Memory, Visual-Spatial Relationships, Visual Form Constancy, Visual Sequential Memory, Visual Figure-Ground, and Visual Closure. Each of the domains contains an equal number of items (16) arranged in order of difficulty. In addition to yielding standard scores for each of the seven domains, an overall Perceptual Quotient is provided.

Memory. Nearly every neuropsychological domain has evidenced significant advances and expansion in the neuropsychological assessment of preschool children. Equally as striking, however, is the relative lack of growth that has been witnessed in the assessment of memory functions in preschoolers. While the past decade has shown nice additions to the assessment armamentarium of psychologists in the area of memory, there currently are no known preschool memory batteries. A number of well-developed memory batteries, such as the Wide Range Assessment of Memory and Learning–2 (Adams & Sheslow, 2003), Test of Memory and Learning (Reynolds & Bigler, 1994), and the Children's Memory Scale (Cohen, 1997), have improved the state of children's memory assessment, but they only extend downward to the age of 5 years, thus substantially limiting their use with preschool children. To date, nearly all of the memory assessment for preschool children derives either from laboratory measures or subtests of intellectual batteries (e.g., SB–V).

Laicardi and colleagues (Laicardi, Artistico, Battisti, & De-Domenico, 2001, 2002) provided evidence for several new memory tasks for preschoolers. The first task reflected short-term verbal memory by having preschoolers recall a short story immediately after they had listened to it. The story was administered to 106 children, ages 4 to 6 years of age, and was scored by the verbalization of specific semantic and syntactic units from the story. High degrees of reliability and validity were noted for the semantic units of the story, but not for the syntactic units. Preschoolers who obtained higher scores on tests of attention also scored higher on this verbal memory test.

This group of investigators (Laicardi et al., 2002) also developed a short-term visual memory test for preschool children. For this test, memory for everyday pictures (Subscale 1) and for geometric and nonsense pictures (Subscale 2) was assessed. Both subscales were administered to a sample of 106 male and female preschool children ages 4 to 6 years of age. Results indicated that older subjects performed better than younger children, with each subscale representing a single factorial dimension. This latter finding is critical as the field begins to conceptualize a preschool memory battery.

Another test that has been available for children ages 4 to 8 years of age, the Children's Test of Nonword Repetition (CN REP; Gathercole & Baddeley, 1996), provides a measure of short-term verbal memory. The test was standardized and normed on a sample of 612 children in the United Kingdom. Unlike other measures (e.g., digit span tasks), the CN REP was developed using unfamiliar spoken words which the child must repeat. Results have shown that this test is more closely linked to important abilities, such as vocabulary knowledge, understanding of spoken language, and reading achievement, than the digit span task. Further, because the test uses unfamiliar spoken items which are not part of the English language, it does not disadvantage children with a less rich environmental language experience. In addition, the relationship of the CN REP to later school performance makes it a candidate for inclusion in a preschool neuropsychological battery.

Executive Functions.   As noted earlier, few of the preschool neuropsychological assessment models have addressed the constructs of attention and executive functions. While selected measures of executive functions for young children have been available for a number of years (e.g., Children's Category Test; Boll, 1993), similar to some of the IQ and
memory tests available, their downward extension into the preschool years stops around
age 5 years. Since the last edition of this text, however, specific contemporary measures
have evolved within the domain of executive functioning (Espy, Kaufmann, McDiarmid,
& Glisky, 2001; Wright, Waterman, Prescott, & Murdoch-Eaton, 2003).

Espy et al. (2001) tested for developmental differences on tasks of executive function
in a sample of children from 26–66 months of age. A battery of tasks was administered to
98 participants across five age groups: 30 months old ($N = 20$), 36 months old ($N = 21$),
42 months old ($N = 20$), 48 months old ($N = 19$), and 60 months old ($N = 18$). Participants were tested on several tools that had expected associations with different components of executive function: A-no-B, known to measure working memory and inhibition;
Delayed Alternation (DA), a measure of working memory; Spatial Reversal (SR) and
Color Reversal (CR), measures of set-shifting; Self Control (SC), a measure of inhibition;
the Shape School (SS), a measure of both inhibition and control; and the Tower of Hanoi
(TOH), a measure of problem solving and planning. Espy et al. (2001) found significant
main effects of age on four of the tasks administered: A-not-B, DA, SS, and TOH. In both
the A-no-B and DA tasks, significant developmental differences were found on all of the dependent variable measures within each of the tasks such that older participants performed
more efficiently and correctly compared to the younger children. On the SS, significant age
group effects were found on the timed variables such that in the control and inhibition conditions time to complete the tasks decreased as the age of the participants increased. On
the Tower task, age group effects also were found, with older participants performing better than younger participants. Furthermore, only in the TOH task was intelligence, as
measured by the Peabody Picture Vocabulary Test–Revised, related to performance on
the executive function measurement, suggesting a possible dissociation between IQ and executive functions in preschool children. No age group effects were found on the SR, SC, and
CR tasks (Espy et al., 2001).

Espy and colleagues have provided further evidence for use of The Shape School in the
assessment of executive functioning. The Shape School was viewed as an assessment that
could test both inhibition and set-shifting capabilities, and it has shown much promise in
measuring these selective components of executive function (Bull, Espy, & Senn, 2004;
Espy, 1997; 2004; Espy et al., 2001; Senn, Espy, & Kaufmann, 2004). The Shape School
is presented in the form of a colorful storybook and consists of four conditions: control, inhibition, switching, and both. In each of the conditions, circle and square shapes of differing colors are shown playing in a schoolyard. In the control condition, the shape's name is
its color, and children are instructed to call each by name as quickly as possible in the order that they appear. In the inhibition condition, the shapes are shown with one of two facial expressions, either happy or frustrated/sad. The children are then told to quickly name
the shapes that are ready for lunch based on the expression manifested. The final two conditions, switch and both, are commonly administered only to those preschoolers that are
more than 48-months of age considering it involves knowledge of both shapes and colors.
In the switch condition, some of the shapes wear hats and their name is the actual shape
of the figure. All of the figures are faceless and the children are told to quickly provide the
names of the figures, both with (name is shape) and without (name is color) hats. In the
both condition, inhibition and switching skills are assessed as figures with happy/frustrated-

sad faces and with/without hats are included. Participants are asked to name the happy-faced pupils that appear ready for art class (with hats = shape; without hats = color) and to not name the shapes that were not ready for class (frustrated-sad faces) (Espy, 1997; Espy et al., 2001; Bull et al., 2004; Senn et al., 2004).

In an initial study, Espy (1997) divided preschool participants into three age groups (3, 4, & 5-years of age) and found significant age group effects for all of the conditions tested. In the control condition, 4-year-olds were more efficient than 3-year-olds; in the inhibition condition 4-year-olds did significantly better than 3-year-olds (Espy, 1997; Espy et al., 2001); and in the switch and both conditions older children performed better than younger participants. Not only has The Shape School shown an ability to measure different types of executive function separately (switching and inhibition), recent research is beginning to investigate the timetable in which these skills are used and how well the skills can be used as predictors of more advanced cognitive processing (Bull et al., 2004; Senn et al., 2004). Similar procedures have been utilized by Wright et al. (2003) to develop a child version of the Stroop task.

Another task, Tails-P (Espy & Cwik, 2004), was adapted from its more established counterpart, the Trail Making Test from the Halstead-Reitan Neuropsychological Battery for Older Children. In the Espy and Cwik (2004) adaptation, the TRAILS-P employs a developmentally salient storybook format with colorful stimuli in differing conditions with varying executive demands. The TRAILS-P was administered to 103 normally developing preschoolers between 2 and 6 years of age. Initial findings suggested moderate to high correlations among the various test indices (i.e., time and errors) and temporal stability over about 1 month was satisfactory. Furthermore, the youngest children generally required more time to complete all TRAILS-P conditions, with the 3-year-old group being disproportionately slow to complete the set-shifting condition. In contrast, the number of errors differed only in the 5-year-olds relative to younger children. These findings are encouraging with respect to examining set-shifting demands in preschool children.

A final neuropsychological assessment procedure created by researchers to assess executive function is the Behavior Rating Inventory of Executive Functioning-Preschool Version (BRIEF-P; Gioia, Espy, & Isquith, 2003. The BRIEF-P represents one of the first standardized rating scales designed to measure executive function in preschool children. Similar to its parent tool, the BRIEF (Gioia, Isquith, Guy, & Kenworthy, 2000b, the BRIEF-P utilizes parent and/or teacher behavioral report to describe a full range of executive functions. The BRIEF-P is a 63-item questionnaire for preschool children between the ages of 2 and 6 that allows for the assessment of a child's executive functions within the context of home and preschool environments. Executive functions assessed include Inhibit, Shift, Emotional Control, Working Memory, and Plan/Organize. These clinical scales combine to form three major indices: Inhibitory Self-Control, Flexibility, and Emergent (Metacognition), and one overall composite score (Global Executive Composite). Two validity scales are also derived to measure excessive negativity and inconsistency of response. Excellent reliability and validity has been demonstrated. Further, Isquith, Gioia, and Espy (2004) have reported the BRIEF-P to be capable of identifying differences in executive function between clinical and control samples across all five domains. In addition, while the BRIEF-P has produced revealing information to suggest that behavioral manifestations in day-to-day routines can indicate cognitive capabilities, Gioia and Isquith (2004) recommended using a multi-level approach (i.e., a combination of test-based measurements and everyday behaviors) in evaluating the executive function capabilities of children with developmental disorders, cognitive delay, or clinical/medical conditions.

Other Measures.   When conducting a neuropsychological assessment with preschool children, the Tri-partite model by Rey-Casserly (1999) probably sets the stage for how to begin. In addition to the background history, behavioral observations, and specific neurocognitive assessment strategies discussed thus far, it becomes important for other areas of assessment to be considered as well—especially from the standpoint of functional outcomes. For the preschool child, this may include pre-academic skills, social-behavioral functions, and adaptive behaviors. While the space limitations of this chapter preclude any in-depth discussion of these domains, suffice it to say that there are a variety of tools to address these functional domains.

For example, within the pre-academic domain, the Get Ready to Read! (GRTR; Whitehurst & Lonigan, 2001) screening tool was created to provide both professionals and non-professionals with an efficient, reliable, and valid instrument to identify 4-year-old preschoolers who would benefit from further emergent literacy skills instruction, and to use the GRTR as a possible predictor of children's later reading proficiency. The norm-referenced GRTR consists of 20 items in which each item asks children to point to one correct answer out of a total of four choices to indicate children's understanding of print knowledge, emergent writing, and phonological awareness. Other tasks, such as the Test of Early Reading Ability–3 (TERA–3), Test of Early Math Ability (TEMA–3), Test of Early Written Language–2 (TEWL–2), the Basic School Skills Inventory (Hammill, Leigh, Pearson, & Maddox, 1998), and the Bracken Basic Concept Scale–Revised (Bracken, 1998) also are available to assist in preacademic skill assessment.

Similarly, within the social-behavioral domain, a number of tools have been developed over the past decade specifically for preschoolers. Several of these tools, the Behavior Assessment System for Children–2 (Reynolds & Kamphaus, 2005), the Child Behavior Checklist for Children 11/2 to 5 (Achenbach & Rescorla, 2000), and the Devereux Early Childhood Clinical Form (LeBuff & Naglieri, 1999), employ state-of-the-art multi-rater, multi-setting formats in order to examine findings from different vantage points. Finally, the adaptive behavior assessment of preschool children also could be a component of a larger flexible/informal neuropsychological assessment battery, depending on the referral question, and contemporary tools include the Vineland Adaptive Behavior Scale–II (Sparrow, Balla, & Cicchetti, 2005) and the Adaptive Behavior Assessment System–II (Harrison & Oakland, 2003). A number of these tools have been described elsewhere in this text by Campbell and James (Chapter 6), and by Harrison and Raineri (Chapter 10).

SUMMARY

Informal flexible neuropsychological test batteries will require the child psychologist and neuropsychologist to have a good foundation in child development, a solid background in neurodevelopmental theory and related issues, and an extensive knowledge of relevant tools to use in conjunction with a particular set of constructs. With this in mind, however, the examiner employing an informal assessment approach should be keenly aware of the potential psychometric and interpretive difficulties posed by using multiple instruments having different normative bases. Further, when using subtests from larger batteries, the examiner should be aware of the psychometric properties of those tasks (e.g., subtest specificities) in order to understand the limits of their interpretability. Since the last edition of this text, there have been significant advances in the area of preschool neuropsychological assessment, with the availability of attention and executive function tasks being most noteworthy in that regard.

ISSUES IN PRESCHOOL NEUROPSYCHOLOGICAL ASSESSMENT

As noted by Nagle earlier in this text (Chapter X), testing with preschool children tends to present a unique set of challenges and issues that can influence neuropsychological results. Many of these issues have been presented in an earlier chapter in this text (Nagle); however, some of issues are particularly pertinent to preschool neuropsychological assessment. First and foremost is the young age of the child. Preschoolers have precious little stamina for sitting still and concentrating for prolonged periods of time. In fact, these typical developmental observations likely will be exacerbated in a child manifesting neurological or neurodevelopmental challenges. Consequently, subjecting a preschool child to a long testing regimen actually could prove counterproductive. The clinician should attempt to modify the assessment battery to address the referral questions thoroughly, but efficiently, and to fit the needs of the child (e.g., perhaps employing multiple sessions, shorter tasks, etc.).

Second, and related to the age of the child and his/her developmental status, is the issue of testing protocol. Just because an examiner instructs a youngster to work quickly, or as fast as they can, does not mean that they will. Concepts related to speed, following directions, and waiting for the next instruction are just coming into the awareness of the preschool child, and these "test savvy" behaviors actually may be nonexistent in a child who has not participated in some kind of preschool setting. Temperamental issues may be present as well, and these issues need to be addressed by the examiner. Although these issues may seem trite to the experienced examiner, they can be devastating to obtaining reliable neuropsychological test data.

The reliability of a preschooler's responses also is a constant issue. In this regard, and in tandem with Lezak's (2004) suggestions for developing an informal battery, it will be critical for a certain amount of redundancy and task repetition to be built into a neuropsychological battery in an effort to account for these "normal" response inconsistencies. This becomes particularly important in profile interpretation and in the planning of intervention strategies. The response inconsistencies of the preschool child also may contribute to lowering the magnitude of predictor-criterion relationships in this population which, in turn, will interfere with prognostic implications.

Finally, the brain-behavior relationships in this population need to continue to receive investigation. Little is known about these relationships at present, although the interjection of a neurodevelopmental framework will provide a vehicle for increasing the understanding of these relationships. The development of specific assessment models, such as with the utilization of the CHC model by major IQ tests (Carroll, 1993), and the increased availability of attention and executive function models, also should fuel this area of inquiry. The interaction and possible synergistic effects between biological and psychosocial factors in a child's (neuro)development also need to be incorporated into any neuropsychological assessment paradigm that might be utilized. In fact, the psychologist or neuropsychologist providing neuropsychological assessment to the preschool child should have a strong foundation in central nervous system development and neurodevelopmental theory, and it should be this foundation that helps to guide test selection and interpretation for any particular preschool child (Kolb & Fantie, 1997).

CONCLUSIONS

This chapter has provided a contemporary overview of neuropsychological assessment procedures for the preschool child, with a particular focus on the recent increase of assessment tools associated with the preschool years. In addition to discussing relevant issues supporting the use of a neuropsychological perspective with preschool children, a variety of assessment procedures were presented. Noteworthy among these procedures are the publication of a comprehensive neuropsychological battery for children that has a downward extension into the preschool years and the relatively recent availability of specific neuropsychological measures for constructs such as attention and executive functions. Conversely, the area of memory assessment appears to be lagging behind at this point in time. When the previous version of this chapter was published approximately 5 years ago (Hooper, 2000), the NEPSY had only been recently published and many other procedures were nonexistent. Although the clinical and research utility of these preschool-specific procedures still remain to be determined, their neurodevelopmental theoretical foundation and good psychometric properties make them strong candidates to advance the field of child neuropsychology with preschoolers. The recent utilization of CHC in other batteries also should provide additional neurodevelopmental information for a preschool neuropsychological assessment.

Although the recent availability of formal preschool neuropsychological batteries is a welcomed addition to the field of child neuropsychology, the informal/flexible battery approach to preschool neuropsychological assessment remains highly utilized. Several models are available for formulation of broad-band constructs; however, despite the recent advances noted, more work is still needed with respect to providing a comprehensive array of constructs for the preschool years. These models require the examiner to be familiar with a wide variety of assessment tasks, and the interpretation of the informal battery demands knowledge of normal and abnormal brain development along with the application of neurodevelopmental theory.

Finally, it is important to recognize that a preschool neuropsychological assessment should go beyond what might be obtained from more traditional psychological assessments at this age level, and it should have the potential to address the specific needs of a preschooler with exceptionalities in a thorough manner. With the development of neuropsychological tasks sensitive to the various aspects of brain development, and the increased understanding of the impact of various neuropathological processes during these critical years, the development of preschool neuropsychological assessment also will continue to move forward. In particular, the next decade undoubtedly will bring tighter assessment-treatment linkages, in conjunction with IDEA and response-to-treatment needs, and the field of child neuropsychology should facilitate many of these connections. It will be exciting to see what advances have emerged in the neuropsychological assessment of preschool children upon the next edition of this text.

ACKNOWLEDGMENTS

This chapter was supported from grants from the Maternal Child Health Bureau (MCJ379154A) and the Administration on Developmental Disabilities (90DD043003).

REFERENCES

Achenbach, T. M., & Rescorla (2000). *Manual for the ASEBA Preschool Forms & Profiles*. Burlington, VT: University of Vermont Research Center for Children, Youth & Families.

Adams, W., & Sheslow, D. (1995). *Wide Range Assessment of Visual-Motor Ability*, Wilmington, DE: Jastak.

Adams, W., & Sheslow, D. (2003). *Wide Range Assessment of Memory and Learning–2*. Wilmington, DE: Jastak.

American Psychiatric Association (2000). Diagnostic and statistical manual of mental disorders Fourth Edition (text Revision) (DSM–IV–TR).Washington, DC: American Psychiatric Association.

Aunola, K., Leskinen, E., Lerkkanen, M. K., & Nurmi, J. E. (2004). *Journal of Educational Psychology, 96*, 699–713.

Aylward, G. P. (1988). Infant and early childhood assessment. In M. G. Tramontana & S. R. Hooper (Eds.), *Assessment issues in child neuropsychology* (pp. 225–248). New York: Plenum Publishing Company.

Aylward, G. P. (1997). *Infant neuropsychology*. New York: Guilford Press.

Aylward, G. P., Gustafson, N., Verhulst, S. J., & Colliver, J. A. (1987). Consistency in the diagnosis of cognitive, motor, and neurologic function over the first three years. *Journal of Pediatric Psychology, 12*, 77–98.

Bagnato, S. J., & Dickerson-Mayes, S. (1986). Patterns of developmental and behavioral progress for young brain-injured children during interdisciplinary intervention. *Developmental Neuropsychology, 2*, 213–240.

Baker, D. B., Taylor, C. J., & Leyva, C. (1995). Continuous performance tests: A comparison of modalities. *Journal of Clinical Psychology, 51*, 548–551.

Bayley, N. (2005). *Bayley Scales of Infant and Toddler Development, Third Edition*. San Antonio, TX: Harcourt Assessment.

Behr, S., & Gallagher, J. J. (1981). Alternative administrative strategies for young handicapped children. A policy analysis. *Journal of the Division for Early Childhood, 2*, 113–122.

Beery, K. E., Buktenica, N. A., & Beery, N. A. (2003). *Developmental Test of Visual Motor Integration, 5th Edition*. Minneapolis, MN: NCS Pearson.

Billard, C. (2002). The BREV neuropsychological test: I. Results from 500 normally developing children. *Developmental Medicine & Child Neurology, 44*, 391–397.

Blair, C., Ramey, C. T., & Hardin, J. M. (1995). Early intervention for low birth weight, premature infants: Participation and intellectual development. *American Journal on Mental Retardation, 99*, 542–554.

Boll, T. J. (1993). *Children's Category Test*. San Antonio, TX: The Psychological Corporation.

Bracken, B. A. (1998). *Basic Concept Scale–Revised*. San Antonio, TX: The Psychological Corporation.

Bull, R., Espy, K. A., & Senn, T. E. (2004). A comparison of performance on the Towers of London and Hanoi in young children. *Journal of Child Psychology and Psychiatry, 45*, 743–754.

Butler, M., Retzloff, P., & Vanderploeg, R. (1991). Neuropsychological test usage. *Professional Psychology, 22*, 510–512.

Carroll, J. B. (1993). *Human cognitive abilities: A survey of factor-analytic studies*. New York: Cambridge University Press.

Carter, A. S., Briggs-Gowan, M. J., & Davis, N. O. (2004). Assessment of young children's social-emotional development and psychopathology: Recent advances and recommendations for practice. *Journal of Child Psychology, 45*, 109–134.

Chelune, G. J., & Edwards, P. (1981). Early brain lesions. Ontogenetic-environmental considerations. *Journal of Consulting and Clinical Psychology, 49*, 777–790.

Cohen, M. (1997). *Children's Memory Scale*. San Antonio, TX: The Psychological Corporation.

Conners, C. K. (2001). *Conners' Kiddie Continuous Performance Test*. Toronto, Ontario, Canada: Multi-Health Systems.

Conners, C. K. (2000). *Conner's Continuous Performance Test II Version 5 for Windows*. Toronto: MHS.

Craft, A., Shaw, D., & Cartlidge, N. (1972). Head injuries in children. *British Medical Journal, 4*, 200–203.

Dean, R. S., & Woodcock, R. W. (2003). *Dean-Woodcock Sensory-Motor Battery*. Itasca, IL: Riverside Publishing Company.

Dennis, M. (1985a). Intelligence after early brain injury. I. Predicting IQ scores from medical variables. *Journal of Clinical and Experimental Neuropsychology, 7*, 526–554.

Dennis, M. (1985b). Intelligence after early brain injury. II. IQ scores of subjects classified on the basis of medical history variables. *Journal of Clinical and Experimental Neuropsychology, 7*, 555–576.

Dennis, M., Edelstein, K., Hetherington, R., Copeland, K., Frederick, J., Blaser, S. E., Kramer, L. A., Drake, J. M., Brandt, M., & Fletcher, J. M. (2004). Neurobiology of perceptual and motor timing in children with spina bifida in relation to cerebellar volume. *Brain, 127*, 1292–1301.

Deysach, R. E. (1986). The role of neuropsychological assessment in the comprehensive evaluation of preschool-age children. *School Psychology Review, 15*, 233–244.

Dunn, L. M., & Dunn, L. M. (1997). *PPVT–III: Peabody Picture Vocabulary Test–3rd edition*. Circle Pines, MN: AGS Publishing.

Ellison, P. H. (1983). The relationship of motor and cognitive function in infancy, preschool and early school years. *Journal of Clinical Child Psychology, 12*, 81–90.

Epstein, J. N., Erkanli, A., Conners, C. K., Klaric, J., Costello, J. E., & Angold, A. (2003). Relations between continuous performance test performance and ADHD behaviors. *Journal of Abnormal Child Psychology, 31*, 543–554.

Espy, K. (2003). Executive functions in preschool children born preterm: Application of cognitive neuroscience paradigms. *Child Neuropsychology, 8*, 83–92.

Espy, K. A. (1997). The Shape School: Assessing executive function in preschool children. *Developmental Neuropsychology, 13*, 495–499.

Espy, K. A. (2004). Using developmental, cognitive, and neuroscience approaches to understand executive control in young children. *Developmental Neuropsychology, 26*, 379–384.

Espy, K. A., & Cwik, M. F. (2004). The development of a trial making test in young children: The TRAILS-P. *Clinical Neuropsychologist, 18*, 411–422.

Espy, K. A., & Kaufmann, P. M. (2001). Individual differences in the development of executive function in children: Lessons from delayed response and A-not-B tasks. In D. L. Molfese & V. J. Molfese (Eds.), *Developmental Variations in Learning: Applications to Social, Executive Function, Language, and Reading Skills*. Mahwah, NJ: Lawrence Erlbaum Associates.

Espy, K. A., Kaufmann, P. M., McDiarmid, M. D., & Glisky, M. L. (2001). New procedures to assess executive functions in preschool children. *The Clinical Neuropsychologist, 15*, 46–58.

Espy, K. A., McDiarmid, M. D., Cwik, M. F., Senn, T. E., Hamby, S., & Stalets, M. M. (in press). The contributions of executive functions to emergent mathematic skills in preschool children. *Developmental Neuropsychology*.

Ewing-Cobbs, L., Prasad, M. R., Landry, S. H., Kramer, L., DeLeon, R. (2004). Executive functions following traumatic brain injury in young children: A preliminary analysis. *Developmental-Neuropsychology, 26*, 487–512.

Fletcher, J. M., Dennis, M., Northrup, H., Barnes, M. A., Hannay, H. J., Landry, S. H., Copeland, K., Blaser, S. E., Kramer, L. A., Brandt, M. E., & Francis, D. J. (2004). Spina bifida, genes, brain, and development. In L. M. Glidden (Ed.), *International review of research in mental retardation* (Vol. 29, pp. 63–117). San Diego, CA: Elsevier Academic Press.

Folio, M. R., & Fewell, R. R. (2000). *Peabody Developmental Motor Scales–2*. Austin, TX: PRO-ED.

Gardener, M. F. (1996). *Test of Visual-Perceptual Skills–Revised*. Hydesville, CA: Psychological and Educational Test Publishers.

Gathercole, S., & Baddeley, A. (1996). *The children's test of nonword repetition*. London: The Psychological Corporation Europe.

Geary, D. C., Hamson, C. O., & Hoard, M. K. (2000). Numerical and arithmetical cognition: A longitudinal study of process and concept deficits in children with learning disability. *Journal of Experimental Child Psychology, 77*, 236–263.

Gioia, G. A., Espy, K. A., & Isquith, P. K. (2003). Behavior Rating Inventory of Executive Function-Preschool Version (BRIEF-P). Odessa, FL: Psychological Assessment Resources Inc.

Gioia, G. A., Isquith, P. K., Guy, S. C., & Kenworthy, L. (2000a). Behavior rating inventory of executive function. *Child Neuropsychology, 6*, 235–238.

Gioia, G. A., Isquith, P. K., Guy, S. C., & Kenworthy, L. (2000b). *The Behavior Rating Inventory of Executive Function*. Lutz, FL: Psychological Assessment Resources.

Gioia, G. A., & Isquith, P. K. (2004). Ecological assessment of executive function in traumatic brain injury. *Developmental Neuropsychology, 25*, 135–158.

Gnys, J. A., & Willis, W. G. (1991). Validation of executive function tasks with young children. *Developmental Neuropsychology, 7*, 487–501.

Hammill, D., Leigh, J., Pearson, N., & Maddox, T. (1998). *Basic School Skills Inventory–3*. Austin, TX: PRO-ED.

Harrison, P., & Oakland, T. (2003). Adaptive Behavior Assessment Systems-Second Edition (ABAS-II). San Antonio, TX: The Psychological Corp.

Hartlage, L. C., & Telzrow, C. F. (1986). Neuropsychological assessment. In K. Paget & B. Bracken (Eds.), *Psychoeducational assessment of preschool children* (pp. 295–320). New York: Grune and Stratton.

Hooper, S. R. (1988). The prediction of learning disabilities in the preschool child: A neuropsychological perspective. In M. G. Tramontana & S. R. Hooper (Eds.), *Assessment issues in child neuropsychology* (pp. 313–335). New York: Plenum Publishing Company.

Hooper, S. R. (1991). Neuropsychological assessment of the preschool child: Issues and procedures. In B. A. Bracken (Ed.), *The psychoeducational assessment of preschool children* (2nd ed., pp. 465–485). Boston: Allyn and Bacon.

Hooper, S. R. (2000). Neuropsychological assessment of the preschool child. In B. A. Bracken (Ed.), *The psychoeducational assessment of preschool children* (3rd ed., pp. 383–398). Boston: Allyn and Bacon.

Hooper, S. R., Roberts, R. E., Zeisel, S. A., & Poe, M. (2003). Core language predictors of behavioral functioning in early elementary school children: Concurrent and longitudinal findings. *Behavior Disorders, 29*, 10–24.

Hooper, S. R., & Umansky, W. (Eds.) (2004). *Young children with special needs* (4th ed.). Upper Saddle River, NJ: Prentice Hall.

Horn, W. G., & Packard, T. (1985). Early identification of learning problems. A meta-analysis. *Journal of Educational Psychology, 77*, 597–607.

Hresko, W. P., Reid, K., & Hammill, D. D. (1999). *Test of Early Language Development–2*. Austin, TX: PRO-ED.

Hughes, C., & Graham, A. (2002). Measuring executive functions in childhood: Problems and solutions. *Child and Adolescent Mental Health, 7*, 131–142.

Individuals with Disabilities Education Improvement Act of 2004, Public Law No. 108–446, §614.

Isquith, P. K., Gioia, G. A., & Espy, K. A. (2004). Executive function in preschool children: Examination through everyday behavior. *Developmental Neuropsychology, 26*, 403–422.

Jansky, J. J. (1970). The contribution of certain kindergarten abilities to second grade reading and spelling achievement. Unpublished doctoral dissertation, Columbia University, New York.

Jordan, N. C., Kaplan, D., & Hanich, L. B. (2002). Achievement growth in children with learning difficulties in mathematics: Findings of a two-year longitudinal study. *Journal of Educational Psychology, 94*, 586–597.

Kolb, B., & Fantie, B. (1997). Development of the child's brain and behavior. In C.R. Reynolds & E. Fletcher-Janzen (Eds.), *Handbook of clinical child neuropsychology* (2nd ed., pp. 17–41). New York: Plenum Press.

Korkman, M., Kirk, U., & Kemp, S. (1998). *NEPSY. A Developmental Neuropsychological Assessment*. San Antonio, TX: The Psychological Corporation.

Korkman, M., & Peltomaa, A. K. (1993). Preventive treatment of dyslexia by a preschool training program for children with language impairments. *Journal of Clinical Child Psychology, 22*, 277–287.

Laicardi, C., Artistico, D., Battisti, A., & De-Domenico, M. (2001). Construction and validation of a visual memory test for preschool children. *Rassegna di Psicologia, 18*, 49–67

Laicardi, C., Artistico, D., Battisti, A., & De-Domenico, M. (2002). Construction and validation of a test of verbal memory for preschool children. *Psicologia Clinica dello Sviluppo, 6*, 235–255.

Laicardi, C., Artistico, D., Passa, M., & Ferrante, A. (2000). Preliminary study on the initial validation of a battery of visual attention tests for preschool children. *Rassegna di Psicologia, 17*, 123–144.

LeBuff, & Naglieri, J. A. (1999). *Devereux Early Childhood Assessment*. Itasca, IL: Riverside Publishing Company.

Lezak, M. D. (2004). *Neuropsychological Assessment* (5th ed.). New York: Oxford University Press.

Luria, A. R. (1980). *The Working Brain*. New York: Basic Books.

Lyytinen, H., Ahonen, T., Eklund, K., Guttorm, T., Kulju, P., Laakso, M. L., Leiwo, M., Leppanen, P., Lyytinen, P., Poikkeus, A. M., Richardson, U., Torppa, M., & Viholainen, H. (2004). Early development of children at familial risk for dyslexia—follow-up from birth to school age. *Dyslexia: An International Journal of Research and Practice, 10*, 146–178.

Mahone, E. M., Cirino, P. T., Cutting, L. E., Cerrone, P. M., Hagelthron, K. M., Hiemenz, J. R., Singer, H. S., & Denckla, M. B. (2002). Validity of the Behavior Rating Inventory of Executive Function in children with ADHD and/or Tourette syndrome. *Archives of Clinical Neuropsychology, 17*, 643–662.

Mahone, E. M., Pillion, J. P., & Hiemenz, J. R. (2001). Initial development of an auditory continuous performance test for preschoolers. *Journal of Attention Disorders, 5*, 93–106.

Mahone, E. M., Pillion, J. P., Hoffman, J., Hiemenz, J. R., & Denckla, M. B. (2005). Construct validity of the auditory continuous performance test for preschoolers. *Developmental Neuropsychology, 27*, 11–33.

Molfese, V. J., & Price, B. (2002). Neuropsychological assessment in infancy. In S. J. Segalowitz & I. Rapin (Eds.), *Handbook of neuropsychology* (2nd ed., Vol. 8, Part 1, pp. 229–249). New York: Elsevier.

Molfese, V. J., Beswick, J., Molnar, A., & Jacobi-Vessels, J. (2006). Alphabetic skills in preschool: A preliminary study of letter naming and letter writing. *Developmental Neuropsychology, 29*, 5–19.

Molfese, V., Modglin, A., & Molfese, D. L. (2003). The role of environment in the development of reading skills: A longitudinal study of preschool and school-age measures. *Journal of Learning Disabilities, 36*, 59–67.

Molfese, D. L., & Molfese, V. J. (1997). Discrimination of language skills at five years of age using event-related potentials recorded at birth. *Developmental Neuropsychology, 13*, 135–156.

Molfese, V. J., Molfese, D. L., & Modglin, A. T. (2001). Newborn and preschool predictors of second grade reading scores: An evaluation of categorical and continuous variables. *Journal of Learning Disabilities, 34*, 545–554.

Molfese, V. J., Molfese, D. L., Modglin, A. T., Walker, J., & Neamon, J. (2004). Screening early reading skills in preschool children: *Get Ready to Read! Journal of Psychoeducational Assessment, 22*, 136–150.

Morrow, C. E., Vogel, A., Anthony, J. C., Ofir, A. Y., Dausa, A. T., & Bandstra, E. S. (2004). Expressive and receptive language functioning in preschool children with prenatal cocaine exposure. *Journal of Pediatric Psychology, 29*, 543–554.

Mullen, E. M. (1995). *Mullen Scales of Early Learning*. Circle Pines, MN: American Guidance Service.

Naglieri, J. A., & Das, J. P. (1997). *Cognitive Assessment System*. Itasca, IL: Riverside Publishing Company.

Pears, K., & Fisher, P. A. (2005). Developmental, cognitive, and neuropsychological functioning in preschool-aged foster children: Associates with prior maltreatment and placement history. *Journal of Developmental and Behavioral Pediatrics, 26*, 112–122.

Puolakanaho, A., Poikkeus, A. M., Ahonen, T., Tolvanen, A., & Lyytinen, H. (2004). Emerging phonological awareness differentiates children with and without familial risk for dyslexia after controlling for general language skills. *Annals of Dyslexia, 54,* 221–243

Ramey, C. T., & Ramey, L. R. (1994). Which children benefit the most from early intervention? *Pediatrics, 94,* 1064–1066.

Reitan, R. M. (1969). *Manual for administration of neuropsychological test batteries for adults and children.* Indianapolis, IN: Author.

Reitan, R. M., & Davison, L. A. (Eds.) (1974). *Clinical neuropsychology: Current status and applications.* New York: John Wiley and Sons.

Rey-Casserly, C. (1999). Neuropsychological assessment of preschool children. In I. Romero & E. V. Nuttall (Eds), *Assessing and screening preschoolers: Psychological and educational dimensions* (2nd ed., pp. 281–295). Needham Heights, MA: Allyn & Bacon.

Reynolds, C. R., & Bigler, E. D. (1994). *Test of Memory and Learning.* Circle Pines, MN: American Guidance Service.

Reynolds, C. R., & Kamphaus, R. W. (2003). *Reynolds Intellectual Assessment Scales.*

Reynolds, C. R., & Kamphaus, R. W (2005). *Behavioral Assessment System for Children–2.* Circle Pines, MN: American Guidance Service.

Rhodes, R. L., Kayser, H., & Hess, R. S. (2000). Neuropsychological differential diagnosis of Spanish-speaking preschool children. In T. L. Strickland & E. Fletcher-Janzen (Eds.), *Critical issues in neuropsychology: Handbook of cross-cultural neuropsychology* (pp. 317–333). Dordrecht, Netherlands: Kluwer Academic Publishers.

Rourke, B. P. (1983). Outstanding issues in research on learning disabilities. In M. Rutter (Ed.), *Developmental Neuropsychiatry* (pp. 564–574). New York: The Guilford Press.

Rourke, B. P., Bakker, D. J., Fisk, J. L., & Strang, J. D. (1983). *Child Neuropsychology.* New York: The Guilford Press.

Satz, P., Taylor, H. G., Friel, J., & Fletcher. J. M. (1978). Some developmental and predictive precursors of reading disabilities. A six year follow-up. In A. L. Benton, & D. Pearl (Eds.), *Dyslexia: An Appraisal of Current Knowledge* (pp. 315–347). New York: Oxford University Press.

Sellers, A. H., & Nadler, J. D. (1992). A survey of current assessment procedures for different age groups. *Psychotherapy in Private Practice, 11,* 47–57.

Selz, M., & Reitan, R. M. (1979). Rules for neuropsychological diagnosis and classification of brain function in older children. *Journal of Consulting and Clinical Psychology, 47,* 258–264.

Senn, T. E., Espy, K. A., & Kaufmann, P. M. (2004). Using path analysis to understand executive function organization in preschool children. *Developmental Neuropsychology, 26,* 445–464.

Silver, A. A., & Hagin, R. A. (1972). Profile of a first grade. A basis for preventive psychiatry. *Journal of the American Academy of Child Psychiatry, 11,* 645–674.

Sommerfelt, K., Markestad, T., & Ellertsen, B. (1998). Neuropsychological performance in low birth weight preschoolers: A population-based, controlled study. *European Journal of Pediatrics, 157,* 53–58.

Sparrow, S. S., Balla, D. A., & Cicchetti, D. V. (2005). *Vineland Adaptive Behavior Scales-II.* Circle Pines, MN: American Guidance Service.

Spreen, O., & Haaf, R. G. (1986). Empirically derived learning disability subtypes. A replication attempt and longitudinal patterns over15 years. *Journal of Learning Disabilities, 19,* 170–180.

Stevenson, H. W., & Newman, R. S. (1986). Long-term prediction of achievement and attitudes in mathematics and reading. *Child Development, 57,* 646–659.

Stoneman, Z., & Rugg, M. E. (2004). Partnerships With Families. In S. R. Hooper & W. Umansky (Eds.), *Young children with special needs* (4th ed.). Upper Saddle River, NJ: Prentice Hall.

Teeter, P. A. (1985). Neurodevelopmental investigation of academic achievement. A report of years 1 and 2 of a longitudinal study. *Journal of Consulting and Clinical Psychology, 53,* 709–717.

Townes, B. D., Turpin, E. W., Martin, D. C., & Goldstein, D. (1980). Neuropsychological correlates of academic success among elementary school children. *Journal of Consulting and Clinical Psychology, 6,* 675–684.

Tramontana, M. G., Hooper, S. R., & Selzer, S. C. (1988). Research on the preschool prediction of later academic achievement. *Developmental Review, 8,* 89–147.

U.S. Department of Education (1986). Education of the handicapped act amendments of 1986. *Federal Register, 51*, 23834–23835.

U.S. Department of Education (1997). Individuals with disabilities education act. *Federal Register, 62*, 55025–55075.

U.S. Department of Education (2004). Individuals with disabilities education improvement act. *Federal Register, 69*, 77968–77969.

Vicari, S., Caravale, B., Carlesimo, G. A., Casadei, A. M., & Allemand, F. (2004). Spatial working memory deficits in children ages 3–4 who were low birth weight, preterm infants. *Neuropsychology, 18*, 673–678.

Walsh, K. K., Kastner, T. A., & Harmon, R. F. (1995). Crack cocaine exposure in preschool children: Focusing on the relevant issues [comment]. *Journal of Developmental and Behavioral Pediatrics, 16*, 418–424.

Wetherington, C. E., & Hooper, S. R. (in press). Preschool Traumatic Brain Injury: A Review for the Early Childhood Special Educator. *Exceptionality.*

Welsh, M. C., Pennington, B. F., & Grossier, D. B. (1991). A normative-developmental study of executive functions: A window on prefrontal function in children. *Developmental Neuropsychology, 7*, 131–149.

Whitehurst, G., & Lonigan, C. (2001). *Get Ready to Read!* Columbus, OH: Pearson Early Learning.

Wiig, E., Semel, E. H., & Secord, W. A. (1992). *Clinical Evaluation of Language Fundamentals-Preschool (CELF-P).* San Antonio, TX: The Psychological Corporation.

Williams, K. T. (1997). *Expressive Vocabulary Test.* Circle Pines, MN: AGS Publishing.

Wilson, B. C. (1986). An approach to the neuropsychological assessment of the preschool child with developmental deficits. In S. B. Filskov & T. J. Boll (Eds.), *Handbook of Clinical Neuropsychology, Volume 2* (pp. 121–171). New York: Wiley.

Wilson, B. C. (1992). The neuropsychological assessment of the preschool child: A branching model. In F. Boller & J. Grafman (Series Eds.), I. Rapin, & S. J. Segalowitz (Section Eds.), *Handbook of neuropsychology: Volume 6. Child neuropsychology* (pp. 377–394). Amsterdam: Elsevier.

Woodcock, R., McGrew, K., & Mather, N. (2001). *Woodcock-Johnson III Cognitive Assessment Battery.* Itasca, IL: Riverside Publishing Company.

Wright, I., Waterman, M., Prescott, H., & Murdoch-Eaton, D. (2003). A new Stroop-like measure of inhibitory function development: Typical developmental trends. *Journal of Child Psychology and Psychiatry and Allied Disciplines, 44*, 561–575.

Wrightson, P., McGinn, B., & Gronwall, D. (1995). Mild head injury in preschool children: Evidence that it can be associated with a persisting cognitive defect. *Journal of Neurology, Neurosurgery, and Psychiatry, 59*, 375–380.

Zimmerman, I. L., Steiner, V. G., & Pond, R. E. (2002). *Preschool Language Scale, fourth edition (PLS-4) English edition.* San Antonio, TX: The Psychological Corporation.

Author Index

Subject Index

Digital Signal Processing Demystified

by James D. Broesch

a volume in the Engineering Mentor™ series

HighText publications
an imprint of

LLH
Technology Publishing
Eagle Rock, Virginia
www.LLH-Publishing.com

ISBN 1-878707-16-7
Library of Congress catalog number: 97-70388

Printed in the United States of America
10 9 8 7 6 5 4 3 2

Cover design: Sergio Villareal, SVGD Design, Vista, CA
Developmental editing: Carol Lewis, LLH Technology Publishing
Interior design and production services: Sara Patton, Maui, HI

LLH
Technology Publishing
Visit us on the web: www.LLH-Publishing.com